An Anthology of Sacred Texts
by and about Women

AN ANTHOLOGY OF SACRED TEXTS BY AND ABOUT WOMEN

EDITED BY
SERINITY YOUNG

CROSSROAD • NEW YORK

In Memory of
Lin Benedict
(1946–1980)

———————

1994
The Crossroad Publishing Company
370 Lexington Avenue, New York, NY 10017

Printed in the United States of America

Library of Congress Cataloging-in-Publication Data

An anthology of sacred texts by and about women / edited by
  Serinity Young.
       p.   cm.
  Includes bibliographical references and index.
  ISBN 0-8245-1143-3; 0-8245-1418-1 (pbk.)
  1. Women and religion. 2. Sacred books. I. Young, Serinity.
BL458.S23   1993
291.8′082—dc20
                                                    92-36343
                                                    CIP

Acknowledgments will be found on pp. 449–452, which constitute an extension of the copyright page.

CONTENTS

INTRODUCTION

Religious traditions in all times and in all places have articulated what it is to be human by explaining humanity's relationship to the sacred. In this connection a great deal has been said about women, some of it good, and some of it bad, but all of it deeply meaningful for those who live or have lived under the influence of religious traditions. Mircea Eliade has pointed out that religious people attempt to live in harmony with their gods by imitating, whenever possible, the actions of the gods. "This faithful repetition of divine models," he explains, "has a two-fold result: (1) by imitating the gods, man [sic] remains in the sacred, hence in reality; (2) by the continuous reactualization of paradigmatic divine gestures, the world is sanctified. Men's [sic] religious behavior contributes to maintaining the sanctity of the world."[1]

While appreciative of Eliade's insights, this book also takes seriously Mary Daly's critique of Eliade's widely-used distinction between the sacred and profane[2] as being a distinction between male and female activities; in other words, what men do is sacred and what women do is profane.[3] Viewing the activities of women as nonreligious, as profane activities, leads to ignoring the significant participation of women in religion. Until fairly recently, the perception that what women do is profane and therefore unimportant has colored most methodologies in the study of religion. These methodologies, by focusing exclusively on the religious activities of men, as if male experience were representative of human experience, lead scholars to distort human experience; that is, they do not tell us how religion functions for all human beings.[4] Recent feminist studies of religion and of other fields have focused on uncovering this bias in scholarly studies.[5]

It still stuns the mind to find little or nothing on women in major books on individual religions or in comparative studies of religion. A cursory survey of the indices of books purporting to be significant and meaningful studies of religion reveals that the interests and concerns of such books are limited to the male half of the human population. We are all the poorer for

---

1. Mircea Eliade, *The Sacred and the Profane* (1956; New York: Harcourt, Brace & World, Inc., 1959), p. 96.

2. The distinction between sacred and profane was actually first formulated by Emile Durkheim in *The Elementary Forms of the Religious Life* (1915; New York: The Free Press, 1965).

3. Mary Daly, *Gyn/Ecology: The Metaethics of Radical Feminism* (Boston: Beacon Press, 1978), pp. 44–51. Eliade himself mentions the activities of women in his works from time to time, but mostly as a leavening for his general points about religion, which remained a male-identified activity. Even though Eliade postulated two separate types of sacrality, male and female (*The Quest* [Chicago: University of Chicago, 1969], pp. 133–134), rather than seeing the distinction of sacred and profane as a male/female distinction, his work continued to privilege male religious activity over female religious activity. See also the remarks of Robert Hertz in "The Pre-eminence of the Right Hand," in *Right & Left: Essays on Dual Symbolic Classification,* ed. Rodney Needham (Chicago: University of Chicago Press, 1973), p. 9, for whom this distinction was obvious.

4. This is certainly not meant to recommend the exclusion of men as subjects for religious studies. On the contrary, studies that specifically take men as their focus can be very insightful. What is being criticized here is scholarly pronouncements about human experience that are based only on male experience.

5. In addition to works that will be cited throughout this essay some early and important studies are the following: *Womanspirit Rising: A Feminist Reader in Religion,* ed. Carol P. Christ and Judith Plaskow (San Francisco: 1979); *Beyond Androcentrism: New Essays on Women and Religion,* ed. Rita M. Gross (Missoula, MT: Scholars Press, 1977); and Gross's recent reflections in "Tribal Religions: Aboriginal Australia" in *Women in World Religions,* ed. Arvind Sharma, pp. 37–40; *The Prism of Sex: Essays in the Sociology of Knowledge,* eds. Julia A. Sherman and Evelyn Torton Beck (Madison, WI: The University of Wisconsin Press, 1979); *Becoming Visible: Women in European History,* eds. Renate Bridenthal and Claudia Koonz (Boston: Houghton Mifflin, 1977); *Woman, Culture & Society,* eds. Michelle Zimbalist Rosaldo and Louise Lamphere (Stanford, CA: Stanford University Press, 1974); *The Outer Circle: Women in the Scientific Community,* ed. Harriet Zuckerman, Jonathan R. Cole, and John T. Bruer (New York: W. W. Norton, 1991); and David Noble, *A World without Women: The Christian Clerical Culture of Western Science* (New York: Alfred A. Knopf, 1992).

this. Even worse, when these texts are used to educate, they miseducate. No religion can be understood in its full complexity when scholars exclude women. It is just wrong-headed. Consequently, the present text is primarily compensatory; it attempts to make available readings by and about women from the primary texts of the world's religions. Moreover, it attempts to give voice to the religious experiences of women. We know how rich the world is in male voices; now we can begin to see the richness of women's religious voices, which are to be found in every religion.

The study of women, however, requires some understanding of humans as gendered beings. That gender is a cultural construction[6] is amply demonstrated by the great variety of social and religious roles assigned to women and men in different cultures. As Frances Dahlberg has shown, even on the simplest level of subsistence, as in hunter/gatherer societies, hunting is not the exclusive activity of men nor is gathering the exclusive activity of women as had been thought: Indeed, some women hunt and some men gather.[7] There are no simple answers. Gender is a highly complex cultural construction.[8]

The terms female and male are essentially symbols[9] and as such are completely void of meaning until they are invested with meaning by society. Significantly, although female and male are imbued with different meanings in different societies, those meanings can and do change within a society and through time. Religion is essential to these interpretations of gender because religion has the authority of the divine or of the ancestors or simply of tradition. Religion teaches people what it means to be female or male when it expands gender symbols into narratives, laws, customs, and rituals, into the sacred texts and ritual acts of the tradition. This is not to say that a society literally acts out these symbolic meanings, although some do,[10] or to deny that meaning varies among individuals, especially among different status groups; but it is to assert that these symbols can be and are called upon to establish order, to ascertain the divine will, or to maintain commitment to the sacred.[11]

Not surprisingly, the interpretation of what it means to be female or male differs for women and men. Religions in which men dominate in sacral roles, will reflect the male interpretation of what it means to be female or male. This suggests that Mary Daly is not far off the mark when she says that patriarchy is the religion of the planet,[12] because many religions are controlled by men. Since religion is a social institution, and given that the social structure has been patriarchal for at least the last six thousand years, religion, with some notable exceptions associated with innovation and revolution, is concerned with supporting patriarchy. The same can and should be said of all other social institutions under patriarchal systems: governments, the military, educational institutions, scientific and medical establishments, the workplace, the

6. Ortner and Whitehead, "Introduction," *Sexual Meanings: The Cultural Construction of Gender and Sexuality,* ed. Sherry B. Ortner and Harriet Whitehead (Cambridge: Cambridge University Press, 1981).

7. "Introduction," in *Woman the Gatherer,* ed. Frances Dahlberg (New Haven, CT: Yale University Press, 1981), pp. 1–33.

8. A thought-provoking study of gender in several cultures can be found in Peggy Reeves Sanday, *Female Power and Male Dominance: On the origins of sexual inequality* (New York: Cambridge University Press, 1981).

9. For further discussions of gender as symbol, see Caroline Bynum, "Introduction," in *Gender and Religion,* ed. Caroline Walker Bynum, Steven Harrell, and Paula Richman (Boston: Beacon Press, 1986), pp. 1–20; and Sherry Ortner and Harriet Whitehead, "Introduction," in *Sexual Meanings,* pp. 1–27.

10. See, for instance, the myths of the origins of cliterodectomies and menstruation. Myths of this type provide explanations and consequently justifications of the practices of clitereodectomy and of menstruation rituals. Even among these examples, however, the relationship between social fact and symbolic meaning remains a highly complex one.

11. See Clifford Geertz's discussion of the relationship between religious symbols and social realities in "Religion as a Cultural System," in *The Interpretation of Cultures: Selected Essays* (New York: Basic Books, Inc., 1973). See also Bynum's critique of Geertz in "Introduction," in *Gender & Religion,* pp. 1–20.

12. Daly, *Gyn/Ecology,* p. 39.

marketplace, the arts, etc. A function of social institutions is to maintain the fabric of society, and if that fabric is patriarchal, then patriarchy is what will be maintained.

This is particularly so where religion participates in a society's distinction between private and public domains.[13] A sharp division between these two realms generally leads to pronounced sexual inequalities.[14] The public realm of religion is usually dominated by men while women hold sway at the private or domestic level. One consequence of male dominance in the public sphere of religion is the allocation and confinement of all positions of prestige within a religion to men. The denial of these positions to women has far-reaching social and spiritual implications, not the least of which is, among the so-called great traditions, that the ideal religious person is always male, that is, the sage, the priest, the monk. Of even greater significance, the primary deities, especially in the monotheistic traditions, are all male. This leaves women with very little social or religious power because no matter how well they fulfill the expectations of their religion, they will remain female and therefore excluded on the ideal level in addition to being excluded on the social level.

However, because gender is a symbol and therefore needs an interpretation, it has some flexibility. For instance, creation myths may proffer stereotypes of female and male roles, but in reality actual women and men may diverge from these assigned roles. A certain amount of deviance from the norm is allowed in most societies and indeed may be necessary.[15]

Finally, male dominance of religious roles is a fairly recent development in the long history of the human race; so in fact is the concept of male divinity. According to recent scholarship, long before men donned sacred attire and began worshiping male gods, women dominated the religious scene as divinities and as religious experts.[16]

My purpose in writing this book has been to make accessible some of the primary texts of world religion that deal specifically with women. To this end I have prepared short introductions to each of the religions represented here which give a historical overview with particular regard to women. Furthermore, there are introductions to the individual selections that provide a historical background and suggest some of their implications for women. I have attempted to choose representative texts about women from works that are central to their respective traditions, such as creation stories, law codes, biographies of founders, and various writings by women. In many cases worthy texts had to be excluded due to limitations of space, and many issues relevant to the study of women in particular religions have not been raised. I hope that the bibliographies at the end of each chapter will enable the reader to continue on her or his own. These bibliographies list works not excerpted within this book, works that are themselves rich in bibliographical resources and representative of scholarship that is stimulating in its approach. Sources for the excerpts are also listed at the end of each chapter.

In organizing the material, I have divided the major traditions into individual chapters, which were then arranged chronologically. Certain chapters group similar traditions, such as

---

13. Of course, these are essentially male constructions that do not reflect the perspective of women. Significantly, within the private realm women educate and socialize the next generation, who will act both in the private and the public realms.

14. Joan Kelly, "The Social Relation of the Sexes: Methodological Implications of Women's History," in *Women, History, and Theory* (Chicago: University of Chicago Press, 1984), pp. 1–18. See also Sherry Ortner, "Is Female to Male as Nature is to Culture?" in *Woman, Culture & Society,* ed. Rosaldo & Lamphere, pp. 67–88; and an important critique of Ortner's essay by Gayle Greene and Coppélia Kahn, "Feminist scholarship and the social construction of woman," in *Making a Difference: Feminist Literary Criticism,* ed. Gayle Greene and Coppélia Kahn (1985; London and New York: Routledge, 1990), pp. 6–12.

15. Kai T. Erickson, *Wayward Puritans: A Study in the Sociology of Deviance* (New York: John Wiley & Sons, Inc., 1966), especially chapter one, pp. 1–29.

16. Marija Gimbutas, *The Goddesses and Gods of Old Europe: Myths and Cult Images* (Berkeley, CA: University of California Press, 1974, 1982) and Merlin Stone, *When God Was a Woman* (1976; New York: Harcourt Brace Jovanovich, 1978).

Shamanism and Tribal Religions, and are necessarily arranged geographically rather than chronologically. Second, all chapters contain similar genres of literature. For instance, wherever possible, chapters begin with the creation story of that tradition and, if that tradition had a founder, then excerpts from that biography follow. Religious laws regarding women also figure prominently among the excerpts. The choice of these genres of sacred literature will be discussed below. The majority of them are the compositions of men, since men wrote the vast majority of the world's religious literature, but the picture they present of their tradition is rounded out by selections from religious works composed by women.

Certain themes persist in these texts which suggest meaningful cross-cultural parallels in women's religious experience. The next section of this introduction will discuss the various kinds of sacred texts I have used and some of the cross-cultural themes that can be found in these texts as well as suggest some interpretations for the persistence of these themes over time and space. Examples used to illustrate a particular theme have been drawn from this anthology and placed in parentheses.

I. Genres of Sacred Literature[17]

As Ninian Smart and Richard Hecht have succinctly put it: "The world's sacred texts are potent sources of inspiration and behaviour and, more importantly, they play a crucial part in the formation of peoples' perception of reality. They may be thought of as somehow revealed, or as expressions of revelatory experiences, and typically they are treated as possessing authority."[18] Sacred texts give people highly valued information about the sacred, information that is evocative, as in myth, story, and ecstatic poetry, or legally and ritually binding, as in law codes and prescribed ceremonies. These texts preserve divine revelations, the teachings of founders and prophets, and the sacred history of a people. Whether oral or written, they are the touchstones of a culture;[19] they tell people who they are, what their place is in the scheme of life—they offer definitions and shape consciousness. Sacred texts vary greatly from tradition to tradition and even within a single tradition. I have attempted to suggest some of this scriptural diversity in the selections that follow. Nevertheless, sacred texts are always perceived as powerful, as an opening into the realm of the sacred. Most sacred texts, especially those texts that have received canonical status, have been composed by men, usually elite men, and the orthodox male view of women tends to dominate these texts. Sacred texts written by women often echo the male view, sometimes in the very ways the authors evade the limitations placed on women. For instance, the majority of religious texts written by women have been written by celibate women, lay and monastic. These women first achieved status in their traditions by giving up their sexuality and only then through their texts. Traditions that valorize celibacy often equate sexuality with women, so only nonsexual women, virgins and widows, are nonthreatening to the religious establishment. That women authors of religious texts have internalized this attitude toward sexuality is shown by their "choice" of celibacy. (At the same time they have also been freed from the domestic chores that attend female sexuality such

---

17. Some comparative discussions of the roles and analysis of sacred texts are: William A. Grahman, "Scripture," in *The Encyclopedia of Religion,* ed. Mircea Eliade, 13: 133–145; *The Holy Book in Comparative Perspective,* ed. Frederick M. Denny and Rodney L. Taylor (Columbia, SC: University of South Carolina Press, 1985); *The Critical Study of Sacred Texts,* ed. Wendy Doniger O'Flaherty (Berkeley, CA: Graduate Theological Union, 1979); *Rethinking Scripture: Essays from a Comparative Perspective,* ed. Miriam Levering (Albany, NY: State University of New York Press, 1989).

18. *Sacred Texts of The World: A Universal Anthology,* ed. Ninian Smart and Richard D. Hecht (New York: Crossroad Publishing Company, 1982), p. xi. See also Levering's critique of Smart and Hecht in *Rethinking Scripture,* pp. 8–11.

19. For an important and accessible discussion of the manifold differences between oral and chirographic cultures see Walter Ong, *Orality and Literacy: The Technologizing of the Word* (London and New York: Methuen, 1982).

as housework and childcare thereby gaining the time to write.) The point is that celibacy does not seem to be a requirement of male religious authors.

Reading sacred texts, especially those familiar texts of one's own tradition, from the perspective of women is a radical activity, an activity that, at its best, subverts male dominance of the texts.[20] In some cases, such a reading can reveal deeper meanings for all, women and men.

a. Creation Myths

Wherever possible I have begun each chapter with the creation myth or myths of that tradition. As Eliade has shown,[21] these are the most pervasive myths of a tradition; they are the schema for understanding reality and what can and cannot be done within that reality. They provide the models, and often the justifications, for a great variety of social actions, including what constitutes correct human behavior. Barbara Sproul explains their primacy in a tradition:

> Not only are creation myths the most comprehensive of mythic statements, addressing themselves to the widest range of questions of meaning, but they are also the most profound. They deal with first causes, the essences of what their cultures perceive reality to be. In them people set forth their primary understanding of man [sic] and the world, time and space. And in them cultures express most directly, before they become involved in the fine points of sophisticated dogma, their understanding of and awe before the absolute reality, the most basic fact of being.[22]

All else follows from the primary understanding of absolute reality that is established in creation myths. They are one of the major building blocks of a tradition and they are universal.

These myths often express explicitly the tradition's understanding of gender, such as the proper labor for each gender (Adam tills the fields and Eve bears children) or the rituals that are necessary for women and men (Dogon).[23] They are also intriguing in their understanding of creation as male activity (Genesis), female activity (Babylonia), a combination of both in the sense of mutual generation (Australia), or initial creation through the male supplemented by the female (Hopi, Amaterasu). This latter type of myth is expressive of the patriarchal view that females are obviously necessary for generation but receive their powers from males. Also, there are myths that postulate androgyny either actual (Buddhism) or in principle (Taoism). And, sometimes these myths reveal antagonisms between the sexes (*Enuma Elish*, Adam and Eve, *Theogony*).

b. Sacred Biography[24]

Frank Reynolds and Donald Capps begin their discussion of sacred biography in world religion by saying: "Eliade's suggestion that myth provides the exemplary pattern to be actualized in human history is central to our own view of biography as the complex interweaving of

---

20. Two excellent introductions to feminist textual analysis are *Making A Difference: Feminist Literary Criticism,* ed. Greene and Kahn; and *The New Feminist Criticism: Essays on Women, Literature and Theory,* ed. Elaine Showalter (New York: Pantheon Books, 1985).

21. *The Sacred and the Profane,* especially pp. 995–99 and passim.

22. Barbara C. Sproul, *Primal Myths: Creating the World* (San Francisco: Harper & Row, Publishers, 1979), pp. 2–3.

23. An important study of gender ideology in creation myths and the connection of such ideology to social reality is contained in Sanday, *Female Power and Male Dominance,* particularly pp. 15–75.

24. For an historical overview of biography in world religion see William R. LaFleur, "Biography," in *The Encyclopedia of Religion,* ed. Eliade, 2: 220–224. Two important book-length studies of this topic are: Frank E. Reynolds & Donald Capps, eds., *The Biographical Process: Studies in the History and Psychology of Religion* (The Hague: Mouton & Company, 1976) and *Charisma and Sacred Biography* (Journal of the American Academy of Religion, Thematic Studies, vol. 48/3 and 4, 1982), ed. Michael A. Williams.

myth and history. Myth and history are not discontinuous, in this view, but manifest a complex interaction."[25] This leads them to recognize that sacred biography, especially the biography of the founder of the tradition, plays a primary role in the creation of religious symbols and images that become basic to the religion.

In contrast to sacred biographies, there is the similar genre of hagiographies, the lives of saints, mystics, and other religious figures, who fulfill a religious ideal or image previously established by the biography of the founder of the tradition. In other words, saints, or their biographers, call upon the biographical images contained in the biographies of the founders.[26] In this and other ways sacred biography and hagiography establish powerful models for the sacred life, and these models are gender specific.

Carolyn Heilbrun has shown that biographical and autobiographical narratives are different for women; they do not follow male models but have an integrity of their own.[27] For instance, Heilbrun makes the point that in all types of literature women are limited to narratives of either the conventional marriage or the erotic plot. She explains that "[f]or women who wish to live a quest plot, as men's stories allow, indeed encourage, them to do, some event must be invented to transform their lives, all unconsciously, apparently 'accidentally,' from a conventional to an eccentric story."[28] Seeking the divine is just such a quest plot. The biographies and writings of women who have gone on such quests need to be read differently from seemingly similar male quests.[29] Particular attention needs to be paid not simply to the relationship such women had to the divine, the establishment of which was often the transformative event of their lives, but also to individual women's reaction to such an appearance or call from the divine. Given the gender specific understandings of appropriate reactions to the sacred in most societies, women and men react differently to such stimulus. Most importantly, since women frequently have less control over their lives than men, the way in which women answer a call from the sacred can be quite radical. Heilbrun's point is demonstrated in the lives of women saints who went to extremes to avoid both the marital and erotic expectations of their societies: stories of disfigurement (Ryōnen Genso), extreme punishment for refusing to marry (Yeshe Tsogyel), escape from marriage (Mahādevīyakka), abandonment of female roles and assumption of male disguises (Joan of Arc), abound.

---

25. Reynolds and Capps, eds., *The Biographical Process,* p. 2.

26. For more on this point see Charles F. Keyes, "Introduction: Charisma: From Social Life to Sacred Biography," in *Charisma and Sacred Biography,* ed. Williams, pp. 1–22.

27. Carolyn G. Heilbrun, *Writing a Woman's Life* (1988, New York: Ballantine Books, 1989). See especially pp. 23–24 for comments on spiritual biography. Additional studies of women and biography can be found in the following: *Revealing Lives: Autobiography, Biography, and Gender,* eds. Susan Grog Bell and Marilyn Yalom (Albany, NY: State University of New York Press, 1990) contains some excellent essays on the topic of gender and biography while the introduction raises pertinent issues and has an extensive bibliography in the notes. *Biography East and West: Selected Conference Papers* (Honolulu, HI: The College of Languages, Linguistics and Literature, University of Hawaii and the East-West Center, 1989), ed. Carol Ramelb, contains a section on autobiography and third world women.

28. *Writing a Woman's Life,* p. 48.

29. Carol Christ has pointed out important gender differences in the lives of mystics connected to the gender expectations of their society. Carol Christ, *Diving Deep and Surfacing: Women Writers on Spiritual Quest* (Boston: Beacon Press, 1980), especially pp. 17–18. See also Ramanujan's study of Hindu saints, which unknowingly confirms Christ's thesis, in A. K. Ramanujan, "On Women Saints" in *The Divine Consort: Rādhā and the Goddesses of India,* ed. John Stratton Hawley and Donna Marie Wulff (Boston: Beacon Press, 1982), pp. 316–324. Ramunjan has established different stages of life for Hindu women saints based on his comparative studies of the biographical literature of Hindu male and female saints. See also David Weinstein and Rudolph M. Bell, *Saints and Society: The Two Worlds of Western Christendom, 1000–1700* (Chicago: University of Chicago Press, 1982) for their analysis of gender among Christian saints, pp. 220–238 and Caroline Bynum's brief but highly evocative remarks in "Introduction," *Gender and Religion,* pp. 13–14.

Significant information about the role of women in a tradition can be gleaned from sacred biographies and hagiographies whether they take a woman or a man as their subject.[30] Women figure in the lives of male saints, not only as temptresses, though they are frequent enough, but also in positive, if very controlled, ways such as devoted patrons, mothers, daughters, and sisters. It is extremely rare to find a male saint who has saintly female companions, especially in anything resembling a relationship of spiritual equality (Clare of Assisi, the female companion of Francis of Assisi, is interesting in this context). With the understanding that saints' lives are often extreme models of piety, it is frequently in these extremes that the values of a tradition receive their clearest expression. Given the frequency with which these stories are told, the clear and dramatic depictions of women in the lives of male saints convey significant information about women, and men, to the tradition's adherents.

The lives of women saints, of course, provide additional data on women from all periods of a tradition, although usually these are the ideal women, the honored women. Their lives must seem inaccessible to other women who, in traditional societies, generally marry and have children before such alternative choices can be acted upon. In this sense these stories limit women's religious experience because few have the courage of these god-possessed women, or really want to completely abandon their connections to family and community while risking public humiliation and censure. Yet these stories, however limiting, also do inspire women in their daily lives, fortifying them in their self-understanding, simply by being powerful and positive images of women.

c. Law Books[31]

Religions are the first givers of law and all religious laws are divinely given, from the Ten Commandments to the Laws of Manu. Law codes function in highly complex ways that vary from tradition to tradition, but all religious law codes are at the very least a reference point for their tradition; when in doubt, the law books are consulted. The ideal function of religious law is to provide a guide for humans to live in accordance with divine wishes, to help them live in harmony with the sacred. Gender-specific laws are a first step in this process. Often these codes are idealizations that may not be followed to the letter in practice, but they can be and were cited against challengers. Generally speaking, women and men know what the law codes require of them, and they shape their lives accordingly.

With regard to women, the religious law books are primarily concerned with ordering their sexuality: They define taboos about menstruation and childbirth; they define with whom and under what circumstances women, and sometimes men, can have sexual relations; and they define the proper behavior for nonsexual women, widows and unmarried girls (that they not be sexually active). Often the law books define inheritance, particularly stating a woman's portion in relation to a man's. Whether the law books in defining the rights of women are limiting those rights or acting to protect them is a controversial subject. For instance, the Qur'ān states that a daughter's inheritance should be half that of her brother's. Whether this imposed a limitation on preexisting inheritance rights of women or introduced such rights is still being

---

30. Max Weber has noted the prominence of women in the lives of founders and he draws some conclusions from this. See Max Weber, *The Sociology of Religion*, trans. Ephraim Fischoff (1922; Boston: Beacon Press, 1963, p. 104). Weber's comments are best read in connection with Joan Kelly's important discussion of the issue of periodization for the study of women and history and the effects of social change on women. See "Did Women Have a Renaissance?" in Joan Kelly, *Women, History, and Theory*, pp. 19–50.

31. For a discussion of various religious legal systems see Weber's *Sociology of Law* in *Max Weber: Economy and Society*, ed. Guenther Roth and Claus Wittick (Berkeley, CA: University of California Press, 1978) vol. II, especially pp. 809–838.

debated. On the other hand, protection is clearly suggested in admonishments to fathers not to sell or prostitute their daughters.

d. Folklore[32]

The popularity of folk and fairy tales is attested to by their repetition, generation after generation. These tales are used to teach important lessons about the world, especially to children, and it should come as no surprise that these lessons are gender specific.[33] Folklore and fairy tales also reveal the religious beliefs of the "little tradition" in contrast to the "great tradition." It is this little tradition, or the popular level of religion, that is often in the hands of women, while the great tradition is represented by the male-dominated forms of orthodoxy.[34] The orthodox realm of the great tradition controls the sacred texts of the tradition, especially its canonical works, which provide a common framework for diverse local practices, while the little tradition exists in a primarily oral culture. This leads to a further distinction, which until quite recent times was the norm, between the religious practices of a literate clergy and an illiterate laity. The practices of the laity can be as diverse as Christians encouraging their children to bob for apples on Halloween (a form of divination practiced by the ancient Celts on All Hallow's Eve, their New Year)[35] or as Muslim women falling into states of possession that exert control over the behavior of their husbands.[36] Both these practices take place, respectively, at the popular or folk level of Christianity and Islam. Further, folk and fairy tales can provide access to long suppressed practices, because they often contain survivals of extinct religious practices, for instance, pre-Christian practices in Europe, or archaic woman-centered practices in China. Another example can be found among the numerous witches and evil old women of the tales, which may very well refer to women who continued ancient religious practices away from the watchful eyes of male orthodoxy. Understood in this way, they can be read as deeply subversive texts. Yet, these stories taught children to be wary of old women, especially those living on the fringes of patriarchal society. Deviance of any kind among women was rarely tolerated.

In reading these tales, particular attention needs to be paid not only to gender specific images but also to the distinction between the folklore of women and that of men.[37] The stories women tell each other are different from the stories men tell each other; and what is important, women's stories are told in different expressive genres. For instance, men tell "yarns" while women "gossip."

---

32. See Alexander H. Krappe, *The Science of Folklore* (1929; New York: W. W. Norton & Company, Inc. 1964); and Stith Thompson, *The Folktale* (New York: Dryden Press, 1946). For a general introduction to this literature. See also Stith Thompson, *Motif-Index of Folk-Literature* (Bloomington, IN: Indiana University Press, 1955–1958), a six-volume guide to the motifs in this literature.

33. Ruth Bottigheimer, *Grimms' Bad Girls and Bold Boys: The Moral and Social Vision of the Tales* (New Haven, CT: Yale University Press, 1987). For an overview of the debate surrounding gender issues in fairy tales, see Kay F. Stone, "The Misuses of Enchantment: Controversies on the Significance of Fairy Tales," in *Women's Folklore, Women's Culture,* ed. Rosan A. Jordan and Susan J. Kalčik (Philadelphia: University of Pennsylvania Press, 1985), pp. 125–145.

34. For more information on the complex topic of folk and popular religion see "Folk Religion: An Overview" by William A. Christian, Jr. in *Encyclopedia of Religion,* ed. Eliade, 5: 372; and "Popular Religion," by Charles H. Long, ibid., vol. 11, especially pp. 442–452.

35. Leonard Norman Primiano, "Halloween," *Encyclopedia of Religion,* ed. Eliade, 6: 176–177.

36. For more on the subject of women and possession, in Islam and other traditions, see I. M. Lewis, *Ecstatic Religion: An Anthropological Study of Spirit Possession and Shamanism* (Harmondsworth, England: Penguin Books Ltd., 1971).

37. See *Journal of American Folklore,* vol. 88, no. 347, January–March, 1975, which is a special issue on "Women and Folklore," edited by Claire R. Farber. While limited to American folklore, the articles raise significant methodological issues that can be applied to the study of non-American folklore. See also *Women's Folklore,* ed. Jordan and Kalčik.

Significantly, scholars of this literature, though heavily indebted to the stories collected from women, have tended to preference stories told by men, which are defined as being more legitimate. This skewers the picture of women in this literature in at least two different ways: First, the vast majority of stories told by men have men as their main characters while the stories told by women are equally divided between female and male main characters. Second, when men do tell stories that have female main characters they cast them into masculine roles, thereby revealing the male preoccupation with male social roles as well as their inability to either perceive or value female social roles. In other words, when men tell stories about women they transform them into men.[38]

e. *The Texts of Tribal Peoples*[39]

The texts of tribal peoples present particular challenges to an anthologist. First and foremost, this literature was originally oral and much of it that has been recorded was done so by people from outside the culture, usually anthropologists but also missionaries and colonialists, or people from within the culture who adhered to the values of those outsiders. Until quite recently the great majority of this recording was done by men who showed a preference for information about men and who did not understand or were denied access to information about women.[40] Tribal women, especially among a conquered people, tended not to reveal their sacred lore to outsiders. Today anthropologists are trained to put aside whatever sectarian preferences they may have and to record what they see and hear as accurately as possible.[41] Many of the excerpts contained herein were gathered by hard working and sympathetic anthropologists under trying conditions; often they present the last vestiges of a destroyed or greatly reduced culture.

f. *Works By Women*

The vast majority of religious texts have been written by men, for other men, and are considered the normative texts of the tradition. They convey an astonishing variety of religious expressions. Though more limited in the actual number of texts, those composed by women present us with equally complex and diverse experiences.

The works by women contained in this anthology take many forms. There are the ecstatic poems of mystics such as Mahādevīyakka and Rābi'āh as well as poems of mourning for a

---

38. See Margaret Mills, "Sex Role Reversals, Sex Changes, and Transvestite Disguise in the Oral Tradition of a Conservative Muslim Community in Afghanistan," in *Women's Folklore,* ed. Jordan and Kalčik, pp. 187–189 and passim.

39. A discussion of important issues for literate peoples who seek to understand to religious life of nonliterate tribal people is contained in Sam D. Gill's thoughtful and provocative essay, "Nonliterate Traditions and Holy Books: Toward a New Model" in *The Holy Book,* eds. Denny and Taylor, pp. 224–239.

40. A brief discussion of some of the field work done by women in the British empire and the issues they faced is contained in Margaret Strobel, "Gender and Race in the Nineteenth- and Twentieth-Century British Empire" in *Becoming Visible,* eds. Bridenthal, Koonz, and Stuard, pp. 387–389. A significant study of the effects of their own gender on anthropologists is Ruby Rohrlich-Leavitt, Barbara Sykes, and Elizabeth Weatherford, "Aboriginal Woman: Male and Female Anthropological Perspectives," in *Toward an Anthropology of Women,* ed. Rayna R. Reiter (New York: Monthly Review Press, 1975), pp. 110–126.

41. See *Fieldnotes: The Makings of Anthropology,* ed. Roger Sanjek (Ithaca and London: Cornell University Press, 1990) for a general introduction to the training of anthropologists and James Clifford's essay "Notes on (Field)notes," ibid. , pp. 47–70, for recording in the field. Feminist approaches to anthropology are well represented in *Woman the Gatherer,* ed. Dahlberg; *Woman, Culture and Society,* ed. Rosaldo and Lamphere; *Sexual Meanings: The Cultural Construction of Gender and Sexuality,* ed. Sherry B. Ortner and Harriet Whitehead (Cambridge: Cambridge University Press, 1981); and *Toward an Anthropology of Women,* ed. Reiter.

dead child or husband, the theological subtleties of Catherine of Sienna, the matter-of-fact statements about their religious lives by tribal women, such as Nisa, which express the uncertainties of any religious knowing. Women may envision the divine in different terms than men, as in Ann Lee's understanding of God as mother, and this leads them to formulate different kinds of relationships to the divine. Sometimes they are the stories women tell each other: the myths about women, their autobiographies, both oral and written, accounts of their religious experiences ranging from drug-induced possession to adventures during a pilgrimage. All speak with a female-centered voice that is deeply located in women's religious experience. Carol Christ has eloquently written of women's need for the stories of other women as well as the consequences of inauthentic stories in women's lives. She says:

> Women's stories have not been told and without stories there is no articulation of experience. Without stories a woman is lost when she comes to make the important decisions of her life. She does not learn to value her struggles, to celebrate the strengths, to comprehend her pain. Without stories she cannot understand herself. Without stories she is alienated from the deeper experiences of self and world that have been called spiritual or religious. She is closed in silence.[42]

Women listen carefully to the words of other women; they search out meanings for themselves as women, meanings that are often missing from the works of men of faith. They have an inherent value in and of themselves and an additional meaning because of their scarcity amidst the cacophony of male voices.

II. Cross-cultural Themes

What follows are suggestive themes for the comparative study of women in world religion. These are not meant to be exhaustive of even the materials contained herein, but rather to highlight some topics and encourage further research. It is hoped that the citations in this chapter will prove helpful in this regard. In addition, the reader is directed to the index for further examples to be found under the topical headings. This discussion has, however, been limited to the materials that are included in this anthology. Many more examples of the individual themes can be found, some quite obvious, and there are many more themes to be explored.

Importantly, we must distinguish between the function of women in religious imagination from that of women in religious reality. In other words, we must distinguish between metaphysical and abstract concepts of "woman" such as truth, beauty, wisdom, the source of immortality, and so on, and women in actual religious law, which imposes ritual restrictions upon them, especially of access to positions of prestige and power in the majority of religious hierarchies, or which defines women as irrelevant and unnecessary to religious practice when not actually threatening to it. The problem is that male imaginative understandings of women often blind one to the realities of women's lives within religious contexts, which were, and in many cases remain, the defining reality of women's lives. Religious realities are social realities.[43]

Further, concepts such as "the feminine" distance us from the actual lives of women; we are prepared for "feminine imagery" but not for flesh and blood women. In this context, Sherry Ortner's wide cultural vision proves helpful when she explains: "Feminine symbolism, far more often than masculine symbolism, manifests the propensity toward polarized ambiguity— sometimes utterly exalted, sometimes utterly debased, rarely within the normal range of human

---

42. Christ, *Diving Deep and Surfacing*, p. 1.
43. For further discussion of the pervasiveness of religious ideas in so-called secular societies and its effect on women's lives, see Christ and Plaskow, "Introduction," in *Womanspirit Rising*, pp. 1–3.

possibilities."[44] The effect of this ambiguity on the lives of women who cannot live up to the imagery has been and continues to be devastating.

a. *Women as Evil*[45]

Representations of women as evil are a particularly complex issue in world religion and one that ties together several themes important to the study of women and religion.

1. *Body and Sexuality.*[46]   Almost every major religion associates women with evil, especially through gender specific dualities such as associating women with the body and materiality while associating men with spirit. In these systems spirit is closer to the divine and therefore good (Aristotle, Aquinas, Ibn 'Arabī), the idea being that it is materiality, especially the body, which keeps people from god. This point is dramatized in the many traditions that link women with sexuality by representing women as sexual temptresses who deflect men from their spiritual goals. This notion receives its fullest development in religions which, while enjoining celibacy on its religious specialists, male or female, particularly empower a male priesthood. Buddhism and Christianity offer dramatic examples of this, but Hinduism, in its valorization of the powers of celibate male sages, also contains many negative sexual images of women. This notion can be seen elsewhere as early as the Gilgamesh story, in which Enkidu loses his innocence by having sex with a woman and in which Gilgamesh rejects the sexual overtures of the goddess Isthar.[47] All of this serves to justify the control of women by men, a justification that is perceived to be divinely given in most sacred law books. Essentially, women are represented as inadequate moral agents who, for their own protection and the protection of their victims (men), must remain under the moral supervision and social constraint of men. Their moral weakness also makes women particularly susceptible to the influence of demonic beings.[48] Inherent in all of this, of course, is a fear and denigration of sexuality.

In the West this begins with Eve[49] and her mistake, which cost human beings paradise. In Judaism this theme is elaborated upon in the story of Lilith, Adam's first wife. In Christianity Eve — and consequently women in general — remains a convenient scapegoat for evil in contrast to the salvational powers of the Virgin Mary. Interestingly, in Islam Eve receives a more even-handed treatment. Traditions from other parts of the world also attribute the earthly problems of human beings to some primordial mistake by a woman (Pandora), a mistake which

---

44. Ortner, "Is Female to Male?" in *Woman, Culture and Society,* eds. Rosaldo and Lamphere, p. 86.

45. See Nel Noddings *Women and Evil* (Berkeley, CA: University of California Press, 1989). The historical presentation of the early chapters of this study is somewhat clouded by the frequent interjection of quotes from Jungian analysts, but it remains useful. Carol Gilligan's *In a Different Voice* (Cambridge, MA: Harvard University Press, 1982) is relevant for its ground-breaking analysis of gender and morality. Two good introductions to feminist ethics are *Women's Consciousness, Women's Conscience: A Reader in Feminist Ethics,* ed. Barbara Hilkert Andolsen, Christine E. Gudorf, and Mary D. Pellauer (1985; San Francisco: Harper & Row, Publishers, 1987) and *Women and Values: Readings in Recent Feminist Philosophy,* ed. Marilyn Pearsall (Belmont, CA: Wadsworth Publishing Company, 1986), especially chapter 8, which is devoted to feminist ethics.

46. An intriguing discussion of metaphors and representations of the female body in the ancient world can be found in Page duBois, *Sowing the Body: Psychoanalysis and Ancient Representations of Women* (Chicago: University of Chicago Press, 1988). For an insightful feminist discussion of sexuality see Gayle Rubin, "Thinking Sex: Notes for a Radical Theory of the Politics of Sexuality," in *Pleasure and Danger: Exploring Female Sexuality,* ed. Carole S. Vance (Boston: Routledge & Kegan Paul, 1984), pp. 267–319.

47. For an important discussion of the religious valorization of female sexuality see Frédérique Apffel Marglin "Hierodouleia" in *Encyclopedia of Religion,* ed. Eliade, 6: 309–313.

48. The connection of women with the demonic, either women's supposed relations with male demons or as female demons, speaks of deep seated fears about women and is an area worthy of further study.

49. For more on Eve, see John A. Phillips, *Eve: The History of an Idea* (San Francisco: Harper & Row, 1984).

requires a set of controls or limitations on the activities of women. Often creation is brought about by a cosmic battle in which a young male sky god kills a primordial water or earth goddess associated with chaos and establishes law and order (Indra, Marduk).

Eastern religions also contain this idea. In China the cosmic duality of yin and yang which, for example, associates the male with heaven (spirit) and the female with earth (materiality), pervaded religious thought, and eventually this thinking spread throughout Asia. Stories abound of female sexual temptresses who try to prevent men from reaching their spiritual goals (The Biography of the Buddha, Shakuntala's mother).

2. *Menstruation Taboos.*   Myths of female evil combined with the association of women with the body and sexuality bring us to menstruation taboos.[50] Such taboos occur all over the world: Muslim women are forbidden to pray while menstruating; many tribal women withdraw to the outskirts of their villages while menstruating; in Shinto, menstruating women are denied access to sacred sites; a menstruating woman can render a Jewish man ritually unclean; and Pliny stated that menstrual blood does everything harmful, from blighting crops to rusting iron and bronze. From the male point of view, menstruation is seen as a powerful time for women, albeit in the negative sense that it enables women to pollute men, in some cases rendering men into women, thereby making them unfit to communicate with the divine. From the female point of view, it is often a time for women to celebrate their formidable (to themselves and to men) powers of fertility and creation. For young girls especially, their time of separation from the general community is also the time for their instruction by older women, who teach them the rituals and stories that prepare them for productive lives as women.

Pollution is not always gender specific. Pollution can be caused by contact with the dead, whether male or female, by eating a forbidden food, performing a proscribed act, etc.[51] Moreover, both men and women can be sexually polluted, men by semen and women by vaginal fluids. Frequently urine and feces pollute both women and men. But, by far, the major sources of pollution are specifically connected to women's bodies, especially, but not limited to, menstruation and childbirth. Sherry Ortner has noted in several cultures a connection between male honor and female pollution.[52] In other words, the more dependent men are on women for preserving male honor, usually through sexual fidelity but also through women's productive and reproductive abilities, the more women are perceived as threatening and polluting. Peggy Reeves Sanday notes that menstruation taboos can lead to the rigid separation of the sexes, and she finds the separation of the sexes to be a prerequisite for the domination of one sex over the other.[53]

3. *Witches.*[54]   In the West all these ideas about women as being evil, dangerous, sexual, and somewhat demonic merge in the concept of the witch. In antiquity witches were beautiful,

50. A somewhat dated but nonetheless useful overview of menstruation practices around the world can be found under the entry "Menstruation" in *Funk and Wagnalls Standard Dictionary of Folklore, Mythology, and Legend,* ed. Maria Leach (San Francisco: Harper & Row, 1972, 1949), pp. 706–707. For cautionary insights on women and pollution outside the Judeo/Christian traditions see Rohrlich-Leavitt, et al., "Aboriginal Women" in *Toward an Anthropology of Women,* ed. Reiter, pp. 117–118. See also Margaret Mead, *Male and Female: A Study of the Sexes in a Changing World* (1949; New York: William Morrow and Company, Inc., 1975), chapter eight, pp. 163–182 for a discussion of menstruation in five different tribal societies and its relationship to gender-specific labor.

51. A wide-ranging discussion of nonmenstrual sources of pollution is contained in Mary Douglas, *Purity and Danger: An analysis of the concepts of pollution and taboo* (London: Routledge & Kegan Paul, 1966, 1978).

52. Ortner, "Introduction," in *Sexual Meanings,* pp. 20–21.

53. Sanday, *Female Power and Male Dominance,* passim but especially pp. 91–110.

54. For further information on witches, see Serinity Young, "A Brief History of Witchcraft," *The Quest,* Summer, 1989, pp. 34–44; Julio Caro Baroja, *The World of the Witches,* trans. O.N.V. Glendinning (1961; Chicago: University of Chicago Press, 1964); *Witchcraft and Sorcery,* ed. Max Marwick (Harmondsworth, England: Penguin Books Ltd., 1970).

seductive, and very dangerous women, such as Circe and Medea. These were sexually active women living outside the binding structures of patriarchal society who could and did bring havoc into men's lives. European folklore continues some of these images, most notably in the figure of Morgan Le Fey; but in these tales witches live in isolated places, though they continue to possess forbidden knowledge about sexuality and fertility, and they are often old and ugly women. During four centuries of madness in Europe enormous numbers of women were tortured and killed in an attempt to stamp out feminine evil. Sometimes these were simple country women innocently repeating the actions of their ancestors (pagan practices), midwives pursuing their profession, Jewish women, heretics, etc. They were accused of being witches, which meant that they were understood to be women who had sex with the devil, killed children either in their rituals or through the practice of abortion, consorted with the dead, and were generally vindictive.

4. *Death*.[55]   Women are clearly associated with death in many cultures through their biological connection to birth, which inevitably leads to death, and through menstruation, where the shedding of blood does not kill the menstruating women but does threaten the males around her. Where burial in the earth is practiced, the earth or the grave is often spoken of as the womb, the idea being that after a brief time in this earth/womb one will be reborn, as from the mother's womb. Women were often in charge of burial rites (this is part of Antigone's story) and their lamentations are essential to death rituals.[56] Part of the secret lore attributed to women is knowledge of the land of the dead: Male heroes often must go to the land of the dead as one of their trials, and they are usually guided by a woman (Circe, Sybil in the *Aeneid*). In Norse legends the Valkyries choose which warriors will die and then take them to Valhalla. Additionally, female witches and other female diviners were believed to get their information about the past and the future from the dead. Goddesses of the dead and goddesses associated with death abound (Kālī/Durgā, Isthar/Inanna, Hathor, Isis, the Furies). In many cultures the origin of death is attributed to a mistake or the breaking of a taboo by a woman (Eve, Pandora) or to the appearance of sexual desire, where sexuality is associated with women.[57]

On the positive side, this association of the female with death frequently also means the association of females with immortality (Isis). This is to suggest that women have control over life and death to such a degree that they can free one from death. Also, returning to women's ability to give birth, women are seen as the source of their husband's immortality because they provide the sons so essential to the continuation of ancestor worship.

b. *Wisdom as Feminine*

Most religions value wisdom,[58] whether understood to be a practical knowledge of the right way to live or an esoteric knowledge of the secret workings of the universe. From the Sophia

55. See Th. P. van Baaren, "Death," in *Encyclopedia of Religion,* ed. Eliade, 4: 251–259 for a general overview of death in world religions.

56. Mary R. Lefkowitz, "Influential Women," in *Images of Women in Antiquity,* eds. Averil Cameron and Amélie Kuhrt (London and Canberra: Croom Helm, 1983), especially pp. 50–52. For ancient Egyptian practices see C. J. Bleeker, "Isis and Hahor: Two Ancient Egyptian Goddesses," in *The Book of the Goddess: Past and Present,* ed. Carl Olson (New York: Crossroad Publishing Company, 1989), pp. 34–35.

57. For a discussion of these associations and connections in the Hindu and Buddhist traditions, see Wendy Doniger O'Flaherty, *The Origins of Evil in Hindu Mythology,* pp. 27–35 and passim.

58. For an overview of the meaning of wisdom in world religion, see Kurt Rudolph, "Wisdom" in *Encyclopedia of Religion,* ed. Eliade, 15: 393–401. Though the author does not discuss wisdom in terms of its female symbolism, the thoughtful reader will find useful ideas.

of the ancient Greeks and Gnostics to the Prajñā of the Buddhists, wisdom is frequently referred to in feminine terms. That this is more than just a linguistic conceit based on the word wisdom being a feminine noun in several languages (e.g., *prajñā, sophia*) can be seen in the iconographic and literary developments of wisdom in explicitly feminine terms (Proverbs and sometimes Shekhinah). Significantly, more goddesses than gods are associated with wisdom and learning (Athena, Metis, Isis, Sarasvatī, Tārā). This feminization of wisdom is connected to the male need for the female (Steiner), as even the often woman-denying hero cycles[59] express when they require the male hero to win or coerce the aid (wisdom) of a female, who can be either an actual woman (Medea) or a goddess (Prajñā, the Valkyries). The overall idea is that woman can transform men, either negatively as witches do, or positively through wisdom.

c. *Dualities*[60]

Some traditions posit a primordial duality as the fundamental causal principle that underlies the universe and they describe this duality in terms of gender. Yin/yang is a leading example of this type. The creation stories of the Confucians as well as the Taoists reflect this understanding: from one primal something two emerged, yin and yang, female and male; and from the interaction of these two all else comes into being. This understanding, which can and did become explicitly hierarchical in Confucianism, suggests a necessary complementarity; you need both in order to have anything. Something of this idea is contained in Tantric Buddhist practices which emphasize achieving a balance between wisdom (*prajñā*), stated to be feminine, and skillful means (*upāya*), stated to be masculine. The Tantric adept must balance both in order to achieve enlightenment. A similar notion appears in Christian Science, which equates the female with life and love while the male is equated with intelligence and truth.

Equally often, though, such pairings are oppositional, rather than complimentary. The following is a list of some of the dualities that frequently appear in religious texts and which are represented in terms of gender:

Male	*Female*
good	evil
heaven	earth
powerful	yielding
light	dark
active	passive
strong	weak
spirit/soul	body/sexuality
order	chaos
reason	emotion
sacred	profane
the living	the dead
right	left[61]

---

59. Though his view of the female is limited, see Joseph Campbell, *The Hero With A Thousand Faces* (1949; New York: The World Publishing Company, 1956), pp. 116, 342–345; and *In Quest of the Hero,* compiled by Robert A. Segal (Princeton, NJ: Princeton University Press, 1990).

60. For an excellent introduction to the anthropological and sociological study of duality see *Right & Left: Essays on Dual Symbolic Classifications,* ed. Rodney Needham (Chicago: University of Chicago Press, 1973), especially the introduction and the articles by Hertz and Evans-Pritchard.

61. The dualities in this list have somewhat static assignments in contrast to, for example, auspicious/inauspicious: While women may be inauspicious more often than men, they can at different times be one or the other — for instance,

Because these dualities are cultural constructions, they are laden with value. Whether complementary or oppositional, dualities tend to be hierarchical; one is inevitably better thought of than the other. Further, when one values, for instance, spirituality over materiality, and these have gendered associations, the duality becomes a subtle, and sometimes not so subtle, support for the control and/or oppression of one gender by the other.

d. Goddesses[62]

Most religions include various feminine aspects of the divine such as independent goddesses, female consorts of male gods,[63] highly valued concepts such as Justice and Wisdom, or deified parts of nature (the earth, the moon, water), and indeed, nature itself.[64] It seems clear that when the earliest understanding of the divine included gender, it was female first and foremost.[65] In addition to the archaeological evidence of cave paintings and sculptures,[66] there are several creation myths that describe the slaying of a primordial goddess, often associated with chaos, by a young, male, thunder-wielding sky god (Indra, Marduk). Primordial battles such as these are also recorded in the historical conquests of goddess-worshiping people by god-worshiping people. This frequently resulted in the marriage, and consequent subjugation, of the goddess to the god and the transfer of cultic control from women to men (Delphi, Eleusis).[67]

Married or not, goddesses can be fierce and warlike (Athena, Brunhilde, Kālī/Durgā, Hathor), passive and compassionate (Pārvartī, the Virgin Mary[68]), virginal[69] (Aphrodite, the Virgin Mary), or sexual (Isthar, Cihuacoatl, Circe). They are powerful creators of the universe (Kālī/Durgā, ancient Near Eastern goddesses), the source of life and death and of the means to rebirth and transformation. Often they are associated with wisdom, learning, literacy, and culture (Athena, Umā, Saraswatī, Inanna, Isis, Sophia, Prajñā). Some goddesses have demonic and destructive aspects in their nature (Cihuacoatl, Kālī/Durgā, Hathor) but almost all are attributed with the life-giving and life-affirming powers of fertility associated with motherhood.

---

an auspicious bride versus an inauspicious widow. It is the same with pollution (in contrast to purity), which, while a constant possibility, is a temporary state that can be ritually reversed. For a clear statement about the analytical limitations, advantages, and dangers of such binary lists, see *Right & Left,* ed. Needham, pp. xxiii–xxx.

62. Two good recent collections of essays on the goddesses are *The Book of the Goddess: Past and Present,* ed. Carl Olson (New York: Crossroad Publishing Company, 1989) and *Mother Worship: Theme and Variations,* ed. James J. Preston (Chapel Hill, NC: University of North Carolina Press, 1982). A problematic but interesting study of European and Near Eastern goddesses is Miriam Robbins Dexter's *Whence the Goddesses: A Source Book* (New York: Pergamon Press, 1990). David Kinsley's *The Goddesses' Mirror: Visions of the Divine from East and West* (Albany, NY: State University of New York Press, 1989) is well researched and has a thoughtful introduction. Especially recommended is James J. Preston's "Goddess Worship: Theoretical Perspectives," in *Encyclopedia of Religion,* ed. Eliade, 6: 53–59, which provides a clear perspective for the study of goddesses.

63. An excellent study of consort goddesses in Hinduism is *The Divine Consort: Rādhā and the Goddesses of India,* ed. John Stratton Hawley and Donna Marie Wulff (1982; Boston: Beacon Press, 1986). For the ancient Greeks, see Philip E. Slater, *The Glory of Hera: Greek Mythology and the Greek Family* (Boston: Beacon Press, 1968, 1971).

64. For additional discussion on the feminine and divine aspects of nature, see Mircea Eliade, *Patterns in Comparative Religion,* trans. Rosemary Sheed (New York: New American Library, 1963, 1974), passim; and Nancy F. Auer Falk, "Feminine Sacrality," in *Encyclopedia of Religion,* ed. Eliade, 5: 303–308.

65. Merlin Stone, *When God Was a Woman* (1976; New York: Harcourt Brace Jovanovich, 1978).

66. Gimbutas, *The Goddesses and Gods of Old Europe.*

67. For a discussion of such events in ancient Greece, see Jane Harrison's *Prolegomena to the Study of Greek Religion,* especially p. 272, and passim (1903; Princeton, NJ: Princeton University Press, 1991).

68. Churches dedicated to Mary were frequently built on the same sites as sacred places of earlier goddesses, whose functions she assumed.

69. M. Esther Harding, *Woman's Mysteries: Ancient and Modern* (1971; Boston: Shambhala Publications, Inc. 1990); chapter nine is a discussion of the virgin goddess from a Jungian perspective.

The goddess is the Great Mother, the source of all life. In short, individual goddesses often manifest contradictory aspects. (In this they do not differ from their male counterparts; divinity is an unpredictable thing.)

The status of actual women in goddess worshiping societies, or societies that attribute certain aspects of the divine as feminine, is problematic.[70] For instance, Jewish Kabbalists spoke of and honored wisdom as feminine but did not include women in their circles; the Virgin Mary was worshiped throughout medieval Europe at a time when European women had few actual rights and could not be priests in her churches; widespread worship of the goddess in India did little to improve the lives of Indian women and, in fact, two prominent women in Hinduism, Mahādevīyakka and Mīrābāī, achieved their religious status while worshiping a male god. A recent study of goddess worshipers among the Hindus of Nepal reveals an interesting gender distinction: The men worship the fierce goddess Durgā in ceremonies designed to reveal what terrifies them about Durgā, and perhaps about women, and then resolve those fears through ritual appeasement of the goddess. Meanwhile, the women worship Pārvatī, the gentle, obedient, and long-suffering wife of the god Shiva.[71] Bennett suggests that such worship helps women to reconcile themselves to their own status and lived reality in patriarchal households.[72] The important point here is that the wild, fierce, and independent goddess Durgā is not a role model for these women; they take Pārvatī as their model, the goddess whose story describes their own reality.

The fact that some of the most independent and warlike goddesses are the product of male generation suggests the male control of their cults (Athena from the head of Zeus, Aphrodite from the sea foam that arose from Uranus's severed genitals, Kālī/Durgā from the combined energy of the male gods). For instance, the ancient Greeks believed that the goddesses and gods preferred being served by a priestess or priest who was like them. Thus, Mars was thought to want a warrior priest, Hera to want a married woman as her priestess, and so on. However, when it came to the powerful (in the political as well as in the religious sense) cults of Athena at Athens and Demeter at Eleusis, to cite only two examples, these centers were under the control of a powerful male priesthood with women limited to attending roles.

The worship of goddesses continues today in many traditional societies and is also a growing movement in the United States and Western Europe. Carol Christ,[73] Starhawk,[74] Margo Adler,[75] and Christine Downing[76] are a few of the authors who have inspired women to explore goddess spirituality.[77]

---

70. For some further discussion, see Sarah B. Pomeroy, *Goddesses, Whores, Wives, and Slaves: Women in Classical Antiquity* (New York: Schocken Books, 1975), especially chapter one.

71. Lynn Bennett, *Dangerous Wives and Sacred Sisters: Social and Symbolic Roles of High Caste Women in Nepal* (New York: Columbia University Press, 1983).

72. Ibid., pp. 273–274.

73. Carol Christ, "Why Women Need the Goddess: Phenomenological, Psychological and Political Reflections," in *Womanspirit Rising*, pp. 273–287; and *Laughter of Aphrodite: Reflections on a Journey to the Goddess* (San Francisco: Harper & Row, Publishers, 1988).

74. Starhawk, *The Spiral Dance: A Rebirth of the Ancient Religion of the Great Goddess* (San Francisco: Harper & Row, Publishers, 1979); and *Dreaming the Dark: Magic, Sex and Politics* (Boston: Beacon Press, 1982).

75. Margo Adler, *Drawing Down the Moon: Witches, Druids, Goddess-Worshipper, and Other Pagans in America Today* (Boston: Beacon Press, 1979, rev. ed., 1986).

76. Christine Downing, *The Goddess: Mythological Images of the Feminine* (New York: Crossroad Publishing Company, 1988).

77. In addition to various works cited at the beginning of this section, two very different but interesting studies are Sylvia Brinton Perera, *Descent to the Goddess: A Way of Initiation for Women* (Toronto: Inner City Books, 1981), a Jungian study; and Judith Gleason *Oya: In Praise of the Goddess* (Boston and London: Shambhala Publications, Inc., 1987), a study of the goddess Oya in Yoruba religion and in the Santeria movement of the Americas.

e. The Exceptional Woman/The Ideal Woman

Because men are represented as the normative models in religious texts and are the most frequent characters in such texts, men are offered a fairly wide range of religious role models. Women, on the other hand, have two problems with role models in religious texts: First, they must make do with the few women who are included in sacred texts. Second, most of the women who are represented in a positive light are exceptional or ideal. The danger, always, of such exceptional women is that they lead one to believe that actual women are represented in the text. They are not. The exceptional woman does not represent women; in fact, they often point to the absence of women, and they do women great harm by establishing an extreme model that normal women are unable to live up to. This is further complicated when these women suffer. All those female Christian martyrs, in the absence of other role models, could lead one to suspect that the only good woman is a dead woman; in the Hebrew Bible, Miriam gets leprosy while Aaron only receives an admonishment for the same act; in the Hindu tradition, after enduring exile and captivity, Sītā must undergo a trial by fire to prove her chastity. Sometimes, though, these women point to the earlier, powerful roles available to women that have disappeared from their tradition and their society.[78] One must bear in mind, however, that these were in all probability elite women. Always they speak of the power of the charismatic, female or male, to break boundaries (Joan of Arc, Mahādevīyakka). On the positive side they can inspire women to excellence and create an opening in gender roles, but they do not necessarily improve the general status of women.

f. Sex Change/Sex Disguise[79]

Sex changes most often reflect culturally perceived notions of prestige associated with gender.[80] In general, when women change into or disguise themselves as men they become heroic, but when men reverse their gender it often leads to powerlessness and humiliation. To say in patriarchal cultures that a woman is like a man is to say that she is more than or better than a woman.[81] One implication to be drawn from religious women being referred to as men is that to be heroic, to achieve success in religious terms, women must become men, they must abandon their female sexuality. Interestingly, both men and women do this, abandon their sexuality, when they take vows of celibacy, but with different consequences for women than for men. Few men are then perceived as women[82] but often celibate women are perceived as men (Rābi'āh, the Gospel of Thomas), or encouraged to actually become men (Tārā, Sāgara's daughter), or perceive themselves through this more prestigious term (Perpetua). In other words,

---

78. For a brief discussion of the various kinds of power available to women, see Jo Ann Hackett, "In the Days of Jael: Reclaiming the History of Women in Ancient Israel," in *Immaculate and Powerful: The Female in Sacred Image and Social Reality,* ed. Clarissa W. Atkinson, Constance H. Buchanan and Margaret R. Miles (Boston: Beacon Press, 1985), pp. 21–22.

79. For a comparative study of sex change and transvestism in religion, among both men and women, see Priscilla Rachun Linn, "Gender Roles" in *Encyclopedia of Religion,* ed. Eliade, 5: 495–502.

80. For more on this point see Ortner, "Introduction," in *Sexual Meanings,* pp. 13–24.

81. Significantly, Margaret Mills has found that the narrators of stories about women changing into or disguising themselves as men are usually men, not women. See "Sex Role Reversals," in *Women's Folklore,* ed. Jordan and Kalčik, pp. 187–213.

82. Notable exceptions appear among male worshipers of Dionysus and the male bhakta saints of India. The point, of course, is the converse: for a man to become a woman is to lose prestige, which is exactly what these god-drenched male mystics seek to do. An extreme example of sex change for men is found among the self-emasculated priests of the goddess Cybele.

religious women are asked to repudiate their gender, their womanhood, in ways that religious men are not. More frequently, however, as discussed above, male celibates persist in perceiving women as sexual temptresses, that is, as threats to their celibacy. The unnamed goddess in the Vimalakīrti Sūtra plays with these preconceptions in a highly creative way.[83]

Conferring masculinity upon women is not something restricted to ancient times and places. According to Ludwig Wittgenstein's latest biographer, the philosopher Elizabeth Anscombe became

> one of Wittgenstein's closest friends and one of his most trusted students, an exception to his general dislike of academic women and especially of female philosophers. She became, in fact, an honorary male, addressed by him affectionately as "old man." "Thank God we've got rid of the women!" he once said to her at a lecture, on finding, to his delight, that no (other) female students were in attendance.[84]

Sex disguise, for women at least, is often a matter of safety when traveling, or for convenience's sake, while ritual reversals of dress and gender roles are fairly common around the world.[85] In the normal course of affairs, though, most cultures discourage cross-dressing. For example, Joan of Arc's inquisitors kept insisting that she change back into women's clothes, and in pre-Christian Iceland cross-dressing was grounds for divorce (*Laxdaela Saga*).

g. *Women Religiosi*[86]

Women have acted as priests in the religious traditions of the ancient Near East, ancient Greece,[87] ancient Rome, the Celts, and in Shinto.[88] There were deaconesses in early Christianity and until quite recently in Greek Orthodoxy. Buddhism and Christianity have large numbers of nuns, as did Taoism, while Islam and Hinduism have orders of ascetic women. The earliest shamans seem to have been exclusively women, and many women, in all parts of the world, still function as shamans (Nisa, Yongsul's Mother).[89] Wherever there has been religion, women have had sacred functions. By this I mean that women have been religious experts, *religiosi,* in ways that, like their male counterparts, have set them apart, to a lesser or greater degree, from their society. In other words, as religious experts, whether male or female, they were, and are, understood by the members of their society to participate more fully in the sacred than the average person. They have taken sacred vows, been ordained or dedicated to the deity: some have received calls to serve through dreams and mystical experiences of

---

83. Another example of a divinity changing sex is Kuan Yin, who begins as a male deity but eventually becomes a female deity.
84. Ray Monk, *Wittgenstein: The Duty of Genius* (New York: The Free Press, 1990), p. 498.
85. See Linn, "Gender Roles," *Encyclopedia of Religion,* ed. Eliade, 5: 495–502, for some examples.
86. For an overview of various kind of *religiosi* in world religions, though one which emphasizes men, see Joachim Wach, *The Sociology of Religion* (Chicago: University of Chicago Press, 1944), pp. 331–374. Prehistoric evidence for the existence of priestesses and priests in Europe is discussed in Johannes Maringer, "Priests and Priestesses in Prehistoric Europe," in *The History of Religions,* vol. 17, 1979, pp. 101–120.
87. Herbert Jennings Rose, "Priests" in *The Oxford Classical Dictionary* (Oxford: The Clarendon Press, 2nd ed. 1970), pp. 876–877. Quite a bit of this article actually discusses the priestesses of Athena.
88. A recent study of ancient priestesses is Norma Loore Goodrich, *Priestesses* (New York: Franklin Watts, 1989). This needs to be read with a grain of salt, since the author often stretches the sources beyond reasonable limits.
89. Weston La Barre, *The Ghost Dance: The Origins of Religion* (New York: Dell Publishing Co., Inc., 1970, 1972), chapter three, contains an intriguing discussion, based on Freudian psychology, in which he suggests that the shaman is a product of the preoedipal stage of human development, and therefore is mother centered, while the priest is a product of the postoedipal stage, and therefore is father centered.

various kinds, and some have inherited their positions. Usually they have gone through a period of training, a novitiate, an initiation, an ordeal. Quite frequently they are believed to be in direct communication with the divine. However, male control of female *religiosi* is widespread from the ancient world to the present day, while female control of male *religiosi* is extremely rare.

As individual saints or mystics, women have achieved the highest goals of their faiths, though their lives frequently reveal opposition and disapproval that is gender specific. Individual women have also functioned as diviners and healers, who straddle the divine and profane realms in ways that enable them to transmit highly valued information from one realm to the other. Often, but not always, these women are celibate.

h. *Myths and Stories of Gender Conflict*

Many myths describe a primordial conflict between the sexes in which men wrest power from women (Australia, the Amazon, the *Eumenides*), often by gaining control of sacred implements or, as in the case of the god Apollo, by taking over a sacred site (Delphi). Apollo is one of many young male sky gods who are renowned for killing a primordial female dragon or snake. (See also Marduk and Indra.) In many cultures snakes, reptiles, and other terrestrial and subterranean creatures such as dragons[90] are frequently associated with the goddess, particularly with the goddess's powers of regeneration and rebirth.[91] Snakes are especially convenient symbols for representing regeneration and rebirth because of their ability to shed their skins and thereby renew themselves. Such associations give rise to new questions about Eve's relationship with the snake in the Garden of Eden: Could the snake represent an ancient goddess cult that honored knowledge and sexuality?

Women do not always lose in these conflicts (Tārā). Women mystics in particular seem to be able to turn around any arguments used against them through their powerful command of language and their ability to get at the core of the traditions where gender is not an issue (Mahādevīyakka, Somā, the *Vimalakīrti*). Quite often, though, victory is gained through women denying their gender (Perpetua) or in men denying it for them (*Gospel of Thomas,* 'Aṭṭār on Rābi'āh). Joan of Arc is a tragic example of a woman mystic who lost a gender conflict.

These myths and stories can be understood as dramatizations of psychological conflicts between gendered beings or as records of historical events, such as the conquest of a goddess-worshiping people by a god-worshiping people, which are historically well documented in many cultures.[92] The fact that these stories continue to be told demonstrates their enduring meaning for humanity. At the same time, these stories also can be, and have been, used as explanations of the will of the gods, or the ancestors, who want social realities of inequality to remain as they are.

Conclusion

I have tried to suggest some of the ways one can look at women in world religion—now I would like to suggest some of the implications of such study. First and foremost, the study

---

90. Interestingly, Euripides said dragons drove Medea's chariot, and Jane Harrison discusses the Furies who pursue Orestes, the Erinys, as snakes and even as dragons, *Prolegomena,* pp. 232–238.

91. For an excellent overview of connections between snakes and goddesses, see Miriam Robbins Dexter, *Whence the Goddesses,* pp. 3–11. See also two works by Marija Gimbutas: *The Language of the Goddess* (San Francisco: Harper San Francisco, 1991), chapter 14, pp. 121–137, for a discussion of snakes and snake goddesses, and chapters 18–24, pp. 187–275, for a discussion of the goddess and regeneration; and her earlier work, *The Goddesses and Gods of Old Europe,* especially chapters 7 and 8, pp. 112–200.

92. The way the hero Gilgamesh insults the goddess Ishtar and her inability to revenge herself is in this genre.

of women in world religion radically alters our understanding of religion: not only our understanding of who participates in religion, but also our understanding of what constitutes religious actions and how we read religious texts.

Further, such a study requires a response or reaction because it is value laden for each and every one of us on the most basic and essential human level, that of our spiritual life. Religion is much more than Whitehead's formulation that "Religion is what the individual does with his [sic] own solitariness." Religion, through its cultural ramifications, is done to us willing or no. Feminist challenges to religion, by both women and men, are changing contemporary religious life as is the modern goddess movement in the West with its resurrection of ancient models of female divinity. As in the past, such changes in spiritual life will lead to changes in cultural life. In other words, the overturning of traditional religious ideas that have been sources of oppression for women can lead to the overturning of one of the major sources of that oppression.[93]

★ ★ ★

Any work sustained over a long period of time, as this book has been, ends up involving scores of people who provided encouragement, made casual suggestions that proved helpful, found sources, read various parts in manuscript form, and offered their insights. First and foremost thanks go to Claude B. Conyers, who early on in this project offered enthusiastic support and concrete advice and who suggested some of the themes this work explores. Many scholars and friends have been of inestimable assistance by sharing their expertise with me. I would like to thank Diana and Arthur Altschul, Peter Banos, Paul Bernabeo, Jean Rhys Bram, Charles Eagan, Robley Evans, Richard Freedman, Eugene Gallagher, Barbara Gombach, Richard Grigg, Susannah Heschel, Ada-Maria Isasi-Diaz, Lozang Jamspal, Laurel Kendall, Adele McCollum, Richard Moorton, Vivian-Lee Nyitray, Jane O'Reilly, Aracelia Pearson-Brok, Irene Schneyder, Barbara C. Sproul, Stuart Smithers, Richard Stein, Vernie J. Taylor, and Dennis Washburn. Students who have taken my courses, especially at Hunter College where I first taught women and world religion, challenged and inspired me. Their responses have contributed a great deal to this book.

Three women's groups have provided abundant amounts of emotional, intellectual, and spiritual support. Since the early 1980s, Feminist Scholars of Religion has been a core group for me. The shared excitement and enthusiasm for the feminist study of religion has been both enlightening and inspiring. Among this group Beverly Wildung Harrison has never wavered in her support of me and has always kept me thinking. Of more recent vintage are the Dreadful Dakinis, an anarchistic and far-flung group of women involved in the study and practice of Buddhism. I want to particularly thank Lu Lu Hamlin, April Wolff, and Pirjo Squillante, who are always there. The Third Thursdays Women Writers' Group has been and remains incredible: wonderful, warm, wickedly funny women writers full out.

Special thanks to Carol Dysinger, Rawn Harding, Tim Harwood, Marguerite Holloway, and Mary Larkin Hughes, long-time friends who listened to me, prodded me along, and generally made life great.

Library staffs at the following institutions made this book possible: Connecticut College, the American Museum of Natural History, the Butler and Lehman Libraries at Columbia University, and Union Theological Seminary.

Finally, to my editor Frank Oveis for his faith in this project, encouragement, and formidable editorial skills.

---

93. See Sanday, *Female Power and Male Dominance,* pp. 11–12 and passim.

JUDAISM

Introduction

Historically Judaism began during what is called the Age of the Patriarchs (c. 2000 B.C.E.-1600 B.C.E.) in the area of the Middle East around the present day state of Israel from where it spread throughout the world. Faithful Jews believe that God, most often referred to as Yahweh, acts in history and that historical events reveal the Jews to be Yahweh's chosen people, whether he chooses to chastise them for their transgressions or to affirm their righteousness with victory. Consequently, history is a key theological issue and a source of revelation for God's will.

The sacred book of the Jews is the Hebrew Bible, or Tanakh, a collection of texts believed to have been divinely inspired and which is authoritative for Jewish practice and faith. The first five books are called the Torah or the Five Books of Moses, and they contain laws and ritual prescriptions as well as descriptions of the early period of Jewish history and of God's part in that history. This includes the migration into Egypt, the exodus back to Canaan and the establishment of the Israelite monarchy. Other books of the Hebrew Bible continue the history of the Jews.

Of great importance to Jewish self-understanding and messianic hope is the fact that since the final fall of the Israelite monarchy to Babylonia in 586 B.C.E. until the founding of the modern state of Israel in 1948 Jews have been ruled by non-Jews. A formative event from this ancient period was the exile in Babylonia in the sixth century B.C.E. when conquering Babylonian kings forcibly took the leading Jewish citizens to Babylonia where they remained for approximately seventy years. This was a defining period in Jewish history and for Jewish consciousness, consequently sections of the Hebrew Bible are referred to as preexilic or post-exilic. This period of exile and the Roman destruction of Jerusalem and expulsion of the Jews from Jerusalem in 70 C.E. mark the beginning of the Jewish *diaspora,* the dispersion.

One way the Jewish tradition survived was through Rabbinic Judaism, or the Judaism of the rabbis, which originated perhaps as early as the fifth century B.C.E. and which eventually became the normative form of Jewish practice. While non-Jews and the Jewish tradition itself spoke of the dignity and bravery of individual Jewish women, in general the rabbinic tradition perceives women, going back to Eve, as wholly other than men. This notion is most vividly expressed in the daily prayer of Jewish men who thank God for not making them a gentile, a slave, or a woman.

Women were essentially excluded or at least limited in their access to two major aspects of Jewish spiritual life, Torah study and the public rituals of the synagogue. A third aspect of Jewish spiritual life, domestic rituals, was and is very much the realm of Jewish women. First and foremost, women have traditionally been more knowledgeable than men with regard to the kosher laws governing diet. Of equal importance are the domestic rituals performed once a week, on the Sabbath, especially the lighting of the candles by the women, which affirm family life as central to Judaism.

The *mikvah,* the ritual bath women take after menstruating, has been and remains an important focus of women's spirituality and women's community. Through this shared ritual women can come together in a woman-centered environment which renews them, by reestablishing their purity, and by connecting them with the generations of women who preceded them in this practice.

Both men and women are enjoined to marry—celibacy has never held a prominent place in Judaism. Sexuality and procreation are essential parts of the Jewish faith and are carefully regulated to keep them in harmony with the divine will. There is, however, something of a double message in Judaism regarding sex because, on the one hand, a main source of impurity is any issue from the sexual organs, but at the same time marital relations are in general considered good and are most auspicious on Sabbath evening. Divorce was controlled by the husband, not the wife, and while there were protections for wives in case of divorce there was little recourse for an unhappily married woman.

The mystical tradition of Judaism, especially as formulated around the Kabbala movement that began in Spain during the Middle Ages, drew on Biblical feminine symbols such as wisdom and the Shekhinah, the visible and/or audible manifestations of God's presence among his people. Various mystical writings develop these and other concepts more fully and stress their feminine aspects. As with all idealizations, this did not necessarily gain actual women entry into mystical circles and the concept of feminine evil is also powerfully alive in these texts in the form of the demon Lilith.

Biblical Period

CREATION

GENESIS 1–3

The creation story of the Jews, and later of the Christians and the Muslims, is contained in the first book of the Hebrew Bible. These five books of the Bible were compiled and edited over five centuries. The first book was called Genesis by its third century B.C.E. Greek translators, but its Hebrew name is Bereshit which means "in the beginning," the opening words of the first chapter.

In actuality, there are two versions of creation, Genesis 1:1–2:4a, c. 400 B.C.E., and Gen. 2:4b–3:24, c. 850 B.C.E. During the time these two versions were being compiled and edited Israel was conquered by Assyria (c. 722 B.C.E.), followed by the conquest of Jerusalem by the Babylonians (c. 598 B.C.E.), the exile in Babylonia, and the gradual return to Jerusalem (c. 598–458 B.C.E.). The two creation stories reflect these historical events in several ways. For instance, Genesis 2:4b–3:24, composed during the confident period of kingdom, emphasizes the creation of human beings (God created them on the same day as the earth and the heavens) while Genesis 1:1–2:4a, composed after the loss of kingdom and the Babylonian exile, emphasizes creation itself (human beings are not created until the sixth day). Additionally, Gen. 1:1–2:4a shows some parallels to the Babylonian story of creation, the *Enuma Elish,* in which a male sky god conquers and puts into order the dark and watery chaos represented by a primordial goddess.

The following table brings out a few of the differences between these two stories:

Gen. 1:1–2:4a (c. 400 B.C.E.)	Gen. 2:4b–3:24 (c. 850 B.C.E.)
Creation of universe	Creation of human beings
Simultaneous creation of Adam & Eve (Eve equal)	Eve created from Adam's rib (as his helper)
Made in God's image	Made from dirt
Both given dominion over all other creatures	No dominion but Adam names the other creatures
No Eden, no Fall	Garden of Eden, Tree of Knowledge, the Fall

Chapter 3 of Genesis continues the story of Gen. 2:4ff. and introduces the character of the serpent who encourages Eve to eat of the Tree of Knowledge in order to become wise.

She does so and then offers some of this fruit to Adam, who accepts it. When God questions them about eating this fruit each blames another: Adam blames Eve and Eve blames the serpent. However, God's wrath comes down on all of them and defines the sufferings that will be associated with each sex for all time: Eve (women) will give birth in pain and be ruled by men while Adam (men) shall rule over women and struggle for their food; both lose their immortality.

Genesis 1–3

When God began to create heaven and earth — the earth being unformed and void, with darkness over the surface of the deep and a wind from God sweeping over the water — God said, "Let there be light"; and there was light. God saw that the light was good, and God separated the light from the darkness. God called the light Day, and the darkness He called Night. And there was evening and there was morning, a first day.

God said, "Let there be an expanse in the midst of the water, that it may separate water from water." God made the expanse, and it separated the water which was below the expanse from the water which was above the expanse. And it was so. God called the expanse Sky. And there was evening and there was morning, a second day.

God said, "Let the water below the sky be gathered into one area, that the dry land may appear." And it was so. God called the dry land Earth and the gathering of waters He called Seas. And God saw that this was good. And God said, "Let the earth sprout vegetation: seed-bearing plants, fruit trees of every kind on earth that bear fruit with the seed in it." And it was so. The earth brought forth vegetation: seed-bearing plants of every kind, and trees of every kind bearing fruit with the seed in it. And God saw that this was good. And there was evening and there was morning, a third day.

God said, "Let there be lights in the expanse of the sky to separate day from night; they shall serve as signs for the set times — the days and the years; and they shall serve as lights in the expanse of the sky to shine upon the earth." And it was so. God made the two great lights, the greater light to dominate the day and the lesser light to dominate the night, and the stars. And God set them in the expanse of the sky to shine upon the earth, to dominate the day and the night, and to separate light from darkness. And God saw that this was good. And there was evening and there was morning, a fourth day.

God said, "Let the waters bring forth swarms of living creatures, and birds that fly above the earth across the expanse of the sky." God created the great sea monsters, and all the living creatures of every kind that creep, which the waters brought forth in swarms, and all the winged birds of every kind. And God saw that this was good. God blessed them, saying, "Be fertile and increase, fill the waters in the seas, and let the birds increase on the earth." And there was evening and there was morning, a fifth day.

God said, "Let the earth bring forth every kind of living creature: cattle, creeping things, and wild beasts of every kind." And it was so. God made wild beasts of every kind and cattle of every kind, and all kinds of creeping things of the earth. And God saw that this was good. And God said, "Let us make man in our image, after our likeness. They shall rule the fish of the sea, the birds of the sky, the cattle, the whole earth, and all the creeping things that creep on earth." And God created man in His image, in the image of God He created him; male and female He created them. God blessed them and God said to them, "Be fertile and increase, fill the earth and master it; and rule the fish of the sea, the birds of the sky, and all the living things that creep on earth."

God said, "See, I give you every seed-bearing plant that is upon all the earth, and every tree that has seed-bearing fruit; they shall be yours for food. And to all the animals on land, to all the birds of the sky, and to everything that creeps on earth, in which there is the breath of life, [I give] all the green plants for food." And it was so. And God saw all that He had made, and found it very good. And there was evening and there was morning, the sixth day.

The heaven and the earth were finished, and all their array. On the seventh day God finished the work that He had been doing, and He ceased on the seventh day from all the work that He had done. And God blessed the seventh day and declared it holy, because on it God ceased from all the work of creation that He had done. Such is the story of heaven and earth when they were created.

When the LORD God made earth and heaven — when no shrub of the field was yet on earth and no grasses of the field had yet sprouted, because the LORD God had not sent rain upon the earth and there was no man to till the soil, but a flow would well up from the ground and water the whole surface of the earth — the LORD God formed man from the dust of the earth. He blew into his nostrils the breath of life, and man became a living being.

The LORD God planted a garden in Eden, in the east, and placed there the man whom He had formed. And from the ground the LORD God caused to grow every tree that was pleasing to the sight and good for food, with the tree of life in the middle of the garden, and the tree of knowledge of good and bad.

A river issues from Eden to water the garden, and it then divides and becomes four branches. The name of the first is Pishon, the one that winds through the whole land of Havilah, where the gold is. The gold of that land is good; bdellium is there, and lapis lazuli. The name of the second river is Gihon, the one that winds through the whole land of Cush. The name of the third river is Tigris, the one that flows east of Asshur. And the fourth river is the Euphrates.

The LORD God took the man and placed him in the garden of Eden, to till it and tend it. And the LORD God commanded the man, saying, "Of every tree of the garden you are free to eat; but as for the tree of knowledge of good and bad, you must not eat of it; for as soon as you eat of it, you shall die."

The LORD God said, "It is not good for man to be alone; I will make a fitting helper for him." And the LORD God formed out of the earth all the wild beasts and all the birds of the sky, and brought them to the man to see what he would call them; and whatever the man called each living creature, that would be its name. And the man gave names to all the cattle and to the birds of the sky and to all the wild beasts; but for Adam no fitting helper was found. So the LORD God cast a deep sleep upon the man; and while he slept, He took one of his ribs and closed up the flesh at that spot. And the LORD God fashioned the rib that He had taken from the man into a woman; and He brought her to the man. Then the man said,

"This one at last
Is bone of my bones
And flesh of my flesh.
This one shall be called Woman,
For from man was she taken."

Hence a man leaves his father and mother and clings to his wife, so that they become one flesh. The two of them were naked, the man and his wife, yet they felt no shame.

Now the serpent was the shrewdest of all the wild beasts that the LORD God had made. He said to the woman, "Did God really say: You shall not eat of any tree of the garden?" The woman replied to the serpent, "We may eat of the fruit of the other trees of the garden. It is only about fruit of the tree in the middle of the garden that God said: 'You shall not eat of it or touch it, lest you die.'" And the serpent said to the woman, "You are not going to die, but God knows that as soon as you eat of it your eyes will be opened and you will be like divine beings who know good and bad." When the woman saw that the tree

was good for eating and a delight to the eyes, and that the tree was desirable as a source of wisdom, she took of its fruit and ate. She also gave some to her husband, and he ate. Then the eyes of both of them were opened and they perceived that they were naked; and they sewed together fig leaves and made themselves loincloths.

They heard the sound of the LORD God moving about in the garden at the breezy time of day; and the man and his wife hid from the LORD God among the trees of the garden. The LORD God called out to the man and said to him, "Where are you?" He replied, "I heard the sound of You in the garden, and I was afraid because I was naked, so I hid." Then He asked, "Who told you that you were naked? Did you eat of the tree from which I had forbidden you to eat?" The man said, "The woman You put at my side—she gave me of the tree, and I ate." And the LORD God said to the woman, "What is this you have done!" The woman replied, "The serpent duped me, and I ate." Then the LORD God said to the serpent,

"Because you did this,
More cursed shall you be
Than all cattle
And all the wild beasts:
On your belly shall you crawl
And dirt shall you eat
All the days of your life.
I will put enmity
Between you and the woman,
And between your offspring and hers;
They shall strike at your head,
And you shall strike at their heel."

And to the woman He said,

"I will make most severe
Your pangs in childbearing;
In pain shall you bear children.
Yet your urge shall be for your husband,
And he shall rule over you."

To Adam He said, "Because you did as your wife said and ate of the tree about which I commanded you, 'You shall not eat of it,'

Cursed be the ground because of you;
By toil shall you eat of it
All the days of your life:
Thorns and thistles shall it sprout for you.
But your food shall be the grasses of the field;
By the sweat of your brow
Shall you get bread to eat,
Until you return to the ground—
For from it you were taken.
For dust you are,
And to dust you shall return."

The man named his wife Eve, because she was the mother of all the living. And the LORD God made garments of skins for Adam and his wife, and clothed them.

And the LORD God said, "Now that the man has become like one of us, knowing good and bad, what if he should stretch out his hand and take also from the tree of life and eat, and live forever!" So the LORD God banished him from the garden of Eden, to till the soil from which he was taken. He drove the man out, and stationed east of the garden of Eden the cherubim and the fiery ever-turning sword, to guard the way to the tree of life.

LILITH AND EVE IN THE LATER TRADITION

Lilith. In his seven volume work *The Legends of the Jews* (1909) Louis Ginzberg compiled various Jewish legends, some of which date back to antiquity. The following excerpt fills in the details of the two creation stories of Genesis by having two separate women created: Lilith, who was created simultaneously with Adam (Gen. 1), and Eve, who was created later, from Adam's rib (Gen. 2). Lilith leaves Adam because he will not treat her as an equal, though variants on this legend say that Lilith insisted on being on top when they had sex. As Lilith is demonized by the tradition her sexuality is exploited and she becomes a succubus, a female night demon who lies on top of sleeping men and forces them to copulate with her. Such nightly emissions of semen were believed to be particularly dangerous because they led to the birth of even more demons. Another part of Lilith's demonic aspect is that she becomes a killer of newborn infants and a threat to women during childbirth. With the creation of Eve, the legend shows that the separate natures of women and men hearken back to the time of creation and affirms marriage because God himself performs the first wedding ceremony.

The Divine resolution to bestow a companion on Adam met the wishes of man, who had been overcome by a feeling of isolation when the animals came to him in pairs to be named. To banish his loneliness, Lilith was first given to Adam as wife. Like him she had been created out of the dust of the ground. But she remained with him only a short time, because she insisted upon enjoying full equality with her husband. She derived her rights from their identical origin. With the help of the Ineffable Name, which she pronounced, Lilith flew away from Adam, and vanished in the air. Adam complained before God that the wife He had given him had deserted him, and God sent forth three angels to capture her. They found her in the Red Sea, and they sought to make her go back with the threat that, unless she went, she would lose a hundred of her demon children daily by death. But Lilith preferred this punishment to living with Adam. She takes her revenge by injuring babes—baby boys during the first night of their life, while baby girls are exposed to her wicked designs until they are twenty days old. The only way to ward off the evil is to attach an amulet bearing the names of the three angel captors to the children, for such had been the agreement between them.

The woman destined to become the true companion of man was taken from Adam's body, for "only when like is joined unto like the union is dissoluble."

The creation of woman from man was possible because Adam originally had two faces, which were separated at the birth of Eve.

When God was on the point of making Eve, He said: "I will not make her from the head of man, lest she carry her head high in arrogant pride; not from the eye, lest she be wanton-eyed; not from the ear, lest she be an eavesdropper; not from the neck, lest she be insolent; not from the mouth, lest she be a tattler; not from the heart, lest she be inclined to envy; not from the hand, lest she be a meddler; not from the foot, lest she be a gadabout. I will form her from a chaste portion of the body," and to every limb and organ as He formed it, God said, "Be chaste! Be chaste!" Nevertheless, in spite of the great caution used, woman has all the faults God tried to obviate. The daughters of Zion were haughty and walked with stretched forth necks and wanton eyes; Sarah was an eavesdropper in her own tent, when the angel spoke with Abraham; Miriam was a talebearer, accusing Moses; Rachel was envious of her sister Leah; Eve put out her hand to take the forbidden fruit, and Dinah was a gadabout.

The physical formation of woman is far more complicated than that of man, as it must be for the function of childbearing, and likewise the intelligence of woman matures more quickly than the intelligence of man. Many of the physical and psychical differences between the two sexes must be attributed to the fact that man was formed from the ground and woman from bone. Women need perfumes, while men do not; dust of the ground remains the same no matter how long it is kept; flesh, however, requires salt to keep it in good condition. The voice of women is shrill, not so the voice of men; when soft viands are cooked, no sound is heard, but let a bone be put in a pot, and at once it crackles. A man is easily placated, not so a woman; a few drops of water suffice to soften a clod of earth; a bone stays hard, even if it were to soak in water for days. The man must ask the woman to be his wife, not the woman the man to be her husband, because it is man who has sustained the loss of his rib, and he sallies forth to make good his loss again. The very differences between the sexes in garb and social forms go back to the origin of man and woman for their reasons. Woman covers her hair in token of Eve's having brought sin into the world; she tries to hide her shame; and women precede men in a funeral cortege, because it was woman who brought death into the world. And the religious commands addressed to women alone are connected with the history of Eve. Adam was the heave offering of the world, and Eve defiled it. As expiation, all women are commanded to separate a heave offering from the dough. And because woman extinguished the light of man's soul, she is bidden to kindle the Sabbath light.

Adam was first made to fall into deep sleep before the rib for Eve was taken from his side. For, had he watched her creation, she would not have awakened love in him. To this day it is true that men do not appreciate the charms of women they have known and observed from childhood up. Indeed, God has created a wife for Adam before Eve, but he would not have her, because she had been made in his presence. Knowing well all the details of her formation, he was repelled by her. But when he roused himself from his profound sleep, and saw Eve before him in all her surprising beauty and grace, he exclaimed, "This is she who caused my heart to throb many a night!" Yet he discerned at once what the nature of woman was. She would, he knew, seek to carry her point with man either by entreaties and tears, or flattery and caresses. He said, therefore, "This is my never-silent bell!"

The wedding of the first couple was celebrated with pomp never repeated in the whole course of history since. God Himself, before presenting her to Adam, attired and adorned Eve as a bride. Yea, He appealed to the angels, saying: "Come, let us perform services of friendship for Adam and his helpmate, for the world rests upon friendly services, and they are more pleasing in my sight than the sacrifices Israel will offer upon the altar." The angels accordingly surrounded the marriage canopy, and God pronounced the blessings upon the bridal couple, as the Hazan does under the Huppah. The angels then danced and played upon musical instruments before Adam and Eve in their ten bridal chambers of gold, pearls, and precious stones, which God had prepared for them.

[From Louis Ginzberg, *The Legends of the Jews*, pp. 65–68.

Eve. Eve remains a touchstone for the religious understanding of women both in Judaism and Christianity and, to a somewhat lesser extent, in Islam. The rabbinic literature explicitly describes three routine aspects of Jewish women's spiritual life as reminders of Eve's transgression, which they believe led to Adam's death. These are the lighting of the Sabbath lamp (Adam was the light of the world), the ritual connected with making the Sabbath bread (Adam was the pure bread or leaven), and menstruation practices (Adam was the blood of life). (P. *Shabbat*, 2, 5b, 34; *Genesis Rabbah* 17:7)

The following excerpts from "The Books of Adam and Eve," a first- or second-century work contained in the Pseudepigrapha, elaborate upon Eve's transgression and later life.

When they were driven out from paradise, they made themselves a booth, and spent seven days mourning and lamenting in great grief.

But after seven days, they began to be hungry and started to look for victual to eat, and they found it not. Then Eve said to Adam 'My lord, I am hungry. Go, look for (something) for us to eat. Perchance the Lord God will look back and pity us and recall us to the place in which we were before.'

And Adam arose and walked seven days over all that land, and found no victual such as they used to have in paradise. And Eve said to Adam: 'Wilt thou slay me that I may die, and perchance God the Lord will bring thee into paradise, for on my account hast thou been driven thence.' Adam answered: 'Forbear, Eve, from such words, that peradventure God bring not some other curse upon us. How is it possible that I should stretch forth my hand against my own flesh?

Nay, let us arise and look for something for us to live on, that we fail not.'

And they walked about and searched for nine days, and they found none such as they were used to have in paradise, but found only animals' food. And Adam said to Eve: 'This hath the Lord provided for animals and brutes to eat; but we used to have angels' food. But it is just and right that we lament before the sight of God who made us. Let us repent with a great penitence: perchance the Lord will be gracious to us and will pity us and give us a share of something for our living.'

And we sat together before the gate of paradise, Adam weeping with his face bent down to the earth, lay on the ground lamenting. And seven days passed by and we had nothing to eat and were consumed with great hunger, and I Eve cried with a loud voice: 'Pity me, O Lord, My Creator; for my sake Adam suffereth thus!'

And I said to Adam: 'Rise up! my lord, that we may seek us food; for now my spirit faileth me and my heart within me is brought low.' Then Adam spake to me: 'I have thoughts of killing thee, but I fear since God created thine image and thou showest penitence and criest to God; hence my heart hath not departed from thee.'

And Adam arose and we roamed through all lands and found nothing to eat save nettles (and) grass of the field. And we returned again to the gates of paradise and cried aloud and entreated: 'Have compassion on thy creature. O Lord Creator, allow us food.'

And for fifteen days continuously we entreated. Then we heard Michael the archangel and Joel praying for us, and Joel the archangel was commanded by the Lord, and he took a seventh part of paradise and gave it to us. Then the Lord said: 'Thorns and thistles shall spring up from under thy hands; and from thy sweat shalt thou eat (bread), and thy wife shall tremble when she looketh upon thee.'

The archangel Joel said to Adam: 'Thus saith the Lord; I did not create thy wife to command thee, but to obey; why art thou obedient to thy wife?' Again Joel the archangel bade Adam separate the cattle and all kinds of flying and creeping things and animals, both wild and tame; and to give names to all things. Then indeed he took the oxen and began to plough.

[From *"The Books of Adam and Eve," The Apocrypha and Pseudepigrapha*, p. 134]

And Eve said to Adam: 'Live thou, my Lord, to thee life is granted, since thou hast committed neither the first nor the second error. But I have erred and been led astray for I have not kept the commandment of God; and now banish me from the light of thy life and I will go to the sunsetting, and there will I be, until I die.' And she began to walk towards the western parts and to mourn and to weep bitterly and groan aloud. And she made there a booth, while she had in her womb offspring of three months old.

And when the time of her bearing approached, she began to be distressed with pains, and she cried aloud to the Lord and said: 'Pity me, O Lord, assist me.' And she was not heard and the mercy of God did not encircle her. And she said to herself: 'Who shall tell my lord Adam? I implore you, ye luminaries of heaven, what time ye return to the east, bear a message to my lord Adam.

But in that hour, Adam said: 'The complaint of Eve hath come to me. Perchance, once more hath the serpent fought with her.' And he went and found her in great distress. And Eve said: 'From the moment I saw thee, my lord, my grief-laden soul was refreshed. And now entreat the Lord God on my behalf to hearken unto thee and look upon me and free me from my awful pains.' And Adam entreated the Lord for Eve.

And behold, there came twelve angels and two 'virtues', standing on the right and on the left of Eve; and Michael was standing on the right; and he stroked her on the face as far as to the breast and said to Eve: 'Blessed art thou, Eve, for Adam's sake. Since his prayers and intercessions are great, I have been sent that thou mayst receive our help. Rise up now, and prepare thee to bear. And she bore a son and he was shining; and at once the babe rose up and ran and bore a blade of grass in his hands, and gave it to his mother, and his name was called Cain.

[From "The Books of Adam and Eve," *The Apocrypha and Pseudepigrapha*, p. 137–138]

SARAH

Traditionally Judaism begins with the first patriarch, Abraham, and his experience of God, Yahweh, and the establishment of the covenant between Yahweh and Abraham that Abraham shall found a great nation. Yahweh also announces that the mother of nation will be Abraham's wife, Sarah (Gen. 17:15–16), even though she is barren (Gen. 11:30).

One of the most peculiar incidents in this narrative occurs when Abraham and Sarah go to Egypt and Sarah ends up in the Pharaoh's harem. Yahweh shows his favor toward Sarah by punishing Pharaoh who then sets her free.

Genesis 12:10–20

There was a famine in the land, and Abram went down to Egypt to sojourn there, for the famine was severe in the land. As he was about to enter Egypt, he said to his wife Sarai, "I know what a beautiful woman you are. If the Egyptians see you, and think, 'She is his wife,' they will kill me and let you live. Please say that you are my sister, that it may go well with me because of you, and that I may remain alive thanks to you."

When Abram entered Egypt, the Egyptians saw how very beautiful the woman was. Pharaoh's courtiers saw her and praised her to Pharaoh, and the woman was taken to Pharaoh's palace. And because of her, it went well with Abram; he acquired sheep, oxen, asses, male and female slaves, she-asses, and camels.

But the LORD afflicted Pharaoh and his household with mighty plagues on account of Sarai, the wife of Abram. Pharaoh sent for Abram and said, "What is this you have done to me! Why did you not tell me that she was your wife? Why did you say, 'She is my sister,' so that I took her as my wife? Now, here is your wife; take her and begone!" And Pharaoh put men in charge of him, and they sent him off with his wife and all that he possessed.

In a second, related incident, Abraham again fails to protect Sarah from unwanted sexual attentions and once again Yahweh intervenes on her behalf. In both cases, however, Abraham profits. These incidents reveal the tentative position of women and perhaps also shed light on Sarah's cruel treatment of Hagar, Abraham's concubine, which God supports, because even with Yahweh's favor, Sarah's security in the patriarchal family was easily threatened.

Genesis 20:1–21:14

Abraham journeyed from there to the region of the Negeb and settled between Kadesh and Shur. While he was sojourning in Gerar, Abraham said of Sarah his wife, "She is my sister." So King Abimelech of Gerar had Sarah brought to him. But God came to Abimelech in a dream by night and said to him, "You are to die because of the woman that you have taken, for she is a married woman." Now Abimelech had not approached her. He said, "O Lord, will you slay people even though innocent? He himself said to me, 'She is my sister!' And she also said, 'He is my brother.' When I did this, my heart was blameless and my hands were clean." "And God said to him in the dream, "I knew that you did this with a blameless heart, and so I kept you from sinning against Me. That was why I did not let you touch her. Therefore, restore the man's wife—since he is a prophet, he will intercede for you—to save your life. If you fail to restore her, know that you shall die, you and all that are yours."

Early next morning, Abimelech called his servants and told them all that had happened; and the men were greatly frightened. Then Abimelech summoned Abraham and said to him, "What have you done to us? What wrong have I done that you should bring so great a guilt upon me and my kingdom? You have done to me things that ought not to be done. What, then," Abimelech demanded of Abraham, "was your purpose in doing this thing?" "I thought," said Abraham, "surely there is no fear of God in this place, and they will kill me because of my wife. And besides, she is in truth my sister, my father's daughter though not my mother's; and she became my wife. So when God made me wander from my father's house, I said to her, 'Let this be the kindness that you shall do me: whatever place we come to, say there of me: He is my brother.'"

Abimelech took sheep and oxen, and male and female slaves, and gave them to Abraham; and he restored his wife Sarah to him. And Abimelech said, "Here, my land is before you; settle wherever you please." And to Sarah he said, "I herewith give your brother a thousand pieces of silver; this will serve you as vindication before all who are with you, and you are cleared before everyone." Abraham then prayed to God, and God healed Abimelech and his wife and his slave girls, so that they bore children; for the LORD had closed fast every womb of the household of Abimelech because of Sarah, the wife of Abraham.

The LORD took note of Sarah as He had promised, and the LORD did for Sarah as He had spoken. Sarah conceived and bore a son to Abraham in his old age, at the set time of which God had spoken. Abraham gave his newborn son, whom Sarah had borne him, the name of Isaac. And when his son Isaac was eight days old, Abraham circumcised him, as God had commanded him. Now Abraham was a hundred years old when his son Isaac was born to him. Sarah said, "God has brought me laughter; everyone who hears will laugh with me." And she added,

"Who would have said to Abraham
That Sarah would suckle children!
Yet I have borne a son in his old age."

The child grew up and was weaned, and Abraham held a great feast on the day Isaac was weaned.

Sarah saw the son whom Hagar the Egyptian had borne to Abraham playing. She said to Abraham, "Cast out that slave-woman and her son, for the son of that slave shall not share in the inheritance with my son Isaac." The matter distressed Abraham greatly, for it concerned a son of his. But God said to Abraham, "Do not be distressed over the boy or your slave; whatever Sarah tells you, do as she says, for it is through Isaac that offspring shall be continued for you. As for the son of the slave-woman, I will make a nation of him, too, for he is your seed."

Early next morning Abraham took some bread and a skin of water, and gave them to Hagar. He placed them over her shoulder, together with the child, and sent her away. And she wandered about in the wilderness of Beer-sheba.

MIRIAM

Miriam, the prophetess and older sister of Moses and Aaron, is a significant participant in the liberation of her people from Egypt, which she celebrates in song and dance (Exod. 15:20). The following excerpt sets the tone of female heroism in the example of the midwives who disobey and lie to the Pharaoh. Their shrewdness and courage continues in Miriam, who secures Moses' future.

Exodus 1:15–2:10

The king of Egypt spoke to the Hebrew midwives, one of whom was named Shiphrah and the other Puah, saying, "When you deliver the Hebrew women, look at the birthstool: if it is a boy, kill him; if it is a girl, let her live." The midwives, fearing God, did not do as the king of Egypt had told them; they let the boys live. So the king of Egypt summoned the midwives and said to them, "Why have you done this thing, letting the boys live?" The midwives said to Pharaoh, "Because the Hebrew women are not like the Egyptian women: they are vigorous. Before the midwife can come to them, they give birth." And God dealt well with the midwives; and the people multiplied and increased greatly. And because the midwives feared God, He established households for them. Then Pharaoh charged all his people, saying, "Every boy that is born you shall throw into the Nile, but let every girl live."

A certain man of the house of Levi went and married a Levite woman. The woman conceived and bore a son; and when she saw how beautiful he was, she hid him for three months. When she could hide him no longer, she got a wicker basket for him and calked it with bitumen and pitch. She put the child into it and placed it among the reeds by the bank of the Nile. And his sister stationed herself at a distance, to learn what would befall him.

The daughter of Pharaoh came down to bathe in the Nile, while her maidens walked along the Nile. She spied the basket among the reeds and sent her slave girl to fetch it. When she opened it, she saw that it was a child, a boy crying. She took pity on it and said, "This must be a Hebrew child." Then his sister said to Pharaoh's daughter, "Shall I go and get you a Hebrew nurse to suckle the child for you?" And Pharaoh's daughter answered, "Yes." So the girl went and called the child's mother. And Pharaoh's daughter said to her, "Take this child and nurse it for me, and I will pay your wages." So the woman took the child and nursed it. When the child grew up, she brought him to Pharaoh's daughter, who made him her son. She named him Moses, explaining, "I drew him out of the water."

Miriam's courage and frankness lead to a great humiliation by Yahweh when she challenges Moses' spiritual authority. It is important to note that Miriam receives the heavy punishment of leprosy while Aaron, who also challenged Moses, does not. There is a message in this for all women who want to question male authority.

Numbers 12

When they were in Hazeroth, Miriam and Aaron spoke against Moses because of the Cushite woman he had married: "He married a Cushite woman!"

They said, "Has the LORD spoken only through Moses? Has He not spoken through us as well?" The LORD heard it. Now Moses was a very humble man, more so than any other man on earth. Suddenly the LORD called to Moses, Aaron, and Miriam, "Come out, you three, to the Tent of Meeting." So the three of them went out. The LORD came down in a pillar of cloud, stopped at the entrance of the Tent, and called out, "Aaron and Miriam!" The two of them came forward; and He said, "Hear these My words: When a prophet of the LORD arises among you, I make Myself known to him in a vision, I speak with him in a dream. Not so with My servant Moses; he is trusted throughout My household. With him I speak mouth to mouth, plainly and not in riddles, and he beholds the likeness of the LORD. How then did you not shrink from speaking against My servant Moses!" Still incensed with them, the LORD departed.

As the cloud withdrew from the Tent, there was Miriam stricken with snow-white scales! When Aaron turned toward Miriam, he saw that she was stricken with scales. And Aaron said to Moses, "O my lord, account not to us the sin which we committed in our folly. Let her not be as one dead, who emerges from his mother's womb with half his flesh eaten away." So Moses cried out to the LORD, saying, "O God, pray heal her!"

But the LORD said to Moses, "If her father spat in her face, would she not bear her shame for seven days? Let her be shut out of camp for seven days, and then let her be readmitted." So Miriam was shut out of camp seven days; and the people did not march on until Miriam was readmitted. After that the people set out from Hazeroth and encamped in the wilderness of Paran.

DEBORAH AND JAEL

The Book of Judges refers to events that occurred in the eleventh century B.C.E., a period when the Hebrews were ruled by Judges and were still in the process of resettling in Canaan. Chapters 4 and 5 preserve the story of Deborah, a woman who was a judge and a prophet. The whole sequence exalts the courage and cleverness of women especially since Deborah's prophecy is fulfilled by another woman, Jael.

Judges 4–5

The Israelites again did what was offensive to the LORD—Ehud now being dead. And the LORD surrendered them to King Jabin of Canaan, who reigned in Hazor. His army commander was Sisera, whose base was Harosheth-goiim. The Israelites cried out to the LORD; for he had nine hundred iron chariots, and he had oppressed Israel ruthlessly for twenty years.

Deborah, wife of Lappidoth. was a prophetess; she led Israel at that time. She used to sit under the Palm of Deborah, between Ramah and Bethel in the hill country of Ephraim, and the Israelites would come to her for decisions.

She summoned Barak son of Abinoam, of Kedesh in Naphtali, and said to him, "The LORD, the God of Israel, has commanded: Go, march up to Mount Tabor, and take with you ten thousand men of Naphtali and Zebulun. And I will draw Sisera, Jabin's army commander, with his chariots and his troops, toward you up to the Wadi Kishon; and I will deliver him into your hands." But Barak said to her, "If you will go with me, I will go; if not, I will not go." "Very well, I will go with you," she answered. "However, there will be no glory for you in the course you are taking, for then the LORD will deliver Sisera into the hands of a woman." So Deborah went with Barak to Kedesh. Barak then mustered Zebulun and Naphtali at Kedesh; ten thousand men marched up after him; and Deborah also went up with him.

Now Heber the Kenite had separated from the other Kenites, descendants of Hobab, father-in-law of Moses, and had pitched his tent at Elon-bezaanannim, which is near Kedesh.

Sisera was informed that Barak son of Abinoam had gone up to Mount Tabor. So Sisera ordered all his chariots—nine hundred iron chariots—and all the troops he had to move from Harosheth-goiim to the Wadi Kishon. Then Deborah said to Barak, "Up! This is the day on which the LORD will deliver Sisera into your hands: the LORD is marching before you." Barak charged down Mount Tabor, followed by the ten thousand men, and the LORD threw Sisera and all his chariots and army into a panic before the onslaught of Barak. Sisera leaped from his chariot and fled on foot as Barak pursued the chariots and the soldiers as far as Harosheth-goiim. All of Sisera's soldiers fell by the sword; not a man was left.

Sisera, meanwhile, had fled on foot to the tent of Jael, wife of Heber the Kenite; for there was friendship between King Jabin of Hazor and the family of Heber the Kenite. Jael came out to greet Sisera and said to him, "Come in, my lord, come in here, do not be afraid." So he entered her tent, and she covered him with a blanket. He said to her, "Please let me have some water; I am thirsty." She opened a skin of milk and gave him some to drink; and she covered him again. He said to her, "Stand at the entrance of the tent. If anybody comes and asks you if there is anybody here, say 'No.'" Then Jael wife of Heber took a tent pin and grasped the mallet. When he was fast asleep from exhaustion, she approached him stealthily and drove the pin through his temple till it went down to the ground. Thus he died.

Now Barak appeared in pursuit of Sisera. Jael went out to greet him and said, "Come, I will show you the man you are looking for." He went inside with her, and there Sisera was lying dead, with the pin in his temple.

On that day God subdued King Jabin of Hazor before the Israelites. The hand of the Israelites bore harder and harder on King Jabin of Canaan, until they destroyed King Jabin of Canaan.

JEPHTHAH'S DAUGHTER

The following excerpt from the Book of Judges reveals a darker side of life for women. The story begins when the Ammonites set up camp in Gilead to prepare for war against Israel. The people of Gilead are hard pressed to find a war leader since they had exiled their best warrior, Jephthah, some time before. But, when appealed to, Jephthah agrees to become their leader and begins his march on the Ammonites. Even though on the way "the Spirit of the Lord" came upon him (11:29) Jephthah makes the unnecessary vow that he will offer a human sacrifice if victory is his. He offers the first person who greets him when he returns home. This turns out to be his only child who Jephthah then blames for what he will do (11:35). She accepts her fate and only asks for a short respite in which to "bewail her virginity" (11:38). After this Jephthah offers her as a sacrifice and the chapter ends with the hint of a lost women's ceremony in which the women of Israel lamented for her during a four-day ceremony once a year.

The story of Jephthah's daughter, who is not named, contrasts in important ways with the story of Abraham's forestalled sacrifice of his son Isaac (Gen. 22) and it raises a question about the greater value placed on sons than on daughters. God *commands* Abraham to make such a sacrifice and then intervenes in its execution. In Judges 11 it is Jephthah who offers to perform such a sacrifice while God remains silent, a textual indication that God did not necessarily agree to the terms Jephthah offered. However, God does not intervene to save her nor does Jephthah appeal to God to do so. Finally, even though Jephthah is guilty of unrighteous behavior that leads to terrible consequences, he is not criticized by the tradition, on the contrary he is spoken of highly.

Judges 11

Jephthah the Gileadite was an able warrior, who was the son of a prostitute. Jephthah's father was Gilead; but Gilead also had sons by his wife, and when the wife's sons grew up, they drove Jephthah out. They said to him, "You shall have no share in our father's property, for you are the son of an outsider." So Jephthah fled from his brothers and settled in the Tob country. Men of low character gathered about Jephthah and went out raiding with him.

Some time later, the Ammonites went to war against Israel. And when the Ammonites attacked Israel, the elders of Gilead went to bring Jephthah back from the Tob country. They said to Jephthah, "Come be our chief, so that we can fight the Ammonites." Jephthah replied to the elders of Gilead, "You are the very people who rejected me and drove me out of my father's house. How can you come to me now when you are in trouble?" The elders of Gilead said to Jephthah, "Honestly, we have now turned back to you. If you come with us and fight the Ammonites, you shall be our commander over all the inhabitants of Gilead." Jephthah said to the elders of Gilead, "[Very well,] if you bring me back to fight the Ammonites and the LORD delivers them to me, I am to be your commander." And the elders of Gilead answered Jephthah, "The LORD Himself shall be witness between us: we will do just as you have said."

Jephthah went with the elders of Gilead, and the people made him their commander and chief. And Jephthah repeated all these terms before the LORD at Mizpah.

* * *

Then the spirit of the LORD came upon Jephthah. He marched through Gilead and Manasseh, passing Mizpeh of Gilead; and from Mizpeh of Gilead he crossed over [to] the Ammonites. And Jephthah made the following vow to the LORD: "If you deliver the Ammonites into my hands, then whatever comes out of the door of my house to meet me on my safe return from the Ammonites shall be the LORD's and shall be offered by me as a burnt offering."

Jephthah crossed over to the Ammonites and attacked them, and the LORD delivered them into his hands. He utterly routed them—from Aroer as far as Minnith, twenty towns—all the way to Abel-cheramim. So the Ammonites submitted to the Israelites.

When Jephthah arrived at his home in Mizpah, there was his daughter coming out to meet him, with timbrel and dance! She was an only child; he had no other son or daughter. On seeing her, he rent his clothes and said, "Alas, daughter! You have brought me low; you have become my troubler! For I have uttered a vow to the LORD and I cannot retract." "Father," she said, "you have uttered a vow to the LORD; do to me as you have vowed, seeing that the LORD has vindicated you against your enemies, the Ammonites." She further said to her father, "Let this be done for me: let me be for two months, and I will go with my companions and lament upon the hills and there bewail my maidenhood." "Go," he replied. He let her go for two months, and she and her companions went and bewailed her maidenhood upon the hills. After two months' time, she returned to her father, and he did to her as he had vowed. She had never known a man. So it became a custom in Israel for the maidens of Israel to go every year, for four days in the year, and chant dirges for the daughter of Jephthah the Gileadite.

ESTHER

The Book of Esther is a story about the Persian period of Jewish history when the Persian King Ahasuerus (i.e. Xerxes I, ruled 486–465 B.C.E.) chose a Jewish wife, Esther. It is also an explanation of the origin of the joyful feast of Purim which is celebrated every Spring.

The villain of the story is the prime minister Haman who obtains the King's consent to a decree that all the Jews in the empire will be killed on an appointed day. Esther successfully pleads with the king for her people and Haman is executed but the first decree cannot be changed. The king then permits Esther's guardian Mordecai to issue a second decree authorizing the Jews to defend themselves when attacked. After the Jews successfully defend themselves Esther and Mordecai institute the annual observance of these events, Purim.

Esther 2:2–18

The king's servants who attended him said, "Let beautiful young virgins be sought out for Your Majesty. Let Your Majesty appoint officers in every province of your realm to assemble all the beautiful young virgins at the fortress Shushan, in the harem under the supervision of Hege, the king's eunuch, guardian of the women. Let them be provided with their cosmetics. And let the maiden who pleases Your Majesty be queen instead of Vashti." The proposal pleased the king, and he acted upon it.

In the fortress Shushan lived a Jew by the name of Mordecai, son of Jair son of Shimei son of Kish, a Benjaminite. [Kish] had been exiled from Jerusalem in the group that was carried into exile along with King Jeconiah of Judah, which had been driven into exile by King Nebuchadnezzar of Babylon. He was foster father to Hadassah—that is, Esther—his uncle's daughter, for she had neither father nor mother. The maiden was shapely and beautiful; and when her father and mother died, Mordecai adopted her as his own daughter.

When the king's order and edict was proclaimed, and when many girls were assembled in the fortress Shushan under the supervision of Hegai, Esther too was taken into the king's palace under the supervision of Hegai, guardian of the women.

* * *

Esther was taken to King Ahasuerus, in his royal palace, in the tenth month, which is the month of Tebeth, in the seventh year of his reign. The king loved Esther more than all the other women, and she won his grace and favor more than all the virgins. So he set a royal diadem on her head and made her queen instead of Vashti. The king gave a great banquet for all his officials and courtiers, "the banquet of Esther." He proclaimed a remission of taxes for the provinces and distributed gifts as befits a king.

Esther 3:1–5:4

Some time afterward, King Ahasuerus promoted Haman son of Hammedatha the Agagite; he advanced him and seated him higher than any of his fellow officials. All the king's courtiers in the palace gate knelt and bowed low to Haman, for such was the king's order concerning him; but Mordecai would not kneel or bow low. Then the king's courtiers who were in the palace gate said to Mordecai, "Why do you disobey the king's order?" When they spoke to him day after day and he would not listen to them, they told Haman, in order to see whether Mordecai's resolve would prevail; for he had explained to them that he was a Jew. When Haman saw that Mordecai would not kneel or bow low to him, Haman was filled with rage. But he disdained to lay hands on Mordecai alone; having been told who Mordecai's people were, Haman plotted to do away with all the Jews, Mordecai's people, throughout the kingdom of Ahasuerus.

In the first month, that is, the month of Nisan, in the twelfth year of King Ahasuerus, *pur*—which means "the lot"—was cast before Haman concerning every day and every month, [until it fell on] the twelfth month, that is, the month of Adar. Haman then said to King Ahasuerus, "There is a certain people, scattered and dispersed among the other peoples in all the provinces of your realm, whose laws are different from those of any other people and who do not obey the king's laws; and it is not in Your Majesty's interest to tolerate them. If it please Your Majesty, let an edict be drawn for their destruction, and I will pay ten thousand talents of silver to the stewards for deposit in the royal treasury." Thereupon the king removed his signet ring from his hand and gave it to Haman son of Hammedatha the Agagite, the foe of the Jews. And the king said, "The money and the people are yours to do with as you see fit."

* * *

When Mordecai learned all that had happened, Mordecai tore his clothes and put on sackcloth and ashes. He went through the city, crying out loudly and bitterly, until he came in front of the palace gate; for one could not enter the palace gate wearing sackcloth. Also, in every province that the king's command and decree reached, there was great mourning among the Jews, with fasting, weeping, and wailing, and everybody lay in sackcloth and ashes. When Esther's maidens and eunuchs came and informed her, the queen was greatly agitated. She sent clothing for Mordecai to wear. so that he might take off his sackcloth; but he refused. Thereupon Esther summoned Hathach, one of the eunuchs whom the king had appointed to serve her, and sent him to Mordecai to learn the why and wherefore of it all. Hathach went out to Mordecai in the city square in front of the palace gate; and Mordecai told him all that had happened to him, and all about the money that Haman had offered to pay into the royal treasury for the destruction of the Jews. He also gave him the written text of the law that had been proclaimed in Shushan for their destruction. [He bade him] show it to Esther and inform her, and charge her to go to the king and to appeal to him and to plead with him for her people. When Hathach came and delivered Mordecai's message to Esther, Esther told Hathach to take back to Mordecai the following reply: "All the king's courtiers and the people of the king's provinces know that if any person, man or woman, enters the king's presence in the inner court without having been summoned, there is but one law for him—that he be put to death. Only if the king extends the golden scepter to him may he live. Now I have not been summoned to visit the king for the last thirty days."

When Mordecai was told what Esther had said, Mordecai had this message delivered to Esther: "Do not imagine that you, of all the Jews, will escape with your life by being in the king's palace. On the contrary, if you keep silent in this crisis, relief and deliverance will come to the Jews from another quarter, while you and your father's house will perish. And who knows, perhaps you have attained to royal position for just such a crisis." Then Esther sent back this answer to Mordecai: "Go, assemble all the Jews who live in Shushan, and fast in my behalf; do not eat or drink for three days, night or day. I and my maidens will observe the same fast. Then I shall go to the king, though it is contrary to the law; and if I am to perish, I shall perish!" So Mordecai went about [the city] and did just as Esther had commanded him.

On the third day, Esther put on royal apparel and stood in the inner court of the king's palace, facing the king's palace, while the king was sitting on his royal throne in the throne room facing the entrance of the palace. As soon as the king saw Queen Esther standing in the court, she won his favor. The king extended to Esther the golden scepter which he had in his hand, and Esther approached and touched the tip of the scepter. "What troubles you, Queen Esther?" the king asked her. "And what is your request? Even to half the kingdom, it shall be granted you." "If it please Your Majesty," Esther replied, "let Your Majesty and Haman come today to the feast that I have prepared for him."

Esther 7:1–8:4

So the king and Haman came to feast with Queen Esther. On the second day, the king again asked Esther at the banquet. "What is your wish, Queen Esther? It shall be granted you. And what is your request? Even to half the kingdom, it shall be fulfilled." Queen Esther replied: "If Your Majesty will do me the favor, and if it pleases Your Majesty, let my life be granted me as my wish, and my people as my request. For we have been sold, my people and I, to be destroyed, massacred, and exterminated. Had we only been sold as bondmen and bondwomen, I would have kept silent; for the adversary is not worthy of the king's trouble."

Thereupon King Ahasuerus demanded of Queen Esther, "Who is he and where is he who dared to do this?" "The adversary and enemy," replied Esther, "is this evil Haman!" And Haman cringed in terror before the king and the queen. The king, in his fury, left the wine feast for the palace garden, while Haman remained to plead with Queen Esther for his life; for he saw that the king had resolved to destroy him. When the king returned from the palace garden to the banquet room, Haman was lying prostrate on the couch on which Esther reclined. "Does he mean," cried the king, "to ravish the queen in my own palace?" No sooner did these words leave the king's lips than Haman's face was covered. Then Harbonah, one of the eunuchs in attendance on the king, said, "What is more, a stake is standing at Haman's house, fifty cubits high, which Haman made for Mordecai—the man whose words saved the king." "Impale him on it!" the king ordered. So they impaled Haman on the stake which he had put up for Mordecai, and the king's fury abated.

That very day King Ahasuerus gave the property of Haman, the enemy of the Jews, to Queen Esther. Mordecai presented himself to the king, for Esther had revealed how he was related to her. The king slipped off his ring, which he had taken back from Haman, and gave it to Mordecai; and Esther put Mordecai in charge of Haman's property.

Esther spoke to the king again, falling at his feet and weeping, and beseeching him to avert the evil plotted by Haman the Agagite against the Jews. The king extended the golden scepter to Esther, and Esther arose and stood before the king. "If it please Your Majesty," she said, "and if I have won your favor and the proposal seems right to Your Majesty, and if I am pleasing to you—let dispatches be written countermanding those which were written by Haman son of Hammedatha the Agagite, embodying his plot to annihilate the Jews throughout the king's provinces. For how can I bear to see the disaster which will befall my people! And how can I bear to see the destruction of my kindred!"

Then King Ahasuerus said to Queen Esther and Mordecai the Jew, "I have given Haman's property to Esther, and he has been impaled on the stake for scheming against the Jews. And you may further write with regard to the Jews as you see fit. [Write it] in the king's name and seal it with the king's signet, for an edict that has been written in the king's name and sealed with the king's signet may not be revoked."

So the king's scribes were summoned at that time, on the twenty-third day of the third month, that is, the month of Sivan; and letters were written, at Mordecai's dictation, to the Jews and to the satraps, the governors and the officials of the one hundred and twenty-seven provinces from India to Ethiopia: to every province in its own script and to every people in its own language, and to the Jews in their own script and language. He had them written in the name of King Ahasuerus and sealed with the king's signet. Letters were dispatched by mounted couriers, riding steeds used in the king's service, bred of the royal stud, to this effect: The king has permitted the Jews of every city to assemble and fight for their lives; if any people or province attacks them, they may destroy, massacre, and exterminate its armed force together with women and children, and to plunder their possessions — on a single day in all the provinces of King Ahasuerus, namely, on the thirteenth day of the twelfth month, that is, the month of Adar. The text of the document was to be issued as a law in every single province: it was to be publicly displayed to all the peoples, so that the Jews should be ready for that day to avenge themselves on their enemies. The couriers, mounted on royal steeds, went out in urgent haste at the king's command; and the decree was proclaimed in the fortress Shushan.

Esther 9:23–32

The Jews accordingly assumed as an obligation that which they had begun to practice and which Mordecai prescribed for them.

For Haman son of Hammedatha the Agagite, the foe of all the Jews, had plotted to destroy the Jews, and had cast *pur* — that is, the lot — with intent to crush and exterminate them. But when [Esther] came before the king, he commanded: "With the promulgation of this decree, let the evil plot, which he devised against the Jews, recoil on his own head!" So they impaled him and his sons on the stake. For that reason these days were named Purim, after *pur*.

In view, then, of all the instructions in the said letter and of what they had experienced in that matter and what had befallen them, the Jews undertook and irrevocably obligated themselves and their descendants, and all who might join them, to observe these two days in the manner prescribed and at the proper time each year. Consequently, these days are recalled and observed in every generation: by every family, every province, and every city. And these days of Purim shall never cease among the Jews, and the memory of them shall never perish among their descendants.

Then Queen Esther daughter of Abihail wrote a second letter of Purim for the purpose of confirming with full authority the aforementioned one of Mordecai the Jew. Dispatches were sent to all the Jews in the hundred and twenty-seven provinces of the realm of Ahasuerus with an ordinance of "equity and honesty:" These days of Purim shall be observed at their proper time, as Mordecai the Jew — and now Queen Esther — has obligated them to do, and just as they have assumed for themselves and their descendants the obligation of the fasts with their lamentations.

And Esther's ordinance validating these observances of Purim was recorded in a scroll.

MARRIAGE AND PROCREATION

Marriage and procreation are enjoined on both men and women. Given this emphasis, the Hebrew Bible contains instructions and laws regarding the proper performance of marital duties and sexuality in general. For instance, Deuteronomy, the fifth and last book of the Torah, which is a collection of laws, admonitions, and songs dating back to at least the eighth century B.C.E., sets out in 22:13–30 laws governing sexuality within marriage and cases of rape. While heavily weighted in favor of men, primarily in order to ensure certain paternity, women have some protection from false accusations of sexual impropriety.

Deuteronomy 22:13–29

A man marries a woman and cohabits with her. Then he takes an aversion to her and makes up charges against her and defames her, saying, "I married this woman; but when I approached her, I found that she was not a virgin." In such a case, the girl's father and mother shall produce the evidence of the girl's virginity before the elders of the town at the gate. And the girl's father shall say to the elders, "I gave this man my daughter to wife, but he has taken an aversion to her; so he has made up charges, saying, 'I did not find your daughter a virgin.' But here is the evidence of my daughter's virginity!" And they shall spread out the cloth before the elders of the town. The elders of that town shall then take the man and flog him, and they shall fine him a hundred [shekels of] silver and give it to the girl's father; for the man has defamed a virgin in Israel. Moreover, she shall remain his wife; he shall never have the right to divorce her.

But if the charge proves true, the girl was found not to have been a virgin, then the girl shall be brought out to the entrance of her father's house, and the men of her town shall stone her to death; for she did a shameful thing in Israel, committing fornication while under her father's authority. Thus you will sweep away evil from your midst.

If a man is found lying with another man's wife, both of them—the man and the woman with whom he lay—shall die. Thus you will sweep away evil from Israel. In the case of a virgin who is engaged to a man—if a man comes upon her in town and lies with her, you shall take the two of them out to the gate of that town and stone them to death: the girl because she did not cry for help in the town, and the man because he violated his neighbor's wife. Thus you will sweep away evil from your midst. But if the man comes upon the engaged girl in the open country, and the man lies with her by force, only the man who lay with her shall die, but you shall do nothing to the girl. The girl did not incur the death penalty, for this case is like that of a man attacking another and murdering him. He came upon her in the open; though the engaged girl cried for help, there was no one to save her.

If a man comes upon a virgin who is not engaged and he seizes her and lies with her, and they are discovered, the man who lay with her shall pay the girl's father fifty [shekels of] silver, and she shall be his wife. Because he has violated her, he can never have the right to divorce her.

Numbers, the fourth book of the Torah, covers the forty-year period of wandering in the desert after the exodus from Egypt and before settling in Canaan. Chapter 5:11–31 enjoins the sexual fidelity of women, but not of men, and describes the ritual ordeal required of a woman whose husband doubts her. The psychological strain of this, the only specification for trial by ordeal in the Hebrew Bible, must have been enormous.

Numbers 5:11–31

The LORD spoke to Moses, saying: Speak to the Israelite people and say to them: If any man's wife has gone astray and broken faith with him in that a man has had carnal relations with her unbeknown to her husband, and she keeps secret the fact that she has defiled herself without being forced, and there is no witness against her—but a fit of jealousy comes over him and he is wrought up about the wife who has defiled herself; or if a fit of jealousy comes over one and he is wrought up about his wife although she has not defiled herself—the man shall bring his wife to the priest. And he shall bring as an offering for her one-tenth of an *ephah* of barley flour. No oil shall be poured upon it and no frankincense shall be laid on it, for it is a meal offering of jealousy, a meal offering of remembrance which recalls wrongdoing.

The priest shall bring her forward and have her stand before the LORD. The priest shall take sacral water in an earthen vessel and, taking some of the earth that is on the floor of the Tabernacle, the priest shall put it into the water. After he has made the woman stand before the LORD, the priest shall bare the woman's head and place upon her hands the meal offering of remembrance, which is a meal offering of jealousy. And in the priest's hands shall be the water of bitterness that induces the spell. The priest shall adjure the woman, saying to her, "If no man has lain with you, if you have not gone astray in defilement while married to your husband, be immune to harm from this water of bitterness that induces the spell. But if you have gone astray while married to your husband and have defiled yourself, if a man other than your husband has had carnal relations with you"—here the priest shall administer the curse of adjuration to the woman, as the priest goes on to say to the woman—"may the LORD make you a curse and an imprecation among your people, as the LORD causes your thigh to sag and your belly to distend; may this water that induces the spell enter your body, causing the belly to distend and the thigh to sag." And the woman shall say, "Amen, amen!"

The priest shall put these curses down in writing and rub it off into the water of bitterness. He is to make the woman drink the water of bitterness that induces the spell, so that the spell-inducing water may enter into her to bring on bitterness. Then the priest shall take from the woman's hand the meal offering of jealousy, elevate the meal offering before the LORD, and present it on the altar. The priest shall scoop out of the meal offering a token part of it and turn it into smoke on the altar. Lastly, he shall make the woman drink the water.

Once he has made her drink the water—if she has defiled herself by breaking faith with her husband, the spell-inducing water shall enter into her to bring on bitterness, so that her belly shall distend and her thigh shall sag; and the woman shall become a curse among her people. But if the woman has not defiled herself and is pure, she shall be unharmed and able to retain seed.

This is the ritual in cases of jealousy, when a woman goes astray while married to her husband and defiles herself, or when a fit of jealousy comes over a man and he is wrought up over his wife: the woman shall be made to stand before the LORD and the priest shall carry out all this ritual with her. The man shall be clear of guilt; but that woman shall suffer for her guilt.

Proverbs, a postexilic work composed perhaps as late as the fourth century B.C.E., contains a chapter on the duties of a wife, which are rather numerous, as well as some of her privileges: she can trade on her own, buy property, etc. These teachings are credited to Lemuel who, in turn, credits his mother. It is she who speaks in this chapter, warning her son against women and then defining a good wife.

Proverbs 31

The words of Lemuel, king of Massa, with which his mother admonished him:

No, my son!
No, O son of my womb!
No, O son of my vows!
Do not give your strength to women,
Your vigor to those who destroy kings.
Wine is not for kings, O Lemuel;
Not for kings to drink,
Nor any strong drink for princes,
Lest they drink and forget what has been ordained
And infringe on the rights of the poor.
Give strong drink to the hapless
And wine to the embittered.
Let them drink and forget their poverty,
And put their troubles out of mind.
Speak up for the dumb,
For the rights of all the unfortunate.
Speak up, judge righteously,
Champion the poor and the needy.

What a rare find is a capable wife!
Her worth is far beyond that of rubies.
Her husband puts his confidence in her,
And lacks no good thing.
She is good to him, never bad,
All the days of her life.
She looks for wool and flax,
And sets her hand to them with a will.
She is like a merchant fleet,
Bringing her food from afar.
She rises while it is still night,
And supplies provisions for her household,

The daily fare of her maids.
She sets her mind on an estate and acquires it;
She plants a vineyard by her own labors.
She girds herself with strength,
And performs her tasks with vigor.
She sees that her business thrives;
Her lamp never goes out at night.
She sets her hand to the distaff;
Her fingers work the spindle.
She gives generously to the poor;
Her hands are stretched out to the needy.
She is not worried for her household because of snow,
For her whole household is dressed in crimson.
She makes covers for herself;
Her clothing is linen and purple.
Her husband is prominent in the gates,
As he sits among the elders of the land.
She makes cloth and sells it,
And offers a girdle to the merchant.
She is clothed with strength and splendor;
She looks to the future cheerfully.
Her mouth is full of wisdom,
Her tongue with kindly teaching.
She oversees the activities of her household
And never eats the bread of idleness.
Her children declare her happy;
Her husband praises her,
"Many women have done well,
But you surpass them all."
Grace is deceptive,
Beauty is illusory;
It is for her fear of the LORD
That a woman is to be praised.
Extol her for the fruit of her hand,
And let her works praise her in the gates.

Leviticus, the third book of the Torah, is a completely preexilic text and therefore contains some very old material. Chapter 12 not only defines the pollution of women through menstruation and childbirth but emphasizes that it is more polluting to give birth to a daughter than to a son. Leviticus 15:16–32 continues in this vein and offers a telling comparison of the polluting effects of semen (impure until evening) and menstrual blood (impure for seven days).

Leviticus 12

The LORD spoke to Moses, saying: Speak to the Israelite people thus: When a woman at childbirth bears a male, she shall be unclean seven days; she shall be unclean as at the time of her menstrual infirmity. On the eighth day the flesh of his foreskin shall be circumcised. She shall remain in a state of blood purification for thirty-three days: she shall not touch any consecrated thing, nor enter the sanctuary until her period of purification is completed. If she bears a female, she shall be unclean two weeks as during her menstruation, and she shall remain in a state of blood purification for sixty-six days.

On the completion of her period of purification, for either son or daughter, she shall bring to the priest, at the entrance of the Tent of Meeting, a lamb in its first year for a burnt offering, and a pigeon or a turtledove for a sin offering. He shall offer it before the LORD and make expiation on her behalf; she shall then be clean from her flow of blood. Such are the rituals concerning her who bears a child, male or female. If, however, her means do not suffice for a sheep, she shall take two turtledoves or two pigeons, one for a burnt offering and the other for a sin offering. The priest shall make expiation on her behalf, and she shall be clean.

Leviticus 15:16–32

When a man has an emission of semen, he shall bathe his whole body in water and remain unclean until evening. All cloth or leather on which semen falls shall be washed in water and remain unclean until evening. And if a man has carnal relations with a woman, they shall bathe in water and remain unclean until evening.

When a woman has a discharge, her discharge being blood from her body, she shall remain in her impurity seven days; whoever touches her shall be unclean until evening. Anything that she lies on during her impurity shall be unclean; and anything that she sits on shall be unclean. Anyone who touches her bedding shall wash his clothes, bathe in water, and remain unclean until evening; and anyone who touches any object on which she has sat shall wash his clothes, bathe in water, and remain unclean until evening. Be it the bedding or be it the object on which she has sat, on touching it he shall be unclean until evening. And if a man lies with her, her impurity is communicated to him; he shall be unclean seven days, and any bedding on which he lies shall become unclean.

When a woman has had a discharge of blood for many days, not at the time of her impurity, or when she has a discharge beyond her period of impurity, she shall be unclean, as though at the time of her impurity, as long as her discharge lasts. Any bedding on which she lies while her discharge lasts shall be for her like bedding during her impurity; and any object on which she sits shall become unclean, as it does during her impurity: whoever touches them shall be unclean; he shall wash his clothes, bathe in water, and remain unclean until evening.

When she becomes clean of her discharge, she shall count off seven days, and after that she shall be clean. On the eighth day she shall take two turtledoves or two pigeons, and bring them to the priest at the entrance of the Tent of Meeting. The priest shall offer the one as a sin offering and the other as a burnt offering; and the priest shall make expiation on her behalf, for her unclean discharge, before the LORD.

You shall put the Israelites on guard against their uncleanness, lest they die through their uncleanness by defiling My Tabernacle which is among them.

Such is the ritual concerning him who has a discharge: concerning him who has an emission of semen and becomes unclean thereby, and concerning her who is in menstrual infirmity, and concerning anyone, male or female, who has a discharge, and concerning a man who lies with an unclean woman.

WISDOM

The Book of Proverbs is part of the Hebrew Wisdom literature and, although this book of the Bible is traditionally ascribed to King Solomon, it is in large part a postexilic work, perhaps composed as late as the fourth century B.C.E. This is particularly the case with chapters

1–9, which praise wisdom, described as a female, and encourages men to find her. Indeed, wisdom herself speaks and explains that God created her at the beginning of creation (8:22–31). This raising up of wisdom as a female image is contrasted throughout the text with attacks on loose women, on adventuresses, on those women who lead men astray. This is, in fact, a textbook for young men, and as such it establishes polar opposites of female imagery: ethereal wisdom contrasts sharply with living, sexual women.

Proverbs 7–9

My son, heed my words;
And store up my commandments with you.
Keep my commandments and live,
My teaching, as the apple of your eye.
Bind them on your fingers;
Write them on the tablet of your mind.
Say to Wisdom, "You are my sister,"
And call Understanding a kinswoman.
She will guard you from a forbidden woman;
From an alien woman whose talk is smooth.

From the window of my house,
Through my lattice, I looked out
And saw among the simple,
Noticed among the youths,
A lad devoid of sense.
He was crossing the street near her corner,
Walking toward her house
In the dusk of evening,
In the dark hours of night.
A woman comes toward him
Dressed like a harlot, with set purpose.
She is bustling and restive;
She is never at home.
Now in the street, now in the square,
She lurks at every corner.
She lays hold of him and kisses him;
Brazenly she says to him,
"I had to make a sacrifice of well-being;
Today I fulfilled my vows.
Therefore I have come out to you,
Seeking you, and have found you.
I have decked my couch with covers
Of dyed Egyptian linen;
I have sprinkled my bed
With myrrh, aloes, and cinnamon.
Let us drink our fill of love till morning.
Let us delight in amorous embrace.
For the man of the house is away;
He is off on a distant journey.
He took his bag of money with him
And will return only at mid-month."

She sways him with her eloquence,
Turns him aside with her smooth talk.
Thoughtlessly he follows her,
Like an ox going to the slaughter,

Like a fool to the stocks for punishment
Until the arrow pierces his liver.
He is like a bird rushing into a trap,
Not knowing his life is at stake.
Now, sons, listen to me;
Pay attention to my words;
Let your mind not wander down her ways;
Do not stray onto her paths.
For many are those she has struck dead,
And numerous are her victims.
Her house is a highway to Sheol
Leading down to Death's inner chambers.

It is Wisdom calling,
Understanding raising her voice.
She takes her stand at the topmost heights,
By the wayside, at the crossroads,
Near the gates at the city entrance;
At the entryways, she shouts,
"O men, I call to you;
My cry is to all mankind.
O simple ones, learn shrewdness;
O dullards, instruct your minds.
Listen, for I speak noble things;
Uprightness comes from my lips;
My mouth utters truth;
Wickedness is abhorrent to my lips.
All my words are just,
None of them perverse or crooked;
All are straightforward to the intelligent man,
And right to those who have attained knowledge.
Accept my discipline rather than silver,
Knowledge rather than choice gold.
For wisdom is better than rubies;
No goods can equal her.
"I, Wisdom, live with Prudence;
I attain knowledge and foresight.
To fear the LORD is to hate evil;
I hate pride, arrogance, the evil way,
And duplicity in speech.
Mine are counsel and resourcefulness;
I am understanding; courage is mine.
Through me kings reign
And rulers decree just laws;
Through me princes rule,
Great men and all the righteous judges.
Those who love me I love,
And those who seek me will find me.
Riches and honor belong to me,

Enduring wealth and success.
My fruit is better than gold, fine gold,
And my produce better than choice silver.
I walk on the way of righteousness,
On the paths of justice.
I endow those who love me with substance;
I will fill their treasuries.

"The LORD created me at the beginning of His course
As the first of His works of old.
In the distant past I was fashioned,
At the beginning, at the origin of earth.
There was still no deep when I was brought forth,
No springs rich in water;
Before [the foundation of] the mountains were sunk,
Before the hills I was born.
He had not yet made earth and fields,
Or the world's first clumps of clay.
I was there when He set the heavens into place;
When He fixed the horizon upon the deep;
When He made the heavens above firm,
And the fountains of the deep gushed forth;
When He assigned the sea its limits,
So that its waters never transgress His command;
When He fixed the foundations of the earth,
I was with Him as a confidant,
A source of delight every day,
Rejoicing before Him at all times,
Rejoicing in His inhabited world,
Finding delight with mankind.
Now, sons, listen to me;
Happy are they who keep my ways.
Heed discipline and become wise;
Do not spurn it.
Happy is the man who listens to me,
Coming early to my gates each day,
Waiting outside my doors.
For he who finds me finds life
And obtains favor from the LORD.
But he who misses me destroys himself;
All who hate me love death."

Wisdom has built her house,
She has hewn her seven pillars.
She has prepared the feast,
Mixed the wine,
And also set the table.
She has sent out her maids to announce
On the heights of the town,
"Let the simple enter here";
To those devoid of sense she says,
"Come, eat my food
And drink the wine that I have mixed;
Give up simpleness and live,
Walk in the way of understanding."

To correct a scoffer,
Or rebuke a wicked man for his blemish,
Is to call down abuse on oneself.
Do not rebuke a scoffer, for he will hate you;
Reprove a wise man, and he will love you.
Instruct a wise man, and he will grow wiser;
Teach a righteous man, and he will gain in learning.
The beginning of wisdom is fear of the LORD,
And knowledge of the Holy One is understanding.
For through me your days will increase,
And years be added to your life.
If you are wise, you are wise for yourself;
If you are a scoffer, you bear it alone.
The stupid woman bustles about;
She is simple and knows nothing.
She sits in the doorway of her house,
Or on a chair at the heights of the town,
Calling to all the wayfarers
Who go about their own affairs,
"Let the simple enter here";
And to those devoid of sense she says,
"Stolen waters are sweet,
And bread eaten furtively is tasty."
He does not know that the shades are there,
That her guests are in the depths of Sheol.

Rabbinic Period

PHILO

Philo Judaeus, also called Philo of Alexandria (c. 20 B.C.E.–50 B.C.E.), was an important Hellenistic Jewish philosopher, who constructed an elaborate synthesis of Jewish religious thought and Greek philosophy.

In the following excerpt from his *On the Creation of the World,* he emphasizes that Adam was created separately and before Eve and that it was the creation of women which led to decline.

But since nothing in creation lasts for ever, but all mortal things are liable to inevitable changes and alterations, it was unavoidable that the first man should also undergo some disaster. And the beginning of his life being liable to reproach, was his wife. For, as long as he was single, he resembled, as to his creation, both the world and God and he represented in his soul the characteristics of the nature of each, I do not mean all of them, but such as a mortal constitution was capable of admitting. But when woman also was created, man perceiving a closely connected figure and a kindred formation to his own, rejoiced at the sight, and approached her and embraced her. And she, in like manner, beholding a creature greatly resembling herself, rejoiced also, and addressed him in reply with due modesty. And love being engen-

dered, and, as it were, uniting two separate portions of one animal into one body, adapted them to each other, implanting in each of them a desire of connection with the other with a view to the generation of a being similar to themselves. And this desire caused likewise pleasure to their bodies, which is the beginning of iniquities and transgressions, and it is owing to this that men have exchanged their previously immortal and happy existence for one which is mortal and full of misfortune.

But while man was still living a solitary life, and before woman was created, the history relates that a paradise was planted by God in no respect resembling the parks which are seen among men now.

[From "On the Creation of the World (LIII–LIV)," in *The Essential Philo*, p. 34]

In the following excerpts from *On the Contemplative Life,* Philo describes a monastic Jewish community on the outskirts of Alexandria in which Jewish women and men pursued the spiritual life.

The vocation of these philosophers is at once clear from their title of Therapeutae [m. pl.] and Therapeutrides [f. pl.].

This common sanctuary in which they meet every seventh day is a double enclosure, one portion set apart for the use of the men, the other for the women. For women too regularly make part of the audience with the same ardour and the same sense of their calling. The wall between the two chambers rises up from the ground to three or four cubits built in the form of a breast work, while the space above up to the roof is left open. This arrangement serves two purposes; the modesty becoming to the female sex is preserved, while the women sitting within earshot can easily follow what is said since there is nothing to obstruct the voice of the speaker.

The feast is shared by women also, most of them aged virgins, who have kept their chastity not under compulsion, like some of the Greek priestesses, but of their own free will in their ardent yearning for wisdom. Eager to have her for their life mate they have spurned the pleasures of the body and desire no mortal offspring but those immortal children which only the soul that is dear to God can bring to the birth unaided because the Father has sown in her spiritual rays enabling her to behold the verities of wisdom. The order of reclining is so apportioned that the men sit by themselves on the right and the women by themselves on the left.

After the supper they hold the sacred vigil which is conducted in the following way. They rise up all together and standing in the middle of the refectory form themselves first into two choirs, one of men and one of women, the leader and precentor chosen for each being the most honoured amongst them and also the most musical. Then they sing hymns to God composed of many measures and set to many melodies, sometimes chanting together, sometimes taking up the harmony antiphonally, hands and feet keeping time in accompaniment, and rapt with enthusiasm reproduce sometimes the lyrics of the procession, sometimes of the halt and of the wheeling and counterwheeling of a choric dance. Then when each choir has separately done its own part in the feast, having drunk as in the Bacchic rites of the strong wine of God's love they mix and both together become a single choir, a copy of the choir set up of old beside the Red Sea in honour of the wonders there wrought. For at the command of God the sea became a source of salvation to one party and of perdition to the other. This wonderful sight and experience, an act transcending word and thought and hope, so filled with ecstasy both men and women that forming a single choir they sang hymns of thanksgiving to God their savior, the men led by the prophet Moses and the women by the prophetess Miriam.

It is on this model above all that the choir of the Therapeutae and Therapeutrides, note in response to note, the treble of the women blending with the bass of the men, create an harmonious concert music in the truest sense.

[From *The Special Laws*, in *Maenads, Martyrs, Matrons*, pp. 27–28.]

Philo shows a stricter attitude toward women in the following excerpt from *The Special Laws.*

Market-places and council-halls and law-courts and gatherings and meetings where a large number of people are assembled, and open-air life with full scope for discussion and action—all these are suitable to men both in war and peace. The women are best suited to the indoor life which never strays from the house, within which the middle door is taken by the maidens as their boundary, and the outer door by those who have reached full womanhood. Organized communities are of two sorts, the greater which we call cities and the smaller which we call households. Both of these have their governors; the government of the greater is assigned to men under the name of statesmanship, that of the lesser, known as household management, to women. A woman, then, should not be a busybody, meddling with matters outside her household concerns, but should seek a life of seclusion. She should not shew herself off like a vagrant in the streets before the eyes of other men, except when she has to go to the temple, and even then she should take pains to go, not when the market is full, but when most people have gone home, and so like a freeborn lady worthy of the name, with everything quiet around her, make her oblations and offer her prayers to avert the evil and gain the good. The audacity of women who when men are exchanging angry words or blows hasten to join in, under the pretext of assisting their husbands in the fray, is reprehensible and shameless in a high degree. And so in wars and campaigns and emergencies which threaten the whole country they are not allowed to take their place according to the judgement of the law, having in view the fitness of things, which it was resolved to keep unshaken always and everywhere and considered to be in itself more valuable than victory or liberty or success of any kind. If indeed a woman learning that her husband is being outraged is overcome by the wifely feeling inspired by her love for him and forced by the stress of the emotion to hasten to his assistance, she must not unsex herself by a boldness beyond what nature permits but limit herself to the ways in which a woman can help. For it would be an awful catastrophe if any woman in her wish to rescue her husband from outrage should outrage herself by befouling her own life with the disgrace and heavy reproaches which boldness carried to an extreme entails. What, is a woman to wrangle in the market-place and utter some or other of the words which decency forbids? Should she not when she hears bad language stop her ears and run away? As it is, some of them go to such a length that, not only do we hear amid a crowd of men a woman's bitter tongue venting abuse and contumelious words, but see her hands also used to assault—hands which were trained to weave and spin and not to inflict blows and injuries like pancratiasts and boxers. And while all else might be tolerable, it is a shocking thing, if a woman is so lost to a sense of modesty, as to catch hold of the genital parts of her opponent. The fact that she does so with the evident intention of helping her husband must not absolve her. To restrain her overboldness she must pay a penalty which will incapacitate herself, if she wishes to repeat the offence, and frighten the more reckless members of her sex into proper behaviour. And the penalty shall be this—that the hand shall be cut off which has touched what decency forbids it to touch.

[From *On the Contemplative Life*, in *Maenads, Martyrs, Matrons*, pp. 27–28.]

MISHNAH

The Mishnah is a compilation of laws dating from as early as the second century C.E. but parts of the text go back to a much earlier period. It was compiled after the fall of the Temple as one of the means for Jews, who were living under foreign rulers and were just one religious group among several others, for maintaining not only their identity but a proper relationship with the divine order.

The third division, or chapter, of the Mishnah is devoted to women and it provides the most thoroughgoing systematic model for women to be found in all of Jewish literature. It is mainly concerned with the marital transitions of women, from her father's home to her husband's and from her husband's through death or divorce. In almost all cases women are understood in relationship to some male, not as individuals. Within this context, and in addition to obligations placed upon them, women are guaranteed certain rights.

4:4   A. The father retains control of his daughter [younger than twelve and a half] as to effecting any of the tokens of betrothal: money, document, or sexual intercourse.

B. And he retains control of what she finds, of the fruit of her labor, and of abrogating her vows.

C. And he receives her writ of divorce [from a betrothal].

D. But he does not dispose of the return [on property received by the girl from her mother] during her lifetime.

E. [When] she is married, the husband exceeds the father, for he disposes of the return [on property received by the girl from her mother] during her lifetime.

F. But he is liable to maintain her, and to ransom her, and to bury her.

G. R. Judah says, "Even the poorest man in Israel should not hire fewer than two flutes and one professional wailing woman."

4:5   A. For all purposes is she in the domain of the father, until she enters the domain of the husband through marriage.

I B. [If] the father handed her over to the agents of the husband, lo, she [from that point on] is in the domain of the husband.

II C. [If] the father went along with the agents of the husband, or [if] the agents of the father went along with the agents of the husband, lo, she is in the domain of the father.

III D. [If] the agents of the father handed her over to the agents of the husband, lo, she is in the domain of the husband.

[From *The Mishnah*, 4:4.4:5, pp. 385–386.]

★ ★ ★

5:5   A. These are the kinds of labor which a woman performs for her husband:

B. she (1) grinds flour, (2) bakes bread, (3) does laundry, (4) prepares meals, (5) feeds her child, (6) makes the bed, (7) works in wool.

C. [If] she brought with her a single slave girl, she does not (1) grind, (2) bake bread, or (3) do laundry.

D. [If she brought] two, she does not (4) prepare meals and does (5) not feed her child.

E. [If she brought] three, she does not (6) make the bed for him and does not (7) work in wool.

F. If she brought four, she sits on a throne.

G. R. Eliezer says, "Even if she brought him a hundred slave girls, he forces her to work in wool,

H. "for idleness leads to unchastity."

I. Rabban Simeon b. Gamaliel says, "Also: He who prohibits his wife by a vow from performing any labor puts her away and pays off her marriage contract.

J. "For idleness leads to boredom."

[From *The Mishnah*, 5:5, p. 388.]

★ ★ ★

7:4 III A. He who prohibits his wife by a vow from going home to her father's house—

B. when he [father] is with her in [the same] town,

C. [if it is] for a month, he may persist in the marriage.

D. [If it is] for two, he must put her away and pay off her marriage contract.

E. And when he is in another town, [if the vow is in effect] for one festival season he may persist in the marriage. [But if the vow remains in force] for three, he must put her away and pay off her marriage contract.

[From *The Mishnah*, 7:4, p. 392.]

★ ★ ★

12:3   A. A widow who said, "I don't want to move from my husband's house"—

B. the heirs cannot say to her, "Go to your father's house and we'll take care of you [there]."

C. But they provide for her in her husband's house,

D. giving her a dwelling in accord with her station in life.

E. [If] she said, "I don't want to move from my father's house,"

F. the heirs can say to her, "If you are with us, you will have support. But you are not with us, you will not have support."

G. If she claimed that it is because she is a girl and they are boys, they do provide for her while she is in her father's house.

[From *The Mishnah*, 12:3, p. 403.]

★ ★ ★

2:6   A. Two women who were taken captive—

B. this one says, "I was taken captive, but I am pure,"

C. and that one says, "I was taken captive, but I am pure"—

D. they are not believed.

E. And when they give evidence about one another, lo, they are believed.

[From *The Mishnah*, 2:6, p. 381.]

★ ★ ★

3:4   A. The one who seduces a girl pays on three counts, and the one who rapes a girl pays on four:

B. the one who seduces a girl pays for (1) the shame, (2) the damage, and (3) a fine,

C. and the one who rapes a girl adds to these,

D. for he in addition pays for (4) the pain [which he has inflicted].

E. What is the difference between the one who rapes a girl and the one who seduces her?

F. (1) The one who rapes a girl pays for the pain, and the one who seduces her does not pay for the pain.

G. (2) The one who rapes a girl pays the financial penalties forthwith, but the one who seduces her pays the penalties when he puts her away.

H. (3) The one who rapes the girl [forever after] drinks out of his earthen pot, but the one who seduces her, if he wanted to put her away, does put her away.

3:5   A. How does he "drink from his earthen pot"?

B. Even if she is lame, even if she is blind, and even if she is afflicted with boils, [he must remain married to her].

C. [If] a matter of unchastity turned out to pertain to her, or if she is not appropriate to enter into the Israelite congregation, he is not permitted to confirm her as his wife [but, if he has married her, he must divorce her],

D. since it is said, *And she will be a wife to him* (Dt. 22:29)—a wife appropriate for him.

[From *The Mishnah*, 3:4–3:5, p. 383.]

The sixth division deals with all impurities and the Niddah section of this deals specifically with women's impurities which result primarily from menstruation, miscarriage and childbirth (Leviticus 12 and 15). Menstruation renders women impure for the time they bleed plus one week. They then take a ritual bath which restores them to a pure state. Childbirth renders the mother impure for forty days after the birth of a son and eighty days after the birth of a daughter. A woman's impurity can be transmitted to others and therefore contact with her is to be carefully controlled.

1:1   A. Shammai says, "[For] all women [it is] sufficient for them [to reckon uncleanness from] their time [of discovering a flow]."

[From *The Mishnah*, 1:1, p. 1077.]

3:3   A. She who aborts a sac filled with water, filled with blood, filled with dry matter, does not take thought that this is a valid birth.

B. And if it [a limb] was formed, let her sit [out the days of uncleanness and cleanness] for both male and female.

3:4   A. She who aborts [an abortion shaped like] a sandal or a placenta—

B. let her sit [out the days of uncleanness and cleanness] for both male and female.

C. [If] there is a placenta in a house, the house is unclean.

D. Not that the placenta is the child, but because there is no placenta which does not contain part of the child.

E. R. Simeon says, "The child was mashed before it [the afterbirth] came out."

3:5   A. She who produces a *tumtom* [an infant of doubtful sex] or an androgyne [of double sex]—

B. let her sit [out the days of uncleanness and cleanness] for both male and female.

C. [If she bore twins—] a *tumtom* and a male child, an androgyne and a male child—

D. let her sit [out the days of uncleanness] for both male and female.

E. [If she bore] a *tumtom* and a female, an androgyne and a female—let her sit [out the days of uncleanness] for a female only.

F. [If] it emerged in pieces or feet foremost—once the greater part of it has gone forth, lo, it is as if it were fully born.

G. [If] it came forth in the normal way, [it is not deemed born] until the greater part of its head has come forth.

H. And what is the greater part of its head?

I. Once its forehead has come forth.

3:6   A. She who aborts and what it is is not known [masculine or feminine]—

B. let her sit [out the days of uncleanness and cleanness] for both male and female.

C. [If] it is not known whether or not it was a human foetus,

D. let her sit [out the days of uncleanness and cleanness] for a male and for female and for menstruation.

3:7 A. She who miscarries on the fortieth day does not take account of the possibility that it is a human foetus.

B. [If this takes place] on the forty-first day [after intercourse], let her sit [out the days of uncleanness] for a male, for a female, and for menstruation.

C. R. Ishmael says, "[If it takes place] on the forty-first day, let her sit [out the days of uncleanness] for the male and for menstruation.

D. "If it takes place on the eighty-first day, let her sit [out the days of uncleanness] for male, for female, and for menstruation,

E. "for the male is completed on the fortieth day, and the female on the eighty-first."

F. And sages say, "All the same is the process of the formation of the male and female—both are completed on the forty-first day."

[From *The Mishnah*, 3:3–3:7, pp. 1081-1082.]

5:7 A. Sages have made a parable in regard to the woman: (1) an unripe fig, (2) a ripening fig, and (3) a fully ripe fig.

B. An unripe fig—she is still a little girl.

C. And a ripening fig—these are the days of her girlhood.

D. In both periods her father is entitled to whatever she finds and to her wages and to annul her vows.

E. A fully ripe fig—once she has grown up, her father has no further right over her.

[From *The Mishnah*, 5:7, p. 1085.]

BERURIAH

Talmudic studies were and are a mainstay of Judaism but until quite recently they have been the domain of men. While women have been associated with wisdom, and while folk tradition preserves stories about wise and clever women, only one woman stands out in Jewish history as a great Talmudic scholar, and that is Beruriah, a second-century woman believed to have been married to the famous and beloved Rabbi Meir. Documents containing her story go back to the third century C.E. In the eleventh century, however, an additional story was introduced in which Beruriah mocks the rabbinic attitude toward women, commits adultery with one of her husband's students, and then kills herself.

The following excerpts reveal Beruriah's faith and wisdom.

Rabbi Simlai came before Rabbi Yohanan and said to him, "Let the master teach me the Book of Genealogies (*sefer yuhasin*)." He said to him, "Where are you from?" He answered, "From Lod." "And where is your residence?" "In Nehardea." He said to him, "One engages in discussion neither with Lodites nor with Nehardeans. How much more so with you who are from Lod and whose residence is in Nehardea." He pressed him, and he consented. He [Simlai] said to him, "Let the master teach me [the material] in three months." He [Yohanan] picked up a clod, threw it at him, and said to him, "If Beruriah, the wife (*devethu*) of Rabbi Meir, the daughter of Rabbi Hananyah ben Teradyon, learned 300 traditions in a day from 300 masters, and even so did not fulfill her obligations in three years—how can you say in three months?" As he [Simlai] was getting up to go he said to him,

"Master, what is [the difference] between 'for its own sake' and 'not for its own sake,' [between] 'for those who eat it' and 'not for those who eat it' [referring to Mishnah Pesahim 5:2-3]?" He said to him, Since you are a disciple of the masters (*surba merabbanan*), come and I will tell you. . . ."

[From "The Beruriah Traditions," pp. 208-9.]

It once happened that Rabbi Meir was sitting and lecturing in the house of study on Sabbath afternoon, and his two sons died. What did their mother do? She laid the two of them on the bed and spread a sheet over them. After the departure of the Sabbath, Rabbi Meir came home from the house of study. He said to her, "Where are my two sons?" She said, "They went to the house of study." He said, "I was watching the house of study, and I did not see them." She gave him a cup for *havdalah,* and he recited the *havdalah* prayer. He again said, "Where are my two sons?" She said to him, "They went to another place and will soon come." She set food before him, and he ate and blessed. After he blessed, she said, "Master, I have a question to ask you." He said to her, "Ask your question." She said to him, "Master, some time ago a man came and gave me something to keep for him. Now he comes and seeks to take it. Shall we return it to him or not?" He said to her, "Daughter, whoever has an object in trust must return it to its owner." She said to him, "Master, I would not have given it to him without your knowledge." What did she do? She took him by the hand and led him up to the room. She led him to the bed and removed the sheet that was on them. When he saw the two of them lying dead on the bed, he began to cry and say, "My sons, my sons. . . ." At that time she said to Rabbi Meir, "Master, did you not say to me that I must return the trust to its master?" He said, "The Lord gave and the Lord has taken away; blessed be the name of the Lord (Job 1:21)."

R. Hanina said, "In this way she comforted him, and his mind was set at ease.

[From "The Beruriah Traditions," pp. 217–18.]

A certain Sadducee said to Beruriah, "It is written [Is. 54:1], 'Sing, O barren one, who did not bear.' Because she did not bear [should she] sing?" She said to him, "Fool! Cast your eyes to the end of the verse where is written, 'For the children of the desolate one will be more than the children of her that married, says the Lord.' What then does 'barren one who did not bear' mean? [It means,] rejoice, sons of the assembly of Israel, who resemble a barren woman who did not bear sons of gehenna like you."

[From "The Beruriah Tradition," p. 219.]

The story added in the eleventh century is as follows.

One time she [Beruriah] mocked what the sages said, "Women are flighty." He [Meir] said to her, "By your life! You will eventually concede [the correctness of] their words." He instructed one of his disciples to tempt her to infidelity. He [the disciple] urged her for many days, until she consented. When the matter became known to her, she strangled herself, while Rabbi Meir fled because of the disgrace.

[From "The Beruriah Traditions," p. 221.]

Medieval Period

RABBI MEIR OF ROTHENBURG

Rabbi Meir (1215?–1293) was one of the greatest Talmudic authorities of the thirteenth century and for almost fifty years he settled community disputes in his native Germany and those from surrounding countries. In the last years of his life, due to political upheavals, Rabbi Meir, and many other Jews, left Germany. He was, however, arrested in Lombardy as an apostate and spent the last seven years of his life in the prison where he died.

The following excerpts are from his responses to various inquiries about points of Talmudic law regarding menstruation, sexuality, rape, widow remarriage, and wife beating.

Those who throw keys or money into the hands of their wives during their menstruation period, should be sharply rebuked. Throughout this period until her immersion in a ritual bath, the wife should put down such articles for the husband to pick up, and the husband should put them down for the wife to pick up, but, throwing articles to each other at this period is prohibited.

[From *Rabbi Meir of Rothenburg,* p. 231.]

★ ★ ★

A woman is permitted to cohabit with her husband immediately after her immersion in the ritual bath [following her menstruation], even if such immersion took place in the daytime [of the eighth day]. However, R. Tam holds that a woman is not permitted to immerse herself in a ritual bath during the daylight time of Sabbath even if it be her eighth day.

Q. I have heard that you permit a woman to attend the bathhouse for further lavation, after her required immersion in a ritual bath.

A.   I can find no reason for prohibiting such practice. For the original prohibition against washing in ordinary water after immersion in a ritual bath, was directed only against persons preparing themselves for sacred duties; while a woman prepares herself for a secular purpose. My teacher R. Isaak of Vienna, was wont to prohibit such practice; nevertheless, when I once presented my point of view discussing the matter at length in his presence, he did not contradict me. I also heard from young men from Mantua, that when he (?) inquired about the matter from Rabbi Isaiah of Burgundy [of Trani], the latter also permitted the practice.

[From *Rabbi Meir of Rothenburg,* p. 237.]

* * *

Q.   Are the women among the group of forced converts from Rockenhausen who escaped from their captors, permitted to resume their marital relations with their husbands?

A.   Nowadays that the Gentiles are all powerful, a Jewish woman who was held captive by them, even though only for the purpose of extortion, is not permitted to live with her husband (Ket. 27b). But, since in this case many Jews were held captive together, they are now able to testify which women were not violated by their captors; such women who can furnish this testimony, even by a single witness and even by a woman witness, are permitted to resume their marital relations with their husbands. The fact that the captives did not give their lives for their religion does not disqualify them as witnesses. Although a Jew is enjoined to choose death rather than be forced to worship idols, should he violate this law he would not become disqualified as a witness though he would be guilty of having committed a sin. Moreover, according to the account given by the captives, they never actually embraced Christianity, but merely listened without comment to the priest's recitation of his senseless ritual in the presence of the Gentiles. Thus, the captives never committed a sin; for a Jew is not enjoined to choose death rather than allow the Christians to deceive themselves into believing that they have converted him.

[From *Rabbi Meir of Rothenburg,* pp. 279–280.]

Q.   A, of priestly lineage, married a woman within three months [of the death of her husband]. The authorities would have forced A to divorce her—even though he was of priestly lineage and would not be able to remarry her once he divorced her—had he not postponed asking them about the matter till long after the three months had expired and after it had become definitely certain that she had not been pregnant by her former husband. What is your opinion on this subject?

A.   The ban that is pronounced against a person who marries a widow within three months of her husband's death, is not a punitive measure, but is a means of forcing such a person to divorce her in order that he should not live with her within the three months of her former husband's death [so that the child born seven, eight, or nine, months later would not be of doubtful parentage]. After the three months have passed, therefore, there is no longer any reason for pronouncing the ban, and persons already married prior to the expiration of that period may be permitted to continue their married life undisturbed. The same rule applies to a person who married a nursing widow before her child was twenty-four months old. If no action was taken against him before the expiration of the twenty-four months, none should be taken against him after the expiration of that period. At the same time we make no distinction between a person who married a nursing widow because he was ignorant of the transgression involved, and the person who did so fully aware that he was doing wrong, since forcing a person to divorce his wife whom he married in a forbidden period, as referred to above, is not a punitive measure.

[From *Rabbi Meir of Rothenburg,* pp. 286–87.]

* * *

Q.   A often strikes his wife. A's aunt, who lives at his home, is usually the cause of their arguments, and adds to the vexation and annoyance of his wife.

A.   A Jew must honor his wife more than he honors himself. If one strikes one's wife, one should be punished more severely than for striking another person. For one is enjoined to honor one's wife but is not enjoined to honor the other person. Therefore, A must force his aunt to leave his house, and must promise to treat his wife honorably. If he persists in striking her, he should be excommunicated, lashed, and suffer the severest punishments, even to the extent of amputating his arm. If his wife is willing to accept a divorce, he must divorce her and pay her the *ketubah.*

Q.   A often beats his wife. She begged him to promise not to beat her any more, but he refused to make any such promise. Even when she appeared in the Synagogue to demand that A pay the debts she had contracted in order to pay for her sustenance [probably during a period of separation], A stubbornly refused to promise that in the future he would refrain from beating her.

A.   A must pay for his wife's sustenance since by his action he has shown that he had not decided to desist from his shameful practice. One deserves greater punishment for striking his wife than for striking another person, for he is enjoined to respect her. Far be it from a Jew to do such a thing. Had a similar case come before us we should hasten to excommunicate him. Thus, R. Paltoi Gaon rules that a husband who constantly quarrels with his wife must remove the causes of such quarrels, if possible, or divorce her and pay her the *ketubah;* how much more must a husband be punished, who not only quarrels but actually beats his wife.

[From *Rabbi Meir of Rothenburg,* pp. 326–27.]

MYSTICAL WRITINGS

THE ZOHAR

The *Zohar* is one of the main texts of the international religious movement of Judaism known as Kabbala. It was written in Spain by Moses de Leon (c. 1240–1305) who attributed it to Shimeon ben Yohai, a second century Palestinian mystic. The text is a mystical commentary on the first five books of the Hebrew Bible and was mainly studied by a small esoteric group until the expulsion of the Jews from Spain in 1492. After this time the teachings of the Kabbala as expressed in the *Zohar* spread throughout the Jewish world. The main ideas of these teachings center on the mystical and secret nature of God and the complex relationship that exists between God, humanity, and the world. An important aspect of these relationships is Shekhinah, a female term often translated as wisdom. While Shekhinah contains within itself this meaning of wisdom, frequently it is more specifically referred to as the manifestations of God, one of which is wisdom.

The following excerpts from the *Zohar* describe the gentle and the fierce aspects of Shekhinah. The first is a commentary on Leviticus 26 in which God promises to be present among his people as the *mishkan* or Shekhinah. Here it refers to God's manifestations which are conceived in female terms, particularly as the female lover.

A parable:
One person loved another, and said
"My love for you is so high I want to live with
    you!"
The other said, "How can I be sure that you will
    stay with me?"
So he took all his most precious belongings
and brought them to the other, saying
"Here is a pledge to you that I will never part
    from you."

So, the Blessed Holy One desired to dwell with
    Israel.

What did He do?
He took His most precious possession
and brought it down to them, saying
"Israel, now you have My pledge; so I will never
    part from you."

Even though the Blessed Holy One has removed
    Himself from Us,
He has left a pledge in our hands,
and we guard that treasure of His.
If He wants His pledge, let Him come and dwell
    among us!

[From *The Zohar,* p. 154.]

The second excerpt reveals God's manifestations as chastisement represented as Justice in female form.

One who is not loved by the Blessed Holy One, one who is hated by Him—

the correction is removed from him, the rod is removed.

It is written:
'I have loved you, says *YHVH* . . .'
(Malachi 1:2).
Because of His love, there is always a rod in His
    hand to guide him.
'But Esau I hated'
(Malachi 1:3);
so I removed the rod from him, removed the
    correction,
so as not to share Myself with him.
He is far from My soul,
but as for you, 'I have loved you!'

Therefore, 'My son, do not spurn the discipline of
    YHVH,
do not dread His correction.'
What does this mean: 'do not dread'?
Do not bristle from it, like one who flees from thorns,
for those things are like thorns in the flesh.

Come and see:
When Justice is aroused with Her powers
flashing forces arise on the right and on the left.
Many shafts fly forth from them:
shafts of fire, shafts of coal, shafts of flame!
They materialize to strike at human beings.
Under them are other deputies,
sparklers charged with forty-minus-one.
They hover and swoop down, strike and dart up.
Empowered, they enter the Hollow of the Great
    Abyss.
Here their sparks are dyed red;
a blazing fire is fused to them.
Embers explode,
flying, falling, befalling human beings!
Just as it is written:
'I will discipline you more!'
I will give something more to the Masters of
    Judgment
over and above their claim!
Whereas after the Flood, God said:
'I shall not doom the world any more because of
    humankind'
(Genesis 8:21).
What does this mean: 'any more'?
I will not give more to the Masters of Judgment
lest they destroy the world,
but only as much as the world can endure.
So 'I will discipline you more' means 'I will give
    them more.'
Why more?
To discipline you 'seven for your sins.'
Seven?
But if the Blessed Holy One collected His due,
the world could not endure for even a moment,
as it is written:

'If you kept account of sins, *YHVH*,
    who would survive?'
(Psalms 130:3).
How can you say: 'seven for your sins'?
Rather, what does 'seven' mean?
Seven is confronting you!
Who is She?
Release, who is seven, and called Seven,
as it is said:
'At the end of seven years enact a release'
(Deuteronomy 15:1).
Therefore 'Seven for your sins'. . . ."

Rabbi Abba said
"'I will discipline you Myself, seven for your sins.'
I disciplined you through other deputies,
as has been established.
'Myself'
Now I will confront you!
Seven will be aroused against you!

Come and see the pure love of the Blessed Holy
    One for Israel.
A parable:
There was a king who had a single son who kept
    misbehaving.
One day he offended the king.
The king said, 'I have punished you so many times
and you have not received.
Now look, what should I do with you?
If I banish you from the land and expel you from
    the kingdom,
perhaps wild beasts or wolves or robbers will
    attack you
and you will be no more.
What can I do?
The only solution is that I and you together leave
    the land!'

So, 'Myself': I and you together will leave the land!
The Blessed Holy One said as follows:
'Israel, what should I do with you?
I have already punished you, and you have not
    heeded Me.
I have brought fearsome warriors and flaming
    forces to strike at you
and you have not obeyed.
If I expel you from the land alone,
I fear that packs of wolves and bears will attack you
and you will be no more.
But what can I do with you?
The only solution is that I and you together leave
    the land
and both of us go into exile.
As it is written:
"I will discipline you,"
forcing you into exile;

but if you think that I will abandon you—
"Myself" too, along with you!'

'Seven for your sins'
This means Seven, who will be banished along
    with you.
Why? 'For your sins,'
as it is written:
'For your crimes, your Mother was sent away'
(Isaiah 50:1).
The Blessed Holy One said
'You have made Me homeless as well as yourselves,
for the Queen has left the palace along with you.
Everything is ruined, My palace and yours!
For a palace is worthless to a king unless he can
    enter with his queen.
A king is only happy when he enters the queen's
    palace
and finds her with her son;
they all rejoice as one.
Now neither the son nor the queen is present;
the palace is totally desolate.
What can I do?
I Myself will be with you!'

So now, even though Israel is in exile,
the Blessed Holy One is with them and has not
    abandoned them.
And when Israel comes out of exile
the Blessed Holy One will return with them,
as it is written:
'YHVH your God will return'
(Deuteronomy 30:3),
He Himself will return!
This has already been said."

Rabbi Ḥiyya and Rabbi Yose were walking on
    the road.
They happened upon a certain cave in a field . . .
Rabbi Ḥiyya said
"I have heard a new word said by Rabbi El'azar:
"'I will not spurn them or abhor them so as to
    destroy them."

The verse should read:
"I will not strike them or kill them so as to destroy
    them."
But instead we find: "I will not spurn them or
    abhor them."
Usually, one who is hated by another
is repulsive and utterly abhorrent to him;
but here "I will not spurn them or abhor them."
Why?
Because My soul's beloved is among them
and because of Her, all of them are beloved to Me,
as it is written:
le-khallotam,
spelled: le-khalltam, without the o.
Because of Her, "I will not spurn them or abhor
    them,"
because She is the love of My life.

A parable:
A man loved a woman.
She lived in the tanners' market.
If she were not there,
he would never enter the place.
Since she is there, it appears to him as a market of
    spice-peddlers
with all the world's finest aromas in the air.

Here too:
"Yet even at this point, when they are in the land
    of their enemies,"
which is a tanners' market,
"I will not spurn them or abhor them."
Why?
Le-khallatam, "Because of their bride,"
for I love Her!
She is the beloved of My soul dwelling there!
It seems filled with all the finest aromas of the
    world
because of the bride in their midst.' "
Rabbi Yose said
"If I have come here only to hear this word,
    it is enough for me!"
        [From The Zohar, pp. 158–62.]

The next two excerpts explore additional feminine themes in Zohar such as the following
commentary on Genesis 5, which emphasizes the simultaneous creation of male and female,
drawing positive conclusions from this divine act.

This is the book of the generations of Adam.
On the day that God created Adam,
in the likeness of God He created him;

male and female He created them.
He blessed them and called their name Adam
on the day they were created. (Genesis 5:1–2)

Rabbi Shim'on said
"High mysteries are revealed in these two verses.
'Male and female He created them'
to make known the Glory on high,
the mystery of faith.
Out of this mystery, Adam was created.

Come and see:
With the mystery by which heaven and earth were
    created
Adam was created.
Of them it is written:
'These are the generations of heaven and earth'
(Genesis 2:4).
Of Adam it is written:
'This is the book of the generations of Adam.'
Of them it is written:
'when they were created.'
Of Adam it is written:
'on the day they were created.'

'Male and female He created them.'

From here we learn:
Any image that does not embrace male and
    female
is not a high and true image.
We have established this in the mystery of our
    Mishnah.

Come and see:
The Blessed Holy One does not place His abode
in any place where male and female are not found
    together.
Blessings are found only in a place where male and
    female are found,
as it is written:
'He blessed them and called their name Adam
on the day they were created.'
It is not written:
'He blessed him and called his name Adam.'
A human being is only called Adam
when male and female are as one."
    [From *The Zohar*, pp. 55–56.]

A STORY

The following story from *Reshith Hokmah* shows how love for a woman can transform a man by leading him to God.

. . . there were great saints so absorbed in the Object of their longing that they did not feel any distraction besetting them. He who longs and yearns destroys all thought in himself which excludes the object of his desire; he is alive only to the fire burning within him. So full of longing that he eats, drinks and sleeps totally absorbed in his beloved. In the same way man ought to deport himself with G-d. This we can learn from the following tale told by Rabbi Yitzchak of Acco, of blessed memory, in his *Ma'assitoh Hap'rushim:*

"A princess went to bathe in the river and was observed by a low-born man, one of the slum dwellers. The thought which first flashed into his mind—'When will I be able to deal with her as I please?'—became an obsession. His desire for her grew mightily within him and finally he managed to have a word with her.

"Confessing his love—more in frustrated gestures and deep sighing than in well-put words—he proposed to her. The immensity of his love filled her with compassion and she answered that only in the cemetery could she meet him and be his own. She meant by this that the only place where rich and poor, aristocrat and beggar, are equals is in the cemetery. Their love would have to wait for death before it could be consummated.

"But he understood this only as being an appointment for a tryst. He sold all his possessions. What would he need of his own when he became the princess's squire? And he went to the cemetery, making it his home.

"He meditated on the form of his beloved and day by day his fervor increased. The image of her became more lovely and bold. Whenever impatience took hold of him, he would tell himself: 'How difficult it must be for the princess to leave her palace—she gave me her word. If not today, tomorrow. She will come.' Thus he waited, beholding her constantly with his inner eye.

"From time to time he saw how they brought corpses to the cemetery and soon he became aware of the transitoriness of existence. It can not be the fleshly form of the princess which I love he decided. There is something else about her, something very special and unique, something enduring and divine. And thus he began to contemplate the divine spark in forms which gives them such beauty and grace.

"In time he turned from the divine, which clothes itself in forms, to the loveliness of the eternally divine, which is without form or name. Daily he beheld the preciousness of the King, yearning to be absorbed into His very Being, rather than in any of His manifestations.

"No other thought entered his mind, so absorbed did he keep it on the object of his love. One can not be preoccupied with such single-minded yearning without being transformed into the very substance and being of the beloved object. And so, the former slum dweller, the low-born man, realized G-d. A G-d realized person, a Tzaddik, is soon felt by those who seek one. He attracts those who need him in the same manner as a flower attracts bees. Soon the cemetery became a place of pilgrimage for those who sought his blessings and direction. He was spoken of as the 'Tzaddik of the House of Life.'

"It so happened that the princess, who had already married, was barren. Like many others, she came to seek the blessing of the Tzaddik. When she stood before him, he greeted her and thanked her from the bottom of his heart. For all that he had realized he owed to his initial love for her. The Tzaddik freely bestowed his blessing upon her.

"Soon thereafter, he became so absorbed in His Being that he forgot to return to his flesh.

"At first, the people who came to seek him did not wish to disturb him. They thought him to be in devekuth [absorption]. Only later did they understand he had 'left life for the living.'"

★ ★ ★

Rabbi Yitzchak of Acco continues: "He who has never loved a woman is likened to an ass or worse. For all service to G-d must begin with the discrimination and further sublimation of lofty feelings . . ."

And the *Reshith Hokhmah* continues, saying: "Thus the words 'desire' and 'learning' must be understood. He who fastens his desire exclusively to one thing in the Torah—so that day and night he thinks of nothing else—will surely attain to the highest and most amazing levels of the soul. Such a one needs no fasts and austerities. All depends on the steadfastness and intensity of his longing for Torah, which must be like one who longs for his beloved . . ."

[From "Reshith Hokhmah," translated by Zalman M. Schachter, in *The Secret Garden,* pp. 207–9.]

Works by Women

SARA COPIA SULLAM OF VENICE

Sara Copia Sullam (1590–1641) was a well-known poet of Venice, whose home was a meeting place for talented Jews and Christians. Almost all of her writings have been lost, but the following excerpts from a surviving pamphlet reveal both her deep faith in Judaism and her wide knowledge. The pamphlet was written in response to the public accusation by a Catholic priest that she did not believe in the immortality of the soul.

The human soul, Signor Baldassare, is incorruptible, immortal, and divine, and infused by God into our body at that time when the organism is formed and able to receive it within the maternal womb: and this truth is so certainly, infallibly, and indubitably impressed on me, as I believe it is impressed on every Jew and Christian, that the title of your book, in which you have dared to deal in a farcical way with this matter, reminded me of the saying of that brave Roman who, having been invited to deliver an oration in praise of Hercules, exclaimed, 'Eh, who has said anything against Hercules?' And

in a similar spirit I, too, said: 'Is there any need for a tract like this, particularly in Venice, and what is the purpose of printing such treatises among Christians? When, however, I read the treatise properly later on, I discovered that it was addressed to me on the entirely false assumption that I cherish an opinion opposed to this clear truth. I was astonished and indignant at the shameless calumny which you have thus cast directly upon me, just as if you were the true investigator of the human heart. You must know that my soul is known to God only. . . .

Since, therefore, your calumny is without any

foundation I should have been entitled to use against you quite a different means of defense than that of the pen, by an indictment for open libel. But pity, which is embodied in your law, makes me merciful also towards your simplicity, which made you believe that you could gain immortal fame by saying something about the immortality of the soul. And as you had no better opportunity, you have yourself invented one. But instead of dealing with more important matters I felt that I had to spend two nights in countering your intrigue, on the plotting of which you have wasted night work for two years. I shall prove by this writing how false, unjust and senseless is your imputation that I deny the immortality of the soul. I do this in order to clear myself before those who do not know me, and who perhaps might believe your charge. . . .

Tell me then for God's sake, Signor Baldassare, what has induced you to write and print this tract and to involve my name in it. You say in Virgilian verses that God has chosen you for this purpose. This is ignorance indeed! So the Lord had at his disposal for such a sublime and important purpose no other more illuminated spirit and no more learned servant than just you! Of the host of all scholars He has chosen nobody but you to deal with such a worthy matter! If the belief in the immortality of the soul were not implanted in the human spirit by other means than rational grounds, it would be served badly if there were not other than yours which, although they emanate from learned authors, have been misunderstood and reproduced so badly by you. Such a worthless treatment of so important a matter serves rather to strengthen the arguments of the opposition. You will say, perhaps, that God often chooses vile and abject instruments to do great works, that His omnipotence reveals itself particularly in this way, and that, after all, Balaam's ass spoke once—yes, in those cases the effects were obviously divine, and the baseness of their instruments did no harm to them. You, who have pretended to prophesy without any inspiration but that of an extreme arrogance, have in the upshot shown more of ignorance than of any wonderful divine virtue! You would, therefore, have done better if you had applied to yourself instead of the verses of Virgil those of Dante:

Midway upon the journey of our life
I found myself within a forest dark
For the straightforward pathway had been lost.

You want to deal with the soul? with immortality? with the most difficult and arduous question in all philosophy, which would perhaps have been obscure to you in various aspects if theology had not come to your aid? You are certainly well aware of the fact that you are neither a philosopher nor a theologian, and, if I am not mistaken, I have heard from your own mouth that these sciences do not belong to your profession. And in spite of this you have dared to touch with your fingers such a sublime matter. . . .

It is not enough, my dear Sir, to possess the title 'Juris utriusque Doctor' to deal with the immortality of the soul. And in order to convince you how little skill you possess in theological writing as well as in philosophical reasoning, it may be sufficient to remind you of that nice little calumny you threw at my head in the beginning of your book, in which, after having falsely supposed that I deny the immortality of the soul, you declare that I am the only one who, after so many centuries, has fallen into such an error. That you have not read Scripture nor the historian Josephus Flavius, who reports the various opinions of the Jewish people, I can forgive you; but I cannot forgive you that you have not present in your mind the Gospel of your own creed; otherwise you would have remembered that in St. Matthew, chapter 22, the Sadducees, a Jewish sect that denied the immortality of the soul, came to Christ to submit their objections, and he answered them wisely and reduced them to silence.

You add that I do not believe in the infallible autograph written by God: I do not know that there is to be found in Holy Scripture another autograph written by the hand of God than the Decalogue, to which I cling with my faith and also with works as much as is in my power. If you have another writing made by the hand of God I would be delighted to see it. But let us see how well and with what linguistic skill and knowledge of Hebrew you have used the word 'ruach' in order to produce an argument for your purpose. You declare that the proper meaning of this expression is human, or rather the angelic and Divine spirit. I would be entitled to ask you for the strictest evidence of this interpretation, if you had spoken out of your understanding of this language. As I, however, know that you are without the slightest knowledge of Hebrew, and that this was only whispered to you by other people, I clearly see that you are an ignoramus concerning other matters about which you have spoken as well. You would have acted wisely if in this case, especially when you are engaged in an controversy with a Jewess, you had consulted an expert, because 'ruach' means originally nothing else than atmospheric wind or the air which we breathe; thus it can clearly be seen how incorrect are the conclusions drawn by you from that word. Where you pretend that you can prove by that expression that the soul is bodiless and immaterial, it would be necessary for one inclined to follow your conclusions to resort to another logic than that of Aristotle. But if you are so eager to defend the immortality of the soul, why do you attack a woman who, although somewhat versed in studies, has not made this science her profession? If you wish to show yourself fearless and brave, it would have been necessary to attack the Empedocleses, the Anaxagorases, the Epicuruses, the Aristotles, the Alessandri Afrodisei, the Averrhoi. . . . But as far as I can see you wanted to play the gallant man by withdrawing behind a barricade where nobody is present who would raise your glove. . . . Oh, you valiant fighter against women, the battlefield is entirely yours. Pass from one end to the other, batter the air with your magnificent strokes, and listen, since no other noise is heard, to nothing but the sound of your own hoarse trumpet! . . .

I repeat what I have said already: this is not an answer to your challenge, but a simple manifesto to excuse my not making my appearance. There is no reason for a combat where no resistance exists, neither in words nor deeds. As far as I am concerned, you may remove your armour, but even if you provoke me again with insults, I have no more intention of answering you, first because I do not want to waste my time, and then because I have no desire whatever to attract the attention of the public by my writings as you have shown yourself so ambitious to do. Live happy! You will attain the immortality which you preach so eloquently, if you observe your Christian teaching as well as I observe the law of Judaism. . . .

[From *Letters of the Jews Through the Ages*, pp. 443–47.]

GLÜCKEL OF HAMELN

Glückel of Hameln (1646–1724) was a German Jew who wrote the story of her life for her children. In it she offers them advice both in secular and religious matters.

In my great grief and for my heart's ease I begin this book in the year of Creation 5451 — God soon rejoice us and send us His redeemer soon. Amen. With the help of God, I began writing this, my dear children, upon the death of your good father in the hope of distracting my soul from the burdens laid upon it, and the bitter thought that we have lost our faithful shepherd. In this way I have managed to live through many wakeful nights, and springing from my bed have shortened the sleepless hours.

I do not intend, my dear children, to compose and write for you a book of morals. Such I could not write, and our wise men have already written many. Moreover, we have our holy Torah in which we may find and learn all that we need for our journey through this world to the world to come. Of our beloved Torah we may seize hold. . . . We sinful men are in the world as if swimming in the sea and in danger of being drowned. But our great, merciful and kind God, in his great mercy, has thrown ropes into the sea that we may take hold of them and be saved. These are our holy Torah where is written what are the rewards and punishments for good and evil deeds. . . .

Dear children, I do not want to speak at length upon this, for if I would penetrate too deeply into this matter ten books were not sufficient. Read in the German 'Brandspiegel,' in 'Leb Tob,' or, for those who can study, in books of morals; there you will find everything.

I pray you this, my children: be patient, when the Lord, may He be praised, sends you a punishment, accept it with patience and do not cease to pray to Him; perhaps He will have mercy upon you. . . . Therefore, my dear children, whatever you lose, have patience, for nothing is our own, everything is only a loan. . . . We men have been created for nothing else but to serve God and to keep His commandments and to obey the Torah, for 'He is thy life, and the length of thy life.'

The kernel of the Torah is: 'Thou shalt love thy neighbour as thyself.' But in our days we seldom find it so, and few are they who love their fellowmen with all their heart. On the contrary, if a man can contrive to ruin his neighbour nothing pleases him more. . . .

The best thing for you, my children, is to serve God from your heart without falsehood or deception, not giving out to people that you are one thing while, God forbid, in your heart you are another. Say your prayers with awe and devotion. During the time for prayers do not stand about and talk of other things. While prayers are being offered to the Creator of the world, hold it a great sin to engage another man in talk about an entirely different mater — shall God Almighty be kept waiting until you have finished your business?

Moreover, set aside a fixed time for the study of the Torah, as best you know how. Then diligently go about your business, for providing your wife and children with a decent livelihood is likewise a mitzwah — the command of God and the duty of man. We should, I say, put ourselves to great pains for our children, for on this the world is built, yet we must bear in mind that if children did as much for their parents, the children would quickly tire of it.

A bird once set out to cross a windy sea with its three fledglings. The sea was so wide and the wind so strong that the father bird was forced to carry his young, one by one, in his claws. When he was half-way across with the first fledgling the wind turned to a gale, and he said: 'My child, look how I am struggling and risking my life in your behalf. When you are grown up, will you do as much for me and provide for my old age?' The fledgling replied: 'Only bring me to safety, and when you are old I shall do everything you ask of me.' Whereat the father bird dropped his child into the sea, and it drowned, and he said: 'So shall be done to such a liar as you.' Then the father bird returned to the shore, set forth with his second fledgling, asked the same questions, and receiving the same answer, drowned the second child with the cry 'You, too, are a liar!' Finally he set out with the third fledgling, and when he asked the same question, the third and last fledgling replied: 'My dear father, it is true you are struggling mightily and risking your life in my behalf, and I shall be wrong not to repay you when you are old, but I cannot bind myself. This though I can promise: when I am grown up and have children of my own, I shall do as much for them as you have done for me.' Whereupon the father bird said: 'Well spoken, my child, and wisely; your life I will spare and I will carry you to shore in safety.'

Above all, my children, be honest in money matters, with both Jews and Gentiles, lest the name of Heaven be profaned. If you have in hand money or goods belonging to other people, give more care to them than if they were your own, so that, please God, you do no one a wrong. The first question put to a man in the next world is, whether he was faithful in his business dealings. Let a man work ever so hard amassing great wealth dishonestly, let him during his lifetime provide his children fat dowries and upon his death a rich heritage—yet woe, I say, and woe again to the wicked man who for the sake of enriching his children has lost his share in the world to come! For the fleeting moment he has sold Eternity.

When God sends evil days upon us, we shall do well to remember the remedy contrived by the physician in the story told by Rabbi Abraham ben Sabbati ha-Levi. A great king, he tells us, once imprisoned his physician, and had him bound hand and foot with chains, and fed on a small dole of barley-bread and water. After months of this treatment, the king dispatched relatives of the physician to visit the prison and learn what the unhappy man had to say. To their astonishment he looked as hale and hearty as the day he entered his cell. He told his relatives he owed his strength and well-being to a brew of seven herbs he had taken the precaution to prepare before he went to prison, and of which he drank a few drops every day. 'What magic herbs are these?' they asked; and he answered: 'The first is trust in God, the second is hope, and the others are patience, recognition of my sins, joy that in suffering now I shall not suffer in the world to come, contentment that my punishment is not worse, as well it could be, and, lastly, knowledge that God who thrust me into prison can, if He will, at any moment set me free.'

However, I am not writing this book in order to preach to you, but, as I have already said, to drive away the melancholy that comes with the long nights. So far as my memory and the subject permit, I shall try to tell everything that has happened to me from my youth upward. Not that I wish to put on airs or pose as a good and pious woman. No, dear children, I am a sinner. Every day, every hour, and every moment of my life I have sinned, nearly all manner of sins. God grant that I may find the means and occasion for repentance. But, alas, the care of providing for my orphaned children, and the ways of the world, have kept me far from that state.

If God will that I may live to finish them, I shall leave you my Memoirs in seven little books. And so, as it seems best, I shall now begin with my birth.

[From *Letters of Jews Through the Ages,* pp. 565–68.]

Folktales

RACHEL AND AKIBA

The following popular story about Rabbi Akiba's wife Rachel reveals important values of Jewish society: the faithful wife who knows what is important in a man and who, regardless of the price, encourages her husband in his study of Talmud.

In Jerusalem there once lived a very rich man whose name was Kalba Sabua. He had an only daughter, Rachel, who was beautiful and clever. The sons of the best families in the land proposed to her in marriage but she rejected them all.

"Neither riches nor good family concern me," she said. "The man I will marry must, above all, have a noble character and a good heart."

Among the shepherds who watched over her father's flocks and herds was a youth whose name was Akiba. Rachel fell in love with him and one day said to her father, "I want Akiba for my husband."

"Have you gone out of your mind?" cried her father. "How can you expect me to become the father-in-law of my servant? Never mention this to me again!"

"Father, give me Akiba for my husband!" pleaded Rachel. "I will not marry another."

"If you insist on marrying him you must leave my house!" threatened her father.

Rachel said no more but her mind was made up. She left her father's house and a life of luxury and fled with Akiba.

When Kalba Sabua heard of this he took a solemn oath: "My daughter shall not inherit even the least of my possessions."

Outside the city Akiba and his wife put up a tent. Having but little money they suffered privation and lived on dry bread alone. None the less, Rachel was happy and sustained the spirit of Akiba.

"I would rather live with you in poverty than without you in riches," she told him.

Their bed consisted only of a straw pallet. If a strong wind began to blow at night it would scatter the straw about. Rachel noticed that Akiba no longer slept but was wrapped in gloom.

"Why are you so sad, my husband?" she asked.

"It's on your account, Rachel," he replied. "You must suffer so, and all on account of me!"

At that very moment someone called from outside their tent.

"What is it you wish?" asked Rachel.

"Have pity on me!" answered the voice. "My wife has fallen sick and I have no straw to make a bed for her. Give me some, if you can."

And Rachel gave him some straw. Then she said to Akiba, "Just see—you consider us unfortunate but there are people who are even poorer than we."

"Bless you for your words! They have consoled me!" cried Akiba. Often Akiba had expressed the wish to attend the Houses of Study in Jerusalem in order to acquire learning. One day Rachel said to him, "You must carry out your plan to become an educated man. I know it will be very difficult for you but I will gladly remain behind and not stand in your way. I will patiently wait for your return."

Thereupon Akiba arose and made ready for his journey to Jerusalem. His wife accompanied him on the way for a distance. Then she bade him fond farewell and turned sadly back.

As he walked along the road Akiba said to himself, "I'm almost forty years old and now it may be too late for me to study the Word of God. Who knows if I will ever be able to achieve my goal!"

Suddenly he came upon several shepherds sitting near a spring. At the mouth of the spring lay a stone which had many grooves.

"What caused these grooves?" he asked the shepherds.

"They were made by drops of water that steadily trickled upon the stone."

Hearing this Akiba rejoiced. He said to himself, "If a stone may be softened how much easier will it be to soften my mind!"

And he continued on his journey until he came to a school for children. There he learned how to read and write and was not ashamed to study with children. After that he entered the Houses of Study. He became a pupil of Rabbi Nahum Ish Gamru. Afterwards he studied with Rabbi Eliezer ben Hyrkanos and Rabbi Joshua ben Hananiah.

Each day, before he went to the House of Study, Akiba would go into the forest to chop some wood. A part of it he sold in order to nourish himself, a part he kept for his own use, and the rest he used to pillow his head at night.

When Rachel heard of his hard manner of living she wished to help him. She cut off her hair which she sold, and sent him the money.

Despite his poverty, Akiba studied night and day. Before long he outdistanced all the other students in knowledge and in wisdom. When they met with a difficult problem they asked him to solve it.

Once Akiba stood outside the House of Study. At that time his comrades were discussing a very difficult question in a matter of Law. Akiba suddenly heard one say, "The solution is outside."

By that he clearly meant Akiba, who was capable of answering the question.

Akiba heard him but he did not stir from his place.

The students then continued to discuss another passage of the Torah but soon discovered that they did not understand it.

"The Torah is outside!" called another student.

Akiba heard him but pretended he did not understand the words. And still he did not enter the House of Study.

Once again the students met with a knotty problem.

"Is Akiba outside?" one of them cried. "Do come in, Akiba!"

This time Akiba, since he had been addressed, entered and sat himself at the feet of Rabbi Eliezer and his face was filled with the radiance of illumination.

For twelve long years Akiba stayed away from his

wife. One day he said to himself, "It is high time that I return to her and give her some happiness."

As he reached her door he heard a woman's voice saying, "What has happened to you, Rachel, happens to all disobedient children. Your husband has been away twelve years. All this time you have been living in solitude and poverty. Who knows whether he'll ever come back again! Had you but listened to your father you would have been rich and happy today!"

"Were my husband here to take my advice," replied Rachel, "he'd remain away another twelve years and continue his studies, undisturbed."

When Akiba heard her speak thus he suppressed his bitter yearning for her and turned away.

For twelve more years he continued his studies, this time away from Jerusalem. His fame became so great that the number of his students grew to twenty-four thousand.

When the second twelve years were completed Akiba decided to return to Jerusalem. The multitude of his students accompanied him there.

Soon the report of his return spread throughout Jerusalem. All the inhabitants streamed into the streets to welcome him back. Among them, unknown to each other, were also Kalba Sabua and Rachel; they had not met for twenty-four years.

Rachel was so poorly dressed that her neighbors had said to her, "Let us lend you some good clothes. You cannot go forth dressed like a beggar to meet such a great man as Akiba."

"A man such as Akiba is unconcerned with the way people are dressed!" replied Rachel.

When Akiba appeared among his students Rachel elbowed her way through the throng. She fell at his feet and with streaming eyes kissed the hem of his robe. Akiba's students wished to drive the intruder away.

"Let her be, she is my wife!" cried Akiba. "Know that had it not been for her I would never have been your teacher. It was she who urged me on to devote myself to learning. She has waited for me for twenty-four long years!"

And speaking thus he raised her from the ground, kissed her and went with her into her poor hut.

In the meantime, Kalba Sabua, who did not know that Rabbi Akiba, the foremost sage in Israel, was his former shepherd and his son-in-law, was determined to see him. He wished to ask Rabbi Akiba to release him from the solemn oath he had once taken to disinherit his daughter. So he went to Rabbi Akiba and laid the matter before him.

"And why did you reject the shepherd?" asked the sage, without making his identity known.

"He was an ignorant man!"

"And where is your daughter now, and where is her husband?"

"I do not know, Master. I haven't seen them for twenty-four years. If you will release me from my oath I will go and seek them to the ends of the earth."

All this Rachel heard from an adjoining room. Unable to restrain her feelings any longer she burst into the room, crying to her father, "I am your daughter, Rachel, and Rabbi Akiba is your son-in-law!"

Amazed and overawed, Kalba Sabua regarded his children. Then he embraced them and cried, "My good daughter, you were right when you married Akiba against my wishes. Blessed be both of you!"

[From *A Treasury of Jewish Folklore,* pp. 33–35.]

A CLEVER WOMAN

The following tale is fairly common in world literature. It is the story of a clever woman who manages to secure a tentative status for herself by marrying a powerful man.

The Innkeeper's Clever Daughter

Once there was a nobleman and he had three Jewish tenants on his estate. One held the forest concession, another operated the mill, the third, the poorest of them, ran the inn.

One day the nobleman summoned the three and said to them, "I am going to put to you three questions: 'Which is the swiftest thing in the world? Which is the fattest? Which is the dearest?' The one who answers correctly all of these questions won't have to pay me any rent for ten years. And whoever fails to give me the correct answer, I'll send packing from my estate."

The Jew who had the forest concession and the one who operated the mill did not think very long and decided between them to give the following answers: "The swiftest thing in the world is the nobleman's horse, the fattest is the nobleman's pig, and the dearest is the nobleman's wife."

The poor innkeeper, however, went home feeling very much worried. He had only three days' time to answer the nobleman's questions. He racked his brains. What answers could he give?

Now the innkeeper had a daughter. She was pretty and clever.

"What is worrying you so, father?" she asked.

He told her about the nobleman's three questions.

"Why shouldn't I worry?" he cried. "I've thought and thought but I cannot find the answers!"

"There is nothing to worry about, father," she told him. "The questions are very easy: The swiftest thing in the world is thought, the fattest is the earth, the dearest is sleep."

When the three days were up the three Jewish tenants went to see the landowner. Pridefully the first two gave the answers they had agreed upon beforehand, thinking that the landowner would feel flattered by them.

"You're wrong!" cried the nobleman. "Now pack up and leave my estate right away and don't you dare to come back!"

But, when he heard the innkeeper's answers he was filled with wonder.

"I like your answers very much," he told him, "but I know you didn't think them up by yourself. Confess—who gave you the answers?"

"It was my daughter," the innkeeper answered.

"Your daughter!" exclaimed the nobleman in surprise. "Since she is so clever I'd very much like to see her. Bring her to me in three days' time. But listen carefully: she must come here neither walking nor riding, neither dressed nor naked. She must also bring me a gift that is not a gift."

The innkeeper returned home even more worried than the first time.

"What now, father?" his daughter asked him. "What's worrying you?"

He then told her of the nobleman's request to see her and of his instructions.

"Well, what is there to worry about?" she said. "Go to the market-place and buy me a fishing net, also a goat, a couple of pigeons and several pounds of meat."

He did as she told him and brought to her his purchases.

At the appointed time she undressed and wound herself in the fishing net, so she was neither dressed nor naked. She then mounted the goat, her feet dragging on the ground, so that she was neither riding nor walking. Then she took the two pigeons in one hand and the meat in the other. In this way she arrived at the nobleman's house.

The nobleman stood at the window watching her arrival. As soon as he saw her he turned his dogs on her, and, as they tried to attack her, she threw them

the meat. So they pounced on the meat and let her pass into the house.

"I've brought you a gift that is not a gift," she said to the nobleman, stretching out her hand holding the two pigeons. But suddenly she released the birds and they flew out of the window. The nobleman was enchanted with her.

"What a very clever girl you are!" he cried. "I want to marry you, but only on one condition, never must you interfere in my affairs!"

She gave him her promise and he made her his wife.

One day, as she stood at the window, she saw a weeping peasant pass by.

"Why do you weep?" she asked him.

"My neighbor and I own a stable in partnership," he told her. "He keeps a wagon there and I a mare. Last night the mare gave birth to a pony under my neighbor's wagon. Whereupon, my neighbor insisted that the pony rightfully belonged to him. So I haled him before the nobleman who upheld him and said the pony was his. How unjust, I say!"

"Take my advice," the nobleman's wife said. "Get a fishing-rod and station yourself before my husband's window. Nearby you'll find a sand-heap. Pretend you're catching fish there. My husband will surely be amazed and will ask you: 'How can you catch fish in a sand-heap?' So you will answer him: 'If a wagon can give birth to a pony then I can catch fish in a sand-heap.'"

The peasant did as she told him and it happened exactly as she said it would.

When the nobleman heard the peasant's answer he said to him, "You didn't think this up out of your own head. Confess, who told you?"

"It was your wife."

Angrily the nobleman went to look for his wife.

"You have broken your promise not to interfere in my affairs!" he stormed at her. "Go and choose from all my possessions that which you deem the most precious and return to your father's house!"

"Very well," she answered, "I will go, but before I do I would like to dine with you for the last time."

He consented, and during dinner she plied him with much wine. When he had drunk a great deal he became drowsy and fell asleep. Thereupon she ordered that his carriage be made ready. She then drove him, as he slept, to her father's house.

When he sobered up and discovered where he was he asked in surprise, "How did I ever get here?"

"It was I who brought you here," his wife confessed. "Don't you remember telling me to choose the most precious possession you owned and then to return to my father's house? So I looked over all your possessions, and, not finding any of them as precious as you,

I carried you away with me to my father's house."
The nobleman was overjoyed.
"Since you love me so, let's go home!" he said.

So they were reconciled and lived in prosperity and in honor for the rest of their lives.

[From *A Treasury of Jewish Folklore*, pp. 95–97.]

Sources

Selections from the Hebrew Bible are from *Tanakh — The Holy Scriptures: The New JPS Translation According to the Traditional Hebrew Text,* copyright 1985 by the Jewish Publication Society.

The Apocrypha and Pseudepigrapha of the Old Testament in English, with introductions and critical and explanatory notes to the several books, ed. R. H. Charles, Volume II, *Pseudepigrapha.* Oxford: The Clarendon Press, 1913.

"The Beruriah Traditions," by David Goodblatt, in *Persons and Institutions in Early Rabbinic Judaism,* ed. William Scott Green. Missoula, MT: Scholars Press, 1977, pp. 207–36.

The Essential Philo, by Philo Judaeus, ed. Nahum N. Glatzer. New York: Schocken Books, 1971.

The Legends of the Jews, vol. 1, by Louis Ginzberg. Philadelphia: Jewish Publications Society, 1956.

Letters of Jews Through the Ages: From Biblical Times to the Middle of the Eighteenth Century, Volume 2, edited, with an introduction, biographical notes, and historical comments by Franz Kobler. London: Ararat Publishing Society, 1952.

Maenads, Martyrs, Matrons, Monastics: A Sourcebook on Women's Religion in the Greco-Roman World, ed. Ross S. Kraemer. Philadelphia: Fortress Press, 1988.

The Mishnah: A New Translation, by Jacob Neusner. New Haven and London: Yale University Press, 1988.

Rabbi Meir of Rothenburg, by Irving A. Agus, volume 1. New York: Ktav Publishing House, Inc., 1970.

The Secret Garden: An Anthology in the Kabbalah, ed. David Meltzer. New York: The Seabury Press, 1976.

A Treasury of Jewish Folklore: Stories, Traditions, Legends, Humor, Wisdom, and Folk Songs of the Jewish People, ed. Nathan Ausbel. New York: Crown, 1948.

Zohar: The Book of Enlightenment, trans. Daniel C. Matt. New York: Paulist Press, 1982.

Bibliography

Introductory Works on Judaism

Jacob Neusner, *The Way of the Torah: An Introduction to Judaism.* 4th ed. Belmont, CA: Wadsworth Publishing Company, 1988, 1979.

Encyclopedia Judaica. New York: The Macmillan Company, 1971–1972.

The Interpreter's One-Volume Commentary on the Bible, ed. Charles M. Laymon. Nashville, TN: Abingdon Press, 1971.

Works on Women and Judaism

Judith Baskin, "The Separation of Women in Rabbinic Judaism," in *Women, Religion and Social Change,* ed. Yvonne Yazbeck Haddad and Ellison Banks Findly. Albany, NY: State University Press of New York, 1985.

Phyllis Bird, "Images of Women in the Old Testament," in *Religion and Sexism: Images of Women in the Jewish and Christian Traditions,* ed. Rosemary Radford Ruether. New York: Simon and Schuster, 1974.

Bernadette J. Brooten, *Women Leaders in the Ancient Synagogue.* Chico, CA: Scholars Press, 1982.

Denise L. Carmody, "Judaism," in *Women in World Religions,* ed. Arvind Sharma. Albany, NY: State University of New York Press, 1987.

Steve Davies, "The Canaanite-Hebrew Goddess," in *The Book of the Goddess Past and Present,* ed. Carl Olson. New York: Crossroad, 1989.

Shlomo Deshen, "Domestic Observances: Jewish Practices," in *The Encyclopedia of Religion,* ed. Mircea Eliade. 4: 400–402.

Jo Ann Hackett, "In the Days of Jael: Reclaiming the History of Women in Ancient Israel," in *Immaculate and Powerful: The Female in Sacred Image and Social Reality,* ed. Clarissa W. Atkinson, Constance H. Buchanan, and Margaret R. Miles. Boston: Beacon Press, 1985.

Judith Hauptman, "Images of Women in the Talmud," in *Religion and Sexism: Images of Women in the Jewish and Christian Traditions,* ed. Rosemary Radford Ruether. New York: Simon and Schuster, 1974.

Susannah Heschel, ed. *On Being a Jewish Feminist: A Reader.* New York: Schocken Books, 1983.

Jacob Neusner, *A History of Mishnaic law of Women.* Leiden: Brill, 1980.

——, *Method and Meaning in Ancient Judaism: Second Series.* Chico, CA: Scholars Press, 1981, pp. 127–142, 173–186.

Raphael Patai, *The Hebrew Goddess.* New York: Ktav, 1967.

Judith Plaskow, *Standing Again at Sinai: Judaism from a Feminist Perspective.* San Francisco: Harper & Row, 1990.

Gershom Scholem, *Kabbalah.* New York: Quadrangle/
The New York Times Book Co., 1974.

Leonard Swidler, *Women in Judaism: The Status of Women in Formative Judaism.* Metuchen, NJ: The Scarecrow Press, 1976.

Phyllis Trible, *God and the Rhetoric of Sexuality.* Philadelphia: Fortress Press, 1978.

——, *Texts of Terror: Literary-Feminist Readings of Biblical Narratives.* Philadelphia: Fortress Press, 1984.

Ellen M. Umansky, "Lilith," in *The Encyclopedia of Religion,* ed. Mircea Eliade. 8: 554–555. New York: Macmillan Publishing Company, 1987.

——, and Diane Ashton, eds. *Four Centuries of Jewish Women's Spirituality.* Boston: Beacon Press, 1992.

CHRISTIANITY

Introduction

Christianity began with the teachings of Jesus of Nazareth, called the Christ, meaning the anointed one, in the early part of the first century C.E. and it took shape as a formal tradition under the guidance of Paul of Tarsus. Pre-Pauline Christianity, sometimes referred to as the Jesus movement, was an egalitarian movement in which women figured prominently. The life of Jesus, as recorded in the gospels, brings out the importance of his mother Mary, his female disciples, and the many women he taught. As the tradition took shape, the role of women was reduced and the early equalitarian spirit was somewhat diminished. This is not a process unique to Christianity, other religions such as Buddhism and many smaller religious movements begin with the teachings of a charismatic male who attracts a large number of active and vocal female followers. Generally these movements challenge the norms of their society and when the founder dies, in order to survive, the movement usually modifies its more radical views and begins to conform to their society's practices, especially with regard to women. Early Christianity was not an exception to this rule. Consequently, the images of women in the history of Christianity vary wildly from the bravery of the female disciples who remained at the site of the crucifixion while the male disciples hid, to various diatribes about the inherent evilness of women due to their connection to Eve, the cause of all sin. This picture of early Christianity is further complicated by the varieties of Christianity that were practiced, especially by the Gnostic Christians, in which women seem to have continued in leadership roles longer than in other forms of Christianity and by some of the misogynist polemics of church fathers such as Tertullian and Irenaeus.

Other important images of women are contained in the stories of the martyrs, especially the virgin martyrs, who were often stripped naked and humiliated before suffering horrible deaths. These stories and other forms of Christian affirmation and indeed exaltation of female virginity became an essential part of the ascetic practices which continued to gain in popularity after the legalization of Christianity. These are just a few of the complex of female images that were passed on to women in later Christianity.

Over time monastic opportunities for women continued to grow and, during the so-called Dark Ages, monasteries were the centers of culture and learning; often they possessed the only significant libraries. In these environments women were able to receive and give educations as well as to develop whatever talents they had whether these were spiritual, literary, or administrative. Many of the founders and abbesses of religious communities for women were noblewomen who had exercised some degree of power in their secular lives and they brought their organizational abilities to the monasteries. Several were outstanding scholars who not only knew scripture and the classics, but were also familiar with canon law and church politics. Most contributed significantly to the Christianization of Europe either through their influence on a frequently still pagan populace or by actually being among the first missionaries in areas such as Germany and among the Franks.

With the successful Christianization of Europe the power and prestige of these monasteries was assured. The monastic life was seen by many women as a more viable alternative to secular life and it is in these communities of women that much of the great flowering of writing by medieval women takes place. Much of this literature was written in the form of devotional narratives, most of which were didactic in that they were offered as models for others, especially women, to emulate. These works were written by women who were free of domestic responsibilities and had some education, financial support, and the leisure to pursue their writing.

For women, these requisites were most often met in the nunneries of medieval Europe or similar religious settings. Some of these women were illiterate and consequently dictated descriptions of their visions and their biographies to male clerics.

Many of these medieval women gained religious authority through their visions, but they had to meet certain criteria in order to have their visions taken seriously, most often this meant that they be celibate and preferably virgins, though celibate widows were also accepted.

Equally important for the spiritual life of Christian women were the more loosely knit forms of religious community that began to take shape in the early part of the thirteenth century, especially the Beguines. These were groups of women from all over Europe who gathered into smaller or larger groups, or lived alone. They continued to work at various secular occupations and purposefully avoided being cloistered. Most of these women were given to deep mystical experiences and their movement lasted in northern Europe until the French Revolution. Additionally, throughout the medieval period there were also individual women who lived as anchoresses. For the most part these women led contemplative lives on or near church grounds where they had access to a confessor and many of these women were sought out for their spiritual advice. Certain orders, such as the Dominicans and the Franciscans, created tertiary orders for both women and men who for various reasons were unable to fully leave the secular world. For the most part these were penitential groups who, like the Beguines, practiced spiritual discipline combined with practical works of mercy such as caring for the poor and the sick. Since they were not cloistered they had great freedom of movement along with the support of a religious community. As time went on dissension increased between the hierarchical structures of the church and these various popular and monastic movements.

While the Reformation generally refers to the Protestant Reformation, a full picture of the religious life of European women at this time involves the Catholic counter-Reformation which also changed the religious opportunities available to Catholic women, both lay and clerical.

The Reformation created cataclysmic changes in the religious and political life of Europe. When Luther posted his 95 Theses in 1517 his intention was to reform the decadent and politically entangled church of Rome. Instead he set off a series of upheavals that lasted for most of the century. Periods of intense change often bring to the fore people who normally do not have a voice in their society: the poor, the disenfranchised, and women. This is the case in the Reformation period. At the same time, reform frequently means redefining values and morality in all spheres of life. When the Protestant Reformers turned their attention to family life they ended up redefining the status of women.

While for both Luther and Calvin women and men were spiritual equals, they also believed that women's subordination to men was ordained at the time of creation and must be maintained in order to fulfill God's will. The reformers believed women's vocation was as wife and mother and further that family life was the cornerstone of society. Consequently, they were very serious in their views of women's role in the family. When Protestant leaders focused on women in relation to family, it was to enjoin women to be chaste and obedient to their husbands, thereby fully embracing the patriarchal ideas of their time as well as the patriarchal ideas they saw in the Bible. The Protestant emphasis on marriage was communicated through marriage manuals (Luther himself wrote two of these), sermons, and dramas which centered on married life rather than the popular pre-Reformation plays about virgin martyrs.

Perhaps most significantly, the rejection of clerical celibacy had profound reverberations in the lives of Protestant women. On the one hand they had status within their family but on the other they no longer had the option to choose a non-domestic life. In turning away from the great nunneries of the Catholics, Protestant women lost an important source of women's spirituality. Religious orders of nuns and Beguines came under fire from both the Protestants, who wanted them to disband and marry, and the counter-reformation Catholics who wanted them to be completely cloistered. While there were several notable and successful holdouts, female autonomy in religious life was pretty much at an end. The only formal religious role open to Protestant women was that of the pastor's wife. This was and remains a difficult role in which women are expected to be models of the ideal Christian wife.

The essential point of the Protestant Reformation was that all Christians, through their faith in Christ's work, are equal participants and are equally able to be priests although this priestly equality was not extended to women. Many Protestant women, however, had their own ideas about the meaning and shape of their spiritual lives and they acted upon them. Without the support and bravery of these women, especially the powerful noblewomen who sheltered many religious refugees and influenced political decisions about religious issues, the Protestant Reformation would not have succeeded.

The Early Church

NEW TESTAMENT

THE LIFE OF JESUS

The life of Jesus is told in the four Gospels of the New Testament. The earliest, Mark, was written between 64–75 C.E. and both Matthew, written between 80–85 C.E., and Luke, written between 85–95 C.E., drew on it as a source. The final Gospel to be written was John, sometime after 90 C.E. The last chapters of each of these Gospels deal with the resurrection of Jesus, an event of critical importance to Christians for several reasons. First, the resurrection of Jesus is seen by Christians to contain the promise that, like Jesus, they too shall conquer death and be resurrected into eternal life in heaven. Second, those people who were accepted as witnesses of the resurrection, or those people who saw the resurrected Jesus, were the main source of authority in the early church. In fact, such a vision was one source of Paul's authority, the main organizer of the diverse and far-flung community of early Christians, even though Paul's witnessing occurred three years after Jesus's death. In other words, those who saw the resurrected Jesus were accepted as divinely chosen leaders. Some of these witnesses were women.

In three of the Gospels (Matthew, Luke, and John) women, especially Mary Magdalene, were witnesses to the resurrected Jesus. In Mark women are instructed by an angel to announce the resurrection and later Mary Magdalene sees the resurrected Jesus. Other books of the New Testament reveal that hundreds of early Christians had visions of the resurrected Christ (e.g., 1 Cor 15:6), many of whom understood the vision to be a call or commission to preach. (See, for instance, Paul's experience on the road to Damascus in which he sees a blinding light and hears the voice of Jesus, Acts 9:3–9.) Consequently, additional criteria were necessary in order to limit the number of people who had spiritual authority and this second criteria was that Jesus had constituted them to be public witnesses to his resurrection. A close reading of the following excerpts reveals that in Matthew the women saw the resurrected Jesus and were commissioned to announce the resurrection by Jesus himself (Matthew 28:9–10) while in John Jesus appears first to Mary Magdalene who then tells the disciples (John 20:14–18).

So, while women have spiritual authority in the Gospels, it is either ignored or later revised (e.g., 1 Cor 15 which says that Jesus appeared to Peter and then to the twelve disciples with no mention of the women witnesses). The important question, and the one thus far left unanswered by scholars, is how the version of events preserved in Luke became authoritative.

These excerpts from the Gospels are followed by readings which demonstrate the variety of practices that existed in the early Church and show that the Church was in a constant state of transformation. The role of women was one of the many things that kept changing. As time went by the activities of women continued to be curtailed and one is left to suspect that Luke became the preferred version of the resurrection because it was consistent with the lesser role of women.

What is most important is that it was the women who remained faithful, who were present at the tomb, while the male disciples were in hiding.

Matthew 28

After the sabbath, as the first day of the week was dawning, Mary Magdalene and the other Mary went to see the tomb. And suddenly there was a great earthquake; for an angel of the Lord, descending from heaven, came and rolled back the stone and sat on it. His appearance was like lightning, and his clothing white as snow. For fear of him the guards shook and became like dead men. But the angel said to the women, "Do not be afraid; I know you are looking for Jesus who was crucified. He is not here; for he has been raised, as he said. Come, see the place where he lay. Then go quickly and tell his disciples, 'He has been raised from the dead, and indeed he is going ahead of you to Galilee; there you will see him. This is my message for you.'" So they left the tomb quickly with fear and great joy, and ran to tell his disciples. Suddenly Jesus met them and said, "Greetings!" And they came to him, took hold of his feet, and worshiped him. Then Jesus said to them, "Do not be afraid; go and tell my brothers to go to Galilee, there they will see me."

John 20

Early on the first day of the week, while it was still dark, Mary Magdalene came to the tomb and saw that the stone had been removed from the tomb. So she ran and went to Simon Peter and the other disciple, the one whom Jesus loved, and said to them, "They have taken the Lord out of the tomb, and we do not know where they have laid him." Then Peter and the other disciple set out and went toward the tomb. The two were running together, but the other disciple outran Peter and reached the tomb first. He bent down to look in and saw the linen wrappings lying there, but he did not go in. Then Simon Peter came, following him, and went into the tomb. He saw the linen wrappings lying there, and the cloth that had been on Jesus' head, not lying with the linen wrappings but rolled up in a place by itself. Then the other disciple, who reached the tomb first, also went in, and he saw and believed; for as yet they did not understand the scripture, that he must rise from the dead. Then the disciples returned to their homes.

But Mary stood weeping outside the tomb. As she wept, she bent over to look into the tomb; and she saw two angels in white, sitting where the body of Jesus had been lying, one at the head and the other at the feet. They said to her, "Woman, why are you weeping?" She said to them, "They have taken away my Lord, and I do not know where they have laid him." When she had said this, she turned around and saw Jesus standing there, but she did not know that it was Jesus. Jesus said to her, "Woman, why are you weeping? Whom are you looking for?" Supposing him to be the gardener, she said to him, "Sir, if you have carried him away, tell me where you have laid him, and I will take him away." Jesus said to her, "Mary!" She turned and said to him in Hebrew, "Rabbouni!" (which means Teacher). Jesus said to her, "Do not hold on to me, because I have not yet ascended to the Father. But go to my brothers and say to them, 'I am ascending to my Father and your Father, to my God and your God.'" Mary Magdalene went and announced to the disciples, "I have seen the Lord"; and she told them that he had said these things to her.

1 CORINTHIANS 7 and 11

Paul's first letter to the church at Corinth was written c. 55 C.E., some four years after his stay in that city, and was a reply to questions contained in a letter he had received from that church as well as instructions on other matters. In chapter seven Paul expresses his views on marriage and general contact with women. It should be remembered that Paul, along with most early Christians, believed that the Second Coming of Christ was imminent; as Paul himself says in this chapter, he felt there was only a limited amount of time left (vv. 27, 29, 31) and, therefore, his prescriptions should be understood within that urgent context. Within the tradition, even though the meaning and timing of the Second Coming of Christ has reinterpreted, Paul's words have an enduring authority.

In chapter eleven Paul, following Gen. 2:8–9, stresses the inferiority of women. He expresses his belief that as God is the head of Christ, Christ is the head of man, and man is the head of woman. This leads Paul to instruct the men of Corinth to pray with their heads uncovered, to show their glory, while the women should cover their heads, to show their subordination to men.

1 Corinthians 7

Now concerning the matters about which you wrote: "It is well for a man not to touch a woman." But because of cases of sexual immorality, each man should have his own wife and each woman her own husband. The husband should give to his wife her conjugal rights, and likewise the wife to her husband. For the wife does not have authority over her own body, but the husband does; likewise the husband does not have authority over his own body, but the wife does. Do not deprive one another except perhaps by agreement for a set time, to devote yourselves to prayer, and then come together again, so that Satan may not tempt you because of your lack of self-control. This I say by way of concession, not of command. I wish that all were as I myself am. But each has a particular gift from God, one having one kind and another a different kind.

To the unmarried and the widows I say that it is well for them to remain unmarried as I am. But if they are not practicing self-control, they should marry. For it is better to marry than to be aflame with passion.

To the married I give this command—not I but the Lord—that the wife should not separate from her husband (but if she does separate, let her remain unmarried or else be reconciled to her husband), and that the husband should not divorce his wife.

* * *

Now concerning virgins, I have no command of the Lord, but I give my opinion as one who by the Lord's mercy is trustworthy. I think that, in view of the impending crisis, it is well for you to remain as you are. Are you bound to a wife? Do not seek to be free. Are you free from a wife? Do not seek a wife. But if you marry, you do not sin, and if a virgin marries, she does not sin. Yet those who marry will experience distress in this life, and I would spare you that. I mean, brothers and sisters, the appointed time has grown short; from now on, let even those who

have wives be as though they had none, and those who mourn as though they were not mourning, and those who rejoice as though they were not rejoicing, and those who buy as though they had no possessions, and those who deal with the world as though they had no dealings with it. For the present form of this world is passing away.

I want you to be free from anxieties. The unmarried man is anxious about the affairs of the Lord, how to please the Lord; but the married man is anxious about the affairs of the world, how to please his wife, and his interests are divided. And the unmarried woman and the virgin are anxious about the affairs of the Lord, so that they may be holy in body and spirit; but the married woman is anxious about the affairs of the world, how to please her husband. I say this for your own benefit, not to put any restraint upon you, but to promote good order and unhindered devotion to the Lord.

1 Corinthians 11

Be imitators of me, as I am of Christ.

I commend you because you remember me in everything and maintain the traditions just as I handed them on to you. But I want you to understand that Christ is the head of every man, and the husband is the head of his wife, and God is the head of Christ. Any man who prays or prophecies with something on his head disgraces his head, but any woman who prays or prophecies with her head unveiled disgraces her head—it is one and the same thing as having her head shaved. For if a woman will not veil herself, then she should cut off her hair; but if it is disgraceful for a woman to have her hair cut off or to be shaved, she should wear a veil. For a man ought not to have his head veiled, since he is the image and reflection of God; but woman is the reflection of man. Indeed, man was not made from woman, but woman from man. Neither was man created for the sake of woman, but woman for the sake of man. For this reason a woman ought to have a symbol of authority on her head, because of the angels. Nevertheless, in the Lord woman is not independent of man or man independent of woman. For just as woman came from man, so man comes through woman; but all things come from God. Judge for yourselves: is it proper for a woman to pray to God with her head unveiled. Does not nature itself teach you that if a man wears long hair, it is degrading to him, but if a woman has long hair, it is her glory? For her hair is given to her for a covering.

TERTULLIAN

Tertullian (160?–225?) was foundational for western theology due to the wide number of issues he addressed and because he was the first Christian theologian to write extensively in Latin. In the following excerpt from "On the Apparel of Women" Tertullian connects all women to Eve and enjoins them to dress modestly.

CHAP. I.—INTRODUCTION. MODESTY IN APPAREL BECOMING TO WOMEN, IN MEMORY OF THE INTRODUCTION OF SIN INTO THE WORLD THROUGH A WOMAN.

If there dwelt upon earth a faith as great as is the reward of faith which is expected in the heavens, no one of you at all, best beloved sisters, from the time that she had first "known the Lord," and learned (the truth) concerning her own (that is, woman's) condition, would have desired too gladsome (not to say too ostentatious) a style of dress; so as not rather to go about in humble garb, and rather to affect meanness of appearance, walking about as Eve mourning and repentant, in order that by every garb of penitence she might the more fully expiate that which she derives from Eve,—the ignominy, I mean, of the first sin, and the odium (attaching to her as the cause) of human perdition. "In pains and in anxieties dost thou bear (children), woman; and toward thine husband (is) thy inclination, and he lords it over thee." And do you not know that you are (each) an Eve? The sentence of God on this sex of yours lives in this age: the guilt must of necessity live too. *You* are the devil's gateway: *you* are the unsealer of that (forbidden) tree: *you* are the first deserter of the divine law: *you* are she who persuaded him whom the devil was not valiant enough to attack. *You* destroyed so easily God's image, man. On account of *your* desert—that is, death—even the Son of God had to die. And do you think about adorning yourself over and above your tunics of skins? Come now; if from the beginning of the world the Milesians sheared sheep, and the Serians spun trees, and the Tyrians dyed, and the Phrygians embroidered with the needle, and the Babylonians with the loom, and pearls gleamed, and onyx-stones flashed; if gold itself also had already issued, with the cupidity (which accompanies it), from the ground; if the mirror, too, already had license to lie so largely, Eve, expelled from paradise, (Eve) already dead, would also have coveted *these* things, I imagine! No more, then, ought she *now* to crave, or be acquainted with (if she desires to live again), what, when she *was* living, she had neither had nor known. Accordingly these things are all the baggage of woman in her condemned and dead state, instituted as if to swell the pomp of her funeral.

[From *The Ante-Nicene Fathers*, vol. 4, p. 8.]

THE MARTYRDOM OF PERPETUA

The following excerpts are taken from a first-person account of martyrdom that took place in Carthage on March 7, 203. This is one of the very few extant works by a Christian woman of this period. In it Perpetua records her fears for the child she is still nursing, the pressures of her non-Christian father who wants her to save herself, and the visions which sustain her.

A few days later we were imprisoned. I was terrified because never before had I experienced such darkness. What a terrible day! Because of crowded conditions and rough treatment by the soldiers the heat was unbearable. My condition was aggravated by my anxiety for my baby. Then Tertius and Pomponius, those kind deacons who were taking care of our needs, paid for us to be moved for a few hours to a better part of the prison where we might refresh ourselves. Leaving the dungeon we all went about our own business. I nursed my child, who was already weak from hunger. In my anxiety for the infant I spoke to my mother about him, tried to console my brother, and asked that they care for my son. I suffered intensely because I sensed their agony on my account. These were the trials I had to endure for many days. Then I was granted the privilege of having my son remain with me in prison. Being relieved of my anxiety and concern for the infant, I immediately regained my strength. Suddenly the prison became my palace, and I loved being there rather than any other other place.

Then my brother said to me, "Dear sister, you already have such a great reputation that you could ask for a vision indicating whether you will be condemned or freed." Since I knew that I could speak with the Lord, whose great favors I had already experienced, I confidently promised to do so. I said I would tell my brother about it the next day. Then I made my request and this is what I saw.

There was a bronze ladder of extraordinary height reaching up to heaven, but it was so narrow that only one person could ascend at a time. Every conceivable kind of iron weapon was attached to the sides of the ladder: swords, lances, hooks, and daggers. If anyone climbed up carelessly or without looking upwards, he/she would be mangled as the flesh adhered to the weapons. Crouching directly beneath the ladder was a monstrous dragon who threatened those climbing up and tried to frighten them from ascent.

Saturus went up first. Because of his concern for us he had given himself up voluntarily after we had been arrested. He had been our source of strength but was not with us at the time of the arrest. When he reached the top of the ladder he turned to me and said, "Perpetua, I'm waiting for you, but be careful not to be bitten by the dragon." I told him that in the name of Jesus Christ the dragon could not harm me. At this the dragon slowly lowered its head as though afraid of me. Using its head as the first step, I began my ascent."

At the summit I saw an immense garden, in the center of which sat a tall, grey-haired man dressed like a shepherd, milking sheep. Standing around him were several thousand white-robed people. As he raised his head he noticed me and said, "Welcome, my child." Then he beckoned me to approach and gave me a small morsel of the cheese he was making. I accepted it with cupped hands and ate it. When all those surrounding us said "Amen," I awoke, still tasting the sweet cheese. I immediately told my brother about the vision, and we both realized that we were to experience the sufferings of martyrdom. From then on we gave up having any hope in this world.

A few days later there was a rumor that our case was to be heard. My father, completely exhausted from his anxiety, came from the city to see me, with the intention of weakening my faith. "Daughter," he said, "have pity on my grey head. Have pity on your father if I have the honor to be called father by you, if with these hands I have brought you to the prime of your life, and if I have always favored you above your brothers, do not abandon me to the reproach of men. Consider your brothers; consider your mother and your aunt; consider your son who cannot live without you. Give up your stubbornness before you destroy all of us. None of us will be able to speak freely if anything happens to you."

These were the things my father said out of love, kissing my hands and throwing himself at my feet. With tears he called me not daughter, but woman. I was very upset because of my father's condition. He was the only member of my family who would find no reason for joy in my suffering. I tried to comfort him saying, "Whatever God wants at this tribunal will happen, for remember that our power comes not from ourselves but from God." But utterly dejected, my father left me.

One day as we were eating we were suddenly rushed off for a hearing. We arrived at the forum and the news spread quickly throughout the area near the forum, and a huge crowd gathered. We went up to the prisoners' platform. All the others confessed when they were questioned. When my turn came my father appeared with my son. Dragging me from the step, he begged: "Have pity on your son!"

Hilarion, the governor, who assumed power after the death of the proconsul Minucius Timinianus, said, "Have pity on your father's grey head; have pity on your infant son; offer sacrifice for the emperors' welfare." But I answered, "I will not." Hilarion asked, "Are you a Christian?" And I answered, "I am a Christian." And when my father persisted in his attempts to dissuade me, Hilarion ordered him thrown out, and he was beaten with a rod. My father's injury hurt me as much as if I myself had been beaten, and I grieved because of his pathetic old age. Then the sentence was passed; all of us were condemned to the beasts. We were overjoyed as we went back to the prison cell. Since I was still nursing my child who was ordinarily in the cell with me, I quickly sent the deacon

Pomponius to my father's house to ask for the baby, but my father refused to give him up. Then God saw to it that my child no longer needed my nursing, nor were my breasts inflamed. After that I was no longer tortured by anxiety about my child or by pain in my breasts.

[From *A Lost Tradition*, pp. 20–22.]

During her stay in prison Perpetua than has two more visions, both of her dead brother. Her fourth and final vision is of her coming martyrdom, during which she sees herself transformed into a man.

The day before the battle in the arena, in a vision I saw Pomponius the deacon coming to the prison door and knocking very loudly. I went to open the gate for him. He was dressed in a loosely fitting white robe, wearing richly decorated sandals. He said to me, "Perpetua, come. We're waiting for you!" He took my hand and we began to walk over extremely rocky and winding paths. When we finally arrived short of breath, at the arena, he led me to the center saying, "Don't be frightened! I'll be here to help you." He left me and I stared out over a huge crowd which watched me with apprehension. Because I knew that I had to fight with the beasts, I wondered why they hadn't yet been turned loose in the arena. Coming towards me was some type of Egyptian, horrible to look at, accompanied by fighters who were to help defeat me. Some handsome young men came forward to help and encourage me. I was stripped of my clothing, and suddenly I was a man. My assistants began to rub me with oil as was the custom before a contest, while the Egyptian was on the opposite side rolling in the sand. Then a certain man appeared, so tall that he towered above the amphitheater. He wore a loose purple robe with two parallel stripes across the chest; his sandals were richly decorated with gold and silver. He carried a rod like that of an athletic trainer, and a green branch on which were golden apples. He motioned for silence and said, "If this Egyptian wins, he will kill her with the sword; but if she wins, she will receive this branch." Then he withdrew.

We both stepped forward and began to fight with our fists. My opponent kept trying to grab my feet but I repeatedly kicked his face with my heels. I felt myself being lifted up into the air and began to strike at him as one who was no longer earthbound. But when I saw that we were wasting time, I put my two hands together, linked my fingers, and put his head between them. As he fell on his face I stepped on his head. Then the people began to shout and my assistants started singing victory songs. I walked up to the trainer and accepted the branch. He kissed me and said, "Peace be with you, my daughter." And I triumphantly headed towards the Sanavivarian Gate. Then I woke up realizing that I would be contending not with wild animals but with the devil himself. I knew, however, that I would win. I have recorded the events which occurred up to the day before the final contest. Let anyone who wishes to record the events of the contest itself, do so."

[From *A Lost Tradition*, pp. 24–25.]

SAINT AUGUSTINE – THE CONFESSIONS

St. Augustine (354–439) was one of the most influential theologians in the Christian church as well as a model of piety. His *Confessions,* which recount his conversion from Manichaeism to Christianity, was and remains an enduring popular document. In it Augustine gives first place to his mother Monica for her part in his conversion, and consequently the *Confessions* includes details of her life. The story of Monica and her unstinting devotion to the spiritual welfare of her son became a model for Christian women, especially a model of Christian motherhood. Monica also echoes the powerful cult of the Virgin Mary: The self-sacrificing mother is a particularly safe female image for male celibates and she offered comfort to women with difficult children and husbands. Monica's cult became increasingly popular from the fifteenth century onward.

The following excerpts reveal Augustine's and Monica's attitude toward a wife's duty, which is to serve her husband even if he beats her, and describe a shared vision they had after Augustine's conversion to Christianity. It is at this point that Monica makes her famous speech that the meaning of her life has been to secure her son's salvation; consequently she has no further need of earthly life. It concludes with Monica's death and Augustine's deep mourning for her.

Chapter 8
Monica's Youth

★ ★ ★

I omit many things, as I am making great haste. Accept my confessions and acts of thanksgiving, O my God, for countless things, even those I pass over in silence. But I will not pass over whatever my soul brings to birth concerning that handmaiden of yours, who brought me to birth, both in her flesh, so that I was born into this temporal light, and in her heart, that I might be born into eternal light. Not of her gifts, but of your gifts in her, will I speak. She neither made herself nor did she educate herself: you created her. Neither her father nor her mother knew what sort of woman would be made from them. The rod of your Christ, the rule of your only Son, in a faithful home, in a good member of your Church, instructed her "in your fear."

★ ★ ★

Chapter 9
Monica, Wife of Patricius

Brought up modestly and soberly in this manner and made subject by you to her parents rather than by her parents to you, when she arrived at a marriageable age, she was given to a husband and served "him as her lord." She strove to win him to you, speaking to him about you through her conduct, by which you made her beautiful, an object of reverent love, and a source of admiration to her husband. She endured offenses against her marriage bed in such wise that she never had a quarrel with her husband over this matter. She looked forward to seeing your mercy upon him, so that he would believe in you and be made chaste. But in addition to this, just as he was remarkable for kindness, so also was he given to violent anger. However, she had learned to avoid resisting her husband when he was angry, not only by deeds but even by words. When she saw that he had curbed his anger and become calm and that the time was opportune, then she explained what she had done, if he happened to have been inadvertently disturbed.

In fine, when many wives, who had better-tempered husbands but yet bore upon their faces signs of disgraceful beatings, in the course of friendly conversation criticized their husbands' conduct, she would blame it all on their tongues. Thus she would give them serious advice in the guise of a joke. From the time, she said, they heard what are termed marriage contracts read to them, they should regard those documents as legal instruments making them slaves. Hence, being mindful of their condition, they should not rise up in pride against their lords. Women who knew what a sharp-tempered husband she had to put up with marveled that it was never reported or revealed by any sign that Patricius had beaten his wife or that they had differed with one another in a family quarrel, even for a single day. When they asked her confidentially why this was so, she told them of her policy, which I have described above. Those who acted upon it, found it to be good advice and were thankful for it; those who did not act upon it, were kept down and abused.

★ ★ ★

Finally, towards the very end of his earthy life, she gained her husband for you. After he became one of the faithful, she did not have to complain of what she had endured from him when he was not yet a believer. She was also a servant of your servants. Whosoever among them knew her greatly praised you, and honored you, and loved you in her, because they recognized your presence in her heart, for the fruit of her holy life bore witness to this. She had been the wife of one husband; she repaid the duty she owed to her parents; she had governed her house piously; she had testimony for her good works; she had brought up children, being as often in labor in birth of them as she saw them straying from you. Lastly Lord, of all of us, your servants—for out of your gift you permit us to speak—who, before she fell asleep in you already lived together, having received the graces of your baptism, she took care as though she had been mother to us all, and she served us as though she had been a daughter to all of us.

Chapter 10
The Vision at Ostia

With the approach of that day on which she was to depart from this life, a day that you knew, although it was unknown to us, it came about, as you yourself ordered it, so I believe, in your secret ways, that she and I stood leaning out from a certain window, where we could look into the garden within the house we had taken at Ostia on the Tiber, where, removed from crowds, we were resting up, after the hardships of a long journey, in preparation for the voyage. We were alone, conversing together most tenderly, "forgetting those things that are behind, and stretching forth to those that are before." We inquired of one another "in the present truth," which truth you are, as to what the eternal life of the saints would be like, which eye has not seen, nor ear heard, nor has it entered into the heart of a man." But we were straining out with the heart's mouth for those supernal streams flowing from your fountain, "the fountain of life," which is "with you," so that, being sprinkled with it according to our capacity, we might in some measure think upon so great a subject.

When our discourse had been brought to the point that the highest delight of fleshly senses, in the brightest corporeal light, when set against the sweetness of that life seemed unworthy not merely of comparison with it, but even of remembrance, then, raising ourselves up with a more ardent love to the Selfsame, we proceeded step by step through all bodily things up to that heaven whence shine the sun and the moon and the stars down upon the earth. We ascended higher yet by means of inward thought and discourse and admiration of your works, and we came up to our own minds. We transcended them, so that we attained to the region of abundance that never fails, in which you feed Israel forever upon the food of truth, and where life is that Wisdom by which all these things are made, both which have been and which are to be. And this Wisdom itself is not made, but it is such as it was, and so it will be forever. Nay, rather, to have been and to be in the future do not belong to it, but only to be, for it is eternal. And while we discourse of this and pant after it, we attain to it in a slight degree by an effort of our whole heart. And we sighed for it, and we left behind, bound to it "the first-fruits of the spirit," and we turned back again to the noise of our mouths, where a word both begins and ends. But what is there like to your Word, our Lord, remaining in himself without growing old, and yet renewing all things?

Therefore we said: If for any man the tumult of the flesh fell silent, silent the images of earth, and of the waters, and of the air; silent the heavens; silent for him the very soul itself, and he should pass beyond himself by not thinking upon himself; silent his dreams and all imagined appearances, and every tongue, and every sign; and if all things that come to be through change should become wholly silent to him—for if any man can hear, then all these things say to him, "We did not make ourselves, but he who endures forever made us—if when they have said these

words, they then become silent, for they have raised up his ear to him who made them, and God alone speaks, not through such things but through himself, so that we hear his Word, not uttered by a tongue of flesh, nor by an angel's voice, "nor by the sound of thunder," nor by the riddle of a similitude, but by himself whom we love in these things, himself we hear without their aid,—even as we then reached out and in swift thought attained to that eternal Wisdom which abides over all things—if this could be prolonged, and other visions of a far inferior kind could be withdrawn, and this one alone ravish, and absorb, and hide away its beholder within its deepest joys, so that sempiternal life might be such as was that moment of understanding for which we sighed, would it not be this: "Enter into the joy of your Lord?" When shall this be? When we shall all rise again, but we shall not all be changed."

Such things I said, although not in this manner and in these words. Yet, O Lord, you know that on that day when we were speaking of such things, and this world with all its delights became contemptible to us in the course of our words, my mother said: "Son, for my own part, I now find no delight in anything in this life. What I can still do here, and why I am here, I do not know, now that all my hopes in this world have been accomplished. One thing there was, for which I desired to linger a little while in this life, that I might see you a Catholic Christian before I died. God has granted this to me in more than abundance, for I see you his servant, with even earthly happiness held in contempt. What am I doing here?"

Chapter 11
The Death of St. Monica

What I said to her in answer to this I do not entirely recall, for scarcely five days later, or not much more, she fell sick of fever. One day, as she lay ill, she lost consciousness and for a little while she was withdrawn from all present things. We rushed to her, but she quickly regained her sense. She looked at me and my brother as we stood there, and said to us, after the manner of one seeking something. "Where was I?" Then, gazing at us who were struck dumb with grief, she said, "Here you put your mother." I remained silent and stopped my weeping. But my brother said, as if wishing a happier lot for her, that she should die not in a foreign land but in her own country. When she heard this, she stared reproachfully at him with an anxious countenance, because he was concerned about such things. Then she looked at me and said, "See what he says!" Presently she said to both of us: "Put this body away anywhere. Don't let care about it disturb you. I ask only this of you, that you remember me at the altar of the Lord, wherever you may be." When she had expressed this wish in what words she could manage, she fell silent and was racked with increasing sickness.

* * *

So, on the ninth day of her illness, in the fifty-sixth year of her life and in the thirty-third year of mine, this devout and holy soul was set loose from the body.

Chapter 12
Monica's Burial; Augustine's Grief

I closed her eyes, and a mighty sorrow welled up from the depths of my heart and overflowed into tears. At the same time, by a powerful command of my mind, my eyes drank up their source until it was dry. Most ill was it with me in such an agony! When she breathed her last, the boy Adeodatus burst out in lamentation, but he was hushed by all of us and fell silent. In like manner, something childish in me, which was slipping forth in tears, was by a youthful voice, my heart's own voice, checked, and it grew silent. We did not think it fitting to solemnize that funeral with tearful cries and groans, for it is often the custom to bewail by such means the wretched lot of those who die, or even their complete extinction. But she did not die in agony, nor did she meet with total death. This we knew by sure evidence and proofs given by her good life and by her "unfeigned faith."

What was it, therefore, that grieved me so heavily, if not the fresh wound wrought by the sudden rupture of our most sweet and dear way of life together? I took joy indeed from her testimony, when in that last illness she mingled her endearments with my dutiful deeds and called me a good son. With great love and affection she recalled that she had never heard me speak a harsh or disrespectful word to her. Yet, O my God who made us! what comparison was there between the honor she had from me and the services that she rendered to me? When I was bereft of such great consolation, my heart was wounded through and my life was as if ripped asunder. For out of her life and mine one life had been made.

* * *

Little by little, I regained my former thoughts about your handmaid, about the devout life she led in you, about her sweet and holy care for us, of which I was so suddenly deprived. I took comfort in weeping in your sight over her and for her, over myself and for myself. I gave way to the tears that I had held back, so that they poured forth as much as they wished. I spread them beneath my heart, and it rested upon them, for at my heart were placed your ears, not the ears of a mere man, who would interpret with scorn my weeping.

Now, Lord, I confess to you in writing. Let him read it who wants to, let him interpret it as he wants. If he finds a sin in it, that I wept for my mother for a small part of an hour, for that mother now dead to my eyes who for so many years had wept for me so that I might live in your eyes, let him not laugh me to scorn. But rather, if he is a man of large charity, let him weep over my sins before you, the Father of all brothers of your Christ.

[From *The Confessions of St. Augustine,* book 9, chapters 8–12, pp. 216–26.]

EGERIA—ACCOUNT OF HER PILGRIMAGE

Very little is known about the author of the following text except for what she says about herself within it. The text reveals her to have been an upper-class woman who went on pilgrimage to Jerusalem in the early part of the fifth century. She was a member of a circle of religious women, for whom she wrote this account of her journey, although their exact role in the church is not clear. Her descriptions of the places she visited often reveal a deep knowledge of the Bible and she is treated with respect by the various holy men she meets along the way.

Then on Sabbath we went up the mountain, and coming to some monastic cells, where the monks living there received us very hospitably, providing us every courtesy. A church with a presbyter is there. There we remained for the night, and on the morning of the Lord's Day, with the priests and monks who lived there, one by one we began to climb the mountain.

These mountains are climbed with infinite labor, because you do not go up them very slowly in a circular path, as we say "in a spiral," but you go straight up the whole way as if climbing over a wall. Then one must directly descend each one of these mountains until you reach the very base of the central mountain which is called Sinai. So by the will of Christ our God, helped by the prayers of holy men who were going with us, and with great labor, it was done. I had to go up on foot because one cannot go straight up riding. Nonetheless one does not feel the labor, because I saw the desire which I had being completed through the will of God.

At the fourth hour we arrived at the top of the holy mountain of God, Sinai, where the Law was given, in the place where the majesty of God descended on that day when the mountain of God smoked. [Ex. 19:18] Now in this place the summit of the mountain is not very large. Nonetheless the church itself is very graceful. When therefore by the help of God we had ascended to the height and arrived at the door of the church, there was the presbyter assigned to that church coming to meet us from his monastic cell. He was a healthy old man, and, as they say here, an "ascetic," and — what more can I say — quite worthy to be in this place. Then also other presbyters met us, and all the monks who live around the mountain, that is, if they were not prevented by age or weakness. In fact no one stays on the summit of the central mountain, for there is nothing there except the church and the cave where Saint Moses was. [Ex. 33:22] The reading in this place was all from the book of Moses, the Oblation was made in due order and here we communicated. Now as we left the church the presbyters gave us eulogia from this place, fruits which grow on this mountain. Even though the holy mountain Sinai is all rocky, not having even a bush, still there is a bit of earth down by the foot of these mountains, both around the central one and those which surround it. There the holy monks through their diligence put bushes and establish orchards or cultivated plots, and next to them their dwellings, so that they may seem to gather fruits from the soil of the mountain itself, but nonetheless they have cultivated it with their own hands.

After we had communicated and the holy men had given us the eulogia and we had come through the church door, then I immediately asked them to show us each place. The holy men kindly agreed to show us all the sites. They pointed out to us the cave where Saint Moses was when he ascended into the mountain of God that he might receive again the tables of the Law, after he had broken the first one when the people had sinned. [Ex. 34; 32:19] Then they showed us other places which we wanted to see, and also ones which they knew better than we.

But I would like you to know, venerable ladies my sisters, that from the place where we were standing, the area around the church, the summit of the middle,

it seemed to us that those mountains which we had first ascended with difficulty were like little hills. Nonetheless they seemed boundless and I do not think that I have seen any higher, except for the middle mountain which greatly exceeds them. From that place we saw Egypt, Palestine, the Red Sea, and the Parthenian Sea which goes all the way to Alexandria, and finally the infinite Saracen lands. It is scarcely possible to believe it, but these holy men pointed out each place to us.

[From *A Lost Tradition*, pp. 86–88.]

★ ★ ★

When we returned from the mountains to that place, we came out into the place we had entered the mountains originally, and we returned again to the sea. So too the children of Israel, returning from Sinai the mountain of God went back through the route we took, even to the place where we came out from the mountains and reached the Red Sea. From this point we went back again by the path we had taken. The children of Israel made their own way from this same place as it is written in the book of holy Moses. [Num. 10:12; 33:16ff.] But we remained to Clysma by the same road and rest-stations. In Clysma we had to rest again, and to resume the journey from there, for our route through the desert had been very sandy.

I already knew about the land of Goshen from the first time I was in Egypt. Nonetheless I wished to see all the places where the children of Israel had been going out from Ramesses until they reached the Red Sea, to the place which now, from the camp which is there, is called Clysma. [Ex. 12:37ff.] We wanted to go from Clysma to the land of Goshen, to the city in the land of Goshen called Arabia. It is so called from the territory, that is "the land of Arabia, the land of Goshen"; it is a part of the land of Egypt, but is much better than all of Egypt. [Gen. 46:34 (Septuagint)] It is four days through the desert from Clysma, that is, from the Red Sea, to the city of Arabia, and even though it is through the desert, each resting place has a fort, with soldiers and officers, who always led us from fort to fort.

During this journey the holy men who were with us, the clergy and monks, showed us every single thing which I was seeking from the Scriptures. Some things were on the left of us, others on the right of the route, others were a long way on the trip, yet others were quite near. I wish your affection to believe me, that as far as I would perceive it, the children of Israel went some distance to the right, then they returned to the left, then they went a bit ahead, then they came back again; and thus they made their way until at length they reached the Red Sea.

[From *A Lost Tradition*, pp. 91–92.]

Gnosticism

Gnosticism was a widespread religious movement in the Greco-Roman world that had sects among Jews, Christians, and pagans. Its fundamental idea was that only knowledge, or gnosis, leads to salvation. It postulated a cosmos in which the forces of delusion, or ignorance, associated with darkness and materiality, battled the forces of wisdom and knowledge associated with light and spirituality.

CREATION, WISDOM, AND EVE

The following creation myth was probably composed c. 400 C.E. in Alexandria. It incorporates parts of the Genesis story, but from a Gnostic point-of-view. Primarily it emphasizes the role of Sophia, wisdom, both at the beginning of creation and as a means of salvation. It is she who gives Adam breath, a soul, and her daughter, Eve, to be his instructor. The forces of delusion, in the form of seven archangels, interfere violently in order to keep humans in ignorance and tell Adam and Eve not to eat from the Tree of Knowledge. The myth also describes the eventual conquest of the forces of darkness by the forces of light, especially wisdom.

On the Origin of the World
II 97,24–127,17

Since everyone—the gods of the world and men—says that nothing has existed prior to Chaos, I shall demonstrate that [they] all erred, since they do not know the [structure] of Chaos and its root. Here [is the] demonstration:

If it is [agreed by] all men concerning [Chaos] that it is a darkness, then it is something derived from a shadow. It was called darkness.

But the shadow is something derived from a work existing from the beginning.

So it is obvious that it (the first work) existed before Chaos came into being, which followed after the first work.

Now let us enter into the truth, but also into the first work, from whence Chaos came; and in this way the demonstration of truth will appear.

After the nature of the immortals was completed out of the boundless one, then a likeness called "Sophia" flowed out of Pistis. ⟨She⟩ wished ⟨that⟩ a work ⟨should⟩ come into being which is like the light which first existed, and immediately her wish appeared as a heavenly likeness, which possessed an incomprehensible greatness, which is in the middle between the immortals and those who came into being after them, like what is above, which is a veil which separates men and those belonging to the (sphere) above.

Now the aeon of truth has no shadow ⟨within⟩ it because the immeasurable light is everywhere within it. Its outside, however, is a shadow. It was called "darkness." From within it (darkness) a power appeared (as ruler) over the darkness. And (as for) the shadow, the powers which came into being after them called ⟨it⟩ "the limitless Chaos." And out of it [every] race of gods was brought forth, both [one and] the other and the whole place. Consequently, [the shadow] too is posterior to the first work [which] appeared. The abyss is derived from the aforementioned Pistis.

Then the shadow perceived that there was one stronger than it. It was jealous, and when it became self-impregnated, it immediately bore envy. Since that day the origin of envy has appeared in all of the aeons and their worlds. But that envy was found to be a miscarriage without any spirit in it. It became like the shadows in a great watery substance.

Then the bitter wrath which came into being from the shadow was cast into a region of Chaos. Since that day ⟨a⟩ watery substance has appeared, i.e. what was ⟨enclosed⟩ in it (the shadow) flowed forth, appearing in Chaos. Just as all the useless afterbirth of one who bears a little child falls, likewise the matter which came into being from the shadow was cast aside. And it did not come out of Chaos, but matter was in Chaos, (existing) in a part of it.

Now after these things happened, then Pistis came and appeared over the matter of Chaos, which was cast off like a miscarriage since there was no spirit in ⟨her⟩. For all of that is a boundless darkness and water of unfathomable depth. And when Pistis saw what came into being from her deficiency, she was disturbed. And the disturbance appeared as a fearful work. And it fled [in order to dwell] in the Chaos.

Then she turned to it and [breathed] into its face in the abyss, [which is] beneath all of the heavens.

Now when Pistis Sophia desired [to cause] the one who had no spirit to receive the pattern of a likeness and rule over the matter and over all its powers, a ruler first appeared out of the waters, lion-like in appearance, androgynous, and having a great authority within himself, but not knowing whence he came into being.

Then when Pistis Sophia saw him moving in the depth of the waters, she said to him, "O youth, pass over here," which is interpreted "Yaldabaoth." Since that day, the first principle of the word which referred to the gods and angels and men has appeared. And the gods and angels and men constitute that which came into being by means of the word. Moreover, the ruler Yaldabaoth is ignorant of the power of Pistis. He did not see her face, but the likeness which spoke with him he saw in the water. And from that voice he called himself "Yaldabaoth." But the perfect ones call him "Ariael" because he was a lion-likeness. And after this one came to possess the authority of matter, Pistis Sophia withdrew up to her light.

When the ruler saw his greatness—and he saw only himself; he did not see another one except water and darkness—then he thought that [he] alone existed. His [thought was] made complete by means of the word, and it appeared as a spirit moving to and fro over the waters. And when that spirit appeared, the ruler separated the watery substance to one region, and the dry (substance) he separated to another region. And from the (one) matter he created a dwelling place for himself. He called it "heaven." And from the (other) matter the ruler created a footstool. He called it "earth."

* * *

But on the fortieth day Sophia sent her breath into Adam, who was without soul. He began to move upon the earth. And he was not able to rise. Now when the seven rulers came and saw him, they were very much disturbed. They walked up to him and seized him, and he (Yaldabaoth) said to the breath which was in him, "Who are you? And from whence have you come hither?" He answered and said, "I came through the power of the (light)-man because of the destruction of your work." ‹› When they heard, they glorified him because he gave them rest from the fear and concern in which they were. Then they called that day "the rest," because they rested themselves from their troubles. And when they saw that Adam was not able to rise, they rejoiced. They took him and left him in Paradise, and withdrew up to their heavens.

After the day of rest, Sophia sent Zoe, her daughter, who is called "Eve (of Life)," as an instructor to raise up Adam, in whom there was no soul, so that those

whom he would beget might become vessels of the light. [When] Eve saw her co-likeness cast down, she pitied him, and she said, "Adam, live! Rise up on the earth!" Immediately her word became a deed. For when Adam rose up, immediately he opened his eyes. When he saw her, he said, "You will be called 'the mother of the living' because you are the one who gave me life."

Then the authorities were informed that their molded body was alive, and had arisen. They were very much disturbed. They sent seven archangels to see what had happened. They came to Adam. When they saw Eve speaking with him, they said to one another, "What is this (female) light-being? For truly she is like the likeness which appeared to us in the light. Now come, let us seize her and let us cast our seed on her, so that when she is polluted she will not be able to ascend to her light, but those whom she will beget will serve us. But let us not tell Adam that ‹she› is not derived from us, but let us bring a stupor upon him, and let us teach him in his sleep as though she came into being from his rib so that the woman will serve and he will rule over her."

Then (the Life)-Eve, since she existed as a power, laughed at their (false) intention. She darkened their eyes and left her likeness there stealthily beside Adam. She entered the tree of knowledge, and remained there. But they (tried to) follow her. She revealed to them that she had entered the tree and become tree. And when ‹the blind ones› fell into a great fear, they ran away.

Afterward, when they sobered up from the stupor, they came to [Adam. And] when they saw the likeness of that (woman) with him, they were troubled, thinking that this was the true Eve. And they acted recklessly, and came to her and seized her and cast their seed upon her. They did it with a lot of tricks, not only defiling her naturally but abominably, defiling the seal of her first voice, which (before) spoke with them, saying, "What is it that exists before you?"— ‹But it is impossible› that they might defile those who say that they are begotten in the consummation by the true man by means of the word. And they were deceived, not knowing that they had defiled their own body. It was the likeness which the authorities and their angels defiled in every form.

* * *

Then the seven took counsel. They came to Adam and Eve timidly. They said to him, "Every tree which is in Paradise, whose fruit may be eaten, was created for you. But beware! Don't eat from the tree of knowledge. If you do eat, you will die." After they gave them a great fright, they withdrew up to their authorities.

Then the one who is wiser than all of them, this one who was called "the beast," came. And when he saw the likeness of their mother Eve, he said to her, "What is it that god said to you? 'Don't eat from the tree of knowledge'?" She said, "He not only said 'Don't eat from it,' but 'Don't touch it lest [you] die.'" He said to her, "Don't be afraid! You certainly shall [not die]. For [he knows] that when you eat from it your mind will be sobered and you will become like god, knowing the distinctions which exist between evil and good men. For he said this to you, lest you eat from it, since he is jealous."

Now Eve believed the words of the instructor. She looked at the tree. And she saw that it was beautiful and magnificent, and she desired it. She took some of its fruit and ate, and she gave to her husband also, and he ate too. Then their mind opened. For when they ate, the light of knowledge shone for them. When they put on shame, they knew that they were naked with regard to knowledge. When they sobered up, they saw that they were naked, and they became enamored of one another. When they saw their makers, they loathed them since they were beastly forms. They understood very much.

★ ★ ★

Before the consummation [of the aeon], the whole place will be shaken by a great thunder. Then the rulers will lament, [crying out on account of their] death. The angels will mourn for their men, and the demons will weep for their times, and their men will mourn and cry out on account of their death. Then the aeon will begin to ‹ . . . and› they will be disturbed. Its kings will be drunk from the flaming sword and they will make war against one another, so that the earth will be drunk from the blood which is poured out. And the seas will be troubled by that war. Then the sun will darken and the moon will lose its light. The stars of the heaven will disregard their

course and a great thunder will come out of a great power that is above all the powers of Chaos, the place where the firmament of woman is situated. When she has created the first work, she will take off her wise flame of insight. She will put on a senseless wrath. Then she will drive out the gods of Chaos whom she had created together with the First Father. She will cast them down to the abyss. They will be wiped out by their (own) injustice. For they will become like the mountains which blaze out fire, and they will gnaw at one another until they are destroyed by their First Father. When he destroys them, he will turn against himself and destroy himself until he ceases (to be). And their heavens will fall upon one another and their powers will burn. Their aeons will also be overthrown. And his (the First Father's) heaven will fall and it will split in two. Likewise (the place of) his joy, [however], will fall down to the earth, [and the earth will not] be able to support them. They will fall [down] to the abyss and the [abyss] will be overthrown.

The light will [cover the] darkness, and it will wipe it out. It will become like one which had not come into being. And the work which the darkness followed will be dissolved. And the deficiency will be plucked out at its root (and thrown) down to the darkness. And the light will withdraw up to its root. And the glory of the unbegotten will appear, and it will fill all of the aeons, when the prophetic utterance and the report of those who are kings are revealed and are fulfilled by those who are called perfect. Those who were not perfected in the unbegotten Father will receive their glories in their aeons and in the kingdoms of immortals. But they will not ever enter the kingless realm.

For it is necessary that every one enter the place from whence he came. For each one by his deed and his knowledge will reveal his nature.

[From *The Nag Hammadi Library,* pp. 162–179.]

THE GOSPEL OF MARY

The date of this text is uncertain, but a Greek fragment existed as early as the third century C.E. It begins with a dialogue between the resurrected Jesus and his disciples in which Jesus instructs them to preach the gospel. The male disciples feel unequal to this task until Mary Magdalene strengthens their courage. At the request of Peter she also tells them of some private teaching she received from Jesus. (Unfortunately several pages of her speech have been lost.) Some disciples then challenge what Mary said, not believing that Jesus spoke to her on such matters, but Levi affirms her place with Jesus.

This text is an indication that while Gnostic women seem to have maintained positions as teachers and church leaders that were in many cases better than the position of women among other Christian groups, they too had their battles.

The Gospel of Mary
BG 7,1–19,5

... will matter then be [destroyed] or not?" The Savior said, "All natures, all formations, all creatures exist in and with one another, and they will be resolved again into their own roots. For the nature of matter is resolved into (the roots of) its nature alone. He who has ears to hear, let him hear."

Peter said to him, "Since you have explained everything to us, tell us this also: What is the sin of the world?" The Savior said, "There is no sin, but it is you who make sin when you do the things that are like the nature of adultery, which is called 'sin.' That is why the Good came into your midst, to the essence of every nature, in order to restore it to its root." Then he continued and said, "That is why you [become sick] and die, for [. . .] of the one who [. . . He who] undertands, let him understand. [Matter gave birth to] a passion that has no equal, which proceeded from (something) contrary to nature. Then there arises a disturbance in the whole body. That is why I said to you, 'Be of good courage,' and if you are discouraged (be) encouraged in the presence of the different forms of nature. He who has ears to hear, let him hear."

When the blessed one had said this, he greeted them all, saying, "Peace be with you. Receive my peace to yourselves. Beware that no one lead you astray, saying, 'Lo here!' or 'Lo there!' For the Son of Man is within you. Follow after him! Those who seek him will find him. Go then and preach the gospel of the kingdom. Do not lay down any rules beyond what I appointed for you, and do not give a law like the lawgiver lest you be constrained by it." When he had said this, he departed.

But they were grieved. They wept greatly, saying, "How shall we go to the Gentiles and preach the gospel of the kingdom of the Son of Man? If they did not spare him, how will they spare us?" Then Mary stood up, greeted them all, and said to her brethren, "Do not weep and do not grieve nor be irresolute, for his grace will be entirely with you and will protect you. But rather let us praise his greatness, for he has prepared us (and) made us into men." When Mary said this, she turned their hearts to the Good, and they began to discuss the words of the [Savior].

Peter said to Mary, "Sister, We know that the Savior loved you more than the rest of women. Tell us the words of the Savior which you remember—which you know (but) we do not nor have we heard them." Mary answered and said, "What is hidden from you I will proclaim to you." And she began to speak to them these words: "I," she said, "I saw the Lord in a vision and I said to him, 'Lord, I saw you today in a vision.' He answered and said to me, 'Blessed are you, that you did not waver at the sight of me. For where the mind is, there is the treasure.' I said to him,

'Lord, now does he who sees the vision see it ‹through› the soul ‹or› through the spirit?' The Savior answered and said, 'He does not see through the soul nor through the spirit, but the mind which [is] between the two—that is [what] sees the vision and it is [. . .].' (pp. 11–14 missing)

"[. . .] it. And desire said, 'I did not see you descending, but now I see you ascending. Why do you lie, since you belong to me?' The soul answered and said, 'I saw you. You did not see me nor recognize me. I served you as a garment, and you did not know me.' When it had said this, it went away rejoicing greatly.

"Again it came to the third power, which is called ignorance. [It (the power)] questioned the soul, saying, 'Where are you going? In wickedness are you bound. But you are bound; do not judge!' And the soul said, 'Why do you judge me, although I have not judged? I was bound, though I have not bound. I was not recognized. But I have recognized that the All is being dissolved, both the earthly (things) and the heavenly.'

"When the soul had overcome the third power, it went upwards and saw the fourth power, (which) took seven forms. The first form is darkness, the second desire, the third ignorance, the fourth is the excitement of death, the fifth is the kingdom of the flesh, the sixth is the foolish wisdom of flesh, the seventh is the wrathful wisdom. These are the seven [powers] of wrath. They ask the soul, 'Whence do you come, slayer of men, or where are you going, conqueror of space?' The soul answered and said, 'What binds me has been slain, and what turns me about has been overcome, and my desire has been ended, and ignorance has died. In a [world] I was released from a world, [and] in a type from a heavenly type, and (from) the fetter of oblivion which is transient. From this time on will I attain to the rest of the time, of the season, of the aeon, in silence.'"

When Mary had said this, she fell silent, since it was to this point that the Savior had spoken with her. But Andrew answered and said to the brethren, "Say what you (wish to) say about what she has said. I at least do not believe that the Savior said this. For certainly these teachings are strange ideas." Peter answered and spoke concerning these same things. He questioned them about the Savior: "Did he really speak privately with a woman (and) not openly to us? Are we to turn about and all listen to her? Did he prefer her to us?"

Then Mary wept and said to Peter, "My brother Peter, what do you think? Do you think that I thought this up myself in my heart, or that I am lying about the Savior?" Levi answered and said to Peter, "Peter, you have always been hot-tempered. Now I see you contending against the woman like the adversaries. But if the Savior made her worthy, who are you indeed to reject her? Surely the Savior knows her very well. That is why he loved her more than us. Rather let us be ashamed and put on the perfect man, and separate as he commanded us and preach the gospel, not laying down any other rule or other law beyond what the Savior said." When [. . .] and they began to go forth [to] proclaim and to preach.

[From *The Nag Hammadi Library,* pp. 471–474.]

THE GOSPEL OF THOMAS

The last lines of The Gospel of Thomas, composed c. 200 C.E., also reveal some conflict surrounding Mary Magdalene's position with Jesus. Here the solution is to transform her into a male.

The Gospel of Thomas 112–114

Jesus said, "Woe to the flesh that depends on the soul; woe to the soul that depends on the flesh."

His disciples said to Him, "When will the Kingdom come?" ⟨Jesus said,⟩ "It will not come by waiting for it. It will not be a matter of saying 'Here it is' or 'There it is.' Rather, the Kingdom of the Father is spread out upon the earth, and men do not see it."

Simon Peter said to them, "Let Mary leave us, for women are not worthy of Life."

Jesus said, "I myself shall lead her in order to make her male, so that she too may become a living spirit resembling you males. For every woman who will make herself male will enter the Kingdom of Heaven."

[From *The Nag Hammadi Library,* pp. 129–30.]

Eastern Orthodoxy

Christianity began and flourished in the Middle East long before it came to prominence in Western religious life. Through the centuries, various schisms have separated the Eastern church and the Western church as well as created sects in both. Generally speaking, the position of women in Eastern Orthodoxy differed from that of Western Christian women in that orthodox women had a liturgical role as deaconesses while orthodox priests could and often did marry. Additionally, Mary, the mother of Jesus, is called the *theotokos,* the "Godbearer" or "Mother of God," and holds a central place in official church doctrine and among the faithful. In fact Constantinople, the center of Eastern orthodoxy, gloried in the title "City of the Theotokos" and claimed that Mary had several times miraculously intervened to save the city from enemy attack.

GREGORY OF NYSSA—LIFE OF MACRINA

Gregory of Nyssa wrote the biography of his sister (c. 327–379), *The Life of St. Macrina,* to serve as a model for all Christians. As a means of explaining Macrina, he often compares her to the virgin martyr and teacher St. Thecla, who was a disciple and companion of Paul. Macrina was the oldest of nine children and she was educated by her mother. She was betrothed at age twelve, but the man died and Macrina decided not to marry. Instead she established first a women's religious community and then a religious community for men. She was a superior organizer and a subtle philosophical thinker. Gregory recorded her deathbed teachings entitled *Dialogue on the Soul and the Resurrection.*

The Life offers insights into Eastern Christianity (Macrina lived in Cappadocia, Greece) even though the break between the Western and Eastern church had not yet taken place, and it tells us quite a bit about the day-to-day life of a community of Christian women and about the leadership roles of women.

The following excerpt describes Macrina's decision to establish a convent and the days preceding her death.

In a variety of ways, therefore, her mother was distracted by worries. (By this time her father had left this life.) In all of these affairs, Macrina was a sharer of her mother's toils, taking on part of her cares and lightening the heaviness of her griefs. In addition, under her mother's direction, she kept her life blameless and witnessed in everything by her, and, at the same time, because of her own life, she provided her mother with an impressive leadership to the same goal; I speak of the goal of philosophy, drawing her on little by little to the immaterial and simpler life. After the mother had skillfully arranged what seemed best for each of Macrina's sisters, her brother, the distinguished Basil, came home from school where he had had practice in rhetoric for a long time. He was excessively puffed up by his rhetorical abilities and disdainful of all great reputations, and considered himself better than the leading men in the district, but Macrina took him over and lured him so quickly to the goal of philosophy that he withdrew from the worldly show and began to look down upon acclaim through oratory and went over to this life full of labors for one's own hand to perform, providing for himself, through his complete poverty, a mode of living that would, without impediment, lead to virtue. But his life and the outstanding activities through which he became famous everywhere under the sun and eclipsed in reputation all those conspicuous in virtue, would make a long treatise and take much time, and my attention must be turned back to the subject at hand. When there was no longer any necessity for them to continue their rather worldly way of life, Macrina persuaded her mother to give up her customary mode of living and her more ostentatious existence and the services of her maids, to which she had long been accustomed, and to put herself on a level with the many by entering into a common life with her maids, making them her sisters and equals rather than her slaves and underlings.

[From *Saint Gregory of Nyssa*, pp. 167–68.]

When the prayer and blessing were finished and the women had responded to the blessing by bowing their heads, they removed themselves from our presence and went off to their own quarters. Since not one of them remained with me, I correctly surmised that their Superior [Macrina] was not among them. An attendant led me to the house where the Superior was and opened the door, and I entered that sacred place. She was already very ill, but she was not resting on a couch or bed, but upon the ground; there

was a board covered with a coarse cloth, and another board supported her head, designed to be used instead of a pillow, supporting the sinews of her neck slantwise and conveniently supporting the neck. When she saw me standing at the door, she raised herself on her elbow; her strength was already so wasted by fever that she was not able to come towards me, but she fixed her hands on the floor and, stretching as far forward as she could, she paid me the honor of a bow. I ran to her and, lifting her bowed head, I put her back in her accustomed reclining position. But she stretched out her hand to God and said: 'You have granted me this favor, O God, and have not deprived me of my desire, since you have impelled your servant to visit your handmaid.' And in order not to disturb me, she tried to cover up her groans and to conceal somehow the difficulty she had in breathing, and, through it all, she adjusted herself to the brighter side. She initiated suitable topics of conversation and gave me an opportunity to speak by asking me questions. As we spoke, we recalled the memory of the great Basil [their brother] and my soul was afflicted and my face fell and tears poured from my eyes. But she was so far from being downcast by our sorrow that she made the mentioning of the saint a starting point towards the higher philosophy. She rehearsed such arguments, explaining the human situation through natural principles and disclosing the divine plan hidden in misfortune, and she spoke of certain aspects of the future life as if she was inspired by the Holy Spirit, so that my soul almost seemed to be lifted up out of its human sphere by what she said and, under the direction of her discourse, take its stand in the heavenly sanctuaries.

And just as we hear in the story of Job, that when the man was wasting away and his whole body was covered with erupting and putrefying sores, he did not direct attention to his pain but kept the pain inside his body, neither blessing his own activity nor cutting off the conversation when it embarked upon higher matters. Such a thing as this I was seeing in the case of this Superior also; although the fever was burning up all her energy and leading her to death, she was refreshing her body as if by a kind of dew, she kept her mind free in the contemplation of higher things and unimpeded by the disease. If my treatise were not becoming too long, I would put down everything in order: how she was lifted up by her discourse on the soul; how she explained the reason for life in the flesh, why man exists; how he is mortal, whence death comes; and what release there is from death back again into life. In all of this, she went on as if inspired by the power of the Holy Spirit, explaining it all clearly and logically. Her speech flowed with complete ease, just as a stream of water goes down a hill without obstruction.

[From *Saint Gregory of Nyssa*, pp. 174–76.]

ANNA COMNENA—THE ALEXIAD

Anna Comnena (1083–1153) was the highly educated daughter of Emperor Alexius Comnenus, ruler of the Eastern Empire at Constantinople. Anna's hopes of succeeding her father as ruler were thwarted first by the birth of a brother and finally by her failed assassination attempt on her brother's life. Her punishment was a comfortable exile during which she pursued more literary ambitions of which *The Alexiad,* a history of her father's reign, is the fruit. She was fifty-five years old when she began writing *The Alexiad,* and it remains one of the foremost histories of the First Crusade and indeed of the period in which she lived.

In the following excerpt from book 14 Anna Comnena describes one of her father's battles involving, from the orthodox point-of-view, the heretical Manichaeans in the form of the Paulicians (so named after their seventh-century founder Paul). In her descriptions she reveals the subtlety of her own theological training and represents her father as the "thirteenth apostle" because of his efforts, both military and verbal, to bring people into the true faith.

Once upon a time, it seems, Philippopolis must have been a large and beautiful city, but after the Tauroi and Scyths enslaved the inhabitants in ancient times it was reduced to the condition in which we saw it during my father's reign. Even so we conjectured that it must have been, as I said, a really great city once. It had certain disadvantages; among them was the fact that many heretics lived there. Armenians had taken over the place and also the so-called Bogomils. We shall speak of the latter and of their heresy later on at the appropriate time. Apart from them there were in the city the Paulicians, an utterly godless sect were the Manichaeans. As the name implies, their sect was founded by Paul and John, who having drunk at the well of Manes' profaneness handed on the heresy undiluted to their adherents. I would have liked to outline the Manichaean doctrine with a concise explanation and then hasten to refute their atheistic teachings, but as I know that everyone regards them as absurd and at the same time I am anxious to press on with the history, the disproof of their dogma must be omitted. In any case, I am aware that others, not only men of our own faith, but also Porphyrius, our great adversary, have already refuted them. Porphyrius in several chapters reduced their foolish tenets to the point of insanity when he examined in his most learned fashion the two principles. I must add, though, that his one, absolute and supreme deity compels his readers to accept the Platonic Unity, or the One. We ourselves revere one Deity, but not a Unity limited to one Person; nor do we accept the One of Plato (the Greek *Ineffable* and the Chaldaean *Mystery* for according to them other powers, in great numbers, dependent on their One, powers both cosmic and supracosmic. These disciples of Manes, of Paul and John (the sons of Callinice), who were of a savage and unusually cruel disposition and were prepared to hazard all, even at the cost of bloodshed, met defeat at the hands of that admirable ruler John Tzimisces. He removed them as slaves from Asia, carrying them off from the lands of the Chalybes and Armenians to Thrace. They were forced to dwell in the district of Philippopolis, for two reasons: first, Tzimisces wanted to drive them out of the heavily fortified towns and strongpoints which they ruled as tyrants; and secondly, he used them as a very efficient barrier against Scythian incursions, from which the area had often suffered. The barbarians had been in the habit of crossing the mountain passes of Haemus and overrunning the plains below, but John Tzimisces turned our opponents, these Manichaean heretics, into allies; so far as fighting was concerned they formed a considerable and powerful bulwark against the nomadic Scyths and thereafter the cities, protected now from most of their raids, breathed freely again. The Manichaeans, however, being by nature an independent people, not amenable to discipline, followed their normal customs; they reverted to type. Practically all the inhabitants of Philippopolis were in fact

Manichaeans, so that they lorded it over the Christians there and plundered their goods, paying little or no attention to the emperor's envoys. Their numbers increased until all the people round the city were of their persuasion. They were joined by another flood of immigrants. These newcomers were Armenians — a brackish stream — and they were succeeded by others from the foulest springs of James. Philippopolis was a meeting place, so to speak, of all polluted waters. And if the immigrants differed from the Manichaeans in doctrine, they agreed to join in their rebellious activities. Nevertheless my father pitted against them his long experience of soldiering. Some were taken without a fight; others were enslaved by force of arms. The work that he did there and the labours he courageously endured were truly worthy of a great apostle — for surely there is no reason why he should not be praised. If someone objected that he neglected his military duties, I would point out that both East and West were the scenes of numberless military exploits. Again if he were blamed for treating literature with scant respect, my reply would be this: no man, I am sure, more zealously searched the Holy Scriptures than he, in order to have a ready answer in his debates with the heretics. He alone made use of arms and words alike, for with arms he conquered them and by his arguments he subdued the ungodly. On this occasion it was for an apostolic mission, not for operations of war, that he armed against the Manichaeans. And I myself would call him 'the thirteenth apostle'— though some ascribe that honour to Constantine the Great. However it seems to me that either Alexius ought to be ranked with the Emperor Constantine, or, if someone quarrelled with that, he should follow immediately after Constantine in both roles — as emperor and as apostle. As we were

saying, Alexius arrived at Philippopolis for the reasons I gave, but as the Cumans had not yet appeared, the secondary object of the expedition became more important: he turned away the Manichaeans from their religion with its bitterness and filled them with the sweet doctrines of our Church. From early morning till afternoon or evening, sometimes till the second or third watch of the night, he invited them to visit him and he instructed them in the orthodox faith, refuting their corrupt heresy. He had with him Eustratios, the Bishop of Nicaea, and also the Archbishop of Philippopolis himself. The former was a man learned in the Scriptures and with a wide knowledge of profane literature, more confident in his powers of rhetoric than philosophers of Stoa or Academy. The emperor's chief assistant at all these interviews, however, was my husband, the Caesar Nicephorus, whom he had trained in the study of the Sacred Books. Thus many heretics at this time unhesitatingly sought out the priests in order to confess their sins and receive Holy Baptism. On the other hand, there were many at this same time who clung to their own religion with a passionate devotion surpassing that of the famous Maccabees, quoting from the Sacred Books and using them as evidence to support (as they imagined) their contemptible doctrine. Yet the majority even of these fanatics were persuaded by the emperor's untiring arguments and his frequent admonitions. They too were baptized. The talks went on often from the first appearance of the sun's rays in the east until far into the night, and for him there was no rest, generally no food, although it was summer-time and he was in an open tent.

[From *The Alexiad of Anna Comnena*, pp. 463–467.]

Ordination of a Deaconess

The following excerpt is a prayer to be recited at the ordination of a deaconess. It affirms the spiritual place of women within the tradition and hearkens back to Phoebe, who was called a deaconess in Romans 16:1, 2.

*Prayer at the Ordination
of a Deaconess*

After the Holy Oblation is made, and the doors have been opened, before the Deacon says: Making mention of all Saints, the Candidate for ordination is brought to the Bishop, and he, reciting the Divine Grace, while she bows her head, lays his hand on her

head, and making three signs of the Cross, prays as follows:

Holy and Almighty GOD, Who hast hallowed woman by the birth of Thine Only-Begotten SON our GOD from a Virgin after the flesh, and Who hast given the grace and visitation of Thy HOLY SPIRIT not to men alone, but to women also, look now, O LORD, on this Thy servant, and call her to the work of Thy ministry, and send down on her the rich gift of Thy HOLY SPIRIT, keep her in Thy orthodox faith, and always fulfilling her office in blameless conversation according to Thy good pleasure. For Thee befits etc.

And after the Amen, one of the Deacon prays as follows:

In peace etc. (as for the Deacon, but with this suffrage). For her who is now appointed Deaconess, and for her salvation, let us etc.

While the Deacon is repeating this prayer the Bishop, still keeping his hand on the head of the Candidate prays as follows:

O LORD GOD, Who dost not reject women Who offer themselves in accordance with the Divine Will to minister in Thy holy places, but admittest them into the rank of ministers, give the grace of Thy HOLY SPIRIT to this Thy servant, who desires to offer herself to Thee and to fulfill the grace of the Diaconate, as Thou didst give the grace of Thy Diaconate unto Phoebe whom Thou calledst to the work of the ministry. Grant to her, O GOD, to abide blamelessly in Thy holy temples, to be mindful of her own conversation, and especially of continence, and make Thy servant perfect, that she, standing at the judgment-seat of CHRIST, may receive the reward of her good conversation. Through the mercy and loving-kindness of Thine Only-Begotten SON etc.

And after the Amen, he puts the diaconal stole on her neck, under the wimple, bringing the two ends forward, and then the Deacon who stands on the ambon says:

Making mention of All Saints etc.

After she has partaken of the Holy Body and the Holy Blood, the Archbishop gives her the Holy Chalice, which she receives and places on the Holy Table.

[From *Offices from the Service Books of the Holy Eastern Church*, pp. 152–53.]

Mary

Mary, the mother of Jesus, has a long and elaborate history in Christianity. Her popularity was enhanced by the devotion of early (fourth century) male celibates and remained an essential part of both Roman Catholicism and Eastern Orthodoxy. Her cult spread rapidly during the Middle Ages, was debunked by most Protestant Reformers, and in recent centuries has spread as a source of inspiration and comfort to many through reported appearances, such as at Lourdes, and through Marian pilgrimages.

THE AKATHISTOS

The first excerpt is from the oldest hymn to Mary, the Akathistos of Eastern Orthodoxy. It was composed by an unknown author to celebrate the deliverance of Constantinople from a siege by barbarians in 626. This deliverance was attributed to Mary and the hymn emphasizes her ability to save one from all kinds of dangers, including the ultimate danger of sin. It also lists many more of her attributes such as her wisdom and her ability to inspire; it is a litany of her qualities.

To thee, unconquered Queen, I thy city from danger freed an offering of thanks inscribe. O Forth-bringer of God! Yet for thy unconquerable might free me from all hurt that I may sing to thee:
HAIL! BRIDE UNBRIDED.

An angel chieftain was sent from Heaven to greet the Forth-bringer of God with Hail! Then seeing thee, O Lord, take flesh he is wonder-rapt, and standing crieth out with no lips of flesh to her:
Hail! by whom true hap had dawned.
Hail! by whom mishap has waned.
Hail! sinful Adam's recalling.
Hail! Eve's tears redeeming.

Hail! height untrodden by thought of men.
Hail! depth unscanned by angels' ken.
Hail! for the kingly throne thou art.
Hail! for who beareth all thou bearest?
Hail! O star that bore the Sun.
Hail! the womb of God enfleshed.
Hail! through whom things made are all new made.
Hail! through whom becomes a Babe their Maker.
Hail! through whom the Maker is adored.
HAIL! BRIDE UNBRIDED.

Hail! of Apostles never-silent mouthpiece.

Hail! of the Martyrs strength undaunted.
Hail! of Faith the firm foundation.
Hail! of Grace the shining token.
Hail! by whom hell is despoiled.
Hail! by whom we are clothed with glory.

★ ★ ★

Hail! casket of God's wisdom.
Hail! treasury of his providence.
Hail! confounder of the wisdom of the wise.
Hail! making babble of men's eloquence.
Hail! for the deep thinkers are made foolish.

Hail! barque for those who seek salvation.
Hail! harbour of this life's seafarers.

★ ★ ★

Hail! by whom was loosed our sin.
Hail! by whom was opened Paradise.
Hail! Key of Christ's Kingdom.
Hail! hope of eternal boons.
HAIL! BRIDE UNBRIDED.
[From *Ode in Honour of the Holy Immaculate Most Blessed Glorious Lady Mother of God and Ever Virgin Mary.*]

IRENAEUS

Irenaeus (c. 130–c. 200), the bishop of Lyons, remains an important theologian from the early days of the Church, when it was confronted by Gnostic forms of Christianity. Irenaeus vigorously opposed the Gnostics in his *Against Heresies,* which is a presentation and refutation of their ideas.

In the following two excerpts from *Against Heresies* (3.24.4. and 5.19.1) Irenaeus contrasts the obedient Mary, the bringer of salvation, with Eve, who he says brought death into the world through her disobedience. Eve and Mary endure as contrasting poles of Christian womanhood, the one virginal and obedient, the other sexual and willful.

Against Heresies 3.24.4

In accordance with this design, Mary the Virgin is found obedient, saying, "Behold the handmaid of the Lord; be it unto me according to thy word." But Eve was disobedient; for she did not obey when as yet she was a virgin. And even as she, having indeed a husband, Adam, but being nevertheless as yet a virgin (for in Paradise "they were both naked, and were not ashamed," inasmuch as they, having been created a short time previously, had no understanding of the procreation of children: for it was necessary that they should first come to adult age, and then multiply from that time onward, having become disobedient, was made the cause of death, both to herself and to the entire human race; so also did Mary, having a man betrothed [to her], and being nevertheless a virgin, by yielding obedience, become the cause of salvation, both to herself and the whole human race. And on this account does the law term a woman betrothed to a man, the wife of him who had betrothed her, although she was as yet a virgin; thus indicating the back-reference from Mary to Eve, because what is joined together could not otherwise be put asunder than by inversion of the process by which these bonds of Union had arisen; so that the former ties be cancelled by the latter, that the latter

may set the former again at liberty. And it has, in fact, happened that the first compact looses from the second tie, but that the second tie takes the position of the first which has been cancelled. For this reason did the Lord declare that the first should in truth be last, and the last first. And the prophet, too, indicates the same, saying, "Instead of fathers, children have been born unto thee." For the Lord, having been born "the First-begotten of the dead," and receiving into His bosom the ancient fathers, has regenerated them into the life of God, He having been made Himself the beginning of those that live, as Adam became the beginning of those who die. Wherefore also Luke, commencing the genealogy with the Lord, carried it back to Adam, indicating that it was He who regenerated them into the Gospel of life, and not they Him. And thus also it was that the knot of Eve's disobedience was loosed by the obedience of Mary. For what the virgin Eve had bound fast through unbelief, this did the virgin Mary set free through faith.
[From *The Ante-Nicene Fathers,* p. 455.]

Against Heresies 5.19.1

A COMPARISON IS INSTITUTED BETWEEN THE DISOBEDIENT AND SINNING EVE AND THE VIRGIN MARY, HER

PATRONESS. VARIOUS AND DISCORDANT HERESIES ARE
MENTIONED.

I.   That the Lord then was manifestly coming to
His own things, and was sustaining them by means
of that Creation which is supported by Himself, and
was making a recapitulation of that disobedience
which had occurred in connection with a tree,
through the obedience which was [exhibited by
Himself when He hung] upon a tree, [the effects] also
of that deception being done away with, by which
that Virgin Eve, who was already espoused to a man,
was unhappily misled,—was happily announced,
through means of the truth [spoken] by the angel to
the Virgin Mary, who was [also espoused] to a man.
For just as the former was led astray by the word of
an angel, so that she fled from God when she had
transgressed His word; so did the latter, by an angelic
communication, receive the glad tidings that she
should sustain (*portaret*) God, being obedient to His
word. And if the former did disobey God, yet the
latter was persuaded to be obedient to God, in order
that the Virgin Mary might become the patroness
(*advocata*) of the virgin Eve. And thus, as the human
race fell into bondage to death by means of a virgin,
so is it rescued by a virgin; virginal disobedience
having been balanced in the opposite scale by virginal
obedience. For in the same way the sin of the first
created man (*protoplasti*) receives amendment by the
correction of the First-begotten, and the coming of
the serpent is conquered by the harmlessness of the
dove, those bonds being unloosed by which we had
been fast bound to death.

[From *The Ante-Nicene Fathers,* p. 547.]

THE HAIL MARY

The best known and most frequent prayer to Mary is the Hail Mary, the first part of which
is taken from the words of the angel who announces Mary's conception in the Gospel of Luke.
As such it was in use quite early and became a frequent prayer in Europe by the twelfth century.
The second part, the supplication, was added around the fifteenth century. The simplicity of
this prayer contributed to its popularity. It states Mary's uniqueness as the Mother of God
and seeks her intercession for eternal salvation.

Hail, Mary,
full of grace,
the Lord is with you.
Blessed are you among women
and blessed is the fruit of your womb, Jesus.

Holy Mary,
Mother of God,
pray for us sinners,
now and at the hour of our death.

THE ANGELUS

The pervasiveness of Mary's popularity among Christians is partly shown by the custom
of the Angelus. During the Middle Ages the recitation of three Hail Marys three times a day
as part of the Angelus became popular. Church bells would ring out in the morning, at noon,
and in the evening, calling the faithful to prayer as follows:

The Angel of the Lord declared unto Mary,
And she conceived of the Holy spirit.
Hail Mary . . .

Behold the handmaid of the Lord.
Be it done unto me according to your word.
Hail Mary . . .

And the Word was made flesh,
And dwelt among us.
Hail Mary . . .

Pray for us, O holy Mother of God,
That we may be made worthy of the promises of Christ.
Let us pray. Pour forth, we beg You, O Lord,
Your grace into our hearts:
that we, to whom the Incarnation of Christ Your Son
was made known by the message of an Angel,
may by His Passion and Cross
be brought to the glory of His Resurrection.
Through the same Christ our Lord. Amen.

The Middle Ages

The Middle Ages was an astounding period for women's spiritual writings and the handful of women included here are a small representation of this rich tradition. Almost all had visionary experiences which gave them enough religious authority to have their views accepted and their work preserved. Several were cloistered but many found ways to move about in the secular world. They lived in various countries and had different class and educational backgrounds. All, in one way or another, led heroic lives by being women with formidable wills who overcame significant obstacles and stayed true to their own visions.

At the same time, negative views of women, primarily of a sexual nature, were continually restated.

HILDEGARD OF BINGEN

Hildegard of Bingen (1098–1179) began the religious life when she was only seven or eight years old when she went to live with her aunt who was a religious recluse. A few years later they turned their retreat into a convent and Hildegard became a nun at fourteen. She managed to receive a broad enough education to be familiar with scripture, the sciences, the classics, and philosophy. Her extant works, which she dictated, include letters, songs, prophecies, visions (which began in her childhood), a play, and a book on medicine. Her prophecies were taken seriously by everyone, including the pope. Her major work was the *Scivias,* a record of her life and visions, which she began dictating when she was forty-three. Through all this she was an able manager of a large and complex convent.

The following excerpt is taken from the fourth vision of the *Scivias* in which Hildegard describes the relationship between the soul and the body.

Vision Four: Soul and Body

Then I saw a most great and serene splendor, flaming, as it were, with many eyes, with four corners pointing toward the four parts of the world, which was manifest to me in the greatest mystery to show me the secret of the Supernal Creator; and in it appeared another splendor like the dawn, containing in itself a brightness of purple lightning. And behold! I saw on the earth people carrying milk in earthen vessels and making cheeses from it; and one part was thick, and from it strong cheeses were made; and one part was thin, and from it weak cheeses were curdled; and one part was mixed with corruption and from it bitter cheeses were formed. And I saw the image of a woman who had a perfect human form in her womb. And behold! By the secret design of the Supernal Creator that form moved with vital motion, so that a fiery globe that had no human lineaments possessed the heart of that form and touched its brain and spread itself through all its members.

But then this human form, in this way vivified, came forth from the woman's womb and changed its color according to the movement the globe made in that form.

And I saw that many whirlwinds assailed one of these globes in a body and bowed it down to the ground; but, gaining back its strength and bravely raising itself up, it resisted them boldly and said with a groan:

[From *Hildegard of Bingen*, p. 109.]

★ ★ ★

An infant is vivified in the womb and confirmed by a soul on leaving it

And you see the image of a woman who has a perfect human form in her womb. This means that after a woman has conceived by human semen, an infant with all its members whole is formed in the secret chamber of her womb. And behold! *By the secret design of the Supernal Creator that form moves with vital motion;* for, by God's secret and hidden command and will, fitly and rightly at the divinely appointed time the infant in the maternal womb receives a spirit, and shows by the movements of its body that it lives, just as the earth opens and brings forth the flowers of its use when the dew falls on it. *So that a fiery globe which has no human lineaments possesses the heart of that form;* that is, the soul, burning with a fire of profound knowledge, which discerns whatever is within the circle of its understanding, and, without the form of human members, since it is not corporeal or transitory like a human body, gives strength to the heart and rules the whole body as its foundation, as the firmament of Heaven contains the lower regions and touches the higher. *And it also touches the person's brain;* for in its powers it knows not only earthly but also heavenly things, since it wisely knows God; *and it spreads itself through all the person's members;* for it gives vitality to the marrow and veins and members of the whole body, as the tree from its root gives sap and greenness to all the branches. *But then this human form, in this way vivified, comes forth from the woman's womb, and changes its color according to the movement the globe makes in that form;* which is to say that after the person has received the vital spirit in the maternal womb and is born and begins his actions, his merits will be according to the works his soul does with the body, for he will put

on brightness from the good ones and darkness from the evil ones.

How the soul shows its powers according to the powers of the body

The soul now shows its powers according to the powers of the body, so that in a person's infancy it produces simplicity, in his youth strength, and in adulthood, when all the person's veins are full, it shows its strongest powers in wisdom; as the tree in its first shoots is tender and then shows that it can bear fruit, and finally, in its full utility, bears it. But then in human old age, when the marrow and veins start to incline to weakness, the soul's powers are gentler, as if from a weariness at human knowledge; as when winter approaches the sap of the tree diminishes in the branches and the leaves, and the tree in its old age begins to bend.

[From *Hildegard of Bingen*, pp. 119–20.]

That the soul is the mistress and the flesh the handmaid

The soul is the mistress, the flesh the handmaid. How? The soul rules the body by vivifying it, and the body is ruled by this vivification, for if the soul did not vivify the body it would fall apart and decay. But when a person does an evil deed and the soul knows it, it is as bitter for the soul as poison is for the body when it knowingly takes it. But the soul rejoices in a sweet deed as the body delights in sweet food. And the soul flows through the body like sap through a tree. What does this mean? By the sap, the tree grows green and produces flowers and then fruit. And how is this fruit matured? By the air's tempering. How? The sun warms it, the rain waters it, and thus by the tempering of the air it is perfected. What does this mean? The mercy of God's grace, like the sun, will illumine the person, the breath of the Holy Spirit, like the rain, will water him, and so discernment, like the tempering of the air, will lead him to the perfection of good fruits.

Analogy of a tree to the soul

The soul in the body is like sap in a tree, and the soul's powers are like the form of the tree. How? The intellect in the soul is like the greenery of the tree's branches and leaves, the will like its flowers, the mind like its bursting firstfruits, the reason like the perfected mature fruit, and the senses like its size and shape. And so a person's body is strengthened and sustained by the soul. Hence, O human, understand what you are in your soul, you who lay aside your good intellect and try to liken yourself to the brutes.

[From *Hildegard of Bingen*, pp. 123–24.]

CLARE OF ASSISI

The life of St. Clare (1193–1254) dramatizes, among other things, the whole issue of cloistering women. She herself as a follower of Francis of Assisi and the leader of the female order of Franciscans sought to lead the same religious life as Francis and his male followers: She wished to be free enough in her movements to minister to the poor and infirm. However, within four years of her establishment of the order of women Franciscans church authorities compelled the cloistering of Clare and the women who had joined her. Even the vow of poverty so essential to this order was denied to women although it was granted to Clare and a few of the women around her until Clare's death.

The first excerpt is from *The Testament of St. Clare* and it describes the life of poverty that Clare and her sisters sought to lead and their devotion to Francis.

After the most high heavenly Father saw fit in His mercy and grace to enlighten my heart to do penance according to the example and teaching of our most blessed Father Francis, shortly after his own conversion, I, together with the few sisters whom the Lord had given me soon after my conversion, voluntarily promised him obedience, since the Lord had given us the Light of His grace through his holy life and teaching.

But when the Blessed Francis saw that, although we were physically weak and frail, we did not shirk deprivation, poverty, hard work, distress, or the shame or contempt of the world—rather, as he and his brothers often saw for themselves, we considered [all such trials] as great delights after the example of the saints and their brothers—he rejoiced greatly in the Lord. And moved by compassion for us, he promised to have always, both through himself and through his Order, the same loving care and special solicitude for us as for his own brothers.

And thus, by the will of God and our most blessed Father Francis, we went to dwell at the Church of San Damiano. There, in a short time, the Lord increased our number by His mercy and grace so that what He had predicted through His saint might be fulfilled. We had stayed in another place [before this], but only for a little while.

Later on he wrote a form of life for us, [indicating] especially that we should persevere always in holy poverty. And while he was living, he was not content to encourage us by many words and examples to love and observe holy poverty; [in addition] he also gave us many writings so that, after his death, we should in no way turn away from it. [In a similar way] the Son of God never wished to abandon this holy poverty while He lived in the world, and our most blessed Father Francis, following His footprints, never departed, either in example or teaching, from this holy poverty which he had chosen for himself and for his brothers.

Therefore, I, Clare, the handmaid of Christ and of the Poor Sisters of the Monastery of San Damiano— although unworthy—and the little plant of the holy Father, consider together with my sisters our most high profession and the command of so great a father. [We also take note] in some [sisters] of the frailty which we feared in ourselves after the death of our holy Father Francis, [He] who was our pillar of strength and, after God, our one consolation and support. [Thus] time and again, we bound ourselves to our Lady, most holy Poverty, so that, after my death, the Sisters present and to come would never abandon her.

And, as I have always been most zealous and solicitous to observe and to have the other sisters observe the holy poverty which we have promised the Lord and our holy Father Francis, so, too, the others who will succeed me in office should be bound always to observe it and have it observed by the other sisters. And, for even greater security, I took care to have our profession of most holy poverty, which we promised our Father [Francis], strengthened with privileges by the Lord Pope Innocent, during whose pontificate we had our beginning, and by his other successors. [We did this] so that we would never nor in any way depart from it.

[From *Francis and Clare*, pp. 228–29.]

The second excerpt is from *The Rule of St. Clare* which she wrote toward the end of her life. It describes the order's commitment to poverty and its desire to imitate the life of Jesus.

CHAPTER I: IN THE NAME OF THE LORD BEGINS THE FORM OF LIFE OF THE POOR SISTERS.

The form of life of the Order of the Poor Sisters which the Blessed Francis established, is this: to observe the holy Gospel of our Lord Jesus Christ, by living in obedience, without anything of one's own, and in chastity.

Clare, the unworthy handmaid of Christ and the little plant of the most blessed Father Francis, promises obedience and reverence to the Lord Pope Innocent and to his canonically elected successors, and to the Roman Church. And, just as at the beginning of her conversion, together with her sisters she promised obedience to the Blessed Francis, so now she promises his successors to observe the same [obedience] inviolably. And the other sisters shall always be obliged to obey the successors of the blessed Francis and [to obey] Sister Clare and the other canonically elected Abbesses who shall succeed her.

CHAPTER II: THOSE WHO WISH TO ACCEPT THIS LIFE AND HOW THEY ARE TO BE RECEIVED.

If, by divine inspiration, anyone should come to us with the desire to embrace this life, the Abbess is required to seek the consent of all the sisters; and if the majority shall have agreed, having had the permission of our Lord Cardinal Protector, she can receive her. And if she judges [the candidate] acceptable, let [the Abbess] carefully examine her, or have her examined, concerning the Catholic faith and the sacraments of the Church. And if she believes all these things and is willing to profess them faithfully and to observe them steadfastly to the end; and if she has no husband, or if she has [a husband] who has already entered religious life with the authority of the Bishop of the diocese and has already made a vow of continence; and if there is no impediment to the observance of this life, such as advanced age or some mental or physical weakness, let the tenor of our life be clearly explained to her.

And if she is suitable, let the words of the holy Gospel be addressed to her: that she should *go and sell* all that she has and take care to distribute the proceeds *to the poor* (cf. Mt 19:21). If she cannot do this, her good will suffices. And let the Abbess and her sisters take care not to be concerned about her temporal affairs, so that she may freely dispose of her possessions as the Lord may inspire her. If, however, some counsel is required, let them send her to some prudent and God-fearing men, according to whose advice her goods may be distributed to the poor.

Afterward, once her hair has been cut off round her head and her secular dress set aside, she is to be allowed three tunics and a mantle. Thereafter, she may not go outside the monastery except for some useful, reasonable, evident, and approved purpose. When the year of probation is ended, let her be received into obedience, promising to observe always our life and form of poverty.

During the period of probation no one is to receive the veil. The sisters may also have small cloaks for convenience and propriety in serving and working. Indeed, the Abbess should provide them with clothing prudently, according to the needs of each person and place, and seasons and cold climates, as it shall seem expedient to her by necessity.

Young girls who are received into the monastery before the age established by law should have their hair cut round [their heads]; and, laying aside their secular dress, should be clothed in religious garb as the Abbess has seen [fit]. When, however, they reach the age required by law, in the same way as the others, they may make their profession. The Abbess shall carefully provide a Mistress from among the more prudent sisters of the monastery both for these and the other novices. She shall form them diligently in a holy manner of living and proper behavior according to the form of our profession.

In the examination and reception of the sisters who serve outside the monastery, the same form as above is to be observed. These sisters may wear shoes. No one is to live with us in the monastery unless she has been received according to the form of our profession.

And for the love of the most holy and beloved Child Who *was wrapped in* the poorest of *swaddling clothes and laid in a manger* (cf. Lk 2:7-12), and of His most holy Mother, I admonish, entreat, and exhort my sisters that they always wear the poorest of garments.

[From *Francis and Clare,* pp. 211-13.]

THOMAS AQUINAS—SUMMA THEOLOGICA

Thomas Aquinas (1225-1274) is one of the most important and influential theologians in the Roman Catholic tradition; his works are required reading in Catholic colleges and seminaries. In his own thought Aquinas was greatly influenced by Aristotle and he wrote numerous commentaries on his work. A prominent place is also given to the church fathers, whom he often quotes. His great work, the *Summa Theologica,* a survey of Catholic theology, was written for beginning theology students. His own Dominican order was the first to require the study of his works and to follow his line of reasoning, but by the sixteenth century most of the outstanding Catholic theologians were Thomists. He was somewhat eclipsed after the Reformation but was revived in the late nineteenth century and continues to be an important influence on Catholic theology today.

In the following excerpt from his *Summa Theologica* he discusses the creation of woman by listing various arguments regarding the nature of woman taken from Aristotle, sometimes just referred to as "the Philosopher," as well as the church fathers. He then elaborates upon these arguments in order to refine their meanings. His position is that woman is secondary to man, though necessary for procreation, should be subjugated to man, and has less reason than man. Some of the arguments have been elided in order to highlight Aquinas' position.

QUESTION XCII
THE PRODUCTION OF THE WOMAN.
(In Four Articles)

We must next consider the production of the woman. Under this head there are four points of inquiry (1) Whether the woman should have been made in that first production of things? (2) Whether the woman should have been made from man? (3) Whether of man's rib? (4) Whether the woman was made immediately by God?

FIRST ARTICLE
WHETHER THE WOMAN SHOULD HAVE BEEN MADE IN THE FIRST PRODUCTION OF THINGS?

We proceed thus to the First Article:

Objection 1. It would seem that the woman should not have been made in the first production of things. For the Philosopher says (*De Gener. Animal.* ii. 3), that the *female is a misbegotten male.* But nothing misbegotten or defective should have been in the first production of things. Therefore woman should not have been made at that first production.

Obj. 2. Further, subjection and limitation were a result of sin, for to the woman was it said after sin (Gen. iii. 16): *Thou shalt be under the man's power;* and Gregory says that, *Where there is no sin; there is no inequality.* But woman is naturally of less strength and dignity than man; *for the agent is always more honourable than the patient,* as Augustine says (*Gen. ad lit.* xii. 16). Therefore woman should not have been made in the first production of things before sin.

Obj. 3. Further, occasions of sin should be cut off. But God foresaw that the woman would be an occasion of sin to man. Therefore He should not have made woman.

On the contrary, It is written (Gen. ii, 18): *It is not good for man to be alone; let us make him a helper like to himself.*

I answer that, It was necessary for woman to be made, as the Scripture says, as a *helper* to man; not, indeed, as a helpmate in other works, as some say, since man can be more efficiently helped by another man in other works; but as a helper in the work of generation. This can be made clear if we observe the mode of generation carried out in various living things. Some living things do not possess in themselves the power of generation, but are generated by some other specific agent, such as some plants and animals by the influence of the heavenly bodies, from some fitting matter and not from seed: others possess the active and passive generative power together; as we see in plants which are generated from seed; for the noblest vital function in plants is generation. Wherefore we observe that in these the active power of generation invariably accompanies the passive power. Among perfect animals the active power of generation belongs to the male sex, and the passive power to the female. And as among animals there is a vital operation nobler than generation, to which their life is principally directed; therefore the male sex is not found in continual union with the female in perfect animals, but only at the time of coition; so that we may consider that by this means the male and female are one, as in plants they are always united; although in some cases one of them preponderates, and in some the other. But man is yet further ordered to a still nobler vital action, and that is intellectual operation. Therefore there was greater reason for the distinction of these two forces in man; so that the female should be produced separately from the male; although they are carnally united for generation. Therefore directly after the formation of woman, it was said: *And they shall be two in one flesh* (Gen. ii. 24).

Reply Obj. 1. As regards the individual nature, woman is defective and misbegotten, for the active force in the male seed tends to the production a perfect likeness in the masculine sex; while the production of woman comes from defect in the active force or from some material indisposition, or even from some external influence; such as that of a south wind, which is moist, as the Philosopher observes (*De Gener. Animal.* iv. 2). On the other hand, as regards human nature in general, woman is not misbegotten, but is included in nature's intention as directed to the work of generation. Now the general intention of nature depends on God, Who is the universal Author of nature. Therefore, in producing nature, God formed not only the male but also the female.

Reply Obj. 2. Subjection is twofold. One is servile, by virtue of which a superior makes use of a subject for his own benefit; and this kind of subjection began after sin. There is another kind of subjection, which is called economic or civil, whereby the superior makes use of his subjects for their own benefit and good; and this kind of subjection existed even before sin. For good order would have been wanting in the human family if some were not governed by others wiser than themselves. So by such a kind of subjection woman is naturally subject to man, because in man the discretion of reason predominates. Nor is inequality among men excluded by the state of innocence, as we shall prove (Q. XCVI., A. 3).

Reply Obj. 3. If God had deprived the world of all those things which proved an occasion of sin, the universe would have been imperfect. Nor was it fitting for the common good to be destroyed in order that individual evil might be avoided; especially as God is so powerful that He can direct any evil to a good end.

SECOND ARTICLE.
WHETHER WOMAN SHOULD HAVE BEEN MADE FROM MAN?

I answer that, When all things were first formed, it was more suitable for the woman to be made from the man than (for the female to be from the male) in other animals. First, in order thus to give the first man a certain dignity consisting in this, that as God is the principle of the whole universe, so the first man, in likeness to God, was the principle of the whole human race. Wherefore Paul says that *God made the whole human race from one* (Acts xvii. 26). Secondly, that man might love woman all the more, and cleave to her more closely, knowing her to be fashioned from himself. Hence it is written (Gen. ii.23, 24): *She was taken out of man, wherefore a man shall leave father and mother, and shall cleave to his wife.* This was most necessary as regards the human race, in which the male and female live together for life; which is not the case with other animals. Thirdly, because, as the Philosopher says (*Ethic.* viii. 12), the human male and female are united, not only for generation, as with other animals, but also for the purpose of domestic life, in which each has his or her particular duty, and in which the man is the head of the woman. Wherefore it was suitable for the woman to be made out of man, as out of her principle. Fourthly, there is a sacramental reason for this. For by this is signified that the Church takes her origin from Christ. Wherefore the Apostle says (Eph. v. 32): *This is a great sacrament; but I speak in Christ and in the Church.*

* * *

THIRD ARTICLE.
WHETHER THE WOMAN WAS FITTINGLY MADE FROM THE RIB OF MAN?

I answer that, It was right for the woman to be made from a rib of man. First, to signify the social union of man and woman, for the woman should neither *use authority over man,* and so she was not made from his head; nor was it right for her to be subject to man's contempt as his slave, and so she was not made from his feet. Secondly, for the sacramental signification; for from the side of Christ sleeping on the Cross the Sacraments flowed—namely, blood and water—on which the Church was established.

* * *

FOURTH ARTICLE.
WHETHER THE WOMAN WAS FORMED IMMEDIATELY BY GOD?

I answer that, As was said above (A. 2, *ad* 2), the natural generation of every species is from some determinate matter. Now the matter whence man is naturally begotten is the human semen of man or woman. Wherefore from any other matter an individual of the human species cannot naturally be generated. Now God alone, the Author of nature, can produce an effect into existence outside the ordinary course of nature. Therefore God alone could produce either a man from the slime of the earth, or a woman from the rib of man.

[From *The "Summa Theologica"* of St. Thomas Aquinas, pp. 274–81.]

THE GOLDEN LEGEND

The Golden Legend was one of the most popular books of the Middle Ages. The stories contained in this collection of saints' lives represent an important and popular aspect of Christianity; these stories were meant to inspire Christians to emulate the virtues personified by the saints. It was compiled from a variety of sources by Jacobus de Voragine (c. 1228–1298) who rose from a modest background to become the bishop of Genoa.

One important and private element in the veneration of saints is that Christians are named after saints and are encouraged to feel a strong spiritual connection with their namesakes. Consequently, they want to know all they can about their lives. Another is the widely held medieval belief that the saints could intercede in all aspects of life, such as curing illness (each saint had his or her own speciality ranging from childbirth to fevers) and protecting crops and livestock. Finally, the saints are the heroes and heroines who engage the imagination of the people.

In these stories the saints are not so much clearly drawn individuals as they are ideal types, perfect women and men who emulate Christian ideals even while enduring the appalling tortures leading to their martyrdom. Some features do emerge though, when one compares the experiences of women saints and men saints, as in the following excerpts of Saints Lucy and Agnes. Women martyrs, usually described as virgins, undergo different tortures than men. They are inevitably stripped nude, threatened with rape (when not actually raped), and frequently have their breasts torn off. These stories of martyrdom, for both women and men, express a contempt for the body in favor of the eternal soul, yet the bodies of women are exploited for their sexuality. Erotic imagery is not absent from the stories of male saints in this collection. On the contrary, they contain many female temptresses who independently and freely flaunt their bodies and their sexuality before stalwart male celibates. In this collection, in most cases, sexuality resides with women whether they are virgin martyrs or pagan temptresses.

SAINT LUCY
December 13

Lucy means light. Light has beauty in its appearance; for by its nature all grace is in it, as Ambrose writes. It has also an unblemished effulgence; for it pours its beams on unclean places and yet remains clean. It has a straight way without turning, and goes a long way without halting. By this we are to understand that the virgin Lucy was endowed with a stainless purity of life; that in her was an effusion of heavenly love without any unclean desire; that she followed a straight way in her devotion to God, and a long way in daily good works without weakening and without complaint. Or again. Lucy means *lucis via,* the way of light.

Lucy, the daughter of a noble family of Syracuse, saw how the fame of Saint Agatha was spreading throughout the whole land of Sicily. She went to the tomb of this saint with her mother Euthicia, who for four years had suffered from an incurable issue of blood. The two women arrived at the church during the Mass, at the moment when the passage of the Gospel was being read which narrates the miraculous cure which Jesus worked upon a woman afflicted with an issue of blood. Then Lucy said to her mother: 'If thou believest what has just now been read, thou shouldst also believe that Agatha is now with Him for Whose name she suffered martyrdom. And if thou believest that also, thou shalt recover thy health by touching the saint's tomb in good faith.' And when all the people had left the church, the mother and her daughter remained and approached the tomb, and kneeling down devoutly began to pray. And it happened that the maiden suddenly fell asleep, and dreamt that she saw Saint Agatha standing amidst the angels, decked with precious stones; and Agatha said to her: 'My sister Lucy, virgin consecrated to God, why dost thou ask of me something which thou thyself canst straightaway grant to thy mother? Go, thy faith hath cured her!' Lucy, awakening, said to her mother: 'Mother, thou art healed! But in the name of her to whose prayers thou owest thy cure, I beg of thee to release me from my espousals, and to give to the poor the dowry thou hast saved for me.' Her mother answered: 'Wilt thou not rather wait until thou hast closed my eyes, and then do as it pleases thee with our goods?' But Lucy said: 'That which thou givest at death, thou givest because thou canst not bear it away with thee. But if thou givest it in thy lifetime, thou shalt have thy recompense in the world to come.'

When they returned home, Lucy and her mother

began little by little to give away all their goods to the poor. And Lucy's betrothed, hearing this, inquired about it of the maiden's nurse. This woman put him off by answering that Lucy had found a better property, which she wished to buy, and for that reason was selling a portion of her goods. Being a dull-witted, greedy fellow, he foresaw a material gain, and encouraged them to sell their goods. But when all was sold and it became known that everything had gone to the poor, the betrothed, enraged, made a complaint to the consul Paschasius, saying that Lucy was a Christian and did not obey the laws of the empire.

Paschasius summoned her forthwith, and commanded her to offer sacrifice to the idols. But Lucy answered him: 'The sacrifice which is pleasing to God is to visit the poor and to help them in their needs. And since I have nothing else to offer, I shall offer myself to the Lord.' Said Paschasius: 'Those are words fit to be spoken to fools like thyself; but to me, who keep the decrees of my masters, thou speakest them in vain!' Lucy answered: 'Thou keepest the decrees of thy masters, and I, for my part, wish to keep the law of my God. Thou fearest thy masters, and I fear God. Thou art careful not to offend them; I am wary of offending God. Thou desirest to please them, and I wish to please Christ. Do then what thou thinkest useful to thee, and I shall do what I think is useful to me.' Then said Paschasius: 'Thou hast squandered thine heritage with seducers, and therefore thou speakest like a vile woman.' But Lucy replied: 'As to my heritage, I have put it in a safe place; and never have I allowed near me any seducers, either of the body or of the soul.' Paschasius said to her: 'And who are these seducers of the body and of the soul?' And Lucy answered: 'You and those like you are the seducers of the soul, because you lead souls to turn away from their Creator; as for the seducers of the body, they are those who would have us put fleshly pleasures ahead of eternal joys.' Said Paschasius: 'Thy words will cease when thou feelest the blows of the lash.' Lucy responded: 'The words of God will never cease!' 'Pretendest thou to be God?' asked Paschasius. Lucy answered: 'I am the handmaid of God, Who said to His disciples, "You shall be brought before governors and before kings for my sake . . . but when they shall deliver you up, take no thought how or what to say . . . for it is not you that speak but the Holy Ghost that speaketh in you."' Then said Paschasius: 'Dost thou claim to have the Holy Ghost in thee?' Said Lucy: 'He who lives chastely is the temple of the Holy Ghost!' 'Then l shall send thee to a house of ill fame! There thy body will be violated, and thou wilt lose thy Holy Ghost.' But Lucy answered: 'The body is not soiled unless the soul consents; and if in my despite my body is ravished, my chastity will thereby be doubled. Thus thou canst not ever force my will. And as for my body, here it is, ready for every torture.

Why delayest thou? Son of the Devil, begin! Carry out thy heinous design!'

Then Paschasius summoned panders, and said to them: 'Invite the crowd to have pleasure with this woman, and let them abuse her body until she dies.' But when the panderers tried to carry her off, the Holy Ghost made her so heavy, that they were unable to move her. Paschasius called for a thousand men, and had her hands and her feet bound; but they still did not succeed in lifting her. He sent for yokes of oxen; but the virgin could not be moved. Magicians were called, but their incantations were powerless. Then he said: 'What is this witchery, which makes a thousand men unable to move a lone maiden?' And Lucy replied: 'It is no witchery, but the beneficence of Christ. And you could add another thousand men, and they still would fail to move me.' Then the consul, beside himself with rage, commanded that a great fire be built around her, and that pitch, resin, and boiling oil be thrown upon her. And Lucy said: 'God has granted that I should bear these delays in my martyrdom, in order to free the faithful from the fear of suffering, and to take away from unbelievers any reason for denying His power!'

The friends of Paschasius, seeing him grow more and more furious, plunged a sword into the saint's throat. But, far from losing the power of speech, she said: 'I make known to you that peace is restored to the Church! This very day Maximian has died, and Diocletian has been driven from the throne. And just as God has bestowed my sister Agatha upon the city of Catania as its protectress, so He has this moment entitled me to be the patroness of the city of Syracuse.' And in good truth, while she was still speaking, envoys from Rome arrived to seize Paschasius, and take him as a prisoner before the Senate; for the Senate had learned that he was guilty of innumerable thieveries throughout the province. He was therefore brought to Rome, bound over to the Senate, convicted, and put to death. As for the virgin Lucy, she did not stir from the spot where she had suffered, but remained alive until the priests came to bring her Holy Communion, the whole populace piously assisting. There also she was buried, and a church was raised in her honour. Her martyrdom took place about the year of the Lord 310.

[From *The Golden Legend of Jacobus de Voragine*, pp. 34-37.]

SAINT AGNES
January 21

Agnes is the same as *agna*, which means lamb; for she was gentle and humble like a little lamb. Or it may come from *agnon*, which is Greek and means pious; for she was pious and compassionate. Or it comes from *agnoscere,* meaning to know; for she knew the way of truth. But Augustine opposes truth to three vices, namely vanity, lying, and doubt: and she overcame these three by means of the great virtues which were hers.

Agnes, a maiden of great wisdom, was thirteen years of age when she lost death and found life. She was young in years, but mature of mind and soul: she was fair of visage, but fairer of heart.

The son of a prefect, seeing her on the way home from school, fell in love with her. He promised her diamonds and great riches if she would consent to be his wife. But Agnes answered him: 'Begone, sting of sin, food of crime, poison of the soul, for I am already given to another lover!' She began to vaunt her lover and betrothed, praising in him the five qualities which an espoused maiden esteems most highly in him whom she loves: namely, nobility, beauty, wealth, courage blended with strength, and lastly love. And she said: 'He whom I love is nobler than thou. The sun and the moon wonder at His beauty, His riches are inexhaustible, He is mighty enough to bring the dead to life, and His love surpasses all love. He has placed His ring upon my finger, has given me a necklace of precious stones, and has clothed me in a gown woven with gold. He has graven a sign upon my face, to keep me from loving any other than Himself, and He has sprinkled my cheeks with His blood. Already I have been embraced by His pure arms, already His body is with my body. And He has shown me an incomparable treasure, and has promised to give it to me if I persevere in His love.'

Hearing this, the young man sickened with his love, and was in danger of death. His father came to call upon the maiden in his son's behalf: but Agnes made answer that she could not break faith with her Bridegroom. Then the prefect asked who this lover might be, and when someone told him that it was Christ whom she called her lover, he began at first to question her gently, and then threatened to punish her if she refused to answer. But Agnes said to him: 'Do whatever pleases thee, I shall not give up my secret!' Then said the prefect: 'Make thy choice! If thou prizest thy virginity, offer sacrifice to Vesta with the virgins of the Goddess; otherwise I shall lock thee up with prostitutes!' But she replied: 'I will not sacrifice to thy gods, and yet I shall not be defiled, for

I have with me a guardian of my body, an angel of the Lord!' Then the prefect had her stripped of her garments, and led naked to a house of debauch. But God made her hair to grow in such abundance that it covered her better than any garments. And when she entered the house of shame, she found an angel awaiting her, holding a tunic of dazzling whiteness. Thus the place became for her a house of prayer, and the angel cast about her a supernatural light.

Then the prefect's son came to the place with other youths, and invited his companions first to have their pleasure of the maiden. But when they entered the room where Agnes was, they were so terrified that they fled back to the prefect's son; and he, calling them cowards, rushed madly into the room. But the Devil throttled him on the spot, because he had not honoured God. Then the prefect, in tears, came to Agnes, and questioned her about the death of his son. And Agnes said: 'He whose designs he sought to carry out has received power over him, and killed him.' And the prefect said to her: 'If thou dost not wish me to think that thou thyself hast killed him by some magic art, ask and obtain that he come back to life!' And at Agnes' prayer the young man returned to life, and began to confess Christ publicly.

But then the priests of the gods stirred up the populace, and cried out: 'Death to the witch, who changes men's souls and bewitches their minds!' Meanwhile the prefect, at the sight of the miracle, would gladly have released the maiden: but, fearing that he would be proscribed, he withdrew sadly, and left her under guard with a lieutenant. This man, whose name was Aspasius, had the young girl thrown into a raging fire, but the flames, dividing, consumed the pagans, and left Agnes untouched. Then, by the order of Aspasius, a dagger was thrust into her throat, and in this manner her heavenly Spouse claimed her for His bride, having decked her with the crown of martyrdom. All this is believed to have taken place under the reign of Constantine the Great, who reigned about the year 309. And the parents of Saint Agnes, with the other Christians, buried her with great joy; and they barely escaped the shower of stones which the pagans hurled at them.

[From *The Golden Legend of Jacobus de Voragine,* pp. 110–13.]

A curious exception to these patterns of female sexuality is the story of the great sinner and penitent, Mary Magdalene. The story presents her as the rich sister of Lazarus and Martha, only briefly alluding to her hedonistic past. Perhaps because she did not suffer martyrdom, which for women occasioned specific and vivid sexual attention, and because she was and remains one of the greatest and most popular female saints, her earlier sexual activity needed to be played down. (Other stories, however, and some artistic renderings do emphasize her role as the repentant sinner, specifically suggesting sexual sins.) *The Golden Legend* concentrates on her long life after her conversion. In this story Mary Magdalene never gets punished, and in particular she never gets punished as a woman. On the contrary, the story presents her in a very different light from the rest of the women saints in this collection: It confirms her apostolic mission, which she received at the tomb of Jesus, and it shows her preaching and having disciples.

SAINT MARY MAGDALEN
July 22

Mary Magdalen was born of parents who were of noble station, and came of royal lineage. Her father was called Syrus, and her mother Eucharia. Together with her brother Lazarus and her sister Martha, she was the possessor of the fortified town of Magdala near Genezareth, of Bethany close by Jerusalem, and of a large section of Jerusalem itself; but these vast possessions were so divided that Lazarus held the section of Jerusalem, Martha retained Bethany, and Magdala belonged to Mary, who thus came by the surname of Magdalen. And since Magdalen gave herself wholly to the pleasures of the senses, and Lazarus served in the army, the prudent Martha was entrusted with the stewardship of her brother's and sister's properties. All three, moreover, sold their goods after Our Lord's Ascension, and laid the price at the feet of the apostles.

As rich as Mary was, she was no less beautiful; and so entirely had she abandoned her body to pleasure that she was no longer called by any other name than 'the sinner.' But when Jesus was journeying about the country preaching, she learned one day, by divine inspiration, that He sat at meat in the house of Simon the Leper. Thither she ran at once, but, not daring to mingle with His disciples, she stayed apart. And she washed the Lord's feet with her tears, and wiped them with the hair of her head, and anointed them with precious ointment: for the warmth of the climate compelled the people of this region to use water and ointment several times a day. And when Simon the Pharisee was astonished to see that a prophet suffered himself to be touched by a woman of evil life, Our Lord reproached him for his proud righteousness, and said that all this woman's sins were forgiven her, because she loved much.

And thenceforward there was no grace that He refused her, nor any mark of affection that He withheld from her. He drove seven devils out of her, admitted her to His friendship, condescended to dwell in her house, and was pleased to defend her whenever occasion arose. He defended her before the Pharisee who accused her of being unclean, and before her sister Martha, who charged her with idleness, and

before Judas, who reproached her for her prodigality. And He could not see her in tears without Himself weeping. For love of her, He restored her brother to life after he had been dead four days, He cured Martha of an issue of blood which she had suffered for seven years, and He chose Martha's serving-maid, Martilla, to utter the memorable words: 'Blessed is the womb that bore thee, and the paps that gave thee suck!' Magdalen also had the honour of being present at the death of Jesus, standing at the foot of the Cross: and it was she that anointed His body with sweet spices after His death, and who stayed at the sepulchre when all the disciples went away. And to her first the risen Jesus appeared, and made her apostle to the apostles.

In the fourteenth year after the Passion and Ascension of Our Lord, the disciples went out into the diverse regions of the earth to sow the word of God; and Saint Peter entrusted Mary Magdalen to Saint Maximinus, one of the seventy-two disciples of the Lord. Then Saint Maximinus, Mary Magdalen, Lazarus, Martha, Martilla, and Saint Cedonius, the man born blind who had been cured by Jesus, together with still other Christians, were thrown by the infidels into a ship without a rudder and launched into the deep, in the hope that in this way they would all be drowned at once. But the ship was guided by the power of God, and made port in good estate at Marseilles. There no one would give shelter to the newcomers, who were forced to take refuge beneath the porch of a pagan temple. And when Mary Magdalen saw the pagans going into their temple to offer sacrifice to their gods, she arose with calm mien and prudent tongue, and began to draw them away from the worship of the idols and to preach Christ to them. And all wondered at her, not only for her beauty but for her eloquence, which eloquence was not indeed a matter of surprise on lips that had touched the Lord's feet.

Now the ruler of the province came to the temple to sacrifice to the idols, hoping to obtain a child, for his marriage had been without fruit. But Magdalen, by her preaching, deterred him from offering sacrifice to the false gods. And some days later she appeared to the ruler's wife and said to her: 'Why do you, who are rich, leave the servants of God to die of cold and hunger?' And she threatened her with the wrath of

God if she did not persuade her spouse to be more charitable. But the woman was afraid to speak of this vision to her husband. Again Magdalen appeared to her on the following night, and again she failed to speak of it to her husband. Finally, on the third night, Magdalen appeared with her face aflame with just ire, and upbraided the woman vehemently for her hardness of heart. The woman awoke all atremble, and saw that her spouse trembled likewise. 'My lord,' she said to him, 'hast thou also seen the dream that I have seen?' And he replied: 'I have seen the Christian woman, and she has reproached me for my want of charity, and threatened me with the wrath of God. What shall we do?' 'It were better to obey her,' said the woman, 'than to bring down upon us the anger of her God!' They therefore gave welcome to the Christians, and promised to provide for all their needs.

One day when Magdalen was preaching, this same ruler said to her: 'Thinkest though that thou canst give proof of the faith which thou preachest?' And she answered: 'Of a certain I can defend a faith that is confirmed day by day through miracles, and through the preaching of Peter, my master, the bishop of Rome!' Then the ruler and his wife said: 'We shall obey thee in all things if thou succeedest in obtaining from thy God that a son be born to us.' And Mary Magdalen besought the Lord for them, and her prayer was granted, for in a little time the woman was with child.

* * *

Then the citizens of Marseilles tore down all the temples of the idols, and built Christian churches in their stead; and by common consent they chose Lazarus to be bishop of Marseilles. Then Mary Magdalen and her followers went to Aix, where by many miracles they converted the people to the faith of Christ; and Saint Maximinus was elected bishop.

In the meantime Saint Mary Magdalen, moved by her wish to live in contemplation of the things of God, retired to a mountain cave which the hands of angels had made ready for her, and there she dwelt for thirty years, unknown to anyone. There she found neither water nor herb nor tree, whereby she knew that Jesus wished to sustain her with naught but heavenly meats, allowing her no earthly satisfaction. But every day the angels bore her aloft at the seven canonical hours, and with her bodily ears she heard the glorious chants of the heavenly hosts. Then, being filled with this delightful repast, she came down to her grotto, and needed no bodily food. Now a certain priest who wished to live in solitude had built a cell at a distance of twelve stadia from Magdalen's grotto. And one day Our Lord opened his eyes and made him to see the angels entering the grotto, lifting the saint into the air, and bearing her back after the space of an hour. Thereupon the priest, desiring to

be sure that his vision was real, ran to the place where she had appeared to him. But when he came within a stone's throw of the spot, all his members were paralyzed. He was able to use them to withdraw from the place, but when he sought to go toward it, his legs refused to carry him. Thus he understood that here was a sacred mystery, surpassing human ken. Calling upon Christ, he cried out: 'I adjure thee by the Lord, if thou who dwellest in this grotto art a human being, answer me and tell me the truth!' And after he had thrice repeated his adjuration, Saint Mary Magdalen responded: 'Come nearer, and thou shalt know what thou desirest to know!' Then, when the favour of Heaven had allowed the priest to take some steps forward, the saint said: 'Dost thou recall having read in the Gospel the story of Mary, the notorious sinner who washed the Saviour's feet, wiped them with the hairs of her head, and obtained pardon for all her sins?' And the priest replied: 'Well do I recall it! And for thirty years our holy Church has honoured her memory!' Then said the saint: 'I am that sinner. For thirty years I have lived here unknown to anyone. And every day the angels bear me up to Heaven seven times, where for my joy I hear the songs of the heavenly company with my own ears. But now the moment is at hand when I shall leave this earth forever. Go therefore to the Bishop Maximinus, and say to him that on the day of the Resurrection, as soon as he rises, he is to go to his oratory; and there he shall find me, led thither by the angels.' And while she spoke, the priest could not see her, but only heard a voice of angelic sweetness.

He ran straight to Maximinus, to whom he related all that he had seen and heard. On the appointed day and hour the holy bishop repaired to his oratory, and there saw Mary Magdalen, as yet surrounded by the angels who had brought her thither. She was raised two cubits above the earth, and held her arms extended. And as Saint Maximinus feared to draw near, she said to him: 'Father, do not flee thy daughter!' And Maximinus himself tells in his writings that the saint's visage, long used to the sight of the angels, had become so radiant that one might more easily have looked into the rays of the sun than into her face. Then the bishop, summoning the aforesaid priest and his clergy, gave the Body and Blood of the Lord to Saint Mary Magdalen: and no sooner had she taken the Communion than her body fell lifeless before the altar, and her soul took its flight to the Lord. And such was the perfume of her sanctity that for seven days the oratory was filled with it. Saint Maximinus cause her body to be interred with great pomp, and commanded that he himself be buried near her after his death.

[From *The Golden Legend of Jacobus de Voragine*, pp. 355–64.]

* * *

CATHERINE OF SIENA

Catherine of Siena (1347–1380) had her first visionary experiences while still a child and by the time she was fifteen she had privately vowed her virginity to Jesus. Her parents preferred that she marry and when Catherine continued to resist marriage she was treated rather badly by them. At seventeen she fell ill with smallpox, which disfigured her. This, however, led to the achievement of her ultimate goal, which was to be accepted as the first virgin Dominican tertiary. Prior to this all female tertiaries had been mature widows. Since these women were not cloistered they felt unable to protect a young woman, but Catherine's disfigurement seems to have been severe enough to have reduced their fears on that account. That and Catherine's determination gained her entry.

Although she did not learn to read until she was seventeen years old, Catherine became the trusted advisor of popes and indeed was instrumental in getting Pope Gregory XI to leave Avignon and return to Rome.

The following excerpt is from sections 73 and 74 of *The Dialogue,* a book she wrote as a guide for others on the spiritual path. In it she describes the concluding stages of the perfection of the soul which ultimately abides in perfect love.

Up to now I have shown you in many ways how the soul rises up from imperfection and comes to perfect love, and what she does after she has attained the love of friendship and filial love.

I told you that she came this far by dint of perseverance and shutting herself up in the house of self-knowledge. (But this self-knowledge must be seasoned with knowledge of me, or it would end in confusion.) For through self-knowledge the soul learns contempt for her selfish sensual passion and for pleasure in her own consolation. And from contempt grounded in humility she draws patience, which will make her strong in the face of the devil's attacks and other people's persecutions, and strong in my presence when for her own good I take away her spiritual pleasure. With this power she will endure it all.

And if difficulties make her selfish sensuality want to rise up against reason, her conscience must use [holy] hatred to pronounce judgment and not let any impulse pass uncorrected. Indeed the soul who lives in [holy] hatred finds self-correction and self-reproach in everything—not only in those [movements] which are against reason but often even in those which come from me. This is what my gentle servant Gregory meant when he said that a holy and pure conscience makes sin where there is no sin. In other words, the soul in the purity of her conscience sees guilt even where there was no guilt.

Now the soul who would rise up from imperfection by awaiting my providence in the house of self-knowledge with the lamp of faith ought to do and does just as the disciples did. They waited in the house and did not move from there, but persevered in watching and in constant humble prayer until the coming of the Holy Spirit.

This, as I have told you, is what the soul does when she has risen from imperfection and shuts herself up at home to attain perfection. She remains watching, gazing with her mind's eye into the teaching of my Truth. She is humbled, for in constant prayer (that is, in holy and true desire) she has come to know herself, and in herself she has come to know my affectionate charity. Now it remains to say how one can tell that a soul has attained perfect love. The sign is the same as that given to the holy disciples after they had received the Holy Spirit. They left the house and fearlessly preached my message by proclaiming the teaching of the Word, my only-begotten Son. They had no fear of suffering. No, they even gloried in suffering. It did not worry them to go before the tyrants of the world to proclaim the truth to them for the glory and praise of my name.

So it is with the soul who has waited for me in self-knowledge: I come back to her with the fire of my charity. In that charity she conceived the virtues through perseverance when she stayed at home, sharing in my power. And in that power and virtue she mastered and conquered her selfish sensual passion.

In that same charity I shared with her the wisdom of my Son, and in that wisdom she saw and came to know, with her mind's eye, my truth and the delusions of spiritual sensuality, that is, the imperfect love of one's own consolation. And she came to know the malice and deceit the devil works on the soul who is bound up in that imperfect love. So she rose up in contempt of that imperfection and in love for perfection.

I gave her a share in this love, which is the Holy Spirit, within her will by making her will strong to endure suffering and to leave her house in my name to give birth to the virtues for her neighbors. Not that she abandons the house of self-knowledge, but the virtues conceived by the impulse of love come forth from that house. She gives birth to them as her neighbors need them, in many different ways. For the fear she had of not showing herself lest she lose her own consolations is gone. After she has come to perfect, free love, she lets go of herself and comes out, as I have described.

And this brings her to the fourth stage. That is, after the third stage, the stage of perfection in which she both tastes and gives birth to charity in the person of her neighbor, she is graced with a final stage of perfect union with me. These two stages are linked together, for the one is never found without the other any more than charity for me can exist without charity for one's neighbors or the latter without charity for me. The one cannot be separated from the other. Even so, neither of these two stages can exist without the other.

[From *Catherine of Siena*, pp. 135–37.]

CHRISTINE DE PIZAN

Christine de Pizan (c. 1365–1430) was supported and encouraged in her education and literary efforts first by her father and then by her husband. Widowed at age twenty-five, she found herself without funds and with three children to support. She turned to writing, receiving some royal patronage, and became the first professional female writer in France. In her works she confronted and undid many of the medieval constraints put on women and was the first woman to speak out on behalf of women in the vernacular. She was a thoughtful Christian, who believed that a correct understanding of Christianity would help overcome the oppression of women. The last decade of her life was spent in the religious community where her daughter was a nun.

The following excerpts are from her *The Book of the City of Ladies,* which is an erudite and thought-provoking attack on the misogynist writings abounding in her time. The book is in the form of a dialogue between Christine de Pizan and three ladies, Reason, Rectitude, and Justice.

CHRISTINE ASKS REASON WHETHER GOD HAS EVER WISHED TO ENNOBLE THE MIND OF WOMAN WITH THE LOFTINESS OF THE SCIENCES; AND REASON'S ANSWER.

After hearing these things, I replied to the lady who spoke infallibly: "My lady, truly has God revealed great wonders in the strength of these women whom you describe. But please enlighten me again, whether it has ever pleased this God, who has bestowed so many favors on women, to honor the feminine sex with the privilege of the virtue of high understanding and great learning, and whether women ever have a clever enough mind for this. I wish very much to know this because men maintain that the mind of women can learn only a little."

She answered, "My daughter, since I told you before, you know quite well that the opposite of their opinion is true, and to show you this even more clearly, I will give you proof through examples. I tell you again—and don't fear a contradiction—if it were customary to send daughters to school like sons, and

if they were then taught the natural sciences, they would learn as thoroughly and understand the subtleties of all the arts and sciences as well as sons. And by chance there happen to be such women, for, as I touched on before, just as women have more delicate bodies than men, weaker and less able to perform many tasks, so do they have minds that are freer and sharper whenever they apply themselves."

"My lady, what are you saying? With all due respect, could you dwell longer on this point, please. Certainly men would never admit this answer is true, unless it is explained more plainly, for they believe that one normally sees that men know more than women do."

She answered, "Do you know why women know less?"

"Not unless you tell me, my lady."

"Without the slightest doubt, it is because they are not involved in many different things, but stay at home, where it is enough for them to run the household, and there is nothing which so instructs a reasonable creature as the exercise and experience of many different things."

"My lady, since they have minds skilled in conceptualizing and learning, just like men, why don't women learn more?"

She replied, "Because, my daughter, the public doesn't require them to get involved in the affairs which men are commissioned to execute, just as I told you before. It is enough for women to perform the usual duties to which they are ordained. As for judging from experience, since one sees that women usually know less than men, that therefore their capacity for understanding is less, look at men who farm the flatlands or who live in the mountains. You will find that in many countries they seem completely savage because they are so simple-minded. All the same, there is no doubt that Nature provided them with the qualities of body and mind found in the wisest and most learned men. All of this stems from a failure to learn, though, just as I told you, among men and women, some possess better minds than others. Let me tell you about women who have possessed great learning and profound understanding and treat the question of the similarity of women's minds to men's."

[From *The Book of the City of Ladies*, pp. 62– 65.]

★ ★ ★

HERE BEGINS THE THIRD PART OF THE BOOK OF THE CITY OF LADIES, WHICH TELLS HOW THE HIGH ROOFS OF THE TOWERS WERE COMPLETED AND BY WHOM AND WHICH NOBLE LADIES WERE CHOSEN TO RESIDE IN THE GREAT PALACES AND LOFTY MANSIONS.

1. THE FIRST CHAPTER TELLS HOW JUSTICE LED THE QUEEN OF HEAVEN TO LIVE IN THE CITY OF LADIES.

Lady Justice then turned to me in her sublime manner and said, "Christine, to tell the truth, it seems to me that you have worked extraordinarily well at building the City of Ladies, according to your capacities and with the aid of my sisters which you have put to excellent use. Now it is time for me to undertake the rest, just as I promised you. That is, to bring and to lodge here the most excellent Queen, blessed among women, with her noble company, so that she may rule and govern the City, inhabited by the multitude of noble ladies from her court and household, for I see the palaces and tall mansions ready and furnished, the streets paved to receive her most excellent and honorable company and assembly. Let princesses, ladies, and all women now come forward to receive her with the greatest honor and reverence, for she is not only their Queen but also has ministry and dominion over all created powers after the only Son whom she conceived of the Holy

Spirit and carried and who is the Son of God the Father. And it is right that the assembly of all women beg this most lofty and excellent sovereign princess to reside here below in her humility with them in their City and congregation without disdain or spite because of their insignificance compared to her highness. Yet, there is no need to fear that her humility, which surpasses all others, and her more than angelic goodness will allow her to refuse to inhabit and reside in the City of Ladies, and above all, in the palace already prepared for her by my sister Rectitude, which is constructed solely of glory and praise. Let all women now accompany me, and let us say to her:

"'We greet you, Queen of Heaven, with the greeting which the Angel brought you, when he said, *Hail Mary,* which pleased you more than all other greetings. May all the devout sex of women humbly beseech you that it please you well to reside among them with grace and mercy, as their defender, protector, and guard against all assaults of enemies and of the world, that they may drink from the fountain of virtues which flows from you and be so satisfied that every sin and vice be abominable to them. Now come to us, Heavenly Queen, Temple of God, Cell and Cloister of the Holy Spirit, Vessel of the Trinity, Joy of the Angels, Star and Guide to those who have gone astray, Hope of the True Creation. My Lady, what man is so brazen to dare think or say that the feminine sex is vile in beholding your dignity? For if all other women were bad, the light of your goodness so surpasses and transcends them that any remaining evil would vanish. Since God chose His spouse from among women, most excellent Lady, because of your honor, not only should men refrain from reproaching women but should also hold them in great reverence.'"

The Virgin replied as follows: "O Justice, greatly beloved by my Son, I will live and abide most happily among my sisters and friends, for Reason, Rectitude, and you, as well as Nature, urge me to do so. They serve, praise, and honor me unceasingly, for I am and will always be the head of the feminine sex. This arrangement was present in the mind of God the Father from the start, revealed and ordained previously in the council of the Trinity."

Here Justice answered, while all the women knelt with their heads bowed, "My Lady, may honor and praise be given to you forever. Save us, our Lady, and pray for us to your Son who refuses you nothing."

1. CONCERNING THE SISTERS OF OUR LADY AND MARY MAGDALENE.

"Now the incomparable Empress resides with us, regardless of whether it pleases the malicious slanderers. Her blessed sisters and Mary Magdalene must also dwell with her, for they stayed steadfastly with her, next to the Cross, during the entire Passion of her Son. What strong faith and deep love those women possess who did not forsake the Son of God who had been abandoned and deserted by all His Apostles. God has never reproached the love of women as weakness, as some men contend, for He placed the spark of fervent love in the hearts of the blessed Magdalene and of other ladies, indeed His approval of this love is clearly to be seen."

[From *The Book of the City of Ladies*, pp. 217–19.]

★ ★ ★

18. JUSTICE SPEAKS OF MANY NOBLE WOMEN WHO WAITED ON AND LODGED THE APOSTLES AND OTHER SAINTS.

"What more do you want me to tell you, my fair friend, Christine? I could recall other similar examples to you without stop. But because I see that you are surprised—for you said earlier, that every classical author attacked women—I tell you that, in spite of what you may have found in the writings of pagan authors on the subject of criticizing women, you will find little said against them in the holy legends of Jesus Christ and His Apostles; instead, even in the histories of all the saints, just as you can see yourself, you will find through God's grace many cases of extraordinary firmness and strength in women. Oh, the beautiful service, the outstanding charity which they have performed with great care and solicitude, unflinchingly, for the servants of God! Should not such hospitality and favors be considered? And even if some foolish men deem them frivolous, no one can deny that such works in accordance with our faith are the ladders leading to Heaven. So it is written regarding Drusiana, an honest widow who received Saint John the Evangelist in her home and waited on him and served him meals. It happened when this same Saint John returned from exile that the city dwellers held a large feast for him just as Drusiana was being led to burial, for she had died from grief over his long absence. And the neighbors said, 'John, here is Drusiana, your good hostess, who died from sorrow at your absence. She will never wait on you again.' Whereupon Saint John addressed her, 'Drusiana, get up and go home and prepare my meal for me.' And she came back to life.

"Likewise, a valiant and noble lady from the city of Limoges, named Susanna, was the first to give lodging to Saint Martial, who had been sent there by Saint Peter in order to convert the country. And this lady did many good things for him.

"Similarly, the good lady Maximilla removed Saint Andrew from the cross and buried him and in so doing risked death.

"The holy virgin Ephigenia in like manner followed Saint Matthew the Evangelist with great devotion and waited upon him. And after his death she had a church built in his honor.

"Similarly, another good lady was so taken with holy love for Saint Paul that she followed him everywhere and served him diligently.

"Likewise, during the time of the Apostles, a noble Queen named Helen (not the mother of Constantine but the queen of Adiabene, in Assyria) went to Jerusalem, where there was a terrible shortage of foodstuffs because of the famine there. And when she learned that the saints of our lord, who were in the city to preach to the people and to convert them, were dying of hunger, she had enough food purchased to provide them food as long as the famine lasted.

"Similarly, when Saint Paul was led to be beheaded at Nero's command, a good lady named Plautilla, who had customarily waited on him, walked ahead of him, weeping profoundly. And Saint Paul asked her for the scarf which she had on her head. And she gave it to him, whereupon the evil men who were there taunted her, saying that it was a fine thing for her to forfeit such a beautiful scarf. Saint Paul himself tied it around his eyes, and when he was dead, the angels gave it back to the woman, and it was completely smeared with blood, for which she cherished it dearly. And Saint Paul appeared to her and told her that because she had served him on Earth, he would serve her in Heaven by praying for her. I will tell you many more similar cases.

"Basilissa was a noble lady by virtue of her chastity. She was married to Saint Julian, and both of them took a vow of virginity on their wedding night. No one could conceive of the holy way of life of this virgin, nor the multitude of women and maidens who were saved and drawn to a holy life through her sacred preaching. And, in short, she was so deserving of grace because of her great chastity that our Lord spoke to her as she was dying.

"I do not know what more I could tell you, Christine, my friend. I could tell of countless ladies of different social backgrounds, maidens, married women, and widows, in whom God manifested His virtues with amazing force and constancy. But let this suffice for you, for it seems to me that I have acquitted myself well of my office in completing the high roofs of your City and in populating it for you with outstanding ladies, just as I promised. These last examples will serve as the doorways and gates into our City. And even though I have not named all the holy ladies who have lived, who are living, and who will live—for I could name only a handful!—they can all be included in this City of Ladies. Of it may be said, '*Gloriosa dicta sunt de te, civitas Dei.*' So I turn it over to you, finished perfectly and well enclosed, just as I promised. Farewell and may the peace of the Lord be always with you."

[From *The Book of the City of Ladies*, pp. 252–54.]

THE MALLEUS MALEFICARUM

The *Malleus Maleficarum* (*The Hammer of Witches*) became the authoritative handbook describing the activities of witches and how to convict them. It was written by two Dominican Inquisitors, Heinrich Kramer and James Sprenger. The misogyny of this text is hysterical in tone and its authors are fixated on sexuality. Its publication in 1486 helped to accelerate the killing of so-called witches in three ways: (1) by increasing the number of people who could be accused of witchcraft, (2) by increasing the geographical area of the persecution to include most of Europe, and (3) by focusing attention especially on women. As the following excerpt from Part I, Question 6 shows, the text specifies that women are more prone to witchcraft than men for a variety of reasons: women are more credulous than men, more impressionable, less intelligent, more carnal, etc.; they are also weaker and seek vengeance. Note the blame placed on Eve and the saving influence of Mary.

The third reason is that they have slippery tongues, and are unable to conceal from their fellow-women those things which by evil arts they know; and, since they are weak, they find an easy and secret manner of vindicating themselves by witchcraft. See *Ecclesiasticus* as quoted above: I had rather dwell with a lion and a dragon than to keep house with a wicked woman. All wickedness is but little to the wickedness of a woman. And to this may be added that, as they are very impressionable, they act accordingly.

There are also others who bring forward yet other reasons, of which preachers should be very careful how they make use. For it is true that in the Old Testament the Scriptures have much that is evil to say about women, and this because of the first temptress, Eve, and her imitators; yet afterwards in the New Testament we find a change of name, as from Eva to Ave (as S. Jerome says), and the whole sin of Eve taken away by the benediction of MARY. Therefore preachers should always say as much praise of them as possible.

But because in these times this perfidy is more often found in women than in men, as we learn by actual experience, if anyone is curious as to the reason, we may add to what has already been said the following: that since they are feebler both in mind and body, it is not surprising that they should come more under the spell of witchcraft.

For as regards intellect, or the understanding of spiritual things, they seem to be of a different nature from men; a fact which is vouched for by the logic of the authorities, backed by various examples from the Scriptures. Terence says: Women are intellectually like children. And Lactantius (*Institutiones*, III): No woman understood philosophy except Temeste. And *Proverbs* xi, as it were describing a woman, says: As a jewel of gold in a swine's snout, so is a fair woman which is without discretion.

But the natural reason is that she is more carnal than a man, as is clear from her many carnal abominations. And it should be noted that there was a defect in the formation of the first woman, since she was formed from a bent rib, that is, a rib of the breast, which is bent as it were in a contrary direction to a man. And since through this defect she is an imperfect animal, she always deceives. For Cato says: When a woman weeps she weaves snares. And again: When a woman weeps, she labours to deceive a man. And this is shown by Samson's wife, who coaxed him to tell her the riddle he had propounded to the Philistines, and told them the answer, and so deceived him. And it is clear in the case of the first woman that she had little faith; for when the serpent asked why they did not eat of every tree in Paradise, she answered: Of every tree, etc.—lest perchance we die. Thereby she showed that she doubted, and had little faith in the word of God. And all this is indicated by the etymology of the word; for *Femina* comes from *Fe* and *Minus*, since she is ever weaker to hold and preserve the faith. And this as regards faith is of her very nature; although both by grace and nature faith never failed in the Blessed Virgin, even at the time of Christ's Passion, when it failed in all men.

Therefore a wicked woman is by her nature quicker to waver in her faith, and consequently quicker to abjure the faith, which is the root of witchcraft.

[From *The Malleus Maleficarum* of Heinrich Kramer and James Sprenger, p. 44.]

* * *

To conclude. All witchcraft comes from carnal lust, which is in women insatiable. See *Proverbs* xxx: There are three things that are never satisfied, yea, a fourth thing which says not, It is enough; that is, the mouth of the womb. Wherefore for the sake of fulfilling their lusts they consort even with devils. More such reasons could be brought forward, but to the understanding it is sufficiently clear that it is no matter for wonder that there are more women than men found infected with the heresy of witchcraft. And in consequence of this, it is better called the heresy of witches than of wizards, since the name is taken from the more powerful party. And blessed be the Highest Who has so far preserved the male sex from so great a crime: for since He was willing to be born and to suffer for us, therefore He has granted to men this privilege.

What sort of Women are found to be above all Others Superstitious and Witches.

As to our second inquiry, what sort of women more than others are found to be superstitious and infected with witchcraft; it must be said, as was shown in the preceding inquiry, that three general vices appear to have special dominion over wicked women, namely, infidelity, ambition, and lust. Therefore they are more than others inclined towards witchcraft, who more than others are given to these vices. Again, since of these three vices the last chiefly predominates, women being insatiable, etc., it follows that those among ambitious women are more deeply infected who are more hot to satisfy their filthy lusts; and such are adulteresses, fornicatresses, and the concubines of the Great.

Now there are, as it is said in the Papal Bull, seven methods by which they infect with witchcraft the venereal act and the conception of the womb: First, by inclining the minds of men to inordinate passion; second, by obstructing their generative force; third, by removing the members accommodated to that act; fourth, by changing men into beasts by their magic art; fifth, by destroying the generative force in women; sixth, by procuring abortion; seventh, by offering children to devils, besides other animals and fruits of the earth with which they work much harm.

[From *The Malleus Maleficarum* of Heinrich Kramer and James Sprenger, p. 47.]

The *Malleus Maleficarum* served to put a large number of women into immediate jeopardy by stating that the activities of midwives can reveal signs of witchcraft (Part I, Question 11). At this time in history the great majority of births were attended by midwives, women familiar with childbirth and herbal cures. In other words these women were healers. They were also the confidants of women who wanted to have children and those who did not want children, so they had some knowledge of birth control and abortion. They were experts in sexual matters in a society dominated by a celibate clergy, a clergy that had confounded sexuality with devil worship. Once the *Malleus Maleficarum* made the association of midwives with witchcraft these women could be brought before the Inquisition for questioning. Few were found innocent.

Thus begun, the witch burning craze continued into the eighteenth century. No certain figures exist for the exact number of people who were killed but some scholars put it as high as four million. Significantly, 85 percent of those killed were women, varying in age from young children to old women. Certainly some of these women were witches or thought they were, but by far the larger number were victims of false accusations based on an excessive misogyny sanctioned by Christianity.

QUESTION XI

That Witches who are Midwives in Various Ways Kill the Child Conceived in the Womb, and Procure an Abortion; or if they do not this Offer New-born Children to Devils.

Here is set forth the truth concerning four horrible crimes which devils commit against infants, both in the mother's womb and afterwards. And since the devils do these things through the medium of women, and not men, this form of homicide is associated rather with women than with men. And the following are the methods by which it is done.

The Canonists treat more fully than the Theologians of the obstructions due to witchcraft; and they say that it is witchcraft, not only when anyone is unable to perform the carnal act, of which we have spoken above; but also when a woman is prevented from conceiving, or is made to miscarry after she has conceived. A third and fourth method of witchcraft is when they have failed to procure an abortion, and then either devour the child or offer it to a devil.

There is no doubt concerning the first two methods, since, without the help of devils, a man can by natural means, such as herbs, savin for example, or other emmenagogues, procure that a woman cannot generate or conceive, as has been mentioned above. But with the other two methods it is different; for they are effected by witches. And there is no need to bring forward the arguments, since very evident instances and examples will more readily show the truth of this matter.

The former of these two abominations is the fact that certain witches, against the instinct of human nature, and indeed against the nature of all beasts, with the possible exception of wolves, are in the habit of devouring and eating infant children. And concerning this, the Inquisitor of Como, who has been mentioned before, has told us the following: that he was summoned by the inhabitants of the County of Barby to hold an inquisition, because a certain man had missed his child from its cradle, and finding a congress of women in the night-time, swore that he saw them kill his child and drink its blood and devour it. Also, in one single year, which is the year now last passed, he says that forty-one witches were burned, certain others taking flight to the Lord Archduke of Austria, Sigismund. For confirmation of this there are certain writings of John Nider in his *Formicarius,* of whom, as of those events which he recounts, the memory is still fresh in men's minds; wherefore it is apparent that such things are not incredible. We must add that in all these matters witch midwives cause yet greater injuries, as penitent witches have often told to us and to others, saying: No one does more harm to the Catholic Faith than midwives. For when they do not kill children, then, as if for some other purpose, they take them out of the room and, raising them up in the air, offer them to devils.

[From *The Malleus Maleficarum of Heinrich Kramer and James Sprenger,* p. 66.]

JOAN OF ARC

Joan's short life (1412?–1431) offers a dramatic example of the religious and political issues of her day. At the time of her first visions, when she was about thirteen years old, France was engaged in both a civil war and a war with England. Through her visions and voices Joan came to believe that she was called by God to drive the English out of France and she set out to do so. Though initially successful in her military exploits Joan was eventually captured by the British who turned her over to an ecclesiastical court to try her as a heretic and a witch. Since Joan had grown up in a peasant family with stronger ties to the folk religion of her region of France than to the orthodox church that would judge her, she was particularly vulnerable. This complicated religious background came out during her trial when she admitted she may have danced with other young girls at a 'fairies' tree' which was located near a spring believed to heal sickness. Unknowingly Joan was probably referring to ancient Celtic practices that survived among their French descendants. In their minds, Joan and her neighbors were just doing what they had done for generations but, for the church, these were pagan practices. This is brought out in the excerpts when she is questioned about her Godmother who was said to have seen fairies.

Joan was accused of three crimes. The first involved her "voices," voices she said came from St. Catherine and St. Margaret but which her inquisitors thought were coming from evil spirits. Essentially Joan was convicted of witchcraft because she listened to these voices, in other words she consorted with the 'familiar' spirits associated with witches, the fairies of the Celtic Tradition. Secondly, she refused to submit to the authority of the church saying her voices had a higher authority. Her third crime was that she, a woman, dressed as a man. The transcript of her trial contains frequent references to the issues of her attire and demands that she return to women's clothes. Joan's clothes were a constant reminder to the inquisitors that she was not conforming to their ideas of proper behavior for a woman. The issue for Joan was that she refused to wear women's clothes while she continued to be held in a military prison with male guards constantly in her cell.

Joan was burned at the stake on May 30, 1431. In 1456, after a lengthy retrial, the verdict of 1431 was nullified. Nearly 500 years later, in 1920, Joan was canonized as a saint in the church that had executed her.

"When you asked to hear Mass, did it not seem to you that it would be more proper to be in female dress? Which would you like best, to have a woman's dress to hear Mass, or to remain in a man's dress and not hear it?"

"Give me assurance beforehand that I shall hear Mass if I am in female attire, and I will answer you this."

"Very well, I give you assurance of it: you shall hear Mass if you put on female attire."

"And what say you, if I have sworn and promised to our King my Master, not to put off this dress? Well, I will answer you this: Have made for me a long dress down to the ground, without a train; give it to me to go to Mass, and then on my return I will put on again the dress I have."

"I say it to you once again, do you consent to wear female attire to go and hear Mass?"

"I will take counsel on this, and then I will answer you: but I beseech you, for the honour of God and Our Lady permit me to hear Mass in this good town."

"You consent simply and absolutely to take female attire?"

"Send me a dress like a daughter of your citizens— that is to say, a long 'houppeland.' I will wear it to go and hear Mass. I beseech you as earnestly as I can, permit me to hear it in the dress I wear at this moment and without changing anything!"

"Will you submit your actions and words to the decision of the Church?"

"My words and deeds are all in God's Hands: in all, I wait upon Him. I assure you, I would say or do nothing against the Christian Faith: in case I have done or said anything which might be on my soul and which the clergy could say was contrary to the Christian Faith established by Our Lord, I would not maintain it, and would put it away."

"Are you not willing to submit yourself in this to the order of the Church?"

"I will not answer you anything more about it now. Send me a cleric on Saturday; and, if you do not wish to come yourself, I will answer him on this, with God's help; and it shall be put in writing."

"When your Voices come, do you make obeisance to them as to a Saint?"

"Yes; and if perchance I have not done so, I have afterwards asked of them grace and pardon. I should not know how to do them such great reverence as belongs to them, for I believe firmly they are Saint Catherine and Saint Margaret. I believe the same of Saint Michael."

[From *Jeanne d'Arc,* pp. 81–82.]

* * *

"Will you, in respect of all your words and deeds, whether good or bad, submit yourself to the decision of our Holy Mother the Church?"

"The Church! I love it, and would wish to maintain it with all my power, for our Christian Faith; it is not I who should be prevented from going to Church and hearing Mass! As to the good deeds I have done and my coming to the King, I must wait on the King of Heaven, who sent me to Charles, King of France, son of Charles who was King of France. You will see that the French will soon gain a great victory, that God will send such great doings that nearly all the Kingdom of France will be shaken by them. I say it, so that, when it shall come to pass, it may be remembered that I said it."

"When will this happen?"

"I wait on Our Lord."

"Will you refer yourself to the decision of the Church?"

"I refer myself to God Who sent me, to Our Lady, and to all the Saints in Paradise. And in my opinion it is all one, God and the Church; and one should make no difficulty about it. Why do you make a difficulty?"

"There is a Church Triumphant in which are God and the Saints, the Angels, and the Souls of the Saved. There is another Church, the Church Militant, in which are the Pope, the Vicar of God on earth, the Cardinals, Prelates of the Church, the Clergy and all good Christians and Catholics: this Church, regularly assembled, cannot err, being ruled by the Holy Spirit. Will you refer yourself to this Church which we have thus just defined to you?"

"I came to the King of France from God, from the Blessed Virgin Mary, from all the Saints of Paradise, and the Church Victorious above, and by their command. To this Church I submit all my good deeds, all that I have done or will do. As to saying whether I will submit myself to the Church Militant, I will not now answer anything more."

"What do you say on the subject of the female attire, which is offered to you, to go and hear Mass?"

"I will not take it yet, until it shall please Our Lord. And if it should happen that I should be brought to judgment, [and that I have to divest myself in Court,] I beseech the lords of the Church to do me the grace to allow me a woman's smock and a hood for my head; I would rather die than revoke what God has made me do; and I believe firmly that God will not allow it to come to pass that I should be brought so low that I may not soon have succour from Him, and by miracle."

"As you say that you bear a man's dress by the command of God, why do you ask for a woman's smock at the point of death?"

"It will be enough for me if it be long."

"Did your Godmother who saw the fairies pass as a wise woman?"

"She was held and considered a good and honest woman, neither divineress nor sorceress."

"You said you would take a woman's dress, that you might be let go: would this please God?"

"If I had leave to go in woman's dress, I should soon put myself back in man's dress and do what God has commanded me: I have already told you so. For nothing in the world will I swear not to arm myself and put on a man's dress; I must obey the orders of Our Lord."

"What age and what dress had Saint Catherine and Saint Margaret?"

"You have had such answers as you will have from me, and none others shall you have: I have told you what I know of it for certain."

"Before today, did you believe fairies were evil spirits?"

"I know nothing about it."

[From *Jeanne d'Arc*, pp. 86–88.]

The Reformation and Counter-Reformation

The Protestant Reformers' emphasis on the value of marriage and family life over against clerical celibacy has had an enduring impact on the lives of Protestant women in that women were primarily defined within the contexts of the roles of wife and mother. Several of the readings that follow present the Protestant understanding of marriage and consequently the Protestant understanding of women.

MARTIN LUTHER

Martin Luther (1483–1546), the great German theologian and reformer, was very concerned about the ordering of family life, which he saw as central to the organizing of Christian life. Though he himself married quite late, he was adamant about marriage for the Protestant clergy. In 1525 he married Katherine von Bora, a former nun, which gave ample fuel to his opponents, though their marriage provided a model for generations of Protestant ministers and their wives. Luther's writings on marriage and family life were almost definitive for the Protestant tradition and remain an enduring legacy in our time.

TABLE TALK

The following excerpts are taken from *Table Talk*, a collection of notes written down by visitors to Luther's home as they were all gathered at the dining room table. Luther's wife, Katherine von Bora, whom he calls Katy, often appears in these conversations which give some feeling for their marriage. The excerpts are grouped together under the name of the recorder or collector.

RECORDED BY DIETRICH

Marriage Should Begin with Prayer
Between February and March, 1532   No. 185

"Marriage consists of these things: the natural desire of sex, the bringing to life of offspring, and life together with mutual fidelity. Yet the devil can so rupture marriage that hate is never more bitter than here. This comes from our beginning everything without prayer and with presumption. A God-fearing young man who is about to be married should pray, 'Dear God, add thy blessing!' But this is not done. Everybody is like Dolzig, and the most important things are begun presumptuously. What is our Lord God to do under the circumstances? It is implied that his name is false: Almighty, Creator, the Giver of all things. Accordingly, dear Master Veit, do as I did. When I wished to take my Katy I prayed to God earnestly. You ought to do this too. You have never yet prayed to God earnestly for a wife."

[From *Luther's Works*, vol. 54, pp. 125–126.]

★ ★ ★

RECORDED BY SCHLAGINHAUFEN

Luther Jests with His Wife About Monogamy
Between April 7 and May 1, 1532   No. 1461

[Martin Luther said,] "The time will come when a man will take more than one wife."

The doctor's wife responded, "Let the devil believe that!"

The doctor said, "The reason, Katy, is that a woman can bear a child only once a year while her husband can beget many."

Katy responded, "Paul said that each man should have his own wife" [I Cor. 7:2].

To this, the doctor replied, "Yes, 'his own wife' and not 'only one wife,' for the latter isn't what Paul wrote."

The doctor spoke thus in jest for a long time, and finally the doctor's wife said, "Before I put up with this, I'd rather go back to the convent and leave you and all our children."

[From *Luther's Works*, vol. 54, p. 153.]

COLLECTED BY CORDATUS

When Women Try to Run Everything
Between December 11, 1532,
and January 2, 1533   No. 2847b

When he [Martin Luther] was arguing with his wife he said, "You convince me of whatever you please. You have complete control. I concede to you the control of the household, provided my rights are preserved. Female government has never done any good. God made Adam master over all creatures, to rule over all living things, but when Eve persuaded him that he was lord even over God she spoiled everything. We have you women to thank for that! With tricks and cunning women deceive men, as I, too, have experienced."

[From *Luther's Works*, vol. 54, pp. 174–175.]

RECORDED BY LAUTERBACH AND WELLER

In Praise of Women and Marriage
Between January 14 and 31, 1537   No. 3528

Martin Luther looked admiringly at a painting of his wife and said, "I think I'll have a husband added

to that painting, send it to Mantua [where a Catholic Council was to meet], and inquire whether they prefer marriage [to celibacy]."

Then he began to speak in praise of marriage, the divine institution from which everything proceeds and without which the whole world would have remained empty and all creatures would have been meaningless and of no account, since they were created for the sake of man. "So Eve and her breasts would not have existed, and none of the other ordinances would have followed. It was for this reason that, in the power of the Holy Spirit, Adam called his wife by that admirable name Eve, which means mother. He did not say 'wife,' but 'mother,' and he added 'of all living.' Here you have the ornament that distinguishes woman, namely, that she is the fount of all living human beings. These words were very few, but neither Demosthenes nor Cicero ever composed such an oration. This is the oration of the very eloquent Holy Spirit, fitted to our first parent. He is the one who declaims here, and since this orator defines and praises [marriage] it is only right that we put a charitable construction on everything that may be frail in a woman. For Christ, our Savior, did not hold woman in contempt but entered the womb of a woman. Paul also reflected on this [when he wrote], 'Woman will be saved through bearing children,' etc. [I Tim. 2:15]. This is admirable praise, except that he uses the little word 'woman' and not 'mother.'"

[From *Luther's Works*, vol. 54, pp. 222–223.]

RECORDED BY LAUTERBACH

The Tyranny and Burden of Celibacy
February 24, 1538   No. 3777

Then he [Luther] spoke at length about the tyranny of celibacy, how great a burden celibacy was. "When he was quite old, Augustine still complained about nocturnal pollutions. When he was goaded by desire Jerome beat his breast with stones but was unable to drive the girl out of his heart. Francis made snowballs and Benedict lay down on thorns. Bernard macerated his harassed body until it stank horribly. I believe that virgins also have temptations and enticements, but if there are fluxes and pollutions the gift of virginity is no longer there; then the remedy of marriage which God has given should be taken hold of.

"People who occupied stations at least as high as ours lived in the estate of marriage. Peter had a mother-in-law, and therefore had a wife too. So James, the brother of the Lord, and all the apostles were married, except John. Paul counted himself among the unmarried and widowers, but it appears that he was married in his youth according to the custom of the Jews. Spyridion, bishop of Cyprus, was married. Bishop Hilary had a wife, for when he was in exile he wrote a letter to his little daughter in which he urged her to be obedient and to learn to pray. He wrote that he had been at the home of a rich man who promised that if Hilary's daughter behaved he would send her a golden cloak. In such a childlike way, Hilary wrote to his little daughter. I marvel that the holy fathers contended with such juvenile temptations and did not feel the loftier ones when they occupied such high offices."

[From *Luther's Works,* vol. 54, pp. 270–71.]

LECTURES ON GENESIS

The following excerpts are from Luther's lectures on Genesis, particularly Gen. 2.18. In it Luther affirms marriage and procreation while also emphasizing the inferiority and subjection of women because of Eve's sin. Essentially wives are useful for continuing the species, managing households, and avoiding the sin of fornication.

The Lord God also said: It is not good that man is alone; I shall make him a help which should be before him.

We have the church established by the Word and a distinct form of worship. There was no need of civil government, since nature was unimpaired and without sin. Now also the household is set up. For God makes a husband of lonely Adam and joins him to a wife, who was needed to bring about the increase of the human race. Just as we pointed out above in connection with the creation of man that Adam was created in accordance with a well-considered counsel, so here, too, we perceive that Eve is being created according to a definite plan. Thus here once more Moses points out that man is a unique creature and that he is suited to be a partaker of divinity and of immortality. For man is a more excellent creature than heaven and earth and everything that is in them.

But Moses wanted to point out in a special way that the other part of humanity, the woman, was created by a unique counsel of God in order to show that this sex, too, is suited for the kind of life which Adam was expecting and that this sex was to be useful for procreation. Hence it follows that if the woman had not been deceived by the serpent and had not sinned, she would have been the equal of Adam in all respects. For the punishment, that she is now subjected to the man, was imposed on her after sin and because of sin, just as the other hardships and dangers were: travail, pain, and countless other vexations. Therefore Eve was not like the woman of today; her state was far better and more excellent, and she was in no respect inferior to Adam, whether you count the qualities of the body or those of the mind.

But here there is a question: "When God says: 'It is not good that man should be alone,' of what good could He be speaking, since Adam was righteous and had no need of a woman as we have, whose flesh is leprous through sin?"

My answer is that God is speaking of the common good or that of the species, not of personal good. The personal good is the fact that Adam had innocence. But he was not yet in possession of the common good which the rest of the living beings who propagated their kind through procreation had. For so far Adam was alone; he still had no partner for that magnificent work of begetting and preserving his kind. Therefore "good" in this passage denotes the increase of the human race. In this way, although Adam was innocent and righteous, he did not yet have that good for which he was created, namely, immortality, into which he would have been translated in due time if he had remained in innocence. Hence the meaning is that Adam as the most beautiful creature is well provided for so far as his own person is concerned but still lacks something, namely, the gift of the increase and the blessing—because he is alone.

Today, after our nature has become corrupted by sin, woman is needed not only to secure increase but also for companionship and for protection. The management of the household must have the ministration of the dear ladies. In addition—and this is lamentable—woman is also necessary as an antidote against sin. And so, in the case of the woman, we must think not only of the managing of the household which she does, but also of the medicine which she is. In this respect Paul says (1 Cor. 7:2): "Because of fornication let each one have his own wife." And the Master of the *Sentences* declares learnedly that matrimony was established in Paradise as a duty, but after sin also as an antidote. Therefore we are compelled to make use of this sex in order to avoid sin. It is almost shameful to say this, but nevertheless it is true. For there are very few who marry solely as a matter of duty.

But the rest of the animals do not have this need. Consequently, for the most part they copulate only once a year and then are satisfied with this as if by their very action they wanted to indicate that they were copulating because of duty. But the conduct of human beings is different. They are compelled to make use of intercourse with their wives in order to avoid sin. As a result, we are begotten and also born in sin, since our parents did not copulate because of duty but also as an antidote or to avoid sin.

And yet, in the presence of this antidote and in so wretched a state, the Lord fulfilled His blessing; and people are begotten, though in sin and with sin. This would not have been the case in Paradise. The act of begetting would have been a most sacred one without any passion or lust such as there is now, and children would have been in original righteousness and up-rightness. Immediately, without any instruction, they would have known God; they would have praised Him; they would have given thanks to Him, etc. All this has now been lost; and yet it serves a purpose to think of these things that we may gain some idea of the difference between that state in which we now are, that is, original sin, and that one in which Adam was, that is, original righteousness, for which we hope when all things are restored (Acts 3:21).

In connection with the expression "Let Us make" I suggested that Eve was created according to a unique counsel that it might be clear that she has a share in immortality, a life better than that of the remaining animals, which live only their animal life, without hope of eternal life.

What appears in the Latin text as "like unto himself" is in Hebrew "which should be about him." With this expression the text also makes a difference between the human female and the females of all the remaining animals, which are not always about their mates: the woman was so created that she should everywhere and always be about her husband. Thus imperial law also calls the life of married people an inseparable relationship. The female of the brutes has a desire for the male only once in a whole year. But after she has become pregnant, she returns to her home and takes care of herself. For her young born at another time she has no concern, and she does not always live with her mate.

But among men the nature of marriage is different. There the wife so binds herself to a man that she will be about him and will live together with him as one flesh. If Adam had persisted in the state of innocence, this intimate relationship of husband and wife would have been most delightful. The very work of procreation also would have been most sacred and would have been held in esteem. There would not have been that shame stemming from sin which there is now, when parents are compelled to hide in darkness to do this. No less respectability would have attached to cohabitation than there is to sleeping, eating, or drinking with one's wife.

Therefore was this fall not a terrible thing? For truly in all nature there was no activity more excellent and more admirable than procreation. After the proclamation of the name of God it is the most important activity Adam and Eve in the state of innocence could carry on—as free from sin in doing this as they were in praising God. Although this activity, like the other wretched remnants of the first state, continues in nature until now, how horribly marred it has become! In honor husband and wife are joined in public before the congregation; but when they are alone, they come together with a feeling of the utmost shame. I am not speaking now about the hideousness inherent in our flesh, namely, the bestial desire and lust. All these are clear indications of original sin.

So the woman was a helper for Adam; for he was unable to procreate alone, just as the woman was also unable to procreate alone. Moreover, these are the highest praises of sex, that the male is the father in procreation, but the woman is the mother in procreation and the helper of her husband. When we look back to the state of innocence, procreation, too, was better, more delightful, and more sacred in countless ways.

[From *Luther's Works*, vol. 1, pp. 115–18.]

JOHN CALVIN

John Calvin (1509–1564), the great systematic theologian of the Protestant Reformation, was born in Noyon, France. In 1533 he was forced to flee his native country because of his involvement in the spread of Luther's ideas and he spent the rest of his life in exile, primarily in Geneva, which became an important center of the Protestant Reformation. It was here that Calvin struggled, rather successfully, to establish a society that enforced a biblical worldview and a strict moral code for all.

The following excerpts are taken from Calvin's magnum opus, *The Institutes of the Christian Religion,* completed in 1536 and revised by him in 1559. The first excerpt (II.VIII.41–43) is his commentary on the Seventh Commandment, "You shall not commit adultery." This leads Calvin, following Paul, into a general discussion of marriage primarily as a means of avoiding the sin of fornication. In the second excerpt (IV.XV.20–22) Calvin upholds the position that women cannot baptize, no matter how extreme the circumstances. Significantly, he concludes by explaining that the absence of baptism does not prevent an infant from entering heaven. So, on the one hand, he is reducing one of the most urgent causes of women performing baptisms, to save the soul of a dying infant, and on the other hand he is confining this power to a male clergy.

The Institutes II.VIII.41–43

Man has been created in this condition that he may not lead a solitary life, but may enjoy a helper joined to himself [cf. Gen. 2:18]; then by the curse of sin he has been still more subjected to this necessity. Therefore, the Lord sufficiently provided for us in this matter when he established marriage, the fellowship of which, begun on his authority, he also sanctified by his blessing. From this it is clear that any other union apart from marriage is accursed in his sight; and that the companionship of marriage has been ordained as a necessary remedy to keep us from plunging into unbridled lust. Let us not delude ourselves, then, when we hear that outside marriage man cannot cohabit with a woman without God's curse.

Celibacy?

Now, through the condition of our nature, and by the lust aroused after the Fall, we, except for those whom God has released through special grace, are doubly subject to women's society. Let each man, then, see what has been given to him. Virginity, I agree, is a virtue not to be despised. However, it is denied to some and granted to others only for a time. Hence, those who are troubled with incontinence and cannot prevail in the struggle should turn to matrimony to help them preserve chastity in the degree of their calling. For those who do not receive this precept [cf. Matt. 19:11], if they do not have recourse to the remedy offered and conceded them for their intemperance, are striving against God and resisting his ordinance. Let no one cry out against me — as many do today — that with God's help he can do all things. For God helps only those who walk in his ways, that is, in his calling [cf. Ps. 91:1, 14?]. All who, neglecting God's help, strive foolishly and rashly to overcome and surmount their necessities, depart from their calling. The Lord affirms that continence is a special gift of God, one of a kind that is bestowed not indiscriminately, not upon the body of the church as a whole, but upon a few of its members. For first of all, the Lord distinguishes a class of men who have castrated themselves for the sake of the Kingdom of Heaven [Matt. 19:12] — that is, to permit them to devote themselves more unreservedly and freely to the affairs of the Kingdom of Heaven. Yet lest anyone think that such castration lies in a man's power, he pointed out just before that not all men can receive this precept, but only those to whom it is especially "given" from heaven [Matt. 19:11]. From this he concludes: "He who is able to receive this, let him receive it" [Matt. 19:12]. Paul declares it even more clearly when he writes: "Each has his own special gift from God, one of one kind and one of another" [I Cor. 7:7].

Marriage as related to this commandment

We are informed by an open declaration, that it is not given to every man to keep chastity in celibacy, even if he aspires to it with great zeal and effort, and that it is a special grace which the Lord bestows only upon certain men, in order to hold them more ready for his work. Do we not, then, contend against God and the nature ordained by him, if we do not accommodate our mode of life to the measure of our ability? Here the Lord forbids fornication. He therefore requires purity and modesty of us. There is but one way to preserve it: that each man measure himself by his own standard. Let no man rashly despise marriage as something unprofitable or superfluous to him; let no man long for celibacy unless he can live without a wife. Also, let him not provide in this state for the repose and convenience of the flesh, but only that, freed of this marriage bond, he may be more prompt and ready for all the duties of piety. And since this blessing is conferred on many persons only for a time, let every man abstain from marriage only so long as he is fit to observe celibacy. If his power to tame lust fails him, let him recognize that the Lord has now imposed the necessity of marriage upon him. The apostle proves this when he enjoins that to flee fornication "each man should have his own wife, and each woman her own husband" [I Cor. 7:2]. Again: "If they cannot exercise self-control, they should marry" in the Lord [I Cor. 7:9]. First, he means that the greater part of men are subject to the vice of incontinence; secondly, of those who are so subject he enjoins all without exception to take refuge in that sole remedy with which to resist unchastity. Therefore if those who are incontinent neglect to cure their infirmity by this means, they sin even in not obeying this command of the apostle. And let him who does not touch a woman not flatter himself, as if he could not be accused of immodesty, while in the meantime his heart inwardly burns with lust. For Paul defines modesty as "purity of heart joined with chastity of body." "The unmarried woman," he says, "is anxious about the affairs of the Lord, how to be holy in body and spirit" [I Cor. 7:34]. Thus while he confirms by reason that precept mentioned above, he says not only that it is better to take a wife than to pollute oneself by associating with a harlot [cf. I Cor. 6:15 ff.], but he says that "it is better to marry than to burn" [I Cor. 7:9].

[From *Calvin: Institutes of the Christian Religion*, vol. 1, pp. 407–8.]

Institutes IV.XV.20–22

Against "emergency" baptism

It is also pertinent here to know that it is wrong for private individuals to assume the administration of baptism; for this as well as the serving of the Supper is a function of the ecclesiastical ministry. For Christ did not command women, or men of every sort, to baptize, but gave this command to those whom he had appointed apostles. And when he ordered his disciples to do in the ministering of the Supper [Matt. 28:19] what they had seen him do—while he was performing the function of a lawful steward [Luke 22:19]—he doubtless willed that they should follow his example in it.

For many ages past and almost from the beginning of the church, it was a custom for laymen to baptize those in danger of death if a minister was not present at the time. I do not see, however, how this can be defended with sound reasoning. Not even the ancient writers themselves, who either followed this practice or condoned it, were certain whether it was right to do it. Now Augustine displays this doubt when he says: "Even if a layman compelled by necessity should give baptism, I do not know whether anyone might piously say that it should be repeated. For if no necessity compels it to be done, it is a usurping of another's office; but if necessity urges it, it is either no sin at all or a venial one." Concerning women, it was decreed without exception in the Council of Carthage that they should not presume to baptize at all.

* * *

Women not permitted to baptize

The practice before Augustine was born is first of all inferred from Tertullian, who held that a woman was not allowed to speak in the church, and also not to teach, to baptize, or to offer. This was that she might not claim for herself the function of any man, much less that of a priest. Epiphanius also is a trustworthy witness of this matter when he upbraids Marcion for having given women permission to baptize.

And I am well aware of the answer of those who think otherwise: that there is a great difference between common usage and an extraordinary remedy required by dire necessity. But since Epiphanius declares that it is a mockery to give women the right to baptize and makes no exception, it is clear enough that he condemns this corrupt practice as inexcusable under any pretext. Also in the third book, where he teaches that permission was not even given to the holy mother of Christ, he adds no reservation.

* * *

But this principle will easily and immediately settle the controversy: infants are not barred from the Kingdom of Heaven just because they happen to depart the present life before they have been immersed in water. Yet we have already seen that serious injustice is done to God's covenant if we do not assent to it, as if it were weak of itself, since its effect depends neither upon baptism nor upon any additions. Afterward, a sort of seal is added to the sacrament, not to confer efficacy upon God's promise as if it were invalid of itself, but only to confirm it to us. From this it follows that the children of believers are baptized not in order that they who were previously strangers to the church may then for the first time become children of God, but rather that, because by the blessing of the promise they already belonged to the body of Christ, they are received into the church with this solemn sign.

[From *Calvin: The Institutes of the Christian Religion*, vol. 2, pp. 1320–23.]

ARGULA VON GRUMBACH

Argula von Grumbach (1492–after 1563) was one woman of the Reformation who has left some heated and articulate writings. She was an impoverished noblewoman, fairly well educated in German, and an enthusiastic follower of and correspondent with Luther. Her first public writing, in 1523, was a letter to the University of Ingolstadt, which, under threat of the stake, had exacted a recantation of Luther's theology from a member of the faculty. Many more of her letters were to come. She wrote as follows:

"To the honorable, worthy, highborn, erudite, noble, stalwart Rector and all the Faculty of the University of Ingolstadt: When I heard what you had done to Arsacius Seehofer under terror of imprisonment and the stake, my heart trembled and my bones quaked. What have Luther and Melanchthon taught save the Word of God? You have condemned them. You have not refuted them. Where do you read in the Bible that Christ, the apostles, and the prophets imprisoned, banished, burned, or murdered anyone? You tell us that we must obey the magistrates. Correct. But neither the pope, nor the Kaiser, nor the princes have any authority over the Word of God. You need not think you can pull God, the prophets and the apostles out of heaven with papal decretals drawn from Aristotle, who was not a Christian at all. I am not unacquainted with the word of Paul that women should be silent in church (1 Tim. 1:2) but, when no man will or can speak, I am driven by the word of the Lord when he said, 'He who confesses me on earth, him will I confess and he who denies me, him will I deny,' [Matt. 10, Luke 9], and I take comfort in the words of the prophet Isaiah [3:12, but not exact], 'I will send you children to be your princes and women to be your rulers.' You seek to destroy all of Luther's works. In that case you will have to destroy the New Testament, which he has translated. In the German writings of Luther and Melanchthon I have found nothing heretical, and there are a goodly number of Luther's works of which Spalatin has sent me a list. Even if Luther should recant, what he has said would still be the Word of God. I would be willing to come and dispute with you in German and you won't need to use Luther's translation of the Bible. You can use the one written 31 years ago [actually the Koburger of 1483]. You have the key of knowledge and you close the kingdom of heaven. But you are defeating yourselves. The news of what has been done to this lad of 18 has reached us and other cities in so short a time that soon it will be known to all the world. The Lord will forgive Arsacius, as he forgave Peter, who denied his master, though not threatened by prison and fire. Great good will yet come from this young man. I send you not a woman's ranting, but the Word of God. I write as a member of the Church of Christ against which the gates of hell shall not prevail, as they will against the Church of Rome. God give us his grace that we may all be blessed. Amen."

[From *Women of the Reformation*, pp. 97–100.]

MARGUERITE OF NAVARRE

Marguerite of Navarre (1492–1549) is a prime example of a noblewoman using her influence to support the Reformation and to protect its adherents. She was the older sister of King Francis I of France and one of the main supporters of Guillaume Briconnet, the bishop of Meaux, who sought to reform the church throughout France and who was her spiritual director. She corresponded with Calvin, though they did not always agree, and her region of Navarre became the focal point of the Huguenot movement. She was a highly educated and erudite woman, familiar with contemporary as well as classical works. A passionate Christian, she was determined to reform the excesses of the church, and in her writings she concentrated on God's Love.

The first three of her poems excerpted below are on theological themes that dominated the Reformation.

The Primacy of Scripture

Encased in lambskin is the sacred Word
Embossed with markings of a deep blood red,
Sealed with seven seals may now be heard
By those who find that law and grace are wed.

Justification by Faith

To you I testify
That God does justify
Through Christ, the man who sins.
But if he does not believe
And by faith receive
He shall have no peace,
From worry no surcease.
God will then relieve,
If faith will but believe
Through Christ, the gentle Lord.

The Doctrine of Election

God has predestined His own
That they should be sons and heirs.
Drawn by a gentle constraint
A zeal consuming is theirs.
They shall inherit the earth
Clad in justice and worth.
    [From *Women of the Reformation in France and England*, p. 21.]

The next excerpt is from a long poem entitled *Prisons* which Marguerite wrote at the end of her life. The title itself conveys her point of view that this world, for all its delights, is a prison and that true freedom exists only in the final union with God that comes at death, a union she eagerly awaits.

Lord, when shall come the festal day
So ardently desired
That I shall be by love upraised
And seated at Thy side,
The rapture of this nuptial joy
Denudes me quite.
Seductions of love and fame

No more delight.
Assuage my streaming eyes
And hear my sigh.
And may I have a gentle sleep
When I shall die.
    [From *Women of the Reformation in France and England*, p. 21.]

TERESA OF AVILA

The great Spanish mystic and reformer Teresa of Avila (1515–1582) was a nun in the order of Carmelites. She lived in a time when the Spanish Inquisition was vigorously persecuting what it perceived to be heresies in what proved to be a successful attempt to prevent the Protestant Reformation from taking root in Spain. Many women had been convicted as heretics and suffered imprisonment and death. Against this background, when Teresa began to describe her ecstasies, her confessors insisted she write down her experiences for their judgment. From this evolved her exquisite *Life*. While it is true that Teresa wrote under the command of her confessors, she also took great pleasure in her writing and thought of it as important. The following excerpt from chapter 36 of her *Life* describes the obstacles she faced in founding a reformed Carmelite convent. Prior to this Teresa had lived for twenty-eight years in a convent that followed a modified Carmelite rule. At age forty-eight Teresa underwent a conversion experience, while reading Augustine's *Confessions,* that led her to seek the stricter observances of the original Carmelite rule, which involved fasting, silence, limited contact with outsiders, and poverty.

CHAPTER XXXVI

Continues the subject already begun and describes the completion of the foundation of this convent of the glorious Saint Joseph, and the great opposition and numerous persecutions which the nuns had to endure after taking the habit, and the great trials and temptations which she suffered, and how the Lord delivered her from everything victoriously, to His glory and praise.

After leaving that city I went on my way very happily, resolved to suffer with the greatest willingness whatever it might please the Lord to send me. On the very night of my arrival in these parts there arrived our patent for the convent and the Brief from Rome. I was astonished at this, and so were those who knew how the Lord had hastened my coming here, when they found how necessary it had proved to be and how the Lord had brought me here just in the nick of time. For here I found the Bishop and the saintly Fray Peter of Alcántara, and another gentleman, a great servant of God, in whose house this saintly man was staying—he was one with whom God's servants could always find hospitality.

Between them, these two persuaded the Bishop to sanction the foundation of the convent. This was by no means easy, as it was to be founded in poverty, but he was so much drawn to people whom he saw determined to serve the Lord that he at once inclined to the idea of helping it. The whole thing was due to the approval of this saintly old man and the way he urged first one person and then another to come to our aid. If, as I have already said, I had not arrived at this particular moment, I cannot see how it could have been done, for this saintly man was here only for a few days—not more than a week, I believe—and during that time he was very ill: not long afterwards the Lord took him to Himself. It seems as if His Majesty had prolonged his life until this business was settled, for he had for some time been in very poor health—I fancy for over two years.

Everything was done with great secrecy: had it been otherwise, nothing could have been done at all, for, as appeared later, the people were opposed to the plan. The Lord had ordained that a brother-in-law of mine should fall ill, and, his wife not being with him, should be in such need of me that I was given leave to go and stay with him. This prevented anything from being discovered, and, though a few people must have been rather suspicious, they did not think there was anything in it. The remarkable thing was that his illness lasted only for just the time we needed for our negotiations, and, when it was necessary for him to be better so that I could be free again and he could go away and leave the house, the Lord at once restored him to health, and he was amazed at it.

What with one person and what with another, I had a great deal of trouble in getting the foundation sanctioned. Then there was my patient, and there were the workmen—for the house had to be got ready very quickly, so that it would be suitable for a convent, and there was a great deal which had to be done to it. My companion was not here, for we thought it advisable that she should be away so that the secret might be the better kept. I saw that speed was of the first importance, and this for many reasons, one of them being that I was in hourly fear of being sent back to my own convent. So many were the trials I had to suffer that I began to wonder if this was my cross, though I thought it very much lighter than the heavy one which I had understood the Lord to say I should have to bear.

When everything had been arranged, the Lord was pleased that some of the sisters should take the habit on Saint Bartholomew's Day and on that day too the Most Holy Sacrament was placed in the convent. So with the full weight of authority this convent of our most glorious father Saint Joseph was founded in the year 1562. I was there to give the habit, with two other nuns of our own house, who chanced to be absent from it. As the house in which the convent was established belonged to my brother-in-law, who, as I have said, had bought it in order to keep the matter secret, I was there by special permission, and I did nothing without asking the opinion of learned men, lest in any way whatever I should act against obedience. As they saw what benefits, in numerous ways, were being conferred upon the whole Order, they told me I might do what I did, although it was being done in secret and I was keeping it from my superiors' knowledge. Had they told me that there was the slightest imperfection in this, I think I would have given up a thousand convents, let alone a single one. Of that I am sure; for, though I desired to make the foundation so that I could withdraw more completely from everything and fulfill my profession and vocation with greater perfection and in conditions of stricter enclosure, I desired it only with the proviso that if I found that the Lord would be better served by my abandoning it entirely, I should do so, as I had done on a former occasion, with complete tranquility and peace.

* * *

When this was over, I wanted to get a little rest after dinner. (All the previous night I had had hardly any peace of mind; and on several of the preceding nights I had been continuously troubled and worried; so that during each day I had felt worn out. For now what we had done became known in my convent and in the city, and for the reasons I have given there was a great deal of commotion—not, it seemed, without some cause.) But the Superior sent for me to come to her immediately. On receiving the order, I went at once, leaving my nuns terribly upset. I was well aware that there was ample trouble in store for me, but, as the thing was now done, I cared very little about that. I prayed to the Lord and begged Him to help me and besought my father Saint Joseph to bring me back to his house. I offered up to God all I should have to suffer, very happy at having some suffering to offer Him and some service to render. I went in the belief that I should at once be put in prison. This,

I think, would have been a great joy to me, as I should not have had to talk to anyone and should have been able to rest for a little and be alone—and I needed that very badly, for all this intercourse with people had worn me to pieces.

When I got there and gave the Superior my version of the affair, she relented a little, and they all sent for the Provincial and laid the case before him. He came, and I went to hear his judgment with the utmost happiness, thinking that there would now be something for me to suffer for the Lord. I could not discover that I had committed any offense either against His Majesty or against the Order—indeed, I was striving with all my might to strengthen the Order and to do this I would willingly have died, for my whole desire was that its Rule should be observed with all perfection. But I remembered the trial of Christ and realized that all this, by comparison, was nothing at all. I acknowledged my fault, as if I had acted very wrongly, and so in fact I must have appeared to have done to anyone who did not know all the reasons. The Provincial gave me a severe rebuke, though its severity was less than would have been justified by the report which many people had given him of my delinquency. I would not excuse myself, for I had already resolved not to do so, but begged him to forgive me, to punish me and not to be annoyed with me any longer.

In some ways I knew quite well that they were condemning me unjustly, for they told me that I had done this so as to win esteem for myself, to get well known, and so on. But in other ways it was clear to me that they were speaking the truth—in saying that I was more wicked than other nuns, and in asking how, if I had not kept all the numerous rules observed in that house, I could consider keeping stricter rules in another: I should be scandalizing the people, they said, and setting up new ideas. None of this caused me the least trouble or distress, though I gave the impression that it did, lest I should appear to be making light of what they were saying. Finally, I was commanded to state my version of the matter in the presence of the nuns, so I had to do so.

I was inwardly calm and the Lord helped me, my account of the affair gave neither the Provincial nor the others present any reason for condemning me. Afterwards, when I was alone with him, I spoke to him more plainly, and he was quite satisfied, and promised me, if my foundation succeeded, to give me permission to go there as soon as the city was quiet—for there had been a great commotion in the city.

* * *

When the city was finally somewhat calmed, the Dominican Father-Presentado who was helping us managed things for us very well. He had not previously been there, but the Lord brought him at a time which was very convenient for us, and His Majesty seems to have done so for that end alone, for he told me afterwards that he had had no reason for coming and had only heard of the matter by accident. He stayed with us for as long as was necessary. When he left, he managed somehow—it seemed impossible that he could have done this in so short a time—to get our Father Provincial to give me leave to go and live in the new house and to take some other nuns with me so that we might say the Office and instruct the sisters who were there. It was the happiest of days for me when we went in.

While at prayer in the church, before entering the convent, I all but went into a rapture, and saw Christ, Who seemed to be receiving me with great love, placing a crown on my head and thanking me for what I had done for His Mother. On another occasion, after Compline, when we were all praying in choir, I saw Our Lady in the greatest glory, clad in a white mantle, beneath which she seemed to be sheltering us all. From this I learned what a high degree of glory the Lord would give to the nuns in this house.

When we had started to say the Office, the people began to be very much devoted to the convent. More nuns were received and the Lord started to move the people who had persecuted us most to help us and give us alms. So they now found themselves approving what previously they had so strongly condemned and gradually they abandoned the lawsuit and said they now realized the work was of God, since His Majesty had seen well to further it despite so much opposition. There is no one now who thinks it would have been right to give up the foundation, so they are very anxious to provide for us with their alms; and, without our making any appeals or asking anyone for money, the Lord inspires people to send it. We get on very well, then, and have no lack of necessaries; I hope in the Lord that this will be the case always. As the nuns are few in number I am sure His Majesty will never fail them if they do their duty, as at present He is giving them grace to do; nor will they ever have to be burdensome or importunate, for the Lord will take care of them as He has done until now. It is the greatest happiness to me to find myself among souls with detachment.

Their life consists in learning how to advance in the service of God. They find their greatest happiness in solitude and it troubles them to think of seeing anyone—even a near relative—unless doing so will help to enkindle them in the love of their Spouse. So none come to this house save with that aim; were they to do so it would give pleasure neither to themselves nor to the sisters. They speak only of God, and they understand no one who speaks of anything else, nor does such a person understand them. We observe the rule of Our Lady of Carmel, and we keep it without mitigation, in the form drawn up by Fray Hugo, Cardinal of Santa Sabina, and given in the year 1248, in the fifth year of the pontificate of Pope Innocent IV.

All the trials that we have suffered will, I believe, have been endured to good purpose. The rule is rather strict, for meat is never eaten except in cases of necessity, there is an eight-months' fast, and there are other ascetic practices, as may be seen in the primitive

Rule. Yet many of these things seem to the sisters very light and they observe other rules which we have thought it necessary to make so that our own Rule may be kept the more perfectly. I hope in the Lord that what we have begun will prosper, as His Majesty told me it would.

[From *The Complete Works of Saint Teresa of Jesus,* pp. 248–59.]

Sources

Selections from the New Testament are from the New Revised Standard Version Bible, copyright 1989, Division of Christian Education of the National Council of Churches of Christ in the United States of America.

The Alexiad of Anna Comnena, trans. E. R. A. Sewter. Harmondsworth, Middlesex, England: Penguin Books, 1969.

The Ante-Nicene Fathers, Volume 1, *The Apostolic Fathers, Justin Martyr, Irenaeus,* ed. Alexander Roberts and James Donaldson, Reprint. Grand Rapids, MI: Wm. B. Eerdmans Publishing Co., 1977.

The Ante-Nicene Fathers, Volume 4, *Fathers of the Third Century: Tertullian, Part Fourth; Minucius Felix; Commodian; Origen, Parts First and Second,* ed. Alexander Roberts and James Donaldson. Reprint. Grand Rapids, MI: Wm. B. Eerdmans Publishing Co., 1977.

The Book of the City of Ladies, by Christine de Pizan, trans. Earl Jeffrey Richards. New York: Persea Books, 1982.

Calvin: Institutes of the Christian Religion, ed. John T. McNeill, translated and indexed by Ford Lewis Battles. 2 vols. The Library of Christian Classics, Vols. 20 and 21. Philadelphia: Westminster Press, 1960.

Catherine of Siena: The Dialogue, translation and introduction by Suzanne Noffke. New York: Paulist Press, 1980.

The Complete Works of Saint Teresa of Jesus, Volume 1: *General Introduction, Life, Spiritual Relations,* trans. and ed. E. Allison Peers. New York: Sheed & Ward, 1946.

The Confessions of St. Augustine, translated, with an introduction and notes, by John K. Ryan. Garden City, NY: Image Books, Doubleday & Co., 1960.

Francis and Clare: The Complete Works, translation and introduction by Regis J. Armstrong and Ignatius C. Brady. New York: Paulist Press, 1982.

The Golden Legend of Jacobus de Voragine, translated and adapted from the Latin by Granger Ryan and Helmut Ripperger. New York: Arno Press, 1969.

Hildegard of Bingen: Scivias, trans. Mother Columba Hart and Jane Bishop, New York: Paulist Press, 1990.

Jeanne d'Arc, Maid of Orleans: As set forth in the Original Documents, trans. T. Douglas. New York: McClure, Phillips & Co., 1902.

A Lost Tradition: Women Writers of the Early Church, by Patricia Wilson-Kastner et al. Lanham, MD: University Press of America, 1981.

Luther's Works, Volume 1: *Lectures on Genesis, Chapters 1–5,* ed. Jaroslav Pelikan. Saint Louis, MO: Concordia, 1958.

Luther's Works, Volume 54: *Table Talk,* ed. and trans. Theodore G. Tappert. Philadelphia: Fortress Press, 1967.

The Malleus Maleficarum of Heinrich Kramer and James Sprenger, trans. Montague Summers. London: John Rodker, 1928. repr. New York: Dover Publications, 1971.

The Nag Hammadi Library: In English, trans. Members of the Coptic Gnostic Library Project of the Institute for Antiquity and Christianity, James M. Robinson, Director. New York: Harper & Row, 1977.

Ode in Honour of the Holy Immaculate Most Blessed Glorious Mother of God and Ever Virgin Mary, Written on the Occasion of the Deliverance of Constantinople from the Barbarians, A.D. 626, trans. Vincent McNabb. Oxford: Blackfriars Publications, 1947.

Offices from the Service Books of the Holy Eastern Church, trans. Richard Frederick Littledale. London: Williams and Norgate, 1863.

Saint Gregory of Nyssa: Ascetical Works, trans. Virginia Woods Callahan. Washington, DC: Catholic University of America Press, 1967.

The "Summa Theologica" of St. Thomas Aquinas, Part I. QQ. XXXV.-CII., trans. Fathers of the English Dominican Province. London: Burns Oates & Washbourne, 1912.

Women of the Reformation in France and England, by Roland H. Bainton. Minneapolis, MN: Augsburg Publishing House, 1973.

Women of the Reformation in Germany and Italy, by Roland H. Bainton. Minneapolis: MN: Augsburg Publishing House, 1971.

Bibliography

Introductory Texts

Jaroslav Pelikan, *The Christian Tradition: A History of the Development of Doctrine,* 5 vols. Chicago: University of Chicago Press, 1971–1974.

Mary Jo Weaver, *Introduction to Christianity,* 2nd ed. Belmont, CA: Wadsworth Publishing Company, 1991, 1984.

The Interpreter's One-Volume Commentary on The Bible, ed. Charles M. Laymon. Nashville, TN: Abingdon Press, 1971.

Works on Women and Christianity

Roland H. Bainton, *Women of the Reformation in France and England.* Minneapolis, MN: Augsburg Publishing House, 1973.

——, *Women of the Reformation in Germany and Italy.* Minneapolis, MN: Augsburg Publishing House, 1971.

Jorunn Jacobsen Buckley, "Two Female Gnostic Revealers," in *History of Religions,* February 1980, vol. 19, No. 3, pp. 259–269.

Elizabeth Clark and Herbert Richardson, eds., *Women and Religion: A Feminist Source Book of Christian Thought.* New York: Harper & Row, Publishers, 1977.

Elisabeth Schüssler Fiorenza, *In Memory of Her: A Feminist Theological Reconstruction of Christian Origins.* New York: Crossroad, 1983.

Sherrin Marshall, ed., *Women in Reformation and Counter-Reformation Europe.* Bloomington, IN: Indiana University Press, 1989.

Joann McNamara and Suzanne Wemple, "Sanctity and Power: The Dual Pursuit of Medieval Women" in *Becoming Visible: Women in European History,* ed. Renate Bridenthal and Claudia Koonz. Boston: Houghton Mifflin, 1977.

Michael O'Carroll, *Theotokos: A Theological Encyclopedia of the Blessed Virgin Mary.* Wilmington, DE: Michael Glazier, Inc., 1982.

Elaine Pagels, *Adam, Eve, and the Serpent.* New York: Random House, 1988.

——, *The Gnostic Gospels.* New York: Random House, 1979.

Elizabeth Alvilda Petroff, ed. *Medieval Women's Visionary Literature.* New York: Oxford University Press, 1986.

Rosemary Radford Ruether, ed. *Religion and Sexism: Images of Woman in the Jewish and Christian Traditions.* New York: Simon and Schuster, 1974.

Rosemary Ruether and Eleanor McLaughlin., eds., *Women of Spirit: Female Leadership in the Jewish and Christian Traditions.* New York: Simon and Schuster, 1979.

Lucy Rushton, "Doves & Magpies: Village Women in the Greek Orthodox Church" in *Women's Religious Experience,* ed. Pat Holden. Totowa, NJ: Barnes & Noble Books, 1983.

Marcelle Thiebaux, *The Writings of Medieval Women.* Vol. 14, Series B, Garland Library of Medieval Literature. New York: Garland Publishing, Inc., 1987.

Katharina M. Wilson, ed., *Medieval Women Writers.* Athens, GA: The University of Georgia Press, 1984.

ISLAM

Introduction

Islam began in the seventh century C.E. in Arabia with the revelations received by the Prophet Muḥammad (c. 570–632 C.E.). Eventually these revelations were written down and organized as the sacred book of the Muslims, the Qur'ān (sometimes transliterated as the Koran). Though Muḥammad's message was not readily accepted when he first began to preach, by the end of his lifetime Islam had been accepted by the majority of nomadic tribes in Arabia and treaties had been made with various Christian and Jewish groups within Arabia which allowed them to retain religious autonomy in return for payment of tribute. This is an important point for the understanding of Islam: Muḥammad was the only founder of a major world religion who lived to see it become a world power. His private visions of the angel Gabriel bringing him the word of God became the shared visions of a conquering people who then became the rulers of a diverse society. Consequently, Muḥammad had to seek guidance not only in matters of personal conscience but in matters pertaining to war and governing a society—all of which had to be done as ordained by God. Whether in ordering their personal lives or running their governments, faithful Muslims want to follow God's revelations. Most importantly, they do this within highly diverse cultural settings in all parts of the world. Islam is a religion of many parts.

The Qur'ān is considered to be the very words of God and therefore it is the first source of spiritual authority for the Muslim community. After the Qur'ān, due to the special role Muḥammad played as the messenger of God, religious authority is found in the Hadīth, documented collections of Muḥammad's words and stories about his life. Much of this material is contained in his biographies. The last source of spiritual authority is analogy or legal reasoning. All these sources deal with women at length.

As will be seen in the excerpts from Muḥammad's biography, some women had position and prestige in the early days of Islam. Gradually, however, the religious practices of men and women, became distinct. Men fulfill their religious obligations at the mosques, which are centers of community worship as well as political, social, and cultural activities. While women generally have access to the mosques in separate sections from the men, periodically they are denied access when they are perceived to be ritually unclean, e.g. menstruating, after childbirth, etc. At the same time, women can fulfill their religious obligations in the home, in magical practices and, later in the tradition, at the shrines of saints. In effect, the first level of Islam, the great tradition of orthodoxy, is almost exclusively in the hands of men and is authoritative for both men and women while a second level, the folk tradition of Islam, which is of less certain orthodoxy, is primarily in the hands of women, though some men are involved. This folk tradition also has an impact on the lives of both women and men. While men control the lives of women through orthodoxy women can control or at least coerce men through the folk tradition. For instance, Muslim men seem to be particularly wary of the magical procedures available to women. Checks and balances exist that give Muslim women a degree of control over their lives in a way that is not apparent in the orthodox system of Islam.

An important distinction that needs to be made regarding Muslim women is whether they are urban or rural women. This is particularly relevant to issues of veiling and seclusion. (See Sura 24.30 and 33.53–59 for Qur'anic authority for the veiling of women.) Generally speaking, in the countryside Muslim women move about quite freely, without veils. In the cities they are veiled and their movements more circumscribed.

Due to the lack of written records from Pre-Islamic times it is hard to ascertain whether Islam improved or weakened the status of Arab women. As the selections from the Qur'ān show, Islam certainly clarified their position.

Sunnī and Shī'ī

Equally important for the understanding of women in Islam are the distinctions to be made between Sunnī and Shī'ī Islam. When Muḥammad died in 632 he had not declared who should succeed him as the leader of the Muslim community. After a brief period the first of the Caliphs, Abū Bakr (one of the earliest converts to Islam and the father of A'isha, Muḥammad's youngest wife) assumed this position. Herein lies the division of Islam into two branches: the majority of Muslims are Sunnī who accept the caliphate of Abū Bakr and the minority are Shī'ī who claim that Muḥammad appointed 'Alī, his cousin and the husband of his daughter Fāṭima, as successor. The Shī'ī are supporters of the family of Muḥammad, and consequently have a great reverence for Fāṭima around whom important religious practices developed, while the Sunnī emphasize the need for a ruler who will preserve the unity of the Muslim community whether he is a physical descendant of the Prophet or not. 'Ali did become the fourth Caliph with the support of the Shī'ī, but he was murdered in 661 and his son Ḥasan was forced to abdicate in the same year after a brief reign. Ḥasan died in 671. The Shī'ī believe he was poisoned which makes him a martyr for the faith. 'Ali's second son Ḥusayn, who the Shī'ī hoped would become Caliph, was killed with his family in 680 so he too became a martyr. Soon after this mourning for Ḥusayn became an institutionalized form of religious expression for the Shī'ī. Pilgrimage to his tomb is one of their most important religious rituals.

Sufism

Sufism is the mystical tradition of Islam. In most world religions individual women, and/or feminine concepts, are more prominent in the mystical than in the orthodox tradition and this is somewhat the case in Sufism as well. Sufis first and foremost seek union with God. They emphasize leading a simple and self-disciplined life devoted to God which almost anyone who is willing can follow. One of the foremost Sufi saints was an impoverished slave woman, Rābi'ah.

Sufi movements began to arise in various parts of the Muslim empire during the eighth century, eventually developing into particular schools claiming descent from individual Sufi masters, many of which still exist today. Some of these Sufi masters were married, but large numbers of Sufis chose celibacy in the belief that this enabled them to be closer to God. Monasteries and convents were established to support their pursuit of the spiritual life. In this environment, which freed them from domestic and social obligations, many women rose to prominence as spiritual guides and were renown for their devotion. As with their male counterparts, some of these women were venerated as saints both before and after their deaths. Pilgrimages to and worship at the tombs of saints, male and female, remains an integral part of Islam to this day and is a popular form of devotion among Muslim women.

The Classical Period

THE QUR'ĀN

Muslims believe that the Qur'ān is the final word of God which was revealed to Muḥammad by the angel Gabriel over a twenty-two year period beginning in 610 and ending with the death of the Prophet in 632. Consequently, Muḥammad is referred to as the "Seal of the Prophet." This means that Muḥammad is the last in a long line of prophets who have preached God's word stretching back through Jesus and the prophets of the Bible to Abraham.

Consequently Muslims accept the Genesis story of creation and the story of Adam and Eve. They do this, however, through their retelling of these stories.

CREATION—ADAM AND EVE

The Qur'ān is arranged into 114 Suras or chapters. The Sura on Women opens by making reference to the creation of women from the soul of man. (See also Sura 7.187.) This cosmic secondary status of women is elaborated upon in this Sura which sets forth how women are to be treated by men.

Sura IV
Women

In the Name of God, the Merciful, the Compassionate

Mankind, fear your Lord, who created you
of a single soul, and from it created
Its mate, and from the pair of them scattered
abroad many men and women; and fear God
by whom you demand one of another,
and the wombs; surely God ever
   watches over you.

Give the orphans their property, and do not
exchange the corrupt for the good; and devour
not their property with your property; surely
   that is a great crime.
If you fear that you will not act justly
towards the orphans, marry such women
as seem good to you two, three, four;
but if you fear you will not be equitable,
then only one or what your right hands own;
so it is likelier you will not be partial.
And give the women their dowries as a gift
spontaneous; but if they are pleased
to offer you any of it, consume it
   with wholesome appetite.
But do not give to fools their property
that God has assigned to you to manage;
provide for them and clothe them out of it,
and speak to them honourable words.
Test well the orphans until they reach
the age of marrying; then, if you perceive
in them right judgment, deliver to them
their property; consume it not wastefully
   and hastily
ere they are grown. If any man is rich,
let him be abstinent; if poor, let him
   consume in reason.
And when you deliver to them their property,
take witnesses over them; God suffices
   for a reckoner.

To the men a share of what parents and kinsmen
leave, and to the women a share of what

parents and kinsmen leave, whether it be
little or much, a share apportioned;
and when the division is attended by
kinsmen and orphans and the poor,
make provision for them out of it,
and speak to them honourable words.
And let those fear who, if they left
behind them weak seed, would be afraid
on their account, and let them fear
God, and speak words hitting the mark.
Those who devour the property of orphans
unjustly, devour Fire in their bellies,
and shall assuredly roast in a Blaze.

God charges you, concerning your children:
to the male the like of the portion
of two females, and if they be women
above two, then for them two-thirds
of what he leaves, but if she be one
then to her a half; and to his parents
to each one of the two the sixth
of what he leaves, if he has children;
but if he has no children, and his
heirs are his parents, a third to his
mother, or, if he has brothers, to his
mother a sixth, after any bequest
he may bequeath, or any debt.
Your fathers and your sons—you know not
which out of them is nearer in profit
to you. So God apportions; surely God is
   All-knowing, All-wise.

And for you a half of what your wives
leave if they have no children; but
if they have children, then for you of what
they leave a fourth, after any bequest
they may bequeath, or any debt.
And for them a fourth of what you leave,
if you have no children; but if you
have children, then for them of what
you leave an eighth, after any bequest
you may bequeath, or any debt.
If a man or a woman have no heir
direct, but have a brother or a sister,

to each of the two a sixth; but if they
are more numerous than that, they share
equally a third, after any bequest
he may bequeath, or any debt not
prejudicial; a charge from God. God is
     All-knowing, All-clement.

★ ★ ★

Such of your women as commit indecency,
call four of you to witness against them;
and if they witness, then detain them
in their houses until death takes them
or God appoints for them a way.
And when two of you commit indecency,
punish them both; but if they repent
and make amends, then suffer them to be;
God turns; and is All-compassionate.

O believers, it is not lawful for you
to inherit women against their will;
neither debar them, that you may go off
with part of what you have given them,
except when they commit a flagrant indecency.
Consort with them honourably; or if
you are averse to them, it is possible
you may be averse to a thing, and God set
   in it much good.
And if you desire to exchange a wife
in place of another, and you have given
to one a hundredweight, take of it nothing.
What, will you take it by way of calumny
   and manifest sin?
How shall you take it, when each of you has been
privily with the other, and they have taken from you
   a solemn compact?
And do not marry women that your fathers
married unless it be a thing of the past;
surely that is indecent and hateful,
   an evil way.

Forbidden to you are your mothers and daughters
your sisters, your aunts paternal and maternal,
your brother's daughters, your sister's daughters,
your mothers who have given suck to you,
your suckling sisters, your wives' mothers,
your stepdaughters who are in your care
being born of your wives you have been in to—
but if you have not yet been in to them
it is no fault in you—and the spouses
of your sons who are of your loins,
and that you should take to you two sisters
together, unless it be a thing of the past;
God is All-forgiving, All-compassionate;
and wedded women, save what your right hands own.
So God prescribes for you. Lawful for you,
beyond all that, is that you may seek,
using your wealth, in wedlock and not
in license. Such wives as you enjoy thereby,
give them their wages apportionate; it is no
fault in you in your agreeing together,
after the due apportionate. God is
     All-knowing, All-wise.

★ ★ ★

Men are the managers of the affairs of women
for that God has preferred in bounty
one of them over another, and for that
they have expended of their property.
Righteous women are therefore obedient,
guarding the secret for God's guarding.
And those you fear may be rebellious
admonish; banish them to their couches,
and beat them. If they then obey you,
look not for any way against them; God is
     All-high, All-great.
And if you fear a breach between the two,
bring forth an arbiter from his people
and from her people an arbiter, if they
desire to set things right; God will
compose their differences; surely God is
     All-knowing, All-aware.
     [From Sura IV, *The Koran Interpreted*, pp.
100–106]

Interestingly, in the Muslim telling of the story of Adam and Eve, the blame for the Fall
is shared equally by them—Eve is not singled out as the tempter of Adam.

Sura VII
The Battlements

'O Adam, inherit, thou and thy wife,
the Garden, and eat of where you will,
but come not nigh this tree, lest you be
   of the evildoers.'
Then Satan whispered to them, to reveal

to them that which was hidden from them
of their shameful parts. He said, 'Your Lord
has only prohibited you from this tree
lest you become angels, or lest you
   become immortals.'
And he swore to them, 'Truly, I am for you
   a sincere adviser.'
So he led them on by delusion; and when

they tasted the tree, their shameful parts
revealed to them, so they took to stitching
upon themselves leaves of the Garden.
And their Lord called to them, 'Did not I
prohibit you from this tree, and say
to you, "Verily Satan is for you a manifest foe"?'
They said, 'Lord, we have wronged ourselves,
and if Thou dost not forgive us, and have
mercy upon us, we shall surely be among the lost.'

Said He, 'Get you down, each of you
an enemy to each. In the earth a sojourn
shall be yours, and enjoyment for a time.'
Said He, 'Therein you shall live, and
therein you shall die, and from there you
    shall be brought forth.'
    [From Sura VII, *The Koran Interpreted*, pp.
172–173.]

In fact, in another Sura blame is placed squarely on Adam, not Eve.

Sura XX Ta Ha

    And We made covenant with Adam before,
but he forgot, and We found in
    him no constancy.
And when We said to the angels, 'Bow
yourselves to Adam'; so they bowed
themselves, save Iblis [Satan]; he refused.
Then We said, 'Adam, surely this
is an enemy to thee and thy wife.
So let him not expel you both
from the Garden, so that thou art unprosperous.
It is assuredly given to thee

neither to hunger therein, nor to go naked,
neither to thirst therein, nor to
    suffer the sun.' Then Satan whispered to him
saying, 'Adam, shall I point thee to
the Tree of Eternity, and a Kingdom
    that decays not?'
So the two of them ate of it, and
their shameful parts revealed to them,
and they took to stitching upon
themselves leaves of the Garden. And
Adam disobeyed his Lord, and so he erred.
    [From Sura XX, *The Koran Interpreted*, pp.
347–48]

EVE IN THE LATER TRADITION

    The later tradition contains many versions of the story of creation. The following excerpt
is taken from al-Kisā'ī's *Qiṣaṣ al-Anbiyā'*, a work of the eleventh century. In it Eve is second
in creation, being formed from Adam's rib, and made to be his companion. Allah himself
performs their wedding ceremony and stresses the importance of marriage and sexuality which
offends Iblīs (Satan), not God.

The Story of the Creation of Eve

While Adam slept Allah Most High created Eve from
one of the ribs of his left side, namely that crooked
rib. She is called Eve (*Hawwā'*) because she was created
from a live person (*hayy*). This is as Allah has said (IV,
1): "O ye people, show piety towards your Lord, who
created you from a single person, and from that person created his spouse." Eve was of the same height
as Adam and equally splendid and beautiful. She had
seven hundred locks of hair intertwined with jacinths
and sprinkled with musk, was auburn haired, of even
stature, with wide black eyes, thin skinned, white
complexioned, with henna-dyed palms, and hanging

locks so long you could hear their rustling. She had
ears pierced for earrings, was so plump her thighs
chafed as she walked, and was of the same form as
Adam save that her skin was more tender, her colouring lighter, her voice sweeter, her eyes wider and
darker, her nose more hooked, her teeth whiter. When
Allah Most High had created her He sat her by
Adam's head. Now Adam had seen her in his dream
that day and love for her had taken possession of his
heart, so [when he woke up and saw her] Adam said:
"O Lord, who is this?" The Most High answered:
"This is My handmaid Eve." Said he: "O Lord, for
whom hast Thou created her?" He answered: "For
him who will take her in faithfulness and be joined

with her in thankfulness." Said he: "O Lord, I will take her under those conditions, so marry me to her." So He married him to her before He let him enter the Garden.

It is related that ʿAlī b. Abī Ṭālib—with whom may Allah be pleased—said that Adam saw her in a dream in which she spoke with him, saying: "I am Allah's handmaid and you are Allah's servant, so ask my hand in marriage from your Lord." ʿAlī—with whom may Allah be pleased—said: "Make your marriages a good thing, for women in themselves have neither benefit nor harm, they are but a trust from Allah to you, so do not be contentious with them." Kaʿb al-Aḥbār—with whom may Allah be pleased—said that Adam saw her in a dream and when he woke up he said: "O Lord, who is this Thou hast delighted me by bringing near?" The Most High replied: "This is My handmaid and thou art My servant, O Adam. Nothing I have created is dearer to Me than you two if you obey Me and serve Me. Now I have created for you two a dwelling which I have named My Garden. Whosoever enters it is truly My friend, and he who does not enter it My enemy." At this Adam was seized with fear and said: "O Lord, do you have an enemy, when you are Lord of the heavens and the earths?" The Most High replied: "Had I wished that all creatures be My friends I could have had it so, but I do what I will and withhold what I wish." Said Adam: "O Lord, this maidservant of Thine, Eve, for whom hast Thou created her?" Allah Most High replied: "O Adam, I have created her for thee, that thou mayest dwell along with her and not be alone in My Garden." Said Adam: "O Lord, marry her to me." The Most High replied: "O Adam, I will marry her to thee on condition that thou dost teach her the principles of My religion and be thankful to Me for her." Adam was content with this, so a chair made of a jewel was set for Adam, on which he sat while the

angels gathered together, and Allah signified to Gabriel that he should be the affiancer. So the Lord of the worlds was the *walī*, Gabriel the *khāṭib*, the angels the witnesses, Adam was the bridegroom and Eve the bride, and thus Eve was married to Adam under covenant of obedience and piety and good works, while the angels showered down upon them celestial confetti (*nuthār*).

ʿAbdallah b. ʿAbbās—with whom may Allah be pleased—said: "Make public your wedding ceremonies, for that is a custom from your father Adam. Nothing is more pleasing to Allah than marriage, and nothing so moves Him to anger as divorce. Whenever a true believer bathes after accomplishing the marital act Iblīs weeps, saying: 'This person has removed his sin, has satisfied his desire, and has continued in the custom of his father Adam.'" Then the Most High said to Adam: "Now remember My favours to you, for I have made you the masterpiece of My creation, have fashioned you a man according to My will, have breathed into you of My own spirit, made My angels do obeisance to you and carry you on their shoulders, have made you the preacher to them, have loosened your tongue to all languages, had you up on the pulpit of approval where you were preacher to the Ṣāffūn, the Ḥāffūn, the Cherubs, the Rūḥānīs and those who draw near. All this I have done for you as glory and honour, so beware of this Iblīs whom I have made to despair, and whom I have made accursed since he refused with disdain to do obeisance to you. Now as a special honour I have joined you with My hand-maid Eve, and there is no greater blessing, O Adam, than a pious wife. Moreover, two thousand years before I created you I had built for the pair of you a dwelling place which you may enter under covenant and pledge to Me."

[From *A Reader On Islam,* pp. 185–187.]

However, as the following excerpt from an eleventh century text on politics shows, Muslims also looked back to Eve for justifications to limit women's social roles.

The king's underlings must not be allowed to assume power. This particularly applies to women, for they are wearers of the veil and have not complete intelligence. Their purpose is the continuation of the lineage, and the more chaste (and veiled) their bearing the more admirable they are. But when the king's wives begin to assume the part of rulers they are not able to see things with their own eyes. . . . They give orders following what they are told by such as chamberlains and servants. In all ages, nothing but

disgrace, infamy, discord and corruption have followed when kings have been dominated by their wives. The first man who suffered loss and underwent pain and trouble for obeying a woman was Adam, who did the bidding of Eve.

[From *"The Art of Muslim Kingship: The Sultanate," from The Book of Politics,* Nizām al-Mulk (d. A.H. 485/A.D. 1092), in *Themes of Islamic Civilization,* p. 105]

Women

According to tradition, the youngest wife of the Prophet, Āʾisha, mentioned to Muḥammad that he was only speaking of men, that he was not including women. Thereafter he began to specifically say "men and women." Though much of the Qurʾān seems to be directed toward men, an argument for the equal position of women can be made from excerpts such as the following. (See also Sura 4.122.)

Men and woman who have surrendered,
believing men and believing women,
obedient men and obedient women,
truthful men and truthful women,
enduring men and enduring women,
humble men and humble women,
men and women who give in charity,
men who fast and women who fast,
men and women who guard their private parts,
men and women who remember God oft—

for them God has prepared forgiveness
and a mighty wage.

It is not for any believer, man or
woman, when God and His Messenger
have decreed a matter, to have the choice
in the affair. Whosoever disobeys
God and His Messenger has gone astray
into manifest error.

[From Sura XXXIII, *The Koran Interpreted*, p. 125]

There is also an equal concern that believers, both female and male, marry among themselves as is shown in the following excerpt which enjoins first men and then women not to marry outside the faith. The excerpt continues however in an uneven vein with regard to women. It declares women to be ritually unclean while menstruating and allows for women to be divorced after a four month waiting period. (This is to allow time for a reconciliation and to make sure the women are not pregnant before they are free to remarry, which indeed they are allowed to do.) Women are also allowed not to nurse their children if they so desire. The final word though is that "men have a degree above them [women]."

Sura II
The Cow

Do not marry idolatresses, until
they believe; a believing slavegirl
is better than an idolatress, though
you may admire her. And do not marry
idolaters, until they believe. A believing
slave is better than an idolater, though
    you may admire him.
Those call unto the Fire; and God calls unto
Paradise, and pardon, by His leave, and He
makes clear His signs to the people; haply
    they will remember.

They will question thee concerning
the monthly course. Say: 'It is hurt;
so go apart from women during
the monthly course, and do not approach them
till they are clean. When they have cleansed
themselves, then come unto them as God

has commanded you.' Truly, God loves
those who repent, and He loves those
    who cleanse themselves.
Your women are a tillage for you; so come
unto your tillage as you wish, and forward
for your souls; and fear God, and know that
you shall meet Him. Give thou good tidings
    to the believers.

Do not make God a hindrance, through your oaths,
to being pious and godfearing, and putting
things right between men. Surely God is
    All-hearing, All-knowing.
God will not take you to task for a slip
in your oaths; but He will take you to task
for what your hearts have earned; and God is
    All-forgiving, All-clement.

For those who forswear their women
a wait of four months; if they revert,
God is All-forgiving, All-compassionate;

but if they resolve on divorce, surely God is
    All-hearing, All-knowing.
Divorced women shall wait by themselves
for three periods; and it is not lawful
for them to hide what God has created
in their wombs; if they believe in God
and the Last Day. In such time their mates
have better right to restore them, if they
desire to set things right. Women have
such honourable rights as obligations, but
their men have a degree above them; God is
    All-mighty, All-wise.
Divorce is twice; then honourable retention
or setting free kindly. It is not lawful
for you to take of what you have given them
unless the couple fear they may not maintain
God's bounds; if you fear they may not maintain
God's bounds, it is no fault in them for her
to redeem herself. Those are God's bounds;
do not transgress them. Whosoever
transgresses the bounds of God—those
    are the evildoers.
If he divorces her finally, she shall not
be lawful to him after that, until she
marries another husband. If he divorces her,
then it is no fault in them to return
to each other, if they suppose that they will
maintain God's bounds. Those are God's bounds;
He makes them clear unto a people
    that have knowledge.
When you divorce women, and they have reached
their term, then retain them honourably
or set them free honourably; do not retain them
by force, to transgress; whoever does that
has wronged himself. Take not God's signs

in mockery, and remember God's blessing
upon you, and the Book and the Wisdom He
has sent down on you, to admonish you.
And fear God, and know that God has knowledge
    of everything.
When you divorce women, and they have reached
their term, do not debar them from marrying
their husbands, when they have agreed together
honourably. That is an admonition for
whoso of you believes in God and the Last Day;
that is cleaner and purer for you; God knows,
    and you know not.

Mothers shall suckle their children two years
completely, for such as desire to fulfil
the suckling. It is for the father to provide them
and clothe them honourably. No soul is charged
save to its capacity; a mother shall not be pressed
for her child, neither a father for his child.
The heir has a like duty. But if the couple
desire by mutual consent and consultation
to wean, then it is no fault in them.
And if you desire to seek nursing
for your children, it is no fault in you
provide you hand over what you have given
honourably; and fear God, and know that God sees
    the things you do.

And those of you who die, leaving wives,
they shall wait by themselves for four months
and ten nights; when they have reached their term
then it is no fault in you what they may do
with themselves honourably. God is aware of
    the things you do.
[From Sura II, *The Koran Interpreted*, pp. 58–61]

THE BIOGRAPHY OF MUHAMMAD

The earliest full biography of Muḥammad is the *Sīrat Rasūl Allāh* written by Ibn Isḥāq (707–773 C.E.). Though Ibn Isḥāq leaned somewhat toward the Shī'ī position his biography is widely accept among the Sunnī. He records Muḥammad's life as honestly as he can by making a serious attempt to be historically accurate; he cites his sources by saying "*x* or *y* told me" and frequently offers more than one version of the same incident. Ibn Isḥāq often cited two women as sources: Ā'isha, the youngest wife of Muḥammad, and Fāṭima, the wife of Hishām b. 'Urwa.

Three women are particularly prominent in Muḥammad's life and all have an enduring influence on Islam. Muḥammad married Ā'isha, his youngest wife, while she was still a child, so she was only eighteen years old when he died. Her influence on Islam has been enormous in that Muḥammad spoke so highly of her and because she holds such a prominent place in the Hadīth collections: She is the source of 1,210 hadīth she heard directly from Muḥammad. There seems to have been some conflict between her and Muḥammad's daughter Fāṭima which accelerated over the issue of the succession after Muḥammad's death. Āʾisha opposed the succession of Fāṭima's husband ʿAlī and supported the caliphate. Her father Abū Bakr was the first Caliph.

Fāṭima is the daughter of Muḥammad and his first wife Khadīja and the only one of Muḥammad's children to provide him with direct descendants. She is especially important to Shīʿī Islam because of the belief that, after Muḥammad's death, the leadership of the Muslim community passed to her husband ʿAlī and then to their sons Ḥasan and Ḥusayn. Muḥammad often praised her and went so far as to deny permission for her husband ʿAlī to take a second wife, saying: "Fāṭima is a part of my body, and I hate what she hates to see, and what hurts her, hurts me." (al-Bukhārī 62.110)

Khadīja, Muḥammad's first wife, was a wealthy widow who proposed to the young and impoverished Muḥammad first that he work for her and then that he marry her. Although Khadīja seems to have been in her forties when she married Muḥammad, she bore him several children and Muḥammad did not take a second wife until after her death. Tradition says he mourned deeply for her and al-Bukhārī records Āʾisha saying of Khadīja: "I never felt so jealous of any wife of Allah's Apostle as I did of Khadīja because Allah's Apostle used to remember and praise her too often and because it was revealed to Allah's Apostle that he should give her the glad tidings of her having a palace of Qaṣab in Paradise." (62.109)

The following excerpts from Muḥammad's biography describe Khadīja, her confirmation of his message as coming from God and her acceptance of his teachings. She, in fact, was the first Muslim.

The Apostle of God Marries Khadīja

Khadīja was a merchant woman of dignity and wealth. She used to hire men to carry merchandise outside the country on a profit-sharing basis, for Quraysh were a people given to commerce. Now when she heard about the prophet's truthfulness, trustworthiness, and honourable character, she sent for him and proposed that he should take her goods to Syria and trade with them, while she would pay him more than she paid others. He was to take a lad of hers called Maysara. The apostle of God accepted the proposal, and the two set forth until they came to Syria.

The apostle stopped in the shade of a tree near a monk's cell, when the monk came up to Maysara and asked who the man was who was resting beneath the tree. He told him that he was of Quraysh, the people who held the sanctuary; and the monk exclaimed: 'None but a prophet ever sat beneath this tree.'

Then the prophet sold the goods he had brought and bought what he wanted to buy and began the return journey to Mecca. The story goes that at the height of noon when the heat was intense as he rode his beast Maysara saw two angels shading the apostle from the sun's rays. When he brought Khadīja her property she sold it and it amounted to double or thereabouts. Maysara for his part told her about the two angels who shaded him and of the monk's words. Now Khadīja was a determined, noble, and intelligent

woman possessing the properties with which God willed to honour her. So when Maysara told her these things she sent to the apostle of God and—so the story goes—said: 'O son of my uncle I like you because of our relationship and your high reputation among your people, your trustworthiness and good character and truthfulness.' Then she proposed marriage. Now Khadīja at that time was the best born woman in Quraysh, of the greatest dignity and, too, the richest. All her people were eager to get possession of her wealth if it were possible.

Khadīja was the daughter of Khuwaylid b. Asad b. ʿAbdu'l-ʿUzzā b. Quṣayy b. Kilāb b. Murra b. Kaʿb b. Luʾayy b. Ghālib b. Fihr. Her mother was Fāṭima d. Zāʾida b. al-Aṣamm b. Rawāḥa b. Ḥajar b. ʿAbd b. Maʿīṣ b. ʿĀmir b. Luʾayy b. Ghālib b. Fihr. Her mother was Hāla d. ʿAbdu Manāf b. al-Ḥārith b. ʿAmr b. Munqidh b. ʿAmr b. Maʿīṣ b. ʿĀmir b. Luʾayy b. Ghālib b. Fihr. Hāla's mother was Qilāba d. Suʿayd b. Saʿd b. Sahm b. ʿAmr b. Ḥuṣays b. Kaʿb b. Luʾayy b. Ghālib b. Fihr.

The apostle of God told his uncles of Khadīja's proposal, and his uncle Ḥamza b. ʿAbdu'l-Muṭṭalib went with him to Khuwaylid b. Asad and asked for her hand and he married her.

She was the mother of all the apostle's children except Ibrāhīm, namely al-Qāsim (whereby he was known as Abu'l-Qāsim); al-Ṭāhir, al-Ṭayyib, Zaynab, Ruqayya, Umm Kulthūm, and Fāṭima.

Al-Qāsim, al-Ṭayyib, and al-Ṭāhir died in paganism. All his daughters lived into Islam, embraced it, and, migrated with him to Medina.

Khadīja had told Waraqa b. Naufal b. Asad b. 'Abdu'l-'Uzzā, who was her cousin and a Christian who had studied the scriptures and was a scholar, what her slave Maysara had told her that the monk had said and how he had seen the two angels shading him. He said, 'If this is true, Khadīja, verily Muhammad is the prophet of this people. I knew that a prophet of this people was to be expected. His time has come,' or words to that effect.

[From *The Life of Muhammad*, pp. 82–83.]

The Prophet's Mission

When it was the night on which God honoured him with his mission and showed mercy on His servants thereby, Gabriel brought him the command of God. 'He came to me,' said the apostle of God, 'while I was asleep, with a coverlet of brocade whereon was some writing, and said, "Read!" I said, "What shall I read?" He pressed me with it so tightly that I thought it was death; then he let me go and said, "Read!" I said, "What shall I read?" He pressed me with it again so that I thought it was death; then he let me go and said "Read!" I said, "What shall I read?" He pressed me with it the third time so that I thought it was death and said "Read!" I said, "What then shall I read?"— and this I said only to deliver myself from him, lest he should do the same to me again. He said:

"Read in the name of thy Lord who created,
Who created man of blood coagulated.
Read! Thy lord is the most beneficent,
Who taught by the pen,
Taught that which they knew not unto men."

So I read it, and he departed from me. And I awoke from my sleep, and it was as though these words were written on my heart. (T. Now none of God's creatures was more hateful to me than an (ecstatic) poet or a man possessed: I could not even look at them. I thought, Woe is me poet or possessed—Never shall Quraysh say this of me! I will go to the top of the mountain and throw myself down that I may kill myself and gain rest. So I went forth to do so and then) when I was midway on the mountain, I heard a voice from heaven saying, "O Muhammad! thou art the apostle of God and I am Gabriel." I raised my head towards heaven to see (who was speaking), and lo, Gabriel in the form of a man with feet astride the horizon, saying, "O Muhammad! thou art the apostle of God and I am Gabriel." I stood gazing at him, (T. and that turned me from my purpose) moving neither forward nor backward; then I began to turn my face away from him, but towards whatever region of the sky I looked, I saw him as before. And I continued standing there, neither advancing nor turning back,

until Khadīja sent her messengers in search of me and they gained the high ground above Mecca and returned to her while I was standing in the same place; then he parted from me and I from him, returning to my family. And I came to Khadīja and sat by her thigh and drew close to her. She said, "O Abū'l-Qāsim, where hast thou been? By God, I sent my messengers in search of thee, and they reached the high ground above Mecca and returned to me." (T. I said to her, "Woe is me poet or possessed." She said, "I take refuge in God from that O Abū'l-Qāsim. God would not treat you thus since he knows your truthfulness, your great trustworthiness, your fine character, and your kindness. This cannot be, my dear. Perhaps you did see something." "Yes, I did," I said.) Then I told her of what I had seen; and she said, "Rejoice, O son of my uncle, and be of good heart. Verily, by Him in whose hand is Khadīja's soul, I have hope that thou wilt be the prophet of this people." Then she rose and gathered her garments about her and set forth to her cousin Waraqa b. Naufal b. Asad b. 'Abdu'l-'Uzzā b. Quṣayy, who had become a Christian and read the scriptures and learned from those that follow the Torah and the Gospel. And when she related to him what the apostle of God told her he had seen and heard, Waraqa cried, 'Holy! Holy! Verily by Him in whose hand is Waraqa's soul, if thou hast spoken to me the truth, O Khadīja, there hath come unto him the greatest Nāmūs (T. meaning Gabriel) who came to Moses aforetime, and lo, he is the prophet of this people. Bid him be of good heart.' So Khadīja returned to the apostle of God and told him what Waraqa had said. (T. and that calmed his fears somewhat.) . . .

Ismā'il b. Abū Ḥakīm, a freedman of the family of al-Zubayr, told me on Khadīja's authority that she said to the apostle of God, 'O son of my uncle, are you able to tell me about your visitant, when he comes to you?' He replied that he could, and she asked him to tell her when he came. So when Gabriel came to him, as he was wont, the apostle said to Khadīja, 'This is Gabriel who has just come to me.' 'Get up, O son of my uncle,' she said, 'and sit by my left thigh'. The apostle did so, and she said, 'Can you see him?' 'Yes,' he said. She said, 'Then turn round and sit on my right thigh.' He did so, and she said, 'Can you see him?' When he said that he could she asked him to move and sit in her lap. When he had done this she again asked if he could see him, and when he said yes, she disclosed her form and cast aside her veil while the apostle was sitting in her lap. Then she said, 'Can you see him?' And he replied, 'No.' She said, 'O son of my uncle, rejoice and be of good heart, by God he is an angel and not a satan.'

I told 'Abdullah b. Ḥasan this story and he said, 'I heard my mother Fāṭima, daughter of Ḥusayn, talking about this tradition from Khadīja, but as I heard it she made the apostle of God come inside her shift, and thereupon Gabriel departed, and she said to the apostle of God, "This verily is an angel and not a satan."

[From *The Life of Muhammad*, pp. 106–107.]

Khadīja, Daughter of Khuwaylid, Accepts Islam

Khadīja believed in him and accepted as true what he brought from God, and helped him in his work. She was the first to believe in God and His apostle, and in the truth of his message. By her God lightened the burden of His prophet. He never met with contradiction and charges of falsehood, which saddened him, but God comforted him by her when he went home. She strengthened him, lightened his burden, proclaimed his truth, and belittled men's opposition. May God Almighty have mercy upon her!

The Prescription of Prayer

The apostle was ordered to pray and so he prayed. Ṣāliḥ b. Kaisān from 'Urwa b. al-Zubayr from 'Ā'isha told me that she said, 'When prayer was first laid on the apostle it was with two prostrations for every prayer: then God raised it to four prostrations at home while on a journey the former ordinance of two prostrations held.'

A learned person told me that when prayer was laid on the apostle Gabriel came to him while he was on the heights of Mecca and dug a hole for him with his heel in the side of the valley from which a fountain gushed forth, and Gabriel performed the ritual ablution as the apostle watched him. This was in order to show him how to purify himself before prayer. Then the apostle performed the ritual ablution as he had seen Gabriel do it. Then Gabriel said a prayer with him while the apostle prayed with his prayer. Then Gabriel left him. The apostle came to Khadīja and performed the ritual for her as Gabriel had done for him, and she copied him. Then he prayed with her as Gabriel had prayed with him, and she prayed his prayer.

[From *The Life of Muhammad*, pp. 111–112.]

HADĪTH

Hadīth are collections of anecdotes about the life of Muhammad which serve as guides for Muslim religious practices and jurisprudence that are not covered directly or fully by the *Qur'ān*. Muslim scholars developed criteria for distinguishing accurate hadīth, that is hadīth which had been preserved through various reliable sources. Consequently, each hadīth includes its record of transmission, its *isnād*, e.g. "Ā'isha, the wife of Muhammad, who heard it from Muhammad, told it to 'x' who told it to 'y'," etc. Six such collections are important to Sunnī Muslims and the following excerpts are taken from one of the earliest collections, that of al-Bukhārī (810–870 C.E.).

The first selections discuss the general condition of women as well as menstruation taboos.

Narrated Ibn 'Abbās: The Prophet said: "I was shown the Hell-fire and that the majority of its dwellers were women who were ungrateful." It was asked, "Do they disbelieve in Allāh?" (or are they ungrateful to Allāh?) He replied, "They are ungrateful to their husbands and are ungrateful for the favours and the good (charitable deeds) done to them. If you have always been good (benevolent) to one of them and then she sees something in you (not of her liking), she will say, 'I have never received any good from you.'"

[From *The Translation of the Meanings of Sahih Al-Bukhari*, 2.21.]

Narrated Abū Sa'īd Al-Khudrī: Once Allāh's Apostle went out to the Muṣallā (to offer the prayer) of 'Id-al-Adha or Al-Fitr prayer. Then he passed by the women and said, "O women! Give alms, as I have seen that the majority of the dwellers of Hell-fire were you (women)." They asked, "Why is it so, O Allāh's Apostle?" He replied, "You curse frequently and are ungrateful to your husbands. I have not seen anyone more deficient in intelligence and religion than you. A cautious sensible man could be led astray by some of you." The women asked, "O Allāh's Apostle! What is deficient in our intelligence and religion?" He said, "Is not the evidence of two women equal to the witness of one man?" They replied in the affirmative. He said, "This is the deficiency in her intelligence. Isn't it true that a woman can neither pray nor fast during her menses?" The women replied in the affirmative. He said, "This is the deficiency in her religion."

[ibid., 6.8]

* * *

A woman should ask her husband's permission (on wishing) to go to the mosque.

Narrated Sālim bin 'Abdullāh: My father said, "The Prophet said, 'If the wife of any one of you asks permission (to go to the mosque) do not forbid her.'"

[ibid., 12.84]

* * *

The witness of women and the Statement of Allāh:— 'And if there are not two men (available as witnesses), then a man and two women.'

* * *

Narrated Abū Sa'īd Al-Khudrī: The Prophet said, "Isn't the witness of a woman equal to half of that of a man?" The women said, "Yes." He said, "This is because of the deficiency of a woman's mind."

[ibid., 48.12]

* * *

And the Statement of Allāh: "They ask you (O Muhammad) concerning menstruation. Say: It is a filthy (thing), so keep away from women during menses and go not in unto them until they have been purified (from Menses and washed their bodies). And when they have purified themselves, then go in unto them as Allāh has ordained for you (go in unto them in any manner as long as it is in their vagina). Truly, Allāh loves those who repent to Him and loves those who purify themselves."

[ibid., 6.1]

* * *

There is no prayer to be offered by a menstruating woman in lieu of the missed prayers during her menses. And the Prophet said, "The lady (in her menses) must leave her prayers."

[ibid., 6.22]

As faithful Muslims, however, women were enjoined to perform the *hajj*, or the pilgrimage to Mecca.

Hajj of women. Narrated Ibrahim from his father from his grandfather that 'Umar in his last Hajj allowed the wives of the Prophet to perform Hajj and he sent with them 'Uthmān bin 'Affān and 'Abdur-Rahmān bin 'Auf as escorts.

Narrated 'Aisha (mother of the faithful believers): I said, "O Allāh's Apostle! Shouldn't we participate in Holy battles and Jihād along with you?" He replied, "The best and the most superior Jihād (for women) is Hajj which is accepted by Allāh." 'Aisha added: Ever since I heard that from Allāh's Apostle I have determined not to miss Hajj.

[Ibid., 29.26]

*Performing Hajj for a person
who cannot sit firmly on the Mount.*

Narrated Ibn 'Abbās: A woman from the tribe of Khath'am came in the year (of Hajjat-ul-wadā' of the Prophet) and said, "O Allāh's Apostle! My father has come under Allāh's obligation of performing Hajj but he is a very old man and cannot sit properly on his Mount. Will the obligation be fulfilled if I perform Hajj on his behalf?" The Prophet replied in the affirmative.

[Ibid., 29.23]

PILGRIMAGE

The pilgrimage to Mecca (the *hajj*) is one of the Five Pillars of Islam, obligatory religious acts for all Muslims, female and male. (The other four are the profession of faith, alms giving, prayer, and fasting. The religious obligation of the pilgrimage, however, is not required of those who do not have the money to make the journey.) Originally the pilgrimage to Mecca was an ancient pre-Islamic practice centering then, as it does today, on the Ka'bah, a sacred black stone. Abraham and his son Ishmael were believed to have founded the original shrine in honor of the one God. Honoring the Ka'bah is therefore a symbolic act of allegiance to God. After his conquest of Mecca, Muhammad refused admittance to the pagan Arabs and he himself made the pilgrimage in 632 which established its main forms.

An important effect of religious pilgrimage is that it defines, however temporarily, the ideal religious society and consequently ideal gender relations. This is certainly the case in the pilgrimage to Mecca. The following excerpt is taken from a pilgrim's guide for proper behavior while on pilgrimage. The author is a Sunnī Muslim and it was published by a leading Shī'ī press with an approving preface. Therefore it expresses fairly widespread views among Muslims. It explains the *ihram,* the proper clothing to be worn, and also the particular rules for women regarding menstruation, the need for male guardians, and for silence.

Ihram and the Sacred Garments of the Hajj

The first of the principal ceremonies of the Pilgrimage is the putting off of conventional garments to don those of Ihram, the traditional habit which distinguishes pilgrims from all others but permits no distinction one from another. All, high-born and humble, wear identical robes and are reminded that in the eyes of God all men are created equal — and that on the Day of Judgment all will be accountable.

Ihram is a state of many sacred prohibitions.

On taking this garb the pilgrim enters into a period of peace and self-denial. Violence in any form is banned. The pilgrim must abstain from luxuries and gratification of the senses, however legitimate, until the rites of the Pilgrimage have been observed and Ihram put aside. Jewelry or other personal adornment is forbidden; so, too, is perfume or scent. It is forbidden for a pilgrim in Ihram to uproot any growing thing or to cut down a tree within the Sanctuary of Makkah. Sexual intercourse must cease temporarily and the sexual impulse is to be sublimated.

During the days in Ihram there may be no wrangling or argument, no rudeness, no discussion of the opposite sex, and no hunting. Bodily, the pilgrim is to be devoted to the acts of Pilgrimage; intellectually, he or she is to be concerned with prayer, aspirations, praise of God, and self-examination.

For Hajj are the months well known. If any one undertakes that duty therein, let there be no obscenity, nor wickedness, nor wrangling, in the Hajj. And whatever good ye do, God knoweth it. And take a provision for the journey, but the best of provisions is right conduct. So fear Me, O ye who are wise! [Qur'an 2:196]

The Period of Ihram

Ihram's garments are worn during —
(I) The pilgrims' arrival at Makkah for the first tawaf and sa'y, the initial rituals by and circuits of the Holy Ka'bah and the visiting of the hills Safa and Marwah, traversing the distance between them seven times.

(II) The stand before the stone mountain 'Arafat on the ninth day of the Pilgrimage Month; then, that night, at the gathering of pebbles and the pause in the darkness for prayer at Muzdalifah, a sacred spot in the wilderness between 'Arafat and the Valley of Mina.

(III) Then, on the tenth day, the casting of stones at the Jamrat al-'Aqabah, the largest of the three crude stone-and-mortar monuments marking the places in Mina where Satan appeared to Isma'il, son of the Prophet Ibrahim.

(IV) And the offering of the blood sacrifice at Mina.

Ihram for Male Pilgrims

For men the Ihram dress is comprised of two large pieces of white fabric, without design, decoration, or seam. Many pilgrims prefer white cotton towelling; this is better than lighter cloth as a protection both from the killing heat of the summer and against the sudden, blade-like winds when Pilgrimage must be made during the winter. Before the time of Muhammad the Hajj ceremonies took place at a fixed time in the autumn. In pagan years the lunar months were kept to their solar setting by the insertion of extra days, a practice abandoned by the Prophet. Today the year is lunar and the time of Pilgrimage changes, passing through every season; pilgrims must remember this and prepare themselves accordingly.

In ancient, pagan times pilgrims approaching the Holy Ka'bah removed all of their clothing as a sign of humility. Naked, they performed the ritual tawaf, kissed the Black Stone, and otherwise did as we do now. Until the time of the Prophet Muhammad it had been the custom to go, naked, in the dark before dawn to the Ka'bah for the rites of absolution. The Prophet did not approve of this nudity, nor of the loud manner in which the worship was performed. He introduced the Ihram dress we wear today and the more subdued manner in which we pray, but the rite is an ancient rite.

One length of the Ihram cloth is worn over the shoulders, covering the upper half of the body. The second length is worn wrapped about the waist and secured with a belt; it should reach to the ankles. Each piece of cloth should measure approximately two and a half meters in length and one and a half meters in breadth. No other garment is to be worn over this or beneath it, but it is common usage to wear a money-pouch on a shoulder sling or a moneybelt; one of these is requisite as the Ihram robes should have no pockets.

Men may not cover their heads during the Pilgrimage, nor are the feet to be shod in other except sandals which do not cover the backs of the heels.

Ihram for Female Pilgrims

Women do not wear the Ihram garments which are worn by men. They may keep to their customary dress, garbing themselves in plain, fresh clothing at the time of entering into Ihram. Though female pilgrims are not to veil their faces during the Pilgrimage, their hair is to be covered. Women's garments should reach to their ankles and the sleeves to their wrists; the neck-line should be high, revealing none of the breast.

Female pilgrims who are menstruating at the time they take Ihram, or who menstruate during the days they are in Ihram, should not perform any of the daily prayers or other ritual *rak'ah* until their menses have left them; but they may read all other forms of prayer except those requiring obeisances.

No woman is to make Pilgrimage unless she is accompanied by her husband or, if she is unwed, by two male members of her immediate family, both of whom must be of such close relationship as to preclude sexual interest or eventual marriage. And no man is to approach his wife sexually, or woman to encourage her husband to enter her, during Ihram.

During periods of prayer only male pilgrims may worship aloud or recite audibly. Female pilgrims may not lift their voices or conduct themselves in such a manner as to attract attention; scrupulously they must avoid distracting males from their devotions.

[From *The Sacred Journey,* pp. 14–17.]

WOMEN POETS

The first four selections are poems of mourning written by Muslim women who lost brothers in the battles to secure the ascendancy of Islam. The names of the poets precede their poems.

Khansá: Two Poems

Tears, ere thy death, for many a one I shed,
But thine are all my tears since thou art dead.
To comforters I lend my ear apart,
While pain sits ever closer to my heart.
    [From *Translations of Eastern Poetry and Prose,*
p. 18.]

When night draws on, remembering keeps me
    wakeful
And hinders my rest with grief upon grief returning
For Şakhr. What a man was he on the day of
    battle,
When, snatching their chance, they swiftly exchange
    the spear-thrusts!
Ah, never of woe like this in the world of spirits
I heard, or of loss like mine in the heart of woman.
What Fortune might send, none stronger than he to
    bear it;

None better to meet the trouble with mind unshaken;
The kindest to help, wherever the need was sorest:
They all had of him a boon—wife, friend, and suitor.
O Şakhr! I will ne'er forget thee until in dying
I part from my soul, and earth for my tomb is cloven.
The rise of the sun recalls to me Şakhr my brother,
And him I remember also at every sunset.
    [Ibid., p. 19]

Şafíya of Báhila

Two boughs, the fairest ever tree possessed,
We sprang and mounted from the selfsame root,
Until men said, "Long are their shoots, and blest
Their shade and sweet the promise of their fruit."

But Time, whose villainy will nothing spare,
Destroyed my dear one. He did us excel
As 'mongst the stars a moon more bright and fair,
And as a moon from forth our midst he fell.
    [Ibid., pp. 26–27.]

Fári'a Daughter of Ṭaríf

At Tallu Nuhākā stands the cairn of a grave set high
As though on a mountain-peak o'ertopping the
mountains,
A grave that doth hold renown most ancient and
chieftainhood
And courage heroical and judgment unshaken.
But why bud ye, O ye trees of Khábúr, with leaves
afresh?
Methinks, ye have never mourned Ṭarif's son, my
brother.
He liked not of food but that he gained in the fear
of God,
Of wealth only what was won by good swords and
lances;
Nor aught would he prize and keep but many a hardy
mare
Sleek-coated, well-used to charge thro' ranks of the
battle.
And now 'tis as though with us thou ne'er hadst been
present here,
Or ta'en 'gainst our foes a stand not soon to be yielded;
Or ever done on, for sake of plunging in loathly
fray,
A hauberk of mail amongst dark-glittering horsemen;
Or striven on a field of War, when big is her womb
with woe
And keen tawny-shafted pikes have pricked her to
fury.
The comrade of Bounty he, his life long: him Bounty
loved,

And since he is dead, no more loves Bounty a
comrade.
We lost thee as Youth, once lost, returns not; and fain
had we
Redeemed thee with thousands of the lives of our
bravest.
For aye was Walíd, till Death drew right forth the soul
of him,
A grief to the foeman or a home to the friendless.
Come weep, O my kin, the doom of death and the
woeful change
And earth trembling after him and quaking beneath
us!
Come weep, O my kin, the turns of fortune, the
perishings,
And pitiless Fate that dogs the noble with ruin!
Alas for the perfect moon fall'n low from amongst
the stars,
Alas for the sun when toward eclipse was his journey!
Alas for the lion, yea, the lion without reproach,
What time to a hollowed grave, roofed over, they bore
him!
Oh, God curse the mounded stones that covered him
out of sight,
A man that was never tired of doing a kindness!
If he by Yazíd the son of Mazyad was done to
death,
Yet many a host he led of warriors to combat.
Upon him the peace of God abide evermore!
Meseems
That fast fall the strokes of Death on all who are noble.
[Ibid., pp. 36–37.]

The following poem shows the author's irreverence for her soft and ambitious husband, then the governor of Syria and soon to be the Caliph, and her longing for the desert life of her youth.

Maisún

A tent with rustling breezes cool
Delights me more than palace high,
And more the cloak of simple wool
Than robes in which I learned to sigh.

The crust I ate beside my tent
Was more than this fine bread to me;
The wind's voice where the hill-path went
Was more than tambourine can be.

And more than purr of friendly cat
I love the watch-dog's bark to hear;
And more than any lubbard fat
I love a Bedouin cavalier!
[Ibid., p. 23]

Sufism

Sufism is the mystical tradition of Islam in which individual Sufis seek union with God. The Sufis take their name from the Arabic word *suf,* meaning wool, referring to their modest attire of coarse woolen cloth. This form of dress served to distinguish the Sufis from their more worldly-minded and more richly-dressed brethren and to evoke the memory of the austere life of the desert followed by Muḥammad and his companions. This emphasis on a simple and self-disciplined life devoted to God reveals Sufism's origins in the early ascetic movements of Islam. Sufi movements began to arise in various parts of the Muslim empire during the eighth century, eventually developing into particular schools claiming descent from individual Sufi masters.

BIOGRAPHIES OF SUFI WOMEN

RĀBI'AH

One of the earliest Sufis, and certainly the most famous woman saint of Islam, was Rābi'ah (d. 801) who lived her life in great poverty. Her name, meaning "four," was given to her by her father because she was his fourth daughter. After the death of her parents she was sold into bondage but later released because of her piety. Rābi'ah had an important and continuing influence on Sufism in that it was she who emphasized the role of love in mystical union with God, often quoting the Qur'anic verse "He loves them and they love him" (Sura 5.59). This pure love for God is a constant theme in the prayers and poems attributed to her as well as in the stories about her. One vivid story describes Rābi'ah racing through the streets with a bucket of water in one hand and a burning torch in the other. When asked where she was going Rābi'ah replied: "To put out the fires of hell and to burn down paradise." Her point is that good Muslims were so concerned about avoiding the sufferings of hell and trying to get into paradise that they forgot about God.

The following excerpts are from 'Aṭṭār's (d. 1221) *Tadhkirat al-awliyā* (Biographies of the Saints). The inclusion of a women in this collection is something that 'Aṭṭār felt he needed to explain. This contrasts with Ibn 'Arabī's collections of saints lives which includes four women as a matter of course. 'Aṭṭār's point about Rābi'ah's gender is ambivalent at best. He is suggesting, first, that her gender is irrelevant; second, if it is relevant then he invokes the precedent of the religious authority of one other important woman, Ā'isha, the wife of Muḥammad and the source of many hadīths; third, he denies her gender and says she has become a man. Significantly, however, 'Aṭṭār used three earlier collections for his own work and none of these included Rābi'ah.

Rabe'a, her birth and early life

If anyone says, "Why have you included Rabe'a in the rank of men?" my answer is, that the Prophet himself said, "God does not regard your outward forms." The root of the matter is not form, but intention, as the Prophet said, "Mankind will be raised up according to their intentions." Moreover, if it is proper to derive two-thirds of our religion from A'esha, surely it is permissible to take religious instruction from a hand-maid of A'esha. When a woman becomes a "man" in the path of God, she is a man and one cannot any more call her a woman.

The night when Rabe'a came to earth, there was nothing whatsoever in her father's house; for her father lived in very poor circumstances. He did not possess even one drop of oil to anoint her navel; there was no lamp, and not a rag to swaddle her in. He already had three daughters, and Rabe'a was his fourth; that is why she was called by that name.

"Go to neighbour So-and-so and beg for a drop of oil, so that I can light the lamp," his wife said to him.

Now the man had entered into a covenant that he would never ask any mortal for anything. So he went out and just laid his hand on the neighbour's door, and returned.

"They will not open the door," he reported.

The poor woman wept bitterly. In that anxious state the man placed his head on his knees and went to sleep. He dreamed that he saw the Prophet.

"Be not sorrowful," the Prophet bade him. "The girl child who has just come to earth is a queen among women, who shall be the intercessor for seventy thousand of my community. Tomorrow," the Prophet continued, "go to Isa-e Zadan the governor of Basra. Write on a piece of paper to the following effect. 'Every night you send upon me a hundred blessings, and on Friday night four hundred. Last night was Friday night, and you forgot me. In expiation for that, give this man four hundred dinars lawfully acquired.'"

Rabe'a's father on awaking burst into tears. He rose up and wrote as the Prophet had bidden him, and sent the message to the governor by the hand of a chamberlain.

"Give two thousand dinars to the poor," the governor commanded when he saw the missive, "as a thanksgiving for the Master remembering me. Give four hundred dinars also to the shaikh, and tell him, 'I wish you to come to me so that I may see you. But I do not hold it proper for a man like you to come to me. I would rather come and rub my beard in your threshold. However, I adjure you by God, whatever you may need, pray let me know.'"

The man took the gold and purchased all that was necessary.

When Rabe'a had become a little older, and her mother and father were dead, a famine came upon Basra, and her sisters were scattered. Rabe'a ventured out and was seen by a wicked man who seized her and then sold her for six dirhams. Her purchaser put her to hard labour.

One day she was passing along the road when a stranger approached. Rabe'a fled. As she ran, she fell headlong and her hand was dislocated.

"Lord God," she cried, bowing her face to the ground, "I am a stranger, orphaned of mother and father, a helpless prisoner fallen into captivity, my hand broken. Yet for all this I do not grieve; all I need is Thy good pleasure, to know whether Thou art well-pleased or no."

"Do not grieve," she heard a voice say. "Tomorrow a station shall be thine such that the cherubim in heaven will envy thee."

So Rabe'a returned to her master's house. By day she continually fasted and served God, and by night she worshipped standing until day. One night her master awoke from sleep and, looking through the window of his apartment, saw Rabe'a bowing prostrate and praying.

"O God, Thou knowest that the desire of my heart is in conformity with Thy command, and that the light of my eye is in serving Thy court. If the affair lay with me, I would not rest one hour from serving Thee; but Thou Thyself hast set me under the hand of a creature."

Such was her litany. Her master perceived a lantern suspended without any chain above her head, the light whereof filled the whole house. Seeing this, he was afraid. Rising up, he returned to his bedroom and sat pondering till dawn. When day broke he summoned Rabe'a, was gentle with her and set her free.

"Give me permission to depart," Rabe'a said.

He gave her leave, and she left the house and went into the desert. From the desert she proceeded to a hermitage where she served God for a while. Then she determined to perform the pilgrimage, and set her face towards the desert. She bound her bundle on an ass. In the heart of the desert the ass died.

"Let us carry your load," the men in the party said.

"You go on," she replied. "I have not come putting my trust in you."

So the men departed, and Rabe'a remained alone.

"O God," she cried, lifting her head, "do kings so treat a woman who is a stranger and powerless? Thou hast invited me unto Thy house, then in the midst of the way Thou hast suffered my ass to die, leaving me alone in the desert."

Hardly had she completed this orison when her ass stirred and rose up. Rabe'a placed her load on its back, and continued on her way. (The narrator of this story reports that some while afterwards he saw that little donkey being sold in the market.) She travelled on through the desert for some days, then she halted.

"O God," she cried, "my heart is weary. Whither am I going? I a lump of clay, and Thy house a stone! I need Thee here."

God spoke unmediated in her heart.

"Rabe'a, thou art faring in the life-blood of eighteen thousand worlds. Hast thou not seen how Moses prayed for the vision of Me? And I cast a few motes of revelation upon the mountain, and the mountain shivered into forty pieces. Be content here with My name!"

Anecdotes of Rabe'a

One night Rabe'a was praying in the hermitage when she was overcome by weariness and fell asleep. So deeply was she absorbed that, when a reed from the reed-mat she was lying on broke in her eye so that the blood flowed, she was quite unaware of the fact.

A thief entered and seized her chaddur. He then

made to leave, but the way was barred to him. He dropped the chaddur and departed, finding the way now open. He seized the chaddur again and returned to discover the way blocked. Once more he dropped the chaddur. This he repeated seven times over; then he heard a voice proceeding from a corner of the hermitage.

"Man, do not put yourself to such pains. It is so many years now that she has committed herself to us. The Devil himself has not the boldness to slink round her. How should a thief have the boldness to slink round her chaddur? Be gone, scoundrel! Do not put yourself to such pains. If one friend has fallen asleep, one Friend is awake and keeping watch."

★ ★ ★

One day Rabe'a's servant girl was making an onion stew; for it was some days since they had cooked any food. Finding that she needed some onions, she said, "I will ask of next door."

"Forty years now," Rabe'a replied, "I have had a covenant with Almighty God not to ask for aught of any but He. Never mind the onions."

Immediately a bird swooped down from the air with peeled onions in its beak and dropped them into the pan.

"I am not sure this is not a trick," Rabe'a commented.

And she left the onion pulp alone, and ate nothing but bread.

★ ★ ★

Once Rabe'a passed by Hasan's house. Hasan had his head out of the window and was weeping, and his tears fell on Rabe'a's dress. Looking up, she thought at first that it was rain; then, realizing that it was Hasan's tears, she turned to him and addressed him.

"Master, this weeping is a sign of spiritual languor. Guard your tears, so that there may surge within you such a sea that, seeking the heart therein, you shall not find it save *in keeping of a King Omnipotent.*"

These words distressed Hasan, but he kept his peace. Then one day he saw Rabe'a when she was near a lake. Throwing his prayer rug on the surface of the water, he called,

"Rabe'a, come! Let us pray two *rak'as* here!"

"Hasan," Rabe'a replied, "when you are showing off your spiritual goods in this worldly market, it should be things that your fellow-men are incapable of displaying."

And she flung her prayer rug into the air, and flew up on it.

"Come up here, Hasan, where people can see us!" she cried.

Hasan, who had not attained that station, said nothing. Rabe'a sought to console him.

"Hasan," she said, "what you did fishes also do, and what I did flies also do. The real business is outside both these tricks. One must apply one's self to the real business."

★ ★ ★

Once Rabe'a saw a man with a bandage tied round his head.

"Why have you tied the bandage?" she asked.

"Because my head aches," the man replied.

"How old are you?" she demanded.

"Thirty," he replied.

"Have you been in pain and anguish the greater part of your life?" she enquired.

"No," the man answered.

"For thirty years you have enjoyed good health," she remarked, "and you never tied about you the bandage of thankfulness. Now because of this one night that you have a headache you tie the bandage of complaint!"

★ ★ ★

A party of men once visited her to put her to the test, desiring to catch her out in an unguarded utterance.

"All the virtues have been scattered upon the heads of men," they said. "The crown of prophethood has been placed on men's heads. The belt of nobility has been fastened around men's waists. No woman has ever been a prophet."

"All that is true," Rabe'a replied. "But egoism and self-worship and 'I am your lord, the Most High' have never sprung from a woman's breast. No woman has ever been a hermaphrodite. All these things have been the speciality of men."

Prayers of Rabe'a

O God, whatsoever Thou hast apportioned to me of worldly things, do Thou give that to Thy enemies; and whatsoever Thou hast apportioned to me in the world to come, give that to Thy friends; for Thou sufficest me.

O God, if I worship Thee for fear of Hell, burn me in Hell, and if I worship Thee in hope of Paradise, exclude me from Paradise; but if I worship Thee for Thy own sake, grudge me not Thy everlasting beauty.

O God, my whole occupation and all my desire in this world, of all worldly things, is to remember Thee, and in the world to come, of all things of the world to come, is to meet Thee. This is on my side, as I have stated; now do Thou whatsoever Thou wilt.

[From *Muslim Saints and Mystics,* pp. 40–51.]

IBN 'ARABĪ'S COLLECTION

Among the numerous works of the great Sufi mystic and philosopher Ibn 'Arabī (1164–1240 C.E.) are two collections of biographies of Sufi masters who lived primarily in Spain from the twelfth to the thirteenth centuries. These two texts are the *Rūḥ al-quds fī munāsaḥat al-nafs* (The Spirit of Holiness in the Counselling of the Soul) and *al-Durrat al-fākhirah fī dhikr man intafa'tu bihi fī ṭarīq al-ākhirah* (The Precious Pearl concerned with the Mention of Those from whom I have derived Benefit in the way of the Hereafter).

Ibn 'Arabī is an important and influential figure in Sufism for two reasons. First, he united the thinking of Eastern and Western Sufism. He was born and raised in Spain, where he first studied Sufism, and he then traveled throughout the Muslim world to the Middle East, where he spent the later half of his life. Second, he was an historical bridge between the rich oral tradition of Spanish Sufism, which he preserved and explained in his writings, and the Sufism that developed after him.

The following excerpts from his two collections of biographies reveal the deep respect Ibn 'Arabī had for these women and for their paranormal powers.

Nunah Fatimah Bint Ibn al-Muthanna

She lived at Seville. When I met her she was in her nineties and only ate the scraps left by people at their doors. Although she was so old and ate so little, I was almost ashamed to look at her face when I sat with her, it was so rosy and soft. Her own special chapter of the Qur'an was 'The Opening.' She once said to me, 'I was given "The Opening" and I can wield its power in any matter I wish.'

I, together with two of my companions, built a hut of reeds for her to live in. She used to say, 'Of those who come to see me, I admire none more than Ibn Al-'Arabī.' On being asked the reason for this she replied, 'The rest of you come to me with part of yourselves, leaving the other part of you occupied with your other concerns, while Ibn al-'Arabī is a consolation to me, for he comes to me with all of himself. When he rises up it is with all of himself and when he sits it is with his whole self, leaving nothing of himself elsewhere. That is how it should be on the Way.'

Although God offered to her His Kingdom, she refused, saying, 'You are all, all else is inauspicious for me.' Her devotion to God was profound. Looking at her in a purely superficial way one might have thought she was a simpleton, to which she would have replied that he who knows not his Lord is the real simpleton. She was indeed a mercy to the world.

Once, on the night of the Festival, Abū 'Āmir, the muezzin, struck her with his whip in the mosque. She gave him a look and left the place feeling very angry with him. In the morning she heard him calling to prayer and said, 'O my Lord, do not rebuke me that I was affected by one who calls Your Name in the darkness of the night while other men sleep, for it is my Beloved who is mentioned on his lips. O God, do not censure him because of my feeling against him.'

The next morning the jurists of the locality went, after the Festival prayer, to convey their respects to the Sultan. This muezzin, full of worldly aspiration, went in with them. When the Sultan enquired who the fellow might be, he was told that it was only the muezzin. Then the Sultan asked who had allowed him to come in with the jurists and ordered him to be thrown out, which he was. However, after someone had pleaded with the Sultan for him he was let off, although the Sultan had intended to punish him. Fāṭimah heard about this incident and said, 'I know about it, and if I had not prayed for leniency for him he would have been executed.' Her spiritual influence was very great indeed. After this she died.'

From the 'Al-Durrat al-Fākhirah'

Some of the believing *Jinn* would sit with her, seeking her companionship, but she would refuse them and ask them to remain hidden and would remind them of what the Apostle of God had said the night he caught the demon, 'I remembered the words of my brother Solomon and used them on it.'

At first she had earned her living on a spindle. Then it occurred to her to earn her keep by hand-spinning, but God caused her spinning finger to become crippled from the moment she started on the work. I had noticed the finger and had asked her about it. She then told me the story and told me that she had, from that day relied upon the scraps of food thrown from people's houses. She came to the Way while still a young girl living in her father's house. I met her when she was already ninety-six years of age.

She had married a righteous man whom God had afflicted with leprosy. She served him happily for twenty-four years until he was taken to God's mercy. When she became hungry and no scraps or offerings of food came her way she would be content and thank God for His favour in that he was subjecting her to that to which He had subjected his prophets and Saints. She would say, 'O Lord, how can I deserve this great position in that You treat me as You treated Your loved ones?'

One day I built a hut for her of palm branches in which to perform her devotions. That same night the oil in her lamp ran out, something which had never happened to her before. I never learned the secret of that from her. She got up to open the door to ask me to bring her some more oil and, in the darkness, plunged her hand into some water in the bucket underneath her. At this she cursed and the water was immediately changed into oil. She then took the jug and filled it with the oil, lit the lamp and came back to see from where the oil had come. When she saw no further trace of oil she realized that it had been a provision from God.

One day when I was with her a woman came to see her to complain of her husband who had gone away to Sidonia, two days' journey from Seville. She told us that her husband wanted to seek another wife in that place, which she found hard to accept. I asked Fāṭimah whether she had heard the woman's plea and begged her to call upon God to restore her husband to her. She said, 'I will make no supplication, but I will cause the chapter "The Opening" (al-fātihah) to follow behind him and bring him back.' I then said, 'In the name of God, the Merciful, the Compassionate,' and she recited the rest of the chapter. Then she said, 'O chapter of "The Opening," go to Jerez de Sidonia to the husband of this woman and drive him back at once from wherever you find him and do not let him delay.' She said this sometime between noon and the late afternoon.

On the third day the man arrived at his home. Then the woman came to inform us of his arrival and to thank us. I then told her to bring her husband to us. When he came we asked him what had brought him back from Jerez, when he had intended to marry and settle down there. He replied that he had left his house in the middle of the afternoon heading towards the municipal building for the marriage and that on the way he had felt a constriction in his heart and everything seemed suddenly very dark to him. At this he became very anxious. Then he left that place and arrived in Triana before sunset, where he had found a boat for Seville. Thus he had sailed the day before and had arrived in Seville that morning, having left all his baggage and effects behind in Jerez. He admitted that he still did not know why he had done it. I have seen various miracles performed by her.
[From *Sufis of Andalusia*, pp. 143–46.]

A Slave Girl of Qasim al-Dawlah

She belonged to our master the Prince of the Faithful. She lived in the neighbourhood of Mecca and died there. She was unique in her time and had attained the power to cover great distances quickly. When she was away on her wanderings she would commune with the mountains, rocks and trees, saying to them, 'Welcome, welcome!' Her spiritual state was strong and she served the Folk and followed the Way with unswerving sincerity. She had the virtues of chivalry and was most strenuous in self-discipline, frequently practising day-and-night fasting. Despite this she was strong and her exertions seemed to suit her well. I have never seen one more chivalrous than her in our time. Dedicated to the exaltation of God's majesty, she attached no worth to herself.
[From *Sufis of Andalusia*, p. 154.]

Zainab al-Qal'iyyah

From the fortress of the Banū Jamād she was of those devoted to the Book of God, the foremost ascetic of her day. Although she possessed both great beauty and considerable wealth she freely abandoned the world and went to live in the region of Mecca, a woman ennobled by God. I had contact with her both in Seville and at Mecca. She was the companion of many eminent men of the Folk, among them, Ibn Qassūm, al-Shubarbulī, Maimūm al-Qirmizī, Abū al-Husain b. al-Ṣa'igh, a Traditionist and a notable ascetic, Abū al-Ṣabr Ayyūb al-Qahrī, and others.

When she sat down to practise Invocation she would rise into the air from the ground to a height of thirty cubits; when she had finished she would descend again. I accompanied her from Mecca to Jerusalem and I have never seen anyone more strict in observing the times of prayer than her. She was one of the most intelligent people of her time.
[From *Sufis of Andalusia*, pp. 154–55.]

Shams, Mother of the Poor

She lived at Marchena of the Olives where I visited her often. Among people of our kind I have never met one like her with respect to the control she had over her soul. In her spiritual activities and communications she was among the greatest. She had a strong and pure heart, a noble spiritual power and a fine discrimination. She usually concealed her spiritual state, although she would often reveal something of it to me in secret because she knew of my own attainment, which gladdened me. She was endowed with many graces. I had considerable experience of her intuition and found her to be a master in this sphere. Her spiritual state was characterized chiefly by her fear of God and His good pleasure in her, the combination of the two at the same time in one person being extremely rare among us.

From the Al-Durat al-Fākhirah

I first met her when she was in her eighties.

One day al-Mawrūrī and I were with her. Suddenly she looked towards another part of the room and called out at the top of her voice, " 'Alī, return and get the kerchief." When we asked to whom she was speaking, she explained that 'Alī was on his way to visit her and that on his way he had sat down to eat by a stretch of water. When he got up to resume his journey he had forgotten the kerchief. This is why she had called out him; he had gone back and had retrieved the kerchief. 'Alī was at that time well over a league away. After an hour he arrived and we asked him what had happened to him on the way. He told us that he had stopped at some water on the way to eat and that he had then got up and left the kerchief behind. He went on to tell us that he had then heard our lady Shams calling him to return and get it, which he had done. She also had the power to voice the thoughts of others. Her revelations were true and I saw her perform many wonders.

[From *Sufis of Andulasia*, pp. 142–43.]

WORKS BY WOMEN

The following is an excerpt from a seventeenth-century Indian work by Fāṭima Jahānārā Begum Ṣāḥib, the daughter of the Mogul emperor Shāhjahān who was deposed by her brother Aurangzeb. Fāṭima chose to remain with her father during his imprisonment but after his death her brother restored her position. Fāṭima, however, preferred to spend her time in devotion to God and she wrote the *Risālat al-Ṣahibiyya*, a treatise of her mystical experiences. In it she describes her sense of union with God and how it transforms all human beings, women or men.

I offer a thousand praises and thanks to God the Incomparable, for it was He Who, when my life was being spent to no purpose, led me to give myself to the great search for Him, and Who, after that, let me attain to the high degree of Union with Himself. He it was Who enabled me to quench my thirst in the ocean of Truth and the fountain of Gnosis and thereby granted me the unending happiness and state of blessedness, which are to be found by one who drinks from these. I pray that God Most High will let me walk in the Path which leads, like *Ṣirāṭ*, to Paradise, with firm step and unfaltering courage, and to taste the delight of continual recollection of Himself.

Praise be to God for His grace in what He has given to me. I have been granted full and perfect apprehension of the Divine Essence, as I had always most earnestly desired. That one who has not attained to knowledge of the Absolute Being is not worthy to be called a man—he belongs to the type of those of whom it is said: "They are like the beasts of the field and are even more ignorant." But he to whom this supreme happiness has been granted has become a perfect man and the most exalted of created beings, for his own existence has become merged in that of the Absolute Being. He has become a drop in the ocean, a mote in the rays of the sun, a part of the whole. In this state, he is raised above death and the fear of punishment, above any regard for Paradise or dread of Hell. Whether woman or man, such a one is the most perfect of human beings. This is the grace of God which He gives to whom He wills.

[From *Readings from the Mystics of Islām*, pp. 131–32.]

The following two poems were written by women of the Ottoman Empire. Little is known about the first poet, Sidqi (died 1703), who wrote mainly in a mystical vein.

He who union with the Lord gains, more delight desireth not!
He who looks on charms of fair one, other sight desireth not.

Pang of love is lover's solace, eagerly he seeks there for,
Joys he in it, balm or salve for younder blight, desireth not.

Paradise he longs not after, nor doth aught beside regard;

Bower and Garden, Mead, and Youth, and Huri bright, desireth not.

From the hand of Power Unbounded draineth he the Wine of Life,

Aye inebriate with Knowledge, learning's light, desireth not.

He who loves the Lord is monarch of an empire, such that he—

King of Inward Mysteries—Suleyman's might, desireth not.

Thou art Sultan of my heart, aye, Soul of my soul e'en art Thou;

Thou art Soul enow, and Sidoj other plight desireth not.

[From *Ottoman Poets,* p. 111.]

The second poet, Zeyneb (died 1481), was educated in both the Arabic and Persian poetic traditions by her father. She was well known and greatly praised within her own lifetime and seems never to have married. The images in the following poem could be directed either to a human beloved or to the divine Beloved, God. In either case, Zeyneb takes an assertive, "manly" posture.

Cast off thy veil, and heaven and earth in dazzling light array!

As radiant Paradise, this poor demented world display!

Move thou thy lips, make play the ripples light of Kevser's pool!

Let loose thy scented locks, and odours sweet through earth convey!

A musky warrant by thy down was traced, and zephyr charged:—

"Speed, with this scent subdue the realms of China and Cathay!"

O heart! should not thy portion be the Water bright of Life,

A thousand times mayst thou pursue Iskender's darksome way.

O ZEYNEB, woman's love of earthly show leave thou behind;

Go manly forth, with single heart, forsake adornment gay!

[From *Ottoman Poets,* p. 18.]

A STORY

Like other great mystical traditions, Sufism frequently makes its point through stories and parables. The following excerpt reveals some of the tensions that exist between the legalistic and mystical aspects of Islam. Importantly, it also affirms women's abilities on the Sufi path. The story was first told in 1174 by Ahmed el-Rifai, the founder of the Rifai Order of Dervishes.

The Wayward Princess

A certain king believed that what he had been taught, and what he believed, was right. In many ways he was a just man, but he was one whose ideas were limited.

One day he said to his three daughters:

'All that I have is yours, or will be yours. Through me you obtained your life. It is my will which determines your future, and hence determines your fate.'

Dutifully, and quite persuaded of the truth of this, two of the girls agreed.

The third daughter, however, said:

'Although my position demands that I be obedient to the laws, I cannot believe that my fate must always be determined by your opinions.'

'We shall see about that,' said the king.

He ordered her to be imprisoned in a small cell, where she languished for years. Meanwhile the king and his obedient daughters spent freely of the wealth which would otherwise have been expended upon her.

The king said to himself:

'This girl lies in prison not by her own will, but by mine. This proves, sufficiently for any logical mind, that it is *my* will, not hers, which is determining her fate.'

The people of the country, hearing of their princess's situation, said to one another:

'She must have done or said something very wrong for a monarch, with whom we find no fault, to treat his own flesh and blood so.' For they had not arrived at the point where they felt the need to dispute the king's assumption of rightness in everything.

From time to time the king visited the girl. Although she was pale and weakened from her imprisonment, she refused to change her attitude.

Finally the king's patience came to an end.

'Your continued defiance,' he said to her, 'will only annoy me further, and seem to weaken my rights, if you stay within my realms. I could kill you; but I am merciful. I therefore banish you into the wilderness adjoining my territory. This is a wilderness, inhabited only by wild beasts and such eccentric outcasts who cannot survive in our rational society. There you will soon discover whether you can have an existence apart from that of your family; and, if you can, whether you prefer it to ours.'

His decree was at once obeyed, and she was conveyed to the borders of the kingdom. The princess found herself set loose in a wild land which bore little resemblance to the sheltered surroundings of her upbringing. But she soon learned that a cave would serve for a house, that nuts and fruit came from trees as well as from golden plates, that warmth came from the Sun. This wilderness had a climate and a way of existing of its own.

After some time she had so ordered her life that she had water from springs, vegetables from the earth, fire from a smouldering tree.

'Here,' she said to herself, 'is a life whose elements belong together, form a completeness, yet neither individually nor collectively do they obey the commands of my father the king.'

One day a lost traveller — as it happened a man of great riches and ingenuity — came upon the exiled princess, fell in love with her, and took her back to his own country, where they were married.

After a space of time, the two decided to return to the wilderness where they built a huge and prosperous city where their wisdom, resources and faith were expressed to their fullest possible extent. The 'eccentrics' and other outcasts, many of them thought to be madmen, harmonized completely and usefully with this many-sided life.

The city and its surrounding countryside became renowned throughout the entire world. It was not long before its power and beauty far outshone that of the realm of the princess's father.

By the unanimous choice of the inhabitants, the princess and her husband were elected to the joint monarchy of this new and ideal kingdom.

At length the king decided to visit the strange and mysterious place which had sprung up in a wilderness, and which was, he heard, peopled at least in part by those whom he and his like despised.

As, with bowed head, he slowly approached the foot of the throne upon which the young couple sat and raised his eyes to meet those whose repute of justice, prosperity and understanding far exceeded his own, he was able to catch the murmured words of his daughter:

'You see, Father, every man and woman has his own fate and his own choice.'

[From *Tales of the Dervishes,* pp. 63–65.]

ON WOMEN AND THE FEMININE

IBN 'ARABĪ

The following excerpt is from Ibn 'Arabī's (1164–1240) *The Bezels of Wisdom,* a work of his later years which he intended to be a summary of his teachings. In it he examines the lives of the prophets, concluding with Muḥammad. It is in this final chapter that he most fully expresses his understanding of the spiritual role of women and the feminine.

The Wisdom of Singularity in the Word of Muhammad

His [Muhammad] is the wisdom of singularity because he is the most perfect creation of this humankind, for which reason the whole affair [of creation] begins and ends with him. He was a prophet when Adam was still between the water and the clay and he is, by his elemental makeup, the Seal of the Prophets, first of the three singular ones, since all other singulars derive from it.

He was the clearest of evidence for his Lord, having been given the totality of the divine words, which are those things named by Adam, so that he was the closest of clues to his own triplicity, he being himself a clue to himself. Since, then, his reality was marked by primal singularity and his makeup by triplicity, he said concerning love, which is the origin of all existent being, "Three things have been made beloved to me in this world of yours," because of the triplicity inherent in him. Then he mentioned women and perfume, and added that he found solace in prayer.

He begins by mentioning women and leaves prayer until last, because, in the manifestation of her essence, woman is a part of man. Now, man's knowledge of himself comes before his knowledge of his Lord, the latter being the result of the former, according to his saying, "Whoso knows himself, knows his Lord." From this one may understand either that one is not able to know and attain, which is one meaning, or that gnosis is possible. According to the first [interpretation] one cannot know oneself and cannot, therefore, know one's Lord, while, according to the second, one may know oneself and therefore one's Lord. Although Muhammad was the most obvious evidence of his Lord, every part of the Cosmos is a clue to its origin, which is its Lord, so understand.

Women were made beloved to him and he had great affection for them because the whole always is drawn toward its part.

* * *

Then God drew forth from him a being in his own image, called woman, and because she appears in his own image, the man feels a deep longing for her, as something yearns for itself while she feels longing for him as one longs for that place to which one belongs. Thus, women were made beloved to him, for God loves that which He has created in His own image and to which He made His angels prostrate, in spite of their great power, rank and lofty nature. From that stemmed the affinity [between God and man], and the [divine] image is the greatest, most glorious and perfect [example of] affinity. That is because it is a syzygy that polarizes the being of the Reality, just as woman, by her coming into being, polarizes humanity, making of it a syzygy. Thus we have a ternary, God, man, and woman, the man yearning for his Lord Who is his origin, as woman yearns for man. His Lord made women dear to him, just as God loves that which is in His own image. Love arises only for that from which one has one's being, so that man loves that from which he has his being, which is the Reality, which is why he says, "were made beloved to me," and not "I love," directly from himself. His love is for his Lord in Whose image he is, this being so even as regards his love for his wife, since he loves her through God's love for him, after the divine manner. When a man loves a woman, he seeks union with her, that is to say the most complete union possible in love, and there is in the elemental sphere no greater union than that between the sexes. It is [precisely] because such desire pervades all his parts that man is commanded to perform the major ablution. Thus the purification is total, just as his annihilation in her was

total at the moment of consummation. God is jealous of his servant that he should find pleasure in any but Him, so He purifies him by the ablution, so that he might once again behold Him in the one in whom he was annihilated, since it is none other than He Whom he sees in her.

When man contemplates the Reality in woman he beholds [Him] in a passive aspect, while when he contemplates Him in himself, being that from which woman is manifest, he beholds Him in an active aspect. When, however, he contemplates Him in himself, without any regard to what has come from him, he beholds Him as passive to Himself directly. However his contemplation of the Reality in woman is the most complete and perfect, because in this way he contemplates the Reality in both active and passive mode, while by contemplating the Reality only in himself, he beholds Him in a passive mode particularly.

Because of this the Apostle loved women by reason of [the possibility of] perfect contemplation of the Reality in them. Contemplation of the Reality without formal support is not possible, since God, in His Essence, is far beyond all need of the Cosmos. Since, therefore, some form of support is necessary, the best and most perfect kind is the contemplation of God in women. The greatest union is between man and woman, corresponding as it does to the turning of God toward the one He has created in His own image, to make him His vicegerent, so that He might behold Himself in him. Accordingly, He shaped him, balanced him, and breathed His spirit into him, which is His Breath, so that his outer aspect is creaturely, while his inner aspect is divine. Because of this He describes it [the spirit] as being the disposer of this human structure by which God *disposes of things from the heaven,* which is elevation, *to the earth,* which is the lowest of the low, being the lowest of the elements.

He calls them women [*nisā'*], a word that has no singular form. The Apostle therefore said, "Three things have been made beloved to me in this world, women . . . ," and not "woman," having regard to the fact that they came into being after him [man]. Indeed, the word *nus'ah* means "coming after." He says, *The postponed month* [*nasī'*] *is an increase in unbelief,* as also selling by *nasī'ah,* that is, "by postponement." Thus he says "women." He loves them only because of their [lower] rank and their being the repository of passivity. In relation to him they are as the Universal Nature is to God in which He revealed the forms of the Cosmos by directing toward it the divine Will and Command, which, at the level of elemental forms, is symbolized by conjugal union, [spiritual] concentration in the realm of luminous spirits, and the ordering of premises toward a conclusion [in the realm of thought], all of which correspond to the consummation of the Primordial Singularity in all these aspects.

Whoever loves women in this way loves with a divine love, while he whose love for them is limited to natural lust lacks all [true] knowledge of that desire. For such a one she is mere form, devoid of spirit, and even though that form be indeed imbued with spirit, it is absent for one who approaches his wife or some other woman solely to have his pleasure of her, without realizing Whose pleasure [really] is. Thus, he does not know himself [truly], just as a stranger does not know him until he reveals his identity to him. As they say,

They are right in supposing that I am in love,
Only they know not with whom I am in love.

Such a man is [really] in love with pleasure itself and, in consequence, loves its repository which is woman, the real truth and meaning of the act being lost on him. If he knew the truth, he would know Whom it is he is enjoying and Who it is Who is the enjoyer; then he would be perfected.

Just as woman [ontologically] is of a lower rank than man, according to His saying, *Men enjoy a rank above them,* so also is the creature inferior in rank to the One who fashioned him in his image, despite his being made in His image. By virtue of the superiority by which He is distinguished from him, He is above all need of the Cosmos and is the primary agent, the form or image being an agent only in a secondary sense, since the image [man] does not have the primacy, which belongs to God. The eternal essences are similarly distinguished according to their ranks, and the gnostic allots to everything its proper due. Thus it is that Muhammad's love for women derives from the divine love and because God *Gives to everything He has created* what is its due, essentially. He gives to them according to a merit fixed in the [eternally predisposed] essence of that which is deserving.

He places women first because they are the repository of passivity, just as the Universal Nature, by its form, comes before those things that derive their being from her. In reality, Nature is the Breath of the Merciful in which are unfolded the forms of the higher and lower Cosmos, because of the pervasion of the expressed Breath in the primordial Substance, particularly in the realm of the celestial bodies, its flow being different in respect of the existence of the luminous spirits and accidents.

Then the Apostle goes on to give precedence to the feminine over the masculine, intending to convey thereby a special concern with and experience of women. Thus he says *thalāth* [three] and not *thalāthah*, which is used for numbering masculine nouns. This is remarkable, in that he also mentions perfume, which is a masculine noun, and the Arabs usually make the masculine gender prevail. Thus one would say, "The Fatimahs and Zaid went out [using the third person masculine plural]," and not the third person feminine plural. In this way they give preference to the masculine noun, even if there is only one such noun together with several feminine nouns. Now, although the Apostle was an Arab, he is here giving special attention to the significance of the love enjoined on him, seeing that he himself did not choose that love. It was God Who taught him what he knew not, and God's bounty on him was abundant. He therefore gave precedence to the feminine over the masculine by saying *thalāth*. How knowledgeable was the Apostle concerning [spiritual] realities and how great was his concern for proper precedence.

Furthermore, he made the final term [prayer] correspond to the first [women] in its femininity, placing the masculine term [perfume] between them. He begins with "women" and ends with "prayer," both of which are feminine nouns, [the masculine noun] perfume coming in between them, as is the case with its existential being, since man is placed between the Essence [a feminine noun] from which he is manifested, and woman who is manifested from him. Thus he is between two feminine entities, the one substantively feminine, the other feminine in reality, women being feminine in reality, while prayer is not. Perfume is placed between them as Adam is situated between the Essence, which is the source of all existence, and Eve, whose existence stems from him. [Other terms] such as *sifah* [attribute] and *qudrah* [capability] are feminine. Indeed, whatever school of thought you adhere to, you will find feminine terms prominent. Even the Causalists say that God is the "Cause" [*'illah*] of the Cosmos, and *'illah* is feminine. As for the wisdom of perfume and his putting it after "women," it is because of the aromas of generation in women, the most delightful of perfumes being [experienced] within the embrace of the beloved, as they say in the well-known saying.

[From *Bezels of Wisdom,* pp. 272–79.]

RŪMĪ

Rūmī (1207–1273), the great mystical poet of Persia, was also the founder of the Mevlevis, the Sufi order of dervishes well known for their whirling and circling dances which Rūmī created out of his ecstatic experiences.

Like many Sufis, Rūmī uses the passionate love of a man and woman and the agony of their separation to express love for and union with God. In Rūmī's mystical vision everything comes from and is of God; therefore union with the beloved, whoever she or he may be, can lead to union with God.

Love in Absence

How should not I mourn, like night, without His day
  and the favour of His day-illuming countenance?
His unsweetness is sweet to my soul: may my soul
  be sacrificed to the Beloved who grieves my heart!
I am in love with grief and pain for the sake of pleas-
  ing my peerless King.
Tears shed for His sake are pearls, though people think
  they are tears.
I complain of the Soul of my soul, but in truth I am
  not complaining: I am only telling.
My heart says it is tormented by Him, and I have long
  been laughing at its poor pretence.
Do me right, O Glory of the righteous, O Thou Who
  art the dais, and I the threshold of Thy door!
Where are threshold and dais in reality? Where the
  Beloved is, where are "we" and "I"?
O Thou Whose soul is free from "we" and "I", O Thou
  Who art the essence of the spirit in men and
  women,
When men and women become one, Thou art that
  One; when the units are wiped out, lo, Thou art
  that Unity.
Thou didst contrive this "I" and "we" in order to play
  the game of worship with Thyself,
That all "I"s and "thou"s might become one soul and
  at last be submerged in the Beloved.
  [From *Rūmī: Poet and Mystic,* pp. 33–34.]

"The Marriage of True Minds"

Happy the moment when we are seated in the palace,
  thou and I,
With two forms and with two figures but with one
  soul, thou and I.

The colours of the grove and the voices of the birds
  will bestow immortality
At the time when we shall come into the garden, thou
  and I.
The stars of Heaven will come to gaze upon us:
We shall show them the moon herself, thou and I.
Thou and I, individuals no more, shall be mingled
  in ecstasy,
Joyful and secure from foolish babble, thou and I.
All the bright-plumed birds of Heaven will devour
  their hearts with envy
In the place where we shall laugh in such a fashion,
  thou and I.
This is the greatest wonder, that thou and I, sitting
  here in the same nook,
Are at this moment both in 'Irāq and Khorāsān, thou
  and I.
  [From *Rūmī: Poet and Mystic,* p. 35.]

The Love of Woman

If you rule your wife outwardly, yet inwardly you are
  ruled by her whom you desire,
This is characteristic of Man: in other animals love
  is lacking, and that shows their inferiority.
The Prophet said that woman prevails over the wise,
  while ignorant men prevail over her; for in them
  the fierceness of the animal is immanent.
Love and tenderness are human qualities, anger and
  lust are animal qualities.
Woman is a ray of God; she is not the earthly beloved.
  She is creative: you might say she is not created.
  [From *Rūmī: Poet and Mystic,* p. 44.]

A Shī'īte Women's Ritual

  The following excerpt is one version of the tale that is told at the beginning of the *Sofreh,* a woman-centered and woman-controlled food ritual practiced by Iranian Shī'īte women. The tale explains the origin of the ritual. It begins with an evil step-mother who encourages her husband to abandon his daughter, which he does. The girl prays for help and eventually comes across three divine women (*houris*) who are cooking a soup. Participants in the *sofreh* ritual identify two of these women as daughters of Muḥammad, but Muḥammad's actual daughter Fāṭima, so important to the Shī'ī, is evoked when these three women tell the girl she must beg the ingredients for the soup from the seven Fatimehs. In other words, the woman who wants to host this ritual must beg the ingredients from homes in which a woman named Fāṭima lives. The women in these homes will then attend the *sofreh.* As the story continues it dramatizes the helplessness of the girl and her eventual vindication and attainment of a measure of control over her own life and the lives of her husband and mother-in-law by virtue of her connection to these three supernatural beings. In effect, the story and the ritual sacralize women's work (cooking), build solidarity between women (by the sharing of the ritual) and establish connections with these three powerful female beings or powerful Muslim saints. The purpose of the ritual is to establish a relationship with a supernatural being by having him or her accept the food offerings of the *sofreh*, thereby obligating him- or herself to be helpful to the hostess and other female participants. Such supernatural assistance is usually sought for healing the sick, curing infertility, success in marriage, etc.

The Story of the Sofreh of Bibi Hur, Bibi Nur, and Bibi Sehshoenbeh

This appendix is a full translation of the narrative included in the description of the rite, in Ibrahim Shokurzadeh's *'Aeqayed o Rosum-e 'Ameh-ye Moerdom-e Khorassan* (Tehran, 1346 A.H.), pp. 29–32. Shokur-zadeh does not quote any single informant, nor does he specify to what extent the text he gives has been edited from one or more oral performances. Lack of information as to the exact provenance and status of the text discourages fine-grained analysis of its contents; nonetheless it is presented in its entirety for the sake of details that contribute further to the themes discussed in general terms in the body of this chapter.

Once there was, once there was not. Long ago there was a man with one daughter. His wife died, and the girl was motherless. In order not to be alone, the man took another wife. His new wife was very cruel and mean toward the girl and had no interest in her, and because the woman was of bad character, she thought about getting rid of her. In order to do this, one day she pretended to be sick and said to her husband, "Your daughter is very inauspicious, her presence in this house has no felicity or good omen for me. If you want me to recover from this illness, and be healthy, you must go as soon as possible and abandon her in the desert for the wolves to eat." This ignorant man, who was very partial to his second wife, saw no alternative to obedience. He put the girl on a horse and took her to a spot very far off in the desert. There he put her down, asleep, under a tree, and returned to the city. Some hours later the girl awoke and called her father, and heard no answer. Solitary and alone she ran in all directions. In a panic, she sought her father, not knowing that her ignoble father had left her in the desert and gone, to let her feed the wolves. Little by little night came on. The girl, out of fear of predatory animals, climbed a tree and stayed there till morning. At dawn she climbed down, put her faith in God, and set out. Tearfully she wandered in all directions, begging God and his Prophet for her deliverance. She walked and walked, till she arrived at a wood, and there she suddenly spied a white tent.

She went up to it and saw three very beautiful women (houris) there, sitting beside a spring, cooking soup, and they had also set a bowl of water down beside the soup pot. She stepped forward and greeted them. The women, who were Bibi Hur, Bibi Nur, and the third, Bibi Sehshaenbeh, politely returned her greeting and asked about her condition. The girl explained her situation to them. After the three holy houris heard her story, they said to her, "If you wish to see repose and reach your goal, make a vow that you will cook the soup of Bibi Hur and Bibi Nur and Bibi Sehshaenbeh." The girl said, "How is this soup cooked?" The houris answered, "Thus, that if you gain your wish, you go and beg from seven Fatimehs a little flour and chick-peas and dried beans and lentils and mung beans, and cook a soup from that, and distribute it to the women of the quarter." Then they taught the girl the manner of cooking the soup and the customs for laying the *sofreh* and the other customs for that vow, and then suddenly disappeared from view. The girl was cheered and vowed to herself that if she were delivered from this wood and free of her stepmother's grip, and gained a comfortable existence, she would lay a *sofreh* for Bibi Hur and Bibi Nur and with this in mind she said to herself,

"Oh, Lord, grant my plea,
From my stepmother's trap set me free."

She had not even finished the verse when she suddenly saw three riders appear from afar, approaching her. One of them was the son of the king of that country, and the other two were the sons of the vizier and the chief justice. As soon as the prince's glance fell on the girl, he fell in love with her, not with one heart but with a hundred. He came forward and said to the girl, "Oh, girl, have you any water that we could drink? We have come far and are thirsty." The girl said "Yes," and took the bowl of water from beside the soup pot and gave it to the prince. When the bowl was empty, she filled it with cold water from the spring and gave that to the prince. The prince asked, "What is the wisdom in this, that you first gave us warm water, then cold?" The girl said, "At first you were freshly arrived from the road and your bodies were hot. I gave you warm water to quench your thirst somewhat, and then I gave you cold, to completely remove your heat and thirst." The prince was very pleased by the ready retort and understanding and accomplishment of the girl. He set her up behind him on the horse and took her to the palace and married her according to custom, and thus the girl's fortune turned.

One day the girl recalled her vow, that whenever she achieved comfort and wealth, she would cook the soup for Bibi Sehshaenbeh. She fell to thinking how she could fulfill her vow as soon as possible. But because she was the daughter-in-law of the king and could not go and beg from seven Fatimehs the flour and the rest of the ingredients, of necessity she put a little flour and chick-peas and lentils in seven of the niches around the room, then put on a *chador* and went "begging" from one niche to the next. At this moment the queen saw her, and went directly and gave the information to her son, and said, "Dear boy, if you want me to hold my milk lawful to you, throw this beggarly girl out! See how lowly she is, that even now she cannot renounce her old beggarly ways!"

The prince came to the girl immediately, to see if this was true. When he came in, he saw that the girl had put a pot on to boil and was making soup. He was very annoyed and gave the pot a good kick, and tipped over the soup. The girl wept and cursed him. The next day the prince went hunting with the vizier's son and the judge's son. The vizier's son and the judge's son carelessly got lost. However much the prince searched for them, he could not find them. Of

necessity he finally turned his horse back toward the city. As he rode along, lost in thought, suddenly he heard a voice from behind him. He turned around, but there was no one there. First he was afraid, then he said to himself, "I must have been mistaken." When he had gone a few more steps, the same sound came to his ears. Again he turned his head and again no one was there. At this moment his glance fell on the rear of the horse, and he saw the severed heads of the vizier's son and the judge's son tied on behind him, one on each side. In a panic he whipped up the horse and raced back to the city with all possible speed. The king assumed that he had killed the vizier's son and the judge's son and ordered him imprisoned. Some days later the queen wanted to go to see her son, and the girl said, "Tell your son, 'If you had not kicked my soup pot, you would not have suffered this affliction. Now if you can find the faith to make a vow to prepare the soup of Bibi Sehshaenbeh, be assured that you will be released from prison.'" The moment the prince heard this from his mother, he knew that this unjust accusation was on account of the girl's curse, and he ordered his mother to go immediately and prepare the pot of soup. The soup was not even ready when the news came that the vizier's son and the judge's son had been found. Everyone was happy and rejoiced, and the prince was released from prison and vowed to himself that after this he would have perfect faith in the soup of Bibi Hur and Bibi Nur and Bibi Sehshaenbeh.

[From *Gender and Religion*, pp. 56–59.]

FOLKTALES

The following tale shows the value placed on clever women.

The Clever Minister's Daughter

A king once wanted to test the sharpness of his minister, the *wazir* who stood on his right. He said, "Here are three questions:

What is the most precious of all stones?
What is the sweetest of all sounds?
What, after God, gives us life?

Then he said, "Bring me the answers by tomorrow morning or I shall have your head."

The minister went home, his face yellow as wax. His daughter came out to meet him, and said, "Are you ill, O my father?" "No," said the minister, "but unless I find the answer to the king's three questions by tomorrow morning, I shall die." "You, who are the king's first minister, who stands on his right, are frightened by three questions? Tell them to me; maybe I can find the answers." And he told her. His daughter

listened, then said, "It is not difficult. Tell the king: the most precious of all stones is the millstone, the sweetest of all sounds is the call to prayer, and the most life-giving after God is water." And so with the help of his daughter, the minister escaped with his life.

But the king wanted to challenge his *wazir* further. He gave him a tray made of gold that held a golden sculpted hen and her golden chicks, all pecking seeds of pearl. "Guess the worth of this golden hen with all her train, and you may keep it," he said. "If you fail to find the answer, you lose it and your head." The minister immediately went to repeat the king's riddle to his daughter. "Don't worry, Father," she said. "When the king questions you, say,

More than the golden hen with all her train—
More than your minister with all his brain—
Is the worth of a shower of April rain.

Astonished at his minister's wit, the king thought of

a new way to trip him up. He gave the *wazir* a lamb and said, "Can you feed me a supper off this lamb and earn me money with this lamb, yet bring it back alive to me tomorrow morning?" This time the poor minister went home with the lamb in his arms and despair in his heart.

His daughter laughed to hear his troubles. She said, "Geld the lamb and I can do it easily." When he had done so, she cut up the gelded parts and roasted them on a skewer over the fire. Next she sheared the lamb's wool and sold it in the market for ten pennies. In the morning she sent her father off with the skewer of meat in one hand and the price of the wool in the other and the lamb trotting on the end of a rope behind him.

The king was impressed. "I shall not ask any questions again," he said, "except this last. How did you find the answers to my riddles?" The minister felt some fear, but also pride. He confessed that it was not he but his daughter who had solved the riddles. The king gave a shout of delight and said, "That is the very woman I have been looking for to be my wife."

And so the first minister continued to stand at the king's right shoulder, and now he was also father of the queen.

[From *Arab Folk Tales,* pp. 354–55.]

The following tale points to the importance of observing God's law, in this case the giving of alms (one of the five pillars of Islam).

Anecdote of a Charitable Woman

It is related that a certain King said to the people of his dominions, if any one of you give aught in alms, I will assuredly cut off his hand. So all the people refrained from alms-giving, and none could bestow upon another. And it happened that a beggar came to a woman one day, and hunger tormented him, and he said to her, Give me somewhat as an alms.—How, said she, can I bestow an alms upon thee when the King cutteth off the hand of every one who doth so? But he rejoined, I conjure thee by God (whose name be exalted!) that thou give me an alms. So when he conjured her by God, she was moved with pity for him, and bestowed upon him two cakes of bread. And the news reached the King; whereupon he gave orders to bring her before him; and when she came, he cut off her hands. And she returned to her house.

Then the King, after a while, said to his mother, I desire to marry: therefore, marry me to a comely woman. And she replied, There is, among our female slaves, a woman than whom none more beautiful existeth; but she hath a grievous defect.—And what is it? he asked. She answered, She is maimed of the two hands. The King however said, I desire to see her. Wherefore she brought her to him, and when he saw her, he was tempted by her beauty, and married her. And that woman was she who bestowed upon the beggar the two cakes of bread, and whose hands were cut off on that account. But when he had married her, her fellow-wives envied her, and wrote to the King, telling him that she was unchaste: and she had given birth to a son. And the King wrote a letter to his mother, in which he commanded her to go forth with her to the desert, and to leave her there, and return.

His mother therefore did so: she took her forth to the desert, and returned. And that woman began to weep for the misfortune that had befallen her, and to bewail violently, with a wailing not to be exceeded. And while she was walking, with the child upon her neck, she came to a river, and kneeled down to drink, because of the violence of the thirst that had affected her from her walking and fatigue and grief; and when she stooped her head, the child fell into the water. So she sat weeping violently for her child; and while she wept, lo, there passed by her two men, who said to her, What causeth thee to weep? She answered, I had a child upon my neck, and he fell into the water. And they said, Dost thou desire that we rescue him, and restore him to thee? She answered, Yes. And upon this they supplicated God (whose name be exalted!), and the child came forth to her safe and unhurt. Then they said to her, Dost thou desire that God should restore to thee thy hands as they were? She answered, Yes. And they supplicated God (whose perfection be extolled, and whose name be exalted!); whereupon her hands returned to her in the most perfect state. After this they said to her, Knowest thou who we are?— God, she replied, is all-knowing. And they said, We are thy two cakes of bread which thou gavest as an alms to the beggar, and which alms occasioned the cutting off of thy hands. Therefore praise God (whose name be exalted!) that He hath restored to thee thy hand and thy child.—And she praised God (whose name be exalted!), and glorified Him.

[From *A Thousand and One Nights,* pp. 455–56.]

The following story blends two popular motifs of Islamic folk literature, the woman warrior and the Christian woman who abjures her faith for the love of a Muslim man.

The Maiden Champion

There lived once in Darishmana two brothers, Fakih Ahmed and Khidder, who had suffered much from the hostility of the Bulbassis, the most powerful people of Pizhder. Fakih Ahmed, who was of a bold and proud spirit, quitted his village in disgust, swearing never to return to it unless he should be in a position to avenge himself. He went to Constantinople, and entered the service of the Sultan.

It so happened that the sultan was at that time at war with the English (or Franks). In those days battles were generally decided by single combat. A champion had come forth from the Frankish host who for five days had kept the field against the flower of the Turkish chivalry, all of whom he had successively overthrown and slain. Fakih Ahmed volunteered to meet this redoubtable foe, upon which the Sultan sent for him, asked him concerning his country, and being satisfied with his appearance, allowed him to undertake the adventure, after first supplying him with a suitable horse and arms. He ran his course, and overthrew the Frankish knight. Upon alighting to cut off his head, he found, to his great astonishment, that his fallen enemy was a young maiden, who besought him to spare her life and she would marry him. He brought her back to the Turkish camp in triumph, and upon the Sultan's asking him what reward he should bestow upon him, he claimed and obtained a *firman*, constituting him Bey, and bestowing on him in perpetuity the village and lands of Darishmana. In this he displayed either his modesty or his ignorance, for, had he claimed the whole of Kūrdistan, he would have obtained it.

Fully satisfied, however, with his new acquisition, he returned in triumph to his native place with his bride, Keighan, by whom he had subsequently two children, Baba Sūliman and Boodakh Keighan. He had frequent contests with the Bulbassis, whom he succeeded in reducing to considerable order.

One day, however, when he was absent, a large party of them came down on a predatory excursion. His wife, Keighan, sallied forth alone, and put the whole of them, amounting to some four or five hundred horsemen, to flight, killing a great number. She then summoned together the people of Darishmana, mounted her horse, and addressed them as follows:

"Men of Darishmana, Fakih Ahmed spared my life when I was in his power, and I have this day requited the service, which was all I wanted or waited for. Now tell Fakih Ahmed what you have seen, and also that I am gone where he shall see me no more. Tell him that I charge him not to follow me, for it would be in vain, and I should do him harm, which, God knows, I would not willingly do." So saying, she turned her horse, and was out of sight in a moment.

As might be supposed, Fakih Ahmed was, on his return, much astonished to hear what had happened, and also deeply grieved at the loss of his beloved Keighan, whom he resolved to follow in spite of her prohibition. He came up with her in the valley of Khidheran, which is in Pizhder, and besought her to return with him.

"It is impossible," she replied. "You are a Moslem, I am a Frank. I go to the land of my fathers. Farewell. Come not near me, or I shall harm you!"

As the enamoured Fakih persisted, she raised her spear, and thrust him through the shoulder. He fell, and she galloped off. But she had not gone far when she bethought herself that she had made but a poor requital for his mercy to her when her life was at his disposal, and that, though he was a Moslem, he was the father of her children. She therefore relented, turned back, and finding him still breathing, applied to his wound a powerful ointment which placed him out of danger till he should receive succour. She then set off again. But the ardent lover and husband, as soon as he had recovered from his wound, nothing abashed by the rough usage he had received at Keighan's hands, still persisted in his design of following and recovering her, and in pursuit of her reached Frenghistan. At nightfall he came to a large city, where he heard the sound of revelry. The *mehter khana* (band) was playing, the *mashalls* (torches) were lighted, and all the other preparations for a *toey* (nuptial feast) were going forward.

Uncertain what to do, or where to take up his abode for the night, he resolved to leave it to chance and remain where his horse might stop. He accordingly gave him the reins, and the animal stopped before the house of an old woman. After making some difficulties, the woman consented to receive Fakih Ahmed as her guest, and he then inquired of her what was the occasion of all the rejoicings. She replied that the daughter of the king had gone to war with the Moslems, and had just returned after having been missing for several years, and also that she was then going to be married to her cousin. Fakih Ahmed begged his hostess to procure him admission as a spectator to the nuptial feast, which she at length agreed to do, provided he would allow her to dress him in woman's attire. This he consented to, and, favoured by his disguise, he contrived to be close at hand during the first interview between the fair Keighan and her proposed spouse.

When the lady came forth, the ungracious bridegroom immediately saluted her with a box on the ear, saying:

"Thou hast been a prisoner in the hands of Moslems; thou hast been dishonoured; and darest thou show thyself before me?"

The bride, in her anguish, exclaimed in the Kūrdish language, which had become familiar to her, "Oh,

Fakih Ahmed, would that thou wert here!"

The person thus invoked immediately rushed forward, slew the bridegroom, and escaped with his wife to Constantinople, where the Sultan bestowed upon him an addition to his former grant. The couple then returned to Pizhder, where they lived happily all their days. Before Fakih Ahmed died, he comple[t]ely subjugated the districts of Pizhder, Mergeh, and Mawutt, and was succeeded by his eldest son, Baba Sūliman, the ancestor of the present princes of Sūlimanieh, who conquered the remaining districts of that part of Kūrdistan now under their authority.

[From *The Women of Turkey and Their Folk-lore,* pp. 174–78.]

Sources

Arab Folk-Tales, trans. and ed. Inea Bushnaq. New York: Pantheon Books, 1986.

The Bezels of Wisdom, by Ibn Al-'Arabi, translation and introduction by R. W. J. Austin, preface by Titus Burckhardt. New York: Paulist Press, 1980.

Gender and Religion: On the Complexity of Symbols, ed. Caroline Walker Bynum, Stevan Harrell, and Paula Richman. Boston: Beacon Press, 1986.

The Life of Muhammad: A Translation of Ibn Ishāq's Sīrat Rasūl Allah, by A. Guillaume. Karachi: Oxford University Press, 1967.

The Koran Interpreted, trans. by A. J. Arberry. New York: Macmillan, 1976.

Muslim Saints and Mystics: Episodes from the Tadhkirat al-Auliya' ('Memorial of the Saints') by Farid al-Din Attar, translated by A. J. Arberry. London: Arkana, 1990.

Ottoman Poems, translated into English verse in the original forms, with introduction, biographical notices, and notes by E. J. W. Gibb. London: N. Trübner & Co., 1882.

A Reader on Islam, ed. Arthur Jeffery. Paris: Mouton, 1962.

Readings from the Mystics of Islām, translations from Arabic and Persian by Margaret Smith. London: Luzac & Company, 1950.

Rūmī: Poet and Mystic, Selections from His Writings, translated from the Persian with introduction and notes by Reynold A. Nicholson. London: Allen & Unwin, 1950.

The Sacred Journey: Being Pilgrimage to Makkah, by Ahmad Kamal. New York: Duell, Sloan and Pearce, 1961.

Sufis of Andalusia: The Rūḥ al-quds and al-Durrat al-fākhirah of Ibn 'Arabī, translated with introduction and notes by R. W. J. Austin, with a foreword by Martin Lings. Berkeley and Los Angeles: University of California Press, 1977.

Tales of the Dervishes: Teaching-stories of the Sufi Masters over the Past Thousand Years, by Idries Shah. New York: E. P. Dutton, 1970.

Themes of Islamic Civilization, edited by John Alden Williams. Berkeley, Los Angeles, and London: University of California Press, 1971.

The Thousand and One Nights, a new translation from the Arabic, with copious notes by Edward William Lane. Volume 2. London: Chatto and Windus, 1883.

Translations of Eastern Poetry and Prose, by Reynold A. Nicholson. London: Curzon Press; New Jersey: Humanities Press, 1987.

The Translation of the Meanings of Sahih Al-Bukhari, volume 1, by Muhammad Muhsin Khan. Chicago: Kazi Publications Inc., 1976.

The Women of Turkey and Their Folk-Lore, by Lucy M. J. Garnett. London: David Nutt, 1891.

Bibliography

Introductory and General Works on Islam

The Encyclopaedia of Islam, ed. H. A. R. Gibb, et al., 4 vols. (Leiden: Brill, 1954–1978).

Hodgson, Marshall G. S., *The Venture of Islam,* 3 vols. (Chicago: University of Chicago Press, 1974).

Schimmel, Annemarie, *Mystical Dimensions of Islam* (Chapel Hill, NC: University of North Carolina Press, 1975).

Works on Women and Islam

Beck, Lois, and Nikki Keddie, eds., *Women in the Muslim World* (Cambridge, Mass.: Harvard University Press, 1978).

Betteridge, Anne H., "Domestic Observances: Muslim Practices," in *The Encyclopedia of Religion,* ed. Eliade. 4: 404–407.

Fernea, Robert A., and Elizabeth W. Fernea, "Variation in Religious Observance among Islamic Women," in *Scholars, Saints, and Sufis: Muslim Religious Institutions in the Middle East since 1500* (Berkeley, CA: University of California Press, 1972).

Sabbah, Fatna A., *Woman in the Muslim Unconscious* (New York: Pergamon Press, 1984).

Smith, Jane I., "Islam," in *Women in World Religions,* ed. Arvind Sharma (Albany, NY: State University of New York Press, 1987).

———, "Women, Religion and Social Change in Early Islam," in *Women, Religion, and Social Change,* ed. Yvonne Yazbeck Haddad and Ellison Banks Findly (Albany, NY: State University of New York Press, 1985).

Smith, Margaret, *Rabi'a the Mystic and Her Fellow-Saints in Islam* (Cambridge: Cambridge University Press, 1928).

Stowasser, Barbara Freyer, "The Status of Women in Early Islam," in *Muslim Women,* ed. Freda Hussain (New York: St. Martin's Press, 1984).

ANCIENT NEAR EAST, GREECE, AND ROME

Ancient Near East

INTRODUCTION

The worldview of the two great river civilizations of the Ancient Near East, Egypt and Mesopotamia, are suggested in the patterns of the rivers that made their lives possible. On the one hand there is the Nile, whose annual inundations were predictable and a continuing source of life because of the fertile soil the waters left on the plain as they receded. The Tigris and Euphrates rivers, on the other hand, were totally unpredictable in their floodings, which were often destructive of life and property. Of equal significance, ancient Egyptian civilization lasted for three thousand years (c. 3100−323 B.C.E.) and fought most of its wars outside of Egypt while the early Mesopotamian civilization, Sumeria, was conquered first by the Akkadians (c. 2350 B.C.E.) and then by the Semitic peoples (c. 1765 B.C.E.), who created the empires of Babylonia and Assyria, both of which were tormented by centuries of warfare. Consequently, the Egyptians felt themselves to be a secure and elect people, while the Mesopotamians were pessimistic and wary.

Historical information for the early periods of these civilizations is sketchy but some conclusions can be drawn. First of all, women seem to have enjoyed a higher status at the beginning of civilization than they do in later historical periods. In other words, in the early stages of city life in the ancient Near East (c. 3000 B.C.E.), in both Egypt and Sumeria, women had the same legal rights as men: They inherited and traded property, made contracts, gave testimony, held prominent positions and, in general, were full economic participants in their societies. The status of Egyptian women, which had been in a slow, continual decline, was sharply reduced after Alexander's conquest of Egypt in 323 B.C.E., while in Mesopotamia the status of women began to decline as early as the conquest of Sumeria by the Akkadians and continued to decline under the military societies of Babylonia and Assyria.

EGYPT

In ancient Egypt, the treatment of women in death reveals a great deal about the treatment of women in life. Egyptian religion begins with the death rituals of the god-king which assure his immortality. In these rituals the body is preserved and buried in elaborate structures along with the possessions the dead might need in the afterlife. Underlying these practices is the common idea in many cultures that unless the dead are properly attended to they will return to the realm of the living. The central myth of Egyptian religious life is that of the dead god-king Osiris and the restorative powers of the goddess-queen Isis. In the Old Kingdom (2686-2181 B.C.E.), which saw the development of pyramids as royal tombs, royal women had tombs of their own which were quite similar to those of royal men. The mothers of kings were particularly honored by memorial cults and records listing the names of the mothers of kings go back for centuries, affirming the importance of matrilineal descent. These records also list professional titles of women who held responsible positions in both the workplace and in religious life. Even so, women's tombs and mummies are far fewer than those of men and nonroyal women are inevitably referred to in relational terms to their husbands.

During this and the Middle Kingdom period (c. 2030-1786 B.C.E.) a great number of women were priestesses, some of whom functioned in important administrative positions. One important priesthood was that of the goddess Hathor, which functioned as a protector of the kingship (the queen was thought to be the embodiment of Hathor), but no women achieved leadership positions in it. There were also priestesses for male gods, and women played various important roles in funerary rituals as priests, mourners, dancers, singers, and as imitators of the sister goddesses Isis and Nephthys (important deities in death rituals). These priestesses could be married or single. The status of women, especially in religious life, started to decline toward the end of this period although the New Kingdom (1567-1085 B.C.E.) saw an increase in the status of royal women which is clearly demonstrated by the impressive reign of the female pharaoh, Hatshepsut. Generally women still have positions in the temples, but fewer of them reach the higher positions.

Over thousands of years and at different cultic centers throughout the kingdom Egyptian religion wore many faces. Much of what is known is based on accidental finds and refers to the royal cults, not popular religion. None of the many different priesthoods attempted to systematize the religious life of the people into a coherent whole. They were satisfied with the literature that pertained to the deities they worshiped and they felt no need to reconcile this literature with the literature of other deities. Consequently, religious life remained fluid and diverse. New elements were added while old beliefs were retained in a complex web of images and concepts that tended toward multiplicity rather than simplicity. All that can be said with certainty is that the ancient Egyptians were a deeply religious and totally undogmatic people, who worshiped many goddesses and gods and who spent a great deal of time and effort in preparing for the afterlife.

CREATION

The creation stories of the ancient Egyptians emphasize the role of male deities. In the following myth the god Atum rises out of a primeval watery chaos (Nu) which is also male. Atum begins creation by masturbating, and when he weeps, human beings are created out of his tears.

I was . . . the creator of what came into being, the creator of what came into being all; after my coming into being many [were] the things which came into being coming forth from my mouth. Not existed heaven, not existed earth, not had been created the things of the earth, (i.e., plants), and creeping things . . . I raised up them from out of Nu (i.e., the primeval abyss of water) from a state of inactivity. . . .

* * *

I . . . had union with my clenched hand, I joined myself in an embrace with my shadow, I poured seed into my mouth, I sent forth issue in the form of Shu, I sent forth moisture in the form of Tefnut. . . . That is from out of myself [and after] I came into being in earth. . . . Were raised up therefore Shu [and] Tefnut in the inert watery mass wherein they were, brought they to me my eye in their train. After therefore I had united my members I wept over them [and] came into being men and women from the tears [which] came forth from my eye.

[From *The Gods of the Egyptians,* 1:308-312.]

Isis

The multifaceted Isis is one of the most important goddesses of ancient Egypt. She was intimately connected with royal power through the pharaohs who referred to themselves as "the son of Isis." On one level, her primary myth involves a problem of royal succession when her husband/brother, the king, is killed by his brother and the kingdom is left without a legitimate heir. Isis eventually gives birth to Horus, the rightful heir, who she nurtures and protects until he is old enough to claim his father's throne. This myth reveals Isis in her role as the protector of the royal succession and therefore as the protector of the pharaohs. Though originally a royal cult that assured the pharaohs an afterlife, from quite early times Isis began to be depicted as a more general salvational goddess, one who could grant an afterlife first to nobles, who had received the proper funerary rites, and eventually to anyone who had these rites. Her powers over life and death and her knowledge of magic led to depictions of her as the goddess of wisdom. Stories about her magical abilities and her restoration of various beings to life are found throughout ancient Egyptian literature and they were frequently depicted on the walls of tombs.

Isis and Osiris

The best known story about Isis involves the murder and dismemberment of her beloved husband and brother Osiris. The various parts of his body were scattered throughout the land and Isis makes a sorrowful journey gathering them together. The last part of his body she finds is his penis which she uses to impregnate herself with their son Horus. Her mourning for and care of the dead Osiris dramatized her feelings for all her devotees who hoped for similar treatment after their deaths.

The following excerpt is taken from the fullest account of the myth of Isis and Osiris extant in Egyptian sources. It was inscribed on a limestone stela dating from the Eighteenth Dynasty (1567–1320 B.C.E.). This myth emphasizes Isis's role as protector of the pharaohs in that she guards Osiris while he is the living king, gives him new life when he is dead, and conceives a legitimate heir, their son Horus.

Hail to you, Osiris.
Lord of eternity, king of gods,
Of many names, of holy forms,
Of secret rites in temples!

★ ★ ★

The joined Two Lands adore him,
When His Majesty approaches,
Mightiest noble among nobles,
Firm of rank, of lasting rule.
Good leader of the Nine Gods,
Gracious, loving to behold,
Awe inspiring to all lands,
That his name be foremost.
All make offering to him,
The lord of remembrance in heaven and earth,
Rich in acclaim at the *wag*-feast,

Hailed in unison by the Two Lands.
The foremost of his brothers,
The eldest of the Nine Gods,
Who set Maat throughout the Two Shores,
Placed the son on his father's seat.
Lauded by his father Geb,
Beloved of his mother Nut,
Mighty when he fells the rebel,
Strong-armed when he slays his foe.
Who casts fear of him on his enemy,
Who vanquishes the evil-plotters,
Whose heart is firm when he crushes the rebels.

Geb's heir (in) the kingship of the Two Lands,
Seeing his worth he gave (it) to him,
To lead the lands to good fortune.
He placed this land into his hand,

Its water, its wind,
Its plants, all its cattle.
All that flies, all that alights,
Its reptiles and its desert game,
Were given to the son of Nut,
And the Two Lands are content with it.
Appearing on his father's throne,
Like Re when he rises in lightland,
He places light above the darkness,
He lights the shade with his plumes.
He floods the Two Lands like Aten at dawn,
His crown pierces the sky, mingles with the stars.
He is the leader of all the gods,
Effective in the word of command,
The great Ennead praises him,
The small Ennead loves him.

His sister was his guard,
She who drives off the foes,
Who stops the deeds of the disturber
By the power of her utterance.
The clever-tongued whose speech fails not,
Effective in the word of command,
Mighty Isis who protected her brother,
Who sought him without wearing.
Who roamed the land lamenting,
Not resting till she found him,

Who made a shade with her plumage,
Created breath with her wings.
Who jubilated, joined her brother,
Raised the weary one's inertness,
Received the seed, bore the heir,
Raised the child in solitude,
His abode unknown.
Who brought him when his arm was strong
Into the broad hall of Geb.

The Ennead was jubilant:
"Welcome, Son of Osiris,
Horus, firm-hearted, justified,
Son of Isis, heir of Osiris!"
The Council of Maat assembled for him
The Ennead, the All-Lord himself,
The Lords of Maat, united in her,
Who eschew wrongdoing,
They were seated in the hall of Geb,
To give the office to its lord,
The kingship to its rightful owner.
Horus was found justified,
His father's rank was given him,
He came out crowned by Geb's command,
Received the rule of the two shores.
[*Ancient Egyptian Literature,* 2:81–84.]

ISIS AND HORUS

The following excerpt reveals one of the early Egyptian stories of her ability to restore life. In the story Isis has given birth to Horus and she raises him in secrecy in a swamp. She briefly leaves him alone to go to a town for food and when she returns he has been killed by the sting of a scorpion. Isis weeps and laments but, with the help of her sister Nephthys and the god Thoth, Horus is restored to life.

I am Isis, who conceived her male child, and was heavy with Horus. A goddess I bore Horus, son of Osiris, within a nest of papyrus plants. I rejoiced over it greatly, twice, because I saw (in him) one who would answer for his father. I hid him, I concealed him having fear of his being bitten. I went to the city Am, (the people) saluted according to custom. I spent the time in seeking for the boy to make his food. I returned to embrace Horus, I found him, Horus, the beautiful one of gold, the boy, the child, he was nothing. He had bedewed the ground with the water of his eye, and with the foam of his lips; his body was motionless, his heart still, not moved the muscles of his body. I sent forth a cry. . . .

Horus was smitten by the wickedness of his brother. . . . Those who were in his service . . . (said) concerning him, "Shall Horus live for his mother?" They found where he was, and a Scorpion stung him, and the slayer of the heart had stabbed him. Placed Isis her nose in his mouth to know if had breath he who was in his coffin. She opened the wound of the heir divine, she found it possessing poison. She embraced him hurriedly and leaped about with him like a fish laid upon a fire . . . (saying) Stung is Horus, O Ra, stung is thy son. Stung is Horus, heir of heir, lord of the [pillars?] of Shu. Stung is Horus, the child of the papyrus swamp, the child in Het-ser. Stung is the child beautiful of gold. The child, the babe, he is nothing. Stung is Horus, son of Un-nefer.

Then came Nephthys weeping, she cried, going about the swamp. . . . What then is to the child Horus,

Isis? pray thou therefore to heaven so that . . . not will travel the boat of Ra (the son). . . . Sent forth Isis her cry to heaven. . . . Stood still the disk [of the sun] at her coming, not moved he on his seat. Thoth came provided with his magic power, possessing command great of *maa-kheru*.

. . . Horus, his protection is from the boat of Ra. I have come today in the boat of the disk from its place of yesterday. When the night cometh the light driveth (it) away to heal Horus for his mother Isis (and) person every who is under the knife likewise.

[*The Gods of the Egyptians*, 2:233–240.]

The Goddess Hathor

Hathor is another important and multifaceted goddess. As the goddess of fertility she is associated with sexuality and with agricultural plenty. In these ways she provides for the living, but she was also a goddess of the dead. She continued to care for her devotees in the land of the dead, renewing their lives and fulfilling their needs. However, her nature is not always benign. An early text inscribed on the walls of three royal tombs between 1465–1165 B.C.E. reveals the destructive side of her nature. Here she is depicted as the eye of the sun god Re. In this myth Re is the creator of the universe, but he is growing old and there are rebellions against him, especially by human beings. Re sends Hathor, his eye, to kill them, which she does, but Hathor wants to continue killing. Re is unable to control her directly, so he resorts to a trick; he creates a flood of beer which Hathor drinks. She gets drunk and forgets about killing. This myth was enacted at one of Hathor's festivals in which the celebrants imbibed copious quantities of alcohol. They believed Hathor's wrathful aspects could be appeased by alcohol.

It happened that . . . Re, the god who came into being by himself, when he was king of men and gods all together. Then mankind plotted something in the (very) presence of Re. Now then, his majesty — life, prosperity, health! — was old. His bones were of silver, his flesh of gold, and his hair of genuine lapis lazuli.

Then his majesty perceived the things which were being plotted against him by mankind. Then his majesty — life, prosperity, health! said to those who were in his retinue: "Pray, summon to me my Eye, Shu, Tefnut, Geb and Nut, as well as the fathers and mothers who were with me when I was in Nun [the waters of creation], as well as my god Nun also. He is to bring his court with him. Thou shalt bring them *secretly*: let not mankind see; let not their hearts escape. Thou shalt come with them to the Great House, that they may tell their plans, since the [*times*] *when* I came from Nun to the place in which I came into being."

Then these gods were brought in, and these gods [*came*] beside him, putting their heads to the ground in the presence of his majesty, so that he might make his statement in the presence of the father of the eldest, he who made mankind, the king of people. Then they said in the presence of his majesty: "Speak to us, so that we may hear it."

Then Re said to Nun: "O eldest god, in whom I

came into being, O ancestor gods, behold mankind, which came into being from my Eye — they have plotted things against me. Tell me what ye would do about it. Behold, I am seeking; I would not slay them until I had heard what ye might say about it." Then the majesty of Nun said: "My son Re, the god greater than he who made him and mightier than they who created him, sitting upon thy throne, the fear of thee is great when thy Eye is (directed) against them who scheme against thee!" Then the majesty of Re said: "Behold, they have fled into the desert, their hearts being afraid because I *might* speak to them." Then they said in the presence of his majesty: "May thy Eye be sent, that it may *catch* for thee them who scheme with evil things. (But) the Eye is not (*sufficiently*) prominent therein to smite them for thee. It should go down as Hat-Hor."

So then this goddess came and slew mankind in the desert. Then the majesty of this god said: "Welcome, Hat-Hor, who hast done for me *the deed for which I came!*" Then this goddess said: "As thou livest for me, I have prevailed over mankind, and it is pleasant in my heart!" Then the majesty of Re said: "I shall prevail over them *as a king* by diminishing them!" That is how Sekhmet came into being, the (beer)-mash of the night, to wade in their blood from Herakleopolis.

Then Re said: "Pray, summon to me swift and speedy messengers, so that they may run like the shadows of a body." Then these messengers were brought immediately. Then the majesty of this god said: "Go ye to Elephantine and bring me red ochre very abundantly." Then this red ochre was brought to him. Then the majesty of this great god caused . . . , [and He-With]-the-Side-Lock who is in Heliopolis ground up this red ochre. When further maidservants crushed barley to (make) beer, then this red ochre was added to this mash. Then (it) was like human blood. Then seven thousand jars of the beer were made. So then the majesty of the King of Upper and Lower Egypt: Re came, together with these gods, to see this beer.

Now when day broke for the slaying of mankind by the goddess at their season of going upstream, then the majesty of Re said: "How good it is! I shall protect mankind with it!" Then Re said: "Pray, carry it to the place in which she expected to slay mankind." Then the majesty of the King of Upper and Lower Egypt: Re went to work early in the depth of the night to have this sleep-maker poured out. Then the fields were filled with liquid for three palms, through the power of the majesty of this god.

Then this goddess went at dawn, and she found this (place) flooded. Then her face (looked) beautiful therein. Then she drank, and it was good in her heart. She came (back) drunken, without having perceived mankind.

[Pritchard, *The Ancient Near East,* 1:3–5.]

Hathor was also the goddess of love and in this context she was often referred to as "the Golden One" or simply as "the Gold." The following love poems, written by unnamed Egyptian women and men of the New Kingdom period (1567–1085 B.C.E.), call upon Hathor in various ways. The first is a song of praise by a man to thank Hathor for having helped him win his lover. The second and third poems are both by women, one of whom appeals to Hathor for help in her love affair while the other makes a claim that Hathor wants the affair to happen. In all these poems the lovers refer to each other as "brother" and "sister," which were terms of endearment in ancient Egypt.

I *praise* the Golden, I worship her majesty,
I extol the Lady of Heaven;
I give adoration to Hathor,
Laudations to my Mistress!
I called to her, she heard my plea,
She sent my mistress to me;
She came by herself to see me,
O great wonder that happened to me!
I was joyful, exulting, elated,
When they said: "See, she is here!"
As she came, the young men bowed,
Out of great love for her.
I make devotions to my goddess,
That she grant me my sister as gift;
Three days now that I pray to her name,
Five days since she went from me!

★ ★ ★

I *passed* before his house,
I found his door ajar;
My brother stood by his mother,
And all his brothers with him.
Love of him captures the heart
Of all who tread the path;

Splendid youth who has no peer,
Brother outstanding in virtues!
He looked at me as I passed by,
And I, by myself, rejoiced;
How my heart exulted in gladness
My brother, at your sight!
If only the mother knew my heart,
She would have understood by now;
O Golden, put it in her heart,
Then will I hurry to my brother!
I will kiss him before his companions
I would not weep before them;
I would rejoice at their understanding
That you acknowledge me!
I will make a feast for my goddess,
My heart leaps to go;
To let me see my brother tonight,
O happiness in *passing*!

★ ★ ★

My *brother* torments my heart with his voice,
He makes sickness take hold of me;
He is neighbor to my mother's house,
And I cannot go to him!
Mother is right in charging him thus:

"Give up seeing her!"
It pains my heart to think of him,
I am possessed by love of him.
Truly, he is a foolish one,
But I resemble him;
He knows not my wish to embrace him,
Or he would write to my mother.

Brother, I am promised to you
By the Gold of women!
Come to me that I see your beauty,
Father, Mother will rejoice!
My people will hail you all together,
They will hail you, O my *brother!*
[*Ancient Egyptian Literature,* 2:182–85.]

QUEEN HATSHEPSUT

Hatshepsut, the daughter of Pharaoh Thutmose I and Queen Ahmose, was one of the very few female Pharaohs to rule Egypt (1486–1468 B.C.E.). She came to the throne after the death of her husband Thutmose II as Regent for her stepson Thutmose III, but eventually she took on all the regalia and powers of the Pharaoh. She had a glorious reign in which she strengthened Egypt's position politically, militarily, and economically. Her wish was that her daughter Neferure succeed her as king but she died while still quite young and Hatshepsut accepted Thutmose III as the heir. Once Hatshepsut was dead, Thutmose III went to great lengths to have her image chiseled from the wall reliefs of the temples she had built—an act of revenge for the years she kept him from full control of the throne.

The following text was engraved on an obelisk standing 97.5 feet high erected by Hatshepsut in the temple of Anum at Karnak. In this text Hatshepsut honors her divine and human fathers, respectively the god Amun and Pharaoh Thutmose I; the obelisk was erected for the glory of Amun and to honor the memory of Thutmose. She mentions the amount of work it involved and the huge amounts of gold she used to gild it. Notice also that when she asserts herself as ruler she speaks of herself as "the son of Isis" and "the son of Nut," though elsewhere in the text she speaks of herself in feminine terms. In much the same way, Hatshepsut had herself depicted in statues, sometimes as a man and sometimes as a woman.

Speech of the Queen

I have done this with a loving heart for my father
    Amun;
Initiated in his secret of the beginning,
Acquainted with his beneficent might,
I did not forget whatever he had ordained.
My majesty knows his divinity,
I acted under his command;
It was he who led me,
I did not plan a work without his doing.
It was he who gave directions,
I did not sleep because of his temple,
I did not stray from what he commanded.
My heart was Sia [filled with understanding] before
    my father,
I entered into the plans of his heart.
I did not turn my back to city of the All-Lord,
Rather did I turn my face to it.
I know that Ipet-sut is the lightland on earth,
The august hill of the beginning,
The Sacred Eye of the All-Lord.
His favored place that bears his beauty,
That gathers in his followers.

It is the King himself who says:
I declare before the folk who shall be in the future,
Who shall observe the monument I made for my
    father,
Who shall speak in discussion,
Who shall look to posterity—
It was when I sat in the palace,
And thought of my maker,
That my heart led me to make for him
Two obelisks of electrum,
Whose summits would reach the heavens,
In the august hall of columns,
Between the two great portals of the King,
The Strong Bull, King Aakheperkare, the Horus
    triumphant.
Now my heart turns to and fro,
In thinking what will the people say,
They who shall see my monument in after years,
And shall speak of what I have done.
Beware of saying, "I know not, I know not:
Why has this been done?
To fashion a mountain of gold throughout,
Like something that just happened."
I swear, as I am loved of Re,

As Amun, my father, favors me,
As my nostrils are refreshed with life and dominion,
As I wear the white crown,
As I appear with the red crown,
As the Two Lords have joined their portions for me,
As I rule this land like the son of Isis,
As I am mighty like the son of Nut,
As Re rests in the evening bark,
As he prevails in the morning bark,
As he joins his two mothers in the god's ship,
As sky endures, as his creation lasts,
As I shall be eternal like an undying star,
As I shall rest in life like Atum—
So as regards these two great obelisks,
Wrought with electrum by my majesty for my father
   Amun,
In order that my name may endure in this temple,
For eternity and everlastingness,
They are each of one block of hard granite,
Without seam, without joining together!

My majesty began work on them in year 15, second
month of winter, day 1, ending in year 16, fourth
month of summer, last day, totaling seven months of
quarry work. I did it for him out of affection, as a
king for a god. It was my wish to make them for him
gilded with electrum. "Their foil lies on their body,"
is what I expect people to say. My mouth is effective
in its speech; I do not go back on my word. Hear ye!
I gave for them of the finest electrum. I measured it
by the gallon like sacks of grain. My majesty summoned a quantity beyond what the Two Lands had
yet seen. The ignorant and the wise know it.

Not shall he who hears it say,
"It is a boast," what I have said;
Rather say, "How like her it is,
She is devoted to her father!"
Lo, the god knows me well,
Amun, Lord of Thrones-of-the-Two-Lands;
He made me rule Black Land and Red Land as reward,
No one rebels against me in all lands.
All foreign lands are my subjects,
He placed my border at the limits of heaven,
What Aten encircles labors for me.
He gave it to him who came from him,
Knowing I would rule it for him.
I am his daughter in very truth,
Who serves him, who knows what he ordains.
My reward from my father is life-stability-rule,
On the Horus throne of all the living, eternally like
   Re.
   [From *Ancient Egyptian Literature*, 2:27–29.]

MESOPOTAMIA *(Sumeria, Akkadia, Assyria and Babylonia)*

The earliest evidence from Sumeria shows a number of rich graves of women and a reverence
for goddesses, especially the goddess Inanna. Women had equivalent rights with men and could
inherit and sell property, act as witnesses, do business, etc. The temple was the center of city
life and its economic center; often temples acted as banks and extended loans. Here priestesses
and priests served the deities in daily public rituals. Initially leaders were temporarily elected
in times of crisis but permanent kingship was eventually established, though a few women
also ruled, such as Ku-baba (c. 2450 B.C.E.), ruler of Kish, the first known woman ruler in
history. Armies were also organized on a temporary basis but in time a standing army became
the main support of the permanent kingship. As the culture continued to urbanize and militarize
this tightening up of society led to increasing restrictions on the activities of women and the
loss of prestige for female deities. In the earliest records it is the goddess Nammu who created
all the gods and the universe but over time she and other female deities are demoted.

Shortly after the city of Akkad came under the rule of Sargon (c. 2350 B.C.E.) he conquered
Sumeria and made his daughter Enheduanna chief priestess. His empire was short lived, it
was conquered by Semitic people, but the custom of a royal woman serving as chief priestess
endured for over five hundred years. Other priestesses came from various classes, could be
married or unmarried, lived a cloistered life or moved about freely in the society. Records
from the Old Babylonian Period (1894-1595 B.C.E.) list various types of priestesses but say
little about their duties or functions in religious life. During this period one type of priestess,
the *naditu,* was a cloistered community of celibate women. The majority of these women came
from upper class families and received dowries, which enabled them to set up independent
households within the cloistered community.

The Semitic people who conquered and eventually controlled all of ancient Sumer and Akkad were a more pessimistic people used to living a harsh desert life. While their famous law codes of Hammurabi (1792-1750 B.C.E.) preserved the rights of women, these rights diminished with the social status of individual women and gave more control to the husband in sexual and economic matters.

Another Semitic people, the Assyrians, were aggressive traders; they often went to war to open up or protect trade routes. Since their extended empire was vulnerable to invasion they were a vigorously military society, which placed little value on women: Women could neither inherit nor trade property and were essentially themselves property that was traded between patriarchal families. Veiling and seclusion were the means of distinguishing between respectable and public women (such as prostitutes).

From the evidence of their earliest religious records the Mesopotamians appear to be a pessimistic people who believed human beings were created by the gods in order to serve them through rituals, sacrifices, and building temples. Each individual was ruled by her or his destiny, which had been decreed by the gods, and the gods were unpredictable and not known for their fairness. Life on earth was at best uncertain and frequently fraught with danger. The afterlife was a dark, dreary nether world without end.

Over its long history, the public religious activities of the Mesopotamians were mainly the daily offerings of food and liquids to the gods in their temples and monthly celebrations such as the New Moon Feast. The most important public ritual was the New Year celebrations which lasted for several days. During this time the creation myth was publicly recited and the king performed the sacred marriage rite with the goddess Inanna/Isthar.

CREATION—THE ENUMA ELISH

The creation story of the Babylonians, The *Enuma Elish,* was inscribed on clay tablets as early as 1000 B.C.E., though it was probably composed during the reign of Hammurabi (1728-1686 B.C.E.). The story focuses on the rise of the god of the Babylonians, Marduk, over the gods of other Mesopotamian cities and reflects the political rise of Babylonia over these kingdoms. It was recited every year by the high priest during the New Year celebrations. As the story goes, Apsu and Tiamat are the parents of all the gods. The younger gods begin to behave badly and Apsu, their father, wants to destroy them but Tiamat, their mother, refuses to do so. One of the gods, Ea, later to become Marduk's father, learns of Apsu's plan and kills Apsu. Tiamat's other children then encourage her to revenge their father. Tiamat appoints Kingu as her war leader but decides to do battle herself with Marduk. After Marduk kills her he carves her body up and begins creating the universe. Tiamat represents the primordial chaos of the female while Marduk is the male bringer of law and order.

Then the lord [raised] the rain flood, his mighty weapon.
[As for T'îamat, who was furious, thus he answered her:
"[In arrogance(?)] thou art risen (and) hast highly exalted thyself(?).
[Thou hast caused] thy heart to plot the stirring-up of conflict.
[. . .] the sons treat their fathers unjustly;
(And) thou, their bearer, dost hate (them) wi[thout cause(?)].

Thou hast exalted Kingu to be [thy] spouse;
Thine illegal [authority] thou hast set up in place of the authority of Anu.
[Against] Anshar, the king of the gods, thou seekest evil,
And hast proven thy wickedness [against the god]s my fathers.
Let thine army be equipped! let them be girded with thy weapons!
Come thou forth (alone) and let us, me and thee, do single combat!"

When T'îamat heard this,
She became like one in a frenzy (and) lost her reason.
T'îamat cried out loud (and) furiously,
To the (very) roots her two legs shook back and forth.
She recites an incantation, repeatedly casting her spell;
As for the gods of battle, they sharpen their weapons.
T'îamat (and) Marduk, the wisest of the gods,
    advanced against one another;
They pressed on to single combat, they approached
    for battle.
The lord spread out his net and enmeshed her;
The evil wind, following after, he let loose in her face.
When T'îamat opened her mouth to devour him,
He drove in the evil wind, in order that (she should)
    not (be able) to close her lips.
The raging winds filled her belly;
Her belly became distended, and she opened wide her
    mouth.
He shot off an arrow, and it tore her interior;
It cut through her inward parts, it split (her) heart.
When he had subdued her, he destroyed her life;
He cast down her carcass (and) stood upon it.
After he had slain T'îamat, the leader,
Her band broke up, her host dispersed.
As for the gods her helpers, who marched at her side,
They trembled for fear (and) faced about.
They tried to break away to save their lives,
(But) they were completely surrounded, (so that) it
    was impossible to flee.
He imprisoned them and broke their weapons.
In the net they lay and in the snare they were;
They hid in the corners (and) were filled with
    lamentation;
They bore his wrath, being confined in prison.
As for the eleven (kinds of) creatures which she had
    laden with terror-inspiring splendor,
The host of demons that marched 'impetuously
    before' her,

He cast (them) into fetters (and) [tied(?)] their arms
    [together(?)];
With (all) their resistance, [he tr]ampled (them)
    underfoot.
As for Kingu, who had become chief among them,
He bound him and counted him among the dead
    gods.
He took from him the tablet of destinies which was
    not his rightful possession.
He sealed (it) with (his) seal and fastened (it) on his
    breast.
After he had vanquished (and) subdued his enemies,
Had overpowered the arrogant foe like a bull(?),
Had fully established Anshar's victory over the
    enemy,
Had attained the desire of Nudimmud, the valiant
    Marduk
Strengthened his hold upon the captive gods;
And then he returned to T'îamat, whom he had
    subdued.
The lord trod upon the hinder part of T'îamat,
And with his unsparing club he split (her) skull.
He cut the arteries of her blood
And caused the north wind to carry (it) to out-of-
    the-way places.
When his fathers saw (this), they were glad and
    rejoiced
(And) sent him dues (and) greeting-gifts.
The lord rested, examining her dead body,
To divide the abortion (and) to create ingenious things
    (therewith).
He split her open like a mussel(?) into two (parts);
Half of her he set in place and formed the sky (there-
    with) as a roof.
He fixed the crossbar (and) posted guards;
He commanded them not to let her waters escape.
    [*The Babylonian Genesis,* pp. 39–42.]

CREATION BY THE GODDESS

The following two myths of the creation of human beings by the goddess Ninhursag, the goddess of the earth, come from Babylonia (c. 1700 B.C.E.) and Assyria (c. 100 B.C.E.). Though parts
of the texts have been destroyed, it is clear that the myths were recited when women went into
labor so that each birth recalled the first birth of the goddess and solicited her protection.

Old Babylonian Text
(obverse)
(preceding column and top of the
present column destroyed)

"That which is slight he shall raise to abundance;
The *burden* of creation man shall bear!"

The goddess they called, [. . .], [the *mot*]*her,*
The most helpful of the gods, the wise Mami:
"Thou art the mother-womb,
The one who creates mankind.
Create, then, Lullu and let him bear the yoke!
The yoke he shall bear, . . . [. . .];
The *burden* of creation man shall bear!"

Nintu opened her mouth,
Saying to the great gods:
"With me is the *doing* of all that is suitable;
With his . . . let Lullu appear!
He who shall *serve* all the gods,
Let him *be formed* out of clay, be *animated* with blood!"
Enki opened his mouth,
Saying to the great gods:
"In the month of *restoration of confidence,*
Cleansing of the land, judgment of its people,
Let them slay one god,
And let the gods be purified in the *judgment.*
With his flesh and his blood
Let Ninhursag mix clay.
God and man
Shall . . . *benefit* jointly *by* the clay!
Unto eternity [. . .] we shall hear."
(remainder of obverse too fragmentary for translation)

(reverse)
[. . .] her breast,
[. . .] the beard,
[. . .] the cheek of the man.
[. . .] and the raising
[. . .] of both eyes, the wife and her husband.
[Fourteen mother]-wombs were assembled
[Before] Nintu.
[At the ti]me of the new moon
[To the House] of Fates they called the *votaries.*
[. . .] Ea came and
[*Kneel]ed down,* opening the womb.
[. . .] . . . and happy was his countenance.
[. . . bent] the knees [. . .],
[. . .] made an opening,
She brought forth her issue,
Praying.
Fashion a clay brick into a core,
Make . . . stone in the midst of [. . .];
Let the vexed rejoice in the house of the one in travail!
As the Bearing One gives birth,

May the mo[ther of the ch]ild bring forth by herself!
(remainder too fragmentary for translation)

Assyrian Version

(beginning mutilated)
[. . . they kis]sed her feet,
[Saying: "The creatress of mankind] we call thee;
[The mistr]ess of all the gods be thy name!"
[They went] to the House of Fate,
[Nin]igiku-Ea (and) the wise Mama.
[Fourteen mother]-wombs were assembled
To tread upon the [c]lay before her.
[. . .] Ea says, as he recites the incantation.
Sitting before her, Ea causes her to recite the
    incantation.
[Mama reci]ted the incantation; when she completed
    [her] incantation,
[. . .] she drew upon her clay.
[Fourteen pie]ces she pinched off; seven pieces she
    placed on the right,
[Seven pie]ces she placed on the left; between them
    she placed a brick.
[E]*a* was kneeling on the *matting;* he opened its navel;
[. . . he c]alled the wise wives.
(Of the) [seven] and seven mother-wombs, seven
    brought forth males,
[Seven] brought forth females.
The Mother-Womb, the creatress of destiny,
In pairs she completed them,
In pairs she completed (them) before her.
The forms of the people Mami forms.
In the house of the bearing woman in travail,
    Seven days shall the brick lie.
. . . from the house of Mah, the wise Mami.
The vexed shall rejoice in the house of the one in
    travail.
As the Bearing One gives birth,
May the mother of the child bring forth by [her]self.
(remainder destroyed)
[From *Ancient Near Eastern Texts,* pp. 99–100.]

THE HERO GILGAMESH AND THE GODDESS ISHTAR

The earliest written version of the epic of *Gilgamesh* is in Sumerian and dates from around the turn of the second millennium, although the story is much older. The events it depicts are set in the third millennium B.C.E. The hero of the epic, King Gilgamesh, is described as being two-thirds divine, because his mother was a minor goddess, and one-third human, because of his human father. He may, in fact, have been based on an historical king of Uruk named Gilgamesh who ruled in the middle of the third millennium. Ishtar (the Sumerian Inanna) is the Akkadian/Babylonian goddess of love and war whose contradictory attributes suggest some of the dangers that lurk in her nature. While she is spoken of as being beautiful and benevolent, the *Gilgamesh* emphasizes the destructive side of her nature.

The following excerpt, translated from the Akkadian, takes place after Gilgamesh has performed many heroic feats. The goddess Ishtar desires him but Gilgamesh rejects her as a lover, taunting her with the miserable fates of her earlier lovers. Two things are of particular interest here: One is that a mortal, even if part divine, boldly insults a divinity; and two, it is a human male who humiliates a divine female. This latter point places the Gilgamesh and Ishtar episode in the genre of stories about male heroes and gods who conquer divine females and suggests the power of a new ideal, the military hero. Of even greater significance, by sexually rejecting the goddess Ishtar Gilgamesh is breaking with the religious ritual of the *hieros gamos,* the sacred marriage in which mortal Mesopotamian kings participated in ritual sexuality with the goddess (actually this was usually a priestess of the goddess called a *hierodule*) in order to ensure the fertility of the land and to receive the endorsement of the goddess of his right to rule. Thus Gilgamesh's rejection of Ishtar has far reaching implications for the status of this goddess in the religious and political life of Mesopotamia. In retaliation for this insult Ishtar sends a divine bull after Gilgamesh, but with the help of his friend Enkidu, the bull is killed, and Ishtar can only lament with the rest of the women. She is powerless against Gilgamesh.

He washed his grimy hair, polished his weapons,
The braid of his hair he shook out against his back.
He cast off his soiled (things), put on his clean ones,
Wrapped a fringed cloak about and fastened a sash.
When Gilgamesh had put on his tiara,
Glorious Ishtar raised an eye at the beauty of Gilgamesh:
"Come, Gilgamesh, be thou (my) lover!
Do but grant me of thy fruit.
Thou shalt be my husband and I will be thy wife.
I will harness for thee a chariot of lapis and gold,
Whose wheels are gold and whose horns are brass.
Thou shalt have storm-demons to hitch on for mighty mules.
In the fragrance of cedars thou shalt enter our house.
When our house thou enterest,
Threshold (and) dais shall kiss thy feet!
Humbled before thee shall be kings, lords, and princes!
The *yield* of hills and plain they shall bring thee as tribute.
Thy goats shall cast triplets, thy sheep twins,
Thy he-ass in lading shall surpass thy mule.
Thy chariot horses shall be famed for racing,
[Thine ox] under yoke shall not have a rival!"

[Gilgamesh] opened his mouth to speak,
[Saying] to glorious Ishtar:
["What am I to give] thee, that I may take thee in marriage?
[Should I give oil] for the body, and clothing?
[Should I give] bread and victuals?
[. . .] food fit for divinity,
[. . .] drink fit for royalty.
(mutilated)

[. . . if I] take thee in marriage?

[Thou art but a brazier which goes out] in the cold;
A back door [which does not] keep out blast and windstorm;
A palace which crushes the valiant [. . .];
A *turban* whose cover [. . .];
Pitch which [soils] its bearers;
A waterskin which [soaks through] its bearer;
Limestone which [*springs*] the stone rampart;
Jasper [which . . .] enemy land;
A shoe which [pinches the foot] of its owner!
Which lover didst thou love forever?
Which of thy shepherds pleased [thee for all time]?
Come, and I will na[me for thee] thy lovers:

Of . . . [. . .] . . .
For Tammuz, the lover of thy youth,
Thou hast ordained wailing year after year.
Having loved the dappled shepherd-bird,
Thou smotest him, breaking his wing.
In the groves he sits, crying 'My wing!'
Then thou lovedst a lion, perfect in strength;
Seven pits and seven thou didst dig for him.
Then a stallion thou lovedst, famed in battle;
The whip, the spur, and the lash thou ordainedst for him.
Thou decreedst for him to gallop seven leagues,
Thou decreedst for him the muddied to drink;
For his mother, Silili, thou ordainedst wailing!
Then thou lovedst the keeper of the herd,
Who ash-cakes ever did heap up for thee,
Daily slaughtered kids for thee;
Yet thou smotest him, turning him into a wolf,
So that his own herd boys drive him off,
And his dogs bite his thighs.
Then thou lovedst Ishullanu, thy father's gardener,
Who baskets of dates ever did bring to thee,
And daily did brighten thy table.

Thine eyes raised at him, thou didst go to him:
'O my Ishullanu, let us taste of thy vigor!
Put forth thy "hand" and touch our "modesty!"'
Ishullanu said to thee:
'What dost thou want with me?
Has my mother not baked, have I not eaten,
That I should taste the food of stench and foulness?
Does reed-work afford cover against the cold?'
As thou didst hear this [his talk],
Thou smotest him and turn[edst] him into a *mole*.
Thou placedst him in the midst of . . [.];
He cannot go up . . . nor can he come down . . .
If thou shouldst love me, thou wouldst [treat me] like
    them."
When Ishtar heard this,
Ishtar was enraged and [mounted] to heaven.
Forth went Ishtar before Anu, her father,
To Antum, her mother, she went and [said]:
"My father, Gilgamesh has heaped insults upon me!
Gilgamesh has recounted my stinking deeds,
My stench and my foulness."
Anu opened his mouth to speak,
Saying to glorious Ishtar:
"But surely, thou didst invite . [. .],
And so Gilgamesh has recounted thy stinking deeds,
Thy stench and [thy] foulness."
Ishtar opened her mouth to speak,
Saying to [Anu, her father]:
"My father, make me the Bull of Heaven [that he smite
    Gilgamesh],
[And] fill Gil[gamesh . . .]!
If thou [dost not make] me [the Bull of Heaven],
I will smash [the doors of the nether world],
I will[. . .],
I will [raise up the dead eating (and) alive],
So that the dead shall outnumber the living!"

Anu [opened his mouth to speak],
Saying [to glorious Ishtar]:
"[If I do what] thou askest [of me],
[There will be] seven years of (barren) husks.
Hast thou gathered [grain for the people]?
Hast thou grown grass [for the beasts]?"

[Ishtar opened her mouth] to speak,
[Saying to A]nu, her father:
"[Grain for the people] I have stored,
[Grass for the beasts] I have provided.
[If there should be seven] years of husks,
[I have ga]thered [grain for the people],
[I have grown] grass [for the beasts]."

(Lines 114–28 are too fragmentary for translation. It
is plain, however, that Anu did Ishtar's bidding, for
the Bull comes down and kills hundreds of men with
his first two snorts.)

With [his] third snort [*he sprang*] at Enkidu.
Enkidu *parried* his onslaught.
Up leaped Enkidu, seizing the Bull of Heaven by the
    horns.
The Bull of Heaven hurled [his] foam in [his] face,
Brushed him with the thick of his tail.

Enkidu opened his mouth to speak,
Saying [to Gilgamesh]:
"My friend, we have gloried [. . .]."

(Lines 137–51 mutilated, but the course of the battle
is made plain by the following:)

Between neck and horns [he thrust] his sword.
When they had slain the Bull, they tore out his heart,
Placing it before Shamash.
They drew back and did homage before Shamash.
The two brothers sat down.

Then Ishtar mounted the wall of ramparted Uruk,
Sprang on the battlements, uttering a curse:
"Woe unto Gilgamesh because he insulted me
    By slaying the Bull of Heaven!"

When Enkidu heard this speech of Ishtar,
He *tore loose* the right thigh of the Bull of Heaven
    And tossed it in her face:
"Could I but get thee, like unto him
I would do unto thee.
His entrails I would hang at thy side!"
(Thereupon) Ishtar assembled the votaries,
The (pleasure-)lasses and the (temple-)harlots.
Over the right thigh of the Bull of Heaven she set
    up a wail.
But Gilgamesh called the craftsmen, the armorers,
All (of them).
The artisans admire the thickness of his horns:
Each is cast from thirty minas of lapis;
The coating on each is two fingers (thick);
Six measures of oil, the capacity or the two,
He offered as ointment to his god, Lugalbanda.
He brought (them) and hung them in his princely
    bed-chamber.
    [From *The Ancient Near East*, 1:51–55.]

ISHTAR'S DESCENT TO THE UNDERWORLD

The following myth makes plain Isthar's connections with death and fertility when she goes
to the land of the dead where she is held captive by her sister Ereshkigal, the Queen of the

Underworld. During this time all fertility on the earth ceases. The god Ea gains Ishtar's release by distracting Ereshkigal with a beautiful male eunuch (emphasizing the lack of fertility in Ereshkigal's realm) who gets the waters of life that free Ishtar. The story is rich in complex meanings among which are the connections between death and fertility as well as Isthar's knowledge of and success in both the realms of the living and the dead. The seven gates at which Ishtar first leaves and then retrieves a possession, symbolizing her loss of divine powers and their restoration, are connected to the planetary symbolism much loved by the Babylonians.

When Ishtar reached the gate of the Land of no
    Return,
She said (these) words to the gatekeeper:
"O gatekeeper, open thy gate,
Open thy gate that I may enter!

★ ★ ★

"Enter, my lady, that Cutha may rejoice over thee,
That the palace of the Land of no Return may be glad
    at thy presence."
When the first door he had made her enter,
    He stripped and took away the great crown on her
    head.
"Why, O gatekeeper, didst thou take the great crown
    on my head?"
"Enter, my lady, thus are the rules of the Mistress of
    the Nether World."
When the second gate he had made her enter,
    He stripped and took away the pendants on her
    ears.
"Why, O gatekeeper, didst thou take the pendants on
    my ears?"
"Enter, my lady, thus are the rules of the Mistress of
    the Nether World."
When the third gate he had made her enter,
    He stripped and took away the chains round her
    neck.
"Why, O gatekeeper, didst thou take the chains round
    my neck?"
"Enter, my lady, thus are the rules of the Mistress of
    the Nether World."
When the fourth gate he had made her enter,
    He stripped and took away the ornaments on her
    breast.
"Why, O gatekeeper, didst thou take the ornaments
    on my breast?"
"Enter, my lady, thus are the rules of the Mistress of
    the Nether World."
When the fifth gate he had made her enter,
    He stripped and took away the girdle of birthstones
    on her hips.
"Why, O gatekeeper, didst thou take the girdle of
    birthstones on my hips?"
"Enter, my lady, thus are the rules of the Mistress of
    the Nether World."
When the sixth gate he had made her enter,

He stripped and took away the clasps round her
    hands and feet.
"Why, O gatekeeper, didst thou take the clasps round
    my hands and feet?"
"Enter, my lady, thus are the rules of the Mistress of
    the Nether World."
When the seventh gate he had made her enter,
    He stripped and took away the breechcloth round
    her body.
"Why, O gatekeeper, didst thou take the breechcloth
    on my body?"
"Enter, my lady, thus are the rules of the Mistress of
    the Nether World."
As soon as Ishtar had descended to the Land of no
    Return,
Ereshkigal saw her and burst out at her presence.
Ishtar, unreflecting, flew at her.
Ereshkigal opened her mouth to speak,
Saying (these) words to Namtar, her vizier:
"Go, Namtar, lock [her] up [in] my [palace]!
Release against her, [against] Ishtar, the sixty
    mis[eries]:
Misery of the eyes [against] her [eyes],
Misery of the sides ag[ainst] her [sides],
Misery of the heart ag[ainst her heart],
Misery of the feet ag[ainst] her [feet],
Misery of the head ag[ainst her head]—
Against every part of her, against [her whole body]!"
After Lady Ishtar [had descended to the nether
    world],
The bull springs not upon the cow, [the ass impreg-
    nates not the jenny],
In the street [the man impregnates not] the maiden.
The man lies [in his (own) chamber, the maiden lies
    on her side],
[. . .l]ies [. . .].
(reverse)

The countenance of Papsukkal, the vizier of the great
    gods,
    Was fallen, his face was [clouded].
He was clad in mourning, long hair he wore.
Forth went Papsukkal before Sin his father, weeping,
[His] tears flowing before Ea, the king:
"Ishtar has gone down to the nether world, she has
    not come up.

Since Ishtar has gone down to the Land of no Return,
The bull springs not upon the cow, the ass impreg-
nates not the jenny,
In the street the man impregnates not the maiden.
The man lies down in his (own) chamber,
The maiden lies down on her side.
Ea in his wise heart conceived an image,
And created Asushunamir, a eunuch:
"Up, Asushunamir, set thy face to the gate of the Land
of no Return;
The seven gates of the Land of no Return shall be
opened for thee.
Ereshkigal shall see thee and rejoice at thy presence.
When her heart has calmed, her mood is happy,
Let her utter the oath of the great gods.
(Then) lift up thy head, paying mind to the life-water
bag:
"Pray, Lady, let them give me the life-water bag
That water therefrom I may drink."
As soon as Ereshkigal heard this,
She smote her thigh, bit her finger:
"Thou didst request of me a thing that should not be
requested.
Come, Asushunamir, I will curse thee with a mighty
curse!
The food of the city's *gutters* shall be thy food,
The *sewers* of the city shall be thy drink.
The shadow of the wall shall be thy station,

The threshold shall be thy habitation,
The besotted and the thirsty shall smite thy cheek!"
Ereshkigal opened her mouth to speak,
. . .
"Sprinkle Ishtar with the water of life and take her
from my presence!"
Forth went Namtar. . . .
Sprinkled Ishtar with the water of life and took her
from her presence.
When through the first gate he had made her go out,
He returned to her the breechcloth for her body.
When through the second gate he had made her go
out,
He returned to her the clasps for her hands and feet.
When through the third gate he had made her go out,
He returned to her the birthstone girdle for her
hips.
When through the fourth gate he had made her go
out,
He returned to her the ornaments for her breasts.
When through the fifth gate he had made her go out,
He returned to her the chains for her neck.
When through the sixth gate he had made her go out,
He returned to her the pendants for her ears.
When through the seventh gate he had made her go
out,
He returned to her the great crown for her head.
[From *The Ancient Near East,* 1: 81–85.]

HYMN TO THE GODDESS INANNA COMPOSED BY A PRIESTESS

Princess Enheduanna was the daughter of the Akkadian king Sargon (rose to power c. 2350 B.C.E.), the high priestess to the moon god Nanna and, as the following indicates, a significant poet. The popularity of her hymns to Inanna, written after she learned the Sumerian language, is attested to by the fact that they were listed in several of the literary catalogs of her time and survive in nearly fifty different samples. Legend says King Sargon was the son of a high priestess of Inanna and later the lover of another of her priestesses. This alliance may have contributed to his successful rise at the court of Kish. Later in his career he solidified his con-quest of the kingdoms of Ur and Uruk by installing Enheduanna as the high priestess and bride of the moon god of Ur, Nanna, and eventually Enheduanna also served in this capacity in the city of Uruk where she was regarded as the personification of Inanna. During a rebellion against Sargon's rule Enheduanna was removed from her priestly office and she complains of this in the hymns, asking Inanna to restore her. Sargon's final act in shaping the religious life of his kingdom was to equate the Sumerian Inanna with the Akkadian Ishtar.

Inanna means "the goddess of heaven" and she is represented in tangible form as the moon and as the morning and evening star (the planet Venus). Her connection with the moon makes plain her dual aspects as goddess of life and fertility (the full moon) as well as the goddess of death and rebirth (the new moon). She has journeyed to the land of the dead and successfully returned. Further, she is also the goddess of love and the goddess of war.

Inanna and Enlil

Devastatrix of the lands,
  you are lent wings by the storm.
Beloved of Enlil,
  you fly about in the nation.

You are at the service
  of the decrees of An.
Oh my lady, at the sound of you
  the lands bow down.

When mankind
  comes before you
In fear and trembling
  at (your) tempestuous radiance,
They receive from you
  their just deserts.

Proffering a song of lamentation,
  they weep before you,
They walk toward you along the path
  of the house of all the great sighs.

The Banishment [of Enheduanna] from Ur

Verily I had entered
  my holy *gipāru* at your behest,
I, the high priestess,
  I, Enheduanna!

I carried the ritual basket,
  I intoned the acclaim.
(But now) I am placed in the leper's ward,
  I, even I, can no longer live with you!

The Indictment of Nanna [the moon god]

As for me, my Nanna
  takes no heed of me.
He has verily given me over to destruction
  in murderous straits.

Ashimbabbar
  has not pronounced my judgment.
Had he pronounced it: what is it to me?
  Had he not pronounced it: what is it to me?

(Me) who once sat triumphant
  he has driven out of the sanctuary.
Like a swallow he made me fly
  from the window, my life is consumed.

He made me walk
  in the bramble of the mountain.
He stripped me of the crown
  appropriate for the high priesthood.
He gave me dagger and sword—
  "it becomes you," he said to me.

The Appeal to Inanna

Most precious lady,
  beloved of An,
Your holy heart is lofty,
  may it be assuaged on my behalf!

Beloved bride
  of Ushumgalanna,
You are the senior queen
  of the heavenly foundations and zenith.

The Anunna
  have submitted to you.
From birth on
  you were the "junior" queen.

How supreme you are over the great gods, the Anunna!
The Anunna kiss the ground with their lips (in obeisance) to you.

(But) my own sentence is not concluded
  a hostile judgment appears before my eyes as my judgment.
(My) hands are no longer folded
  on the ritual couch,
I may no longer reveal
  the pronouncements of Ningal to man.

(Yet) I am the brilliant
  high priestess of Nanna,
Oh my queen beloved of An,
  may your heart take pity on me!

The Exaltation of Inanna

That one has not recited as a "Known! Be it known!" of Nanna,
  that one has recited as a "'Tis Thine!":

"That you are lofty as Heaven—
  be it known!
That you are broad as the earth—
  be it known!
That you devastate the rebellious land—
  be it known!
That you roar at the land—
  be it known!
That you smite the heads—
  be it known!
That you devour cadavers like a dog—
  be it known!
That your glance is terrible—
  be it known!
That you lift your terrible glance—
  be it known!
That your glance is flashing—
  be it known!

That you are ill-disposed toward the . . .
   be it known!
That you attain victory—
   be it known!"

That one has not recited (this) of Nanna,
   that one has recited it as a "'Tis Thine!"—

(That,) oh my lady, has made you great,
   you alone are exalted!

Oh my lady beloved of An,
   I have verily recounted your fury!
      [From *The Exaltation of Inannu*, pp. 17, 23, 29–33.]

Ancient Greece

The polytheistic religion of ancient Greece had no founder and no systematizer. As in most early cultures, no sharp distinction was made between the religious and secular aspects of life. Religious practices varied from community to community while within individual communities there were family cults, and eventually city cults, and pan-Hellenic cults, such as Eleusis. Individuals worshiped the particular goddess or god who might best fulfill their need of the moment: pregnant women might offer sacrifices to Artemis for a safe delivery, while warriors would seek the favor of the war god Ares. At the same time various festivals dedicated to different deities defined the religious calendar.

The main concern of Greek religion was the here and now; the afterlife received little attention, except in the mystery cults, and only the gods were immortal. Knowledge about the divine, the nature of the gods, and their involvement in human affairs was preserved by a rich oral tradition of folktales, poetry, and drama. The central rite was the blood sacrifice, which could be a formal state occasion with an officiating priestess, or priest, or a domestic ceremony which anyone who was not polluted could perform, although such sacrifices were usually performed by men as the heads of households. Almost anyone could be a priestess or priest, though certain offices were hereditary, such as that of the priestess of Athena in Athens, and not all offices were for life—some were as short as one year.

There were several mystery cults, such as those of Eleusis, Dionysus, and Orpheus. Women played a significant part in these cults and were an important element in their mythology. While recognized and often controlled by the city governments, these cults remained on the fringes of society. Additionally, women had their own festivals, such as the Thesmophoria, an annual three-day festival dedicated to Demeter, the goddess of the grain, that was designed to ensure the fertility of the crops.

In general, Greek religion attempted to contain the religious activities of women and to control the most powerful goddesses such as Demeter at Eleusis. Women were perceived as irrational beings which, to most of the Greek men who exalted rationality, made women dangerous and contemptible.

CREATION—THE THEOGONY

The creation story of the Greeks preserved in Hesiod's *Theogony* (c. 700 B.C.E.) is a study in conflict, conflict between the sexes and conflict between the generations. Of paramount importance is male control of female reproduction, as shown in the relationships of Chaos and Gaia, the earth goddess. When her children are born Chaos pushes them back into her until Gaia encourages one of her sons, Kronos, to emasculate his father (vv. 115–182). The next generation of gods repeats this pattern of male control of female fertility when the god Kronos eats the children borne by Rheia, another earth goddess, until she too gets one of her sons, Zeus, to overcome him (vv. 452–468). Zeus, in turn, takes matters a step further by swallowing his first wife Metis, goddess of wisdom, while she is pregnant (vv. 881–901). Full control of female fertility is then demonstrated by Zeus's so-called birth of Athena from his head (vv. 924–926). Athena remains a deeply ambivalent goddess, who is noted for taking the male side in most arguments and who well represents the successful overthrow of the goddesses by the gods. Given Zeus's (highly questionable) pretensions to moral authority, his victory reflects the Greek notion of the need for male moral authority to control female generative powers. Further, it justifies the subjugation of nature to civilization, an equally pervasive theme in Greek civilization.

First of all there came Chaos,
  and after him came
Gaia of the broad beast,
  to be the unshakable foundation
of all the immortals who keep the crests
  of snowy Olympos,
and Tartaros the foggy in the pit
  of the wide-wayed earth,
and Eros, who is love, handsomest among all
  the immortals,
who breaks the limbs' strength,
  who in all gods, in all human beings
overpowers the intelligence in the breast,
  and all their shrewd planning.
From Chaos was born Erebos, the dark,
  and black Night,
and from Night again Aither and Hemera,
  the day, were begotten,
for she lay in love with Erebos
  and conceived and bore these two.
But Gaia's first born was one
  who matched her every dimension,
Ouranos, the starry sky,
  to cover her all over,
to be an unshakable standing-place
  for the blessed immortals.
Then she brought forth the tall Hills,
  those wild haunts that are beloved
by the goddess Nymphs who live on the hills
  and in their forests.

★ ★ ★

After these her youngest-born
  was devious-devising Kronos,
most terrible of her children;
  and he hated his strong father.

★ ★ ★

And still other children were born
to Gaia and Ouranos,

★ ★ ★

and they hated their father
from the beginning, and every time each one
  was beginning

to come out, he would push them back again,
  deep inside Gaia,
and would not let them into the light,
  and Ouranos exulted
in his wicked work; but great Gaia
  groaned within for pressure
of pain; and then she thought of an evil,
  treacherous attack.
Presently creating the element of gray flint
she made of it a great sickle,
  and explained it to her own children,
and spoke, in the disturbance of her heart,
  to encourage them:
"My sons, born to me of a criminal father,
  if you are willing
to obey me, we can punish your father
  for the brutal treatment
he put upon you, for he was first to think
  of shameful dealing."
  So she spoke, but fear took hold of all,
  nor did one of them
speak, but then great devious-devising Kronos
  took courage
and spoke in return,
  and gave his gracious mother an answer:
"My mother, I will promise to undertake
  to accomplish
this act, and for our father,
  him of the evil name, I care
nothing, for he was the first
  to think of shameful dealing."
  So he spoke, and giant Gaia
  rejoiced greatly in her heart
and took and hid him in a secret ambush,
  and put into his hands
the sickle, edged like teeth, and told him
  all her treachery.
And huge Ouranos came on
  bringing night with him, and desiring
love he embraced Gaia and lay over her
  stretched out
complete, and from his hiding place his son
  reached with his left hand
and seized him, and holding in his right
  the enormous sickle

with its long blade edged like teeth,
  he swung it sharply,
and lopped the members of his own father,
  and threw them behind him
to fall where they would,
      [From *Hesiod*, pp. 130–34.]

Rheia, submissive in love to Kronos,
  bore glorious children,
Histia and Demeter,
  Hera of the golden sandals,
and strong Hades, who under the ground
  lives in his palace
and has a heart without pity;
  the deep-thunderous Earthshaker,
and Zeus of the counsels,
  who is the father of gods and of mortals,
and underneath whose thunder
  the whole wide earth shudders;
but, as each of these children
  came from the womb of its mother
to her knees, great Kronos swallowed it down,
  with the intention
that no other of the proud children
  of the line of Ouranos
should ever hold the king's position
  among the immortals.
For he had heard, from Gaia
  and from starry Ouranos,
that it had been ordained for him,
  for all his great strength,
to be beaten by his son,
  and through the designs of great Zeus.
Therefore he kept watch, and did not sleep,
  but waited
for his children, and swallowed them,
  and Rheia's sorrow was beyond forgetting.
      [From *Hesiod*, p. 150.]

Now when the immortal gods had finished
  their work of fighting,
they forced the Titans to share with them
  their titles and privilege.
Then, by the advice of Gaia,

they promoted Zeus, the Olympian
of the wide brows, to be King
  and to rule over the immortals
and he distributed among them their titles
  and privilege.

Zeus, as King of the gods,
  took as his first wife Metis,
and she knew more than all the gods
  or mortal people.
But when she was about to be delivered
  of the goddess, gray-eyed
Athene, then Zeus, deceiving her perception
  by treachery
and by slippery speeches,
  put her away inside his own belly.
This was by the advices of Gaia,
  and starry Ouranos,
for so they counseled,
  in order that no other everlasting
god, beside Zeus, should ever be given
  the kingly position.
For it had been arranged that, from her,
  children surpassing in wisdom
should be born, first the gray-eyed girl,
  the Tritogeneia
Athene; and she is the equal of her father
  in wise counsel
and strength; but then a son to be King
  over gods and mortals
was to be born of her, and his heart
  would be overmastering:
but before this, Zeus put her away
  inside his own belly
so that this goddess should think for him,
  for good and for evil.

                    ★ ★ ★

Then from his head, by himself,
  he produced Athene of the gray eyes,
great goddess, weariless,
  waker of battle noise, leader of armies,
a goddess queen who delights in war cries,
  onslaughts, and battles,
      [From *Hesiod*, pp. 176–79.]

PANDORA—THE FIRST WOMAN

Hesiod (c. 700 B.C.E.) was one of the earliest Greek poets. His telling of the stories of the gods and heroes of ancient Greece are filled with moral advice and practical instruction. The following myth, excerpted from *The Works and Days* (vv. 10–105), is an elaboration on the Greek creation story in which an earlier golden age was disrupted by the appearance of Pandora, the first woman. Much like Eve, Pandora is represented as the woman who transformed man's blissful existence into a life of labor, sickness, and death. Being made from earth and water, however, suggests the earlier Pandora, an indigenous earth deity, whose story is now being retold within the context of the patriarchal pantheon headed by Zeus. According to Hesiod, though, she was fashioned by Zeus as a punishment to mankind because the hero Prometheus had stolen fire from the gods and given it to human beings.

Zeus thought up dismal sorrows
  for mankind.
He hid fire; but Prometheus, the powerful son
  of Iapetos,
stole it again from Zeus of the counsels,
  to give to mortals.
He hid it out of the sight of Zeus
  who delights in thunder
in the hollow fennel stalk. In anger
  the cloud-gatherer spoke to him:
"Son of Iapetos, deviser of crafts beyond all others,
you are happy that you stole the fire,
  and outwitted my thinking;
but it will be a great sorrow to you,
  and to men who come after.
As the price of fire I will give them an evil,
  and all men shall fondle
this, their evil, close to their hearts,
  and take delight in it."
So spoke the father of gods and mortals;
and laughed out loud.
He told glorious Hephaistos to make haste, and plaster
earth with water, and to infuse it with a human voice
and vigor, and make the face
  like the immortal goddesses,
the bewitching features of a young girl;
  meanwhile Athene
was to teach her skills, and how
  to do the intricate weaving,
while Aphrodite was to mist her head
  in golden endearment
and the cruelty of desire and longings
  that wear out the body,
but to Hermes, the guide, the slayer of Argos,
  he gave instructions
to put in her the mind of a hussy,
  and a treacherous nature.

So Zeus spoke. And all obeyed Lord Zeus,
  the son of Kronos.
The renowned strong smith modeled her figure of
  earth,
  in the likeness
of a decorous young girl, as the son of Kronos
  had wished it.
The goddess gray-eyed Athene dressed and arrayed
  her;
  the Graces,

who are goddesses, and hallowed Persuasion
  put necklaces
of gold upon her body, while the Seasons,
  with glorious tresses,
put upon her head a coronal of spring flowers,
[and Pallas Athene put all decor upon her body].
But into her heart Hermes, the guide,
  the slayer of Argos,
put lies, and wheedling words
  of falsehood, and a treacherous nature,
made her as Zeus of the deep thunder wished,
  and he, the gods' herald,
put a voice inside her, and gave her
  the name of woman,
Pandora, because all the gods
  who have their homes on Olympos
had given her each a gift, to be a sorrow to men
who eat bread. Now when he had done
  with this sheer, impossible
deception, the Father sent the gods' fleet messenger,
  Hermes,
to Epimetheus, bringing her, a gift,
  nor did Epimetheus
remember to think how Prometheus had told him
  never
to accept a gift from Olympian Zeus,
  but always to send it
back for fear it might prove
  to be an evil for mankind.
He took the evil, and only perceived it
  when he possessed her.

Since before the time the races of men
  had been living on earth
free from all evils, free from laborious work,
  and free from
all wearing sicknesses that bring
  their fates down on men
[for men grow old suddenly
  in the midst of misfortune];
but the woman, with her hands lifting away the lid
  from the great jar,
scattered its contents, and her design
  was sad troubles for mankind.
Hope was the only spirit that stayed there
  in the unbreakable
closure of the jar, under its rim,
  and could not fly forth

abroad, for the lid of the great jar
  closed down first and contained her;

this was by the will of cloud-gathering Zeus
  of the aegis.
          [From *Hesiod,* pp. 19–31.]

MOTHER RIGHT VS. FATHER RIGHT

The Eumenides, a play by Aeschylus (525/4-456 B.C.E.), was first performed in 458 B.C.E. Aeschylus loved justice and, as *The Eumenides* shows, thought of the gods as a governing force in the universe. The play takes place shortly after the fall of Troy, when the victorious Greeks returned to their homes. The leader of the Greeks was King Agamemnon who, at the beginning of the war, raised a wind for the Greek ships to sail to Troy by sacrificing Iphigenia, the daughter of his wife Queen Clytemnestra. (In some versions of this story Agamemnon is Iphigenia's father, but in others her father was Clytemnestra's first husband.) Agamemnon deceived Clytemnestra by telling her that he planned to arrange for Iphigenia's marriage. Clytemnestra is enraged when she learns of her daughter's death, and she waits ten long years for her revenge while the Greeks do battle at Troy. When Agamemnon returns home, she kills him. The obligation now falls on their son Orestes to avenge his father's murder by killing the murderer, his mother, which he does.

The play opens after these events and focuses on Orestes who is being tormented by the Furies for having killed his mother. These are very ancient female deities associated with death, sometimes represented as snakelike creatures, who fill humans with horror. They are the ones who have brought charges against Orestes and speak as the chorus in the play. A trial by the gods then takes place. When questioned by Athena, who acts as his judge, Orestes freely admits to having killed his mother but argues that he is not guilty of her death because he killed her in order to revenge the death of his father. Orestes is arguing that revenging his father was his primary duty and took precedence over any injunctions against matricide. Next Apollo speaks in Orestes' defense by presenting the biological theory that women are the mere incubators of male seed and offering Athena herself, who was born from her father Zeus' head, as living evidence of his point.

When Athena decides that Orestes is innocent of his mother's murder she openly acknowledges her preference for all things male and connects this preference with the fact that she herself was not born from a woman but from a man. In their protests over this judgment, the Furies reveal their understanding that their time has passed, that a new order has replaced them, an order that supports the rights of the fathers over the rights of the mother.

Athene: Stranger, what answer do you wish to make in your turn?
Tell me what are your country and your family and your fortunes,
and then try to rebut this accusation,
if it is with confidence in justice that you sit
clutching my image near my altar,
a suppliant to be revered after Ixion's fashion.

To all these charges return an answer I can understand!

Orestes: Queen Athene, your last words contain
a great cause of anxiety that I will first remove.

I am no suppliant in need of purifying; nor was it with pollution
upon my hand that I took my seat near your image.
And I will tell you of a powerful proof of this.
It is the custom for the killer to be silent,
till by the action of a purifier of blood-guilt
the slaughter of a suckling victim shall have shed blood upon him.
Long since I have been thus purified at other houses, both by victims and by flowing streams.
This cause for anxiety I thus dispel;
and what is my lineage you shall soon know.
I am an Argive; and my father you know well,

Agamemnon, who marshaled the men of the fleet,
with whom you made Ilium's city a city no more.
He perished by no honorable death, when he came
home; my black-hearted mother
slew him, when she had wrapped him
in a crafty snare, one that bore witness to his murder
   in the bath.
And I returned, having been before in exile,
and killed my mother—I will not deny it—
exacting the penalty of death in return for my dear
   father.
And together with me Loxias is answerable;
for he warned me of pains that would pierce my heart,
if I should fail to act against those who bore the guilt
   of this.
Whether I acted justly or unjustly, you decide the case!
For however I may fare, I shall rest content with your
   decision.
   [From *The Eumenides,* pp. 38–39.]

[Apollo speaks:]
She who is called the child's mother is not
its begetter, but the nurse of the newly sown
   conception.
The begetter is the male, and she as a stranger for a
   stranger
preserves the offspring, if no god blights its birth;
and I shall offer you a proof of what I say.
There can be a father without a mother; near at hand
is the witness, the child of Olympian Zeus . . .
. . . .
and she was not nurtured in the darkness of the
   womb,
but is such an offspring as no goddess might bear.
   [From *The Eumenides,* pp. 38–39.]

   Chorus: Since your youth is riding down my
venerable age,
I wait to hear justice given in this case,

being still in doubt whether to visit my anger on the
   city.

   Athene: It is now my office to give final
judgment;
and I shall give my vote to Orestes.
For there is no mother who bore me;
and I approve the male in all things, short of accepting marriage,
with all my heart, and I belong altogether to my
   father.
Therefore I shall not give greater weight to the death
   of a woman,
one who slew her husband, the watcher of the house;
Orestes is the winner, even should the votes be equal.
Throw out in all speed from the urns the lots,
you among the judges to whom this duty is assigned!
   [From *The Eumenides,* p. 58.]

   Chorus: Ah, you younger gods, the ancient laws
you have ridden down, and snatched them from my
   grasp!
I am bereft of honor, unhappy one! And with grievous
   wrath
against this land, alack,
venom, venom in requital for my grief from my heart
   shall I discharge,
a distillation for the land
intolerable; and after that
a canker, blasting leaves and children—Ah, Justice!—
speeding over the ground
shall cast upon the land infections that destroy its
   people.
I lament! What can I do?
I am mocked! Grievous, I say,
is the fate of the hapless daughters
of Night, who mourn, robbed of their honor!
   [From *The Eumenides,* pp. 60–61.]

APOLLO AND THE PYTHIA (A FEMALE ORACLE)

The conflict between the sexes contained in the *Theogony* continues in the *Homeric Hymns.* This is a collection of hymns to the gods composed by a variety of poets from about the seventh to the fourth centuries B.C.E. The following excerpt from the "Homeric Hymn to Pythian Apollo" describes Apollo's conquest of the indigenous female deity at Delphi. This was the supreme oracle of ancient Greece and consequently a religious site of great importance and influence. The deity Apollo fights is described as a female dragon, in other words a primordial earth deity. The gender conflict in this myth is heightened when the poet also relates an earlier incident in which this deity helped the goddess Hera in her revenge against Zeus for giving birth to the woman-denying goddess Athena, his ultimate cooptation of female power.

It is interesting to note that the oracle at Delphi, who was called the Pythia, had to be a woman, but her ecstatic utterances were interpreted by male priests.

There lord Phoebus Apollo
decided to make his lovely temple.
. . . .
But near this place there was a spring
that was flowing beautifully,
and there the lord, the son of Zeus,
killed the big fat she-dragon,
with his mighty bow.
She was a wild monster
that worked plenty of evil
on the men of earth,
sometimes on the men themselves,
often on their sheep with their thin feet.
She meant bloody misery.
She once received from Hera,
who sits on a golden throne,
the dreaded, cruel, Typhaon,
and raised him, a sorrow for mankind.
Hera had given him birth once
when she was mad at father Zeus,
when the son of Cronos himself
was giving birth to glorious Athena
in his head. The lady Hera
got angry then, and said this

★ ★ ★

How did you dare give birth,
alone, to bright-eyed Athena?
Wouldn't I have given birth for you?
At least I was called your wife
among the gods
who live in this big heaven.
Watch out now that I don't plan
some trouble for you later on:
yes in fact I will plan something,
that a son will be born to me
who will stand out among the immortal gods,
and it won't shame your sacred marriage
or mine. But I won't come to your bed,
I'll go far away from you
and stay with the immortal gods."

She said all this
and went away from the gods,
her heart very angry. The lady Hera,
with her cow-eyes, then prayed,
and struck the ground
with the flat of her hand, and said:
"Listen to me now,

Earth and wide Heaven overhead,
and you Titan gods
who live under the earth
around big Tartarus,
from whom we get both men and gods.
Listen to me now,
all of you, and give me a child
separate from Zeus, and yet one
who isn't any weaker than him
in strength. In fact,
make him stronger than Zeus,
just as Zeus who sees so far
is stronger than Cronos."
She cried this out
and beat the ground
with her thick hand.

★ ★ ★

But when the months and days
were finished, and the seasons
came and went with the turning year,
she bore something
that didn't resemble the gods,
or humans, at all: she bore
the dreaded, the cruel, Typhaon,
a sorrow for mankind.
Immediately the lady Hera,
with her cow-eyes, took it
and gave it to her (the she-dragon),
bringing one wicked thing to another.
And she received it.
And it used to do
plenty of terrible things
to the famous tribes of mankind.

Whoever encountered the she-dragon,
it was doomsday for him,
until the lord Apollo,
who works from a distance,
shot a strong arrow at her.
And she lay there,
torn with terrible pain,
gasping deeply, and rolling around
on the ground.
She made an incredible, wonderful noise.
She turned over again and again,
constantly, in the wood.
And then life left her,
breathing up blood.
[From *The Homeric Hymns,* pp. 166–71.]

THE MAENADS—ECSTATIC WOMEN

The Maenads were female worshipers of the god Dionysus who entered ecstatic trances which gave them great physical strength and a complete indifference to the conventions of their society. These women wandered freely in the countryside celebrating Dionysus in song and dance. Sometimes they were quite gentle, but Euripides brings out their violent aspects in his play *The Bacchants,* written c. 408–406 B.C.E. Women made up the majority of Dionysus's followers, and the men who did join them often dressed as women when they participated in the rites. The cult was not without its critics—in Rome the Senate attempted to repress it. In Euripides' play, King Pentheus also attempts to stamp out the cult in which his mother, Agave, is a celebrant. In the following excerpt a herdsman who has overseen the women reports to the king.

HERDSMAN.   Our herds of pasturing kine had just begun to ascend the steep to the ridge, at the hour when the sun shoots forth his rays to warm the earth. I saw three bands of women dancers: Autonoe was leader of the first choir, your mother Agave of the second, and Ino of the third. They all lay in the sleep of exhaustion. Some were reclining with their backs against branches of fir, others had flung themselves at random on the ground on leaves of oak [modestly, not as you charge, intoxicated with the wine-bowl and the sound of the flute and hunting Cypris in the lonely forest].

Then your mother rose up in the midst of the bacchants and called upon them to bestir their limbs from sleep when she heard the lowing of the horned kine. The women then cast the heavy sleep from their eyes and sprang upright, a sight of wondrous comeliness. There were young women and old women and maids yet unmarried. First they let their hair fly loose about their shoulders and tucked up their fawnskins, those whose fastenings had become unloosed, and girt the speckled skins about them with serpents that licked their cheek. Others held gazelles in their arms, or the untamed whelps of wolves, feeding them with white milk. These were young mothers who had left their infants behind and still had their breasts swollen with milk. Then they put on ivy wreaths and crowns of oak and flowery smilax. One took her thyrsus and struck it against a rock, and there sprang from it a dewy stream of water. Another struck her fennel wand upon the ground, and the god sent up a fountain of wine for her. Those that had a desire for the white drink scraped the earth with the tips of their fingers, and had rich store of milk. From the wands of ivy there dripped sweet streams of honey. If you had been there to see, you would have approached with prayers the god whom you now revile.

We cowherds and shepherds came together to argue and debate with one another on the fearful and wonderful things they did. One fellow who was fond of loafing about town, an experienced talker, spoke out to all and sundry: "You who dwell upon the holy terraces of the mountains, do you vote that we chase Pentheus' mother, Agave, from her bacchic revels and do our king a kindness?" He seemed to us to speak well, and so we set an ambush amidst the leafy thickets and hid ourselves. At the set time they waved the thyrsus for their revelling and all together with one voice, invoked Bacchus, Zeus' offspring Bromius. The whole mountain cried "Bacchus" with them. The animals joined in the revelry. Everywhere there was a stirring as they raced along.

Now Agave happened to come racing by me and I jumped out and made to seize her, evacuating the ambush where I was hiding. But she raised a cry: "Ah, my fleet hounds, we are being hunted by these men! But follow me, follow with your wands in your hands for weapons."

We fled and escaped a rending at the bacchants' hands. But, with naked, unarmed, hands, the women attacked the heifers that were grazing on the grass. You could see one holding wide the legs of a well-fed calf which bellowed and bellowed. Others rent heifers apart. You could see ribs of cloven hooves tossed here and there, and pieces smeared with gore hanging from the firs, dripping blood. The wanton bulls—forgotten the menace of their levelled horns—were tripped and dragged to the ground by the hands of countless young women. Quicker were their coverings of flesh torn asunder than you could close the lids of your royal eyes. Like birds they soared off the ground in their flight as they scoured the spreading plains by the streams of Asopus which grow the fine harvests of Thebes. Like an invading army they fell upon Hysiae and Erythrae, which nestle under Cithaeron's slopes, and everywhere they wrought confusion and havoc. They pillaged homes at random. Their loot they put upon their shoulders, and though it was not tied on, it held fast; nothing fell to the dark earth, neither brass nor iron. They carried fire in their curls and it did not burn them. Some of us, angered by the depredations of the bacchants, resorted to arms. And *there* was a terrible sight to see, O king. Pointed spears drew no blood, whereas the women flung wands from their hands and wounded their assailants till they turned tail and ran. Women defeating men! There was a god with them. Then they went back whence they had started, to the fountains which the god has shot up for them. They washed off the blood, while the serpents licked clean the clots from their cheeks.

[From *Ten Plays by Euripides,* pp. 296–97.]

SAPPHO—A WOMAN POET

Sappho, the most famous woman poet among the Greeks, was born on the island of Lesbos about 612 B.C.E. Sappho was married, but, like the male aristocrats of ancient Greece, preferred the love of her own sex. She was perhaps best known for the erotic poems she wrote about women. Some of her poems suggest that she was in charge of a school for young girls.

The poems below are praises of and supplications to Aphrodite, the goddess of love, fertility, and beauty.

A Prayer to Aphrodite

On your delicate throne, Aphrodite,
sly eternal daughter of Zeus,
I beg you: do not crush me with grief,

but come to me now—as once
you heard my far cry, and yielded,
slipping from your father's house

to yoke the birds to your gold
chariot, and came. Handsome swallows
brought you swiftly to the dark earth,

their wings whipping the middle sky.
Happy, with deathless lips, you smiled:
"What is wrong, why have you called me?

What does your mad heart desire?
Whom shall I make love you, Sappho,
who is turning her back on you?

Let her run away, she'll soon chase you;
refuse your gifts, she'll soon give them.
She will love you, though unwillingly."

Then come to me now and free me
from fearful agony. Labor
for my mad heart, and be my ally.

To Aphrodite of the Flowers, at Knossos

Come to the holy temple of the virgins
where the pleasant grove of apple trees
circles in altar smoking with frankincense.

The roses leave shadow on the ground
and cool springs murmur through apple branches
where shuddering leaves pour down profound sleep.

In that meadow where horses have grown
glossy, and all spring flowers grow wild,
the anise shoots fill the air with aroma

And there our queen Aphrodite pours
celestial nectar in the gold cups,
which she fills gracefully with sudden joy.

To Aphrodite

For you, Aphrodite, I will burn
the savory fat of a white she-goat.
All this I will leave behind for you.
[From *Greek Lyric Poetry,* pp. 70–71, 72.]

CIRCE – GODDESS AND WITCH

Homer lived during the 8th century B.C.E. and his two great works, the *Iliad* and the *Odyssey*, take place during the Trojan War of the thirteenth century B.C.E. In Chapter Ten of the *Odyssey*, the hero, Odysseus, and his men have been wandering for some time since the fall of Troy, unable to reach their homeland of Ithaca. One of the many places they visit is the island of Aeaea, where Circe lives with four maids and assorted animals who are actually men she has transformed into beasts. Odysseus and his men variously describe her as a beautiful woman, a witch, and a goddess (her parents are gods, Helios and Perse). Under the guise of offering Odysseus' men hospitality, Circe transforms some of them into swine. She does this by means of a magic potion, or drug, which she puts in their food, and her magic wand. With the help of the god Hermes, Odysseus successfully avoids Circe's magic and convinces her to transform his men back into their human forms which she does by rubbing them with a magic salve. Odysseus then lives with her in great happiness for about one year.

Circe is a beautiful and dangerous woman, one who enchants men, turning them into beasts, with her potions and her wand. Her sexuality also makes her dangerous, as is shown by Odysseus' need to bind her with an oath before they go to her bed. There are two not un-connected issues here. The first has to do with women whose sexuality is not controlled by a man. This is always problematic in patriarchal societies. The second issue has to do with the fear of being trapped in the body of an animal while remaining conscious of being a human being. In the ancient world this seemed to be a possibility. In Greek mythology the gods have the power to transform themselves into animals (e.g., Zeus, particularly in his amourous quests) and to turn others into animals. Circe also has this power. Her sexuality seems to be con-nected to her ability to transform men into animals, perhaps to 'bring out the beast in men.'

In the following excerpt, under pressure from his crew, Odysseus wants to start his journey home and he asks Circe to fulfill her promise to help him. She tells him that before he can go home he must go to the Land of the Dead in order to consult with a dead prophet. Circe gives Odysseus detailed instructions on how to find the Land of the Dead, how to protect himself once he is there, and the particular rituals he should perform while waiting for the dead prophet to appear. In this way Circe demonstrates her equal familiarity with the Land of the Living and the Land of the Dead. Therefore she can act as a medium or guide between these two realms.

Then I climbed on the beautiful bed of Circe and begged her, clasping her knees, and the divine goddess heard me as I spoke winged words to her:

"O Circe, fulfill the promise which you made to me and send me home. The spirit is already eager in me and in the rest of my companions. They pine away, lamenting around me when you are away somewhere."

So I spoke and the divine goddess answered:

"Zeus-descended son of Laertes, Odysseus of many devices, never remain unwilling in my house. But first it is necessary for you to complete another journey, and come to the house of Hades and dread Persephone, so that you may consult the spirit of Theban Teiresias, the blind seer, whose mind is still steadfast. For to him, though he is dead, Persephone

granted a mind that is understanding. The others flit around like shadows."

So she spoke and my heart was destroyed. Sitting on the bed, I wept. In my heart I no longer wished to live or see the light of the sun. But when I had had my fill of weeping and tossing around, then answer-ing her in words, I said:

"O Circe, who will be the guide on this journey? Whoever sailed to Hades?"

So I spoke and the divine goddess answered me:

"Zeus-descended son of Laertes, Odysseus of many devices, do not let the lack of a pilot be a care to you. Set up the mast, spread the white sails and sit down. The breath of the North Wind will carry the ship for you. When you have passed through Oceanos in your ship, where there is the strand and the fertile grove of Persephone—great poplars and willows shedding their fruit—draw up your ship there by deep-eddying Oceanos and go yourself to the dank house of Hades. There Pyiphlegethon and Cocytos flow in Acheron, which is a branch of the water of Styx—a rock and a meeting of two loud-thundering rivers. Then coming near, as I order you, hero, dig a trench the size of a cubit on each side. Around it pour a libation for all the dead, first of honey mixed with milk, then of wine, and thirdly of water, and sprinkle it with white barley. Make many prayers to the powerless heads of the dead, vowing that when you come to Ithaka, you will sacrifice a sterile cow, the best there is, in your halls, and pile goods on the fire. Sacrifice separately to Teiresias a black sheep, the best in your flock. When

you have prayed to the famous tribes of the dead, sacrifice a ram and a black ewe, turning their heads toward Erebos. And you yourself turn away toward the streams of the river. At that point, many souls of the departed dead will come up. Then urge and command your companions to flay the sheep lying there slaughtered by the pitiless sword. And pray to the gods and the Hades and dread Persephone."

"You yourself, drawing your swords from your thigh, sit there, not allowing the feeble heads of the dead to go near the blood until you hear from Teiresias. Straitaway will come the seer, the leader of the people, who will tell you the measure of the journey and of your return home, how you may go on the fish-breeding seas."

[From *The Odyssey,* Book 10, 480–540.]

ANTIGONE—A HEROINE

The story of Antigone the daughter of Oedipus and his sister Jocasta, was dramatized by Sophocles (c. 496-406 B.C.E.) as the last play in his trilogy about this family. She is one of the great heroines of ancient Greece, a woman who acts according to the dictates of her conscience. When the play begins both Antigone's parents are dead and her uncle, Creon, rules in their place. Her brothers have killed each other in a civil war and now one of them, Polyneices, who fought against Creon, is being denied burial rites. In the following excerpt Antigone requests the aid of her sister, Ismene, in burying their brother.

ANTIGONE:
Listen, Ismenê:
Creon buried our brother Eteoclês
With military honors, gave him a soldier's funeral,
And it was right that he should; but Polyneicês,
Who fought as bravely and died as miserably,—
They say that Creon has sworn
No one shall bury him, no one mourn for him,
But his body must lie in the fields, a sweet treasure
For carrion birds to find as they search for food.
That is what they say, and our good Creon is coming here
To announce it publicly; and the penalty—
Stoning to death in the public Square!
    There it is,
And now you can prove what you are:
A true sister, or a traitor to your family.
ISMENE:
Antigonê you are mad! What could I possibly do?
ANTIGONE:
You must decide whether you will help me or not.

ISMENE:
I do not understand you. Help you in what?
ANTIGONE:
Ismenê, I am going to bury him. Will you come?
ISMENE:
Bury him! You have just said the new law forbids it.
ANTIGONE:
He is my brother. And he is your brother, too.
ISMENE:
But think of the danger! Think what Creon will do!
ANTIGONE:
Creon is not strong enough to stand in my way.
ISMENE:
Ah sister!
Oedipus died, everyone hating him
For what his own search brought to light, his eyes
Ripped out by his own hand; and Iocastê died,
His mother and wife at once: she twisted the cords
That strangled her life; and our two brothers died,
Each killed by the other's sword. And we are left:
But oh, Antigonê,
Think how much more terrible than these. . . .

Our own death would be if we should go against
   Creon
And do what he has forbidden! We are only women,
We cannot fight with men, Antigonê!
The law is strong, we must give in to the law
In this thing, and in worse. I beg the Dead
To forgive me, but I am helpless: I must yield
To those in authority. And I think it is dangerous
   business
To be always meddling.
ANTIGONE:
   If that is what you think,
I should not want you, even if you asked to come.

You have made your choice, you can be what you
   want to be.
But I will bury him; and if I must die,
I say that this crime is holy: I shall lie down
With him in death, and I shall be as dear
To him as he to me.
   It is the dead,
Not the living, who make the longest demands:
We die for ever . . .
   You may do as you like
Since apparently the laws of the gods mean nothing
   to you.
   [From Sophocles, *The Oedipus Cycle,* pp.
   186–188.]

Antigone is caught performing burial rites for her brother and brought before Creon where
a guard describes her actions. Antigone argues that she followed God's law, which is greater
than Creon's law.

[Guard:]
And then she brought more dust
And sprinkled wine three times for her brother's
   ghost.

We ran and took her at once. She was not afraid,
Not even when we charged her with what she had
   done.
She denied nothing.
   And this was a comfort to me,
And some uneasiness: for it is a good thing
To escape from death, but it is no great pleasure
To bring death to a friend.
   Yet I always say
There is nothing so comfortable as your own safe
   skin!
CREON: [*Slowly, dangerously*]
And you, Antigonê,
You with your head hanging,—do you confess this
   thing?
ANTIGONE:
I do. I deny nothing.
CREON: [*To* SENTRY]
You may go.

                                    [*Exit* SENTRY]
                                    [*To* ANTIGONE:]
Tell me, tell me briefly:
Had you heard my proclamation touching this matter?
ANTIGONE:
It was public. Could I help hearing it?

CREON:
And yet you dared defy the law.
ANTIGONE:
   I dared.
   It was not God's proclamation. That final Justice
That rules the world below makes no such laws.

Your edict, King, was strong,
But all your strength is weakness itself against
The immortal unrecorded laws of God.
They are not merely now: they were, and shall be,
Operative for ever, beyond man utterly.

I knew I must die, even without your decree:
I am only mortal. And if I must die
Now, before it is my time to die,
Surely this is no hardship: can anyone
Living, as I live, with evil all about me,
Think Death less than a friend? This death of mine
Is of no importance; but if I had left my brother
Lying in death unburied, I should have suffered.
Now I do not.
   You smile at me. Ah Creon,
Think me a fool, if you like; but it may well be
That a fool convicts me of folly.
CHORAGOS:
Like father, like daughter: both headstrong, deaf to
   reason!
She has never learned to yield.
   [From Sophocles, *The Oedipus Cycle,* pp. 202–203.]

MEDEA

Medea's story is best known through the classical playwright Euripides (c. 485–c. 406 B.C.E.). His Medea was first performed in Athens in 431 B.C.E., though it depicts events thought to have taken place as much as 1,000 years earlier.

The play opens with Medea's nurse briefly recounting the events that have lead up the present situation. Medea fell in love with the Greek hero Jason when he came to her father's kingdom seeking the golden fleece. Out of her passion for Jason, Medea betrayed her father, used her magical powers to aid Jason in stealing the golden fleece, and killed her brother when he pursued them. Jason and Medea fled to the city of Corinth where they lived happily for a time and where Medea bore Jason two sons. As the play opens, it is now Jason who has betrayed Medea by planning to marry the young daughter of the King of Corinth. Through this union Jason will secure a place of prominence for himself, though Medea and her sons will have to be banished. Medea is enraged. Pretending to acquiesce to Jason's marriage, Medea takes her revenge first by killing the bride and her father and then by killing her own children, Jason's children. Jason arrives, screaming curses at her, and accuses her of causing all this destruction simply because he will no longer have sex with her. Medea acknowledges this before she flies off in a chariot drawn by two dragons.

In the following excerpt from the beginning of the play Medea describes her position as a woman in a foreign city abandoned by her husband, and she pleads with King Creon to let her stay in Corinth. Note especially the references to Medea's magical powers and her speech to Hecate, the goddess of witches.

CHORUS. *I hear a cry of grief and deep sorrow. In piercing accents of misery she proclaims her woes, her ill-starred marriage and her love betrayed. The victim of grievous wrongs, she calls on the daughter of Zeus, even Themis, Lady of Vows, who led her through the night by difficult straits across the briny sea to Hellas.*

[*Enter Medea.*]

MEDEA. Women of Corinth, do not criticize me, I come forth from the palace. Well I know that snobbery is a common charge, that may be levelled against recluse and busy man alike. And the former, by their choice of a quiet life, acquire an extra stigma: they are deficient in energy and spirit. There is no justice in the eyes of men; a man who has never harmed them they may hate at sight, without ever knowing anything about his essential nature. An alien, to be sure, should adapt himself to the citizens with whom he lives. Even the citizen is to be condemned if he is too selfwilled or too uncouth to avoid offending his fellows. So I . . . but this unexpected blow which has befallen me has broken my heart.

It's all over, my friends; I would gladly die. Life has lost its savor. The man who was everything to me, well he knows it, has turned out to be the basest of men. Of all creatures that feel and think, we women are the unhappiest species. In the first place, we must pay a great dowry to a husband who will be the tyrant of our bodies (that's a further aggravation of the evil);

and there is another fearful hazard: whether we shall get a good man or a bad. For separations bring disgrace on the woman and it is not possible to renounce one's husband. Then, landed among strange habits and regulations unheard of in her own home, a woman needs second sight to know how best to handle her bedmate. And if we manage this well and have a husband who does not find the yoke of intercourse too galling, our life is a life to be envied. Otherwise, one is better dead. When the man wearies of the company of his wife, he goes outdoors and relieves the disgust of his heart [having recourse to some friend or the companions of his own age], but we women have only one person to turn to.

They say that we have a safe life at home, whereas men must go to war. Nonsense! I had rather fight three battles than bear one child. But be that as it may, you and I are not in the same case. You have your city here, your paternal homes; you know the delights of life and association with your loved ones. But I, homeless and forsaken, carried off from a foreign land, am being wronged by a husband, with neither mother nor brother nor kinsman with whom I might find refuge from the storms of misfortune. One little boon I crave of you, if I discover any ways and means of punishing my husband for these wrongs: your silence. Woman in most respects is a timid creature, with no heart for strife and aghast at the sight of steel;

but wronged in love, there is no heart more murderous than hers.

LEADER. Do as you say, Medea, for just will be your vengeance. I do not wonder that you bemoan your fate. But I see Creon coming, the ruler of this land, bringing tidings of new plans.

[Enter Creon.]

CREON. You there, Medea, looking black with rage against your husband; I have proclaimed that you are to be driven forth in exile from this land, you and your two sons. Immediately. I am the absolute judge of the case, and I shall not go back to my palace till I have cast you over the frontier of the land.

MEDEA. Ah! Destruction, double destruction is my unhappy lot. My enemies are letting out every sail and there is no harbor into which I may flee from the menace of their attack. But ill-treated and all, Creon, still I shall put the question to you: Why are you sending me out of the country?

CREON. I am afraid of you—there's no need to hide behind a cloak of words—afraid you will do my child some irreparable injury. There's plenty logic in that fear. You are a wizard possessed of evil knowledge. You are stung by the loss of your husband's love. And I have heard of your threats—they told me of them— to injure bridegroom and bride and father of the bride. Therefore before anything happens to me, I shall take precautions. Better for me now to be hateful in your eyes than to relent and rue it greatly later.

* * *

MEDEA. Allow me to stay for this one day to complete my plans for departure and get together provision for my children, since their father prefers not to bother about his own sons. Have pity on them. You too are the father of children. It is natural that you should feel kindly. Stay or go, I care nothing for myself. It's them I weep for in their misfortune.

CREON. My mind is not tyrannical enough; mercy has often been my undoing. So now, though I know that it is a mistake, woman, you will have your request. But I give you warning: if to-morrow's divine sun sees you and your children inside the borders of this country, you die. True is the word I have spoken. [Stay, if you must, this one day. You'll not have time to do what I dread.]

[Exit Creon.]

CHORUS. Hapless woman! overwhelmed by sorrow! Where will you turn? What stranger will afford you hospitality?

God has steered you, Medea, into an unmanageable surge of troubles.

MEDEA. Ill fortune's everywhere, who can gainsay it? But it is not yet as bad as that, never think so. There is still heavy weather ahead for the new bride and groom, and no little trouble for the maker of the match. Do you think I would ever have wheedled the king just now except to further my own plans? I would not even have spoken to him, nor touched him either. But he is such a fool that though he might have thwarted my plans by expelling me from the country he has allowed me to stay over for this one day, in which I shall make corpses of three of my enemies, father and daughter and my own husband.

My friends, I know several ways of causing their death, and I cannot decide which I should turn my hand to first. Shall I set fire to the bridal chamber or make my way in stealthily to where their bed is laid and drive a sword through their vitals? But there is one little difficulty. If I am caught entering the palace or devising my bonfire I shall be slain and my enemies shall laugh. Better take the direct way and the one for which I have the natural gift. Poison. Destroy them with poison. So be it.

But suppose them slain. What city will receive me? Whose hospitality will rescue me and afford me a land where I shall be safe from punishment, a home where I can live in security? It cannot be. I shall wait, therefore, a little longer and if any tower of safety shows up I shall carry out the murders in stealth and secrecy. However, if circumstances drive me to my wits' end, I shall take a sword in my own hands and face certain death to slay them. I shall not shirk the difficult adventure. No! by Queen Hecate who has her abode in the recesses of my hearth—her I revere above all gods and have chosen to assist me—never shall any one of them torture my heart with impunity. I shall make their marriage a torment and grief to them. Bitterly shall they rue the match they have made and the exile they inflict on me.

But enough! Medea, use all your wiles; plot and devise. Onward to the dreadful moment. Now is the test of courage. Do you see how you are being treated? It is not right that the seed of Sisyphus and Aeson should gloat over you, the daughter of a noble sire and descendant of the Sun. But you realize that. Moreover by our mere nature we women are helpless for good, but adept at contriving all manner of wickedness.

[From Ten Plays by Euripides, pp. 36–41.]

DIOTIMA—A WOMAN PHILOSOPHER

In the following excerpt from Plato's (429-347 B.C.E.) Symposium (sections 201-212) Socrates, Plato's teacher and spokesperson, describes a conversation he had with the philosopher Diotima, who was his teacher. The topic is the nature of love, which Socrates had been debating with Agathon. This conversation clearly shows that not only did Diotima teach him about the nature of love, she also taught him the so-called "Socratic method" of teaching by questioning. For Diotima love is the mediating spirit or force between the human and the divine. Her parable on the parents of love, Plenty and Poverty, is rich in meaning and suggests the influence love has on both the rich and the poor, as well as the skills it inspires in lovers. For Diotima love is both wise and foolish. Through a combination of careful questioning and exposition she leads Socrates to understand that love, through its pursuit of wisdom and beauty, can be elevated from the particular to the universal, or from the concrete to the abstract.

[Socrates:]

And now, taking my leave of you, I will rehearse a tale of love which I heard from Diotima of Mantineia, a woman wise in this and in many other kinds of knowledge, who in the days of old, when the Athenians offered sacrifice before the coming of the plague, delayed the disease ten years. She was my instructress in the art of love, and I shall repeat to you what she said to me, beginning with the admissions made by Agathon, which are nearly if not quite the same which I made to the wise woman when she questioned me: I think that this will be the easiest way, and I shall take both parts myself as well as I can. As you, Agathon, suggested, I must speak first of the being and nature of Love, and then of his works. First I said to her in nearly the same words which he used to me, that Love was a mighty god, and likewise fair; and she proved to me as I proved to him that, by my own showing, Love was neither fair nor good. 'What do you mean, Diotima,' I said, 'is love then evil and foul?' 'Hush,' she cried; 'must that be foul which is not fair?' 'Certainly,' I said. 'And is that which is not wise, ignorant? do you not see that there is a mean between wisdom and ignorance?' 'And what may that be?' I said. 'Right opinion,' she replied; 'which, as you know, being incapable of giving a reason, is not knowledge (for how can knowledge be devoid of reason? nor again, ignorance, for neither can ignorance attain the truth), but is clearly something which is a mean between ignorance and wisdom.' 'Quite true,' I replied. 'Do not then insist,' she said, 'that what is not fair is of necessity foul, or what is not good evil; or infer that because love is not fair and good he is therefore foul and evil; for he is in a mean between them.' 'Well,' I said, 'Love is surely admitted by all to be a great god.' 'By those who know or by those who do not know?' 'By all.' 'And how, Socrates,' she said with a smile, 'can Love be acknowledged to be a great god by those who say that he is not a god at all?' 'And who are they?' I said. 'You and I are two of them,' she replied. 'How can that be?' I said. 'It is quite intelligible,' she replied; 'for you yourself would acknowledge that the gods are happy and fair — of course you would — would you dare to say that any god was not?'

'Certainly not,' I replied. 'And you mean by the happy, those who are the possessors of things good or fair?' 'Yes.' 'And you admitted that Love, because he was in want, desires those good and fair things of which he is in want?' 'Yes, I did.' 'But how can he be a god who has no portion in what is either good or fair?' 'Impossible.' 'Then you see that you also deny the divinity of Love.'

'What then is Love?' I asked; 'Is he mortal?' 'No.' 'What then?' 'As in the former instance, he is neither mortal nor immortal, but in a mean between the two.' 'What is he, Diotima?' 'He is a great spirit (δαίμων), and like all spirits he is intermediate between the divine and the mortal.' 'And what,' I said, 'is his power?' 'He interprets,' she replied, 'between gods and men, conveying and taking across to the gods the prayers and sacrifices of men, and to men the commands and replies of the gods; he is the mediator who spans the chasm which divides them, and therefore in him all is bound together, and through him the arts of the prophet and the priest, their sacrifices and mysteries and charms, and all prophecy and incantation, find their way. For God mingles not with man; but through Love all the intercourse and converse of god with man, whether awake or asleep, is carried on. The wisdom which understands this is spiritual; all other wisdom, such as that of arts and handicrafts, is mean and vulgar. Now these spirits or intermediate powers are many and diverse, and one of them is Love.' 'And who,' I said, 'was his father, and who his mother?' 'The tale,' she said, 'will take time; nevertheless I will tell you. On the birthday of Aphrodite there was a feast of the gods, at which the god Poros or Plenty, who is the son of Metis or Discretion, was one of the guests. When the feast was over, Penia or Poverty, as the manner is on such occasions, came about the doors to beg. Now Plenty, who was the worse for nectar (there was no wine in those days), went into the garden of Zeus and fell into a heavy sleep; and Poverty considering her own straitened circumstances, plotted to have a child by him, and accordingly she lay down at his side and conceived Love, who partly because he is naturally a lover of the beautiful, and because Aphrodite is herself beautiful, and also because he was born on her birthday, is her follower and attendant. And as his parentage is, so also are his fortunes. In the first place he is always poor, and anything but tender and fair, as the many imagine him; and he is rough and squalid, and has no shoes, nor a house to dwell in; on the bare earth exposed he lies under the open heaven, in the streets, or at the doors of houses, taking his rest; and like his mother he is always in distress. Like his father too, whom he also partly resembles, he is always plotting against the fair and good; he is bold, enterprising, strong, a mighty hunter, always weaving some intrigue or other, keen in the pursuit of wisdom, fertile in resources; a philosopher at all times, terrible as an enchanter, sorcerer, sophist. He is by nature neither mortal nor immortal, but alive and flourishing at one moment when he is in plenty, and dead at another moment, and again alive by reason of his father's nature. But that which is always flowing in is always flowing out, and so he is never in want and never in wealth; and, further, he is in a mean between ignorance and knowledge. The truth of the matter is this: No god is a philosopher or seeker after wisdom, for he is wise already; nor does any man who is wise seek after wisdom. Neither do the ignorant seek after wisdom. For herein is the evil of ignorance, that he who is neither good nor wise is nevertheless satisfied with himself: he has no desire for that of which he feels no want.' 'But who then, Diotima,' I said, 'are the lovers of wisdom, if they are neither the wise nor the foolish?' 'A child may answer that question,' she replied; 'they are those who are in a mean between the two; Love is one of them. For wisdom is a most beautiful thing, and Love is of the beautiful; and therefore Love is also a philosopher or lover of wisdom, and being a lover of wisdom is in a mean between the wise and the ignorant. And of this too his birth is the cause; for his father is wealthy and wise, and his mother poor and foolish. Such, my dear Socrates, is the nature of the spirit Love. The error in your conception of him was very natural, and as I imagine from what you say, has arisen out of a confusion of love and the beloved, which made you think that love was all beautiful. For the beloved is the truly beautiful, and delicate, and perfect, and blessed; but the principle of love is of another nature, and is such as I have described.'

* * *

[Diotima continues:]

'And the true order of going, or being led by another, to the things of love, is to begin from the beauties of earth and mount upwards for the sake of that other beauty, using these as steps only, and from one going on to two, and from two to all fair forms, and from fair forms to fair practices, and from fair practices to fair notions, until from fair notions he arrives at the notion of absolute beauty, and at last knows what the essence of beauty is. This, my dear Socrates,' said the stranger of Mantineia, 'is that life above all others which man should live, in the contemplation of beauty absolute; a beauty which if you once beheld, you would see not to be after the measure of gold, and garments, and fair boys and youths, whose presence now entrances you; and you and many a one would be content to live seeing them only and conversing with them without meat or drink, if that were possible—you only want to look at them and to be with them. But what if man had eyes to see the true beauty—the divine beauty, I mean, pure and clear and unalloyed, not clogged with the pollutions of mortality and all the colours and vanities of human life—thither looking, and holding converse with the true beauty simple and divine? Remember how in that communion only, beholding beauty with the eye of the mind, he will be enabled to bring forth, not images of beauty, but realities (for he has hold not of an image but of a reality), and bringing forth and nourishing true virtue to become the friend of God and be immortal, if mortal man may. Would that be an ignoble life?'

[From *The Dialogues of Plato*, 1:327–35.]

ARISTOTLE ON WOMEN

In the following excerpts from *The Generation of Animals* Aristotle (384–322 B.C.E.) discusses the development of the fetus in humans and animals specifically in terms of the contributions of semen and menstrual blood. Aristotle believed that females provide the body of the fetus, but it is males who provide the soul because the soul is potentially contained in semen, which is pure, and not in menstrual blood, which is impure (Book II, 3 & 4). Also, Aristotle believes people, and other species, are analyzable in terms of hot and cold, wet and moist. These distinctions vary between the sexes: females are cold and wet, while males are hot and dry, and these distinctions influence the sex of the fetus (Book IV, 1 & 2).

It has been settled, then, in what sense the embryo and the semen have soul, and in what sense they have not; they have it potentially but not actually.

Now semen is a residue and is moved with the same movement as that in virtue of which the body increases (this increase being due to subdivision of the nutriment in its last stage). When it has entered the uterus it puts into form the corresponding residue of the female and moves it with the same movement wherewith it is moved itself. For the female's contribution also is a residue, and has all the parts in it potentially though none of them actually; it has in it potentially even those parts which differentiate the female from the male, for just as the young of mutilated parents are sometimes born mutilated and sometimes not, so also the young born of a female are sometimes female and sometimes male instead. For the female is, as it were, a mutilated male, and the menstrual fluids are semen, only not pure; for there is only one thing they have not in them, the principle of soul. For this reason, whenever a wind-egg is produced by any animal, the egg so forming has in it the parts of both sexes potentially, but has not the principle in question, so that it does not develop into a living creature, for this is introduced by the semen of the male. When such a principle has been imparted to the residue of the female it becomes an embryo.

★ ★ ★

To consider now the region of the uterus in the female—the two blood-vessels, the great vessel and the aorta, divide higher up, and many fine vessels from them terminate in the uterus. These become over-filled from the nourishment they convey, nor is the female nature able to concoct it, because it is colder than man's; so the blood is excreted through very fine vessels into the uterus, these being unable on account of their narrowness to receive the excessive quantity, and the result is a sort of haemorrhage. The period is not accurately defined in women, but tends to return during the waning of the moon. This we should expect, for the bodies of animals are colder when the environment happens to become so, and the time of change from one month to another is cold because of the absence of the moon, whence also it results that this time is stormier than the middle of the month. When then the residue of the nourishment has changed into blood, the menstrual discharges tend to occur at the above-mentioned period, but when it is not concocted a little matter at a time is always coming away, and this is why 'whites' appear in females while still small, in fact mere children. If both these discharges of the residues are moderate, the body remains in good health, for they act as a purification of the residues which are the causes of a morbid state of body; if they do not occur at all or if they are excessive, they are injurious, either causing illness or pulling down the patient; hence whites, if continuous and excessive, prevent girls from growing. This residue then is necessarily discharged by females for the reasons given; for, the female nature being unable to concoct the nourishment thoroughly, there must not only be left a residue of the useless nutriment, but also there must be a residue of the blood in the blood-vessels, and this filling the channels of the finest vessels must overflow. Then nature, aiming at the best and the end, uses it up in this place for the sake of generation, that another creature may come into being of the same kind as the former was going to be, for the menstrual blood is already potentially such as the body from which it is discharged.

In all females, then, there must necessarily be such a residue, more indeed in those that have blood and of these most of all in man, but in the others also some matter must be collected in the uterine region. The reason why there is more in those that have blood and most in man has been already given; but why, if all females have such a residue, have not all males one to correspond? For some of them do not emit semen but, just as those which do emit it fashion by the movement in the semen the mass forming from the material supplied by the female, so do the animals in question bring the same to pass and exert the same formative power by the movement within themselves in that part from which the semen is secreted. This is the region about the diaphragm in all those animals which have one, for the heart or its analogue is the first principle of a natural body, while the lower part is a mere addition for the sake of it. Now the reason why it is not all males that have a generative residue, while all females do, is that the animal is a body with soul; the female always provides the material, the male that which fashions it, for this is the power that we say they each possess, and this is what it is for them to be male and female. Thus while it is necessary for the female to provide a body and a material mass, it is not necessary for the male, because it is not within what is produced that the tools or the maker must exist. While the body is from the female, it is the soul that is from the male, for the soul is the substance of a particular body.

[From *The Complete Works of Aristotle*, 1:1144–46.]

★ ★ ★

To recapitulate, we say that the semen has been laid down to be the ultimate residue of the nutriment. By ultimate I mean that which is carried to every part of the body, and this is also the reason why the offspring is like the parent. For it makes no difference whether we say that the semen comes from all the parts or goes to all of them, but the latter is the better.

But the semen of the male differs in that it contains a principle within itself of such a kind as to set up movements also in the embryo and to concoct thoroughly the ultimate nourishment, whereas the secretion of the female contains material alone. If, then, the male element prevails it draws the female element into itself, but if it is prevailed over it changes into the opposite or is destroyed. But the female is opposite to the male, and is female because of its inability to concoct and of the coldness of the sanguineous nutriment. And nature assigns to each of the residues the part fitted to receive it. But the semen is a residue, and this in the hotter animals with blood, i.e. the males, is moderate in quantity, which is why the recipient parts of this residue in males are only passages. But the females, owing to inability to concoct, have a great quantity of blood, for it cannot be worked up into semen. Therefore they must also have a part to receive this, and this part must be unlike the passages of the male and of a considerable size. This is why the uterus is of such a nature, this being the part by which the female differs from the male.

We have thus stated for what reason the one becomes female and the other male. Observed facts confirm what we have said. For more females are produced by the young and by those verging on old age than by those in the prime of life; in the former the heat is not yet perfect, in the latter it is failing. And those of a moister and more feminine state of body are more wont to beget females, and a liquid semen causes this more than a thicker; now all these characteristics come of deficiency in natural heat.

Again, more males are born if copulation takes place when north than when south winds are blowing; for animals' bodies are more liquid when the wind is in the south, so that they produce more residue—and more residue is harder to concoct; hence the semen of the males is more liquid, and so is the discharge of the menstrual fluids in women.

Also the fact that menstruation occurs in the course of nature rather when the month is waning is due to the same causes. For this time of the month is colder and moister because of the waning and failure of the moon; as the sun makes winter and summer in the year as a whole, so does the moon in the month. This is not due to the turning of the moon, but it grows warmer as the light increases and colder as it wanes.

The shepherds also say that it not only makes a difference in the production of males and females if copulation takes place during northern or southerly winds, but even if the animals while copulating look towards the south or north; so small a thing will sometimes turn the scale and cause cold or heat, and these again influence generation.

The male and female, then, are distinguished generally, as compared with one another in connexion with the production of male and female offspring, for the causes stated. However, they also need a certain correspondence with one another; for all things that come into being as products of art or of nature exist in virtue of a certain ratio. Now if the hot preponderates too much it dries up the liquid; if it is very deficient it does not solidify it; for the product we need the due mean between the extremes. Otherwise it will be as in cooking; too much fire burns the meat, too little does not cook it, and in either case the process is a failure. So also there is need of due proportion in the mixture of the male and female elements. And for this cause it often happens to many of both sexes that they do not generate with one another, but if divorced and remarried to others do generate; and these oppositions show themselves sometimes in youth, sometimes in advanced age, alike as concerns fertility or infertility, and as concerns generation of male or female offspring.

One country also differs from another in these respects, and one water from another, for the same reasons. For the nourishment and the condition of the body are of such or such a kind because of the tempering of the surrounding air and of the food entering the body, especially the water; for men consume more of this than of anything else, and this enters as nourishment into all food, even solids. Hence hard waters cause infertility, and cold waters the birth of females.

[From *The Complete Works of Aristotle*, 1:1186–87.]

Ancient Rome

The earliest forms of Roman religion did not have anthropomorphic images of their goddesses and gods nor did they compose detailed myths about them. Instead, specific deities were defined by their powers, e.g., Ceres and the fertility of grain. The ancient Romans had two goals in their religious life. The first was to avoid the wrath of the deities and the second was to win their favor. They believed all things happened through the will of the deities. Consequently, the Romans wanted to know the will of the goddesses and gods, which they learned through the practices of various forms of divinations such as reading divine signs in nature or examining the entrails of sacrificed animals. The Sibylline Books, purportedly going back to the seventh century B.C.E., were another important source for knowing the divine will. These books were thought to have originated from the utterances of the Cumae Sibyl, a woman believed to have the ability to predict the future while in ecstatic trances.

As Rome solidified its power in Italy and began expanding it incorporated the gods of the people it conquered. At the same time, due to Greek influence, Roman religion began anthropomorphizing their deities and synthesizing them with Greek deities. For instance, the Roman goddess of grain, Ceres, was identified with the Greek goddess of grain, Demeter. As Rome continued its conquest of the world it absorbed all aspects of Hellenistic culture.

The Hellenistic period is traditionally dated from the death of Alexander the Great (323 B.C.E.), the man who conquered the known world and was dead by age thirty-three. His armies swept through Greece and the decaying empires of the Middle East, Egypt, Persia, Babylonia, and so on, out to the Indus River of India. His conquests changed the social and religious concepts of all these lands, creating a unified world that responded to the Greek culture left behind by Alexander. The world was now a place where encounters between diverse cultures went on for centuries, encounters that led to an environment of broadened horizons that accepted and even invited the new and the foreign. This was particularly true in religious life, where there was a new respect for the religious beliefs of others and frequently the identification of foreign deities with familiar deities along with a consequent combining of their cults. Further, people began to have new spiritual longings for certainty about the afterlife as well as hopes for salvation, and these longings and hopes were frequently satisfied by mystery religions, many of which were rooted in very ancient religious practices. Mystery religions often had public, esoteric rites, but their main characteristic was that the essential teachings were only revealed to a limited numbers of initiates, women and men who performed a wide range of purifying acts, made various offerings through prayers, sacrifices, and vows, and frequently modified their daily habits, such as changing their diets to exclude meat or wine. These initiates then participated in the esoteric rituals that took place apart from public view, and they swore never to reveal the details of these rituals to the uninitiated. Since most initiates kept their vows of secrecy, we know very little about their esoteric rituals. We do know, however, that these rituals often involved a symbolic encounter with death followed by a rebirth experience. This was thought to prepare the initiate for the experience of death that would lead to a rebirth into eternal life. Mystery religions, especially through these initiations, offered people a personal and elite experience of the sacred that provided reassurance about the afterlife.

A common feature of mystery religions is their connection to agricultural rituals; the seasonal pattern of planting, fruition, decay, and new planting which was a metaphor for the human cycle as well. Devotees hoped that through initiation they entered into an exclusive company who, like the plants that returned every year, would be reborn, though reborn into an eternal afterlife. An important feature of agricultural rituals is that goddesses tend to predominate and this was often the case in the mystery religions that flourished at this time.

Roman religion also gave a prominent place to goddesses from the earliest times, especially to the goddesses Vesta, Juno, and Minerva. Another important goddess, Venus, achieved prominence through the Trojan warrior Aeneas, said to be her son and the founder of Rome.

When Augustus became emperor in 19 B.C.E. he began making changes in Roman religious and moral life. His stated objective was to restore earlier Roman values and strengthen the moral structure of the Roman family. The last involved establishing greater control over women. Augustus saw the decline of family life, demonstrated by a low birth rate and a high divorce rate, as a threat to Roman stability. He therefore instituted new laws regarding women. One law transferred the powers previously held by fathers over their daughters to husbands, while another transferred the father's power to the state, allowing women to be publicly judged. For instance, the *Lex Julia de Adulteriis* established a court to hear cases of women accused of adultery. On the other hand, Augustus instituted a law that gave women who bore three children full control of their persons and property without need of a legal guardian. In effect, the patriarchal family system of the Republic was undermined by the power of the state. One unexpected consequence of this was that women achieved positions of power and influence in both politics and religion. The women of the royal family were more prominent in public life than Republican women, and Roman women found satisfying public and private roles in the new foreign cults.

CREATION

Ovid's (43 B.C.E.-17 C.E.) poem, *The Metamorphoses,* is the first book to organize all the Greek and Roman myths into a cohesive whole. Ovid opens his work with a speculative discussion of creation in which he reveals his uncertainty as to whether the separation from the primordial chaos began through the agency of a god or of nature. But, if it was by divine agency, he is certain that it was a male god and not a female goddess. Essentially, his view is that there was a progression, or metamorphosis, out of chaos into order.

Chaos and Creation

Before land was and sea—before air and sky
Arched over all, all Nature was all Chaos,
The rounded body of all things in one
The living elements at war with lifelessness;
No God, no Titan shone from sky or sea,
No Moon, no Phoebe outgrew slanted horns
And walked the night, nor was Earth poised in air.
No wife of Ocean reached her glittering arms
Into the farthest shores of reef and sand.
Earth, Air, Water heaved and turned in darkness,
No living creatures knew that land, that sea
Where heat fell against cold, cold against heat—
Roughness at war with smooth and wet with
   drought.
Things that gave way entered unyielding masses,
Heaviness fell into things that had no weight.

Then God or Nature calmed the elements:
Land fell away from sky and sea from land,
And aether drew away from cloud and rain.
As God unlocked all elemental things,
Fire climbed celestial vaults, air followed it
To float in heavens below; and earth which carried
All heavier things with it dropped under air;
Water fell farthest, embracing shores and islands.

When God, whichever God he was, created
The universe we know, he made of earth
A turning sphere so delicately poised
That water flowed in waves beneath the wind
And Ocean's arms encircled the rough globe:
At God's touch, lakes, springs, dancing waterfalls
Streamed downhill into valleys, waters glancing
Through rocks, grass and wild-flowered meadows;
Some ran their silver courses underground,
Others raced into seas and broader Ocean—

All poured from distant hills to farthest shores.
Then God willed plain, plateau, and fallen sides
Of hills in deep-leaved forests: over them
He willed rock-bodied mountains against sky.
As highest heaven has two zones on the right,
Two on the left, and a fifth zone in flames,
With celestial fires between the four, so
God made zones on earth, the fifth zone naked
With heat where none may live, at each extreme
A land of snow, and, at their sides, two zones
Of temperate winds and sun and shifting cold.

And air arched over all, air heavier than
Fire in the same measure as water carries
Less weight than the entire weight of earth.
Through gathering air God sent storm clouds and
   rain,
Thunder that shakes the heart, ice in the wind
That pierces all with cold—yet the world's master
Did not give all air's space to fighting ground
Of the Four Winds: each had his home and yet
So wildly the Brothers quarrel, even now
The world is almost torn in a war of winds.
Eurus whose winged breath stirs Araby
Went where the hills of Persia glow with dawn;
And where the western shores are lit with fires
There Zephyrus with the setting sun came home;
While ice-tongued Boreas roared in farthest north,
Auster, the South Wind, gathered summer storms—
Shining above them floated heavenly aether.

As God divided regions of this world
Into their separate parts, then all the stars
Long lost in ancient dark began to light
Pale fires throughout the sky. And as each part
Of universal being came to life,
Each filled with images of its own kind:

Among the stars gods walked the house of heaven
And where the sea opened its waves fish spawned;
Earth gathered beasts, and in the trembling air
The flight of birds.

   Yet world was not complete:
It lacked a creature that had hints of heaven
And hopes to rule the earth. So man was made.
Whether He who made all things aimed at the best,
Creating man from his own living fluid,
Or if earth, lately fallen through heaven's aether,

Took an immortal image from the skies,
Held it in clay which son of Iapetus
Mixed with the spray of brightly running waters
It had a godlike figure and was man.
While other beasts, heads bent, stared at wild earth,
The new creation gazed into blue sky;
Then careless things took shape, change followed change
And with it unknown species of mankind.
   [From Ovid, *Metamorphoses*, pp. 31–33.]

THE CUMAE SIBYL

   The *Aeneid* of Virgil (70–19 B.C.E.) is an epic poem that describes the founding of Rome by the Trojan hero Aeneas. The following excerpt from Book Six takes place seven years after the fall of Troy. Through a vision of his dead father Aeneas is told that he must visit the land of the dead before he sails for Italy and that the Sibyl will be his guide. This is the Sibyl at Cumae, who, according to Virgil, received her inspiration from Apollo (Phoebus), though the goddesses Hecate and Diana are also mentioned. Actually, the Cumae Sibyl predates the cult of the Greek god Apollo in Rome and was the purported source for the Sibylline Books. These books became the source of the state oracle of Rome and as such shaped much of not only Roman political life, but also Roman religious life: They provided affirmative oracles for changes in religious life such as the building of the first temple to the goddess Ceres and for allowing the foreign cults of Asklelpios and Magna Mater into the city. Originally these books were kept in the temple of Jupiter. After this temple burned down in 83 B.C.E. Emperor Augustus ordered a new collection to be placed in the newly built temple of Apollo. Despite their origin from a female oracle, the priesthood which consulted these books was exclusively male. The *Aeneid* vividly describes the ecstatic quality of the Sibyl's trance. She predicts the future for Aeneas and tells him what to expect on the journey to the land of the dead where she will act as his guide.

Then the priestess summoned the men to her lofty temple.
The side of the Euboean cliff is hollowed out
into a cavern with a hundred mouths and tunnels,
through which as many voices emerge—the Sibyl's answers.
And as they reached the temple's threshold the maiden cried:
"Now is the time to consult the oracle. Lo, the god, the god!" and as she spoke her face and color changed,
her hair fell in disorder, her bosom heaved and panted,
her heart swelled with wild frenzy; she seemed to become taller,
her voice no longer sounded human; the god was near her,
touching her with his breath. "Trojan Aeneas," she said,
"Why do you delay with prayer? For until you pray

the temple's mighty mouth will not be afraid and open."
She was silent. An icy shudder ran through the Trojans' limbs.
Aeneas, their king, begins to pray from deep in his heart.
"O Phoebus, you who have always pitied the woes of Troy,
who guided the hand of Paris and the Dardanian shaft
against Achilles, under your leadership I have sailed
to many lands and many seas, from the distant country
of the Massylians to the fields the Syrtes border.
Now at last we have reached the fleeting Italian shore:
may Troy's ill fortune not pursue us any further!
And all you gods and goddesses, who once were offended
by Troy and all her glory, Destiny now permits you

ANCIENT NEAR EAST, GREECE, AND ROME

to spare this people. And you, O holy prophetess,
seer of the future, grant us (for I do not ask
a kingdom not promised by Fate) allow the Trojans
  to settle
in Latium, with the wandering, storm-tossed gods
  of Troy.
And I shall dedicate to Phoebus and Trivia
a solid marble temple, with festal days for Apollo.
You too, O Sibyl, shall have an ample shrine in our
  land,
where I shall place your oracles and mystic responses
that you will give my people, with chosen men as
  priests.
Only, I beg you, do not entrust your verses to leaves,
for they will fly about in wild disorder, the playthings
of greedy winds; but chant them yourself." He finished speaking.
But the prophetess, not yet submitting to Phoebus,
runs wildly through the cave, still trying to shake off
the power of the god. But Phoebus, all the more,
torments her mouth and tames her heart and molds
  her will.
And now the hundred mighty mouths, of their own
  accord,
opened and carried through the air the seer's response:
"You who at last have overcome the sea's great
  perils,
the land holds even worse for you. The Trojans will
  come
into Lavinium's realm—dismiss this care from your
  mind—
but they will live to regret it. Wars, terrible wars
I see for you. The Tiber will run red with blood.
Another Simois and Xanthus and Grecian camp
await you there; and you shall find another Achilles,
also born of a goddess; and Juno still will hound you;
and you shall pray, a suppliant in desperate plight,
to all the peoples, and all the cities of Italy.
The cause of all these woes will again be a foreign
  bride,
again an alien marriage. . . .
But do not yield to troubles, nay, face them even more
  boldly
than Fortune seems to permit you. For the road to
  safety
will come, where you least expect it, from a Grecian
  city."
These are the ambiguous words the Cumaean Sibyl
chants from her shrine, a roaring echo in the cavern,

shrouding truth in riddles. Such is the might of
  Apollo,
holding the reins, applying the goad to the priestess'
  mind.
But when her frenzy had passed and her raging mouth
  was silent,
the hero Aeneas began: "O maiden, no new trials
or unexpected labors are in store for me;
for I have foreseen them all within my mind.
One thing I pray: since this is said to be the entrance
to the Underworld—the gloomy marsh of Acheron
allow me to see again my beloved father's face;
teach me the road and own for me the sacred portals.

* * *

He spoke and clasped the altar;
the priestess then replied: "Trojan son of Anchises,
sprung from blood divine, the descent to Avernus is
  easy.
The doors of gloomy Dis stand open night and day.
But to retrace your steps and escape to the air above,
this is the task, this the toil. To a few, whom Jupiter
  loved,
or who were exalted by their virtuous deeds to
  Heaven
sons of gods, this was permitted. Surrounded by
  forests,
inky Cocytus girds the place with sinuous folds.
But if you have in your heart such longing, such desire
twice to cross the Styx, and twice to see black
  Tartarus,
if you really wish to embark on such an insane
  adventure,
this is what you must do. There is a golden bough
hidden in the forest: both leaves and stem are of gold;
this bough consecrated to infernal Juno,
and deeply hidden by shadows in the gloomy valley.
And no one is allowed to see Earth's hidden domain
who has first plucked the golden foliage from its tree.
The fair Proserpina herself demands this gift.
Now when the branch has been taken away, another
  one
grows in its place, and shines with the same golden
  luster;
so search with lifted eyes, and find it, and pluck it off,
and it will easily come away of its own accord,
provided the Fates are willing; but otherwise, no force
will avail to conquer it—not even a blade of steel.
  [From Virgil, *The Aeneid*, pp. 115–18.]

VESTA AND THE VESTAL VIRGINS

The title of the Vestal Virgins comes from Vesta, the Roman goddess of the hearth, whom
they served. Vesta was one of the most ancient goddess of Rome. She was worshiped from

earliest times to the Fall of Rome. Numa Pompilius, the second king of Rome (traditionally 715–673 B.C.E.), is credited with building the first temple to Vesta and establishing the institution of the Vestal Virgins. The following excerpt from the *Fasti* (vi. 249–334), a poetical calendar of the Roman year written by Ovid (43 B.C.E.-17 C.E.), mentions Numa, explains why Vesta's temple is round rather than the usual four-sided construction of Roman temples, why the Vestals are virgins, and why Vesta is not represented in anthropomorphic form.

O Vesta, grant me thy favour! In thy service now I open my lips, if it is lawful for me to come to thy sacred rites. I was wrapt up in prayer; I felt the heavenly deity, and the glad ground gleamed with a purple light. Not indeed that I saw thee, O goddess (far from me be the lies of poets!), nor was it meet that a man should look upon thee; but my ignorance was enlightened and my errors corrected without the help of an instructor. They say that Rome had forty times celebrated the Parilia when the goddess, Guardian of Fire, was received in her temple; it was the work of that peaceful king, than whom no man of more godfearing temper was ever born in Sabine land. The buildings which now you see roofed with bronze you might then have seen roofed with thatch, and the walls were woven of tough osiers. This little spot, which now supports the Hall of Vesta, was then the great palace of unshorn Numa. Yet the shape of the temple, as it now exists, is said to have been its shape of old, and it is based on a sound reason. Vesta is the same as the Earth; under both of them is a perpetual fire; the earth and the hearth are symbols of the home. The earth is like a ball, resting on no prop; so great a weight hangs on the air beneath it. Its own power of rotation keeps its orb balanced; it has no angle which could press on any part; and since it is placed in the middle of the world and touches no side more or less, if it were not convex, it would be nearer to some part than to another, and the universe would not have the earth as its central weight. There stands a globe hung by Syracusan art in closed air, a small image of the vast vault of heaven, and the earth is equally distant from the top and bottom. That is brought about by its round shape. The form of the temple is similar: there is no projecting angle in it; a dome protects it from the showers of rain.

You ask why the goddess is tended by virgin ministers. Of that also I will discover the true causes. They say that Juno and Ceres were born of Ops by Saturn's seed; the third daughter was Vesta. The other two married; both are reported to have had offspring; of the three one remained, who refused to submit to a husband. What wonder if a virgin delights in a virgin minister and allows only chaste hands to touch her sacred things? Conceive of Vesta as naught but the living flame, and you see that no bodies are born of flame. Rightly, therefore, is she a virgin who neither gives nor takes seeds, and she loves companions in her virginity.

Long did I foolishly think that there were images of Vesta: afterwards I learned that there are none under her curved dome. An undying fire is hidden in that temple; but there is no effigy of Vesta nor of the fire. The earth stands by its own power; Vesta is so called from standing by power (*vi stando*) and the reason of her Greek name may be similar. But the hearth (*focus*) is so named from the flames, and because it fosters (*fovet*) all things; yet formerly it stood in the first room of the house. Hence, too, I am of opinion that the vestibule took its name; it is from there that in praying we begin by addressing Vesta, who occupies the first place: it used to be the custom of old to sit on long benches in front of the hearth and to suppose that the gods were present at table: even now, when sacrifices are offered to ancient Vacuna, they stand and sit in front of her hearths. Something of olden custom has come down to our time: a clean platter contains the food offered to Vesta. Lo, loaves are hung on asses decked with wreaths, and flowery garlands veil the rough mill-stones. Husbandmen used formerly to toast only spelt in the ovens, and the goddess of ovens has her own sacred rites: the hearth of itself baked the bread that was put under the ashes, and a broken tile was laid on the warm floor. Hence the baker honours the hearth and the mistress of hearths and the she-ass that turns the millstones of pumice.

[From Ovid, *Fasti*, 5, 339–343.]

In his biography of Numa, Plutarch (c. 50–120 C.E.) describes the functions and privileges of the Vestal Virgins, the priestesses who kept the sacred fire of Rome burning. Usually at any one time there were six Vestals from aristocratic families. They were chosen between the ages of six and ten by the high priest under whose control they remained for the period of their office. Plutarch also details the prescribed punishments for failing in their duty or breaking their vow of virginity.

The chief of the Pontifices, the Pontifex Maximus, had the duty of expounding and interpreting the divine will, or rather of directing sacred rites, not only being in charge of public ceremonies, but also watching over private sacrifices and preventing any departure from established custom, as well as teaching whatever was requisite for the worship or propitiation of the gods. He was also overseer of the holy virgins called Vestals; for to Numa is ascribed the consecration of the Vestal virgins, and in general the worship and care of the perpetual fire entrusted to their charge. It was either because he thought the nature of fire pure and uncorrupted, and therefore entrusted it to chaste and undefiled persons, or because he thought of it as unfruitful and barren, and therefore associated it with virginity. Since wherever in Greece a perpetual fire is kept, as at Delphi and Athens, it is committed to the charge, not of virgins, but of widows past the age of marriage.

* * *

In the beginning, then, they say that Gegania and Verenia were consecrated to this office by Numa, who subsequently added to them Canuleia and Tarpeia; that at a later time two others were added by Servius, making the number which has continued to the present time. It was ordained by the king that the sacred virgins should vow themselves to chastity for thirty years; during the first decade they are to learn their duties, during the second to perform the duties they have learned, and during the third to teach others these duties. Then, the thirty years being now passed, any one who wishes has liberty to marry and adopt a different mode of life, after laying down her sacred office. We are told, however, that few have welcomed the indulgence, and that those who did so were not happy, but were a prey to repentance and dejection for the rest of their lives, thereby inspiring the rest with superstitious fears, so that until old age and death they remained steadfast in their virginity.

But Numa bestowed great privileges upon them, such as the right to make a will during the life time of their fathers, and to transact and manage their other affairs without a guardian, like the mothers of three children. When they appear in public, the fasces are carried before them, and if they accidentally meet a criminal on his way to execution, his life is spared; but the virgin must make oath that the meeting was involuntary and fortuitous, and not of design. He who passes under the litter on which they are borne, is put to death. For their minor offenses the virgins are punished with stripes, the Pontifex Maximus sometimes scourging the culprit on her bare flesh, in a dark place with a curtain interposed. But she that has broken her vow of chastity is buried alive near the Colline gate. Here a little ridge of earth extends for some distance along the inside of the city-wall; the Latin word for it is "agger." Under it a small chamber is constructed, with steps leading down from above. In this are placed a couch with its coverings, a lighted lamp, and very small portions of the necessaries of life, such as bread, a bowl of water, milk, and oil, as though they would thereby absolve themselves from the charge of destroying by hunger a life which had been consecrated to the highest services of religion. Then the culprit herself is placed on a litter, over which coverings are thrown and fastened down with cords so that not even a cry can be heard from within, and carried through the forum. All the people there silently make way for the litter, and follow it without uttering a sound, in a terrible depression of soul. No other spectacle is more appalling, nor does any other day bring more gloom to the city than this. When the litter reaches its destination, the attendants unfasten the cords of the coverings. Then the highpriest, after stretching his hands toward heaven and uttering certain mysterious prayers before the fatal act, brings forth the culprit, who is closely veiled, and places her on the steps leading down into the chamber. After this he turns away his face, as do the rest of the priests, and when she has gone down, the steps are taken up, and great quantities of earth are thrown into the entrance to the chamber, hiding it away and making the place level with the rest of the mound. Such is the punishment of those who break their vow of virginity.

[From *Plutarch's Lives,* 1: 339–345.]

MAGNA MATER—THE GREAT MOTHER GODDESS

As Rome continued to expand it incorporated the goddesses and gods of the people it conquered. One important instance of this is Magna Mater, the mother goddess of the Roman empire who was originally the Anatolian mother goddess Cybele. Her cult was brought from

Anatolia to Rome in 204 B.C.E. when Hannibal's army threatened the city. Amidst strange portents, such as meteor showers, the Romans consulted the Sibylline Books, where the prophecies of the ancient sibyls were thought to be preserved. There they found an oracle which stated that an invading army could be defeated if this mother goddess were brought to Rome. When the Delphic oracle confirmed this advice, the Romans sent for the goddess. Hannibal was driven out of Italy a few years later, and the goddess was credited with this victory. Thereafter a festival was held on April 4, the day the goddess entered Rome. The following two excerpts from Ovid's *Fasti* (4.179–392), a poetical calendar of the Roman year written early in the first century C.E., describes this festival. In it questions are put to the Muses, here called Cybele's granddaughters, who explain some of the practices of the cult. They begin, appropriately, with creation, when the god Saturn (Kronos) kept eating the children of his wife, the goddess Rhea (Cybele). The eunuchs are men who, in an ecstatic ritual, castrated themselves in order to become priests of Cybele, called Galli. The text also explains the origin of this practice. The second excerpt describes Cybele's arrival in Rome. The boat carrying the image of the goddess gets stuck in the Tiber, provoking a curious incident, in which a patrician woman establishes her virtue. This incident suggests the enthusiasm Roman women of all classes had for this cult, as well as their prominent participation in it.

Let the sky revolve thrice on its never-resting axis; let Titan thrice yoke and thrice unyoke his steeds, straightway the Berecyntian flute will blow a blast on its bent horn, and the festival of the Idaean Mother will have come. Eunuchs will march and thump their hollow drums, and cymbals clashed on cymbals will give out their tinkling notes: seated on the unmanly necks of her attendants, the goddess herself will be borne with howls through the streets in the city's midst. The stage is clattering, the games are calling. To your places, Quirites! and in the empty law-courts let the war of suitors cease! I would put many questions, but I am daunted by the shrill cymbals clash and the bent flute's thrilling drone. "Grant me, goddess, someone whom I may question." The Cybelean goddess spied her learned granddaughters and bade them attend to my inquiry. "Mindful of her command, ye nurslings of Helicon, disclose the reason why the Great Goddess delights in a perpetual din." So did I speak, and Erato did thus reply (it fell to her to speak of Venus' month, because her own name is derived from tender love): "Saturn was given this oracle: 'Thou best of kings, thou shalt be ousted of thy sceptre by thy son.' In fear, the god devoured his offspring as fast as they were born, and he kept them sunk in his bowels. Many a time did Rhea grumble, to be so often big with child, yet never be a mother; she repined at her own fruitfulness. Then Jove was born. The testimony of antiquity passes for good; pray do not shake the general faith. A stone concealed in a garment went down the heavenly throat; so had fate decreed that the sire should be beguiled. Now rang steep Ida loud and long with clangorous music, that the boy might pule in safety with his infant mouth.

Some beat their shields, others their empty helmets with staves; that was the task of the Curetes and that, too, of the Corybantes. The secret was kept, and the ancient deed is still acted in mimicry; the attendants of the goddess thump the brass and the rumbling leather; cymbals they strike instead of helmets, and drums instead of shields; the flute plays, as of yore, the Phrygian airs."

The goddess ended. I began: "Why for her sake doth the fierce breed of lions yield their unwonted manes to the curved yoke?" I ended. She began: "'Tis thought, the wildness of the brute was tamed by her: that she testifies by her (lion-drawn) car." "But why is her head weighted with a turreted crown? Is it because she gave towers to the first cities?" The goddess nodded assent. "Whence came," said I, "the impulse to cut their members?" When I was silent, the Pierian goddess began to speak: "In the woods a Phrygian boy of handsome face, Attis by name, had attached the tower-bearing goddess to himself by a chaste passion. She wished that he should be kept for herself and should guard her temple, and she said, "Resolve to be a boy for ever. He promised obedience, and, "If I lie," quoth he, "may the love for which I break faith be my last love of all." He broke faith; for, meeting the nymph Sagaritis, he ceased to be what he had been before. For that the angry goddess wreaked vengeance. By wounds inflicted on the tree she cut down the Naiad, who perished thus; for the fate of the Naiad was bound up with the tree. Attis went mad, and, imagining that the roof of the chamber was falling in, he fled and ran for the top of Mount Dindymus. And he kept crying, at one moment, 'Take away the torches!' at another. 'Remove the whips!' And oft he swore that the Palaestinian goddesses [the Furies] were on him. He mangled, too, his body with a sharp stone, and trailed his long hair in the filthy dust; and his cry was, 'I have deserved it! With my blood I pay the penalty that is my due. Ah, perish the parts that were my ruin! Ah, let them perish,' still he said. He retrenched the burden of his groin, and of a sudden was bereft of every sign of manhood. His madness set an example, and still his unmanly ministers cut their vile members while they toss their hair." In such words the Aonian Muse eloquently answered my question as to the cause of the madness of the votaries.

★ ★ ★

"She [Cybele] had arrived at Ostia, where the Tiber divides to join the sea and flows with ampler sweep. All the knights and the grave senators, mixed up with the common folk, came to meet her at the mouth of the Tuscan river. With them walked mothers and daughters and brides, and the virgins who tended the sacred hearths. The men wearied their arms by tugging lustily at the rope; hardly did the foreign ship make head against the stream. A drought had long prevailed; the grass was parched and burnt; the loaded bark sank in the muddy shallows. Every man who lent a hand toiled beyond his strength and cheered on the workers by his cries. Yet the ship stuck fast, like an island firmly fixed in the middle of the sea. Astonished at the portent, the men did stand and quake. Claudia Quinta traced her descent from Clausus of old, and her beauty matched her nobility. Chaste was she, though not reputed so. Rumour unkind had wronged her, and a false charge had been trumped up against her: it told against her that she dressed sprucely, that she walked abroad with her hair dressed in varied fashion, that she had a ready tongue for gruff old men. Conscious of innocence, she laughed at fame's untruths; but we of the multitude are prone to think the worst. When she had stepped

forth from the procession of the chaste matrons, and taken up the pure water of the river in her hands, she thrice let it drip on her head, and thrice lifted her palms to heaven (all who looked on her thought that she was out of her mind), and bending the knee she fixed her eyes on the image of the goddess, and with dishevelled hair uttered these words: 'Thou fruitful Mother of the Gods, graciously accept thy suppliant's prayers on one condition. They say I am not chaste. If thou dost condemn me, I will confess my guilt; convicted by the verdict of a goddess, I will pay the penalty with my life. But if I am free of crime, give by thine act a proof of my innocency, and, chaste as thou art, do thou yield to my chaste hands.' She spoke, and drew the rope with a slight effort. My story is a strange one, but it is attested by the stage. The goddess was moved, and followed her leader, and by following bore witness in her favour: a sound of joy was wafted to the stars. They came to a bend in the river, where the stream turns away to the left: men of old named it the Halls of Tiber. Night drew on; they tied the rope to an oaken stump, and after a repast disposed themselves to slumber light. At dawn of day they loosed the rope from the oaken stump; but first they set down a brazier and put incense on it, and crowned the poop, and sacrificed an unblemished heifer that had known neither the yoke nor the bull. There is a place where the smooth Almo flows into the Tiber, and the lesser river loses its name in the great one. There a hoary-headed priest in purple robe washed the Mistress and her holy things in the waters of Almo. The attendants howled, the mad flute blew, and hands unmanly beat the leathern drums. Attended by a crowd, Claudia walked in front with joyful face, her chastity at last vindicated by the testimony of the goddess. The goddess herself, seated in a wagon, drove in through the Capene Gate; fresh flowers were scattered on the yoked oxen. Nasica received her. The name of the founder of the temple has not survived; now it is Augustus; formerly it was Metellus."

[From Ovid, *Fasti*, 5, 201–215.]

WOMEN AND THE LAW

The threat posed by Hannibal's army caused Rome to pass the Oppian Law in 215 B.C.E. This was meant to be a temporary law that limited women's, but not men's, consumption of expensive goods. Twenty years later the danger had long passed but the law remained. The women of Rome publicly demonstrated for its repeal, and there was a public debate about the law. This quickly became a debate about the "traditional" behavior of women. In Book 34 of his history of Rome, Livy (59 B.C.E.-17 C.E.) presents this debate. The following excerpt (34.1-5) describes the activities of the women, the arguments by the conservative Marcus Porcius Cato for the retention of the law, and the counterarguments of Lucius Valerius for its repeal. Cato's argument is that women must be controlled, should have no voice in government, and if they repeal this law, it will only encourage women to interfere with other laws. He calls on the authority of the past, stating that Roman women have never acted on their own behalf, in other words, they had never been persons in the legal sense which was true in Roman law. Lucius Valerius argues against Cato by citing other occasions in Roman history when women demonstrated in public.

Amid the anxieties of great wars, either scarce finished or soon to come, an incident occurred, trivial to relate, but which, by reason of the passions it aroused, developed into a violent contention. Marcus Fundanius and Lucius Valerius, tribunes of the people, proposed to the assembly the abrogation of the Oppian law. The tribune Gaius Oppius had carried this law in the heat of the Punic War, in the consulship of Quintus Fabius and Tiberius Sempronius, that no woman should possess more than half an ounce of gold or wear a parti-coloured garment or ride in a carriage in the City or in a town within a mile thereof, except on the occasion of a religious festival. The tribunes Marcus and Publius Iunius Brutus were supporting the Oppian law, and averred that they would not permit its repeal; many distinguished men came forward to speak for and against it; the Capitoline was filled with crowds of supporters and opponents of the bill. The matrons could not be kept at home by advice or modesty or their husbands' orders, but blocked all the streets and approaches to the Forum, begging the men as they came down to the Forum that, in the prosperous condition of the state, when the private fortunes of all men were daily increasing, they should allow the women too to have their former distinctions restored. The crowd of women grew larger day by day; for they were now coming in from the towns and the rural districts. Soon they dared even to approach and appeal to the consuls, the praetors, and the other officials, but one consul, at least, they found adamant, Marcus Porcius Cato, who spoke thus in favour of the law whose repeal was being urged.

"If each of us, citizens, had determined to assert his rights and dignity as a husband with respect to his own spouse, we should have less trouble with the sex as a whole; as it is, our liberty, destroyed at home by female violence, even here in the Forum is crushed and trodden underfoot, and because we have not kept them individually under control, we dread them collectively. For my part, I thought it a fairy-tale and a piece of fiction that on a certain island all the men were destroyed, root and branch, by a conspiracy of women; but from no class is there not the greatest danger if you permit them meetings and gatherings and secret consultations. And I can scarcely decide in my own mind whether the act itself or the precedent it sets is worse; the act concerns us consuls and other magistrates; the example, citizens, rather concerns you. For whether the proposal which is laid before you is in the public interest or not is a question for you who are soon to cast your votes; but this female madness, whether it is spontaneous or due to your instigation, Marcus Fundanius and Lucius Valerius, but which beyond question brings discredit upon the magistrates — I do not know, I say, whether this madness is more shameful for you, tribunes, or for the consuls: for you, if you have brought these women here to support tribunicial seditions; for us, if we must accept laws given us by a secession of women, as formerly by a secession of plebeians.

★ ★ ★

"Our ancestors permitted no woman to conduct even personal business without a guardian to intervene in her behalf; they wished them to be under the control of fathers, brothers, husbands; we (Heaven help us!) allow them now even to interfere in public affairs, yes, and to visit the Forum and our informal and formal sessions. What else are they doing now on the streets and at the corners except urging the bill of the tribunes and voting for the repeal of the law? Give loose rein to their uncontrollable nature and to this untamed creature and expect that they will themselves set bounds to their licence; unless you act, this is the least of the things enjoined upon women by custom or law and to which they submit with a feeling of injustice. It is complete liberty or, rather, if we wish to speak the truth, complete licence that they desire.

"If they win in this, what will they not attempt? Review all the laws with which your forefathers restrained their licence and made them subject to their husbands; even with all these bonds you can scarcely control them. What of this? If you suffer them to seize these bonds one by one and wrench themselves free and finally to be placed on a parity with their husbands, do you think that you will be able to endure them? The moment they begin to be your equals, they will be your superiors."
[From *Livy*, 9: 413–419.]

★ ★ ★

Then Lucius Valerius argued thus for the measure which he had proposed:

★ ★ ★

"I propose to defend the measure rather than ourselves, at whom the consul directed his insinuation, more to have something to say than to make a serious charge. This gathering of women he called a sedition and sometimes 'a female secession,' because the matrons, in the streets, had requested you to repeal, in a time of peace and in a rich and prosperous commonwealth, a law that was passed against them in the trying days of a war. I know that there is this and still other vigorous language, which has been sought out to make the argument sound more convincing; we all know, too, that Marcus Cato is an orator not only powerful but sometimes even savage, though he is kind of heart. What new thing, pray, have the matrons done in coming out into the streets in crowds in a case that concerned them? Have they never before this moment appeared in public? Let me unroll your own *Origines* against you. Hear how often they have done it and always, indeed, for the general good. Even in the beginning, while Romulus was king, when the Capitoline had been taken by the Sabines and pitched battle was raging in the centre of the Forum, was not the fighting stopped by the rush of the matrons between the two battle-lines? What of this? When,

after the expulsion of the kings, the Volscian legions led by Marcius Coriolanus had encamped at the fifth milestone, did not the matrons turn away from us the army which would have destroyed our city? When the City was later captured by the Gauls, how was it ransomed? Why, the matrons by unanimous consent contributed their gold to the public use. In the recent war (not to go to remoter times), did not the widows, when there was a scarcity of money, aid the treasury with their wealth, and when new gods too were brought in to help us in our crisis, did not the matrons in a body go down to the sea to receive the Idaean Mother? These cases, you say, are different. It is not my purpose to prove them similar; it suffices if I prove that this is nothing new. But what no one wonders that all, men and women alike, have done in matters that concern them, do we wonder that the women have done in a case peculiarly their own? What now have they done? We have proud ears, upon my word, if, although masters do not scorn to hear the petitions of slaves, we complain that we are appealed to by respectable women.

[From *Livy*, 9: 427-431.]

LUCRETIUS ON WOMEN

The Roman poet and philosopher Lucretius (94-55 B.C.E.) was devoted to expounding the ideas of the Greek philosopher Epicurus (341-270 B.C.E.) to the world. When it comes to women though, he fails rather miserably. Epicurus allowed both women and slaves into his school, an almost unheard of practice. Lucretius, on the other hand, in his general attack on sexual passion, represents women not as potential philosophers, but rather as sexual temptresses who ensnare men's reason. In the following excerpts from *The Nature of the Universe* (4.1141-1192) he suggests some cures for such a condition.

For to avoid being lured into the snares of love is not so difficult as, when you are caught in the toils, to get out and break through the strong knots of Venus. Yet you can escape the danger even when involved and entangled, unless you stand in your own way, and begin by overlooking all faults of mind and body in her whom you prefer and desire. For this is what men usually do when blinded with desire, and they attribute to women advantages which they really have not. Thus women that are in many ways crooked and ugly we often see to be thought darlings and to be held in the highest honour. One lover will actually deride another, and bid him propitiate Venus as being the victim of a discreditable love, and often, poor wretch, casts not a glance at his own surpassing misery. The black girl is a nut-brown maid, the dirty and rank is a sweet disorder, the green-eyed is a little Pallas, the stringy and wooden is a gazelle, the squat

little dwarf is one of the Graces, a pinch of embodied wit; the huge virago is a "stunner," and full of dignity; if she stutters and cannot speak, *elle zêzaye;* the dumb is modest; the fiery, spiteful chatterbox is a little squib; when she is too skinny to live, she is his *maigrelette,* his *chérie;* she is *svelte* when she is half dead of consumption. A swollen thing with great bubbies is Ceres herself with Iacchus at the breast, the pug-nosed is Silena or Madame Satyr, the thick-lipped is "all kiss." It would be a long task if I were to try to go through all the list.

But, however, let her be one of the supremest dignity of countenance, let the power of Venus radiate from her whole body, the truth is there are others, the truth is we have lived so far without this one; the truth is she does all the same things as the ugly woman does, and we know it, fumigating herself, poor wretch, with rank odours while her maidservants give her a wide berth and giggle behind her back. But the lover shut out, weeping, often covers the threshold with flowers and wreaths, anoints the proud doorposts with oil of marjoram, presses his love-sick kisses upon the door; but if he is let in, once he gets but one whiff as he comes, he would seek some decent excuse for taking his leave; there would be an end of the complaint so often rehearsed, so deeply felt, and he would condemn himself on the spot of folly, now he sees that he has attributed to her more than it is right to concede to a mortal. Our Venuses are quite well aware of this; so they are at greater pains themselves to hide all that is behind the scenes of life from those whom they wish to detain fast bound in the chains of love; but all is vanity, since you can nevertheless in your minds drag it all into the light of day, and seek the cause of all the merriment, and if she is nice-minded and not a nuisance, you can overlook in your turn and make some concession to human weakness.

[From Lucretius, *De Rerum Natura*, pp. 365–369.]

PREGNANCY AND MENSTRUATION

The Natural History of Pliny (23/24–79 C.E.) is a multivolumed compilation of facts and observations that he derived from numerous ancient authors: His subjects include humanity, animals, geography, botany, medicine, etc. His approach tended to include rather than exclude material, so he has left us a curious assortment of the beliefs of his time.

In the following excerpts from Book VII (vi–ix, xv) Pliny describes the "symptoms" of pregnancy as being different depending on whether the mother is carrying a female child or a male child (vi). He also discusses how unfortunate it is for children who are born feet first, saying nothing of the life-threatening problems the mother experiences during such a birth (viii). These deliveries foretell such dire characteristics in the child that the death of the mother is to be preferred (ix). Pliny concludes by listing some of negative effects of contact with menstrual blood (xv).

On the tenth day from conception pains in the head, giddiness and dim sight, distaste for food, and vomiting are symptoms of the formation of the embryo. If the child is a male, the mother has a better colour and an easier delivery; there is movement in the womb on the fortieth day. In a case of the other sex all the symptoms are the opposite: the burden is hard to carry, there is a slight swelling of the legs and groin, but the first movement is on the ninetieth day. But in the case of both sexes the greatest amount of faintness occurs when the embryo begins to grow hair; and also at the full moon, which period is also specially inimical to infants after birth. The gait in walking and every thing that can be mentioned are so important during pregnancy that mothers eating food that is too salty bear children lacking nails, and that not holding the breath makes the delivery more difficult; indeed, to gape during delivery may cause death, just as a sneeze following copulation causes abortion.

* * *

It is against nature to be born feet foremost; this is the reason why the designation of 'Agrippa' has been applied to persons so born—meaning 'born with difficulty'; Marcus Agrippa is said to have been born in this manner, almost the solitary instance of a successful career among all those so born—although he too is deemed to have paid the penalty which his irregular birth foretold, by a youth made unhappy by lameness, a lifetime passed amidst warfare and ever exposed to the approach of death, by the misfortune caused to the world by his whole progeny but especially due to his two daughters who became the mothers of the emperors Gaius Caligula and Domitius Nero, the two firebrands of mankind; and also by the shortness of his life, as he was cut off at the age of fifty during the agony caused him by his wife's adulteries and during his irksome subjection to his father-in-law Augustus. Nero also, who was emperor shortly before and whose entire rule showed him the enemy of mankind, is stated in his mother Agrippina's memoirs to have been born feet first. It is Nature's method for a human being to be born head first, and it is the custom for him to be carried to burial feet first.

It is a better omen when the mother dies in giving birth to the child; instances are the birth of the elder Scipio Africanus and of the first of the Caesars, who got that name from the surgical operation performed on his mother; the origin of the family name Caeso is also the same. Also Manilius who entered Carthage with his army was born in the same manner.

* * *

Woman is, however, the only animal that has monthly periods; consequently she alone has what are called moles in her womb. This mole is a shapeless and inanimate mass of flesh that resists the point and the edge of a knife; it moves about, and it checks menstruation, as it also checks births: in some cases causing death, in others growing old with the patient, sometimes when the bowels are violently moved being ejected. A similar object is also formed in the stomach of males, called a tumour, as in the case of the praetorian Oppius Capito. But nothing could easily be found that is more remarkable than the monthly flux of women. Contact with it turns new wine sour, crops touched by it become barren, grafts die, seeds in gardens are dried up, the fruit of trees falls off, the bright surface of mirrors in which it is merely reflected is dimmed, the edge of steel and the gleam of ivory are dulled, hives of bees die, even bronze and iron are at once seized by rust, and a hor-rible smell fills the air; to taste it drives dogs mad and infects their bites with an incurable poison. Moreover bitumen, a substance generally sticky and viscous, that at a certain season of the year floats on the surface of the lake of Judaea called the Asphalt Pool, adheres to everything touching it, and cannot be drawn asunder except by a thread soaked in the poisonous fluid in question. Even that very tiny creature the ant is said to be sensitive to it, and throws away grains of corn that taste of it and does not touch them again. Not only does this pernicious mischief occur in a woman every month, but it comes in larger quantity every three months; and in some cases it comes more frequently than once a month, just as in certain women it never occurs at all. The latter, however, do not have children, since the substance in question is the material for human generation, as the semen from the males acting like rennet collects this substance within it, which thereupon immediately is inspired with life and endowed with body. Hence when this flux occurs with women heavy with child, the offspring is sickly or still-born or sanious, according to Nigidius.

[From Pliny, *The Natural History,* 2: 533–549.]

THE CULT OF ISIS

The cult of the ancient Egyptian goddess Isis spread beyond the borders of Egypt in quite early times; she had a sanctuary near Athens by the fourth century B.C.E. As it spread, it also changed. Most important for its later success, it became a mystery religion in which Isis is the savior goddess. Though her cult continued to grow in popularity, it also had setbacks. She had a temple in Pompeii by the first century B.C.E., but while the Romans were fascinated with the esoteric wisdom of the Egyptians, they remained suspicious of all foreign cults. Consequently, as temples continued to spread they were also frequently destroyed. It is only in the time of the later empire that her cult achieves imperial support and therefore security. Isis was particularly popular with women and the peak of her popularity in the Roman world was in the early third century C.E.

Isis According to Plutarch

In the hellenized world of the Roman empire the cult of Isis had daily public rites as well as esoteric rituals limited to the initiated. The primary myth associated with Isis was part of these esoteric rites. In this myth, Isis' beloved husband and brother Osiris is killed and dismembered and various parts of his body are spread all over Egypt. In deep mourning and facing many dangers, Isis journeys throughout the land, reassembling his body. The last part she finds is his penis, and she uses it to impregnate herself with their son Horus. This is powerful salvational imagery in which Isis not only cares for the dead but gives them new life. She herself suffers and is transformed in the course of her journey, a journey that is imitated in her initiation ceremonies. The promise of her cult is that she will care for and restore to life all her devotees. Her story was told in bits and pieces throughout ancient Egyptian art and literature, but it was the Greek author Plutarch (c. 45-120 C.E.) who first composed a coherent version of her story. As the following excerpt from his *Moralia* (356-358) shows, Plutarch supplements the story with explanations of current practices among Isis worshipers.

One of the first acts related of Osiris in his reign was to deliver the Egyptians from their destitute and brutish manner of living. This he did by showing them the fruits of cultivation, by giving them laws, and by teaching them to honour the gods. Later he travelled over the whole earth civilizing it without the slightest need of arms, but most of the peoples he won over to his way by the charm of his persuasive discourse combined with song and all manner of music. Hence the Greeks came to identify him with Dionysus.

During his absence the tradition is that Typhon attempted nothing revolutionary because Isis, who was in control, was vigilant and alert; but when he returned home Typhon contrived a treacherous plot against him and formed a group of conspirators seventy-two in number. He had also the cooperation of a queen from Ethiopia who was there at the time and whose name they report as Aso. Typhon, having secretly measured Osiris's body and having made ready a beautiful chest of corresponding size artistically ornamented, caused it to be brought into the room where the festivity was in progress. The company was much pleased at the sight of it and admired it greatly, whereupon Typhon jestingly promised to present it to the man who should find the chest to be exactly his length when he lay down in it. They all tried it in turn, but no one fitted it; then Osiris got into it and lay down, and those who were in the plot ran to it and slammed down the lid, which they fastened by nails from the outside and also by using molten lead. Then they carried the chest to the river and sent it on its way to the sea through the Tanitic Mouth. Wherefore the Egyptians even to this day name this mouth the hateful and execrable. Such is the tradition. They say also that the date on which this deed was done was the seventeenth day of Athyr, when the sun passes through Scorpion, and in the twenty-eighth year of the reign of Osiris; but some say that these are the years of his life and not of his reign.

The first to learn of the deed and to bring to men's knowledge an account of what had been done were the Pans and Satyrs who lived in the region around Chemmis, and so, even to this day, the sudden confusion and consternation of a crowd is called a panic. Isis, when the tidings reached her, at once cut off one of her tresses and put on a garment of mourning in a place where the city still bears the name of Kopto. Others think that the name means deprivation, for they also express "deprive" by means of "koptein." But Isis wandered everywhere at her wits' end; no one whom she approached did she fail to address, and even when she met some little children she asked them about the chest. As it happened, they had seen it, and they told her the mouth of the river through which the friends of Typhon had launched the coffin into the sea.

* * *

As they relate, Isis proceeded to her son Horus, who was being reared in Buto, and bestowed the chest in a place well out of the way; but Typhon, who was hunting by night in the light of the moon, happened upon it. Recognizing the body he divided it into fourteen parts and scattered them, each in a different place. Isis learned of this and sought for them again, sailing through the swamps in a boat of papyrus. This is the reason why people sailing in such boats are not harmed by the crocodiles, since these creatures in their own way show either their fear or their reverence for the goddess.

The traditional result of Osiris's dismemberment is that there are many so-called tombs of Osiris in Egypt; for Isis held a funeral for each part when she had found it. Others deny this and assert that she caused effigies of him to be made and these she distributed among the several cities, pretending that she was giving them his body, in order that he might receive divine honours in a greater number of cities, and also that, if Typhon should succeed in overpowering Horus, he might despair of ever finding the true tomb when so many were pointed out to him, all of them called the tomb of Osiris.

Of the parts of Osiris's body the only one which Isis did not find was the male member, for the reason that this had been at once tossed into the river, and the lepidotus, the sea-bream, and the pike had fed upon it; and it is from these very fishes the Egyptians are most scrupulous in abstaining. But Isis made a replica of the member to take its place, and consecrated the phallus, in honour of which the Egyptians even at the present day celebrate a festival.

Plutarch's Moralia, 1: 35-47.

ISIS ACCORDING TO APULEIUS

Apuleius (second century C.E.) was born in North Africa, present day Morocco. He came from a well-to-do family, which enabled him to study law at Carthage, Athens, and Rome. He traveled throughout the hellenized world, including Egypt and Asia Minor. After a rather rowdy student life he experienced a conversion to Isis and eventually became one of her priests. His novel, *The Golden Ass,* reveals much of his own spiritual experience, though translated in such a way that it appealed to a popular audience. The main character, Lucius, is a well meaning young man of his time, deeply interested in magic and chasing women. Through a mishap with magic during a sexual adventure, he is transformed into an ass. He remains in this state for one year, during which he suffers a great deal while travelling in the possession of various owners. His journey is meant to reflect Isis's journey to locate the dismembered parts of her husband Osiris's body, and to also amuse his readers. The transformation from animal to human symbolizes getting rid of the bestial aspects of human nature such as sexuality. Celibacy was a highly regarded virtue in the Hellenistic cult of Isis.

In the following excerpt Lucius, still trapped in the body of an ass, prays to Isis to transform him back into a man. He then falls asleep and has a dream which is a detailed description of Isis' physical appearance, her apparel, and her symbols. Additionally, Isis herself speaks and reveals that she is all the goddesses, that she is worshiped in many lands under various names.

When I had finished my prayer and poured out the full bitterness of my oppressed heart, I returned to my sandy hollow, where once more sleep overcame me. I had scarcely closed my eyes before the apparition of a woman began to rise from the middle of the sea with so lovely a face that the gods themselves would have fallen down in adoration of it. First the head, then the whole shining body gradually emerged and stood before me poised on the surface of the waves. Yes, I will try to describe this transcendent vision, for though human speech is poor and limited, the Goddess herself will perhaps inspire me with poetic imagery sufficient to convey some slight inkling of what I saw.

Her long thick hair fell in tapering ringlets on her lovely neck, and was crowned with an intricate chaplet in which was woven every kind of flower. Just above her brow shone a round disc, like a mirror, or like the bright face of the moon, which told me who she was. Vipers rising from the left-hand and right-hand partings of her hair supported this disc, with ears of corn bristling beside them. Her many-coloured robe was of finest linen; part was glistening white, part crocus-yellow, part glowing red and along the entire hem a woven bordure of flowers and fruit clung swaying in the breeze. But what caught and held my eye more than anything else was the deep black lustre of her mantle. She wore it slung across her body from the right hip to the left shoulder, where it was caught in a knot resembling the boss of a shield; but part of it hung in innumerable folds, the tasselled fringe quivering. It was embroidered with glittering stars on the hem and everywhere else, and in the middle beamed a full and fiery moon.

In her right hand she held a bronze rattle, of the sort used to frighten away the God of the Sirocco; its narrow rim was curved like a sword-belt and three little rods, which sang shrilly when she shook the handle, passed horizontally through it. A boat-shaped gold dish hung from her left hand, and along the upper surface of the handle writhed an asp with puffed throat and head raised ready to strike. On her divine feet were slippers of palm leaves, the emblem of victory.

All the perfumes of Arabia floated into my nostrils as the Goddess deigned to address me: 'You see me here, Lucius, in answer to your prayer. I am Nature, the universal Mother, mistress of all the elements, primordial child of time, sovereign of all things spiritual, queen of the dead, queen also of the immortals, the single manifestation of all gods and goddesses that are. My nod governs the shining heights of Heaven, the wholesome sea-breezes, the lamentable silences of the world below. Though I am worshipped in many aspects, known by countless names, and propitiated with all manner of different rites, yet the whole round earth venerates me. The primeval Phrygians call me Pessinuntica, Mother of the gods; the Athenians, sprung from their own soil, call me Cecropian Artemis; for the islanders of Cyprus I am

Paphian Aphrodite; for the archers of Crete I am Dictynna; for the trilingual Sicilians, Stygian Proserpine; and for the Eleusinians their ancient Mother of the Corn.

'Some know me as Juno, some as Bellona of the Battles; others as Hecate, others again as Rhamnubia, but both races of Aethiopians, whose lands the morning sun first shines upon, and the Egyptians who excel in ancient learning and worship me with ceremonies proper to my godhead, call me by my true name, namely, Queen Isis. I have come in pity of your plight, I have come to favour and aid you. Weep no more, lament no longer; the hour of deliverance, shone over by my watchful light, is at hand.

[From Apuleius, *The Transformations of Lucius,* pp. 263–65.]

Once transformed back into human form through the power of Isis, in gratitude Lucius seeks initiation into her priesthood. He lives at her temple, imitating the restraint of the other priests under the guidance of the high priest, while he waits for a sign from Isis that he should become one of her priests. The following excerpt is the primary source of information on the details of an initiation into the cult of Isis.

I accepted his [the High Priest's] advice and learned to be patient, taking part in the daily services of the temple as calmly and quietly as I knew how, intent on pleasing the Goddess. Nor did I have a troublesome and disappointing probation. Soon after this she gave me proof of her grace by a midnight vision in which I was plainly told that the day for which I longed, the day on which my greatest wish would be granted, had come at last. I learned that she had ordered the High Priest Mithras, whose destiny was linked with mine by planetary sympathy, to officiate at my initiation.

These orders and certain others given me at the same time so exhilarated me that I rose before dawn to tell the High Priest about them, and reached his door just as he was coming out. I greeted him and was about to beg him more earnestly than ever to allow me to be initiated, as a privilege that was now mine by right, when he spoke first. 'Dear Lucius,' he said, 'how lucky, how blessed you are that the Great Goddess has graciously deigned to honour you in this way. There is no time to waste. The day for which you prayed so earnestly has dawned. The many-named Goddess orders me to initiate you into her most holy mysteries.'

He took me by the hand and led me courteously to the doors of the vast temple, and when he had opened them in the usual solemn way and performed the morning sacrifice he went to the sanctuary and took out two or three books written in characters unknown to me: some of them animal hieroglyphics, some of them ordinary letters protected against profane prying by having their tops and tails wreathed in knots or rounded like wheels or tangled together in spirals like vine tendrils. From these books he read me out instructions for providing the necessary clothes and accessories for my initiation.

I at once went to my friends the priests and asked them to buy part of what I needed, sparing no expense: the rest I went to buy myself.

In due time the High Priest summoned me and took me to the nearest public baths, attended by a crowd of priests. There, when I had enjoyed my ordinary bath, he himself washed and sprinkled me with holy water, offering up prayers for divine mercy. After this he brought me back to the temple and placed me at the very feet of the Goddess.

It was now early afternoon. He gave me certain orders too holy to be spoken above a whisper, and then commanded me in everyone's hearing to abstain from all but the plainest food for the ten succeeding days, to eat no meat and drink no wine.

I obeyed his instructions in all reverence and at last the day came for taking my vows. As evening approached a crowd of priests came flocking to me from all directions, each one giving me congratulatory gifts, as the ancient custom is. Then the High Priest ordered all uninitiated persons to depart, invested me in a new linen garment and led me by the hand into the inner recesses of the sanctuary itself. I have no doubt, curious reader, that you are eager to know what happened when I entered. If I were allowed to tell you, and you were allowed to be told, you would soon hear everything; but, as it is, my tongue would suffer for its indiscretion and your ears for their inquisitiveness.

However, not wishing to leave you, if you are religiously inclined, in a state of tortured suspense, I will record as much as I may lawfully record for the uninitiated, but only on condition that you believe it. *I approached the very gates of death and set one foot on Proserpine's threshold, yet was permitted to return, rapt through all the elements. At midnight I saw the sun shining as if it were noon; I entered the presence of the gods of the under-world and the gods of the upper-world, stood near and worshipped them.*

Well, now you have heard what happened, but I fear you are still none the wiser.

The solemn rites ended at dawn and I emerged from the sanctuary wearing twelve different stoles, certainly a most sacred costume but one that there can be no harm in my mentioning. Many uninitiated people saw me wearing it when the High Priest ordered me to mount into the wooden pulpit which stood in the centre of the temple, immediately in front of the Goddess's image. I was wearing an outer garment of fine linen embroidered with flowers, and a precious scarf hung down from my shoulders to my ankles with sacred animals worked in colour on every part of it; for instance Indian serpents and Hyperborean griffins, which are winged lions generated in the more distant parts of the world. The priests call this scarf an Olympian stole. I held a lighted torch in my right band and wore a white palm-tree chaplet with its leaves sticking out all round like rays of light.

The curtains were pulled aside and I was suddenly exposed to the gaze of the crowd, as when a statue is unveiled, dressed like the sun. That day was the happiest of my initiation, and I celebrated it as my birthday with a cheerful banquet at which all my friends were present. Further rites and ceremonies were performed on the third day, including a sacred breakfast, and these ended the proceedings. However, I remained for some days longer in the temple, enjoying the ineffable pleasure of contemplating the Goddess's statue, because I was bound to her by a debt of gratitude so large that I could never hope to pay it.

[From Apuleius, *The Transformations of Lucius,* pp. 278–81.]

SOSIPATRA–A WOMAN PHILOSOPHER

Sosipatra was a Neoplatonic philosopher of the third century C.E. of such great fame that Eunapius (b. ca. 345 C.E.) believed it was appropriate to include her, the only woman, in his biography of philosophers (written about 396 C.E.). Another reason for her inclusion can be found in his motives for writing this book: Eunapius was a staunch supporter of paganism and very anti-Christian—he hoped his book would compete favorably with the biographies of Christian saints that were so popular. Since Christian biographies contained the biographies of women, Eunapius may have been compelled to include a woman in his collection.

During the fourth century C.E. Neoplatonism became an important creed in the pagan reaction against Christianity. The Neoplatonists, especially in later periods, were taken with the idea of Fate and were great students of astrology. The two strange men who educate Sosipatra when she is a child claim to be Chaldeans, that is, people trained in astrology and other esoteric doctrines. The extraordinary events of Sosipatra's life show this Chaldean influence, in that her biography focuses on her ability to either predict events or to know what happens to people when they are away from her. The text makes clear that part of her success as a woman philosopher was due to having been born into a wealthy family, having a father who left her to her own devices, and finding a like-minded husband. Her proposal to Eustathius, himself a famous philosopher, and his acceptance of her suggests he was a supportive husband. The rest of her life was spent in a dignified widowhood, raising her sons, teaching philosophy, and living virtuously.

So far did the fame of this woman travel that it is fitting for me to speak of her at greater length, even in this catalogue of wise men. She was born in Asia, near Ephesus, in that district which the river Cayster traverses and flows through, and hence gives its name to the plain. She came of a prosperous family, blessed with wealth, and while she was still a small child she seemed to bring a blessing on everything, such beauty and decorum illumined her infant years. Now she had just reached the age of five, when two old men (both were past the prime of life, but one was rather older than the other), carrying ample wallets and dressed in garments of skins, made their way to a country estate belonging to Sosipatra's parents, and persuaded the steward, as they were easily able to do, to entrust to them the care of the vines. When a harvest beyond all expectation was the result—the owner himself was there, and with him was the little girl Sosipatra—

men's amazement was boundless, and they went so far as to suspect the intervention of the gods. The owner of the estate invited them to his table, and treated them with the highest consideration; and he reproached the other labourers on the estate with not obtaining the same results. The old men, on receiving Greek hospitality and a place at a Greek table, were smitten and captivated by the exceeding beauty and charm of the little girl Sosipatra, and they said: "Our other powers we keep to ourselves hidden and unrevealed, and this abundant vintage that you so highly approve is laughable and mere child's-play which takes no account of our superhuman abilities. But if you desire from us a fitting return for this maintenance and hospitality, not in money or perishable and corruptible benefits, but one far above you and your way of life, a gift whereof the fame shall reach the skies and touch the stars, hand over this child Sosipatra to us who are more truly her parents and guardians, and until the fifth year from now fear no disease for the little girl, nor death, but remain calm and steadfast. But take care not to set your feet on this soil till the fifth year come with the annual revolutions of the sun. And of its own accord wealth shall spring up for you and shall blossom forth from the soil. Moreover, your daughter shall have a mind not like a woman's or a mere human being's. Nay, you yourself also shall have higher than mortal thoughts concerning the child. Now if you have good courage accept our words with outspread hands, but if any suspicions awake in your mind consider that we have said nothing." Hearing this the father bit his tongue, and humble and awestruck put the child into their hands and gave her over to them. Then he summoned his steward and said to him: "Supply the old men with all that they need, and ask no questions." Thus he spoke, and before the light of dawn began to appear he departed as though fleeing from his daughter and his estate.

Then those others—whether they were heroes or demons or of some race still more divine—took charge of the child, and into what mysteries they initiated her no one knew, and with what religious rite they consecrated the girl was not revealed even to those who were most eager to learn. And now approached the appointed time when all the accounts of the revenue of the estate were due. The girl's father came to the farm and hardly recognized his daughter, so tall was she and her beauty seemed to him to have changed its character; and she too hardly knew her father. He even saluted her reverently, so different did she appear to his eyes. When her teachers were there and the table was spread, they said: "Ask the maiden whatever you please." But she interposed: "Nay, father, ask me what happened to you on your journey." He agreed that she should tell him. Now since he was so wealthy he travelled in a four-wheeled carriage,

and with this sort of carriage many accidents are liable to happen. But she related every event, not only what had been said, but his very threats and fears, as though she had been driving with him. Her father was roused to such a pitch of admiration that he did not merely admire her but was dumb with amazement, and was convinced that his daughter was a goddess. Then he fell on his knees before those men and implored them to tell him who they were. Slowly and reluctantly, for such was perhaps the will of heaven, they revealed to him that they were initiates in the lore called Chaldean, and even this they told enigmatically and with bent heads.

* * *

They then departed and went whithersoever it was; but her father took charge of the girl, now fully initiated, and though without pride, filled with divine breath, and he permitted her to live as she pleased and did not interfere in any of her affairs, except that sometimes he was ill pleased with her silence. And as she grew to the full measure of her youthful vigour, she had no other teachers, but ever on her lips were the works of the poets, philosophers, and orators; and those works that others comprehend but incompletely and dimly, and then only by hard work and painful drudgery, she could expound with careless ease, serenely and painlessly, and with her light swift touch would make their meaning clear. Then she decided to marry. Now beyond dispute Eustathius of all living men was alone worthy to wed her. So she said to him and to those who were present: "Do you listen to me, Eustathius, and let those who are here bear me witness: I shall bear you three children, and all of them will fail to win what is considered to be human happiness, but as to the happiness that the gods bestow, not one of them will fail therein. But you will go hence before me, and be allotted a fair and fitting place of abode, though I perhaps shall attain to one even higher. For your station will be in the orbit of the moon, and only five years longer will you devote your services to philosophy—for so your phantom tells me—but you shall traverse the region below the moon with a blessed and easily guided motion. Fain would I tell you my own fate also." Then after keeping silence for a short time, she cried aloud: "No, my god prevents me!" Immediately after this prophecy—for such was the will of the Fates—she married Eustathius, and her words had the same force as an immutable oracle, so absolutely did it come to pass and transpire as had been foretold by her.

I must relate also what happened after these events. After the passing of Eustathius, Sosipatra returned to her own estate, and dwelt in Asia in the ancient city of Pergamon, and the famous Aedesius loved and cared for her and educated her sons. In her own home

Sosipatra held a chair of philosophy that rivalled his, and after attending the lectures of Aedesius, the students would go to hear hers; and though there was none that did not greatly appreciate and admire the accurate learning of Aedesius, they positively adored and revered the woman's inspired teaching.

[From Philostratus and Eunapius, *The Lives of the Sophists,* pp. 401–11.]

HYPATIA—A WOMAN PHILOSOPHER

Hypatia (370–415 C.E.) of Alexandria was a well known and highly regarded Neoplatonist. She equalled her father Theon in his fame as a mathematician and astronomer, and she publicly taught, both in Athens and Alexandria, these subjects as well as the philosophy of Plato and Aristotle. At this time the Bishop of Alexandria, Cyril, was fanatical in his pursuit of so-called heretics. Aside from his persecution of Christian "heretics," he incited a mob to destroy and loot the synagogues of Alexandria, after which he expelled the entire Jewish community. Secular authority could not stand against him; in fact, at Cyril's instigation a mob stoned Orestes, the prefect of Egypt. After the chief assailant against Orestes was killed, Cyril claimed the body and publicly treated him as a martyr. The continued breach between these two men was blamed on Orestes' friend, Hypatia. Once again Cyril incited a Christian mob to violence, this time against Hypatia. Even the church father Socrates (b. 379 C.E.) of Constantinople, when he tells this story in his *Ecclesiastica Historia* (VII.15), is appalled by the wanton death of such an honored woman, though he softens the grisly details of her agonizing death at the hands of the mob.

There was a woman at Alexandria named Hypatia, daughter of the philosopher Theon, who made such attainments in literature and science, as to far surpass all the philosophers of her own time. Having succeeded to the school of Plato and Plotinus, she explained the principles of philosophy to her auditors, many of whom came from a distance to receive her instructions. On account of the self-possession and ease of manner, which she had acquired in consequence of the cultivation of her mind, she not infrequently appeared in public in presence of the magistrates. Neither did she feel abashed in coming to an assembly of men. For all men on account of her extraordinary dignity and virtue admired her the more. Yet even she fell a victim to the political jealousy which at that time prevailed. For as she had frequent interviews with Orestes, it was calumniously reported among the Christian populace, that it was she who prevented Orestes from being reconciled to the bishop. Some of them therefore, hurried away by a fierce and bigoted zeal, whose ringleader was a reader named Peter, waylaid her returning home, and dragging her from her carriage, they took her to the church called *Caesareum,* where they completely stripped her, and then murdered her with tiles. After tearing her body in pieces, they took her mangled limbs to a place called Cinaron, and there burnt them. This affair brought not the least opprobrium, not only upon Cyril, but also upon the whole Alexandrian church. And surely nothing can be farther from the spirit of Christianity than the allowance of massacres, fights, and transactions of that sort. This happened in the month of March during Lent, in the fourth year of Cyril's episcopate, under the tenth consulate of Honorius, and the sixth of Theodosius.

[From Socrates, *Church History,* p. 160.]

Another Christian bishop, Synesius (made bishop of Ptolemais in 410 C.E.), was one of Hypatia's students and several of his letters to her survive. Their tone is intimate and frank. In the following letter, he speaks of his grief at the death of his children and describes what an important influence Hypatia is in his life. It concludes with a request to help some young men with a legal matter while they are in Alexandria, a demonstration of Hypatia's influence in that city.

Even if Fortune is unable to take everything away from me, at least she wants to take away everything that she can, she who has 'bereft me of many excellent sons.' But she can never take away from me the choice of the best, and the power to come to the help of the oppressed, for never may she prevail to change my heart! I abhor iniquity: for one may, and I would fain prevent it, but this also is one of those things which were taken from me; this went even before my children.

There was a time when I, too, was of some use to my friends. You yourself called me the providence of others. All respect which was accorded to me by the mighty of this earth I employed solely to help others. The great were merely my instruments. But now, alas, I am deserted and abandoned by all, unless *you* have some power to help. I account you as the only good thing that remains inviolate, along with virtue. You always have power, and long may you have it and make a good use of that power. I recommend to your care Nicaeus and Philolaus, two excellent young men united by the bond of relationship. In order that they may come again into possession of their own property, try to get support for them from all your friends, whether private individuals or magistrates.

[From *The Letters of Synesius of Cyrene*, p. 174.]

Sources

Apuleius, *The Transformations of Lucius, Otherwise Known as The Golden Ass,* trans. Robert Graves (New York: Farrar, Straus & Giroux, 1951).

Ancient Egyptian Literature: A Book of Readings, Vol. 2, *The New Kingdom,* by Miriam Lichtheim (Berkeley: University of California Press, 1976).

The Ancient Near East: An Anthology of Texts and Pictures, Vol. 1, ed. James B. Pritchard (Princeton, NJ: Princeton University Press, 1958).

Ancient Near Eastern Texts Relating to the Old Testament, ed. James B. Pritchard, 2d ed. (Princeton, NJ: Princeton University Press, 1955).

The Babylonian Genesis: The Story of Creation, by Alexander Heidel, 2d ed. (Chicago: University of Chicago Press, 1951).

The Complete Works of Aristotle: The Revised Oxford Translation, Vol. 1, ed. Jonathan Barnes (Princeton, NJ: Princeton University Press, 1984).

The Dialogues of Plato, trans. B. Jowett, 2 vols., 3d ed. (New York: Random House, 1937).

The Exaltation of Inanna, by William W. Hallo and J. J. A. Van Dijk (New Haven: Yale University Press, 1968).

The Eumenides by Aeschylus, translated with commentary by Hugh Lloyd-Jones (Englewood Cliffs, NJ: Prentice-Hall, 1970).

The Gods of the Egyptians, or Studies in Egyptian Mythology, by E. A. Wallis Budge, 2 vols. (New York: Dover, 1969).

Greek Lyric Poetry, trans. Willis Barnstone (New York: Bantam Books, 1962).

Hesiod: The Works and Days, Theogony, The Shield of Herakles, trans. Richmond Lattimore (Ann Arbor: University of Michigan Press, 1959).

Homer, *The Odyssey,* trans. Robert Fitzgerald (New York: Random House, 1990).

The Homeric Hymns, trans. Charles Boer (Chicago: Swallow Press, 1970).

The Letters of Synesius of Cyrene, trans. Augustine Fitz-Gerald (Cambridge: Oxford University Press, 1926).

Livy, with an English translation in fourteen volumes, Vol. 9, Books 31–34, trans. Evan T. Sage (London: Heinemann; Cambridge: Harvard University Press, 1967).

Lucretius, *De Rerum Natura,* trans. W. H. D. Rouse, revised by Martin Ferguson Smith, 2d ed. (London: Heinemann; Cambridge: Harvard University Press, 1982).

Ovid, in six volumes, Vol. 5, *Fasti,* with an English translation by Sir James George Frazer (London: Heinemann; Cambridge: Harvard University Press, 1976).

Ovid, *The Metamorphoses,* trans. Horace Gregory (New York: New American Library, 1960).

Philostratus and Eunapius, *The Lives of the Sophists,* with an English translation by Wilmer Cave Wright (London: William Heinemann; Cambridge: Harvard University, 1968).

Pliny, *Natural History,* in ten volumes, Vol. 2, Books 3–7, with an English translation by H. Rackham (London: William Heinemann; Cambridge: Harvard University Press, 1969).

Plutarch's Lives, in ten volumes, Vol. 1, Theseus and Romulus, Lycurgus and Numa, Solon and Publicola, with an English translation by Bernadotte Perrin (London: William Heinemann; New York: Macmillan, 1914).

Plutarch's Moralia, in sixteen volumes, Vol. 5, 351c–438e, with an English translation by Frank Cole Babbitt (London: William Heinemann; Cambridge: Harvard University Press, 1969).

Socrates, Sozomenus, *Church Histories,* Vol. 2 of *A Select Library of Nicene and Post-Nicene Fathers of the Christian Church,* ed. Philip Schaff and Henry Wace, 2d series (Grand Rapids, MI: Eerdmans, 1979).

Sophocles, *The Oedipus Cycle,* trans. Dudley Fitts and Robert Fitzgerald (New York: Harcourt, Brace & World, 1949).

Ten Plays by Euripides, trans. Moses Hadas and John McLean (New York: Bantam Books, 1960).

Vergil, *The Aeneid,* trans. James H. Mantinband (New York: Frederick Ungar Publishing Co., 1964).

Bibliography

Introductory Texts

The Ancient Mysteries: A Sourcebook: Sacred Texts of the Mystery Religions of the Ancient Mediterranean World, ed. Marvin W. Meyer (San Francisco: Harper & Row, 1987).

Franz Cumont, *Oriental Religions in Roman Paganism* (1911; New York: Dover Publications, 1956).

The Oxford Classical Dictionary, ed. N. G. L. Hammond and H. H. Scullard (2d ed.; Oxford: The Clarendon Press, 1970).

Jane Harrison, *Prolegomena to the Study of Greek Religion* (1903, 1922; 3d ed.; Princeton, NJ: Princeton University Press, 1991).

Samuel Noah Kramer, *Mythologies of the Ancient World* (New York: Doubleday, 1961).

Texts About Women in the Ancient World

Arethusa, 6/1 (Spring, 1973) and 10/1, 2 (Spring & Fall, 1978). Special issues devoted to women in antiquity.

Marilyn Arthur, "From Medusa to Cleopatra: Women in the Ancient World," in *Becoming Visible: Women in European History* (Boston: Houghton Mifflin Company, 1977; 2d ed., 1987), pp. 79–105.

C. J. Bleeker, "Isis and Hathor, Two Ancient Egyptian Goddesses," in *The Book of the Goddess: Past and Present* (New York: Crossroad, 1989), pp. 29–48.

Images of Women in Antiquity, ed. Averil Cameron and Amelie Kuhrt (London & Canberra: Croom Helm, 1983).

Norma Lorre Goodrich, *Priestesses* (New York: Franklin Watts, 1989).

Ross S. Kraemer, "Bibliography: Women in the Religions of the Greco-Roman World," in *Religious Studies Review* 9/2 (April 1983).

Mary R. Lefkowitz and Maureen B. Fant, *Women's Life in Greece & Rome: A source book in translation* (Baltimore, MD: The Johns Hopkins University Press, 1982).

Barbara S. Lesko, *Women's Earliest Records: From Ancient Egypt and Western Asia* (Proceedings of the Conference on Women in the Ancient Near East, Brown University, Providence, RI, November 5–7, 1987) (Atlanta, GA: Scholars Press, 1989).

——, "Women of Egypt and the Ancient Near East," in *Becoming Visible: Women in European History* (Boston: Houghton Mifflin Company, 1977; 2nd. ed. 1987), pp. 41–77.

Maenads, Martyrs, Matrons, Monastics: A Sourcebook on Women's Religions in the Greco-Roman World, ed. Ross S. Kraemer (Philadelphia: Fortress Press, 1988).

Jo Ann McNamara, "Matres Patriae/Matres Ecclesiae: Women of the Roman Empire," in *Becoming Visible: Women in European History,* ed. Renate Bridenthal, Claudia Koonz, Susan Stuard (Boston, MA: Houghton Mifflin Company, 1977; 2d ed. 1987), pp. 107–29.

Ursule Molinaro, "A Christian Martyr in Reverse: Hypatia: 370–415 A.D." in *Hypatia: A Journal of Feminist Philosophy,* 4/1 (Spring 1989), pp. 6–8.

Christine Pierce, "Equality: *Republic* V," *The Monist* 57/1 (January, 1973), pp. 1–11.

Sarah B. Pomeroy, *Goddesses, Whores, Wives, and Slaves: Women in Classical Antiquity* (New York: Schocken Books, 1975).

M. Renee Salzman, "Magna Mater: Great Mother of the Roman Empire," in *The Book of the Goddess: Past and Present* (New York: Crossroad, 1989), pp. 60–67.

Ilse Seibert, *Women in the Ancient Near East* (New York: Abner Schram, 1974).

Merlin Stone, *When God was a Woman* (1976; New York: Harcourt Brace Jovanovich, 1978).

Diane Wolkstein and Samuel Noah Kramer, *Inanna Queen of Heaven and Earth: Her Stories and Hymns from Sumer* (London: Rider & Company, 1984).

Women in the Ancient World: The Arethusa Papers, ed. John Peradotto and J. P. Sullivan (Albany, NY: State University of New York Press, 1984).

NORTHERN EUROPEAN PAGANISM

Introduction

This chapter deals with an incredibly rich, varied, and controversial literature. First, there are the earliest literary sources for the study of northern European paganism that come from the literature of the Roman empire. Mainly these are documents referring to the military conflicts that arose between Rome and the various tribal peoples of Europe as Rome expanded its empire into their territories. Later literary sources were composed or committed to writing several centuries after the events they describe and after the advent of Christianity, an event often anticipated in this literature. The scribes who wrote down most of these stories were usually Christian converts who wanted to preserve the rich oral culture which was also their pre-Christian history. A third source of information on these people and their beliefs is contained in the folklore and fairy tales of northern Europe. Here the earlier religious ideas of these tribal peoples are subsumed in tales. The witches who populate these stories may, in fact, refer to women living on the outskirts of Christian society, where they continued their ancestral practices referred to by Christians as paganism. These European witches share many of the characteristics of the witches of the classical world: They make potions, transform humans into animals, can themselves change shape, and so on. These sources tend to view women through the social and moral lens of the compiler's culture, be it Roman, Christian, or German Romanticism.

For the most part, all these literary sources are consistent in suggesting a high status for at least some of these pagan women: They are fierce and independent, own property, often choose their sexual partners rather than having one chosen for them, rule countries, and command men. Some are powerful warriors. At the same time these stories often undercut women's power and try to put limits on it. One explanation for this is that much of the literature composed during the medieval period was designed to educate courtiers in proper behavior; courtesy and hospitality are important virtues in them, details about clothing determined fashion and emphasized stylish dressing for both women and men. They instruct rough warriors, female and male, in good manners. An important element in the medieval understanding of courtesy is the relations between women and men. Consequently, this literature emphasizes different aspects of gender; in other words, they are shaping the gender roles of well-bred courtiers.

A second explanation is that northern European women had a higher status in pagan religion than they did under Christianity. Yet, the historical evidence reveals a more complex picture. Essentially, the legal position of northern European women is in conflict with actual practice. For instance, various law codes limit women's ownership and exchange of property, yet surviving deeds, wills, and the oral and literary traditions indicate women frequently inherited and transferred property. Ideally female virginity was prized, and female adultery severely punished; yet women often initiated divorce and chose who they would next marry. The major factor in the high status and self-determination of these women probably had more to do with the scarcity of women than anything else. This scarcity came about for two reasons. First, these were migrating people. In particular, the Scandinavian migrations, especially to Iceland but also to the British isles, appear to have been the migration of men without women. Second, the Scandinavians, like most cultures around the world, practiced various forms of infanticide. Of course, where infanticide is practiced, it is most often female infanticide. The combination of these two factors and the evidence of gravesites and oral and literary traditions suggests an unparalleled shortage of women. The literature reflects this in various ways. Often the action of a saga turns on the conflict of two men over one woman or the willful act of a woman against her father or husband. These are women who knew their value and acted on it. The coming of Christianity, the slow abandonment of infanticide, and the end of the age of migration all combined to increase the number of women and to lower their status.

Finally, the frequent association of women with magic and the supernatural reveals a suspicion of women and a fear of their power. This leads to negative assessments of womenkind in general and the imposition of limitations to their rights and privileges.

The Celts

At the height of their power in the first millennium, the Celts ranged across Europe, from the Caspian mountains to Ireland. These are a varied people who shared artistic and cultural traditions as well as similar languages. Celtic languages continue to be spoken today in parts of Ireland, Scotland, Wales, and Brittany. They were a fierce warrior culture who sacked Rome in 390 B.C.E. and raided Delphi in 279 B.C.E. Eventually, they were crushed between the migrating tribes of Germany and the growing power of Rome. According to Julius Caesar (*The Conquest of Gaul*) there were three classes, the priests (Druids), whose center of learning was in Britain, the warriors, and the common people or serfs. Though literate, the Druids refused to commit their religious teachings to writing, perhaps believing them to be too sacred for any but oral transmission. Consequently, much of their religious practice, especially their rituals, is lost to us. There is some evidence for the belief in reincarnation, and we know they studied the stars and planets. Recent archaeological research shows the Celts to have had an impressive understanding of astronomy and mathematics. There is also evidence for the practice of human sacrifice, not only of captives and slaves, but of young, noble warriors.

The status of Celtic women varied between groups and probably changed over time. In general, they seem to have had few rights or liberties, though they were highly valued. Some women achieved status among the priesthood, especially in the role of the *faith,* or soothsayer. This is consistent with the role of many of the women in Celtic literature, which is to act as intermediaries between the natural and supernatural world or to be from the supernatural world. Other women were impressive warriors and some were political leaders. Essentially, though, their function was to marry, produce the next generation, and leave public life to men. However, a separation after marriage was relatively easy to obtain and women were not only allowed, but encouraged, to remarry.

The Christianization of the Celts began before the fifth century C.E. and was extended to Scotland and Ireland during the fifth century C.E., although it took several centuries to complete. This entailed a change in, among other things, the status of women, a change that is frequently understood to have been a reduction of status.

THE TAIN—QUEEN MEDB

The earliest manuscript version of the Irish epic, the *Tain Bo Cuailnge* (The Cattle Raid of Cuailnge) dates from the twelfth century but its origins in the oral tradition predate the advent of Christianity into Ireland in the fifth century. The setting of the story is the aristocratic warrior society of the province of Ulster, where some aristocratic women, such as Queen Medb, exercise power. The *Tain* begins with a discussion between Queen Medb and King Ailill as to which of them is the greater and the richer. While this chapter demonstrates Medb's power, it also undercuts it and attempts to put limits on it.

The Pillow Talk

Once when the royal bed was laid out for Ailill and Medb in Cruachan fort in Connacht, they had this talk on the pillows:

'It is true what they say, love,' Ailill said, 'it is well for the wife of a wealthy man.'

'True enough,' the woman said. 'What put that in your mind?'

'It struck me,' Ailill said, 'how much better off you are today than the day I married you.'

'I was well enough off without you,' Medb said.

'Then your wealth was something I didn't know or hear much about,' Ailill said. 'Except for your woman's things, and the neighbouring enemies making off with loot and plunder.'

'Not at all,' Medb said, 'but with the high king of Ireland for my father—Eochaid Feidlech the steadfast, the son of Finn, the son of Finnoman, the son of Finnen, the son of Finngoll, the son of Roth, the son of Rigéon, the son of Blathacht, the son of Beothacht, the son of Enna Agnech the son of Aengus Turbech. He had six daughters: Derbriu, Ethne, Ele, Clothru, Muguin, and myself Medb, the highest and haughtiest of them. I outdid them in grace and giving and battle and warlike combat. I had fifteen hundred soldiers in my royal pay, all exiles' sons, and the same number of freeborn native men, and for every paid soldier I had ten more men, and nine more, and eight, and seven, and six, and five, and four, and three, and two, and one. And that was only our ordinary household.

'My father gave me a whole province of Ireland, this province ruled from Cruachan, which is why I am called "Medb of Cruachan." And they came from Finn the king of Leinster, Rus Ruad's son, to woo me, and from Coirpre Niafer the king of Temair, another of Rus Ruad's sons. They came from Conchobor, king of Ulster, son of Fachtna, and they came from Eochaid Bec, and I wouldn't go. For I asked a harder wedding gift than any woman ever asked before from a man in Ireland—the absence of meanness and jealousy and fear.

'If I married a mean man our union would be wrong, because I'm so full of grace and giving. It would be an insult if I were more generous than my husband, but not if the two of us were equal in this. If my husband was a timid man our union would be just as wrong because I thrive, myself, on all kinds of trouble. It is an insult for a wife to be more spirited than her husband, but not if the two are equally spirited. If I married a jealous man that would be wrong, too: I never had one man without another waiting in his shadow. So I got the kind of man I wanted: Rus Ruad's other son—yourself, Ailill, from Leinster. You aren't greedy or jealous or sluggish. When we were promised, I brought you the best wedding gift a bride can bring: apparel enough for a dozen men, a chariot worth thrice seven bondmaids, the width of your face of red gold and the weight of your left arm of light gold. So, if anyone causes you shame or upset or trouble, the right to compensation is mine,' Medb said, 'for you're a kept man.'

'By no means,' Ailill said, 'but with two kings for my brothers, Coirpre in Temair and Finn over Leinster. I let them rule because they were older, not because they are better than I am in grace or giving. I never heard, in all Ireland, of a province run by a woman except this one, which is why I came and took the kingship here, in succession to my mother Mata Muiresc, Mágach's daughter. Who better for my queen than you, a daughter of the high king of Ireland?'

'It still remains,' Medb said, 'that my fortune is greater than yours.'

'You amaze me,' Ailill said. 'No one has more property or jewels or precious things than I have, and I know it.'

Then the lowliest of their possessions were brought out, to see who had more property and jewels and precious things: their buckets and tubs and iron pots, jugs and wash-pails and vessels with handles. Then their finger-rings, bracelets, thumb-rings and gold treasures were brought out, and their cloth of purple, blue, black, green and yellow, plain grey and many-coloured, yellow-brown, checked and striped. Their herds of sheep were taken in off the fields and meadows and plains. They were measured and matched, and found to be the same in numbers and size. Even the great ram leading Medb's sheep, the worth of one bondmaid by himself, had a ram to match him leading Ailill's sheep.

From pasture and paddock their teams and herds of horses were brought in. For the finest stallion in Medb's stud, worth one bondmaid by himself, Ailill had a stallion to match. Their vast herds of pigs were taken in from the woods and gullies and waste places. They were measured and matched and noted, and Medb had one fine boar, but Ailill had another. Then their droves and free-wandering herds of cattle were brought in from the woods and wastes of the province. These were matched and measured and noted also, and found to be the same in number and size. But there was one great bull in Ailill's herd, that had been a calf of one of Medb's cows—Finnbennach was his name, the White Horned—and Finnbennach, refusing to be led by a woman, had gone over to the king's herd. Medb couldn't find in her herd the equal of this bull, and her spirits dropped as though she hadn't a single penny.

Medb had the messenger Mac Roth called, and she told him to see where the match of the bull might be found, in any province in Ireland.

'I know where to find such a bull and better,' Mac

Roth said: 'in the province of Ulster, in the territory of Cuailnge, in Dáire mac Fiachna's house. Donn Cuailnge is the bull's name, the Brown Bull of Cuailnge.'

'Go there, Mac Roth,' Medb said. 'Ask Dáire to lend me Donn Cuailnge for a year. At the end of the year he can have fifty yearling heifers in payment for the loan, and the Brown Bull of Cuailnge back. And you can offer him this too, Mac Roth, if the people of the country think badly of losing their fine jewel, the Donn Cuailnge: if Dáire himself comes with the bull I'll give him a portion of the fine Plain of Ai equal to his own lands, and a chariot worth thrice seven bondmaids, and my own friendly thighs on top of that.'

[From *The Tain*, pp. 52–55.]

MACHA, THE HORSE GODDESS

The following episode is about a horse goddess, Macha, who is associated with both war and fertility. In this story she brings prosperity to the man she lives with until he ignores her injunction not to brag about her. When the men of Ulster are unsympathetic to her labor pains, she curses all the men to suffer such pains when they are in greatest need, thereby making them, as she is, unable to defend themselves.

The Pangs of Ulster

What caused the pangs of the men of Ulster? It is soon told.

There was a very rich landlord in Ulster, Crunniuc mac Agnomain. He lived in a lonely place in the mountains with all his sons. His wife was dead. Once, as he was alone in the house, he saw a woman coming toward him there, and she was a fine woman in his eyes. She settled down and began working at once, as though she were well used to the house. When night came, she put everything in order without being asked. Then she slept with Crunniuc.

She stayed with him for a long while afterward, and there was never a lack of food or clothes or anything else under her care.

Soon, a fair was held in Ulster. Everyone in Ulster, men and women, boys and girls, went to the fair. Crunniuc set out for the fair with the rest, in his best clothes and in great vigour.

'It would be as well not to grow boastful or careless in anything you say,' the woman said to him.

'That isn't likely,' he said.

The fair was held. At the end of the day the king's chariot was brought onto the field. His chariot and horses won. The crowd said that nothing could beat those horses.

'My wife is faster,' Crunniuc said.

He was taken immediately before the king and the woman was sent for. She said to the messenger:

'It would be a heavy burden for me to go and free him now. I am full with child.'

'Burden?' the messenger said. 'He will die unless you come.'

She went to the fair, and her pangs gripped her. She called out to the crowd:

'A mother bore each one of you! Help me! Wait till my child is born.'

But she couldn't move them.

'Very well,' she said. 'A long-lasting evil will come out of this on the whole of Ulster.'

'What is your name?' the king said.

'My name, and the name of my offspring,' she said, 'will be given to this place. I am Macha, daughter of Sainrith mac Imbaith.'

Then she raced the chariot. As the chariot reached the end of the field, she gave birth alongside it. She bore twins, a son and a daughter. The name Emain Macha, the Twins of Macha, comes from this. As she gave birth she screamed out that all who heard that scream would suffer from the same pangs for five days and four nights in their times of greatest difficulty. This affliction, ever afterward, seized all the men of Ulster who were there that day, and nine generations after them. Five days and four nights, or five nights and four days the pangs lasted. For nine generations any Ulsterman in those pangs had no more strength than a woman on the bed of labour. Only three classes of people were free from the pangs of Ulster: the young boys of Ulster, the women, and Cúchulainn. Ulster was thus afflicted from the time of Crunniuc, the son of Agnoman, son of Curir Ulad, son of

Fiatach mac Urmi, until the time of Furc, the son of Dallán, son of Mainech mac Lugdach. (It is from Curir Ulad that the province and people of Ulster — Ulad — have their name.)

[From *The Tain*, pp. 6–8.]

THE BOOK OF LEINSTER

The Story of Deirdre

One of the best known Irish tales is the story of Deirdre, which is preserved in *The Book of Leinster*. Before Deirdre is born a seer predicts that her great beauty will destroy them all. Hearing this, the king, Conor, decides to have her raised in seclusion until he can have her. When she grows up, however, Deirdre chooses for herself one of Conor's warriors, a man named Naisi. She does this with the aid of Levorcham, here described as a witch, but in other versions she is called a satirist, which means she has the power to compose magical poems that could not only destroy someone's reputation but were believed to be life threatening. Such poets were a powerful force in Celtic society. Naisi, though initially reluctant, agrees to run away with her, but he and his men do not always heed Dierdre's warnings and they are eventually killed. Deirdre is captured and punished for choosing her own man.

In the house of Feidlimid, the son of Dall, even he who was the narrator of stories to Conor the king, the men of Ulster sat at their ale; and before the men, in order to attend upon them, stood the wife of Feidlimid, and she was great with child. Round about the board went drinking-horns, and portions of food; and the revellers shouted in their drunken mirth. And when the men desired to lay themselves down to sleep, the woman also went to her couch; and as she passed through the midst of the house, the child cried out in her womb, so that its shriek was heard throughout the whole house, and throughout the outer court that lay about it. And upon that shriek, all the men sprang up; and, head closely packed by head, they thronged together in the house, whereupon Sencha, the son of Ailill, rebuked them: "Let none of you stir!" cried he, "and let the woman be brought before us, that we may learn what is the meaning of that cry." Then they brought the woman before them, and thus spoke to her Feidlimid, her spouse:

What is that, of all cries far the fiercest,
    In thy womb raging loudly and long?
Through all ears with that clamour thou piercest;
    With that scream, from sides swollen and strong;
Of great woe, for that cry, is foreboding my heart;
    That is torn through with terror, and sore with the smart.

Then the woman turned her, and she approached Cathbad the Druid, for he was a man of knowledge. . . .

* * *

And then said Cathbad:

'Tis a maid who screamed wildly so lately,
    Fair and curling shall locks round her flow,
And her eyes be blue-centered and stately;
    And her cheeks, like the foxglove, shall glow.
For the tint of her skin, we commend her,
    In its whiteness, like snow newly shed;
And her teeth are all faultless in splendour;
    And her lips, like to coral, are red:
A fair woman is she, for whom heroes, that fight
In their chariots for Ulster, to death shall be dight.

* * *

Then Cathbad laid his hand upon the body of the woman; and the little child moved beneath his hand: "Aye, indeed," he said, "it is a woman child who is here: Deirdre shall be her name, and evil woe shall be upon her."

* * *

"Let that maiden be slain!" cried out the young men of Ulster; but "Not so!" said Conor; "she shall in the morning be brought to me, and shall be reared according to my will, and she shall be my wife, and in my companionship shall she dwell."

The men of Ulster were not so hardy as to turn him from his purpose, and thus it was done. The maiden was reared in a house that belonged to Conor, and she grew up to be the fairest maid in all Ireland. She was brought up at a distance from the king's court;

so that none of the men of Ulster might see her till the time came when she was to share the royal couch: none of mankind was permitted to enter the house where she was reared, save only her foster-father, and her foster-mother; and in addition to these Levorcham, to whom naught could any refuse, for she was a witch.

Now once it chanced upon a certain day in the time of winter that the foster-father of Deirdre had employed himself in skinning a calf upon the snow, in order to prepare a roast for her, and the blood of the calf lay upon the snow, and she saw a black raven who came down to drink it. And "Levorcham," said Deirdre, "that man only will I love, who hath the three colours that I see here, his hair black as the raven, his cheeks red like the blood, and his body white as snow." "Dignity and good fortune to thee!" said Levorcham; "that man is not far away. Yonder is he in the burg which is nigh; and the name of him is Naisi, the son of Usnach." "I shall never be in good health again," said Deirdre, "until the time come when I may see him."

* * *

Now when this Naisi found himself alone on the plain, Deirdre also soon escaped outside her house to him, and she ran past him, and at first he knew not who she might be.

"Fair is the young heifer that springs past me!" he cried.

"Well may the young heifers be great," she said, "in a place where none may find a bull."

"Thou hast, as thy bull," said he, "the bull of the whole province of Ulster, even Conor the king of Ulster."

"I would choose between you two," she said, "and I would take for myself a younger bull, even such as thou art."

"Not so, indeed," said Naisi, "for I fear the prophecy of Cathbad."

"Sayest thou this, as meaning to refuse me?" said she.

"Yea indeed," he said; and she sprang upon him, and she seized him by his two ears. "Two ears of shame and of mockery shalt thou have," she cried, "if thou take me not with thee."

"Release me, O my wife!" said he.

"That will I."

Then Naisi raised his musical warriorcry, and the men of Ulster heard it, and each of them one after another sprang up: and the sons of Usnach hurried out in order to hold back their brother.

"What is it," they said, "that thou dost? let it not be by any fault of thine that war is stirred up between us and the men of Ulster."

Then he told them all that had been done; and "There shall evil come on thee from this," said they;

"moreover thou shalt lie under the reproach of shame so long as thou dost live; and we will go with her into another land, for there is no king in all Ireland who will refuse us welcome if we come to him."

Then they took counsel together, and that same night they departed, three times fifty warriors, and the same number of women, and dogs, and servants, and Deirdre went with them. And for a long time they wandered about Ireland, in homage to this man or that; and often Conor sought to slay them, either by ambuscade or by treachery; from round about Assaroe, near to Ballyshannon in the west, they journeyed, and they turned them back to Benn Etar, in the north-east, which men to-day call the Mountain of Howth. Nevertheless the men of Ulster drave them from the land, and they came to the land of Alba, and in its wildernesses they dwelled. And when the chase of the wild beasts of the mountains failed them, they made foray upon the cattle of the men of Alba, and took them for themselves; and the men of Alba gathered themselves together with intent to destroy them. Then they took shelter with the king of Alba, and the king took them into his following, and they served him in war. And they made for themselves houses of their own in the meadows by the king's burg: it was on account of Deirdre that these houses were made, for they feared that men might see her, and that on her account they might be slain.

Now one day the high-steward of the king went out in the early morning, and he made a cast about Naisi's house, and saw those two sleeping therein, and he hurried back to the king, and awaked him: "We have," said he, "up to this day found no wife for thee of like dignity to thyself. Naisi the son of Usnach hath a wife of worth sufficient for the emperor of the western world! Let Naisi be slain, and let his wife share thy couch."

"Not so!" said the king, "but do thou prepare thyself to go each day to her house, and woo her for me secretly."

Thus it was done; but Deirdre whatsoever the steward told her, was accustomed straightway to recount it each even to her spouse; and since nothing was obtained from her, the sons of Usnach were sent into dangers, and into wars, and into strifes that thereby they might be overcome. Nevertheless they showed themselves to be stout in every strife, so that no advantage did the king gain from them by such attempts as these.

The men of Alba were gathered together to destroy the son of Usnach, and this also was told to Deirdre. And she told her news to Naisi: "Depart hence!" said she, "for if ye depart not this night, upon the morrow ye shall be slain!" And they marched away that night, and they betook themselves to an island of the sea.

Now the news of what had passed was brought to the men of Ulster. "'Tis pity, O Conor!" said they, "that the sons of Usnach should die in the land of foes, for the sake of an evil woman. It is better that they should come under thy protection, and that the (fated) slaying should be done here, and that they should come into their own land, rather than that they should fall at the hands of foes." "Let them come to us then," said Conor, "and let men go as securities to them." The news was brought to them.

"This is welcome news for us," they said; "we will indeed come, and let Fergus come as our surety, and Dubhtach, and Cormac the son of Conor." These then went to them, and they moved them to pass over the sea.

But at the contrivance of Conor, Fergus was pressed to join in an ale-feast, while the sons of Usnach were pledged to eat no food in Erin, until they had eaten the food of Conor. So Fergus tarried behind with Dubhtach and Cormac; and the sons of Usnach went on, accompanied by Fiacha, Fergus' son; until they came to the meadows around Emain.

Now at that time Eogan the son of Durthacht had come to Emain to make his peace with Conor, for they had for a long time been at Enmity; and to him, and to the warmen of Conor, the charge was given that they should slay the sons of Usnach, in order that they should not come before the king. The sons of Usnach stood upon the level part of the meadows, and the women sat upon the ramparts of Emain. And Eogan came with his warriors across the meadow, and the son of Fergus took his place by Naisi's side. And Eogan greeted them with a mighty thrust of his spear, and the spear brake Naisi's back in sunder, and passed through it. The son of Fergus made a spring, and he threw both arms around Naisi, and he brought him beneath himself to shelter him, while he threw himself down above him; and it was thus that Naisi was slain, through the body of the son of Fergus. Then there began a murder throughout the meadow, so that none escaped who did not fall by the points of the spears, or the edge of the sword, and Deirdre was brought to Conor to be in his power, and her arms were bound behind her back.

Now the sureties who had remained behind, heard what had been done, even Fergus and Dubhtach, and Cormac. And thereon they hastened forward, and they forthwith performed great deeds. Dubhtach slew,

with the one thrust of his spear, Mane a son of Conor, and Fiachna the son of Feidelm, Conor's daughter; and Fergus struck down Traigthren, the son of Traiglethan, and his brother. And Conor was wrath at this, and he came to the fight with them; so that upon that day three hundred of the men of Ulster fell. And Dubhtach slew the women of Ulster; and, ere the day dawned, Fergus set Emain on fire. Then they went away into exile, and betook them to the land of Connaught to find shelter with Ailill and Maev, for they knew that that royal pair would give them good entertainment. To the men of Ulster the exiles showed no love: three thousand stout men went with them; and for sixteen years never did they allow cries of lamentation and of fear among the Ulstermen to cease: each night their vengeful forays caused men to quake, and to wail.

Deirdre lived on for a year in the household of Conor; and during all that time she smiled no smile of laughter; she satisfied not herself with food or with sleep, and she raised not her head from her knee.

★ ★ ★

"Whom dost thou hate the most," said Conor, "of these whom thou now seest?"

"Thee thyself," she answered, "and with thee Eogan the son of Durthacht."

"Then," said Conor, thou shalt dwell with Eogan for a year;" and he gave Deirdre over into Eogan's hand.

Now upon the morrow they went away over the festal plain of Macha, and Deirdre sat behind Eogan in the chariot; and the two who were with her were the two men whom she would never willingly have seen together upon the earth, and as she looked upon them, "Ha, Deirdre," said Conor, "it is the same glance that a ewe gives when between two rams that thou sharest now between me and Eogan!" Now there was a great rock of stone in front of them, and Deirdre struck her head upon that stone, and she shattered her head, and so she died.

This then is the tale of the exile of the sons of Usnach, and of the Exile of Fergus, and of the death of Deirdre.

[From *Heroic Romances of Old Ireland,* 1:91–102.]

THE MABINOGION

RHIANNON, THE HORSE GODDESS

The Mabinogion is a collection of Welsh oral tales that survive in a written manuscript dated to c. 1325, although they contain much earlier oral material. The tales are an almost inseparable blend of myth and history, with a strong Christian overlay.

The following excerpt is taken from the first tale of *The Mabinogion,* which tells the story of Pwyll, who rules over Dyfed, and his meeting with the mysterious and otherworldy woman Rhiannon. She is really one of the important horse goddesses of the Celts associated with sovereignty and plenty and was often depicted as a mare with a foal. Their story has bizarre twists and turns. It begins when Pwyll first sees Rhiannon riding a white horse and attempts to pursue her; but, for all his skill, he cannot overtake her. At his request, though, she stops, and he agrees to help her avoid an unwanted marriage and, instead, marries her himself. Their marriage is happy except for the fact that they do not have a child. When Rhiannon finally gives birth to a son, he disappears, and she is blamed for his death. Her punishment is to act like a horse by carrying guests on her back. Eventually her child is found beside a mare under mysterious circumstances. The child is returned and the ending is happy.

They [Pwyll and Rhiannon] ruled the land successfully that year and the next. But in the third year, the men of the land began to feel sad within themselves at seeing the man they loved so much as their lord and foster-brother without an heir. And they summoned him to them. It was in Presseleu in Dyfed that they met.

"Lord," they said, "we know that you are not the same age as some of the men in this land, and we are afraid that you might not have an heir from the woman who is with you. So for that reason, take another wife that you may have an heir from her. You will not last forever, and though you would like to remain as you are, we will not tolerate it from you."

"Well," said Pwyll, "we have not been together long, and much may happen yet. Be patient with me until the end of the year: we will arrange to meet a year from now, and I will act according to your advice."

The appointment was made, but before the time was up, a son was born to him, and in Arberth he was born. On the night of his birth, women were brought in to watch over the boy and his mother. What the women did, however, was sleep, and Rhiannon, the boy's mother, too. Six was the number of women brought in. They kept vigil for a part of the night, but then, however, before midnight, each fell asleep; toward dawn they awakened. When they awoke, they looked where they had put the boy, but there was no sign of him there.

"Och!" exclaimed one of the women, "the boy is surely lost!"

"Indeed," said another, "it would be a small punishment to burn us or slay us on account of the boy."

"Is there any counsel in the world for that?" one of them asked.

"There is," said another, "I have good counsel."

"What is it?" they asked.

"There is a staghound bitch here," she said, "and she had puppies. Let us kill some of the pups, smear Rhiannon's face and hands with the blood, cast the bones before her, and swear that she herself has destroyed her son. And our affirmation will not yield to her own."

They decided on that. Toward day Rhiannon awoke and said, "Ladies, where is my boy?"

"Lady," they said, "don't ask us for your son. We have nothing but bruises and blows from struggling with you, and we have certainly never seen ferocity in any woman as much as in you. But it did us no good to fight with you; you have destroyed your son yourself, so do not seek him from us."

"You poor things!" exclaimed Rhiannon, "for the sake of the Lord God who knows all things, don't lie to me! God, who knows everything, knows that's a lie. If it is because you are afraid, I confess to God, I will protect you."

"God knows," they said, "we would not suffer harm to befall us for anyone in the world."

"Poor things," she said, "you'll suffer no harm for telling the truth."

But despite what she would say either in reason or with emotion, she would get only the same answer from the women.

Thereupon Pwyll Pen Annwfn rose, along with the retinue and the hosts; it was impossible to conceal what had happened. The news went through the land, and every nobleman heard it. The nobles met and sent emissaries to Pwyll, to ask him to divorce his wife for having committed an outrage as reprehensible as she had done.

"They have no cause to request that I divorce my wife, save that she bear no children," Pwyll told them. "I know she has children, and I will not divorce her. If she has done wrong, let her be punished for it."

Rhiannon, for her part, summoned to her teachers and men of wisdom. And when it seemed more appropriate to her to accept her penance than to haggle with the women, she accepted her punishment. This was the punishment handed down to her: to be in that court in Arberth for seven years, to sit beside the mounting block that was outside the gate each day, to tell her story to all who came whom she thought might not know it, and to offer to those guests and distant travellers who would allow it to carry them on her back to the court; only rarely would one allow himself to be carried. And thus she spent a part of the year.

At that time, Teyrnon Twrf Liant was lord over Gwent Is Coed, and he was the best man in the world. In his house was a mare, and there was neither stallion nor mare fairer than she in his kingdom. On the eve of every May day she would foal, but no one knew what became of her foal. One night, Teyrnon conversed with his wife.

"Wife," he said, "we are remiss in allowing our mare to bear issue each year without us getting any of them."

"What can be done about it?" she asked.

"God's vengeance on me," said he, "if I do not find out what destruction is carrying off the colts: tonight is May eve."

He had the mare brought into the house, armed himself, and began the night's vigil. As night fell, the mare gave birth to a large, handsome colt; it stood immediately. Teyrnon rose to inspect the stoutness of the colt, and as he was so engaged, he heard a great commotion, and after the commotion, a great claw came through the window, and grasped the colt by the mane. Teyrnon drew his sword and cut off the arm from the elbow, so that that part of the arm and the colt remained inside with him. At the same time, he heard a roar and wail together. He opened the door and rushed headlong in the direction of the noise, but he could see nothing because of the night's darkness. He pursued the sound, following it. Then he remembered having left the door open, and went back. At the door there was a small boy all wrapped up in a mantle of silk brocade! He took the boy to him and, indeed, the boy was strong for his age!

[From *The Mabinogi*, pp. 50–52.]

THE LAYS OF MARIE DE FRANCE

Little is known about the life of the woman who simply called herself "Marie of France" other than that she may have been associated with the court of Eleanor of Aquitaine and Henry II. Combined with other evidence, this dates her lays to the late twelfth century.

The stories of Marie de France maintain the rights of women to choose lovers in spite of arranged marriages. Her stories, and indeed most of the courtly romances of this period, harken back to earlier, pre-Christian tales, in which powerful women decided their own fates. Marie herself states that she is retelling stories she read or heard recited from long ago in order that they may not be forgotten. These stories challenged prevailing Christian sentiments that represented sex as exclusively for procreation within marriage by describing adulterous affairs conducted for personal pleasure. Courtly love, by definition, takes place outside the institution of patriarchal marriage.

Marie de France is not the lone female figure in this period; the literature of courtly love was actively shaped by women both as writers such as Marie de France and as patrons such as Eleanor of Aquitaine.

The following excerpt from *The Lay of Sir Launfal* describes the romance of this impoverished Arthurian knight and a beautiful fairy woman endowed with magical powers. While resting in a meadow one day Sir Launfal is approached by two beautiful women who invite him to meet their mistress in a nearby pavilion.

"Launfal," she said, "fair friend, it is for you that I have come from my own far land. I bring you my love. If you are prudent and discreet, as you are goodly to the view, there is no emperor nor count, nor king, whose day shall be so filled with riches and with mirth as yours."

When Launfal heard these words he rejoiced greatly, for his heart was litten by another's torch.

"Fair lady," he answered, "since it pleases you to be so gracious, and to dower so graceless a knight with your love, there is naught that you may bid me do—right or wrong, evil or good—that I will not do to the utmost of my power. I will observe your commandment, and serve in your quarrels. For you I renounce my father and my father's house. This only I pray, that I may dwell with you in your lodging, and that you will never send me from your side."

When the Maiden heard the words of him whom

so fondly she desired to love, she was altogether moved, and granted him forthwith her heart and her tenderness. To her bounty she added another gift besides. Never might Launfal be desirous of aught, but he would have according to his wish. He might waste and spend at will and pleasure, but in his purse ever there was to spare. No more was Launfal sad. Right merry was the pilgrim, since one had set him on the way, with such a gift, that the more pennies he bestowed, the more silver and gold were in his pouch.

But the Maiden had yet a word to say.

"Friend," she said, " hearken to my counsel. I lay this charge upon you, and pray you urgently, that you tell not to any man the secret of our love. If you show this matter, you will lose your friend, for ever and a day. Never again may you see my face. Never again will you have seisin of that body, which is now so tender in your eyes."

Launfal plighted faith, that right strictly he would observe this commandment. So the Maiden granted him her kiss and her embrace, and very sweetly in that fair lodging passed the day till evensong was come.

Right loath was Launfal to depart from the pavilion at the vesper hour, and gladly would he have stayed, had he been able, and his lady wished.

"Fair friend," said she, "rise up, for no longer may you tarry. The hour is come that we must part. But one thing I have to say before you go. When you would speak with me I shall hasten to come before your wish. Well I deem that you will only call your friend where she may be found without reproach or shame of men. You may see me at your pleasure; my voice shall speak softly in your ear at will; but I must never be known of your comrades, nor must they ever learn my speech.

Sir Launfal returns to Arthur's court where he uses the magic purse to reward and help others. Here he catches the eye of Arthur's Queen (Guenevere who, oddly enough, is the villain of this tale) but rejects her overtures, boasting that he is loved by a woman far more beautiful and virtuous than the Queen. Of course, these hasty words shatter his connection with the fairy women, and the Queen has him brought to trial for insulting her. His only chance of acquittal is to have his beloved appear in Court and thus prove he did not insult the Queen but instead spoke the truth. After much tribulation she does indeed appear, saves her knight (a nice reversal of knightly duties to ladies), and takes him away to fairyland.

The Maiden entered in the palace — where none so fair had come before — and stood before the King, in the presence of his household. She loosed the clasp of her mantle, so that men might the more easily perceive the grace of her person. The courteous King advanced to meet her, and all the Court got them on their feet, and pained themselves in her service. When the lords had gazed upon her for a space, and praised the sum of her beauty, the lady spake to Arthur in this fashion, for she was anxious to begone.

"Sire, I have loved one of thy vassals, — the knight who stands in bonds, Sir Launfal. He was always misprized in thy Court, and his every action turned to blame. What he said, that thou knowest; for over hasty was his tongue before the Queen. But he never craved her in love, however loud his boasting. I cannot choose that he should come to hurt or harm by me. In the hope of freeing Launfal from his bonds, I have obeyed thy summons. Let now thy barons look boldly upon my face, and deal justly in this quarrel between the Queen and me.

The King commanded that this should be done, and

looking upon her eyes, not one of the judges but was persuaded that her favour exceeded that of the Queen.

Since then Launfal had not spoken in malice against his lady, the lords of the household gave him again his sword. When the trial had come thus to an end the Maiden took her leave of the King, and made her ready to depart. Gladly would Arthur have had her lodge with him for a little, and many a lord would have rejoiced in her service, but she might not tarry. Now without the hall stood a great stone of dull marble, where it was the wont of lords, departing from the Court, to climb into the saddle, and Launfal by the stone. The Maiden came forth from the doors of the palace, and mounting on the stone, seated herself on the palfrey, behind her friend. Then they rode across the plain together, and were no more seen.

The Bretons tell that the knight was ravished by his lady to an island, very dim and very fair, known as Avalon. But none has had speech with Launfal and his faery love since then, and for my part I can tell you no more of the matter.

[From *Lays of Marie de France*, pp. 62–76.]

LE MORTE D'ARTHUR

MORGAN LE FAY

Morgan le Fay ("fay" means fairy), the sister of King Arthur (traditionally known as a sixth-century king of the Britons), is a dangerous sorceress who enchants men with her magic as well as her beauty, yet who is also known for her wisdom and her abilities as a healer. These conflicting traits derive from her connections to the Irish goddess Morrigan and the Welsh goddess Modron, as well as to the fairies. Her story is part of the Arthurian legends that originated in northern England and were preserved in Welsh, where they later developed into the medieval story cycles, which often added a Christian gloss.

The following excerpt is taken from Sir Thomas Malory's (d. 1471) *Le Morte d'Arthur*. While Arthur is hunting with Morgan's husband, King Uryens, and her lover, Sir Accolon, she causes all of them to fall into an enchanted sleep, from which each one awakens in a different place. King Uryens wakes in Camelot with Morgan. Arthur wakes in a dungeon, where he is coerced into fighting for his captor, Sir Damas. Sir Accolon wakes in the company of a dwarf, who brings him a message from Morgan saying she has stolen Arthur's magical sword, Excalibur, which she gives to Accolon to use against Arthur. Another sorceress, Nyneve, who loves Arthur and like Morgan was instructed in magic by Merlin, learns of Morgan's plans and uses her magic to thwart them. Meanwhile, Morgan attempts to kill her husband but is prevented from doing so by their son. Once again she steals Arthur's magic scabbard and flees north. She then sends Arthur a deadly mantle.

Her persistent efforts to destroy Arthur and thereby win the throne for herself have been read as a struggle against the forces that were undermining the power of royal women, and/or goddesses, to grant the kingship to a male hero of their own choosing. Significantly, when Arthur does die, Morgan reveals the fairy connection to the realm of the dead, as she and three other fairy queens take his body to the mystic island of Avalon, often referred to as the land of the fairies.

"Sir," said the dwarf, "I bring you greetings from your lady, Morgan le Fay. She bids you be of good cheer, for at dawn tomorrow you shall fight and overcome a knight whose death shall enable you to become king of the realm, with Morgan le Fay as your queen. In this way the agreement between you shall be fulfilled; and to assure your success she sends you King Arthur's own sword, Excalibur, together with the magic sheath. Fight bravely and all will be yours."

"Now," said Sir Accolon, "I understand the reason for my enchantment; tell your mistress that I send her my love, and that I vow not to fail her."

The dwarf departed, and not long afterward a knight, a lady, and six squires rode up to the fountain and invited Sir Accolon to their manor. Sir Accolon accompanied them on a spare horse, and when they arrived he was welcomed by Sir Outlake, who was the lord of the manor. Sir Outlake was wounded in both thighs as the result of a spear thrust which he had received while fighting a recent engage-

ment, and when a messenger came to deliver Sir Damas' challenge to fight his champion at dawn the following day, Sir Accolon realized that this must be the knight whom Morgan le Fay intended that he should fight in fulfillment of their agreement; and therefore he at once offered to accept the challenge on Sir Outlake's behalf. Sir Outlake thanked him warmly, accepted the offer, and informed the messenger accordingly. Sir Accolon was not aware, however, that Sir Damas' champion was King Arthur.

After hearing mass and breaking his fast, Arthur was provided with a good horse and set of armor. He was about to enter the tournament field when a maid came to him and presented him with a perfect counterfeit of his own sword, Excalibur, and a message from Morgan le Fay: "Your sister sends you this sword for the sake of the love that she bears you." Arthur was completely deceived.

When the two champions met on the field, neither recognized the other; and amongst the spectators there was only one who knew the identities of both, and this was Nyneve. She loved King Arthur, and had come in order to save him if she could, having discovered Morgan le Fay's plot to have him killed.

★ ★ ★

Once more, Sir Accolon brandished Excalibur; but Nyneve, who had missed nothing, and whose heart was bleeding for Arthur; by means of a magic spell made it fly from his hand. Arthur leaped upon the sword where it fell, and the moment he picked it up, knew it for his own. Seeing the sheath still hanging from Sir Accolon's side, he suddenly wrenched it from him, and flung it far from them both.

"Sir, too long have I suffered from my own sword," he said, "but now you shall have a taste of it."

Therewith he dragged Sir Accolon bodily to the ground, tore off his helmet, and struck with all his might. As from a fountain, the blood flowed from every part of Sir Accolon's head: from mouth, ears, eyes, nostrils, and hair.

"And now," said Arthur, "I shall kill you."

"Sir," Sir Accolon gasped, "you have won the right to."

But at that moment, in spite of Sir Accolon's unnatural disfigurement and voice, Arthur thought that he recognized him.

"Sir, please tell me your name and where you are from, and how you came to possess the magical sword Excalibur."

"Sir, I am called Sir Accolon and I come from the court of King Arthur. My paramour, Morgan le Fay, stole Excalibur from King Arthur and gave it to me to assure my success in killing Sir Outlake's opponent, whose death, she maintained, would clear the way for her to kill both her husband, King Uryens, and King Arthur himself, by which means I should then rule over his realm with her for my queen. But the plan has gone sadly astray; and because of your terrible valor, not only shall I never rule, but I doubt if I shall live to see my paramour again. But please tell me, most invincible knight, who are you?"

"King Arthur."

"Alas, my liege! I should have known. I beg you to forgive me, and to believe that although I agreed to your death, I did not know that it was you whom I was fighting."

"Sir Accolon, although you have plotted against my person, I believe that you have spoken the truth, and I forgive you. But my sister Morgan le Fay, whom I have honored more than any living person except for my queen, I shall never forgive; and on her I swear the most terrible vengeance."

★ ★ ★

King Arthur then took his leave of the company and, together with Sir Accolon and Sir Outlake, rode to the abbey, where their wounds were skillfully treated by a surgeon, and where the nuns nursed them tenderly. Soon Arthur began to recover, but Sir Accolon died four days later from excessive loss of blood. By Arthur's command his corpse was conveyed to Camelot on a horse litter, and taken into the presence of Morgan le Fay, to whom the bearers delivered this message: "Herewith is a gift from King Arthur to his sister. He informs her that he has recovered Excalibur and its sheath and is aware that she stole it from him."

Morgan le Fay, meanwhile, supposing that Arthur would be killed on the appointed day, had sought for an opportunity of getting rid of her husband, King Uryens. Finding him asleep in his bed one afternoon, she ordered her maid to fetch his sword for her. The maid, however, terrified of her mistress' intentions, went first to Sir Uwayne, their son, and after waking him, warned him to go secretly to his father's chamber, in order to prevent his assassination. Sir Uwayne sped to the chamber, and had successfully hidden himself when the maid, still quaking with fear, delivered the sword to her mistress. Sir Uwayne watched his mother raise the sword to behead the sleeping king, then leaped out from his hiding place and seized her.

"Fiend!" he shouted, "how can I recognize in you the mother who bore me? And yet were it anyone else I should kill him this instant."

"My son!" she exclaimed, "spare me, I beg you. For one moment I must have fallen prey to the devil's command; but only forgive me, and keep the secret so that our name shall not be dishonored, and I swear that never again shall I be so tempted."

"And I thought it was Merlin who was the one supposed to be born of the devil! Well, after the oath you have sworn, I must agree to take no action this time, and shall say nothing."

It was just after her attempt to murder her husband that Morgan le Fay received the corpse of her mutilated lover. She could barely control her grief at the sight of it; but then, receiving Arthur's message, she was inspired with a cold and merciless anger. Taking good care to hide her feelings, she presented herself to Queen Gwynevere, and begged in her sweetest tones for leave to ride with an escort to Arthur, for whom, she said, she had important tidings.

The queen gave her consent when Morgan le Fay insisted that the tidings were urgent. Summoning her escort, Morgan le Fay then set off for the abbey, determined to do to Arthur what harm she could.

Riding all day and all night, she reached the abbey at noon the next day, and demanded, as Arthur's sister, to be admitted to Arthur at once. While humbly acknowledging her rank, the sisters pleaded that the king was asleep for the first time in three days and three nights.

Morgan le Fay then commanded that none but herself should be admitted to him before he awoke, and was directed to his chamber. She found him asleep with the naked Excalibur grasped in his right hand. Cursing silently, she looked about for the scabbard, and finding it, concealed it beneath her gown before leaving. Morgan le Fay then summoned her escort and rode away from the abbey.

Arthur was enraged when he discovered that Morgan le Fay had succeeded once more in stealing Excalibur's scabbard, and after complaining that he had not been properly watched over, demanded that the two best available horses should be saddled immediately. The sisters excused themselves on the grounds that they could not countermand his sister's orders, and the horses were prepared.

Taking Sir Outlake with him, Arthur set off in pursuit of his sister. They had not ridden far when they came upon a cowherd taking his ease by a stone cross. In answer to Arthur's question, the cowherd replied that he had seen Morgan le Fay, together with an escort of forty men. Arthur and Sir Outlake galloped off again in the direction he had indicated.

When Morgan le Fay saw that she was being pursued by Arthur and Sir Outlake, and that they were gaining upon her, she rode up to the shore of a lake and threw the scabbard into the water; being heavy with gold and jewels, it sank immediately. When this was done she led her escort into a rocky valley, and by means of an enchantment, made the whole party indistinguishable from the rocks.

When Arthur and Sir Outlake entered the valley and found it apparently deserted, they gave up the pursuit and searched about for the scabbard. Failing to find this too, they rode back sorrowfully to the abbey, and Arthur swore again to revenge himself upon his sister.

★ ★ ★

The next morning a maid arrived at the court, bearing a mantle of magnificent appearance, being wrought throughout with precious stones. Arthur was entranced with it, and the maid said:

"Sire, I bring this mantle to you from Morgan le Fay, who begs you to accept it as a gift; and she promises that you shall be fully recompensed for every offense she has given you."

Before Arthur had time to reply, Nyneve drew him aside and spoke to him privately:

"Sire, I beg you to take my advice and let no man in your court touch this mantle until Morgan le Fay's maid has herself worn it."

"I will do as you advise," Arthur replied, and turning to the maid, commanded her to wear the mantle.

"Sire," she said, "this is a garment intended for a king. Surely it would be unseemly for a servant such as myself to wear it?"

But Arthur insisted, and the maid put the mantle over her shoulders. She had no sooner done so than she burst into flames, and in a moment was reduced to ashes.

[From *Sir Thomas Malory's Le Morte d'Arthur*, pp. 75–82.]

The Germans and the Scandinavians

The earliest sources on the people known as the ancient Germans are in Tacitus, who modern scholarship has shown to be quite reliable. Tacitus is frankly admiring of these tribes. They are a mix of peoples who migrated from southern Scandinavia and northern Germany and various other peoples from the south and east who are known to history through a variety of additional names such as the Teutons and the Saxons. Here we can also include the Normans, or Norsemen (Scandinavians), of French Normandy. They all valued women, but secular and religious power was mainly in the hands of the men. These were warrior societies, and women participated in war mainly by standing on the edge of battles and shouting encouragements to the warriors. If the battle was not going well, the women would shout out the horrors of captivity that awaited them, begging the warriors to spare them such a fate. There is also evidence, though, of women warriors. The Scandinavians who did not migrate continued to prosper as a seafaring people and also through the amber trade, which continually brought them into contact with other peoples.

Later sources for the religious practices of the Germanic and Scandinavian peoples are to be found in their literature of the sixth and later centuries, which was not written down until after the introduction of Christianity; for instance, the Eddas and the sagas. While problematic because of its heavy Christian overlay, this literature contains information not to be found elsewhere.

In sum, Germanic religion refers to the religious practices of a variety of people over a wide and expanding geographical area and for a long period of time. For the most part, these are warrior societies that attempt to gain victory in battle by winning the favor of the gods through sacrifice, often the sacrifice of human captives, and through other cultic practices. The gods are themselves subject to fate, even as human beings are, and this vulnerability is often revealed in the tales in which gods and humans interact. It was a highly complex religious system, most of which is lost to us.

VELEDA, A GERMAN PROPHETESS

In chapter four of his *Historia* (Sections 61 & 65) the Roman historian Tacitus (born ca. 56 C.E.) preserved the name of Veleda, a German woman who participated in the war against Rome in 69–70 C.E. Her status is equal to the war leader Civilis; together they are chosen as arbiters for a treaty among the tribes who fought against Rome. Note, however, that she herself never appears publicly; and like many other female prophets and sibyls such as the Delphic Oracle, her utterances are transmitted through others, usually men.

Then Civilis fulfilled a vow often made by barbarians; his hair, which he had let grow long and coloured with a red dye from the day of taking up arms against Rome, he now cut short, when the destruction of the legions had been accomplished. It was also said that he set up some of the prisoners as marks for his little son to shoot at with a child's arrow and javelins. He neither took the oath of allegiance to Gaul himself, nor obliged any Batavian to do so, for he relied on the resources of Germany, and felt that, should it be necessary to fight for empire with the Gauls, he should have on his side a great name and superior strength. Munius Lupercus, legate of one of the legions, was sent along with other gifts to Veleda, a maiden of the tribe of the Bructeri, who possessed extensive dominion; for by ancient usage the Germans attributed to many of their women prophetic powers and, as the superstition grew in strength, even actual divinity. The authority of Veleda was then at its height, because she had foretold the success of the Germans and the destruction of the legions.
[From *The Complete Works of Tacitus*, p. 636.]

"As arbiters between us we will have Civilis and Veleda; under their sanction the treaty shall be ratified." The Tencteri were thus appeased, and ambassadors were sent with presents to Civilis and Veleda, who settled everything to the satisfaction of the inhabitants of the Colony. They were not, however, allowed to approach or address Veleda herself. In order to inspire them with more respect they were prevented from seeing her. She dwelt in a lofty tower, and one of her relatives, chosen for the purpose, conveyed, like the messenger of a divinity, the questions and answers.
[From *The Complete Works of Tacitus*, p. 639.]

THE EARTH GODDESS

In his *Germania* (40) Tacitus describes a festival of an earth goddess. Though his reference is obscure, modern scholars believes this took place in what is now modern Denmark. During this festival the goddess is driven around the countryside in her chariot in order to fertilize the land and bestow plenty on one and all.

None of these tribes have any noteworthy feature, except their common worship of Ertha, or mother-Earth, and their belief that she interposes in human affairs, and visits the nations in her car. In an island of ocean there is a sacred grove, and within it a con-secrated chariot, covered over with a garment. Only one priest is permitted to touch it. *He* can perceive the presence of the goddess in this sacred recess, and walks by her side with the utmost reverence as she is drawn along by heifers. It is a season of rejoicing, and festivity reigns wherever she deigns to go and be received. They do not go to battle or wear arms; every weapon is under lock; peace and quiet are known and welcomed only at these times, till the goddess, weary of human intercourse, is at length restored by the same priest to her temple. Afterwards the car, the vestments, and, if you like to believe it, the divinity herself, are purified in a secret lake. Slaves perform the rite, who are instantly swallowed up by its waters. Hence arises a mysterious terror and a pious ignorance concerning the nature of that which is seen only by men doomed to die. This branch indeed of the Suevi stretches into the remoter regions of Germany.

[From *The Complete Works of Tacitus,* pp. 728–729.]

THE PROSE EDDA

The following two excerpts are taken from the first section of *The Prose Edda,* the *Gylfa-ginning,* which is a guide to Norse myth. *The Prose Edda,* sometimes also called *The Younger Edda,* was composed by the Icelandic poet and historian Snorri Sturluson (1179–1241) from earlier sources.

The Norns

The Norns are ambiguous female figures who establish laws and control the fate of humans and gods alike. They live at the roots of and care for the world tree, Yggdrasil, which is at the center of the universe and extends through the three worlds of the gods, the giants and elves, and the underworld. Sometimes they are described as beautiful and benign, at other times they are ugly and dangerous. Most often they are thought to be three sisters.

There are many beautiful places in heaven, and they are all under divine protection. There is a beautiful hall near the spring under the ash tree, and from it come three maidens whose names are Urd, Verdandi, Skuld. These maidens shape the lives of men, and we call them Norns. There are, however, more Norns, those that come to every child that is born in order to shape its life, and these are beneficent, others belong to the family of the elves and a third group belongs to the family of the dwarfs as it says here:

Of different origins
are the Norns, I think,
not all of one kindred;
some come from AEsir-kin,
some from the elves,
and some are the daughters of Dvalin.

Then Gangleri said: 'If the Norns decide the fates of men, they appoint very unequal destinies for them; for some have a good and abundant life, but others have little wealth or fame. Some have a long life and others a short one.'

High One said: 'The good Norns who come from good stock shape good lives, but those who meet with misfortune owe it to the evil Norns.'

* * *

It is said further that the Norns who live near the spring of Urd draw water from the spring every day, and along with it the clay that lies round about the spring, and they besprinkle the ash [the world tree] so that its branches shall not wither or decay. But that water is so sacred that everything that comes into the spring becomes as white as the film (which is called "skin") that lies within the eggshell.

[From *The Prose Edda of Snorri Sturluson,* pp. 44–46.]

VARIOUS GODDESSES

Little has been preserved about the Norse goddesses, especially those connected with fertility, perhaps because the Christian scribes were reluctant to discuss fertility rites, which conflicted with Christian sexual morality. The following excerpt describes the attributes of various goddesses, including Freyja, a goddess of war and love, and Hel, the goddess of the underworld.

Then Gangleri asked: 'Who are the gods men ought to believe in?'

High One replied: 'The divine gods are twelve in number.'

Just-as-High added: 'The goddesses are no less sacred and no less powerful.'

* * *

Freyja is the most renowned of the goddesses. She owns that homestead in heaven known as Fólkvangar, and whenever she rides into battle she has half the slain and Ódin half, as it says here:

Fólkvangar's where
Freyja decides
who shall sit where in the hall;
half the slain every day
she chooses
and Ódin has half.

'Her hall Sessrúmnir is large and beautiful. When she goes on a journey she sits in a chariot drawn by two cats. She is most readily invoked, and from her name derives the polite custom of calling the wives of men of rank Frú. She enjoys love poetry, and it is good to call on her for help in love affairs.'

* * *

'Loki had still more children. There was a giantess in Giantland called Angrboda. Loki had three children by her, the first was the wolf Fenrir, the second, Jörmungand — that is the Midgard Serpent — and the third, Hel. Now when the gods knew that these three children were being brought up in Giantland and had gathered from prophecy that they would meet with great harm and misfortune on their account (and they all anticipated evil, first from the mother and still worse from the father), All-father sent some of the gods to capture the children and bring them to him. And when they came to him, he flung the serpent into the deep sea which surrounds the whole world, and it grew so large that it now lies in the middle of the ocean round the earth, biting its own tail. He threw Hel into Niflheim and gave her authority over nine worlds, on the condition that she shared all her provisions with those who were sent to her, namely men who die from disease or old age. She has a great homestead there with extraordinarily high walls and huge gates. Her hall is called Éljúdnir; her plate, Hunger; her knife, Famine; her man-servant, Ganglati; her maid-servant, Ganglöt; the stone at the entrance, Drop-to-destruction; her bed, Sick-bed; its hangings, Glimmering Misfortune. Hel is half black, half flesh-colour, and is easily recognized from this; she looks rather grim and gloomy.

* * *

Then Gangleri asked: 'What goddesses are there?'

High One replied: 'The foremost is Frigg. She owns that dwelling known as Fensalir, and it is most magnificent.

'Sága is another; she lives at Sökkvabekk, and that is a large estate.

'The third is Eir; she is the best of physicians.

'The fourth is Gefjon; she is a virgin, and women who die unmarried serve her.

'The fifth is Fulla; she, too, is a virgin and wears her hair loose and a golden band round her head. She carries Frigg's little box and looks after her shoes and knows her secrets.

'Freyja is as distinguished as Frigg. She is married to a man called Ód; their daughter is Hnoss; she is so lovely that whatever is beautiful and valuable is called "treasure" from her name. Ód went away on long journeys and Freyja weeps for him, and her tears are red gold. Freyja has many names, and the reason for this is that she gave herself several when she went to look for Ód among peoples she did not know. She is called Mardöll and Hörn, Gefn and Sýr. Freyja owns the necklace of the Brísings. She is also called the divinity of the Vanir.

'The seventh goddess is Sjöfn; she is much concerned with turning the minds of people, both men and women, to love. From her name love is called *sjafni*.

'The eighth is Lofn; she is so gentle and good to invoke that she has permission from All-father and Frigg to being together men and women for whom marriage was forbidden or banned. From her name comes the word "permission," also what is much praised by men.

'The ninth is Vár; she listens to the vows and compacts made by men and women with each other; for this reason such agreements are called *várar*. She also takes vengeance on those who break their vows.

'The tenth is Vör; she is so wise and searching that nothing can be concealed from her. It is a proverb that a woman becomes "aware" of what she gets to know.

'The eleventh is Syn; she guards the door of the hall and shuts it against those who are not to enter. She is also appointed defending counsel at trials in cases she wishes to refute, hence the saying that "Syn is brought forward" when anyone denies an accusation.

'The twelfth is Hlín; she is appointed to protect those men Frigg wants to save from dangers, hence the proverb that "he who is protected 'leans.'"

'The thirteenth is Snotra; she is wise and gentle mannered. From her name a man or woman who is self-controlled is called *snotr.*

'The fourteenth is Gná; Frigg sends her on her errands. She has a horse that runs through the air and over the sea called Hoof-flourisher. Once when she was riding, some Vanir saw her riding in the air and one said:

> What is flying there,
> faring there
> and gliding through the air?

She answered:

> I am not flying,
> although I am faring
> gliding through the air

> on Hoof-flourisher
> whom Skinny-sides
> got by Breaker-of-fences.

'From Gná's name what soars high is called towering.

'Sól and Bil are reckoned among the goddesses, but their nature has been described before.

'There are, moreover, others whose duty it is to serve in Valhalla, carry the drink round and look after the table service and ale-cups. Their names in the *Lay of Grímnir* are as follows:

> Hrist and Mist
> I want to bring me the horn,
> Skeggjöld and Skögul,
> Hild and Thrúd,
> Hlökk and Herfjötur,
> Göll and Geirahöd,
> Randgríd and Rádgríd,
> and Reginleif.
> These bear ale to the Einherjar.

These are called Valkyries. Ódin sends them to every battle, and they choose death for the men destined to die, and award victory. Gud and Rota and the youngest norn Skuld always ride to choose the slain and decide [the issue of] battles.

'Earth, the mother of Thór, and Rind, Váli's mother, are reckoned amongst the goddesses.

[From *The Prose Edda of Snorri Sturluson,* pp. 48–61.]

THE POETIC EDDA

The Poetic Edda, also referred to as *The Elder Edda,* is the work of anonymous Christian compilers of the thirteenth century in Iceland. The poems, or lays, contained in it go back to the pre-Christian Norse culture of Norway and Iceland of the tenth century and some are of even earlier composition.

THE SIBYL'S PROPHECY

In *The Sibyl's Prophecy,* or the *Vǫlospá,* the great god Odin (Warfather) seeks the wisdom of an ancient prophetess, who tells him about the creation of the world and predicts the downfall of the gods. The word *vǫlospá* means "soothsaying, or propheticizing, of the *vǫlva*," a shamanlike figure, usually a woman, who sat on a high platform while spells were sung and who entered a trance from which she divined the future. This form of divination was closely associated with the goddess Freyja. The *Vǫlospá* is rich in examples of women who possess secret knowledge, especially of the past and future, and here they are represented by (1) the Norns or the three maidens of Fate (whose names Snorri Sturulson thought meant Past, Present, and Future), (2) Gullveig, and (3) Heid, as well as by the remark that links magic to wicked women.

Grant me silence, you holy gods
and all men everywhere, Heimdal's sons,
while Warfather listens to the ancient lore,
the oldest runes that I remember.

I know giants of ages past,
those who called me one of their kin;
I know how nine roots form nine worlds
below the Earth where the Ash Tree rises.

When Ymir lived, long ages ago,
before there were seas, chill waves or shore,
Earth was not yet nor the high heavens
but a great emptiness nowhere green.

Then Bur's sons lifted up the land
and made Midgard for men to dwell in;
the sun shone out of the south,
and bright grass grew from the ground of stone.

The sun climbed; the moon's companion
raised its right hand over heaven's rim.
The sun did not know where its hall would stand,
the stars did not know where they would be set,
the moon did not know what would be its might.

Then all the gods met to give judgment,
the holy gods took counsel together:
they named night and the waning moon,
they gave names to morning and midday,
afternoon and evening, ordered time by years.

The Aesir met in Idavelli;
they built altars, high timbered halls,
fashioned hearths to forge gold treasure,
strong tools and heavy tongs.

Cheerful, they sat over games of chess—

they never knew any lack of gold—
until three Norns came, loathsome to look at,
giant maidens from Jotunheim.

And of the Aesir assembled there
three of the holy ones left the hall;
they found on land two feeble trees,
the Ash and the Elm, with no fixed fate.

These did not breathe, nor had they feeling,
speech or craft, bearing, color;
Odin gave life's breath, Hoenir gave feeling,
Lodur gave craft, bearing, color.

There is an ash tree— its name is Yggdrasil—
a tall tree sparkling with clear drops of dew
which fall from its boughs down into the valleys;
ever green it stands beside the Norns' spring.

There live three maidens wise in lore
in a hall which stands beneath that tree:
one is Urd, another is Verdandi,
—they have carved out runes— Skuld is the third;
they established laws, decided the lives
men were to lead, marked out their fates.

I remember war, the first in the world:
the Aesir struck Gullveig with spears
and burned her body in Har's hall;
three times burned, three times born,
again and again, yet she is still alive.

She was called Heid in the halls that knew her,
a sibyl skilled at looking into time;
she used magic to ensnare the mind,
a welcome friend to wicked women.

[From *Poems of the Vikings*, pp. 3–5.]

NEVER TRUST A WOMAN

This literature is also shot through with negative statements about women which suggest the fear men had of them. The following excerpt from the *Havamal* vividly depicts the power of women over the men who desire them.

When a man is not wise, he has only to win
  cattle or a woman's caress,
and his self-esteem waxes, unlike his wits,
  he's all puffed up with pride.

He who would read the sacred runes
  given by the gods,
  that Odin set down
  and the sage stained with color,
is well advised to waste no words.

Praise the day at nightfall, a woman when she's dead,

a sword proven, a maiden married,
ice you've crossed, ale you've drunk.
Cut trees when the wind blows, sail in fair weather;
talk with maidens in the dark— the day has many
  eyes.
Ask speed of a ship, protection from a shield,
keenness from a sword, from a maiden kisses.

Drink ale by the fireside, skate on the ice,
buy lean steeds and bloodstained swords,
fatten horses in the stable, a dog in your home.

Never trust what a maiden tells you
　　nor count any woman constant;
their hearts are turned on a potter's wheel,
　　their minds are made to change.

★ ★ ★

Never trust a field sown early
　　or a son too soon;
weather rules crops, sons need wisdom,
　　you run a risk both ways.

Thus you'll find the love of a faithless woman:
like a smooth-shod horse on slippery ice—
a sprightly two-year-old not yet trained,
or sailing with no rudder in a frantic storm
or a lame man on an icy hill running after reindeer.

Believe what I say— I know them both—
　　men don't keep faith with women;

we speak fair words when we think most falsely
　　to bewilder the wits of the wise.

Speak pleasing words and offer presents
　　to win a woman's love,
flatter a lady about her looks:
　　praise will have the prize.

Let no man ever mock another,
　　laughing at his love;
the stupid may be safe where the wise give way
　　to a fair folly.

Let no man ever mock another
　　for what so many suffer:
out of wise men fools are made
　　by the lures of love.
　　　[From Poems of the Vikings, pp. 24–26.]

THE VALKYRIES

　　The Valkyries, a word meaning "chooser of the slain," are a complex configuration of semi-divine warrior women who revel in battle, paralyze their foes with fear, bring death, and act as intermediaries between humans and deities. In their earliest forms they are terrifying, often ugly, deities of death. In their later forms they are benevolent and beautiful warrior women presented in a royal court setting. In this latter form they serve the god Odin by choosing the warriors who will die in battle and then bringing them to Odin's hall, Valhalla. Here the slain warriors are graciously served mead by the Valkyries. What is consistent in their various forms is that the Valkyries are depicted as dressed in armor, often on horseback; they possess wisdom, eloquence, and the ability to prophesy, are gifted with supernatural powers and have the ability to fly. Their connection with the priestesses who officiated at the sacrifice of war captives seems obvious, but there is no clear historical evidence. In the later tradition especially they often form erotic relationships with male heroes. In the medieval literature of the Christian period the Valkyries become human women with greatly diminished powers; for instance, Brunhilde.

　　The following excerpt from *The Lay of Helgi* is a complicated tale of a Valkyrie and her human lover involving reincarnation. The hero, Helgi, receives his name from the Valkyrie Svava. Later in the tale this Valkyrie reincarnates and is called Sigrun. She protects Helgi, and they become lovers.

Hjorvard and Sigrlinn had a strong and handsome son. He never spoke much, and no name would stick to him. He was sitting on a grave-mound when he saw nine valkyries riding. The noblest-looking of them said:

"Helgi the warrior, you'll wait a long time
to own gold rings or Rodulsfells
if you keep silence, though eagles shrieked early,
prince, and of courage you give proof."

Helgi said: "What gift shall I have with the name of
　Helgi

which you, fair woman, have found for me?
Take your time before you tell me!
That name won't be mine unless you are too."

The valkyrie said: "There are swords hidden in
　Sigarsholm,
four more would make them fifty;
one of those blades is the best of all,
the bane of armor, bound with gold.

"On its hilt a peace ring, heart in the steel,
its tip strikes terror— who takes the sword wins
　these—

over the blade winds a bloodstained serpent,
along it twists a snake's long tail."

King Eylimi had a daughter called Svava. She was a valkyrie, and rode through the air and over the sea. It was she who gave Helgi his name, and afterwards she often helped him in battles.
[From *Poems of the Vikings*, pp. 119–20.]

King Hogni had a daughter called Sigrun. She was a valkyrie and rode through the sky and over the sea. She was Svava reborn. Sigrun rode to meet Helgi and said:

"Who brings the swift ships to these shores?
Tell me, warriors, where is your home?
What do you want in Bruna Bay?
Where do you hope to go from here?"

Helgi said:
"Hamal brings the swift ships to these shores;
we have our homes in the Isles of Hle.
Now we are waiting for a fair wind
to bear us eastward from Bruna Bay."

Sigrun said:
"Prince, where have you been waging war,
feeding the geese of Gunn's sisters?
Why is your byrnie stained with blood,
why do men in armor eat raw meat?"

Helgi said:
"Before he came here, the son of kings
was in the Western Isles, if you wish to know,
capturing bears in Bragalund,
sating the eagles with his spear.
Now I've told you, maiden, why our meat was raw:
there isn't much steak far out at sea."

Sigrun said:
"You speak of the battle when Helgi's sword
felled King Hunding dead on the field;
that great combat avenged your kinsmen—
bright blood streamed down your blade."

Helgi said:
"Noble lady, how do you know,
wise as you are, that we're those warriors?
Many are the proud sons of princes,
keen men, akin to us."

Sigrun said:
"I stood close by, prince, when your sword
struck down that warrior yesterday morning,
but I count it clever of Sigmund's son
to speak in runes that conceal his name.

"I've seen you before— you were on a ship;
boldly you stood on a bloodstained prow
while icy waves played wildly about you.
Now the king hopes to keep his secret,
but Hogni's daughter knows Helgi well."

There was a mighty king named Granmar who lived at Svarin's Cairn. He had many sons: one was named Hodbrodd, another Gudmund, a third Starkad. Hodbrodd was at a meeting of kings and was promised the hand of Sigrun, Hogni's daughter. But when she heard about it, she rode with the valkyries through the air and over the sea to find Helgi.

Helgi was at Logafells where he fought against Hunding's sons, killing Alf and Eyjolf, Hjorvard and Hervard. Exhausted from the battle, he was sitting beneath Eagle Rock. There Sigrun found him. She threw her arms around his neck, kissed him, and told him the tidings, as it is related in *The Old Lay of the Volsungs:*

Sigrun came, seeking the prince;
when she found Helgi she took his hand,
kissed and greeted the mail-clad warrior.
Then to her only turned Helgi's heart.

Hogni's daughter held nothing back,
asking Helgi for his affection;
before she had ever seen Sigmund's son,
she had loved him with all her heart.

"All the host heard me promised to Hodbrodd,
but I pledged myself to another prince;
though I fear my kinsmen's fury,
my father shall not have his heart's desire."

Helgi said:
"Pay no heed to Hogni's wrath,
or to your kinsmen's cruel hearts!
From now on, maiden, you shall be mine,
and none of your family do I fear."

Helgi assembled many warships and sailed to Freka Stone. At sea they were in great danger from a violent gale. Lightning flashed from above, striking the ships. Then they saw nine valkyries riding through the sky; one of them was Sigrun. The storm abated, and the ships came safely to land.
[From *The Poems of the Vikings*, pp. 130–33.]

THE NIBELUNGENLIED—BRUNHILDE

The Nibelungenlied was written in Austria about 1200 C.E. by an unknown author. It is based on an earlier tradition of heroic poetry going back to the pre-Christian past of the fifth century

C.E. and contains much of this earlier literature. The following excerpt from chapters 6, 7, and 10 are about Brunhilde, the beautiful Queen of Iceland (Isen-Land), who has vowed to marry only a man who can equal or best her at arms. Gunther, the King of Burgandy, decides to try and win her with the help of his friend, the hero Siegfried. Even after resorting to trickery, deception, and a magic cloak (the Hood of Darkness) that makes him invisible and increases his strength twelvefold, Siegfried barely defeats Brunhilde, though she believes she was bested by Gunther and so agrees to marry him. She is, however, reluctant to consummate the marriage, so Gunther must once again ask Siegfried for help. Interestingly, the loss of her virginity leads to the loss of her great physical strength. In other words, being sexual regularizes her womanhood, yet being sexual does not alter Siegfried's manhood—he retains his great strength.

In other stories Brunhilde is a Valkyrie, one of the divine women warriors who serve the god Odin/Wotan.

Now when the Daughter of Princes looked upon Siegfried's face—
Would ye know of her greeting?—she bespake him with cold and stately grace;
"Now welcome be thou, O Siegfried, in thy coming to this my land.
What meaneth this your journey?—prithee, cause me to understand."
"Exceeding thank do I render, O Daughter of Princes, to thee,
That thou deignest to greet me, Brunhild, Lady of Courtesy,
Before this knight hath been greeted, who standeth before me in place,
For that he is my liege-lord:—Siegfried could well have foregone such grace!
He is the King of Rhineland—what need I say of him more?
All for thy love have we voyaged far overseas to thy shore.
Fixed is his heart to woo thee, whatsoever thereof betide.
While yet there is time, bethink thee:—my lord turns never aside.
He hath to name King Gunther; wide is his royal domain.
For thy love he comes hitherward wooing; nought else he desireth to gain.
Forasmuch as he hath commanded, on this journey have I too come.
If so be he were not my liege-lord, sooth, I had forborne therefrom."

She answered: "If thou be his vassal, and he thy suzerain,
Then must he abide the trial, the tests that I ever ordain.
If he stand at the end the victor, I yield myself his wife;
But if I overcome—bethink you, ye all have staked your life."
Then out spake Hagen of Troneg: "Suffer us, Queen, to see

To what manner of play thou dost challenge. Ere Gunther my lord unto thee
Shall yield up the mastery, surely he shall strive with bitter strain.
A maiden so passing lovely full well to his wife might he gain."
"He shall cast the massy quoit-stone, and far as it flies shall he leap,
And shall hurl against me the javelin—hold not this trial cheap!
Ye may lose not the honor only: your life and limb be at stake.
Therefore, I rede you, bethink you!" So that fair woman spake.

Then Siegfried the battle-helper drew the King apart,
And he prayed him to speak out boldly all that was in his heart
Unto the Queen replying—"Fear not for the end," he said;
"By my cunning devices against her full well will I shield thine head."
Then answered and spake King Gunther: "O child of a royal line,
Lay on me what task thou pleasest: were it harder than this of thine,
Yet for the sake of thy beauty I abide all willingly.
If thou be not won by my wooing, then smite mine head from me."

So soon as the words had been spoken, straightway that Amazon-maid
Commanded, as meet she deemed it, that the trial be not delayed;
And she caused them to bring her armor, and array for the contest grim,
Even a golden hauberk and a shield of ample rim.
A silk-lined battle-tunic about her that maiden drew—
Nor point nor edge of weapon in fight might pierce it through—
Of fine-dressed fells of lions from the land of Libya brought,

With broidery round its borders flashing radiant-
wrought.
Meanwhile her knights were galling those guests with
threat and jeer:
And there stood Dankwart and Hagen exceedingly
heavy of cheer;
For their souls foreboded the issue that might to their
lord betide;
And they said in their hearts: "This journey shall we
knights dearly abide!"

But Siegfried the while, the resourceful, hath hasted
swiftly away,
Ere any was ware of his going, unto where the galley
lay;
And he found the Hood of Darkness in its secret
hiding-place there,
And with speed he did it upon him, and none thereof
was ware.
With speed he returned: of her warriors found he a
great array
In the place by the Queen appointed for the wooer's
perilous play:
But he passed through the midst of them stealthwise,
and still was held of none
Of the multitude there thronging: by magic thus was
it done.
For the lists a wide ring drew they where that grim
sport should be
In the presence of knights of Brunhild, that the trial
all might see,
Bold warriors full seven hundred; and their weapons
of war all bare;
And whoso prevailed in the contest, the truth should
these declare.

Now in the lists stood Brunhild, in her mail of the
adamant rings,
As though she would straight do battle for the land
of all earth's kings.
And all her silken vesture was with gold bands lapped
about;
But thereunder the lilies and roses of her lovely flesh
shown out.

Men into the ring come bearing an exceeding massy
stone,
Most huge, a quoit for a Titan, broad withal and
round.
Scarce twelve of her thanes could bear it into love's
strange battle-ground.
Even this ever hurled she in contest, when the flight
had been sped of the spear.
Thereat were the lords Burgundian thrilled with fore-
boding fear.
'Who is this that my lord would be wooing?—
"Beshrew her!" Hagen cried:

"in the nethermost hell might she fitly be plighted
the Foul Fiend's bride!"'

On her snow-white arms the Maiden her tunic-
sleeves uprolled,
And she stretched forth her hand to the arm-brace
of the shield, and took fast hold:
She hath swung up on high the javelin—lo, the
banners of battle unfold!—
Then the hearts of those two heroes at the fire in her
eyes waxed cold.
And except in that moment Siegfried to his friend's
help had drawn nigh,
She had reft the life from Gunther the King right
certainly;
But he stole to his side all viewless, and softly touched
his hand;
Then, as at a spirit's presence, well-nigh was the King
unmanned;
For the bold knight thought: "Who touched me?—
do I stand on enchanted ground?"
For, look as he would all round him, no man thereby
he found.

Then a whisper came—"It is Siegfried: I, thy companion, am here.
Thou therefore in yon Queen's presence be wholly
void of fear.
Yield up from thy grasp the buckler, and let me bear
it for thee,
And lay up in thine hart the counsel which now thou
hearest of me:—
Be thine all feigning of action, by me shall the work
be done."
Then leapt his heart for gladness, when he know it
was Siegmund's son.
"Ever hide thou my cunning devices, speak word
thereof unto none:
So by the proud King's Daughter shall little enow be
won,
Through thee and thine overthrowing, of the glory
she thinketh to glean.
Behold her, how yonder she standeth with scornful-
arrogant mien!"

Then, then that royal maiden hurled across the field
With her uttermost strength the javelin at the mighty
and broad new shield
Which braced on his left arm firmly the son of
Sigelind bore:
Leapt sparks from the steel, as the wind-blast
sweepeth the chaff from a floor.
The fang of the mighty javelin through the shield's
whole thickness crashed;
And it glanced from the warrior's amour, that the fire
from the ring-mail flashed.
Back from the shock went reeling either stalwart
thane:—

Except for the Hood of Darkness, of a surety had both
been slain!
Yea, from the mouth of Siegfried the valiant burst
forth blood;
But he sprang full-height in a moment; then gripped
that war-thane good
The selfsame spear which the maiden through the rim
of the shield had sped.
Then Siegfried's strong hand backward swung it
above his head.
But he said in his heart: "I will pierce not the maiden
sweet to see."
Backward therefore the deadly point of the lance
turned he;
Then hurled he the spear butt-foremost full at the
rings of her mail:
Loudly they rang at the smiting of the hand that was
strong to prevail.
Flashed out the fire from her hauberk, as flies dust
caught by the wind.
Ha, that was a cast most mightily of the son of
Siegelind!
For all her strength, she prevailed not against that
shock to stand.
In veriest truth, such spear-cast came never from
Gunther's hand!

But the Fairest of fair ones, Brunhild, leapt to her feet
forthright:—
"For thy good spear-cast I thank thee, O Gunther,
noble knight!"
She cried; for she weened that the hero by his own
strength this had done,
Nor dreamed she how that behind him had stolen a
mightier one.
Sped she from that place swiftly, for her fury stung
her as flame:
She grasped the stone, she upheaved it, that royal
Amazon dame.
Far thence from her had that boulder with her utter-
most might she swung,
Then after the cast far leapt she, that her mail-rings
clashed and rung.
Twelve fathoms away from the caster crashed that
stone to the ground;
But farther yet than the quoit-flight did the high-born
maiden bound.
Then strode that swift war-helper, Siegfried, where
lay the stone:—
Men saw but the arm of Gunther, the speeder thereof
saw none.
Mighty of limb was Siegfried, valiant and tall was he;
Farther than Brunhild he hurled it, he leapt yet farther
than she;
And he added thereto a marvel, a deed of magic might,
That he bore in his leap King Gunther, by the power
of the Hood of Night.

Lo, now is the great leap taken; behind on the earth
lay the stone.
Gunther it was, the war-thane, whom men saw there
alone.
Then the face of Brunhild the lovely with helpless
anger burned.
—Lo, Siegfried from King Gunther the imminent
death hath turned!

Then unto the host of her vassals Queen Brunhild
looked, and she cried,
When she saw that hero standing safe on the lists' far
side:
"O ye my friends and liegemen, hitherward come
straightway!
Ye be all unto this King Gunther vassals from this day."
Down laid each valiant warrior his weapons from his
hand,
And low at the feet they bowed them of the Lord of
Burgundia-land;
Yea, unto Gunther the mighty bent many a valiant
knight,
For they weened he had won that contest by his own
unaided might.
With chivalrous grace and in loving wise he greeted
the maid;
And now that Queen of Beauty her hand in his hath
laid,
And to him all rule she yielded over all her wide
domain.
Then glad in his heart was Hagen, that bold and
knightly thane.
She besought that noble chieftain to her palace
builded wide
With her to return, and thither strode Gunther at her
side.
There all men fearing before him in homage lowly
bent.
So the brethren Dankwart and Hagen, thereat were
well content.
[From *The Lay of the Nibelung Men,* pp. 53–64.]

★ ★ ★

[Returning home to Burgundia, Gunther enlists
Siegfried's aid to consummate his marriage with
Brunhilde.]

He [Siegfried] made as though he were Gunther,
Burgundia's mighty King;
And around that peerless maiden a sudden arm did
he fling.
But forth of the couch she hurled him, and against
a high-seat dashed,
That his brows against the footstool thereof full
heavily crashed.
Then leapt to his feet the hero, and he summoned up
all his might

To essay it with better fortune; and these twain closed
    in a fight
Wherein he strove to tame her, and bitter she made
    it for him.
—Never, I ween, of woman was made a defence so
    grim!
Forasmuch as he would not refrain him, the Maiden
    sprang full-height—
"How dar'st thou so much as ruffle the hem of my
    vesture white,
Thou insolent knave, thou ruffian? The deed shalt
    thou dearly abide!
Yea, now will I make thee to know it!" that warrior
    maiden cried.

Arms like unto bands of iron she locked round the
    valiant thane.
She was minded in fetters to lay him even as the King
    had lain,
That still she might lie untroubled in the peace of her
    maiden sleep.
That he touched but her vesture, how fiercely did the
    flame of her fury upleap!
Despite his brawny sinews, in his magic power's
    despite,
She gave dread proof to the hero of her matchless
    bodily might:
She bare him resistlessly backward with overmaster-
    ing stress.
As in vise of steel she crushed him 'twixt the bed and
    an oaken press.
"Out on it!" his heart indignant cried; "if my limb and
    life
Be lost at the hands of a maiden, then every shrewish
    wife—
Who has dreamed not else of rebellion—against her
    lord shall upraise
Malapert brows of defiance through all earth's com-
    ing days!"

Now the King heard all: for his champion with
    exceeding fear was he filled.
Then swift through the heart of Siegfried fierce shame
    and anger thrilled,
With the might of the Dwarfs and the Giants he
    hurled himself on his foe,
And strained his strength against Brunhild as in fury
    of madness-throe.
Yea, even as she thrust him backward, it spurred his
    fury on,
So stinging each mighty sinew, that, spite of her van-
    tage won,
He upwrithed himself against her: the flame of his
    rage outflashed,
And from wall unto wall of the chamber those
    wrestlers hurtled and crashed.
Great fear and tribulation the King endured in that
    hour:

Oft must he flee before them to this side and that of
    the bower.
So furiously they grappled and strained, that a marvel
    it seemed
That out of the hands of each other their very lives
    were redeemed.
In anguish of dread King Gunther trembled for each
    of twain;
But most was his spirit quaking lest Siegfried should
    be slain.
Oft though he, "the life of the hero is well nigh reft
    by the maid!"
Had he but dared to essay it, he would fain have gone
    to his aid.

Long, long between those wrestlers endured that
    desperate strife:
But he slowly at last bare backward to the couch that
    maiden-wife.
How grimly she fought soever, her strength waxed
    faint at the last:
But aye through the heart of Gunther a tumult of wild
    thoughts passed.
Long, long it seemed unto Gunther ere Siegfried
    tamed her mood.
Her grip on his hands was so mighty that from 'neath
    his nails the blood
At her terrible crushing spirted, that his soul was
    wrung with pain:
Yet he wore her down by his stubborn endurance, and
    forced her to refrain
From the fury of eager onset, from the erstwhile
    tiger-leap.
—Ware of all this was Gunther, though he hearkened
    in silence deep.
He crushed her against the bed-beam, that for pain
    aloud she cried;
For the strength of Siegfried the mighty tortured at
    last the bride.
In a desperate hope, at the girdle that around her sides
    she wore
She snatched, if she haply might bind him; but this
    from her grasp he tore.
Her joints are strained unto breaking, on the rack is
    her fainting frame—
Lo, now is the strife's decision: wife to the King is
    the dame.
She moaned, "O king and hero, take not my life from
    me!
Atoned for in wifely duty shall be all scathe done unto
    thee!
Against thy noble embraces myself no more do I
    ward.
At last have I thoroughly proved it, that thou art
    master and lord."

Uprose from the grapple Siegfried—while faint lay
    the panting bride—

Back drew he as though he were minded to put but
   his raiment aside:
Yet first did he draw from her finger a little golden
   ring;
But thereof the Queen outwearied knew not
   anything.
That silken marvel, her girdle, for a trophy withal
   took he:
I know not if haply he did it in pride of victory.
To his wife he gave them thereafter—his own bane
   came thereof!
He is gone; and the King and Brunhild are alone in
   the bed of love.

All in the old sweet fashion he gathered her unto his
   breast:
The erstwhile shame and the anger are for ever laid
   to rest.
As Love the Overcomer prevailed, her cheek waxed
   wan—
There is no more Brunhild the Maiden, and her might
   as a dream is gone!
O yea, she is now no stronger than any woman beside!
He poured out his love upon her, he cherished his
   winsome bride.

   [From *The Lay of the Nibelung Men,* pp. 90–92.]

THE ICELANDIC SAGAS

The Icelandic sagas were composed from the twelfth century on, two hundred years after the introduction of Christianity. Iceland had been settled by Scandinavians late in the ninth centuries, and the sagas were an attempt to record their pre-Christian past and to establish genealogies with Scandinavian families. They are primarily literary creations containing some information on religious practices, but their historical accuracy varies from text to text.

LAXDAELA SAGA—DIVORCE LAWS

The Laxdaela Saga was composed by an unknown author in the early twelfth century but refers to events, with some historical accuracy, taking place in the tenth century, just before the arrival of Christianity in 1000 C.E. The following excerpt from chapter 35 reveals the high status of pagan Icelandic women. These were actually a mix of Norse and Celtic peoples who began settling in Iceland about 870 C.E. onwards. Icelandic women were free to divorce their husbands and had equal rights of property and inheritance. The following excerpt also reveals their fierce and independent natures. Gudrun, the heroine of the saga, has just divorced her husband of two years and now sets her heart on Thord, who is married to Aud. She gets her way and marries Thord, but Aud revenges herself on her former husband. Of some interest is the fact that cross-dressing of either sex was grounds for divorce.

It happened one day as they [Gudrun and Thord] were riding over Blueshaw-heath, the weather being fine, that Gudrun said, "Is it true, Thord, that your wife Aud always goes about in breeches with gores in the seat, winding swathings round her legs almost to her feet?" Thord said, "He had not noticed that." "Well, then, there must be but little in the tale," said Gudrun, "if you have not found it out, but for what then is she called Breeches Aud?" Thord said, "I think she has been called so for but a short time." Gudrun answered, "What is of more moment to her is that she bear the name for a long time hereafter." After that people arrived at the Thing and no tidings befell there. Thord spent much time in Gest's booth and always talked to Gudrun. One day Thord Ingunson asked Gudrun what the penalty was for a woman who went about always in breeches like men. Gudrun replied, "She deserves the same penalty as a man who is dressed in a shirt with so low a neck that his naked breast be seen—separation in either case." Then Thord said, "Would you advise me to proclaim my separation from Aud here at the Thing or in the country by the counsel of many men? For I have to deal with high-tempered men who will count themselves as ill-treated in this affair." Gudrun answered after a while, "For evening waits the idler's suit." Then Thord sprang up and went to the law rock and named to him witnesses, declared his separation from Aud, and gave as his reason that she made for herself gored breeches like a man. Aud's brothers disliked this very much, but things kept quiet. Then Thord rode away from the Thing with the sons of Osvif. When Aud heard these tidings, she said, "Good! Well, that I know that I am left thus single." Then Thord rode, to divide the money, west into Saurby and twelve men with him, and it all went off easily, for Thord made no difficulties as to how the money was divided. Thord drove from the west unto Laugar a great deal of live stock. After that he wooed Gudrun and that matter was easily settled; Osvif said nothing against it. The wedding was to take place in the tenth week of the summer, and that was a right noble feast. Thord and Gudrun lived happily together. What alone withheld Thorkell Whelp and Knut from setting afoot a lawsuit against Thord Ingunson was, that they got no backing up to that end. The next summer the men of Hol had an out-dairy business in Hvammdale, and Aud stayed at the dairy. The men of Laugar had their out-dairy in Lambdale, which cuts westward into the mountains off Salingsdale. Aud asked the man who looked after the sheep how often he met the shepherd from Laugar. He said nearly always as was likely since there was only a neck of land between the two dairies. Then said Aud, "You shall meet the shepherd from Laugar today, and you can tell me who there are staying at the winter-dwelling or who at the dairy, and speak in a friendly way of Thord as it behooves you to do." The boy promised to do as she told him. And in the evening when the shepherd came home Aud asked what tidings he brought. The shepherd answered, "I have heard tidings which you will think good, that now there is a broad bedroom-floor between the beds of Thord and Gudrun, for she is at the dairy and he is swinging at the rear of the hall, he and Osvif being two together alone at the winter-dwelling." "You have espied well," said she, "and see to have saddled two horses at the time when people are going to bed." The shepherd did as she bade him. A little before sunset Aud mounted, and was now indeed in breeches. The shepherd rode the other horse

and could hardly keep up with her, so hard did she push on riding. She rode south over Salingsdale-heath and never stopped before she got to the home-field fence at Laugar. Then she dismounted, and bade the shepherd look after the horses whilst she went to the house. Aud went to the door and found it open, and she went into the firehall to the locked-bed in the wall. Thord lay asleep, the door had fallen to, but the bolt was not on, so she walked into the bedroom. Thord lay asleep on his back. Then Aud woke Thord, and he turned on his side when he saw a man had come in. Then she drew a sword and thrust it at Thord and gave him great wounds, the sword striking his right arm and wounding him on both nipples. So hard did she follow up the stroke that the sword stuck in the bolster. Then Aud went away and to her horse and leapt on to its back, and thereupon rode home. Thord tried to spring up when he got the blow, but could not, because of his loss of blood. Then Osvif awoke and asked what had happened, and Thord told that he had been wounded somewhat. Osvif asked if he knew who had done the deed on him, and got up and bound up his wounds. Thord said he was minded to think that Aud had done it. Osvif offered to ride after her, and said she must have gone on this errand with few men, and her penalty was ready-made for her. Thord said that should not be done at all, for she had only done what she ought to have done. Aud got home at sunrise, and her brothers asked her where she had been to. Aud said she had been to Laugar, and told them what tidings had befallen in her journey. They were pleased at this, and said that too little was likely to have been done by her. Thord lay wounded a long time. His chest wound healed well, but his arm grew no better for work than before (i.e. when it first was wounded).

[From *Laxdaela Saga*, pp. 107–11.]

NJÁL'S SAGA

Njál's Saga was composed by an unknown author around the year 1280 C.E., and it describes events that took place three hundred years earlier, such as the coming of Christianity in the year 1000 C.E. It is broadly based on historical events, and its author drew upon oral traditions as well as the few written records that existed. Chapters 100–102 describe the warrior-evangelist Thangbrand and his experiences in Norway, where he is not always successful at converting people. Here he meets Steinunn, a pagan woman who attempts to convert him. Since this is a Christian text, her argument for paganism is not presented in full. It is significant, however, that a woman would so actively oppose the advance of Christianity.

A change of rulers had taken place in Norway. Earl Hákon had died and Óláf Tryggvason had taken his place. Earl Hákon had met his death at the hands of

the slave Kark who cut the earl's throat at Rimul in Gaulardale.

At the same time it was learned that there had been

a change of faith in Norway. The old faith had been discarded, and King Óláf had christianized the western lands also: the Shetlands, the Orkneys, and the Faroe Islands.

Njál heard many people say that it was a great wickedness to give up the old faith, but he answered: "It seems to me that the new faith is much better, and happy he who accepts it. If those who preach it come here I shall do all I can to further it."

He often went by himself and prayed.

That same autumn a ship arrived in Bear Firth in the east and landed at Gautavík. Its skipper was called Thangbrand. He was the son of Count Vilibald of Saxony. Thangbrand had been sent out by King Óláf Tryggvason to preach the new faith in Iceland.

★ ★ ★

There was a man named Sorcerer-Hedin who lived in Kerlingardale. Heathen men paid him money to put Thangbrand and his followers to death. Sorcerer-Hedin went up to Arnarstakk Heath and offered a great sacrifice there. As Thangbrand rode over the heath from the east the earth burst asunder beneath him, but he leaped from his horse, climbed up to the edge of the chasm, and saved himself. But the horse with all its gear was swallowed up by the earth, so that it was never again seen. Then Thangbrand praised God.

★ ★ ★

Thangbrand's ship, "The Bison," was wrecked off Búlandsness.

Thangbrand traveled through the entire West Quarter. Steinunn, the mother of Skald-Ref, came out

to meet him. She made a long speech and tried to convert him to paganism. Thangbrand remained silent while she spoke, but when she had finished, he spoke at length and confuted everything she had said.

"Have you heard that Thór challenged Christ to the holm and that Christ did not dare to fight against him?" she asked.

"I have heard that Thór would be naught but dust and ashes if God did not permit him to live," answered Thangbrand.

"Do you know who wrecked your ship?" she asked.

"What do you have to say about that?" he asked.

"I'll tell you," she answered.

Was the boat of the bell's warder
beached it angry godheads—
shattered, by the ogres'-offsprings'
awful-slayer wholly.
Crushed was the craft, nor saved your
Christ the iron-hoofed road-steed:
God in nowise guarded
Gylfi's reindeer, ween I.

And she spoke yet another verse:

Thór thrusted then far-off
Thangbrand's ship from harbor—
shook the mast, and shoreward
shoved it on to sandbanks:
never, ween I, will that
wain-of-Atal's-kingdom
sail the swans'-land after
since by him 't was splintered.

Thereupon Thangbrand and Steinunn parted, and Thangbrand and his men traveled west to Bardastrand.

[From Njál's Saga, pp. 211–16.]

THE KALEVALA—CREATION

The national epic of Finland, The Kalevala was compiled and arranged by Elias Lönnrot (1802–1884) from folk songs he and others collected from throughout Finland. The final version was published in 1849 and, while not truly folklore but rather a fictional picture of the ways and beliefs of the ancient Finns, it contains much useful information.

The following excerpt is the creation story. It describes a primordial watery chaos variously called the Water-Mother, the Mother of the Waters, and the maid aërial. A beautiful female bird, a teal, acts as the stimulus for creation by needing a solid place for her nest. The Water-Mother distinguishes part of herself, a knee, for the bird to nest on and thus begins creation.

Short the time that passed thereafter
Scarce a moment had passed over,

Ere a beauteous teal came flying
Lightly hovering o'er the water,

Seeking for a spot to rest in,
Searching for a home to dwell in.

Eastward flew she, westward flew she,
Flew to north-west and to southward,
But the place she sought she found not,
Not a spot, however barren,
Where her nest she could establish,
Or a resting-place could light on.

Then she hovered, slowly moving,
And she pondered and reflected:
"If my nest in wind I 'stablish
Or should rest it on the billows,
Then the winds will overturn it,
Or the waves will drift it from me."

Then the Mother of the Waters,
Water-Mother, maid aërial,
From the waves her knee uplifted,
Raised her shoulder from the billows,
That the teal her nest might 'stablish,
And might find a peaceful dwelling.
Then the teal, the bird so beauteous,
Hovered slow, and gazed around her,
And she saw the knee uplifted
From the blue waves of the ocean,
And she thought she saw a hillock,
Freshly green with springing verdure.
There she flew, and hovered slowly,
Gently on the knee alighting;
And her nest she there established,
And she laid her eggs all golden,
Six gold eggs she laid within it,
And a seventh she laid of iron.

O'er her eggs the teal sat brooding,
And the knee grew warm beneath her;
And she sat one day, a second,
Brooded also on the third day;
Then the Mother of the Waters,
Water-Mother, maid aërial,
Felt it hot, and felt it hotter,
And she felt her skin was heated,
Till she thought her knee was burning,
And that all her veins were melting.
Then she jerked her knee with quickness,
And her limbs convulsive shaking,
Rolled the eggs into the water,
Down amid the waves of ocean;
And to splinters they were broken,
And to fragments they were shattered.

In the ooze they were not wasted,
Nor the fragments in the water,

But a wondrous change came o'er them,
And the fragments all grew lovely.
From the cracked egg's lower fragment,
Now the solid earth was fashioned,
From the cracked egg's upper fragment,
Rose the lofty arch of heaven,
From the yolk, the upper portion,
Now became the sun's bright lustre;
From the white, the upper portion,
Rose the moon that shines so brightly;
Whatso in the egg was mottled,
Now became the stars in heaven,
Whatso in the egg was blackish,
In the air as cloudlets floated.

Now the time passed quickly over,
And the years rolled quickly onward,
In the new sun's shining lustre,
In the new moon's softer beaming.
Still the Water-Mother floated
Water-Mother, maid aërial,
Ever on the peaceful waters,
On the billows' foamy surface,
With the moving waves before her,
And the heaven serene behind her.

When the ninth year had passed over,
And the summer tenth was passing,
From the sea her head she lifted,
And her forehead she uplifted,
And she then began Creation,
And she brought the world to order,
On the open ocean's surface,
On the far extending waters.

Wheresoe'er her hand she pointed,
There she formed the jutting headlands;
Wheresoe'er her feet she rested,
There she formed the caves for fishes;
When she dived beneath the water,
There she formed the depths of ocean;
When towards the land she turned her,
There the level shores extended,
Where her feet to land extended,
Spots were formed for salmon-netting;
Where her head the land touched lightly,
There the curving bays extended.
Further from the land she floated,
And abode in open water,
And created rocks in ocean,
And the reefs that eyes behold not,
Where the ships are often shattered,
And the sailors' lives are ended.
    [From *Kalevala*, pp. 6–8.]

TWO ANGLO-SAXON POEMS

The Anglo-Saxons were a Germanic tribe that began to establish itself in Britain beginning in the fifth century C.E. Their literature is dominated by the male heroic model with the notable exception of the following two poems, which have decidedly female voices — so much so that they could be part of a pan-European literary genre of women's songs referred to as *frauen-lieder*. This was literature on the popular level and was marked by references to nature, the vivid expression of women's pain and sorrow because of separation from a male, and explicit references to sexuality. As with most of Anglo-Saxon poetry, the following two poems are anonymous and were composed sometime between the middle of the seventh century and the end of the tenth.

"WULF AND EADWACER"

The poem "Wulf and Eadwacer" contains a theme often associated with women in Anglo-Saxon poetry, the mourning of a mother for her lost son (Wulf). This poem marks the transitional period between paganism and Christianity during which laws were passed requiring burial in Christian cemeteries rather than in pagan family plots. This may explain the meaning of the line "Wulf is on one island; I on another," suggesting that while the son is interred in a traditional pagan grave site the mother will not be able to join him there. They are separated not only by death but by religion. The image of the wolf carrying away the whelp may refer to the Valkyries, often associated with wolves, who were believed to carry off the dead. The translator tries to capture some of these alternate meanings by including the two possible translations for ambiguous passages.

To my people it is as if someone offered a sacrifice
 for them.
Will they { receive him / devour him } if he comes in their midst?
{ It is otherwise for us: / Our destiny is different.
Wulf is on one island; I on another.
Fast is that island, surrounded by fens.
There are corpse-greedy warriors there on that island;
Will they { receive him / devour him } if he comes in their midst?
{ It is otherwise for us: / Our destiny different.
I suffered from thoughts of my Wulf's journeyings

When it was { rainy weather / the olden days } and I sat sighing,
When the battlebold man laid his arms about me,
What was a joy to me then was likewise my woe.
Wulf, my Wulf, thoughts about you
Have made me sick, your never-coming-back
Made me mournful of mind, it was not lack of
 provision.
Do you hear, Heavenwatcher? The wolf bears
Our wretched whelp away to the woods.
One can easily sever what never was joined:
{ Our tale together / Our elegiac song.
 [From *New Readings on Women in Old English Literature*, pp. 286–87.]

"THE WIFE'S LAMENT"

The poem "The Wife's Lament" poignantly describes a woman's fate. The speaker of this poem enjoyed a happy marriage, but her husband went abroad where he was perhaps killed or was being held captive. In the meantime his family has confined her to a lonely and isolated life, where her only hope is her husband's return and their reconciliation.

The Wife's Lament

A song I sing of sorrow unceasing,
The tale of my trouble, the weight of my woe,
Woe of the present, and woe of the past,
Woe never-ending of exile and grief,
But never since girlhood greater than now.
First, the pang when my lord departed,
Far from his people, beyond the sea;
Bitter the heartache at break of dawn,
The longing for rumor in what far land
So weary a time my loved one tarried.
Far I wandered then, friendless and homeless,
Seeking for help in my heavy need.

With secret plotting his kinsmen purposed
To wedge us apart, wide worlds between,
And bitter hate. I was sick at heart.
Harshly my lord bade lodge me here.
In all this land I had few to love me,
Few that were loyal, few that were friends.
Wherefore my spirit is heavy with sorrow
To learn my beloved, my dear man and mate
Bowed by ill-fortune and bitter in heart,
Is masking his purpose and planning a wrong.
With blithe hearts often of old we boasted
That nought should part us save death alone;
All that has failed and our former love
Is now as if it had never been!
Far or near where I fly there follows
The hate of him who was once so dear.

In this forest grove they have fixed my abode
Under an oak in a cavern of earth,
An old cave-dwelling of ancient days,
Where my heart is crushed by the weight of my woe.
Gloomy its depths and the cliffs that o'erhang it,
Grim are its confines with thorns overgrown—
A joyless dwelling where daily the longing
For an absent loved one brings anguish of heart.

Lovers there are who may live their love,
Joyously keeping the couch of bliss,
While I in my earth-cave under the oak
Pace to and fro in the lonely dawn.
Here must I sit through the summer-long day,
Here must I weep in affliction and woe;
Yet never, indeed, shall my heart know rest
From all its anguish, and all its ache,
Wherewith life's burdens have brought me low.

Ever man's years are subject to sorrow,
His heart's thoughts bitter, though his bearing be
    blithe;
Troubled his spirit, beset with distress—
Whether all wealth of the world be his lot,
Or hunted by Fate in a far country
My beloved is sitting soul-weary and sad,
Swept by the storm, and stiff with the frost,
In a wretched cell under rocky cliffs
By severing waters encircled about—
Sharpest of sorrows my lover must suffer
Remembering always a happier home.
Woeful his fate whose doom is to wait
With longing heart for an absent love.

[From *An Anthology of Old English Poetry*, pp. 10–11.]

BEOWULF—GRENDEL'S MOTHER

Beowulf is an epic poem composed in Britain for public performance sometime in the eighth century C.E., though it is based on much earlier oral folk tales. The setting of the poem is the fifth or sixth century C.E. in pre-Christian southern Scandinavia, and, though a Christian commentary has been grafted onto the poem, it provides insight into the pre-Christian past. This was the world from which the Anglo-Saxons had migrated to Britain beginning in the fifth century C.E., a world which they were slow to repudiate. The only extant manuscript of *Beowulf* was written down about the year 1000 C.E. in Old English.

Since it is a classic epic about a male hero, traditionally *Beowulf* has been studied from the point of view of the male characters. However, a reading of the female characters is quite instructive. Primarily, the human women in the poem function as passive peacemakers, mainly by marrying into enemy groups; but also within these groups they pass out the mead cups during celebrations. By extending such hospitality and having it accepted the women bind the group of warriors together. An example of this is found in Queen Wealhtheow's speech at the celebration that follows the death of Grendel, a man-killing dragon, and that immediately precedes Beowulf's battle with Grendel's mother. During this speech Wealhtheow dispenses gifts and blessing, points out the loyalty that already exists between the men in her hall, and asks Beowulf for his loyalty and to extend his protection to her sons. Grendel's mother, on the other hand, has nothing to do with peace. She has no known ties. It is not even certain that Grendel had a father. Consequently she is unencumbered by the social relations that bind the human women in the poem, and therefore she is free to actively revenge her son's death. Finally, this is the familiar theme in world religions of a young male hero killing a female dragon, perhaps once again representing the passing of a female, earth-centered religion and its replacement by a male, sky-centered religion. The dragon-slaying theme continues, when in his later years Beowulf kills and is in turn killed by another dragon.

Then Wealhtheow, wearing a golden circlet, came forward to where the two leaders, Hrothgar and his nephew, sat; at that time there was still peace between them, each one was true to the other. (Unferth, the speaker, sat at the feet of the Danish lord; each of them trusted his spirit, and believed that he had great courage, although he may not have been honorable in swordplay with his kinsmen.) The Lady of the Danes then spoke: "Take this cup, my dear sovereign lord. Rejoice, generous friend of men, and speak to the Geats with words of friendship, as you should. Be gracious to the Geats, remembering how many gifts you have gathered from far and near.

"Someone has told me that you wish to have this hero as a son. Heorot is cleansed, the bright ring hall; make use of generous rewards while you can, but leave the people and kingdom to your kinfolk when the fated time comes for you to depart. I know my gracious Hrothulf; he will protect our children honorably, if you, my lord, should leave the world before he does. I am sure that if he remembers all the kindnesses we did for him as a child, to his pleasure and honor, he will treat our sons well in turn."

Then she turned to the bench where her sons, Hrethric and Hrothmund, were seated with other young warriors, sons of heroes; there Beowulf, the brave Geat, sat by the two brothers.

The cup was carried to him and cordially offered along with wrought gold, presented graciously.

[From *Beowulf and Other Old English Poems*, pp. 46–47.]

[The hunt for Grendel's mother begins.]

A band on foot advanced, bearing shields. They saw many tracks along the paths of the wood, along the ground where she had journeyed directly forward over the murky moor, bearing the lifeless body of the best thane of all those that ruled at home with Hrothgar. The king went over steep stone cliffs and along narrow paths where it was necessary to go one by one, along unknown ways, over steep bluffs and past many dens of water monsters; with a few experienced men he went on in front to examine the place, until he suddenly found mountain trees leaning over gray stones, a joyless wood. The water stood below, bloody and turbid. It was a painful thing for all the

Danes to suffer, a great grief to every thane, when they encountered Aeschere's head on the waterside cliff.

The water boiled with blood, hot gore, as the people gazed at it. From time to time a horn sounded an eager battle song. The troop all sat down, and saw in the water many serpents, strange sea dragons exploring the brine, and water monsters lying on the slopes of the bluff, like those that many a morning take their ill-omened way on the high sea — such serpents and wild beasts. They rushed away in bitter fury when they heard the clear song of the war horn.

★ ★ ★

Beowulf, son of Ecgtheow, spoke: "Wise and generous prince, glorious son of Healfdene, remember, now that I am ready for the venture, what we two said earlier: that if I should lose my life for your sake you would always stand in a father's place to me when I am gone. Be a protector to my retainers and companions if battle should take me. Also, beloved Hrothgar, send the treasures you gave to me on to Hygelac; then the lord of the Geats, the son of Hrethel, can see, when he looks at the golden treasure, that I found a lord of great munificence and enjoyed it while I could. And let Unferth have my ancient sword, the splendid heirloom with wavy ornament; he may have that hard blade. Either I will gain fame with Hrunting or death shall carry me off."

★ ★ ★

After these words, the leader of the Geats pressed on courageously — he did not wait for an answer. The surging water received the warrior. It was a good part of a day before he could see the bottom. Soon the grim and greedy monster, who had occupied the watery regions for a hundred half-years, found that a man was exploring the alien region from above. She grasped at him, and grabbed the hero in her horrible claws — but nevertheless she could not harm his body, which was unhurt because mail protected it all about; her hostile fingers could not penetrate the war shirt, the intertwined coat of mail.

When she reached the bottom, the she-wolf of the water bore the armed chieftain to her dwelling in such a way that, courageous as he was, he could not use his weapons. Many strange beings afflicted him in the water; many a sea beast tried to break his battle coat with its warlike tusks; many monsters pursued him. Then the hero saw that he was in some sort of enemy hall, where no water harmed him at all and its sudden rush could not touch him because of the roof of the chamber; he saw firelight, brilliant flames shining brightly.

Now the brave man could see the accursed monster, the mighty mere-woman. He did not hold back his blow, but gave a mighty rush with his sword so that the blade sang a fierce war song on her head. But the flashing sword would not bite or do her harm; the edge failed the prince in his need. It had endured many skirmishes before and had often sheared the helmet and mail of a doomed man: this was the first time that the glory of the precious treasure was diminished.

But the kinsman of Hygelac was resolute and intent on achieving brave deeds; his courage did not fail him at all. The angry warrior threw the ornamented sword so that the firm steel edge lay on the earth; he trusted in his own strength, his mighty hand-grip. So must a man do when he hopes to gain long-lasting fame in war — he cannot worry about saving his life. The leader of the Geats did not flinch from the battle: he seized Grendel's mother by the shoulder. In a fury, the bold warrior flung the deadly foe so that she fell to the floor. She quickly retaliated with grim grasps and seized him; weary in spirit, the strongest of champions stumbled and fell down.

The demon pounced on the intruder, drew her knife, broad and bright of edge — she wished to avenge her child, her only son. The woven mail which covered Beowulf's shoulder protected his life and withstood the entry of point and edge. Ecgtheow's son, the Geatish champion, would have perished then under the earth if his armor, the hard war mail, had not given him help; and holy God brought about victory in battle. The wise Lord, Ruler of the heavens, easily decided the issue rightly, after Beowulf stood up again.

Among the armor in that place he saw a victorious sword: an ancient giant's sword, strong of edge, the glory of warriors. It was the choicest of weapons except that this good and splendid work of giants was too huge for any other man to carry in battle. The grim, fierce defender of the Danes seized the chained hilt and drew the ring-marked sword, despairing of life; angrily he struck so that it took her hard against the neck and broke the bone-rings. The sword cut right through her doomed body and she fell to the floor. The sword was bloody; the man rejoiced in his work.

The light gleamed; a glow shone forth within, just as the light of the skies shines brightly from heaven. Beowulf looked around the building and turned along the wall. He raised the weapon firmly by the hilt, angry and determined — that blade was not useless to the warrior, for he wished to repay Grendel at once for the many attacks which he had made on the Danes, many besides that one occasion when he killed Hrothgar's men in their sleep, when he ate fifteen sleeping men of the Danish tribe and carried off as many again, hideous booty! The fierce warrior had repaid him for that and now he found Grendel lying in his resting-place, wearied by war, dead of his injuries at the fight in Heorot. The corpse burst wide open when it suffered a blow after death; Beowulf cut off its head with a hard stroke of the sword.

[From *Beowulf and Other Old English Poems*, pp. 51–55.]

THE GRIMM BROTHERS

The researches of the Grimm brothers, Jakob (1785–1863) and Wilhelm (1786–1859), are the foundational studies of early German language, literature, and religion. They were the first scholars to take seriously the popular tales that they gathered by reading medieval manuscripts and recording oral material. They scrupulously avoided embellishing the tales and carefully documented where, when, and from whom they received a tale. One of their best informants was an elderly woman who lived near Kassel, Katherina Viehmann (1755–1815). The Grimm brothers praised her prodigious memory, which enabled her to not only know a large number of stories but also to be able to repeat them without significantly varying any of their details. The first excerpt, from "The Riddle," is one she told.

Surveying what they had collected, they surmised that some of the content of these tales referred back to the pre-Christian pagan practices of ancient Germany, and, while they understood that the religious significance of these tales had long been forgotten, they believed that people continued to find value in the early mythic elements of the tales, and this is what caused them to be preserved over the centuries.

The depiction of women in these tales is complicated, but several motifs emerge. Good girls are in the main silent and passive. Being young, they can represent new ideas about proper feminine deportment. Evil women are older and often represent earlier ideas about the religious power of women, which is now seen as evil, pre-Christian practices. The witches in these tales can be seen as non–Christian women living outside the controls of society who have some financial independence, their "treasure." In between are young women who act up a bit, somewhat like the older women, until they are taught a lesson, usually by the young hero, and then become good women, accepting male wisdom and authority in place of women's wisdom.

The stories the Grimm brothers collected went through several editions, which were continually sanitized to make them acceptable reading for young children. The final sanitizing was done when they were translated into English for American children; yet, as the following stories show, they have an enduring appeal and continue to reveal meanings from an ancient past.

"THE RIDDLE"

The first excerpt from "The Riddle" is a tale in two parts. It begins with a prince, whose travels bring him to the home of a beautiful, good girl and her evil stepmother, who turns out to be a witch known for poisoning people with her magic potions. Notice that the witch and her stepdaughter live on the fringes of society, that they are women outside the control of society, and that they are connected to treasure — common motifs in these tales about evil women. The prince avoids the witch's poison, which follows after him, but it kills his enemies and the witch. In the second part of the story the prince uses this event as a riddle to win the hand of a princess. This riddle contest recalls ancient contests, usually of arms, in which men had to prove their worth before they could marry. At the same time, the second part of this tale also recalls powerful ancient associations of women with wisdom and divination (through dreams and riddles), but these are now trivialized and represented as the basis for a false pride. Notice also that the good women, the stepdaughter and, once she learns her lesson, the princess, are passive, while the evil women, the witch and initially the princess, are active.

There was once a King's son who was seized with a desire to travel about the world, and took no one with him but a faithful servant. One day he came to a great forest, and when darkness overtook him he could find no shelter, and knew not where to pass the night. Then he saw a girl who was going towards a small house, and when he came nearer, he saw that the maiden was young and beautiful. He spoke to her, and said: "Dear child, can I and my servant find shelter for the night in the little house?" "Oh, yes," said the girl, in a sad voice, "that you certainly can, but I do not advise you to venture it. Do not go in." "Why not?" asked the King's son. The maiden sighed and said: "My stepmother practices wicked arts; she is ill-disposed toward strangers." Then he saw very well that he had come to the house of a witch, but as it was dark, and he could not go farther, and also was not afraid, he entered. The old woman was sitting in an armchair by the fire, and looked at the stranger with her red eyes. "Good evening," growled she, and pretended to be quite friendly. "Take a seat and rest yourselves." She fanned the fire on which she was cooking something in a small pot. The daughter warned the two to be prudent, to eat nothing, and drink nothing, for the old woman brewed evil drinks. They slept quietly until early morning. When they were making ready for their departure, and the King's son was already seated on his horse, the old woman said: "Stop a moment, I will first hand you a parting draught." Whilst she fetched it, the King's son rode away, and the servant who had to buckle his saddle tight, was the only one present when the wicked witch came with the drink. "Take that to your master," said she; but at that instant the glass broke and the poison spirted on the horse, and it was so strong that the animal immediately fell down dead. The servant ran after his master and told him what had happened, but as he did not want to leave his saddle behind, he ran back to fetch it. When he came to the dead horse, however, a raven was already sitting on it devouring it. "Who knows whether we shall find anything better today?" said the servant; so he killed the raven, and took it with him. And now they journeyed onwards into the forest the whole day, but could not get out of it. By nightfall they found an inn and entered it. The servant gave the raven to the innkeeper to prepare for supper. They had stumbled, however, on a den of murderers, and during the darkness twelve of these came, intending to kill the strangers and rob them. But before they set about this work, they sat down to supper, and the innkeeper and the witch sat down with them, and together they ate a dish of soup in which was cut up the flesh of the raven. Hardly had they swallowed a couple of mouthfuls, before they all fell down dead, for the raven had communicated to them the poison from the horse-flesh. There was now no one else left in the house but the innkeeper's daughter, who was and had taken no part in their godless deeds. She opened all doors to the stranger and showed him the store of treasures. But the King's son said she might keep everything, he would have none of it, and rode onwards with his servant.

After they had traveled about for a long time, they came to a town in which was a beautiful but proud princess, who had made it known that whosoever should set her a riddle which she could not guess, that man should be her husband; but if she guessed it, his head must be cut off. She had three days to guess it in, but was so clever that she always found the answer to the riddle given her before the appointed time. Nine suitors had already perished in this manner, when the King's son arrived, and, blinded by her great beauty, was willing to stake his life for it. Then he went to her and laid his riddle before her. "What is this?" said he: "One slew none, and yet slew twelve." She did not know what that was; she thought and thought, but she could not solve it. She opened her riddle-books, but it was not in them—in short, her wisdom was at an end. As she did not know how to help herself, she ordered her maid to creep into the lord's sleeping-

chamber, and listen to his dreams, and thought that he would perhaps speak in his sleep and reveal the riddle. But the clever servant had placed himself in the bed instead of his master, and when the maid came there, he tore off from her the mantle in which she had wrapped herself, and chased her out with rods. The second night the King's daughter sent her maid-in-waiting, who was to see if she could succeed better in listening, but the servant took her mantle also away from her, and hunted her out with rods. Now the master believed himself safe for the third night, lay down in his own bed. Then came the princess herself, and she had put on a misty-grey mantle, and she seated herself near him. And when she thought that he was asleep and dreaming, she spoke to him, and hoped that he would answer in his sleep, as many do, but he was awake, and understood and heard everything quite well. Then she asked: "One slew none, what is that?" He replied: "A raven, which ate of a dead and poisoned horse, and died of it." She inquired further: "And yet slew twelve, what is that?" He answered: "That means twelve murderers, who ate the raven and died of it."

When she knew the answer to the riddle she wanted to steal away, but he held her mantle so fast that she was forced to leave it behind her. Next morning, the King's daughter announced that she had guessed the riddle, and sent for the twelve judges and expounded it before them. But the youth begged for a hearing, and said: "She stole into my room in the night and questioned me, otherwise she could not have discovered it." The judges said: "Bring us a proof of this." Then were the three mantles brought thither by the servant, and when the judges saw the misty-grey one which the King's daughter usually wore, they said: "Let the mantle be embroidered with gold and silver, and then it will be your wedding-mantle."

[From *The Complete Grimm's Fairy Tales*, pp. 128–31.]

"Hansel and Gretel"

"Hansel and Gretel" is a classic tale of evil women who are a threat to children. The tale begins with Hansel and Gretel's evil stepmother, who convinces their father to abandon them in the forest. Here they come upon a wicked witch, an old woman who lives alone on the margins of society, is depicted as a cannibal, especially of children, and has a store of treasure. Gretel shows some gumption, though, and manages to save herself and her brother.

It was now three mornings since they had left their father's house. They began to walk again, but they always came deeper into the forest, and if help did

not come soon, they must die of hunger and weariness. When it was mid-day, they saw a beautiful snow-white bird sitting on a bough, which sang so delightfully that they stood still and listened to it. And when its song was over, it spread its wings and flew away before them, and they followed it until they reached a little house, on the roof of which it alighted; and when they approached the little house they saw that it was built of bread and covered with cakes, but that the windows were of clear sugar. "We will set to work on that," said Hänsel, "and have a good meal. I will eat a bit of the roof, and you Gretel, can eat some of the window, it will taste sweet." Hänsel reached up above, and broke off a little of the roof to try how it tasted, and Gretel leant against the window and nibbled at the panes. Then a soft voice cried from the parlor:

"Nibble, nibble, gnaw,
Who is nibbling at my little house?"

The children answered:

"The wind, the wind,
The heaven-born wind,"

and went on eating without disturbing themselves. Hänsel, who liked the taste of the roof, tore down a great piece of it, and Gretel pushed out the whole of one round window-pane, sat down, and enjoyed herself with it. Suddenly the door opened, and a woman as old as the hills, who supported herself on crutches, came creeping out. Hänsel and Gretel were so terribly frightened that they let fall what they had in their hands. The old woman, however, nodded her head, and said: "Oh, you dear children, who has brought you here? Do come in, and stay with me. No harm shall happen to you." She took them both by the hand, and led them into her little house. Then good food was set before them, milk and pancakes, with sugar, apples, and nuts. Afterwards two pretty little beds were covered with clean white linen, and Hänsel and Gretel lay down in them, and thought they were in heaven.

The old woman had only pretended to be so kind; she was in reality a wicked witch, who lay in wait for children, and had only built the little house of bread in order to entice them there. When a child fell into her power, she killed it, cooked and ate it, and that was a feast day with her. Witches have red eyes, and cannot see far, but they have a keen scent like the beasts, and are aware when human beings draw near. When Hänsel and Gretel came into her neighborhood, she laughed with malice, and said mockingly: "I have them, they shall not escape me again!" Early in the morning before the children were awake, she was already up, and when she saw both of them sleeping and looking so pretty, with their plump and rosy cheeks, she muttered to herself: "That will be a dainty mouthful!" Then she seized Hänsel with her shrivelled hand, carried him into a little stable, and locked him in behind a grated door. Scream

as be might, it would not help him. Then she went to Gretel, shook her till she awoke, and cried: "Get up, lazy thing, fetch some water, and cook something good for your brother, he is in the stable outside, and is to be made fat. When he is fat, I will eat him." Gretel began to weep bitterly, but it was all in vain, for she was forced to do what the wicked witch commanded.

And now the best food was cooked for poor Hänsel, but Gretel got nothing but crab-shells. Every morning the woman crept to the little stable, and cried: "Hänsel, stretch out your finger that I may feel if you will soon be fat." Hänsel, however, stretched out a little bone to her, and the old woman, who had dim eyes, could not see it, and thought it was Hänsel's finger, and was astonished that there was no way of fattening him. When four weeks had gone by, and Hänsel still remained thin, she was seized with impatience and would not wait any longer. "Now, then, Gretel," she cried to the girl, "stir yourself, and bring some water. Let Hänsel be fat or lean, to-morrow I will kill him, and cook him." Ah, how the poor little sister did lament when she had to fetch the water, and how her tears did flow down her cheeks! "Dear God, do help us," she cried. "If the wild beasts in the forest had but devoured us, we should at any rate have died together." "Just keep your noise to yourself," said the old woman, "it won't help you at all."

Early in the morning, Gretel had to go out and hang up the cauldron with the water, and light the fire. "We will bake first," said the old woman, "I have already heated the oven, and kneaded the dough." She pushed poor Gretel out to the oven, from which flames of fire were already darting. "Creep in," said the witch, "and see if it is properly heated, so that we can put the bread in." And once Gretel was inside, she intended to shut the oven and let her bake in it, and then she would eat her, too. But Gretel saw what she had in mind, and said: "I do not know how I am to do it; how do I get in?" "Silly goose," said the old woman. "The door is big enough; just look, I can get in myself!" and she crept up and thrust her head into the oven. Then Gretel gave her a push that drove her far into it, and shut the iron door, and fastened the bolt. Oh! then she began to howl quite horribly, but Gretel ran away, and the godless witch was miserably burnt to death.

Gretel, however, ran like lightning to Hänsel, opened his little stable, and cried: "Hänsel, we are saved! The old witch is dead!" Then Hänsel sprang like a bird from its cage when the door is opened. How they did rejoice and embrace each other, and dance about and kiss each other! And as they had no longer any need to fear her, they went into the witch's house, and in every corner there stood chests full of pearls and jewels. "These are far better than pebbles!" said Hänsel, and thrust into his pockets whatever could be got in, and Gretel said: "I, too, will take something home with me," and filled her pinafore full. "But now we must be off," said Hänsel, "that we may get out of the witch's forest."

[From *The Complete Grimm's Fairy Tales,* pp. 90–93.]

Sources

An Anthology of Old English Poetry, translated by Charles W. Kennedy. New York: Oxford University Press, 1960.

Beowulf and Other English Poems, translated by Constance B. Hieatt. New York: The Odyssey Press, 1967.

The Complete Works of Tacitus, translated by Alfred John Church and William Jackson Brodribb. New York: Random House, 1942.

The Complete Grimm's Fairy Tales, translated by Margaret Hunt, revised by James Stern. New York: Random House, 1944.

Heroic Romances of Ireland, by A. H. Leahy. 2 volumes. London; David Nutt, 1905.

Kalevala: The Land of the Heroes, translated by W. F. Kirby. London and Dover, NH: The Athlone Press, 1907.

The Lay of the Nibelung Men, translated by Arthur S. Way. Cambridge: Cambridge University Press, 1911.

The Lays of Marie de France and Other French Legends, translated by Eugene Mason. London: J. M. Dent & Sons, 1911.

Laxdaela Saga, translated by Muriel A. C. Press. London: J. M. Dent, 1909.

The Mabinogi and Other Medieval Welsh Tales, translated by Patrick K. Ford. Berkeley, CA: University of California Press, 1977.

New Readings on Women in Old English Literature, edited by Helen Damico and Alexandra Hennessey Olsen. Bloomington, IN: Indiana University Press, 1990.

Njál's Saga, trans. Carl F. Bayerschmidt and Lee M. Hollander. New York: New York University Press, 1955.

Poems of the Vikings: The Elder Edda, translated by Patricia Terry. Indianapolis, IN: Bobbs-Merrill, 1969.

The Prose Edda of Snorri Sturluson: Tales from Norse Mythology, translated by Jean I. Young. Berkeley, CA: University of California Press, 1964.

Sir Thomas Malory's Le Morte d'Arthur, a rendition in modern idiom by Keith Raines. New York: Bramhall House, 1962.

The Tain, translated by Thomas Kinsella. 1969. Oxford: Oxford University Press, 1970.

Bibliography

Introductory Texts

Peter Buchholz, "Perspectives for Historical Research in the Germanic Religion," in *The History of Religions,* 8/2 (November 1968) 111–38.

Nora Chadwick, *The Celts.* Harmondsworth, England: Penguin Books Ltd., 1970.

H. R. Ellis Davidson, *Gods and Myths of Northern Europe.* London: Penguin Books, Ltd., 1964, 1990.

Georges Dumézil, *Gods of the Ancient Northmen,* ed. Einar Haugen. 1959. Berkeley, CA: University of California Press, 1973.

W. Y. Evans-Wentz, *The Fairy-Faith in Celtic Countries.* 1911. Atlantic Highlands, NJ: Humanities Press Inc. 1977, 1981.

Jakob Grimm, *Teutonic Mythology,* 4 vols., trans. and ed. James Steven Stallybrass. 1966. Reprint, Gloucester, MA: Peter Smith, 1976.

Roger Sherman Loomis, *Arthurian Traditions and Chretien de Troyes.* New York: Columbia University Press, 1949.

Texts about Women

Gillian Bennett, *Traditions of Belief: Women and the Supernatural.* London: Penguin Books, Ltd., 1987.

Donal O. Cathasaigh, "The Cult of Brigid: A Study of Pagan-Christian Syncretism in Ireland." Pp. 75–94 in *Mother Worship: Theme and Variations,* ed. James J. Preston. Chapel Hill, NC: The University of North Carolina Press, 1982.

Jane Chance, *Woman as Hero in Old English Literature.* Syracuse, NY: Syracuse University Press, 1986.

Helen Damico and Alexandra Hennessey Olsen, eds., *New Readings on Women in Old English Literature.* Bloomington, IN: Indiana University Press, 1990.

Wendy Davies, "Celtic Women in the Early Middle Ages." Pp. 145–66 in *Images of Women in Antiquity,* eds. Averil Cameron and Amélie Kuhrt. London and Canberra: Croom Helm, 1983.

Joan Kelly, "Did Women Have a Renaissance?" in *The Essays of Joan Kelly: Women, History, and Theory.* Chicago: The University of Chicago Press, 1984.

Johannes Maringer, "Priests and Priestesses in Prehistoric Europe," *History of Religions,* 17/2 (November, 1977) 101–20.

Graham Webster, *Boudica: The British Revolt against Rome AD 60.* Totowa, NJ: Rowman and Littlefield, 1978.

SHAMANISM AND TRIBAL RELIGIONS

Introduction

The term shamanism encompasses a great variety of religious practices performed in all parts of the world from the earliest times to the present day. These practices tend to center on the religious expert called a shaman, a term that specifically refers to a religious expert of Siberia and Central Asia. Characteristics of the Siberian shaman, however, appear in almost all other parts of the world, among Native Americans, both northern and southern, Africans, Pacific Islanders, Asians, Australians, etc. Shamanism makes up a significant part of the religious life of tribal peoples, when it is not their exclusive practice. And for tribal peoples religion is not a choice, it is a given: there is no such thing as a secular realm where they are free to put off religious definitions of who they are. Religion is the fabric of tribal life. It tends, however, not to be a textual religion in a literal sense; it has few sacred books, and most of those were written down late in the tradition or recorded by outsiders. Mainly it is an incredibly rich oral tradition of story telling, myth making, and ritual, all of a highly complex nature.

Essentially, future shamans undergo a process that begins with a crisis, often an illness; and this illness can be mental or physical. The illness is often understood to be the call of the spirits, who then cure the future shaman when she or he accepts initiation. Quite often it is not a vocation they willingly choose. Other events that are thought to reveal such a call are surviving an unusual accident, the death of the shaman's child, undergoing an ordeal, strange and dramatic occurrences, or powerful and terrifying dreams. It is generally believed that if they refuse the call they will die and/or bad things will continue to happen to them or their families. When an individual freely chooses to become a shaman, she or he undertakes arduous ascetic practices which they hope will lead to visions or dreams revealing the approval of the spirits and/or ancestors.

During their initiations, future shamans usually have visionary experiences, particularly a vision of the dismemberment of their body followed by its reconstruction. In this way shamans are believed to die to their past life and become new, confident persons empowered by a powerful guardian spirit.

The central ability of the shaman is to enter into alternate states of consciousness in which they travel to other realms, such as the land of the ancestors or the land of the dead, and directly communicate with various spirits. Shamans do this to effect cures, guide the dead to the next world, divine the future, and so on. While in such trances shamans usually wear clothes that partake of the spirit realms by being made of special materials that have symbolic markings on them. Various instruments, most importantly the drum, complete the external details.

Shamans enter other states of consciousness in a variety of ways: Quite often they do so through drumming, dancing, or singing and by ascetic practices such as fasting, going without sleep, and meditation. Some take a variety of mind altering substances, such as the *soma* of the ancient Aryans and the peyote of Native Americans. Most tribal people have a formidable knowledge of pharmacology, and shamans, through their connection to healing, are particularly knowledgeable about such substances.

Evidence from various parts of Asia, especially Korea and Japan, as well as Melanesia, reveals that the earliest shamans were women who, probably through their ability to give life, were perceived to be natural possessors of the sacred and therefore were appropriate intermediaries between the mundane and spiritual realms. Additionally, women seem to have been more active in and to have had greater access to ecstatic practices associated with shamanism such as trance and possession. In some regions there was a gradual and widespread displacement of women's spiritual power from women to men by which politically powerful central cults were controlled by men, though usually some women were retained in decorative capacities, and which left women in charge of the local, folk practices. Where shamanism mixed with one of the so-called great traditions, such as Confucianism, Buddhism, or Christianity, it remained or became the religion of the women, who were its experts, its practitioners, and its supporters, while the dominant religious system remained in the hands of the men.

Gender distinctions are central to tribal religions, as can be seen in the initiation ceremonies that mark the passages of the human life cycle. These distinctions are most often complimentary, but sometimes they are oppositional. Essentially they ritualize, or make sacred, the separate spheres of male and female activities. Women's rites and stories tend to focus on their fertility, as dramatized by menstruation and childbirth. Unfortunately most of the available material on women's practices has been gathered by men from other men, when it has been gathered at all, and so we are limited in our knowledge of how tribal women themselves perceive these gender distinctions. Rather than seeing menstruation taboos and the withdrawal of women at these times as restrictive, they may just as well be times for the assertion of power, for renewal and celebration. They certainly are a break from the endless round of domestic chores, which suggests that such times of separation may have been instituted by women, not men.

ASIA

CHINA

THE *CH'U TZ'Ŭ*

The *Ch'u Tz'ŭ* is an anthology of poems put together by the scholar Fang I in the second century C.E., though the tradition dates some of the poems to the fourth century B.C.E. The following poems were sung by male and female shamans to draw the gods and goddesses down from heaven. The songs are filled with erotic longing for the all too brief encounters with these divine beings.

Tung Huang T'ai I
(The Great One, Lord of the Eastern World)

On a lucky day with an auspicious name,
Reverently we come to delight the Lord on High.
We grasp the long sword's haft of jade,
And our girdle pendants clash and chime.
Jade weights fasten the god's jewelled mat.
Now take up the rich and fragrant flower-offerings,
The meats cooked in melilotus, served on orchid mats,
And libations of cinnamon wine and pepper sauces!
Flourish the drumsticks and beat all the drums!

* * *

The singing begins softly to a slow, solemn measure;
Then, as pipes and zithers join in, the singing grows shriller.
Now the priestesses come, splendid in their gorgeous apparel,

And all the hall is filled with a penetrating fragrance.
The five sounds mingle in a rich harmony;
And the god is merry and takes his pleasure.

Hsiang Fu Jen
(The Lady of the Hsiang)

The Child of God, descending the northern bank,
Turns on me her eyes that are dark with longing.
Gently the wind of autumn whispers;
On the waves of the Tung-t'ing lake the leaves are falling.
Over the white sedge I gaze out wildly;
For a tryst is made to meet my love this evening.
But why should the birds gather in the duckweed?
And what are the nets doing in the tree-tops?
The Yuan has its angelicas, the Li has its orchids:
And I think of my lady, but dare not tell it,
As with trembling heart I gaze on the distance
Over the swiftly moving waters.

Ta Ssŭ Ming
(The Greater Master of Fate)

Open wide the door of heaven!
On a black cloud I ride in splendour,
Bidding the whirlwind drive before me,
Causing the rainstorm to lay the dust.

In sweeping circles my lord is descending:
'Let me follow you over the K'ung-sang mountain'.
See the teeming peoples of the Nine Lands!
'What is the span of man's life to me?'

Shan Kuei
(The Mountain Goddess)

There seems to be some one in the fold of the
    mountain
In a coat of fig-leaves with a rabbit-floss girdle,
With eyes that hold laughter and a smile of pearly
    brightness:
'Lady, your allurements show that you desire me.'

Driving tawny leopards, leading the striped lynxes;
A car of lily-magnolia with banner of woven cassia;
Her cloak of stone-orchids, her belt of asarum:
She gathers sweet scents to give to one she loves.

I am in the dense bamboo grove, which never sees
    the sunlight,
A place of gloomy shadow, dark even in the daytime.

Solitary she stands, upon the mountain's summit:
So steep and hard the way is, that I shall be late.

The clouds' dense masses begin below me:
When the east wind blows up, the goddess sends
    down her showers.
Dallying with the Fair One, I forget about returning.
What flowers can I deck myself with, so late in the
    year?

I shall pluck the 'thrice-flowering herb' among the
    mountains.
The arrowroot spreads creeping over the piled-up
    boulders.
Sorrowing for my lady, I forget that I must go.
My lady thinks of me, but she has no time to come.

The lady of the mountains is fragrant with pollia;
She drinks from the rocky spring and shelters beneath
    the pine trees.

* * *

My lady thinks of me, but she holds back, uncertain.

The thunder rumbles; rain darkens the sky:
The monkeys chatter; apes scream in the night:
The wind soughs sadly and the trees rustle.
I think of my lady and stand alone in sadness.
    [From Ch'u Tz'ŭ, pp. 36–43.]

KOREA

YONGSU'S MOTHER

The following excerpt is taken from Laurel Kendall's recording of the life story of a modern day Korean shaman called Yongsu's Mother. Here she tells of her first encounter in a dream with the spirit who would eventually be one of her guides when she became a shaman. Yongsu's Mother had this dream under the stressful circumstances of being one of the civilian captives the People's Army took from Seoul in the early 1950s.

They took us away in the night. This was probably because the National Army had already crossed the river, so they weren't able to move in broad daylight. I'd planned to escape during the journey, but it was impossible. The boy at the rear of the line got away, but if I tried to leave the middle of the line, they'd see that I was missing. Those at the back of the line could escape; they all got away in the dark without being caught.

We went in a line, forced along all night, and then when it got light, they took us to some abandoned house. Our guards hadn't brought so much as a grain of rice. There wasn't so much as half a sack of grain, maybe three or four *mal*. If there was a pot, then they'd cook some of the grain, no more than a baby's fistful; they'd cook it up in salted water and that's what they gave us to eat. I was hungry; the first thing I thought about was food. The unhusked grain would pierce my stomach, but even so, it was something to eat and I ate. They poured the gruel into our cupped hands because there weren't any bowls; that's how they had us eat.

How many people were there?

Eighty people. During the day, we couldn't budge. Those wretches kept their eyes on everything that went on in the room. They posted a sentry in the doorway. They'd force us inside an empty house and then stand in the doorway. I couldn't escape from there. The sentry would threaten us with a stick of wood and bellow "Go to sleep!" Planes were flying around dropping bombs, so these People's Army bastards led us around at night and kept us inside the houses during the day. The planes were everywhere. So sleep. I lay down to sleep, but I lay down hungry. When it got dark, they'd give us another tiny bit of food in a ball and then lead us into the night and drag us on again. By the night of the third day, they'd run out of grain and didn't give us even that little bit of food. Those bastards were hungry and we were hungry. I was so hungry and cold that I could have died, I mean it.

It was the end of the third day, and I was sleeping. A white-haired grandfather appeared. A long white beard spilled down his chest and he stood up tall, holding a twisted staff, the staff that the Mountain God carries. The grandfather spoke [she draws out her words], "It's getting late; you don't have much time!" What? I woke with a start. It was a dream. Everyone else was asleep. I was the only one awake, and I'd had that dream. My stomach was so empty, but I couldn't do a thing about it. I closed my eyes and settled down again. "It's getting late; you don't have much time!" I woke up the girl who was sleeping beside me and told her my dream. "Let's escape! Whether we die in captivity or whether we die trying to escape, it's all the same. Let's get out of here!"

If they caught us, we would be killed. She didn't even want to try. But if we were killed trying to escape, at least we wouldn't die burdened with regrets for our passivity. But the other girl was afraid. How could we bring it off?

This girl still had some money, People's Army money, the money the reds used, printed with a rake and hoe.

"What money is this?"

"It's what we use now."

"Where did you get it?"

"My grandmother and I were looking after the house [everyone else had fled]. I went out in the evening to see if I could buy some food, rice husks or wheat chaff or barley. Those people grabbed me and brought me here."

"Let's say we'll buy something to eat with this money and get out of here." I said this, but I had no idea where we were. We'd traveled by night and hidden ourselves by day. But I went to work on the other girl and coaxed her into it. We were about to get up when the guard came over with his stick and yelled at us to go to sleep.

"We have this money and we're so hungry that we can't sleep. Let us go out and get some bread."

"Absolutely not. If my superior finds out, then I'll really be in trouble."

"But if we go out and get a large chunk of bread, then you can have some and we can have some. We're so hungry we can't go on. Just let us go and buy bread and we'll come right back."

"No way. You'll just run away."

"Now look here, I was in your headquarters for four days and I've been on this march for four days. It's already been a week, eight days. Have I escaped? Even if you threw me out, I wouldn't go. We'll buy some bread with this money and bring it back so we can all eat." [Arguing, she assumes the relentless nagging logic of the middle-aged woman, Yongsu's Mother. Now she becomes the girl again, back in character.]

The People's Army bastard seemed to think that was a good idea. He was hungry too. "Can you get back quickly?"

"We'll be right back, before anyone finds out about it." I insisted that the two of us would to go together, so he let us both out. It was all because of my dream that I'd gotten up and talked about buying bread. That was why they let me go. It was all because I had Grandfather Mountain God's help, isn't that so?

[From *The Life and Hard Times of a Korean Shaman,* pp. 55–57.]

Japan

SHINTO

Though it has been greatly influenced by both Chinese and Buddhist ideas, Shinto, the indigenous religion of Japan, retains much of its original character. Essentially it is a religion that worships nature and is concerned with avoiding pollution or, failing that, having access to purification. Death is the main source of pollution, but eventually, perhaps through foreign influences, aspects of women's fertility such as menstruation and childbirth also became sources of pollution requiring purification rituals. It seems, however, that originally menstruation and childbirth were times when women demonstrated their awesome powers of fecundity and were thought to be too sacred to approach. As in most parts of the world, the main problem with being polluted is that it denies one access to the sacred. In the Japanese instance it denies one access to the *kami,* the spirits, who are thought to be helpful to human beings.

THE NIHONGI—CREATION

Japanese creation stories tell of the divine origins of the islands of Japan and everything on them: the plants, the animals, the people—all is sacred.

The following creation story is taken from book I, part I of the *Nihongi,* a collection of myths and stories compiled by 720 C.E., which is one of the earliest textual sources for Shinto. It tells of the union of heaven and earth from which comes a series of divine beings: first a group of four males, then four females. Eventually these deities produced the divine pair: Izanagi (male) and Izanami (female) who, among other things, struggle with gender issues such as who approaches whom for sexual purposes.

Of old, Heaven and Earth were not yet separated, and the In and Yō [yin and yang] not yet divided. They formed a chaotic mass like an egg which was of obscurely defined limits and contained germs.

The purer and clearer part was thinly drawn out, and formed Heaven, while the heavier and grosser element settled down and became Earth.

The finer element easily became a united body, but the consolidation of the heavy and gross element was accomplished with difficulty.

Heaven was therefore formed first, and Earth was established subsequently.

Thereafter Divine Beings were produced between them.

Hence it is said that when the world began to be created, the soil of which lands were composed floated about in a manner which might be compared to the floating of a fish sporting on the surface of the water.

At this time a certain thing was produced between Heaven and Earth. It was in the form like a reed-shoot. Now this became transformed into a God, and was called Kuni-toko-tachi no Mikoto.

* * *

These were pure males spontaneously developed by the operation of the principle of Heaven.

* * *

The next Deities which came into being were Izanagi no Mikoto and Izanami no Mikoto.

One writing says:— "These two Deities were the children of Awo-kashiki-ne no Mikoto."

One writing says:— "Kuni no toko-tachi no Mikoto produced Ame kagami no Mikoto, Ame kagami no Mikoto produced Ame yorodzu no Mikoto, Ame yorodzu no Mikoto produced Aha-nagi no Mikoto, and Aha-nagi no Mikoto produced Izanagi no Mikoto."

These make eight Deities in all. Being formed by the mutual action of the Heavenly and Earthly principles, they were made male and female. From Kuni no toko-tachi no Mikoto to Izanagi no Mikoto and Izanami no Mikoto are called the seven generations of the age of the Gods.

* * *

Izanagi no Mikoto and Izanami no Mikoto stood on the floating bridge of Heaven, and held counsel together, saying:

"Is there not a country beneath?"

* * *

Thereupon they thrust down the jewel-spear of Heaven, and groping about therewith found the ocean. The brine which dripped from the point of the spear coagulated and became an island which received the name of Ono-goro-jima.

The two Deities thereupon descended and dwelt in this island. Accordingly they wished to become husband and wife together, and to produce countries.

So they made Ono-goro-jima the pillar of the center of the land.

Now the male deity turning by the left, and the female deity by the right, they went round the pillar of the land separately. When they met together on one side, the female deity spoke first and said:— "How delightful! I have met with a lovely youth." The male deity was displeased, and said:— "I am a man, and by right should have spoken first. How is it that on the contrary thou, a woman, shouldst have been the first to speak? This was unlucky. Let us go round again." Upon this the two deities went back, and having met anew, this time the male deity spoke first, and said: —"How delightful! I have met a lovely maiden."

Then he inquired of the female deity, saying: — "In thy body is there aught formed?" She answered, and said: —"In my body there is a place which is the source of femineity." The male deity said: —"In my body again there is a place which is the source of masculinity. I wish to unite this source place of my body to the source-place of thy body." Hereupon the male and female first became united as husband and wife.

Now when the time of birth arrived, first of all the island of Ahaji was reckoned as the placenta, and their minds took no pleasure in it. Therefore it received the name of Ahaji no Shima.

Next there was produced the island of Oho-yamato no Toyo-aki-tsu-shima.

Here and elsewhere Nippon is to be read Yama'o.

Next they produced the island of Iyo no futa-na, and next the island of Tsukushi. Next the islands of Oki and Sado were born as twins. This is the proto-type of the twin-births which sometimes take place among mankind.

Next was born the island of Koshi, then the island of Oho-shima, then the island of Kibi no Ko.

Hence first arose the designation of the Oho-ya-shima country.

Then the islands of Tsuhima and Iki, with the small islands in various parts, were produced by the coagulation of the foam of the salt-water.

★ ★ ★

They next produced the sea, then the rivers, and then the mountains. Then they produced Ku-ku-no-chi, the ancestor of the trees, and next the ancestor of herbs, Kaya no hime. *Also called Nudzuchi.*

After this Izanagi no Mikoto and Izanami no Mikoto consulted together, saying: — "We have now produced the Great-eight-island country, with the mountains, rivers, herbs, and trees. Why should we not produce someone who shall be lord of the universe? They then together produced the Sun-Goddess, who was called Oho-hiru-me no muchi."

Called in one writing Ama-terasu no Oho kami.

[From *Nihongi*, pp. 1–18.]

THE KOJIKI—AMATERASU

The following excerpts are taken from the *Kojiki,* a collection of myths and stories compiled in 712 C.E. and one of the earliest textual sources for Shinto. In the following story about Amaterasu, the sun goddess, deities perform magical and religious acts that probably have their origins in mid-winter ceremonies to coax the sun back and/or to protect against eclipses. As the sun goddess and the divine ancestress of the imperial family, Amaterasu was at the center of an important cult. Her main priestess was the daughter of the emperor, and one of these royal women was guided by the goddess to Ise, where she founded the main center for the worship of Amaterasu. This religious role of royal women relates Amaterasu to the early female shamans who ruled with administrative help from their brothers.

Through a series of solitary nonsexual acts the male deity Izanagi brings various deities into existence, including Amaterasu. (She is born when Izanagi washes his left eye.) Izanagi gives her the rulership over the heavens. Her brother Susanowo was given rule over the ocean. In the following story Izanagi expels him, and he goes to visit Amaterasu's realm. During this time they have children, Susanowo offends her, and she goes into hiding. The world is plunged into darkness, and the other deities have to find ways to entice her back and to punish Susanowo.

At this time, PAYA-SUSA-NÖ-WO-NÖ-MIKÖTÖ said: "In that case, before I go I will take my leave of AMA-TERASU-OPO-MI-KAMĪ."

When he ascended to the heavens, the mountains and rivers all roared, and the lands all shook.

Then AMA-TERASU-OPO-MI-KAMĪ heard this and was startled, saying:

"It is certainly not with any good intentions that my brother is coming up. He must wish to usurp my lands."

* * *

Thus waiting for him, she asked him:

"Why have you come?"

Then PAYA-SUSA-NÖ-WO-NÖ-MIKÖTÖ replied:

"I have no evil intentions. It is merely that the Great Deity divinely inquired about my weeping and howling. I said that I was weeping because I wished to go to the land of my mother. Then the Great Deity said: 'You may not live in this land,' and expelled me with a divine expulsion. Whereupon I came up intending to take leave upon my departure. I have no other intentions."

Then AMA-TERASU-OPO-MI-KAMĪ said:

"If that is so, how am I to know that your intentions are pure and bright?"

Then PAYA-SUSA-NÖ-WO-NÖ-MIKÖTÖ replied: "Let us swear oaths and bear children."

Whereupon they each stood on opposite sides of [the river] AMË-NÖ-YASU-NÖ-KAPA and swore their oaths.

At this time, AMA-TERASU-OPO-MI-KAMĪ first asked for the sword ten hands long which TAKE-PAYA-SUSA-NÖ-WO-NÖ-MIKÖTÖ wore at his side. Breaking the sword in three pieces, she rinsed them, the jewels making a jingling sound, in [the heavenly well] AMË-NÖ-MANA-WI, chewed them to pieces, and spat them out.

In the misty spray there came into existence a deity named TAKĪRI-BIME-NÖ-MIKÖTÖ, also named OKI-TU-SIMA-PIME-NÖ-MIKÖTÖ; next, IKITI-SIMA-PIME-NÖ-MIKÖTÖ, also named SA-YÖRI-BIME-NÖ-MIKÖTÖ; and next, TAKITU-PIME-NÖ-MIKÖTÖ. (Three deities)

PAYA-SUSA-NÖ-WO-NÖ-MIKÖTÖ, asking for the long string of myriad MAGA-TAMA beads wrapped on the left hair-bunch of AMA-TERASU-OPO-MI-KAMĪ, rinsed them, the jewels making a jingling sound, in [the heavenly well] AMË-NÖ-MANA-WI, chewed them to pieces, and spat them out.

In the misty spray there came into existence a deity named MASA-KATU-A-KATU-KATI-PAYA-PI-AMË-NÖ-OSI-PO-MIMI-NÖ-MIKÖTÖ.

Again, he asked for the beads wrapped on her right hair-bunch, chewed them to pieces, and spat them out.

In the misty spray there came into existence a deity named AMË-NÖ-PO-PI-NÖ-MIKÖTÖ.

* * *

At this time AMA-TERASU-OPO-MI-KAMĪ said to PAYA-SUSA-NÖ-WO-NÖ-MIKÖTÖ:

"The latter-born five male children came into existence from my possessions and are therefore naturally my children. The first-born three female children came into existence from your possessions, and are therefore your children."

Thus saying, she distinguished [the offspring].

* * *

Then PAYA-SUSA-NÖ-WO-NÖMIKÖTÖ said to AMA-TERASU-OPO-MI-KAMĪ:

"It was because my intentions were pure and bright that in the children I begot I obtained graceful maidens. By this it is obvious that I have won."

Thus saying, he raged with victory, breaking down the ridges between the rice paddies of AMA-TERASU-OPO-MI-KAMĪ and covering up the ditches.

Also he defecated and strewed the faeces about in the hall where the first fruits were tasted.

Even though he did this, AMA-TERASU-OPO-MI-KAMĪ did not reprove him, but said:

"That which appears to be faeces must be what my brother has vomited and strewn about while drunk. Also his breaking down the ridges of the paddies and covering up their ditches—my brother must have done this because he thought it was wasteful to use the land thus."

Even though she thus spoke with good intention, his misdeeds did not cease, but became even more flagrant.

When AMA-TERASU-OPO-MI-KAMĪ was inside the sacred weaving hall seeing to the weaving of the divine garments, he opened a hole in the roof of the sacred weaving hall and dropped down into it the heavenly dappled pony which he had skinned with a backwards skinning.

The heavenly weaving maiden, seeing this, was alarmed and struck her genitals against the shuttle and died.

* * *

At this time, AMA-TERASU-OPO-MI-KAMĪ, seeing this, was afraid, and opening the heavenly rock-cave door, went in and shut herself inside.

Then TAKAMA-NÖ-PARA was completely dark, and the Central Land of the Reed Plains was entirely dark.

Because of this, constant night reigned, and the cries of the myriad deities were everywhere abundant, like summer flies; and all manner of calamities arose.

Then the eight-hundred myriad deities assembled in a divine assembly in the river-bed of the AMË-NÖ-YASU-NÖ-KAPA.

* * *

They uprooted by the very roots the flourishing MA-SAKAKĪ trees of the mountain AMË-NÖ-KAGU-YAMA; to the upper branches they affixed long strings of myriad MAGA-TAMA beads; in the middle branches they hung a large-dimensioned mirror; in the lower branches they suspended white NIKITE cloth and blue NIKITE cloth.

These various objects were held in his hands by PUTO-TAMA-NÖ-MIKÖTÖ as solemn offerings, and AMÊ-NÖ-KO-YANE-NÖ-MIKÖTÖ intoned a solemn liturgy.

AMÊ-NÖ-TA-DIKARA-WO-NÖ-KAMĪ stood concealed beside the door, while AMÊ-NÖ-UZUME-NÖ-MIKÖTÖ bound up her sleeves with a cord of heavenly PI-KAGÊ vine, tied around her head a head-band of the heavenly MA-SAKI vine, bound together bundles of SASA leaves to hold in her hands, and overturning a bucket before the heavenly rock-cave door, stamped resoundingly upon it. Then she became divinely possessed, exposed her breasts, and pushed her skirt-band down to her genitals.

Then TAKAMA-NÖ-PARA shook as the eight-hundred myriad deities laughed at once.

Then AMA-TERASU-OPO-MI-KAMĪ, thinking this strange, opened a crack in the heavenly rock-cave door, and said from within:

"Because I have shut myself in, I thought that TAKAMA-NÖ-PARA would be dark, and that the Central Land of the Reed Plains would be completely dark. But why is it that AMÊ-NÖ-UZUME sings and dances, and all the eight-hundred myriad deities laugh?"

Then AMÊ-NÖ-UZUME said:

"We rejoice and dance because there is here a deity superior to you."

While she was saying this, AMÊ-NÖ-KO-YANE-NÖ-MIKÖTÖ and PUTO-TAMA-NÖ-MIKÖTÖ brought out the mirror and showed it to AMA-TERASU-OPO-MI-KAMĪ.

Then AMA-TERASU-OPO-MI-KAMĪ, thinking this more and more strange, gradually came out of the door and approached [the mirror].

Then the hidden AMÊ-NÖ-TA-DIKARA-WO-NÖKAMĪ took her hand and pulled her out. Immediately PUTO-TAMA-NÖ-MIKÖTÖ extended a SIRI-KUMÊ rope behind her, and said:

"You may go back no further than this!"

When AMA-TERASU-OPO-MI-KAMĪ came forth, TAKAMA-NÖ-PARA and the Central Land of the Reed Plains of themselves became light.

At this time the eight-hundred myriad deities deliberated together, imposed upon PAYA-SUSA-NÖ-WO-NÖ-MIKÖTÖ a fine of a thousand tables of restitutive gifts, and also, cutting off his beard and the nails of his hands and feet, had him exorcised and expelled him with a divine expulsion.

[From *Kojiki,* book 1, chaps. 14–17, pp. 74–86.]

EMPRESS JINGU

The next excerpt from the *Kojiki* tells the story of empress Jingu. On one occasion she is possessed by a deity, and she delivers an oracle to the emperor that he can conquer Korea. The emperor ignores her and, as a consequence, dies. Empress Jingu then divines how to cross the ocean, and she conquers Korea herself. After her victory she gives birth to a son, and then fights a battle to ensure his succession to the throne. This story reflects shamanistic practices that continue in Japan today in which women are possessed by deities which enable them to divine events and effect cures.

In those days the Empress OKINAGA-TARASI-PIME-NÖ-MIKÖTÖ often became divinely possessed.

[It was] at the time when the emperor dwelt at the palace of KASIPI in TUKUSI and was about to attack the land of the KUMASÖ. The emperor was playing the cither, and the OPO-OMI TAKESI-UTI-NÖ-SUKUNE abode in the ceremonial place in order to seek the divine will.

Then the empress became divinely possessed and spoke these words of instruction:

"There is a land to the west. Gold and silver, as well as all sorts of eye-dazzling precious treasures, abound in this country. I will now give this country [into your hands]."

Hereupon the emperor replied:

"When one climbs to a high place and looks toward the west, no land is visible. There is only the ocean."

Saying [that this was] a deceiving deity, he pushed away the cither and sat silent without playing it.

Then the deity, greatly enraged, said:

"You are not to rule this kingdom. Go straight in one direction!"

At this time, the OPO-OMI TAKESI-UTI-NÖ-SUKUNE said:

"This is a dreadful thing. My lord, continue to play the cither!"

Finally, then, he drew the cither to him and began to play reluctantly.

After a while, the sound of the cither stopped. When they raised the lights, they saw that he was dead.

Then, astonished and frightened, they moved him to a mortuary palace.

Besides, great offerings were assembled from [throughout] the land; and a thorough search was made for such sins as skinning alive, skinning backwards, breaking down the ridges, covering up the ditches, defecation, incest, and sexual relations with horses, cows, chickens, and dogs; then a great exorcism of the [entire] land was held.

Then again TAKESI-UTI-NÖ-SUKUNE abode in the ceremonial place in order to seek the divine will.

The instructions given then were exactly as [those given] previously, [namely]:

"This land is the land to be ruled by the child who is inside your womb."

Then TAKESI-UTI-NÖ-SUKUNE said:

"O awesome great deity, what is the child who is inside the womb of the deity?"

The answer was:

"[It is] a boy-child."

Then he inquired specifically:

"I should like to know the name of the great deity who is now giving such instructions."

The answer was:

"This is the will of AMA-TERASU-OPO-MI-KAMĪ, also of the three great deities SÖKÖ-DUTU-NÖ-WO, NAKA-DUTU-NÖ-WO, and UPA-DUTU-NÖ-WO.

It was at this time that the names of the three great deities were revealed.

"If at this time you truly wish to seek that land, then present offerings to all the heavenly deities and the earthly deities, as well as to all the deities of the mountains and of the rivers and seas.

"Enshrine our spirit at the top of the ship, and put wood ashes into a gourd; make many chopsticks and flat plates and cast all of them out to float on the ocean, then cross over!"

★ ★ ★

Then, exactly in accordance with these instructions, they put their army in order and marshalled many ships.

As they were crossing [the sea], all the fish of the sea, the small as well as the large, bore the ships across on their backs.

Then a favorable wind began to blow strongly, and the ships moved along with the waves.

These waves washed the ships ashore in the land of SIRAGI, [and they came to rest] halfway across the country.

At this time the king of the country, struck with awe, said:

"From now on I will obey the will of the emperor and will become your royal stable-groom. Every year I will arrange the many ships in line, without giving their bottoms time to dry, and without letting their oars and rudders dry; together with heaven and earth, unceasing will I serve."

In accordance with this, the land of SIRAGI was designated as the royal stable-groom, and the land of KUDARA was designated as the overseas MIYAKË.

Then she stood her staff at the gate of the king of SIRAGI and worshipped the rough spirit of the great deities of SUMI-NÖ-YE, whom she made the tutelary deities of the land. Then she crossed back over [the sea.]

★ ★ ★

Before the completion of this mission, [the child which she] was carrying was about to be born.

In order to delay the birth, she took stones and attached them to her skirt around the waist.

After she had crossed over to the land of TUKUSI, the child was born.

The name of the place where the child was born is UMI.

Also, the stones which she attached to her skirt are in the village of ITO in the land of TUKUSI.

Again, when she reached the hamlet of TAMA-SIMA in the AGATA of MATURA in TUKUSI, she ate a meal by the river.

At the time, it was the early part of the fourth month. She went out on the rocks in the midst of the river, unraveled some threads from her skirt, and using grains of cooked rice as bait, fished for the trout in the river.

The name of this river is WO-GAPA, and the name of this rock is KATI-DO-PIME.

For this reason, in the early part of the fourth month, the custom of women unraveling threads from their skirts and fishing for trout with rice grains as bait has continued until today.

★ ★ ★

At this time, as OKINAGA-TARASI-PIME-NÖ-MIKÖTÖ was returning to YAMATÖ, she prepared a funeral ship and put her son in this funeral ship, because there was doubt about the popular mind.

First of all, she caused rumors to be spread to the effect that the prince had already died.

As she thus proceeded up [to YAMATÖ], KAGO-SAKA-NÖ-MIKO and OSI-KUMA-NÖ-MIKO, hearing of this, plotted to wait and take them; they went out on the TOGA plain and were divining by hunting.

Then KAGO-SAKA-NÖ-MIKO climbed up a KUNUGI tree and looked out; whereupon a huge, enraged boar came and uprooted the KUNUGI tree and ate up KAGO-SAKA-NÖ-MIKO.

His younger brother OSI-KUMA-NÖ-MIKO, not afraid even after this, raised an army and waited for them.

Then he approached the funeral ship and was about to attack [this supposedly] empty ship.

But troops descended from the funeral ship and engaged him in battle.

At this time OSI-KUMA-NÖ-MIKO'S commanding general was ISAPI-NÖ-SUKUNE, the ancestor of the KISIBE of NANIPA.

The crown prince's commanding general was NANIPA-NEKO-TAKE-PURU-KUMA-NÖ-MIKÖTÖ, the ancestor of the OMI of WANI.

When they had pushed them back as far as YAMASIRÖ, they ordered their ranks, and both sides engaged in battle without further retreating.

Then, using cunning, TAKE-PURU-KUMA-NÖ-MIKÖTÖ caused it to be said that OKINAGA-TARASI-PIME-NÖ-MIKÖTÖ was dead and that there was no use in fighting further.

Then, cutting his bowstring, he pretended to surrender.

At this time, the [opposing] general, entirely believing this deception, unstrung his bows and put away his weapons.

Then [the empress' troops] took extra bowstrings from their topknots, restrung their bows, and attacked again.

They fled in retreat as far as [the pass] APU-SAKA, where they again faced each other in battle.

Having pursued them and defeated them at SASANAMI, they completely slaughtered their army.

At this time, OSI-KUMA-NÖ-MIKO, together with ISAPI-NÖ-SUKUNE, was hard pressed in pursuit and went by ship across the lake. He sang this song:

> Come, my lads,
> Rather than receive the wounds
> Inflicted by PURU-KUMA,
> Come, like the NIPO birds,
> Let us dive into the waters
> Of the lake of APUMI!

Then, entering the lake, they died together.

[From *Kojiki,* book 2, chaps. 92–96, pp. 257–67.]

North America

HOPI — CREATION AND SPIDER WOMAN

The creation story of the Hopi is excerpted from Frank Waters's *Book of the Hopi.* This book was a joint effort by Waters, White Bear, who acted as recorder and translator, and thirty Hopi elders. Their goal was to preserve their history and religious beliefs for future generations of Hopis.

While creation begins with two male divinities, the actual creation of life is performed by the important deity Spider Woman.

Spider Woman and the Twins

Sótuknang went to the universe wherein was that to be Tokpela, the First World, and out of it he created her who was to remain on that earth and be his helper. Her name was Kókyangwúti, Spider Woman.

When she awoke to life and received her name, she asked, "Why am I here?"

"Look about you," answered Sótuknang. "Here is this earth we have created. It has shape and substance, direction and time, a beginning and an end. But there is no life upon it. We see no joyful movement. We hear no joyful sound. What is life without sound and movement? So you have been given the power to help us create this life. You have been given the knowledge, wisdom, and love to bless all the beings you create. That is why you are here."

Following his instructions, Spider Woman took some earth, mixed with it some *túchvala* (liquid from mouth: saliva), and molded it into two beings. Then she covered them with a cape made of white substance which was the creative wisdom itself, and sang the Creation Song over them. When she uncovered them the two beings, twins, sat up and asked, "Who are we? Why are we here?"

To the one on the right Spider Woman said, "You are Pöqánghoya and you are to help keep this world in order when life is put upon it. Go now around all the world and put you hands upon the earth so that it will become fully solidified. This is your duty."

Spider Woman then said to the twin on the left, "You are Palöngawhoya and you are to help keep this world in order when life is put upon it. This is your duty now: go about all the world and send out sound so that it may be heard throughout all the land. When this is heard you will also be known as 'Echo,' for all sound echoes the creator."

★ ★ ★

She then created from the earth trees, bushes, plants, flowers, all kinds of seed-bearers and nut-bearers to clothe the earth, giving to each a life and name. In the same manner she created all kinds of birds and animals—molding them out of earth, covering them with her white-substance cape, and singing over them. Some she placed to her right, some to her left, others before and behind her, indicating how they should spread to all four corners of the earth to live.

Sótuknang was happy, seeing how beautiful it all was—the land, the plants, the birds and animals, and the power working through them all. Joyfully he said to Taiowa, "Come see what our world looks like now!"

"It is very good," said Taiowa. "It is ready now for human life, the final touch to complete my plan."

So Spider Woman gathered earth, this time of four colors, yellow, red, white, and black; mixed with *túchvala*, the liquid of her mouth; molded them; and covered them with her white-substance cape which was the creative wisdom itself. As before, she sang over them the Creation Song, and when she uncovered them these forms were human beings in the image of Sótuknang. Then she created four other beings after her own form. They were *wúti*, female partners, for the first four male beings.

When Spider Woman uncovered them the forms came to life. This was at the time of the dark purple light, Qoyangnuptu, the first phase of the dawn of Creation, which first reveals the mystery of man's creation.

They soon awakened and began to move, but there was still a dampness on their foreheads and a soft spot on their heads. This was at the time of the yellow light, Síkangnuqua, the second phase of the dawn of Creation, when the breath of life entered man.

In a short time the sun appeared above the horizon, drying the dampness on their foreheads and hardening the soft spot on their heads. This was the time of the red light, Tálawva, the third phase of the dawn of Creation, when man, fully formed and firmed, proudly faced his Creator.

"That is the Sun," said Spider Woman. "You are meeting your Father the Creator for the first time. You must always remember and observe these three phases of your Creation. Ths time of the three lights, the dark purple, the yellow, and the red reveal in turn the mystery, the breath of life, and warmth of love. These comprise the Creator's plan of life for you as sung over you in the Song of Creation.

[From *Book of the Hopi*, pp. 3–7.]

ESKIMO—SEDNA, A SEA GODDESS

The following Eskimo tale is the story of the transformation of the girl Sedna into the goddess of the sea and the keeper of all the sea creatures. This is one of the most famous Eskimo myths and is found in various versions wherever there are Eskimos. It is ritually important as well because when game is scarce the shaman must go into a trance in which he descends to Sedna's seaworld and gets her to release the animals by cleaning and combing her tangled hair. Being without fingers Sedna cannot perform this task for herself, and in some versions her hair becomes tangled and soiled due to hunters breaking taboos. A significant connection between Sedna and Eskimo women is the taboo that they are not allowed to touch their hair while menstruating or childbearing.

Once upon a time there lived on a solitary shore an Inung with his daughter Sedna. His wife had been dead for some time and the two led a quiet life. Sedna grew up to be a handsome girl and the youths came from all around to sue for her hand, but none of them could touch her proud heart. Finally, at the breaking up of the ice in the spring a fulmar flew from over the ice and wooed Sedna with enticing song. "Come to me," it said; "come into the land of the birds, where there is never hunger, where my tent is made of the most beautiful skins. You shall rest on soft bearskins. My fellows, the fulmars, shall bring you all your heart

may desire; their feathers shall clothe you; your lamp shall always be filled with oil, your pot with meat." Sedna could not long resist such wooing and they went together over the vast sea. When at last they reached the country of the fulmar, after a long and hard journey, Sedna discovered that her spouse had shamefully deceived her. Her new home was not built of beautiful pelts, but was covered with wretched fishskins, full of holes, that gave free entrance to wind and snow. Instead of soft reindeer skins her bed was made of hard walrus hides and she had to live on miserable fish, which the birds brought her. Too soon she discovered that she had thrown away her opportunities when in her foolish pride she had rejected the Inuit youth. In her woe she sang: "Aja. O father, if you knew how wretched I am you would come to me and we would hurry away in your boat over the waters. The birds look unkindly upon me the stranger; cold winds roar about my bed; they give me but miserable food. O come and take me back home. Aja."

When a year had passed and the sea was again stirred by warmer winds, the father left his country to visit Sedna. His daughter greeted him joyfully and besought him to take her back home. The father, hearing of the outrages wrought upon his daughter, determined upon revenge. He killed the fulmar, took Sedna into his boat, and they quickly left the country which had brought so much sorrow to Sedna. When the other fulmars came home and found their companion dead and his wife gone, they all flew away in search of the fugitives. They were very sad over the death of their poor murdered comrade and continue to mourn and cry until this day.

Having flown a short distance they discerned the boat and stirred up a heavy storm. The sea rose in immense waves that threatened the pair with destruction. In this mortal peril the father determined to offer Sedna to the birds and flung her overboard. She clung to the edge of the boat with a death grip. The cruel father then took a knife and cut off the first joints of her fingers. Falling into the sea they were transformed into whales, the nails turning into whalebone. Sedna holding on to the boat more tightly, the second finger joints fell under the sharp knife and swam away as seals; when the father cut off the stumps of the fingers they became ground seals.

Meantime the storm subsided, for the fulmars thought Sedna was drowned. The father then allowed her to come into the boat. But from that time she cherished a deadly hatred against him and swore bitter revenge. After they got ashore, she called her dogs and let them gnaw off the feet and hands of her father while he was asleep. Upon this he cursed himself, his daughter, and the dogs which had maimed him; whereupon the earth opened and swallowed the hut, the father, the daughter, and the dogs. They have since lived in the land of Adlivun, of which Sedna is the mistress.

[From *Tales of the North American Indians*, pp. 3–4.]

YUROK—TALES TOLD BY WOMEN

The following stories were collected by A. L. Kroeber in 1900 from two women: Julia Wilson, a fluent speaker of English very influenced by white culture, and her mother, Kate of Wahsek, who did not speak English and was more traditional than her daughter.

No'ots

A girl and her grandmother were living at Ko'men. Her grandmother told her, "When you dig for roots, do not dig *herlker.*" The girl wondered why. At last she thought she would try. She pulled up one of the roots. At the end was a little child. She ran back to the house and closed the door. But the little boy followed her and walked into the house. Her grandmother took care of him.

He grew up and hunted and killed many deer. But his mother would have nothing to do with him: she would not call him her son. She said that only if he got the woodpecker crest-covered deer, in the sky, would she call him her son. Then he killed that deer: now she went to the sky with him. There they saw many dances and festivals. Then they came back to Ko'men.

Now the young man was about to go away. She did not want him to go, but could not stop him. So, when he had gone, she threw her pestle after him. The pestle struck the stern of his boat, broke in two, and (one piece) became a rock off the coast south of the mouth of the Klamath. But the young man went on and did not come back. His name was No'ots.

Pa'aku

On Oka there lived a man who had two daughters. His house was in the middle. There were ten houses on each side of his. He wanted a son-in-law. Whoever killed the woodpecker-crest-covered deer in the sky, was to marry his daughters. Many tried but failed. Coyote tried.

Then one morning the one at Oka heard shouting. Someone was driving deer before him. He sent his two daughters to look. They found a little boy. He was Pa'aku. They brought him to the house. Next morning the people went out to hunt. They said to

Pa'aku, "Come along!" He said, "I cannot; I am too little."

When they were gone, he started to go to the sky with the old man. They went up by a ladder. He told the old man, "Whatever happens, do not open your eyes." Then there was a high wind, but they climbed on. They went through hail, but the old man did not look. Then they came to the sky. They heard people driving deer. Then the deer came. Pa'aku shot an all-red deer. He told the old man, "You too shoot." Then the old man also killed a (woodpecker-covered) deer. Each of them began to pack his deer home, but it was too heavy for the old man, so Pa'aku carried both. Now they returned, and he married the two girls.
[From *Yurok Myths,* pp. 324–25.]

SIOUX—THE SACRED PIPE

Central to North American spirituality is the sacred pipe, which is used in all the ceremonies of the Sioux, especially as an aid to communicating with the Great Spirit, here called Wakan Tanka. The following story tells how the people first got the sacred pipe and how they were instructed in its use. The excerpt is taken from Joseph Epes Brown's record of his conversations with Black Elk of the Oglala Sioux during the winter of 1947–1948.

Early one morning, very many winters ago, two Lakota were out hunting with their bows and arrows, and as they were standing on a hill looking for game, they saw in the distance something coming towards them in a very strange and wonderful manner. When the mysterious thing came nearer to them, they saw that it was a very beautiful woman, dressed in white buckskin, and bearing a bundle on her back. Now this woman was so good to look at that one of the Lakota had bad intentions and told his friend of his desire, but this good man said that he must not have such thoughts, for surely this is a *wakan* woman. The mysterious person was now very close to the men, and then putting down her bundle, she asked the one with bad intentions to come over to her. As the young man approached the mysterious woman, they were both covered by a great cloud, and soon when it lifted the sacred woman was standing there, and at her feet was the man with the bad thoughts who was nothing but bones, and terrible snakes were eating him.

"Behold what you see!" the strange woman said to the good man." I am coming to your people and wish to talk with your chief *Hehlokecha Najin* [Standing Hollow Horn]. Return to him and tell him to prepare a large tipi in which he should gather all his people, and make ready for my coming. I wish to tell you something of great importance!"

The young man then returned to the tipi of his chief, and told him all that had happened: that this *wakan* woman was coming to visit them and that they must all prepare. The chief, Standing Hollow Horn, then had several tipis taken down, and from them a great lodge was made as the sacred woman had instructed. He sent out a crier to tell the people to put on their best buckskin clothes and to gather imme-diately in the lodge. The people were, of course, all very excited as they waited in the great lodge for the coming of the holy woman, and everybody was wondering where this mysterious woman came from and what it was that she wished to say.

Soon the young men who were watching for the coming of the *wakan* person announced that they saw something in the distance approaching them in a beautiful manner, and then suddenly she entered the lodge, walked around sun-wise, and stood in front of Standing Hollow Horn. She took from her back the bundle, and holding it with both hands in front of the chief, said: "Behold this and always love it! It is *lea wakan* [very sacred], and you must treat it as such. No impure man should ever be allowed to see it, for within this bundle there is a sacred pipe. With this you will, during the winters to come, send your voices to *Wakan-Tanka,* your Father and Grandfather."

After the mysterious woman said this, she took from the bundle a pipe, and also a small round stone which she placed upon the ground. Holding the pipe up with its stem to the heavens, she said: "With this sacred pipe you will walk upon the Earth; for the Earth is your Grandmother and Mother, and She is sacred. Every step that is taken upon Her should be as a prayer. The bowl of this pipe is of red stone; it is the Earth. Carved in the stone and facing the center is this buffalo calf who represents all the four-leggeds who live upon your Mother. The stem of the pipe is of wood, and this represents all that grows upon the Earth. And these twelve feathers which hang here where the stem fits into the bowl are from *Wanbli Galeshka,* the Spotted Eagle, and they represent the eagle and all the wingeds of the air. All these peoples, and all the things of the universe, are joined to you who smoke the pipe—all send their voices to *Wakan-Tanka*, the Great Spirit. When you pray with this pipe, you pray for and with everything."

The *wakan* woman then touched the foot of the pipe to the round stone which lay upon the ground, and said: "With this pipe you will be bound to all your relatives: your Grandfather and Father, your Grandmother and Mother. This round rock, which is made of the same red stone as the bowl of the pipe, your Father *Wakan-Tanka* has also given to you. It is the Earth, your Grandmother and Mother, and it is where you will live and increase. This Earth which he has given to you is red, and the two-leggeds who live upon the Earth are red; and the Great Spirit has also given to you a red day, and a red road. All of this is sacred and so do not forget! Every dawn as it comes is a holy event, and every day is holy, for the light comes from your Father *Wakan-Tanka*; and also you must always remember that the two-leggeds and all the other peoples who stand upon this earth are sacred and should be treated as such.

"From this time on, the holy pipe will stand upon this red Earth, and the two-leggeds will take the pipe and will send their voices to *Wakan-Tanka*. These seven circles which you see on the stone have much meaning, for they represent the seven rites in which the pipe will be used. The first large circle represents the first rite which I shall give to you, and the other six circles represent the rites which will in time be revealed to you directly. Standing Hollow Horn, be good to these gifts and to your people, for they are *wakan*! With this pipe the two-leggeds will increase, and there will come to them all that is good. From above *Wakan-Tanka* has given to you this sacred pipe, so that through it you may have knowledge. For this great gift you should always be grateful! But now before I leave I wish to give to you instructions for the first rite in which your people will use this pipe.

"It should be for you a sacred day when one of your people dies. You must then keep his soul as I shall teach you, and through this you will gain much power; for if this soul is kept, it will increase in you your concern and love for your neighbor. So long as

the person, in his soul, is kept with your people, through him you will be able to send your voice to *Wakan-Tanka*.

"It should also be a sacred day when a soul is released and returns to its home, *Wakan-Tanka*, for on this day four women will be made holy, and they will in time bear children who will walk the path of life in a sacred manner, setting an example to your people. Behold Me, for it is I that they will take in their mouths, and it is through this that they will become *wakan*.

"He who keeps the soul of a person must be a good and pure man, and he should use the pipe so that all the people, with the soul, will together send their voices to *Wakan-Tanka*. The fruit of your Mother the Earth and the fruit of all that bears will be blessed in this manner, and your people will then walk the path of life in a sacred way. Do not forget that *Wakan-Tanka* has given you seven days in which to send your voices to Him. So long as you remember this you will live; the rest you will know from *Wakan-Tanka* directly."

The sacred woman then started to leave the lodge, but turning again to Standing Hollow Horn, she said: "Behold this pipe! Always remember how sacred it is, and treat it as such, for it will take you to the end. Remember, in me there are four ages. I am leaving now, but I shall look back upon your people in every age, and at the end I shall return."

Moving around the lodge in a sun-wise manner, the mysterious woman left, but after walking a short distance she looked back towards the people and sat down. When she rose the people were amazed to see that she had become a young red and brown buffalo calf. Then this calf walked farther, lay down, and rolled, looking back at the people, and when she got up she was a white buffalo. Again the white buffalo walked farther and rolled on the ground, becoming now a black buffalo. This buffalo then walked farther away from the people, stopped, and after bowing to each of the four quarters of the universe, disappeared over the hill.

[From *The Sacred Pipe*, pp. 3–9.]

Sioux Ritual for Preparing a Girl for Womanhood

The following excerpt is also taken from Joseph Epes Brown's record of his conversations with Black Elk.

Isha Ta Awi Cha Lowan:
Preparing a Girl for Womanhood

These rites are performed after the first menstrual period of a woman. They are important because it is

at this time that a young girl becomes a woman, and she must understand the meaning of this change and must be instructed in the duties which she is now to fulfill. She should realize that the change which has taken place in her is a sacred thing, for now she will be as Mother Earth and will be able to bear children, which should also be brought up in a sacred manner. She should know, further, that each month when her period arrives she bears an influence with which she must be careful, for the presence of a woman in this condition may take away the power of a holy man. Thus, she should observe carefully the rites of purification which we shall describe here, for these rites were given to us by *Wakan-Tanka* through a vision.

Before we received these rites it was customary that during each menstrual period the woman or young girl should go to a small tipi apart from the camping circle; food was brought to her, and no one else could go near the tipi. During the first period of a young girl, she was instructed by an older woman in the things a woman should know, even in the making of moccasins and clothes. This older woman who helped the girl should have been a good and holy person, for at this time her virtues and habits passed into the young girl whom she was purifying. Before she was permitted to return to her family and to her people the young girl had to be further purified in the *Inipi* lodge. But now I shall tell you how we received the new rites for preparing our young girls for womanhood.

A Lakota by the name of Slow Buffalo (*Tatanka Hunkeshne*) once had a vision of a buffalo calf who was being cleansed by her mother, and through the power of this vision Slow Buffalo became a holy man (*wichasha wakan*) and understood that he had been given rites which should be used for the benefit of the young women of his nation.

A few moons after Slow Buffalo received his vision, a young girl of fourteen called "White Buffalo Cow Woman Appears," had her first period, and of course her father, Feather on Head, thought immediately of Slow Buffalo's vision, so he took a filled pipe and offered it to Slow Buffalo, who accepted it, saying: "*Hi ho! Hi ho!* For what reason do you bring this sacred pipe?"

"I have a girl who is about to pass through her first period," Feather on Head replied, "and I want you to purify her and prepare her for womanhood, for I know that you have had a very powerful vision through which you have learned how this should be done in a better and more *wakan* manner than that which we have followed."

"Certainly, I shall do as you wish," Slow Buffalo replied. "The buffalo people, who have been taught by *Wakan-Tanka*, and who have given us this rite, are next to the two-leggeds, and are our source of life in many ways. For it was the White Buffalo Cow Woman who, in the beginning, brought to us our most sacred pipe, and from that time we have been

relatives with the four-leggeds and all that moves. Tatanka, the buffalo, is the closest four-legged relative that we have, and they live as a people, as we do. It is the will of our Grandfather, *Wakan-Tanka*, that this be so; it is His will that this rite be done here on earth by the two-leggeds. We shall now establish a sacred rite that will be of great benefit to all the people. It is true that all the four-leggeds and all the peoples who move on the universe have this rite of purification, and especially our relative the buffalo, for, as I have seen, they too purify their children and prepare them for bearing fruit. It will be a sacred day when we do this, and it will please *Wakan-Tanka* and all the people who move. All these peoples, and all the Powers of the universe, you must first place in the pipe, so that with them we may send a voice to the Great Spirit!

"I shall make a sacred place for your daughter, who is pure, and who is about to become a woman. The dawn of the day, which is the light of *Wakan-Tanka*, will be upon this place and all will be sacred.

"Tomorrow you must build a tipi just outside of the camping circle, and it must be built with a sheltered way leading to it, as is done in the *hunkapi* rite, and then you must gather together the following things:

a buffalo skull	a pipe
a wooden cup	some Ree tobacco
some cherries	*kinnikinnik*
water	a knife
sweet grass	a stone hatchet
sage	some red and blue paint

Feather on Head then gave to Slow Buffalo offerings of horses, and other gifts, and then he left to prepare for the next day.

The following day everything had been made ready in the sacred tipi, and all the people gathered around it, except those women who were preparing the feast which would come after the rites. Slow Buffalo was seated at the west of the tipi, and in front of him a place had been scraped in the earth, where a hot coal was placed. Holding sweet grass above the coal, Slow Buffalo prayed.

"Grandfather, *Wakan-Tanka*, Father, *Wakan-Tanka*, I offer to You Your sacred herb. O Grandmother Earth, from whence we come, and Mother Earth, who bears much fruit, listen! I am going to make smoke which will penetrate the heavens, reaching even to our Grandfather, *Wakan-Tanka*; it will spread over the whole universe, touching all things!"

After placing the sweet grass on the coal, Slow Buffalo purified first the pipe and then all the equipment which was to be used in the rite.

"All that will be done today," Slow Buffalo said, "will be accomplished with the aid of the Powers of the universe. May they help us to purify and to make sacred this girl who is about to become a woman. I now fill this sacred pipe, and in doing this I am placing within all the Powers, who are helping us here today!"

★ ★ ★

The pipe, containing now the whole universe, was leaned against the little drying rack, with its "foot" on the earth, and its "mouth" pointing toward the heavens. Then Slow Buffalo prepared to make the sacred place, and only the close relatives of White Buffalo Cow Woman Appears were allowed within the tipi, for the rites which were to follow are too sacred to be seen by all the people.

"*Wakan-Tanka*" has given to the people a fourfold relationship—with their Grandfather, Father, Grandmother, and Mother," Slow Buffalo said. "These are always our closest relatives. Since all that is good is done in fours, the two-leggeds will walk through four ages, being relatives with all things. Our closest relative among the four-leggeds is *tatanka*, the buffalo, and I wish to tell you that they have established a relationship with me. I am about to make a sacred place for this virgin, White Buffalo Cow Woman Appears, and I have been given the power to do this from the buffalo. All things and all beings have been gathered together here today to witness this and to help us. It is so! *Hechetu welo!*"

Smoke was then made from the sweet grass, and, standing over it, Slow Buffalo again purified his whole body. When this was finished it was necessary before making the sacred place that Slow Buffalo demonstrate to all the people that he had truly received a power from the buffalo; so he began to chant his holy song which the buffalo had taught him.

This they are coming to see!
I am going to make a place which is sacred.
That they are coming to see.
While Buffalo Cow Woman Appears
Is sitting in a wakan *manner.*
They are all coming to see her!

Just then, as Slow Buffalo finished this song, he let out a loud *Huh!* like the bellow of a buffalo. As he did this a red dust came out of his mouth, just as a buffalo cow is able to do when she has a calf. This Slow Buffalo did six times, blowing the red smoke on the girl, and on the sacred place; everywhere within the tipi there was nothing but this red smoke, and if there were any children peeping in the door of the tipi, they were frightened and ran quickly away, for it was indeed a very terrible sight.

★ ★ ★

White Buffalo Cow Woman Appears was then told to stand, and, holding this bundle of sacred things over her head, Slow Buffalo said:

"This which is over your head is like *Wakan-Tanka*, for when you stand you reach from Earth to Heaven; thus, anything above your head is like the Great Spirit. You are the tree of life. You will now be pure and holy, and may your generations to come be fruitful! Wherever your feet touch will be a sacred place, for now you will always carry with you a very great influence. May the four Powers of the universe help to purify you, for, as I mention the name of each power, I shall rub this bundle down that side of you. May the cleansing waters from where the sun goes down purify you! May you be as the purifying snow which comes from the place where *Waziah* lives. When the dawn of the day comes upon you, may you receive knowledge from the morning star. May you be made pure by the Power of the place towards which we always face, and may those peoples who have walked this straight and good path help to purify you. May you be as the White Swan who lives at this place there where you face, and may your children be as pure as the children of the Swan!"

★ ★ ★

All the people then said "*Hi ho! Hi ho!*" and everybody was rejoicing and happy because of the great thing which had been done that day. White Buffalo Cow Woman Appears was brought out of the tipi, and all the people rushed up to her and placed their hands upon her, for now she was a woman, and, because of the rites which had been performed for her, there was much holiness in her. There was then a great feast, and a "give away," and those who were poor received much. It was in this manner that the rites for preparing a young girl for womanhood were first begun, and they have been the source of much holiness, not only for our women, but for the whole nation.

[From *The Sacred Pipe,* pp. 116–26.]

COMANCHE–SANAPIA, A MEDICINE WOMAN

The following excerpts are taken from David E. Jones's recording of the life history of Sanapia (1895–1968), a Comanche Eagle Doctor, during a three-year period beginning in 1967. It is a particularly intimate record because Jones is Sanapia's adopted son.

Sanapia's father converted to Christianity shortly before her birth and thereafter dressed and tried to lived as much as possible as a white man. Her mother, on the other hand, was also an Eagle Doctor, and she resisted the influence of white society and maintained her traditional ways. It was she who began Sanapia's training in healing. Being a doctor gives women equal status with men in Comanche society and is the height of prestige and social power available to women.

In the first excerpt Sanapia explains the origin of the Eagle Doctors, which reveals some gender tensions such as the grandmother who is represented as not being attentive enough to her grandson. This does not, as one would expect, preclude women from having sacred power, because at the end of the tale it is a young girl who is the first to receive the healing power. Such a story, of course, provides women with the spiritual authority to assume this role though men also could become Eagle Doctors.

Way back in years there used to be an old woman who was pretty poor. She had a grandson she tried her best to take care of because all her children were gone and all that was left was this grandson. When them people moved their camps, she used to trail behind them. When they set up another camp, the old woman would camp right outside on the edge of that camp place. Sometimes people, men, brought them food, meat, you know. But most times they were poor and hungry. And it went on and went on till one time they were all down south and west among them Navajo and Pueblo peoples. They was all trading each other. Meat and blankets for corn and meal and things. One Comanche young man got a whole pile of that corn meal and brought it to the old woman. That's the only way they could get that stuff them days. The grandson was happy over that, you know, over that young man bringing those things and helping them out. Well, later on the grandmother was cooking that corn and her grandson wanted some. The woman said, "No, I can't get any right this minute. I'm too busy to mess with you." Her grandson asked again but he got that same answer. He ask four times until he just fell over backwards and started crying and hollering real loud. Then he told his grandmother that he was going to be an eagle and leave her. Sure enough, he started growing wings on his shoulders. The grandmother thought he was joking, but soon and soon he had wings. When the old woman saw that she start to cry but the boy said, "No, you been stingy and I'm going to go . . . going to leave you all." The grandmother was crying and beggin' him not to go and soon a bunch of people came around her tepee. She ran out and told them what was happening but they didn't do nothing. I guess they thought she was crazy. But then, all at once, the boy came out and flapped his eagle wings and flew up and up. He went over them four times. He told them, "I'm leaving because that old woman was stingy with me." Then he took a feather from his tail and dropped it and it came down real slow, this way and that way, back and forth and back and forth. Then he said, "I'm going to leave you people this thing. Whoever gets that feather when it lands will have my help whenever he or she needs it to help some other people." And don't you know, the first person to get that feather was just a little girl. She was the first one what had that eagle's power like he said.

[From *Sanapia*, pp. 29–30.]

Initially Sanapia received her spiritual power through transmission from her mother and from her maternal uncle, who was also an Eagle Doctor. The two other people involved in her initial training were her maternal grandmother and paternal grandfather. The following excerpt is Sanapia's description of her maternal grandmother's blessing. She was the first to bless Sanapia and thereby gave her approval to Sanapia becoming a doctor.

One morning she told my mother, "This morning I'm going to bless my granddaughter. I want to fix it. I want my son to go out there and build a fire and when it turns to coals he could bring me some." And she had a little iron bucket, you know, and she said, "Put that big coal in this iron and bring it into my tepee. I want to bless her so she could live a long time and help people. And then she going to have children. And whatever she wants, anything at all, she's going to get it . . . easy way . . . she won't have to work, she won't have to do nothing." That's what she said, and then she blessed me. I was pretty good size, about fourteen I guess. She blessed me with all what she said and then she put cedar on them coals and she pray and sing. Then she put her hand on my head and I inhale that cedar and she fan it on my legs and arms, all over my body. She would sing a song and then she prayed some more. And you know, in them days I never did know how they prayed, but she would

pray and she said, "You, I don't know what you are, but I want you to bless this little girl so she can grow up and live to be an old lady like me. You, the one who go in the night and watch people, I don't know who you are, but you're like that, bless her. And this earth, I want her to walk on you for many, many years. I want her to be strong and healthy and I want her to live many years." And after she got through, she took that red paint and put water in it and rubbed it like that. Just smeared it all on my face, and rubbed it from my knees down to the bottom of my feet. Then she said, "Now, she's going to stand on this earth. This paint comes from the earth and she's going to stand on it. And she's going to live long life after she gets old. Help peoples. And when she gets real old, and her hair turns gray and white and her teeth fall out, well, that's when she's going to die." That's what she told me.

[From *Sanapia*, p. 31.]

ZUNI—THE CORN MAIDENS

In the following story excerpted from Ruth Benedict's collection, *Zuni Mythology*, the divine and beautiful corn maidens are insulted by the sexual overtures of the bow priest and leave the people. Consequently there is a time of famine, and the people have to develop rituals to get the corn to grow.

Then they danced the Corn Dance in Itiwana. They made the shelter of boughs and brought the Corn Maidens in. They were very beautiful. That night the bow priest guarded them in the kiva. He watched them, for they were beautiful. In the night Yellow Corn went out to defecate and the bow priest followed her. As she came back he laid hands on her. Yellow Corn resisted him. She said, "No, we do not know men. Our flesh is food for the people. If we were hot with desire the people's food would be spoiled." She escaped from him and went back into the kiva. She said to her sisters, "My sisters, I must tell you the trouble that has come upon us. We are beautiful, my sisters. When I went outside the bow priest followed me and laid hands on me. He desired me. I repulsed him but he persisted. He lifted my clothes. I told him, 'I am your mother. Shall I lie with my child? Your flesh is formed of my flesh.' What shall we do, my sisters?" Red Corn answered, "My sister, we must go away. If we stay here, someone else will desire us and our flesh will be spoiled. Already they have made us less valuable." Yellow Corn said also, "My sister White Corn, what have you to say?" She said, "There is only one thing for us to do. We must

go." "Blue Corn, what have you to say?" "There is no choice. We must go." They talked together about how they should do this. They said, "We will go immediately. It is dark. We shall escape and no one will know."

They went out. The corn out of all the storerooms followed them. It was their flesh and they took it away when they went. Only a little bit was left in each house. They went toward the east, then far to the southeast, and a long journey to the south till they came to the ocean. It was night when they got there. Yellow Corn said to her sisters, "My sisters, how shall we hide ourselves?" They saw Duck. He greeted them. They said to him, "We are the Corn Maidens. We gave our flesh to our people but the bow priest looked upon us with desire. Therefore we left our people and escaped. We have come to the ocean. How shall we hide ourselves?" Duck answered, "I shall hide you, my children." He spread his wings. Yellow Corn, Red Corn, White Corn, took shelter under his right wing, Blue Corn, Speckled Corn and Black Corn took shelter under his left wing. Duck rose and dived under the waters of the ocean with the Corn Maidens.

That spring people planted their corn fields and all

the plants were killed by the frost. The people were poor. Next year they planted their fields again but there was no rain. No corn grew. The third the people were hungry and the fourth year they had nothing. They lived on cactus and venison and wild seeds. For six years no corn grew. The seventh year people were dying. The priests of the council met every night because their people were starving. They said, "Our corn mothers have disappeared all these years. Their trails went to the east and there are no footprints returning." They planned how they could recover them. Every night and every day they prayed their corn mothers to return. The priests said, "We will ask the birds of prey to look for our mothers." The village priest took shell and coral and turquoise and sent for Eagle. Eagle came. He went to the ceremonial room of the village priest. The priests were sitting there all skin and bones. Eagle said, "What is it you have to say to me that you have sent for me?" The village priest said, "Our father, our son, we want to ask you to find our corn mothers. They gave us our flesh and the bow priest laid hands on Yellow Corn when she went to defecate. They left and we have no corn. I have precious beads with which to pay you." Eagle answered, "Very well, I will try." Early next morning Eagle flew up into the sky. He could not find the corn mothers. At sunset he came back to Itiwana. "Did you find them?" "No. There were no traces of them." He sat down in the corner of the ceremonial room of the village priest. (Repeat for cokapiso, and Chicken Hawk). They sent for Crow. He went all the way to the ocean. He went under the waters of the ocean. Underneath there was lots of corn, yellow corn, blue corn, red corn, white corn, speckled corn, black corn. He ate and ate. White Corn said to him, "What do you eat my flesh for?" "I like it." Red Corn said, "Eat all you want." He ate lots. He came home. The village priest said, "Did you find the corn mothers?" "No." The people did not know what to do. They sent for Hummingbird. That night Crow was sick. He vomited. Everybody saw the corn kernels he had eaten. They said, "Where did you find those?" "I didn't know it was corn. Perhaps I found it to the east, perhaps to the south or the west or the north. I don't know." Next morning Hummingbird came. The priest told him, "Crow found our corn mothers but he did not know it was corn." Hummingbird answered, "All right, I will try." Next morning he went up and down, up and down by the ocean, four times he went the length of the ocean. He saw nothing. He came back. "Did you find them?" "No, I saw nothing." The priests did not know what to do. They sent the birds home.

They said, "We will ask Ne'we·kwe Youth (Ne'paiyatamu)." They sent the bow priest to Ashes Spring to ask him to help them. He greeted him and he said, "Sit down. What is it you have come to ask?" "Our Corn Mothers have disappeared. We are

starving. I have come to ask you to search the world for them. We need you." Ne'we·kwe Youth answered, "Very well, I will try." He came back with the bow priest to Itiwana. He went into the ceremonial room of the village priest. He saw them sitting there all skin and bones. He greeted them. They said, "Sit down." He said, "What is it that you have to ask me that you have sent for me?" "Nine years ago our mothers, the Corn Maidens, disappeared. The bow priest desired them and they left us. We are starving. We have sent Eagle, cokapiso, Chickenhawk, Crow and Hummingbird, but they could not find them. We want you to try. Look all over the world for us."

Ne'we·kwe Youth went up to the Milky Way. Before sunrise he saw Duck dive under the waters of the ocean with the Corn Maidens under his wings. He returned to the ceremonial room of the village priest. He said, "I have seen them, I know where they are. But I cannot bring them back alone. I need your help. Go into retreat. Do not stir, do not urinate, do not drink water, do not eat, do not smoke, do not sleep, do not speak to each other. Sit with your arms crossed on your breasts. We shall try to recover them. Make six prayersticks that I may plant for our Corn Maidens." Next morning Ne'we·kwe Youth took the yellow prayerstick the priests of the council had made and went a little to the southeast and planted it. He came back and sat down in the ceremonial room with the priests. They were still in contemplation. They did not move, they did not speak. He stayed with them a little while. He took the blue prayerstick and went out four or five miles to the southeast and planted it. (Repeat for the red prayerstick which he plants fifteen miles to the southeast after remaining three hours in the ceremonial room; for the white prayerstick which he plants still further to the southeast after a still longer stay, for the black prayerstick which he plants still further in the same direction; and the spotted prayerstick which he plants on the shores of the ocean.) Ne'we·kwe Youth came back to the ceremonial room of the village priest. Still the priests had not moved, they had not smoked, they had drunk no water, they had not spoken. He said in his heart, "Poor people, this is the last time I shall stay with you. Next time I shall surely find the Corn Maidens."

He came up out of the ceremonial room and went to the edge of the ocean. Red Corn and Speckled Corn were standing by the edge of the water. They saw Ne'we·kwe Youth planting his black prayerstick in the water. They disappeared under the ocean. Ne'we·kwe Youth watched them go. They came where their sisters were and said, "A man has come. He will find us here soon." Yellow Corn answered, "We cannot help it. He is Ne'we·kwe Youth. He has been in retreat with the priests. They have not stirred, they have not smoked, they have not drunk water, they have not spoken, they have made themselves poor." Ne'we·kwe

Youth went down under the waters of the ocean. He came where Yellow Corn was. "How have you lived all these days, my mothers, my children?" "Happily, thank you. Sit down." He asked Yellow Corn, "Where are your sisters?" "In the other room." "I want to see them." Yellow Corn brought them. Ne'we·kwe Youth greeted them. Yellow Corn said to him, "What is it you wish to say that you have come this long distance and found us here?" "I want you to come back to Itiwana." "No, we cannot come." "Yes, you must come." Four times Yellow Corn refused and the fourth time she said, "Yes, we will go with you. When we come to Itiwana, if nobody is worried, if everybody is happy all the time, if they always pray as they should, if they always think good thoughts, we shall stay and give our flesh again to the people." "Thank you, it is well." He went out. A little way from the edge of the ocean he found a rabbit. He took it back to Yellow Corn. He said, "This is an animal that is happy all the time. It is good to make the people glad." She said, "Yes, kill it." He hit it a blow behind the ears. He took a sharp stone and slit the skin and drew it off. He took a bone from its foreleg and a bone from its ear and made an incision in them. He bound it with sinew that he took from the rabbit's back. He made the whistle and put it in his mouth. He said, "Now, I shall play for you and you will follow me." He went out and they followed him. They came to the pueblos of the east, San Juan, San Felipe, Laguna. They came on toward Itiwana. They came past Corn Mountain, Matsaka, Red Bank. He came in blowing his whistle. In their ceremonial room the village priest heard. He made four crosses with cornmeal on the roof in the four directions. He came down and made a road for Ne'we·kwe Youth to bring in Yellow Corn. Yellow Corn sprinkled pollen as she followed Ne'we·kwe Youth into Itiwana. The village priest led her to the cross of meal that he had made to the north. He made her stand upon it. He touched her with his eagle feathers and turned her to the four directions. (Repeat for the meal cross to the west, south, east. Repeat for all the corn sisters, each one in turn having a more elaborate ceremony. Yellow Corn's presentation should take "only about half an hour and Sweet Corn's about four hours.") All the corn sisters sat down in a row. Ne'we·kwe Youth prayed and made the sign of blessing with his arms and everybody inhaled from their hands. He said, "The Corn Maidens left us because one man desired them and wished to lay hands on them. We are their flesh and they give us themselves to eat. If they give it to us again and we plant in the spring for the rain to water we shall be fed again with their flesh. They will be our mothers and we shall be their children. If at any time we think evil thoughts or are unhappy they will go away from us again and we shall have nothing. When we dance the Corn Dance we shall carry their flesh in our hands. We shall not see them but they will be there in spirit. They will be among us and when we speak to them they will hear us. The people answered, "It shall be as you have said." Yellow Corn said to the priests, "At the end of the year send for us and we will come to Itiwana. Ne'we·kwe Youth will always lead us. Pekwin will go first (make the road) and Pautiwa will follow Ne'we·kwe, and after him Father Koyemci. My flesh is your flesh. When you put my flesh in the ground it sprouts and does not die. It is like your bodies. When they are buried in the ground they do not die. Our flesh is like your flesh." It is so. The people went home. That night, late, when everyone was asleep, Yellow Corn said to her sisters, "Let us go to give our people corn." They came up out of the kiva and went to each house. Yellow Corn took one grain of yellow corn. She bit it and dropped it in the first house. She went on to the next. Blue Corn took a kernel of blue corn. She bit it and dropped it into the first house and went on to the next. (Repeat for Red Corn, White Corn, Speckled Corn, Black Corn and Sweet Corn.) They went to each house and left the village. Next morning each corn room was bursting with the flesh of the corn mothers. Everyone had plenty to eat but after this corn ears never filled out to the tip. Because the bow priest tried to lay hands on Yellow Corn, Zuni corn is never perfectly kernelled.

[From *Zuni Mythology*, vol. 1, pp. 20–24.]

Central and South America

AZTEC—COATLICUE, THE MOTHER OF THE GODS

Coatlicue, "she of the serpent-skirt," is an earth goddess who gives birth to the sun, Huitzilopochtli, after having given birth to the four hundred gods, who are stars, and one daughter, Coyolxauhqui, the moon. The following myth of this birth makes it very plain that her daughter is active in trying kill her mother rather than be ruled by her brother, the sun. The myth is found in the *Florentine Codex*, book 3, chapter 1.

The Aztecs greatly revered Huitzilopochtli;
they knew his origin, his beginning,
was in this manner:

In Coatepec, on the way to Tula,
there was living,
there dwelt a woman
by the name of Coatlicue.
She was mother of the four hundred gods of the south
and their sister
by name Coyolxauhqui.

And this Coatlicue did penance there,
she swept, it was her task to sweep,
thus she did penance
in Coatepec, the Mountain of the Serpent.
And one day,
when Coatlicue was sweeping,
there fell on her some plumage,
a ball of fine feathers.
Immediately Coatlicue picked them up
and put them in her bosom.
When she finished sweeping,
she looked for the feathers
she had put in her bosom,
but she found nothing there.
At that moment Coatlicue was with child.

The four hundred gods of the south,
seeing their mother was with child,
were very annoyed and said:
"Who has done this to you?
Who has made you with child?
This insults us, dishonors us."
And their sister Coyolxauhqui
said to them:
"My brothers, she has dishonored us,
we must kill our mother,
the wicked woman who is now with child.
Who gave her what she carries in her womb?"

When Coatlicue learned of this,
she was very frightened,
she was very sad.
But her son Huitzilopochtli, in her womb,

comforted her, said to her:
"Do not be afraid,
I know what I must do."
Coatlicue, having heard
the words of her son,
was consoled
her heart was quiet,
she felt at peace.

But meanwhile the four hundred gods of the south
came together to take a decision
and together they decided
to kill their mother,
because she had disgraced them.
They were very angry,
they were very agitated,
as if the heart had gone out of them.
Coyolxauhqui incited them,
she inflamed the anger of her brothers,
so that they should kill her mother.
And the four hundred gods
made ready,
they attired themselves as for war.

Then they began to move,
they went in order, in line,
in orderly squadrons,
Coyolxauhqui led them.

At that moment Huitzilopochtli was born,
he put on his gear,
his shield of eagle feathers,
his darts, his blue dart-thrower.

With the serpent of fire he struck Coyolxauhqui,
he cut off her head,
and left it lying there
on the slope of Coatepetl.
The body of Coyolxauhqui
went rolling down the hill,
it fell to pieces,
in different places fell her hands,
her legs, her body.
   [From *Native Mesoamerican Spirituality*, pp. 220–25.]

INSTRUCTIONS TO A DAUGHTER

The following excerpt from the *Florentine Codex,* book 3, chapter 9, repeats the instructions of first a father and then a mother to their daughter and indicates that daughters were valued by the ancient Aztecs. The instructions focus on the religious duties and household tasks of a woman.

Here it is related how the rulers admonished their daughters when they had already reached the age of discretion.

Here you are, my little girl, my necklace of precious stones, my plumage, my human creation, born of me. You are my blood, my color, my image.

Now listen, understand. You are alive, you have been born; Our Lord, the Lord of the Near and the Close, the maker of people, the inventor of men, has sent you to earth.

Now that you begin to look around you, be aware. Here it is like this: There is no happiness, no pleasure. There is heartache, worry, fatigue. Here spring up and grow suffering and distress.

Here on earth is the place of much wailing, the place where our strength is worn out, where we are well acquainted with bitterness and discouragement. A wind blows; sharp as obsidian it slides over us.

They say truly that we are burned by the force of the sun and the wind. This is the place where one almost perishes of thirst and hunger. This is the way it is here on earth.

Listen well, my child, my little girl. There is no place of well-being on the earth, there is no happiness, no pleasure. They say that the earth is the place of painful pleasure, of grievous happiness.

The elders have always said: "So that we should not go round always moaning, that we should not be filled with sadness, the Lord has given us laughter, sleep, food, our strength and fortitude, and finally the act by which men propagate."

* * *

But now, my little one, listen well, look carefully: Here is your mother, our lady, from whose bosom, from whose womb you appeared, you came forth. As the leaf opens, so you grew, you flowered, as if you had been sleeping and awakened.

Listen, look, understand, for thus it is on earth. Do not be idle, do not walk aimlessly, do not wander without a destination. How should you live? How should you go on for a short time? They say it is very difficult to live on the earth, a place of terrific struggle, my little lady, my little bird, my little one.

Be careful, because you come from a renowned family, you descend from them, you are born from illustrious people. You are the thorn, the offshoot of our lords. The lords have left us, those who govern-ed; they are standing in line there, those who came to take command in the world; they gave renown and fame to the nobility.

Listen. Much do I want you to understand that you are noble. See that you are very precious, even while you are still only a little lady. You are a precious stone, you are a turquoise. You have been formed, shaped; you have the blood, the color; you are the offshoot and the stem; you are a descendant of noble lineage.

And now I am going to tell you this. Perhaps you do not understand very well? Are you still playing with earth and potsherds? Perhaps you are still sitting on the ground? Truly, you must listen a little for you already understand these things; by yourself you are gaining experience.

See that you do not dishonor yourself and our lords, the princes, the governors who preceded us. Do not act like the common people of the village, do not become an ordinary person. As long as you live on the earth, near and close to the people, be always a true little lady.

Look now at your work, that which you have to do: During night and day, devote yourself to the things of God; think often how He is like the night and the wind. Pray to Him, invoke Him, call to Him, beg Him earnestly when you are in the place where you sleep. This way your sleep will be pleasant.

Waken, get up in the middle of the night, prostrate yourself on your knees and your elbows, raise your neck and your shoulders. Invoke Him, call the Lord, our Lord, He who is as the night and the wind. He will be merciful, He will hear you in the night, He will look upon you with compassion; then He will grant you your destiny, what is set aside for you.

And if the destiny should be bad, the portion which they gave you when it was still night, what came with you at birth, when you came into life, with this sup-plication it will be made good, rectified; the Lord will change it, our Lord of the Near and the Close.

Watch for the dawn, get up quickly, extend your hands, extend your arms, raise your face, wash your hands, cleanse your mouth, take up the broom quickly, begin to sweep. Do not be idle, do not stay there close to the fire; wash the mouths of your little brothers; burn copal incense, do not forget it, for thus you will have the mercy of Our Lord.

And this being done, when you will be prepared, what will you do? How will you fulfill your womanly duties? Will you not prepare the food, the drink? Will you not spin and weave? Look well how are the food and drink, how they are made, that they should be good; know how good food and good drink are prepared.

These things that are sometimes called "things appropriate for persons of distinction," they are the duty of the wives of those who govern; for this they are called things that belong to the nobles, the food proper for one who governs, his drink. Be skillful in preparing the drink, in preparing the food. Pay attention, dedicate yourself, apply yourself to see how this is done; thus life will pass, thus you will be at peace. Thus you will be highly esteemed. Let it be not in vain if Our Lord some time may send you misfortune. Sometimes there is poverty among the nobles. Face it; then take hold of it, for this is the duty of a woman: spinning and weaving.

Open well your eyes to see what is the Toltec art, what is the art of feathers; how to embroider in colors and how to interweave the threads; how women dye them, those who are like you, our wives, the noble women. How they place the threads on the loom, how to make the woof of the cloth, how to hold it fast. Pay attention, apply yourself, be not idle, do not stand idly by, be strict with yourself.

* * *

Here it is told how when the father had spoken, the mother then replies. She tells her daughter tender words that she will always keep, will always place in her interior, the discourse of her father.

Dove, little dove, little child, little daughter, my little girl: You have received your father's words, the discourse of your lord and father.

What you have received is nothing common, is not given to the ordinary people: It was treasured and well guarded in your father's heart.

And he has not merely loaned it to you, for you are of his blood and his color, he has made himself known in you. Although you are a young girl, you are his image.

But what can I say further, what remains to tell you? I would gladly give you advice, but he spoke fully on all matters, made you aware of everything, there is nothing left to tell you.

Yet I must give you something, in order to fulfill my duty. You must never reject anywhere the words of your lord and father, because they are excellent and precious things, because only good things come from the word of our lord, since his language is truly that of a great person.

* * *

This is the way you must follow, the way of those who educated you, the way of the ladies, the noble women, the aged, white-haired women that preceded

us. Do not think they left us all their wisdom in their discourses. They gave us only a few words, they told us little. Here is all they said:

Listen well, for now is the time to learn here on the earth, and this is the word. Heed it and learn how your life should be lived, how you should shape it.

We travel through a difficult region here, we wander about on the earth, with an abyss on one side, a ravine on the other. If you do not walk between them you will fall on one side or the other. One can live only in the middle, walk safely only in the middle.

Little daughter, little dove, little child, place this counsel in your heart and treasure it there. Do not forget it, but let it be your torch, your light, during all the time you live here on the earth.

There remains only one other matter, with which I will end my words. If you live for a time, if you go on living on this earth for a time, do not deliver up your body foolishly, my little daughter, my child, my little dove, my little girl. Do not give yourself to this one or that one, for if you surrender yourself so carelessly, you are lost, and will never be under the protection of one who truly loves you.

You will never be able to forget it, you will always be burdened with misery and anguish. You will not be able to live in calmness and in peace. Your husband will always be suspicious of you.

My little daughter, my little dove, if you live here on the earth, do not allow two men to know you. And heed this warning always, keep it in mind all your life.

And when you are a married woman, do not think secret thoughts, but govern yourself, and do not allow your heart to stray foolishly to other men. Do not run risks with your husband. Do not foolishly deceive him, that is, do not be an adulteress.

Because, my little daughter, my little girl, if this occurs there is no remedy, there is no return. If you are seen, if it becomes known, you will be cast out into the streets, you will be dragged about, they will crush your skull with stones, will utterly destroy you.

[From *Native Mesoamerican Spirituality,* pp. 63–70.]

AZTEC—A WOMAN'S POEM

The poet Macuilxochitzin was born c. 1435 and lived through the most splendid years of the Aztec empire. The following poem is a celebration of a military campaign planned by her father, who was a counselor to several Aztec rulers. The last two stanzas tell how a defeated warrior's female relatives interceded on his behalf after he had wounded the Aztec ruler Axayacatzin/Axayacatl.

I raise my songs,
I, Macuilxochitl,
with these I gladden the Giver of Life,
may the dance begin!

There Where-in-some-way-one-exists,
to His house,
may these songs be carried?
Or only here
remain your flowers?
May the dance begin!

The Matlatzincas
are your prey, Lord Itzcoatl.
Axayacatzin, you have conquered
the city of Tlacotepec!
There turned in spiral
your flowers, your butterflies.
With this you brought happiness.
The Matlatzincas are in Toluca, in Tlacotepec.

Slowly he makes offerings
of flowers and feathers
to the Giver of Life.
He puts the eagle shields
on the arms of the men,
there where the war rages,
in the midst of the plain.
Like our songs,
like our flowers,
thus you, warrior of the tonsured head,
give pleasure to the Giver of Life.

The flowers of the eagle
remain in your hands,
Lord Axayacatl.
With divine flowers,
with flowers of war
you are covered,
with these becomes intoxicated

he who is on our side.

Above us open
the flowers of war,
in Ehcatepec, in Mexico,
with these become intoxicated
he who is on our side.

They have shown themselves fearless,
the princes,
those of Acolhuacan,
you, the Tepanecs.
On every side Axayacatl
made conquests,
in Matlatzinco, in Malinalco,
in Ocuillan, in Tequaloya, in Xohcotitlan.
From here he went forth.

There in Xiquipilco was Axayacatl
wounded in the leg by an Otomi,
his name was Tlilatl.
That one went in search of his women,
he said to them:
"Prepare a breech cloth, and elegant cloak,
give these to him, you who are courageous."

And Axayacatl called out:
"Bring the Otomi
who wounded me in the leg!
The Otomi was afraid;
he said:
"Now truly they will kill me!"
Then he brought a large piece of wood
and a deer skin,
with these he bowed before Axayacatl.
He was full of fear, the Otomi.
But then his women
made supplication for him to Axayacatl.
[From *Native Mesoamerican Spirituality*,
pp. 259–61.]

MAYAN—THE POPUL VUH—BLOOD GIRL

The following excerpt from *The Popul Vuh* is taken from a text written down sometime between 1550–1555 by a Quiche Mayan trained by missionaries. The original text, upon which this is based, existed both orally and as a hieroglyphic text. Its age is uncertain, but the Mayans list it as one of the gifts of the god Quetzalcoatl to the human race.

The Popul Vuh is the story of the Quiche Maya people from their creation to the coming of the Spanish. It is part myth and legend, part history. The creation story contained in it takes place over four cycles of creation, with humankind as we know it coming into existence in the fourth cycle. The following story comes from the third cycle, and it tells the adventures of Blood Girl, who becomes the mother of the hero twins Hunter and Jaguar Deer. These two heroes are eventually transformed into the sun and the moon.

And so here are the stories of a maiden,
   Daughter of a lord called Blood Chief.

★ ★ ★

And Blood Girl
   Was the name of the maiden.
When she heard the story of the fruit of the tree
   When it was retold by her father,
Then she marvelled
   When it was told.
"Can't I know
   And see this tree
That is talked about?
   Its fruit is said to be really delicious,
I hear,"
   She said then.
So she went all by herself
   And came there
Under the standing tree
   Standing there at Dusty Court.
"Aha! What is the fruit of this tree?
   Isn't it something delicious that this tree bears?
They mustn't die;
   They mustn't be lost.
What if I should just cut one?"
   Said the maiden then.
And then spoke the skull
   That was there in the tree,
"What do you want with what are just skulls
   That have been made round on the branches of
      trees?"
Was what Hunter's skull said
   When it spoke to the maiden.
"You don't want them,"
   She was told.
"I do want them,"
   Said the maiden then.
"All right, you must reach out your right hand.
   Do you see now?" said the skull.
"Yes,"
   Said the maiden then.
She reached right out
   With her right hand before the skull.
And so the skull spat forth its spittle,
   Which came to rest then on the maiden's hand.
So then she looked at what was on her hand;
   She immediately examined it,
But the skull's spittle was not on her hand.

★ ★ ★

And thus the maiden returned once more
   To her home.
Many warnings
   Were told to her.
And immediately she conceived a child in her womb
   just from the spittle,
   And thus were created
Hunter
   And Jaguar Deer.
Then when the maiden arrived home
   And six months had been fulfilled,
Then it was noticed by her father.
   He who was called the Blood Chief was her father.

★ ★ ★

And so then the maiden was observed by her father;
   Then he saw that she was with child.
And then they gathered together
   In council, all the lords,
1 Death
   And 7 Death together with the Blood Chief.
"Behold, my daughter is with child,
   Oh Lords; it is just her fornication,"
Said the Blood Chief then
   When he met with the lords.
"All right, question her about it,
   Then if she doesn't tell
She must then be sacrificed;
   She must go far off and be sacrificed then."
"Very well, ye Lords,"
   He said then.
And so he asked his daughter,
   "Who is the owner of the children who are in your
      womb, my daughter?" he said then.
"I have no children, oh my father.
   I have not known the face of a man," she said then.
"All right, it is true then that you are a fornicator.
   Take her and sacrifice her, you councillor warriors.
Bring here her heart in a jar
   That the lords may examine it at once,"
The Owls were told,
   The four of them.
Then they went carrying the jar;
   Then they went carrying the maiden,
And taking the white knife
   For sacrificing her.
"It cannot be that you will kill me, oh messengers,
   Because my fornication does not exist.
What is in my womb
   Was just created.

It just came from my admiring the head of 1 Hunter
    That is at Dusty Court.
So therefore don't sacrifice me,
    Oh messengers,"
Said the maiden
    When she spoke.
"What can we put in
    As a substitute for your heart?
We were told
    By your father,
Bring her heart back
So the lords can turn it over,
That they may be reassured;
That they may examine its assurance.
Hurry and put it there in the jar;
Wrap it up and drop the heart there in the jar.
Isn't that what we were told, then?
    Then what shall we give them in the jar?
For really we want you not to die,"
    The messengers said then.
"All right, the heart doesn't have to be theirs then,
    But neither will your homes be here.
And not only can you force people to die,
    But really yours will be the real fornicator.
And then also for 1 Death
    And 7 Death,
Only sap,
    Only croton for him.
Let that be burned before him.
    Let it not be this heart that is burned before him.
Take the fruit of the tree,"
    Said the maiden then.
For red was the sap of the tree
    That she went and gathered in the jar,
And then it swelled up
    And became round
And so then it became an imitation heart,
    The sap of the red tree.
Just like blood the sap of the tree became,
    An imitation of blood.
Then she gathered up there in it
    What was red tree sap
And the bark became just like blood,
    Completely red when placed inside the jar.
When the tree was cut by the maiden
    Cochineal Red Tree it was called,
And so she called it blood
    Because it was said to be the blood of the croton.
"So there you will be loved then;
    On earth there will come to be something of yours,"

★ ★ ★

And there was the mother of 1 Monkey
    And 1 Howler
When the woman arrived
    Called Blood Girl,

And when the woman Blood Girl
    Came to the mother
Of 1 Monkey
    And 1 Howler
Her children were still in her womb.
    It was only a little before there were born
Hunter
    And Jaguar Deer, as they are called.
So then the woman came
    To the grandmother,
And the woman said
    To the grandmother,
"I have come,
    Oh mother-in-law.
I am thy daughter-in-law,
    And I am thy child, oh mother-in-law,"
She said when she got there
    To the grandmother.

★ ★ ★

Very well,
    I understand that you are my daughter-in-law.
Go along then,
    Go and take
Their food then,
    So they can eat.
Go cut a big netful
    And then come
And then I will understand that you are my daughter-
    in-law,"
    The maiden was told then.
"Very well,"
    She said then.
And so then she went to the fields
    Where there was the field
Of 1 Monkey
    And 1 Howler.
Cleared by them
    Was the path,
And the maiden followed it
    And arrived
There
    In the field.
And there was just one stalk of corn;
    There was not another stalk,
A second stalk
    Nor a third stalk.
It was a bearing stalk,
    With the fruit of one stalk.
So then was finished
    The maiden's heart.
"I am such a sinner!
    I am a whore!
Where can I even get
    The one net of food
That is asked?"

She said then.
And then she called upon
 The guardian of food,
"Come and eat here,
 Come and agree here,
Oh Rain Woman,
 Oh Ripeness Woman,
Oh Cacao Woman
 And Corndough,
Oh guardian
 Of the food
Of 1 Monkey
 And 1 Howler," said the maiden.
And then she took the tassel,
 The tassel in the top of the ear, and tore it right out.
She didn't cut the ear.
 Then there were abundant ears.
The food in the net
 Filled up the big net.
So then the maiden came back,
 But it was animals who carried the net.
When she got back
 They went and left the rack.
She perspired as though she had carried it,

And came in to see the grandmother.
So then when the grandmother saw the food,
 One big netful,
"Where could the food come from for you?
 Did you fell them then?
If you have brought our whole corn crop here . . .
 I'm going to see," said the grandmother,
And she went;
 She went and looked at the field.
There was still just one cornstalk,
 And there was still just as clearly the net mark under
 it,
So the grandmother rushed back,
 And then she returned to the house
And said
 To the maiden,
"Actually there is a sign there;
 It must be true that you are my daughter-in-law.
I shall watch whatever
 You do,
Together with these who are my grandchildren.
 They are already magicians," the maiden was told.
 [From *The Book of Counsel,* pp. 75–84.]

AMAZON—HOW WOMEN LOST THEIR POWER

The following myth of an ancient switch in the power relations between the sexes comes from the Mundurucú of Brazil. The function of the myth is to explain the present low status of women, a status Mundurucú women do not fully accept. The myth defines the appropriate labor for each gender, gives control of sexual relations to men, and decrees the sacred musical instruments that originally belonged to women to now be taboo for women. The playing of these instruments is believed to be pleasing to the ancestors.

The sacred trumpets of the Mundurucú, called the karökö, are taboo to the sight of women, but the women once owned them. In fact it was the women who first discovered the trumpets.

There were once three women named Yanyonböri, Tuembirú, and Parawarö. When these women went to collect firewood, they frequently heard music from some unknown source. One day they became thirsty and went off in search of water. Deep in the forest they found a beautiful, shallow, and clear lake, of which they had no previous knowledge. This lake came to be named Karököboapti, or "the place from which they took the karökö." The next time the women heard the music in the forest, they noted that it came from the direction of the lake and went off to investigate. But they found only *jiju* fish in the water, which they were unable to catch.

Back in the village, one of the women hit upon the idea of catching the fish with hand nets. They rubbed the mouths of the nets with a nut which had the effect of making fish sleepy, and returned to the lake properly equipped. Each woman caught one fish, and these fish turned into hollow cylindrical trumpets. The other fish fled. That is why each men's house now has a set of only three instruments. The women hid the trumpets in the forest where no one could discover them and went secretly every day to play them.

The women devoted their lives to the instruments and abandoned their husbands and housework to play them. The men grew suspicious, and Marimarebö, the brother of Yanyonböri, followed them and discovered their secret. He did not, however, actually see the instruments. Marimarebö went back to the village and told the other men. When the women returned, he asked if it was true that they had musical instruments in the forest. The women admitted this and were told, "You can play the instruments, but you have to play them in the house and not in the forest." The women agreed to this.

The women, as possessors of the trumpets, had thereby gained ascendancy over the men. The men had to carry firewood and fetch water, and they also had to make the *beijú* (manioc cakes). To this day their hands are still flat from patting the *beijú* into shape. But the men still hunted, and this angered Marimarebö, for it was necessary to offer meat to the trumpets, and the women were able to offer them only a drink made from sweet manioc. For this reason, Marimarebö favored taking the trumpets from the women, but the other men hesitated from fear of them.

On the day on which the women were to bring the trumpets to the village, they ordered the men out to the forest to hunt while they made the sweet manioc drink. When the men returned from the hunt, the three discoverers of the trumpets led the other women out to get the instruments. The leader of the women, Yanyonböri, sent one of the women back to tell the men that they should all shut themselves securely inside the dwelling houses. The men refused to do this and insisted upon remaining in the men's house. Finally, Yanyonböri herself went back to order the men inside the dwelling houses. Her brother, Marimarebö, replied, "We will go into the house for one night only, but no more. We want the trumpets and

will take them tomorrow. If you do not give them to us, then we will not go hunting, and there will be no meat to offer them." Yanyonböri agreed, for she knew that she could not hunt the food for the trumpets or for the guests at the ceremonies.

The men entered the dwelling houses, and the women marched around and around the village playing the trumpets. They then entered the men's house for the night and installed the instruments there. Then, one by one the women went to the dwelling houses and forced the men to have coitus with them. The men could not refuse, just as the women today cannot refuse the desires of the men. This went on all night, and the women returned to the men's house all slippery inside.

The next day the men took the trumpets from the women and forced them to go back to the dwelling house. The women wept at their loss. When the men took the trumpets from the women they sang this song:

It was I who went and hid
I entered the house and hid
I entered the house and almost hid
Because I did not know I was ashamed
Because I did not know I was ashamed
Because I did not know
I entered the house and hid
I entered the house and almost hid.

[From *University of California Publications in Archaeology and Ethnicity*, vol. 49, pp. 89–91.]

AMAZON—THREE WOMEN'S SONGS

The following excerpts are four songs sung by the women of the Jibaro of Ecuador and Peru.

Song of the Priestess at a Victory Feast

Let us sing and dance!
May all of you come!

Arranged in a file may you come and dance!
Arranged in a file may you come without feeling shame!

Well dressed,
having adjusted your tarachi,
having arranged your ornaments,
may you sing and dance!
Grasping one another by the hands
may you dance!

Like the swallow which is moving his body to and fro,

Like the hawk, which is making his circles in the air, may you sing and dance!

[From *The Head Hunters of Western Amazonas*, p. 355.]

Planting Song of Women to the Earth-Mother

Being daughters of Nungüi, the woman,
we are going to sow.
Nungüi, come thou and help us,
come and help us!
Art not thou, art not thou our mother,
are not we thy children?
Whom should we call upon?

We only behold wood and hills.
Thou art the only one who can help us,
us that are going to plant the fruit.

[From *The Head-Hunters of Western Amazonas*,
p. 128.]

Songs of Dancing Women Personifying Birds

I

Being the wife of the cock-of-the-rock,
being the little wife of the sumga,
I jokingly sing to you thus:
Cock-of-the-rock, my little husband,
wearing your many-coloured dress of feathers,
graceful in your movements!

I know I am useless myself,
but still I rejoice,
for I am the wife of the sumga—
So I jokingly sing!

II

Great pheasant, great pheasant,
pheasant with the long hair and the big tail,
my little son, whom I have intoxicated with the
    beer!
I have made myself like the pheasant,
putting on me your long tail
and dressing myself in your brilliant feathers—
So I jokingly sing.

[From *The Head-Hunters of Western Amazonas*,
pp. 497–98.]

Africa

DOGON—CREATION

The following excerpt from the creation story of the Dogon was recorded by Marcel Griaule in October of 1946. Permission for the telling of this sacred story was given by the elders, the custodians of this knowledge. The narrator was Ogotemmêli, a man who, having lost his eyesight in a hunting accident, was free to devote himself fully to the ancient knowledge of his people.

The myth describes the process of creation by the one god Amma, which involved some blunders, such as having sex with the earth. In order to accomplish this Amma first had to perform a clitoridectomy on the earth. Later the earth is raped by her son, the jackal, and this is the cause of menstruation and an explanation of why it is defiling. Finally the story explains the necessity of circumcision and clitoridectomy as rituals designed to counteract the bisexual nature of human souls; in other words to make women fully women and men fully men.

The God Amma took a lump of clay, squeezed it in his hand and flung it from him, as he had done with the stars. The clay spread and fell on the north, which is the top, and from there stretched out to the south, which is the bottom, of the world, although the whole movement was horizontal. The earth lies flat, but the north is at the top. It extends east and west with separate members like a foetus in the womb. It is a body, that is to say, a thing with members branching out from a central mass. This body, lying flat, face upwards, in a line from north to south, is feminine. Its sexual organ is an ant-hill, and its clitoris a termite hill. Amma, being lonely and desirous of intercourse with this creature, approached it. That was the occasion of the first breach of the order of the universe.

Ogotemmêli ceased speaking. His hands crossed above his head, he sought to distinguish the different sounds coming from the courtyards and roofs. He had reached the point of the origin of troubles and of the primordial blunder of God.

'If they overheard me, I should be fined an ox!'

At God's approach the termite hill rose up, barring the passage and displaying its masculinity. It was as strong as the organ of the stranger, and intercourse could not take place. But God is all-powerful. He cut down the termite hill, and had intercourse with the excised earth. But the original incident was destined to affect the course of things for ever; from this defective union there was born, instead of the intended twins, a single being, the *Thos aureus* or jackal, symbol of the difficulties of God. Ogotemmêli's voice sank lower and lower. It was no longer a question of women's ears listening to what he was saying; other, non-material, ear-drums might vibrate to his important discourse. The European and his African assistant, Sergeant Koguem, were leaning towards the old man as if hatching plots of the most alarming nature.

But, when he came to the beneficent acts of God, Ogotemmêli's voice again assumed its normal tone.

God had further intercourse with his earth-wife, and this time without mishaps of any kind, the excision of the offending member having removed the cause of the former disorder. Water, which is the divine seed, was thus able to enter the womb of the earth and the normal reproductive cycle resulted in the birth of twins. Two beings were thus formed. God created them like water. They were green in colour, half human beings and half serpents. From the head to the loins they were human: below that they were serpents. Their red eyes were wide open like human eyes, and their tongues were forked like the tongues of reptiles. Their arms were flexible and without joints. Their bodies were green and sleek all over, shining like the surface of water, and covered with short green hairs, a presage of vegetation and germination.

These spirits, called Nummo, were thus two homogeneous products of God, of divine essence like himself, conceived without untoward incidents and developed normally in the womb of the earth. Their destiny took them to Heaven, where they received the instructions of their father. Not that God had to teach them speech, that indispensable necessity of all beings, as it is of the world-system; the Pair were born perfect and complete; they had eight members, and their number was eight, which is the symbol of speech.

They were also of the essence of God, since they were made of his seed, which is at once the ground, the form, and the substance of the life-force of the world, from which derives the motion and the persistence of created being. This force is water, and the Pair are present in all water: they *are* water, the water of the seas, of coasts, of torrents, of storms, and of the spoonfuls we drink.

Ogotemmêli used the terms 'Water' and 'Nummo' indiscriminately.

★ ★ ★

He returned to the subject of the Nummo spirits, or (as he more usually put it, in the singular) of Nummo, for this pair of twins, he explained, represented the perfect, the ideal unit.

The Nummo, looking down from Heaven, saw their mother, the earth, naked and speechless, as a consequence no doubt of the original incident in her relations with the God Amma. It was necessary to put an end to this state of disorder. The Nummo accordingly came down to earth, bringing with them fibres pulled from plants already created in the heavenly regions. They took ten bunches of these fibres, corresponding to the number of their ten fingers, and made two strands of them, one for the front and one for behind. To this day masked men still wear these appendages hanging down to their feet in thick tendrils.

But the purpose of this garment was not merely modesty. It manifested on earth the first act in the ordering of the universe and the revelation of the helicoid sign in the form of an undulating broken line.

For the fibres fell in coils, symbol of tornadoes, of the windings of torrents, of eddies and whirlwinds, of the undulating movement of reptiles. They recall also the eight-fold spirals of the sun, which sucks up moisture. They were themselves a channel of moisture, impregnated as they were with the freshness of the celestial plants. They were full of the essence of Nummo: they *were* Nummo in motion, as shown in the undulating line, which can be prolonged to infinity.

When Nummo speaks, what comes from his mouth is a warm vapour which conveys, and itself constitutes, speech. This vapour, like all water, has sound, dies away in a helicoid line. The coiled fringes of the skirt were therefore the chosen vehicle for the words which the Spirit desired to reveal to the earth. He endued his hands with magic power by raising them to his lips while he plaited the skirt, so that the moisture of his words was imparted to the damp plaits, and the spiritual revelation was embodied in the technical instruction.

In these fibres full of water and words, placed over his mother's genitalia, Nummo is thus always present.

Thus clothed, the earth had a language, the first language of this world and the most primitive of all time. Its syntax was elementary, its verbs few, and its vocabulary without elegance. The words were breathed sounds scarcely differentiated from one another, but nevertheless vehicles. Such as it was, this ill-defined speech sufficed for the great works of the beginning of all things.

★ ★ ★

The conversation reverted to the subject of speech. Its function was organization, and therefore it was good; nevertheless from the start it let loose disorder.

This was because the jackal, the deluded and deceitful son of God, desired to possess speech, and laid hands on the fibres in which language was embodied, that is to say, on his mother's skirt. His mother, the earth, resisted this incestuous action. She buried herself in her own womb, that is to say, in the anthill, disguised as an ant. But the jackal followed her.

There was, it should be explained, no other woman in the world whom he could desire. The hole which the earth made in the anthill was never deep enough, and in the end she had to admit defeat. This prefigured the even-handed struggles between men and women, which, however, always end in the victory of the male.

The incestuous act was of great consequence. In the first place it endowed the jackal with the gift of speech so that ever afterwards he was able to reveal to diviners the designs of God.

It was also the cause of the flow of menstrual blood which stained the fibres. The resulting defilement of the earth was incompatible with the reign of God. God rejected that spouse, and decided to create living beings directly. Modelling a womb in damp clay, he placed it on the earth and covered it with a pellet flung out into space from heaven. He made a male organ in the same way and having put it on the ground, he flung out a sphere which stuck to it.

The two lumps forthwith took organic shape; their life began to develop. Members separated from the central core, bodies appeared, and a human pair arose out of the lumps of earth.

At this point the Nummo Pair appeared on the scene for the purpose of further action. The Nummo foresaw that the original rule of twin births was bound to disappear, and that errors might result comparable to those of the jackal, whose birth was single. For it was because of his solitary state that the first son of God acted as he did.

'The jackal was alone from birth,' said Ogotemmêli, 'and because of this he did more things than can be told.'

The Spirit drew two outlines on the ground, one on top of the other, one male and the other female.

The man stretched himself out on these two shadows of himself, and took both of them for his own. The same thing was done for the woman. Thus it came about that each human being from the first was endowed with two souls of different sex, or rather with two principles corresponding to two distinct persons. In the man the female soul was located in the prepuce; in the woman the male soul was in the clitoris.

But the foreknowledge of the Nummo no doubt revealed to him the disadvantages of this makeshift. Man's life was not capable of supporting both beings: each person would have to merge himself in the sex for which he appeared to be best fitted.

The Nummo accordingly circumcised the man, thus removing from him all the femininity of his prepuce. The prepuce, however, changed itself into an animal which is 'neither a serpent nor an insect, but is classed with serpents'. This animal is called a *nay*. It is said to be a sort of lizard, black and white like the pall which covers the dead. Its name also means 'four,' the female number, and 'Sun', which is a female being. The *nay* symbolized the pain of circumcision and the need for the man to suffer in his sex as the woman does.

The man then had intercourse with the woman, who later bore the first two children of a series of eight, who were to become the ancestors of the Dogon people. In the moment of birth the pain of parturition was concentrated in the woman's clitoris, which was excised by an invisible hand, detached itself and left her, and was changed into the form of a scorpion. The pouch and the sting symbolized the organ: the venom was the water and the blood of the pain.

[From *Conversations with Ogotemmêli*, pp. 16–23.]

XHOSA—A TALE TOLD BY A WOMAN

The following is an excerpt from a long tale told by a Xhosa woman to an audience of women in South Africa. It was recorded and translated by Harold Scheub on September 15, 1967. The unnamed heroine of the tale is the young sister of the central character of the story. At this juncture in the story the hero, who is the chief, has just been circumcised, but he refuses to leave the circumcision lodge until he receives the skin of a fabled beast. After baking some bread, his sister decides to go and get the skin.

She said, "I'll go! I'll find the kaross for the son of my father, the kaross that he wants to come out with! I want this thing that eats people to eat me, it should begin with me! I'm going, I'll carry these loaves." They are provisions of people who travel. They journeyed

then. They got up, and this child journeyed then. These loaves were carried, too.

It happened, then, that when they were far off, they saw a large river. They went to this river, which was huge, they arrived there and tossed a loaf of bread into the water, and said, "*Nabulele! Nabulele!* Come out and eat me!" There was silence. They passed by this river. Someone said, "It's not here in this river!"

They journeyed on for a long time, seeking another big river. And again they found a huge river, and they sought a deep pool in that big river. They went to it, and again threw a loaf of corn bread in, again they threw a loaf of corn bread in. When the loaf of corn bread was thrown, someone said, "*Nabulele! Nabulele!* Come out and eat me!" The *nabulele* was not there at all!

They passed on from that river, they traveled again for a long time. Again they sought a huge river. Little rivers were crossed, rivers that had small pools which didn't appear to contain this thing.

Finally they came to another big river, and again they stood above a deep pool. They tossed a loaf of bread into the water and said, "*Nabulele! Nabulele!* Come out and eat me!" The water stirred in that pool, the water rolled, it rolled, it rolled! it rolled! it was brown! red! green!

This girl said, "Run! all of you! And take this bread along! Make sure that you can see me at all times! Keep me in your sight!"

They traveled, then, they traveled. They ran, continually looking, continually looking. Thus it was that the *nabulele* came out. This girl ran, then, when the *nabulele* came out. A thing came out—it was huge in a way that she had never seen! It wasn't like a horse, it was huge! It wasn't like anything, this thing was massive! great! as big as this: if it entered a kraal where cattle stay, it could fill that kraal by itself! This child ran, then. It ran after her, not running with speed, but moving steadily, going well. She ran, she ran and ran. When it was far off, she sat down. Then, when it was near, she put a loaf of bread down on the ground, and she ran. It stopped and chewed it, and swallowed it. Again it picked up and pursued her— but it doesn't run, it just walks. Finally, it happened then, she was a short distance from those men who were waiting for her.

When these men saw this, they said, "Oh! Well, we won't stay here! This thing is getting closer!"

"We're on our way, because of this thing!"

"You remain here with it by yourself—a thing which is so terrible, a thing which is so big! Yo yo yo yo!"

The men went on, they left the child behind. The child said, "Though you leave me behind, would you please do this when you're far off? Try to watch me, so that you'll know when I'm eaten by this thing, so that you'll be able to report at home that, well, I've been eaten! Never lose sight of me! Stay in a place that enables you to watch!"

The men agreed, and they departed. The child traveled on. She waited for the *nabulele*. The *nabulele*

came, it came. When it was a short distance away, she put a loaf of bread on the ground. Again she went on her way. She left the *nabulele* behind, she ran. It came to the loaf, and it chewed that loaf of bread. When it had finished chewing it, it again followed her. As for her, she rested again. When it was a short distance away, she again put a loaf of bread on the ground. Then gradually, in this basket that she carried, there remained just one loaf. She ran. It came along and ate this loaf. She ran, she came to these men. Again she poured some loaves into this basket, and it was full. And so it was; the men traveled on. The thing was frightening to these men; they didn't even want to see it. This thing was dreadful! The child again, when the thing was nearby, put a loaf of bread on the ground. And again she ran, and traveled. She went and sat down, far off. It came to the loaf, and the thing ate it. The child walked on. When this child came to the men, she said, "Travel on! Go home! And say there at home that a gun should be borrowed! A gun should be sought, so that this thing might be shot! But you shouldn't come near it; shoot it from a distance! Even if there are many guns, that's fine! because we don't know if this thing can even be penetrated by a gun!" The men ran, then, they traveled and left that child behind. The child traveled on, she left a loaf of bread on the ground. The thing was a short distance away. Again she ran, she was then not far from home!

When the men got there, they reported the girl's speech. Well then, it happened then that the guns were borrowed. They were loaded, they became heavy; they were cocked *xha xha xha* there at home. All the men were carrying guns; those not carrying guns carried spears. Time passed, then, and the sun set. The girl was seen, appearing, coming a short distance from home. Then it came, that thing came! She arrived at home, she arrived and entered the kraal at home.

She said that the men should go into the house. This thing will enter the kraal because it wants this girl whom it sees. "Go into the house, so that it won't see you! Then, when it enters, when it has turned its back, entering the kraal, coming toward me, come out with your weapons and go to work! I'll come out at the other end of the kraal!"

The men heard, and then they entered the houses there, all of them. The girl arrived then, and when she stood in the courtyard above the kraal, the men saw her, they were peeping through some small holes so that they might see this thing. Then the men cried out, the women also cried out, the dogs cried out, and everything there at home ran when they suddenly saw this thing! The dogs ran and descended on the other side. Everything in this homestead ran! the cattle also ran because of the approach of this thing, because this thing resembled nothing but itself, it never having been seen! The people in the house cried out—they were inside, they had closed the doors!

Well, the *nabulele* didn't bother about them at all, crying out though they were. It was face to face with this girl! It had caught up to the girl now! She went, she entered the kraal, and the thing entered the kraal. She left a loaf of bread, then the girl came out at the other end of the kraal. The people came out, coming out to the girl in the kraal. All of them came out with these weapons of theirs. Twelve men began shooting then, they shot, they went through their ammunition.

The thing stirred, still wanting to move on. Twelve other men came out, and they shot. Those men finished their ammunition. It was obvious that the *nabulele* was wounded. It stirred on the ground, not able to stand up so that it might travel. Those who were the weapon-jabbers threw their weapons, they were some distance away. It was obvious that—well, it couldn't make it, it collapsed now and the kraal was broken down, it was broken.

[From *African Folklore,* pp. 540–43.]

FANG—A WOMAN'S VISION

The following is one of the visionary experiences collected by James W. Fernandez from the Fang people of Gabon. These visions are induced by eating the *eboka* plant, which is a narcotic.

The vision of Mebang Mbe (Ngondo Ekumu). Age 33. Last wife of a Banzie. No children. District of Oyem. Bwiti Chapel at Kwakum.

Reasons given and vision: For a long time I resisted eating *eboka* although my husband encouraged me. But when I became very sick and nearly died, my husband decided to transport me to the Chapel at Kwakum. I was in agony and saw a road going through a house. I followed this road a long way to a crossroads, where a man with a great lance stopped me and said, "Where are you going? You are not dead." And he pointed

back. I found myself in bed in Kwakum. I remained sick for some weeks and my experience decided me to find the solution to this illness in *eboka*. But when I took it a year ago I saw only my father and a woman carrying a basin with various herbs. The woman was washed by my father, and my father turned to me and said, "You must return all the things that are in your stomach." I got up and with the help of my mother of *eboka* went to the river and threw up. I have not been sick since.

[From *African Folklore,* p. 514.]

!KUNG—A WOMAN HEALER

The following excerpt is taken from Marjorie Shostak's *Nisa: The Life and Words of a !Kung Woman,* a life history she recorded in Botswana during 1970 and 1971. Here Nisa describes her experiences with *n/um,* the power to heal.

N/um—the power to heal—is a very good thing. This is a medicine very much like your medicine because it is strong. As your medicine helps people, our n/um helps people. But to heal with n/um means knowing how to trance. Because, it is in trance that the healing power sitting inside the healer's body—the n/um—starts to work. Both men and women learn how to cure with it, but not everyone wants to. Trance-medicine really hurts! As you begin to trance, the n/um slowly heats inside you and pulls at you.

It rises until it grabs your insides and takes your thoughts away. Your mind and your senses leave and you don't think clearly. Things become strange and start to change. You can't listen to people or understand what they say. You look at them and they suddenly become very tiny. You think, "What's happening? Is God doing this?" All that is inside you is the n/um; that is all you can feel.

You touch people, laying on hands, curing those you touch. When you finish, other people hold you and blow around your head and your face. Suddenly your senses go "Phah!" and come back to you. You think, "Eh hey, there are people here," and you see again as you usually do.

My father had the power to cure people with trance medicine, with gemsbok-song trance medicine. Certain animals—gemsbok, eland, and giraffe—have trance songs named after them, songs long ago given by God. These songs were given to us to sing and to work with. That work is very important and good work; it is part of how we live.

It is the same with everything—even the animals of the bush. If a hunter is walking in the bush and God wants to, God will tell him, "There's an animal lying dead over there for you to eat." The person is just walking, but soon sees an animal lying dead in the bush. He says, "What killed this? It must have been God wanting to give me a present." Then he skins it and eats it; that's the way he lives.

But if God hadn't wanted, even if the hunter had seen many animals, his arrows would never strike them. Because if God refuses to part with an animal, the man's arrows won't be able to kill it. Even if the animal is standing close beside him, his arrows will miss every time. Finally he gives up or the animal runs away. It is only when God's heart says that a person should kill something, be it a gemsbok or a giraffe, that he will have it to eat. He'll say "What a huge giraffe! I, a person, have just killed a small something that is God's." Or it may be a big eland that his arrows strike.

That is God's way; that is how God does things and how it is for us as we live. Because God controls everything.

God is the power that made people. He is like a person, with a person's body and covered with beautiful clothes. He has a horse on which he puts people who are just learning to trance and becoming healers. God will have the person in trance ride to where he is, so God can see the new healer and talk to him. There are two different ways of learning how to trance and of becoming a healer. Some people learn to trance and to heal only to drum-medicine songs. My mother knew how to trance to these, although she never learned to heal. There are other people who know how to trance and to heal to drum-medicine songs as well as to ceremony-dance songs. The n/um is the same in both. If a person is lying down, close to death, and someone beats out drum-medicine songs, a healer will enter a trance and cure the sick person until he is better. Both men and women have n/um, and their power is equal. Just as a man brings a sick person back to health, so does a woman bring a sick person back to health.

My father was a very powerful healer. He could trance to both kinds of songs, and he taught n/um to my older brother. He also taught it to my younger brother. But when my father died, he stole Kumsa's medicine from him. He left Dau with it, but not Kumsa. Today, even if someone is lying down sick, Kumsa doesn't try to cure him. Only Dau does that.

My present husband, Bo, doesn't have n/um. He was afraid. People wanted to teach him but he refused. He said it would hurt too much.

N/um is powerful, but it is also very tricky. Sometimes it helps and sometimes it doesn't, because God doesn't always want a sick person to get better. Sometimes he tells a healer in trance, "Today I want this sick person. Tomorrow, too. But the next day, if you try to cure her, then I will help you. I will let you have her for a while." God watches the sick person, and the healer trances for her. Finally, God says, "All right, I only made her slightly sick. Now, she can get up." When she feels better, she thinks, "Oh, if this healer hadn't been here, I would have surely died. He's given me my life back again."

That's n/um—a very helpful thing!

I was a young woman when my mother and her younger sister started to teach me about drum-medicine. There is a root that helps you learn to trance, which they dug for me. My mother put it in my little leather pouch and said, "Now you will start learning this, because you are a young woman already." She had me keep it in my pouch for a few days. Then one day, she took it and pounded it along with some bulbs and some beans and cooked them together. It had a horrible taste and made my mouth feel foul. I threw some of it up. If she hadn't pounded it with the other foods, my stomach would have been much more upset and I would have thrown it all up; then it wouldn't have done anything for me. I drank it a number of times and threw up again and again. Finally I started to tremble. People rubbed my body as I sat there, feeling the effect getting stronger and stronger. My body shook harder and I started to cry. I cried while people touched me and helped me with what was happening to me.

Eventually, I learned how to break out of myself and trance. When the drum-medicine songs sounded, that's when I would start. Others would string beads and copper rings into my hair. As I began to trance, the women would say, "She's started to trance, now, so watch her carefully. Don't let her fall." They would take care of me, touching me and helping. If another woman was also in trance, she laid on hands and helped me. They rubbed oil on my face and I stood there—a lovely young woman, trembling in trance—until I was finished.

I loved when my mother taught me, and after I had learned, I was very happy to know it. Whenever I heard people beating out drum-medicine songs, I felt happy. Sometimes I even dug the root for myself and, if I felt like it, cooked it and drank it. Others would ask for some, but if they hadn't learned how to trance, I'd say, "No, if I gave it to you, you might not handle it well." But once I really knew how to trance, I no longer drank the medicine; I only needed that in the beginning.

When my niece gets older, I'll dig some of the root for her, put it in her kaross for a few days, and then prepare it. She will learn how to drink it and to trance. I will stand beside her and teach her.

Unlike my mother, I know how to cure people to drum-medicine songs. An elderly uncle taught me a few years ago. He struck me with spiritual medicine arrows; that's how everyone starts. Now when the drum starts sounding, "dong . . . dong . . . dong . . . dong," my n/um grabs me. That's when I can cure people and make them better.

Lately, though, I haven't wanted to cure anyone, even when they've asked. I've refused because of the pain. I sometimes become afraid of the way it pulls at my insides, over and over, pulling deep within me. The pain scares me. That's why I refuse. Also, sometimes after I cure someone, I get sick for a while.

That happened not long ago when I cured my older brother's wife. The next day, I was sick. I thought, "I won't do that again. I cured her and now I'm sick!" Recently, Dau cured her again. I sat and sang the medicine songs for him. He asked me to help, but I said, "No, I was so sick the last time I almost died. Today, my medicine is not strong enough."

I am a master at trancing to drum-medicine songs. I lay hands on people and they usually get better. I know how to trick God from wanting to kill someone and how to have God give the person back to me. But I, myself, have never spoken directly to God nor have I seen or gone to where he lives. I am still very small when it comes to healing and I haven't made these trips. Others have, but young healers like myself haven't. Because I don't heal very often, only once in a while. I am a woman, and women don't do most of the healing. They fear the pain of the medicine inside them because it really hurts! I don't really know why women don't do more of it. Men just fear it less. It's really funny—women don't fear childbirth, but they fear medicine!

[From *Nisa*, pp. 299–303.]

WALA—HOW MEN AND WOMEN CAME TO LIVE TOGETHER

The following tale was collected by Mona Fikry-Atallah in Ghana during 1966 and 1967.

There was a hunter who was roaming in the bush. He roamed for some time until he came to a closed-in compound. But he didn't even know that this compound existed! He heard busy noises from inside the house, not knowing that there were women inside. At that time women didn't live with men. They lived alone. They also had a woman chief but the hunter didn't know this. He saw the women come out. He walked around the whole house, went about examining it, and hit upon a small opening, which he made still wider. He opened exactly where the women were sitting cooking. Now, the women had a woman chief, and she never cooked. It means, then, that each woman cooked for her ("for another?"). None had husbands. The hunter said, "Yaa! These women! This is what I will do." He then took his penis—yaa!—and inserted it into that opening. A woman was sitting with her vagina against the opening and was cooking her soup. She took her vagina and put it there—yaa! There were some

named Habiba, others Minata, others Zeinabu, many named Kutuma and Fatima—each of them had a name.

Then one day, one of the women, Mama Hawwa, . . . who was first to stir the soup, was first to start the world. She sang,

Song.
My mother's namesake, put in the flour for me.
Habiba, woi! put in the flour for me. . . .
Minata, woi! put in the flour for me. . . .
Fatima, woi! put in the flour for me. . . .
Sanpagaa, woi! put in the flour for me. . . .

The women said, "Ai!" They took the food and first gave it to the senior woman. The food could not be eaten, because the body of Mama Hawwa had such great pleasure! The one who stirred the food could not stir it well, my friend! The woman chief said, "Ai! Why did you cook it like this? You're useless! Why did you stir it like this?" Not knowing that by putting the hunter's penis in just once, it had given seed to Mama Hawwa, who got up and sat down there. The following day came (to be). "I say! Today, as for this food, this sister of yours who cooked so badly . . . she will cook again and if she cooks it badly again, I will beat her up!" Again at the same time that the food was being prepared, the hunter came and went to the same small opening and took his penis and put it in.

Song. (Repeated)

They said, "Um hum! Again this food that she is cooking is thick and bad." It could not be eaten. The woman chief then became annoyed. All the women— and they were all in all thirty—cooked, but it also was no good . . . not even good enough to be sold. The woman chief then came and said, "You are very useless, hopeless, and can't do anything well. Today, I myself will cook this sau." ("That is the truth!")

The buttocks of the woman were that large and the penis was exactly like this. She took her buttocks and sat in front of the hole and placed there her vagina. Mmapp!! So he stuffed in his thing like this. She said,

Song. (Repeated)

She kept on swaying back and forth and then shouted to the women, "Go, run and see what is behind the house and come back!" They ran out to the back of the house and the cause of the disturbance was discovered, and they caught him.

Men, this is why we bring women home. The hunter brought them. If it were not for him, women would still be living alone and men would be staying by themselves. Like this my story comes to an end.

[From *African Folklore*, pp. 416–18.]

BAMBARA—THE AMBIVALENCE OF WOMEN'S POWER

The following tale was recorded by Charles Bird in Mali in 1967. The reciter was the bard Moulaye Kida of Segou. It is an episode from an extended epic cycle about Da Monson, the renowned eighteenth-century king of the Segou empire, and it is particularly rich in its presentation of the ambivalence of women's power, at least from the male perspective, which can both benefit or destroy men. In the tale Da Monson meets another king, Samanyana Basi, and they exchange insults. Da Monson goes to war but is not successful against Samanyana. Unable to live with this shame, Da Monson seeks the advice of the wisest man.

We have long been told that women have played important roles in establishing the power of many kings. We have also been told that women have played important roles in bringing about their downfall. In this story, told to us by the wise old men of our village, we will find out how the war came about between Da Monson and Samanyana Basi, two powerful kings of small states along the Niger River in what is today Mali. We will find out how Da Monson rose to fame and how Samanyana Basi fell to ruin through the wiles of a woman.

Everyone in those times had heard of Da Monson. His power was well established over the great kingdom of Segou, and his reign had lasted for many years. Not only was he a powerful man, but he knew the secrets of plants, animals, and men as well as many of the best-known wise men. Such was his fame that one could not find a man, woman, or child anywhere who had not heard of him.

Samanyana Basi was a king who reigned over the kingdom of Samanyana, to the south of Segou. He was a well-known king, but he was not as great as Da Monson. Samanyana Basi was a man of average stature, not too tall and not too short. He was, however, perfectly built. The people who had seen him called him an Apollo. In addition to his handsome features, he had a small, attractive beard on his chin.

★ ★ ★

Da Monson took the man [a seer] into his house and said: "I want you to tell me the secret that will let me raise an army, attack Samanyana, besiege it, destroy it, and capture Samanyana Basi."

The old seer . . . said simply: "Samanyana Basi will never be taken unless you can get his first handful of food from his evening meal, the hat on his head, and the old sandals on his feet. If you can't get these things so that I can work on them, we'll never arrive in Samanyana, much less capture Samanyana Basi. It just can't be done!"

Da Monson then called all the men in his kingdom whom he could trust, who would not betray him. He explained the matter to them and asked them to find someone who could get Samanyana Basi's first handful of food from his evening meal, the sandals from his feet, and the hat from his head, and bring them to Da Monson.

Da Monson's advisers searched the country for someone who could do the job, but they had no success. Finally a woman appeared in Segou. She was without doubt the most beautiful woman ever to be seen in the land. To look at her was more than a pleasure. Her figure alone would make men leave their families. Her smile was hypnotizing. If a man only set his eyes on her once, the second time he would have to lower his head to save himself. If a man didn't love her as a relative, he would have to adore her as a lover or even as a wife. This woman declared herself willing to help her king, Da Monson. One of the king's counselors came to him and said:

"There is a woman here in Segou called Ten. She is the daughter of a praise singer. She is without a doubt the most beautiful woman in your kingdom. In addition, she is very crafty and knows every secret for entering men's hearts and destroying their minds."

Da Monson called Ten to his court so that she could explain her plan. Ten arrived and kneeled before the King, surrounded by his counselors, saying:

"This whole country, its trees, its animals, and its people, from the little river far to the south to the great river far to the north, belongs to you. If something is bothering you, it is we who must correct it. If you will allow me, I think that I will be able to solve your problem."

Da Monson listened to her words, nodding his head with approval. When she had finished, he said:

"What do you want me to give you?"

Ten said, "Before I go, I want the best jewelry brought to me, gold, silver, precious stones, cowrie shells, the most beautiful and elegant cloth, and the finest blankets made in Masina. In addition, I want you to call your master brewers to prepare their best beer and wine. When they have finished, I will treat it with spices. Once a man has drunk the beer that I shall prepare, he will no longer be a man. He will lose his reason and I will be able to do what I want to with him. I will go to Samanyana and Samanyana Basi will drink his own downfall."

The brewers brought Ten their finest wine and beer. After putting many secret herbs and spices in it, she sweetened the beer with honey and added both red and black pepper. The brew was so strong and fiery that the average man, such as you or me, could not even smell it without losing his senses.

Now Ten was ready. Da Monson gave her his fastest canoe.

* * *

The news finally reached Samanyana Basi that a woman had arrived who was so magnificent that she surpassed the limits of men's most imaginative desires. Samanyana Basi was very suspicious, but he was also too curious. He said to his counselors, "Whoever this woman is, I think she has come here to do someone's dirty work. However, we do know that, from what people say about her, she is not a woman to be neglected. In any case, if she comes before me, we'll soon find out what she is up to. Go and bring her here."

The messengers went up to Ten's canoe and told her that Samanyana Basi wanted her to be in his reception hall in the wink of an eye. Ten was radiant with jewelry and the finest cloth. She walked up the bank and through the village with such assurance and majesty that the people fell away before her as they would before a great queen. She swept into the reception hall, knelt before Samanyana Basi and greeted him before his courtiers.

It was the custom of the country to offer visitors, whether men or women, a large gourdful of millet beer so that they might first cut their thirst before explaining the purpose of their visit. They filled up a gourd and gave it to Ten. She drank it down as if it were water. They filled up another gourd and she drank that one down even quicker than the first.

"By Allah," they exclaimed, "woman, you must have been about ready to die of thirst to drink our beer like that. It's lucky you came up from the beach when you did, but you'd better not drink any more of our beer like that, if you want to stay on your feet."

"What!" Ten replied. "Was that your beer? Why, in Segou that's what we give to our children when they come in hot and sweaty from an afternoon's play. I surely didn't think that this was the beer that you drank together with your great king here. That's why I drank it the way I did. You certainly must know that it's not very strong and surely you wouldn't call it a man's drink!"

"Well," said some, "the conversation is getting interesting. As our ancestors have said, if a woman goes ahead and swallows a turtle, a man must then swallow a lizard."

Everyone fell quiet, waiting for Samanyana Basi to speak.

"Do you think, woman, that Segou Da Monson's beer is better than this?"

"Why, this doesn't even come near it!" replied Ten. "You just can't even compare them. If you call this stuff beer, just a little sip of Da Monson's would make you dizzy."

"And who," asked Basi, "knows how to make this famous beer?"

"I do," Ten replied quickly.

"All right, then. You're going to stay right here. I

need you in my court. You aren't going to make beer for anyone but me."

"I agree," replied Ten. "I came here looking for the man that I have heard people praising throughout the country. I have heard that Samanyana Basi is greater than any man alive. However, from what I've seen here, I don't think you're the man I was looking for. Nonetheless, if you say I should stay here, I'm like the fruit that has fallen into the basket. I happen to have a sample of Da Monson's beer and some aged honey wine down in the canoe. I'll bring them up and you can try them. If they please you, I'll stay here and make more for you."

Ten had sprung her trap well. Basi's youthful pride was cut by her quick tongue. Not only did he want to show himself better than Da Monson, but already half crazed by the beauty of her face and body, which would quicken the blood of the oldest of men, he wanted to show her that he was the man she had been looking for, who could satisfy her and make her love him.

The servants brought up two great jugs. Samanyana Basi filled his gourd with Ten's beer and drank it down. Although he tried to remain impassive, his eyes could not help but show his pleasure at its sweetness and spicy flavor. He filled his calabash with the honey wine and drank that down. When he emptied the cup, Ten knew that he was now defenseless. Samanyana Basi could now no longer keep his eyes off her.

★ ★ ★

"I'm also a very good cook," she said. "Why don't you let me fix a meal that you will never forget?"

Samanyana Basi, in his present state, could only agree, but bade her be quick since his desire for her left him nearly breathless. Ten prepared a heaping bowl of rice and covered it with a rich meat sauce in which the spices and pepper alone were enough to make a man lose his senses. All the while, she kept her eye on Basi's gourd. As soon as he emptied it, she filled it again for him. The meal prepared, Ten set it down before Samanyana and sat down close to him, brushing temptingly against him and letting his head fill with the aroma of the scented oils she had rubbed into her body. Samanyana Basi reached into the bowl, bringing out a handful of rice and meat. As he was bringing his hand up to his mouth, Ten reached out as if to dip her hand into the bowl and knocked the food from Basi's hand.

"Oh!" she cried. "Look how terrible I am!"

"What's the matter?" asked Samanyana Basi. "What are you crying about?"

"I am so clumsy. I've knocked the food right out of your hand onto the floor."

"So, what's the matter with that?" Basi replied. "Look at all that we have left in the bowl. We have more to do than to eat all that. There's no reason to cry about the little bit that's on the floor."

Basi took another handful and began to eat with great pleasure. Ten reached down, picked up the spilled food, wrapped it in her handkerchief and hid it to one side. The peppery sauce increased Basi's thirst and Ten was quick to fill his gourd. They ate and drank until the food was finished. In the last drink she poured for Basi, Ten slipped a strong sleeping potion. Basi, thinking of the night of adventure, drank down the potion. Moments later, he fell into a deep sleep. Ten quickly wrapped her robes around her, walked over to the helpless Basi and yanked off his sandals and pulled off his hat, as well as the amulets hanging from his neck. She snatched up her handkerchief containing Basi's first handful of food from his evening meal, and, carefully checking to see that no one was about, ran down to the beach, where the canoe and her men were waiting. The canoe flew downstream like a sliver of moonlight on the black water. The waves of its wake washing on Samanyana's shore were Ten's last caress to the young man who was brash enough to confront Da Monson.

As dawn was breaking over Segou, the canoe pulled into the port. Ten leaped out with her prizes and ran to give them directly to Da Monson. Da called the wise man and gave him the objects he had requested. After working a night and a day on them, the wise man discovered the sacrifices and potions that would allow Da Monson's army to break Samanyana Basi's magic charms and defeat him.

Da Monson sent two battalions to attack Samanyana. After one day of siege, they broke through the defenses, scattered Basi's soldiers, and razed the town. Basi, stripped of his magical protection, was just another man, helpless before Da Monson's power. He was captured and summarily beheaded.

There you see the deeds of Ten. By her beauty and her wiles, she helped build the empire of one king and destroy that of another.

A woman can be a beautiful thing, but she can also be evil. What is honey to one man may be poison to another.

May Allah protect us from them and send us only the good ones.

[From *African Folklore*, pp. 457–67.]

Australia and Oceania

AUSTRALIA—HOW WOMEN LOST SACRED POWER

The following myth is the basis for the important Djanggawul cult of north-eastern and north-central Arnhem Land. Ronald M. Berndt recorded the myth during his field work in the late 1940s. According to the myth, among the ancient ancestors it was women who first had the sacred implements and sacred songs, consequently they had sacred power until it was stolen by the men. Their exaggerated sexual organs symbolize their supernatural fertility, for they populate the land with people as they travel, as well as the eventual need for clitoridectomies and circumcision.

There were three of them: Djanggawul himself, his elder Sister, Bildjiwuraroiju, and his younger Sister, Miralaidj. With them, too, was another man, named Bralbral. The Two Sisters and their Brother, however, were nearly always known as the Djanggawul. Djanggawul himself had an elongated penis, and each of the Two Sisters had a long clitoris; these were so long that they dragged upon the ground as they walked.

* * *

At Bralgu, as they walked around with these, they left grooves in the ground from their dragging. And when the Djanggawul Brother had coitus with his Sisters, he lifted aside their clitorises, entering them in the usual way. He was able to have incestuous relations with his Sisters, because at that time there were no marriage rules, no moieties, and no prohibitions. Djanggawul was the lawmaker. There is, however, no mention of Bralbral's having sexual relations with the Two Women. Djanggawul had been having coitus with Bildjiwuraroiju for a long time; her breasts had grown large and 'fallen down' with milk, and she had produced many children. Miralaidj, though, was quite young, having just passed puberty, and her breasts were rounded and firm.

They lived at Bralgu for some little time, putting people there, and leaving 'Dreamings' in the form of totemic designs, sacred emblems and body painting. They also instituted their rituals and ceremonies. The Brother's penis and the Sister's clitorises were sacred emblems, like *ranggsa* poles.

At last they made ready their bark canoe, and loaded it with 'Dreamings', sacred drawings and emblems; the latter were kept in a conically-shaped *ngainmara* mat. When all this was ready they themselves, with their companion Bralbral, climbed into the canoe. Then they paddled out to sea, leaving the island of Bralgu far behind. For days and days they paddled, until they sighted the Arnhem Land mainland. At last

they came to it, landing near Rose River. But they soon left this part of the country, and continued paddling along the coast until they reached Jelangbara, Port Bradshaw.

* * *

Then they dragged their canoe on to the beach and unloaded it, making this a sacred place. Jelangbara is the largest Djanggawul centre in north-eastern Arnhem Land and, today, the most important.

Here the Djanggawul Brother wished to shorten his Sister's clitorises. But the elder Sister said, 'No, wait till we reach Arnhem Bay. We can have a good rest, and put Dreamings there.' So they walked around, still dragging the clitorises and elongated penis, leaving marks on the ground which may be seen to-day.

* * *

Continuing on, the Djanggawul reached Nganmaruwi, where they erected another large 'shade'. During all the time they had been on the Australian mainland, there is no mention of the Brother's having coitus with his Sisters; but while they were living here, he said to Bildjiwuraroiju, 'I want to copulate with you, Sister.'

But the elder Sister was shy. 'Why?' she asked him.

'I want to put a few people in this place,' the Brother replied.

So he lifted her clitoris, and inserted his long penis. He did the same with Miralaidj. So they continued living there, and he copulated as a husband does with his wives.

After some time, Bildjiwuraroiju became pregnant, and her Brother said to her, 'Sister, may I have a look at you?'

'What for?' she asked.

'Because I want to put some people in this place.'

'All right,' she replied. She opened her legs a little,

resting her clitoris on her left leg. The Brother sat before his Sister and placed his index finger into her vagina, up to the first joint. Then he pulled it away, and at the same time a baby boy came out. Bildjiwu-raroiju was careful to open her legs only a little; if she had spread them out, children would have flowed from her, for she kept many people stored away in her uterus. These people (or children) in her uterus were like *rangga* emblems kept in the conical-shaped *ngainmara* mat, for the latter is a uterus symbol.

As the baby boy came out, the Brother stood listening to hear the sound of his cry. As soon as he heard this, he took hold of the child and put him on to the grass near by. Then he returned to his Sister, and saw a baby girl coming out. After she had cried, he lifted her gently and placed her under the *ngainmara* mat, which served to shelter her from the sun. The crying of a male child is *rirakai'dugung,* a forceful 'heavy' sound; while that of a girl is *rirakai njumulgunin,* a 'small' sound."

Then another male child issued from the elder Sister, and was put into the grass by the Brother. She continued giving birth to children of both sexes; when she had finished she closed her legs, and the Djanggawul Brother said to her:

'Sister, these little boys we will put in the grass, so that later, when they grow up, they will have whiskers; those whiskers are from the grass. We will always do that when we remove male children. And these little girls we have put under the *ngainmara* mat, hiding them there. That is because they must be smooth and soft and have no body hair, and because girls are really sacred. They must be kept under the *ngainmara,* just as the *rangga* emblems are kept. We will always do that when we remove female children.'

* * *

While they were living there, the elder Sister said one day to the younger, 'We had better put our dilly bags in this shade, and leave them here for a while.'
'What are we going to do?' asked the other. 'If we put them here, what then are we going to do?'
'Well,' replied the elder Sister, 'we can look around for mangrove shells.'
So they both left their camp to collect *mingaul* and *waluwon* shells. While they were away, the Djanggawul Brother and his companions, men who had come out of the Sisters, but called the Djanggawul 'brother' and 'sisters', were hiding in their big shade. In the myth, these are called the Djanggawul Brothers. The women who came out of the Sisters are assumed to have gone out foraging for food in another direction.
Meantime, the Two Sisters had collected a lot of

shells. When they waded back to dry land, they heard the whistle of the *djunmal* bird (a black, green and yellow mangrove bird), warning them that something was wrong. At once they knew that something had happened to their dilly bags, which contained the sacred *rangga.*
'You know that *djunmal,* Sister,' the younger Sister asked. 'What is it crying for?'
'That bird cries to let us know,' answered the other. 'Perhaps something has happened to our sacred dilly bags. Maybe the fire has burnt them. We had better go back and look.'
They left what they were doing, and ran back towards their shade. The dilly bags were gone, and on the ground about the shade were the tracks of the men who had stolen them.
'Sister, look!' called the younger Sister. 'What are we going to do now? Where are our dilly bags?'
'We had better go down and ask the men,' said the other, 'it's nothing to do with them.'
They hurried off, down towards the men. As they came running, the Djanggawul Brother and his companions looked up from their shade and saw them.
'What shall we do?' thought the Brother. He picked up his *jugulung* singing sticks, and began to beat rhythmically upon them, while they all sang.
As soon as the Sisters heard the beat of the singing sticks, and the sound of the men's singing, they fell down and began to crawl along the ground. They were too 'frightened' to go near that dreaming place, the shade of the Djanggawul Brother. They were fearful not of the men, but of the power of the sacred songs. The men had taken from them not only these songs, and the emblems, but also the power to perform sacred ritual, a power which had formerly belonged only to the Sisters. They had carried the emblems and dreamings in their *ngainmara,* which were really their uteri; and the men had had nothing.
The Two Sisters got up from the ground, and the younger one said to the elder, 'What are we going to do? All our dilly bags are gone, all the emblems, all our power for sacred ritual!
But the other replied, 'I think we can leave that. Men can do it now, they can look after it. We can spend our time collecting bush foods for them, for it is not right that they should get that food as they have been doing. We know everything. We have really lost nothing, for we remember it all, and we can let them have that small part. For aren't we still sacred, even if we have lost the bags? Haven't we still our uteri?' And the younger Sister agreed with her.
In this way, the Two Sisters left all their dreamings at that place. They put a lot of people there too, while the Djanggawul Brother and his companions sang songs and performed ritual of the *dua nara* ceremonies.
[From *Djanggawul,* pp. 24–41.]

NEW ZEALAND—IHUNUI'S LAMENT FOR HER DAUGHTER RANGI

The following song was composed sometime in the sixteenth century by a Maori women of New Zealand.

Ihunui's Lament for Her Daughter Rangi

Oppressed am I with omens and their signs,
Perturbing to my mind.
Who indeed are you who thus afflicts me?
Causing with warning vague and formless fear
This restlessness within me?
And was it you, indeed, O cherished one,—
Who would have thought that you would go, O
    Rangi!
Weariness my body bends, as I,
Here, in Puhirangi sit
Looking lornly forth on Hine-moana
Surging unrestrainedly beyond the headlands.

But you have gone, borne on the ocean stream
To distant Tawhiti-nui, to Tawhiti-pamamao,
To Te Hono-i-wairua on Irihia.
Fare safely on, and enter Hawaiki-rangi;
Seize as it passes that uplifting wind
Upon which Tane of old ascended
To Tikitiki-o-rangi.
That you too may enter Te Rauroha,
To be welcomed by spirit maids in Rangiatea;
There shall remembrance of this world cease,
O maid,—Alas!

[From *Games and Pasttimes of the Maori*, pp. 110–11.]

NEW GUINEA—BROTHER AND SISTER

The following tale was collected by John LeRoy from the Kewa off the southern Highlands Province of Papua, New Guinea. It shows the affectionate relations that can exist between a brother and sister, although there is conflict about her nudity.

Limu and his sister lived together, working in their food gardens. Since the young woman was of marriageable age, once in a while men would come with valuables and offer to take her in marriage. When they came with their shells and pigs, Limu would say to his sister, "Now that men are coming, go to the garden and fetch some sweet potatoes and *padi* greens." She would do so. But later, while Limu and the men were discussing the bridewealth, she would return without her skirt. This made Limu deeply ashamed. He would go to her quickly, hoping others had not seen her, and tell her to put the skirt back on.

Again and again this would happen. Men from many parts had heard that the young woman was ready to marry, and they came to make bridewealth offers. But the sister would always appear naked. Sometimes Limu himself had to go and knot the skirt around her.

One day some men from Erave came with shells. Limu, thinking that his sister's skirt was perhaps poorly made or falling apart, had himself made a new, strong one for her. When the men approached with their shells, he once again told his sister to fetch some food from the garden while he shared some bananas

and sugar cane with the guests. Presently he looked up and saw his sister returning from the garden. Once again she was naked. Limu took the skirt he had made and tied it on her tightly.

When the food was cooked, the siblings and the suitors ate their meal and talked. In the afternoon, when the men were about to return to their home, the sister was again without her skirt. Those men had agreed to give shells and pigs for her, but when they saw this, they gathered up their valuables and departed, as had all the others before them.

Limu, both ashamed and angry, struck his sister on the head and went into the house to sit by the fire.

The woman did not join him there. She went to one side of the house and then away. He did not bother to find out where she might have gone. He did not care, for he had many clansmen there, as many as there are here in Karapere, and he had his dogs, too. So he would stay without her.

But one day sometime later he sat and thought about her, "Ah, this sister of mine, she has gone off someplace and is lost. I must find her," he said to himself. So he took his dogs and set off. First he went to the forest at Apirawalu and hunted possums. From there he went to Karanda, over to Mount Kata, then to the forest at Alamu. In a dense part of that forest he came across a clearing where the daylight penetrated to the forest floor. Trees were lying toppled in different directions, and visible between them were the leaves of food crops. Many sorts of crops grew there in luxuriance—bananas, sugar cane, and taro of the good *binale* variety. Limu tied his dogs and approached quietly to the edge of the garden.

In the middle he saw a young, good looking woman with long hair down to her shoulders, wearing a white skirt. She was busy mounding the soil and planting sweet potato runners. Limu, somewhat fearful, hesitated to go further. Deciding to return home, he took a step backwards. But as he did so, he stepped on a dry branch underfoot. It cracked. "Hey!" the woman called out. "Who's there? Are you someone from a village (*ada ali*) or from the forest (*ra ali*)?" Limu, recognizing his sister's voice, replied, "I am someone from the village."

When she heard his voice, the young woman knew it to be her brother's. But she said only, "All right, come forth if you are really a man of the village." Limu did so, and the two wept because of the sympathy (*yara*) they had for one another.

Then the sister told him, "I have everything I want here except for one thing that I hunger for. Do you still go the forest with your dogs?"

"Yes, I came hunting with them," replied Limu, and he showed her the bag of possums he had left by the edge of the garden. In an earth oven the siblings cooked the meat, with *kuni* greens of the good *palasu* kind and with *binale* taro.

Then the sister said, "I grow many good foods in the gardens, but I do not eat possums or pork. You must continue to kill and cook these for me." So Limu went to kill more possums for her in the forest around the garden, telling her to keep them to cook later.

"Return now," she said, "but first I will give you something to take with you." And she handed him a couple of large pigs, two netbags full of pearl shells, a bushknife, and an axe.

When Limu was about to depart, the woman gave him some advice. "All these things I have given you. In return you must return with more pork for me. Do not bring me fat, however, only the lean meat. Moreover, when you come here, do not do so along the main paths; but take the path I took when I fled from your house after you struck me. Near the edge of your house stands a tall *waria* tree with a mounded base; there you will see my footprints still. Now I am giving you this payment (*pe*). Use these things to marry. Take two wives. One must be from Ialibu land, and one from Erave. Do not take a Palea (Wiru) wife." Limu assented to all this and then departed for home.

First he married an Ialibu woman. Later he was about to marry an Erave wife, but a Palea woman came to stay in his house. She stayed with him even though he offered no payment for her. Limu wondered why she had come. Her presence worried him, for he remembered what his sister had said.

His clan brothers were concerned as well. "Why do you not marry that Erave woman, as your sister told you to do? Even though this woman has come, you must take an Erave wife as well." Limu tried to send this woman off, but she stayed.

On the occasions when people were killing pigs and distributing their meat, he would give much pork to his Ialibu wife, but to this Palea woman, who had come on her own, he gave only a few poor pieces. Then he would set off in secret and give lean meat to his sister. The pieces of fat he always gave to his two wives, the one from Ialibu and the one from Palea land. When he returned from his visits to his sister, Limu would always come back with pigs and shells she had given him.

The Palea wife wondered why she was always given pork fat. Now one day Limu went to where they were killing pigs down in Batire, leaving his two wives to stay at home. While he was away his Palea wife, still desirous of understanding why she received no good meat, went over to Limu's brothers' house.

"When Limu comes and gives you pork, does he give you flesh as well, and meat on the bone?" she inquired.

"No," they replied, "he gives us only fat. See, we are getting *rani* greens ready to cook the fat he will give us when he returns." She heard this, thought for a while, and then went around to the other entrance of the men's house. She asked the other men there, and received the same response. Limu had told her he had to give all the good meat to these clansmen, but now these men told her they received the same as she did, just the fat.

She heard what they said, returned to the house, and then set off along the little-used path that Limu took from the mounded base of the *waria* tree.

On and on she went. To one side of the path she saw an *opo* tree, whose strong wood is used for making digging sticks. Cutting a short length of it, she made a pointed dagger which she hid in her netbag.

Presently she arrived at a forest garden in which grew abundant plantains and sugar cane. In it she saw a long-haired young woman. "Are you Limu's sister?" she asked.

"Yes," replied the other.

"Limu comes here to you, does he?"

The sister heard her accent and thought, "Ah, this is a Palea woman he has married!" and she was troubled. But she asked only. "Why have you come? Do you want to take shells and pigs home?"

"No, I have not come for that," said the Palea woman, looking gravely at her. The two sat. After a short silence, the Palea woman said, "I will pick the lice from your hair, lest your long hair be spoiled." She sat behind the sister, as one does to look for nits. Drawing her *opo* stake from her netbag, she stabbed the other woman in the back, into the kidney, then rose and quickly departed. The sister crawled to the porch of her house, where she lay on her side and murmured, "Only when I have seen my brother shall I die."

Limu returned from the pig kill carrying pork. He saw that his Ialibu wife had brought piles of vegetables to be cooked with the pork, but that the Palea woman was just sitting looking preoccupied. She had not brought food. Limu was troubled. Perceiving his worry, the Ialibu wife whispered to him, "She has been off someplace and has returned just now." Limu thought for a while and told the Ialibu woman to take care of everything; she could cook all the pork and share it out as she wished. "I am sick," he said, "and want to lie down inside the house."

But while the two women were busy preparing the earth oven, he stole out of the house and went quickly along the path that led from the *waria* tree, taking with him some lean meat on the bone.

Presently he came to his sister's house. As he drew close, he noticed flies buzzing around him. Then he saw his sister's body covered with flies. Peering into her half-closed eyes, he saw she was still alive.

"What happened?" he asked her.

"That Palea woman has killed me, the woman I told you not to marry," she replied. "I offered her pigs and shells, the way I did to you. But she didn't want any, and she killed me. Did you wish I should die, that you broke your word and married her?" She said no more.

Limu was grieved. He carried his sister to a place in the forest where rats make their burrows. In that soft earth he dug a deep hole with a piece of *opo* wood. He placed her in the pit, threw dead leaves and twigs on top, and then covered her with earth. That done, he walked slowly back home and lay down inside the house. All this time, the two wives continued to cook the pork. He told them they could give the meat away, for he was still sick. But he sat up, mourning for his sister, his eyes filled with tears.

Then one day he decided to put an end to his mourning and killed a pig. He cooked it and gave out the meat, but ate none himself. After that he lived normally, working in the garden and doing other business.

But he had not forgotten. One day he took out a stone scraper and prepared bamboo-tipped arrows. He took his axe to the sharpening stone in Yopene Stream and honed down the blade's edge. Then he told his two wives, "Since I didn't eat any of that pig, I'm hungry to eat meat. Let's go and kill some rats in the forest."

The Ialibu woman replied, "You know I'm no good at catching rats." The Palea woman, however, agreed to go.

So the two went. Limu led her toward that place where he had buried his sister, and there the woman exclaimed, "Ah, there are rats here; see the burrows!"

He told her to dig for them, and he went and fetched the *opo* stick he had left, saying, "Look, other women have come here to dig for rats. Use this!" She found many rats, digging deeper and deeper.

Then Limu said, "I'll go and stand with my bow and arrow at the ready, lest our enemies surprise us here. Dig quickly and we shall go back." He stood back while she dug down through the loose earth.

Finally she thrust her hand into a rat burrow and suddenly jerked it back.

"Dig on," Limu told her. She uncovered part of the sister's body and recoiled, crying out, "Oh no!"

Limu said, "All right, why did you kill her?" The woman did not answer. "You came to eat, now go ahead and do so," he said, indicating the body. He fitted a *kane* arrow to his bowstring and took aim.

So the woman began to eat, and she ate and ate. Presently her stomach could distend no more; she had eaten all she could. Then Limu shot and killed her.

He took his *wiruapu* bow and broke it in two, stuck the pieces into his rear, and flew off as a *walawe* lorikeet.

His Ialibu wife waited for a long time for the two to return. When they did not, she got many pigs and shells and put them inside the house. Then she burned the house down, and she was consumed as well. She became a *mumakarubi* quail. She had thought, "There's no one to stay with now," so she set fire to herself and all their possessions. The grass grew over the burnt house site, and in such places we sometimes now see these *mumakarubi* quail.

The brother had made *ali kalia* compensation for the death of his sister by killing the Palea woman. We still observe this custom.

[From *Kewa Tales*, pp. 41–46.]

CAROLINE ISLANDS—A MOTHER'S LAMENT FOR HER SON

We all lived together here
Beside the channel between the islands—

I am worn and weary
All through my body.

It is like a fire burning inside me,
A sickness that rises into my head,
A soreness all over me
That wears me down.
Every bit of me is weary.
I picked up my little boy when he was sick;
He said, "Good-bye, I think I must die tonight."
His brother, whose name is like his,
Is here with me still.
They used to play together.
If only both could be here now!
When I see the one, I think of the other;
It nearly drives me mad!
I walk about like a crazy woman.
This house where we all used to live
Reminds me of him too.

If people could see inside me,
If they could know how worn out I am.
People come and go, but I think only of him.
I think I will gird the place about
With coconut leaves for a taboo sign,
So they will not come here all the time,
Stepping in his footprints.
I am always thinking of him.
If only he could come back
And be close beside me, as he used to!

I will go and lie inside his body,
Go down in the sea where they buried him,
And stay with him there.
[From *Flower in My Ear,* pp. 140–45.]

FIJI—THE GODDESS ADI MAILAGU

The following tale is about the complex goddess, Adi Mailagu, sometimes called Adi Mailagi, who is sometimes a beautiful maiden, sometimes an old woman, and sometimes a rat. She takes life, and she is also an oracle.

The Lady of the Sky

The men of Uruone were planting the dalo in the water-terraces when they heard a noise in the sky which sounded as though some object were rushing towards them. They looked up and saw a dark speck which grew larger and larger as it approached. When it was overhead they could see that the strange creature was a goddess. She fell from the sky in front of them, right into the Na Kele Kele stream. The water surged over the bank, and as it began to run back into the bed of the stream, a large grey rat climbed out and ran along the path that leads to Daku.

"It is Adi Mailagi," someone exclaimed, "The Lady of the Sky has come to make her home with us."

They looked at one another fearfully, wondering what would happen next. The rat had disappeared, and there was nothing left to do but to finish their work and return home.

The following day word was brought to the village that the rat had been seen, and had spoken to men at Udu. Shortly afterwards strange stories began to circulate, which proved that a goddess had indeed come to live among men, and that she had an evil spirit. She took many forms; sometimes she showed herself as a beautiful young woman, at others as a withered repulsive old crone, and again as a grey rat. She made her home in an ivi tree, and woe betide anyone if he made a noise as he passed the place.

Soon children began to fall sick, and it was discovered that Adi Mailagi had stolen their shadows, putting them in her palmleaf basket and carrying them away. We know this is true because some of the shadows escaped and came back to their owners; but if they did not return the children died.

The greatest danger came to the young men of the tribe. To them Adi Mailagi appeared as a young woman of beauty so ravishing that they left their houses and gave themselves up to her embraces. After that she would leave them, and they would wander about in a daze, with no thought except of the goddess. Eventually they would be taken sick, and lie on their mats until she came to them and gathered up their souls, like a fisherman catching fish with a net.

It was only the most handsome men whom she afflicted. To women, and to men who did not appeal to her, she appeared as an old hag, dirty and unkempt. Occasionally she injured them, if she was in a spiteful mood.

On one occasion the men of Uruone were bringing a large drum which they had made from the wood of the vesi tree from Daku to their home at Udu. It was heavy, so when in the late afternoon, they reached a place where the path climbed over a steep hill, they decided to leave it there and return for it in the morning. Shortly after they had left, a young woman happened to go past, and noticed the drum sitting on the ground with the drumsticks beside it. She picked up the sticks and beat the drum, listening admiringly to the sound as it rolled across the valley. Adi Mailagi sprang out of a nearby tree and pushed her down so fiercely that her leg was broken.

It was well for Gulia Meli that the goddess had not taken a liking to her. Many tales are told of those whose spirits she captured; many are the stories of those who escaped from her. There was Tui Merike who was riding on his donkey at dusk near Uruone when the goddess appeared from behind a tree and pounced on him, shouting, "Where are you going?"

The poor beast was trembling with fear and Tui Merike knew he was in the presence of Adi Mailagi. He urged his donkey and galloped down the path with the hag close at their heels. Over hill and valley they flew until he came to Mualevu, where she left him, calling after him, "You have escaped, Tui Merike, but it is only because of your speed."

Again, another man came round a bend in the road and surprised the goddess. She was in the form of an old woman, sitting on the ground, while from her mouth her red tongue lay across her knees and trailed on the ground. The man was on her before he realised she was there. For a moment he was petrified as he saw her tongue coil itself up like a snake and dis-appear into her mouth. She shrieked and dived into the water, emerging later at a considerable distance.

It was necessary to appease this goddess. The priests carried wood to the ivi tree where she had made her abode, and made a fire. When the goddess smelled the smoke she emerged as a rat. She jumped across to the branches of a nearby makosoi tree and sat down, answering questions which the priests put to her. Afterwards she descended to the ground, where she allowed the priests to rub her fur until it glistened, and to feed her with tit-bits. The rat goddess became the oracle of the tribe, and would warn them when one of their principal men was about to die.

It was in her manifestations as a woman that Adi Mailagi did so much harm. No one could touch the goddess, whether she appeared as a beautiful young woman or an ugly hag, but in the rat form she was more vulnerable.

It was in modern days that Tui Uruone went with his young men and cut down both the ivi and the makosoi tree; but Adi Mailagu escaped, and it was Tui Uruone who died.

Where is she now? Who can tell? But beware the young woman who comes to embrace you at night, for she will imperil your soul.

[From *Myths and Legends of Fiji*, pp. 48–50.]

HAWAII—THE GODDESS PELE

The following myth tells of the great Hawaiian goddess of fire, Pele. Pele sleeps and dreams of a lover, so the story occurs in both mythic and dream time. This myth is also interesting because of the aggressive role Pele takes in their relationship and for the terms she sets. The myth was recorded by Nathaniel B. Emerson in the first decade of this century.

In her sleep Pele heard the far-off beating of hula drums, and her spirit-body pursued the sound. At first it seemed to come from some point far out to sea; but as she followed, it shifted, moving to the north, till it seemed to be off the beach of Waiakea, in Hilo; thence it moved till it was opposite Lau-pahoehoe. Still evading her pursuit, the sound retreated till it came from the boisterous ocean that beats against the shaggy cliffs of Hamakua. Still going north, it seemed presently to have reached the mid channel of Ale-nui-haha that tosses between Hawaii and Maui.

"If you are from my far-off home-land Kahiki, I will follow you thither, but I will come up with you," said Pele.

To her detective ear, as she flitted across the heaving waters of Ale-nui-haha, the pulsing of the drums now located itself at the famous hill Kauwiki, in Hana; but, on reaching that place, the music had passed on to the west and sounded from the cliffs of Ka-haku-loa.

The fugitive music led her next across another channel, until in her flight she had traversed the length of Moloka'i and had come to the western point of that island, Lae-o-ka-laau. Thence she flew to cape Maka-pu'u, on Oahu, and so on, until, after crossing that island, she reached cape Kaena, whose fingerpoint reaches out towards Kaua'i. In that desolate spot dwelt an aged creature of myth, Pohaku-o-Kaua'i by name, the personal representative of that rock whose body-form the hero Mawi had jerked from its ocean bed ages before, in his futile attempt to draw together the two islands Kaua'i and Oahu and unite them into one mass.

Pele, arguing from her exasperation, said, "It must

be my old grandfather Pohaku-o-Kaua'i who is play-ing this trick with the music. If it's he that's leading me this chase, I'll kill him."

The old fellow saw her approach and, hailing her from a distance, greeted her most heartily. Her answer was in a surly mood: "Come here! I'm going to kill you to-day. So it's you that's been fooling me with deceitful music, leading me a wearisome chase."

"Not I, I've not done this. There they are, out to sea; you can hear for yourself." And, sure enough, on listening, one could hear the throbbing of the music in the offing.

Pele acknowledged her mistake and continued her pursuit, with the parting assurance to the old soul that if he had been the guilty one, it would have been his last day of life.

The real authors of this illusive musical per-formance were two little creatures named Kani-ka-wí and Kani-ka-wá, the former a sprite that was em-bodied in the nose-flute, the latter in the hokeo, a kind of whistle, both of them used as accompaniments to the hula. Their sly purpose was to lure Pele to a place where the hula was being performed.

Pele now plunged into the water—from this point at least she swam—and, guided by the call of the music, directed her course to the little village of Haena that perched like a gull on the cape of the same name, at the northernmost point of the island of Kaua'i. It was but a few steps to the hall of the hula—the *halau*—where throbbed the hula drums and where was a concourse of people gathered from the whole island.

As Pele drew near to the rustic hall where the hula was in full blast, the people in the outskirts of the assembly turned to look in wonder and admiration at the beauty and charm of the stranger who had ap-peared so unexpectedly and whose person exhaled such a fragrance, as if she had been clad with sweet-scented garlands of maile, lehua and hala. One and all declared her to be the most beautiful woman they had ever looked upon. Where was she from? Surely not from Kaua'i. Such loveliness could not have re-mained hidden in any nook or corner of the island, they declared.

Instinctively the wondering multitude parted and offered a lane for her to pass through and enter the halau, thus granting to Pele a full view of the musi-cians and performers of the hula, and, sitting in their midst, Lohiau,—as yet seemingly unconscious of her presence,—on his either hand a fellow drummer; while, flanking these to right and left, sat players with a joint of bamboo in either hand (the kaekeeke). But drummer and kaekeeke-player, musicians and actors—aye, the whole audience—became petrified and silent at the sight of Pele, as she advanced step by step, her eyes fixed on Lohiau.

Then, with intensified look, as if summoning to her aid the godlike gifts that were hers as the mistress of Kilauea, she reached out her hand and, in a clear tone, with a mastery that held the listeners spell-bound, she chanted:

* * *

Tight-pressed is Hanalei's throng,
A tree bent down by heavy rain,
Weighted with drops from the clouds,
When rain columns sweep through Manu'a-kepa,
This throng that has lured on the stranger,
Nigh to downfall, to downfall, was I,
Laid flat by your trick—aye yours!
My quest was for comfort and life,
Just for comfort and life!

The silence became oppressive. In the stillness that followed the song expectant eyes were focused upon Prince Lohiau, awaiting his reply to the address of the stranger who stood in their midst. No one knew who she was; no one imagined her to be Pele. That she was a person of distinction and rank was evident enough, one whom it was the duty and rare privilege of their chief to receive and entertain.

Presently there was wrinkling of foreheads, an exchange of glances, prompting winks and nods, in-clinations of the head, a turning of the eyes—though not a word was spoken—; for his friends thought thus to rouse Lohiau from his daze and to prompt him to the dutiful rites of hospitality and gallantry. Paoa, his intimate friend, sitting at Lohiau's right hand, with a drum between his knees, even ventured to nudge him in the side.

The silence was broken by Pele:

* * *

Bristling, frumpy, sits Hilo,
Drenched by the pouring rain,
Forbidden to murmur,
Or put forth a sound,
Or make utt'rance by speech:
Must all remain breathless,
Nor heave an audible sigh,
Withholding the nod, the wink,
And the glance to one side.
I pray you behold me now:—
Here stand I, your guest,
Your companion, your mate!

Lohiau, once roused from his ecstasy, rose to the occasion and with the utmost gallantry and politeness invited Pele to sit with him and partake of the hospi-talities of the halau.

When Pele had seated herself on the mat-piled dais, Lohiau, following the etiquette of the country, ask-ed whence she came.

"I am of Kaua'i," she answered.

"There is no woman of Kaua'i your equal in beauty," said Lohiau. "I am the chief and I know, for I visit every part of the whole island."

"You have doubtless traveled about the whole island," answered Pele; "yet there remain places you are not acquainted with; and that is where I come from."

"No, no! you are not of Kaua'i. Where *are* you from?"

Because of his importunity, Pele answered him, "I am from Puna, from the land of the sunrise; from Ha'eha'e, the eastern gate of the sun."

Lohiau bade that they spread the tables for a feast, and he invited Pele to sit with him and partake of the food. But Pele refused food, saying, "I have eaten."

"How can that be?" said he, "seeing you have but now come from a long journey? You had better sit down and eat."

Pele sat with him, but she persistently declined all his offers of food, "I am not hungry."

Lohiau sat at the feast, but he could not eat; his mind was disturbed; his eyes were upon the woman at his side. When they rose from the table he led her, not unwilling, to his house, and he lay down upon a couch by her side. But she would favor him only with kisses. In his growing passion for her he forgot his need of food, his fondness for the hula, the obliga-tions that rested upon him as a host: all these were driven from his head.

All that night and the following day, and another night, and for three days and three nights, he lay at her side, struggling with her, striving to overcome her resistance. But she would grant him only kisses.

And, on the third night, as it came towards morning, Pele said to Lohiau, "I am about to return to my place, to Puna, the land of the sunrise. You shall stay here. I will prepare a habitation for us, and, when all is ready I will send and fetch you to myself. If it is a man who comes, you must not go with him; but, if a woman, you are to go with the woman. Then, for five days and five nights you and I will take our fill of pleasure. After that you will be free to go with another woman."

In his madness, Lohiau put forth his best efforts to overcome Pele's resistance, but she would not permit him. "When we meet on Hawaii you shall enjoy me to your fill," said she. He struggled with her, but she foiled him and bit him in the hand to the quick; and he grasped the wound with the other hand to staunch the pain. And he, in turn, in the fierceness of his passion, planted his teeth in her body.

At this, Pele fluttered forth from the house, plunged into the ocean and—was gone.

[From *Pele and Hiiaka,* pp. 3–8.]

HAWAII—A MAGICAL ANCESTRESS

The following is the story of the original ancestress of one Hawaiian family, a magical child who can predict the future. It was told to Laura S. Green by an old woman of the family in the early years of this century.

At the birth of Ke-ahi-a-loa, or "Eternal-fire," she was adopted by her mother's own older sister. When she was seven years old, her adopted mother took her from Hawaii, the land of her birth, to live in Kauai.

After their arrival, the mother was drawn into immoral pleasures and soon gave no thought to the child. She was allowed to wander hungry until her body became weak and emaciated and her eyes like the drawn threads of a spider-web.

One night she crawled to the sweet-potato patch owned by an aged couple and nibbled those potatoes which she could reach. And because of the long road she had traveled, she soon fell asleep.

When the old woman came the next morning to dig the potatoes and found small bits that had been chewed, she thought the garden must have been invaded by a turtle and she called to her husband, "Come, old man, let us hunt for this turtle that has been eating our potatoes!" In their search they found Eternal-fire asleep and great was their joy, for they had no children. They took her home and named her "Turtle."

As the child grew older, it was evident that she possessed gifts of magic and could foretell to her foster-parents events that were to happen. Often she visited the mountain-side and never returned without being adorned with such plants as the sweet-scented *mai-le,* the scarlet *le-hu-a,* and the royal *moki-hana.* Among her favorite pastimes was that of coasting on a grassy hill-slope with the young people of that country.

One day Ke-ahi-a-loa turned to her foster-parents and said, "Listen, grandparents! you have worked hard for me and now that I see I am a woman it is right that I should work for you. If you will listen to my counsel, we shall live like chiefs in the land.

Tomorrow let us go to the mountain for *taro* and *awa*, after that to the sea-shore for every delicacy of the ocean. A stranger is coming who will make me his wife."

Before the dawn of day they ascended the mountain to pull *taro* and *awa* root, and reached home before noon. As day was declining the *taro* was cooked and pounded. Near dark they went to the beach, where they very soon had secured all the fish they desired. When all was in readiness the girl said, "Let us now sleep and in the early morning my stranger will arrive."

Sure enough, at daybreak a stranger made his appearance, the son of the land agent, who had been inspecting the fish-ponds belonging to the chief and in the darkness had wandered out of the path. As it grew light he had tried to find the way which led to the residents of the place, but instead had reached the house of the old couple shivering with cold and half famished.

The old people welcomed the stranger and their daughter prepared food for him. When the youth's hunger was appeased he asked the old people, "Say! is this your daughter?"—"Yes, she is ours."—"I should like her to become my wife; what would you think of it?"—"Oh! we are not the ones to marry you; ask her!"

The girl at once assented to his proposal. When noon-time came, he went to tell his parents that he had found a wife. They immediately began to prepare a new grass house, mats, bark cloth for bed coverings and clothing, and other things necessary for the young people, planning in ten days to go and fetch her.

About this time, while Eternal-fire was living on Kauai in this manner, a certain man came to the home of her own parents on Hawaii and told how the mother's sister had neglected the child and how one day she had wandered off and been lost. Hearing all this, the father beat his wife cruelly and scolded her well, saying, "It was not I who gave my daughter away; it was because of your obstinacy that my only garland was given to your older sister. I told you how it would be. You must now make forty fine mats, forty coarse mats and forty sheets of bark cloth, and if you do not finish them within ten days I will beat you again so as to hurt you badly!"

Sympathetic relatives collectively labored to achieve this task, and before the time appointed everything was ready. The parents at once boarded a canoe and started for Kauai. During the passage, the father dreamed that his guardian spirit came to him in the form of a shark and said, "Listen! proceed on your way and I will be with you. You shall not weary

yourself with search for the child, for I will lead you to her. The house upon which you see a rainbow resting, that is where our garland dwells." So he arose from sleep full of hope that he would again behold his beloved child.

* * *

Ke-ahi-a-loa gazed over the ocean and said, "Today there will come to our marriage the land-agent, his wife, their son, and all their people. And also today will arrive my own parents from Hawaii. When a rainbow cloud stretches from our house to the ocean, we shall see them landing from the canoe. This booth here is prepared for the land-agent, that over there for my parents."

When the sun was in mid-heaven, the land-agent and his family arrived bearing many gifts. As they were seated, a rainbow cloud like smoke glowed above the ridge-pole of the house and soon after the parents of the girl stood before them. Then, as the father beheld his one garland, he wept aloud declaring his love for his child:

"Alas! my garland! my flower!
You were brought hither to this land of strangers
    to be treated cruelly,
To wander like a homeless cloud!
O Ke-ahi-a-loa, listen!
O my daughter, you who have evaded much
    suffering!"

Now this was the first intimation the old couple had had that Ke-ahi-a-loa, that is, "Eternal-fire," was the name of their foster-child and that she was descended from chiefs. They had never called her anything but "Turtle."

The land-agent too stood and wondered whether the parents might not forbid the marriage of the young people; but when Eternal-fire had explained how kindly she had been cared for by the old couple and how because of her great love for them she had consented to become the daughter-in-law of the land-agent, the parents readily consented and they were wedded that very day.

At the close of the feast, Eternal-fire arose and pronounced this edict concerning her future offspring for all time; namely, that children of a younger brother or sister should not be given in adoption to an older brother or sister, lest they die, but only an older brother's or sister's child to a younger, that they might prosper. Hence the descendants of Ke-ahi-a-loa have kept this command of their ancestress until this day.

[From *Folk-tales from Hawaii*, pp. 71–86.]

Sources

African Folklore, by Richard M. Dorson. Bloomington, IN: Indiana University Press, 1972.

The Book of Counsel: The Popul Vuh of the Quiche Maya of Guatemala, by Munro S. Edmonson. New Orleans, LA: Middle American Research Institute, Tulane University, 1971.

Book of the Hopi, by Frank Waters. New York: Ballantine Books, 1969.

Ch'u Tz'ŭ: The Songs of the South: An Ancient Chinese Anthology, by David Hawkes. Oxford: Clarendon Press, 1959.

Conversations with Ogotemmêli: An Introduction to Dogon Religious Ideas, by Marcel Griaule. Oxford: Oxford University Press, 1965.

Djanggawul: An Aboriginal Religious Cult of North-Eastern Arnhem Land by Ronald M. Berndt. London: Routledge & Kegan Paul, 1953.

Flower in My Ear: Arts and Ethos of Ifaluk Atoll, by Edwin Grant Burrows. Seattle: University of Washington Press, 1963.

Folk-tales from Hawaii, collected and translated by Laura S. Green, edited by Martha Warren Beckwith. Poughkeepsie, NY: Vassar College, 1926.

Games and Pastimes of the Maori . . . including some information concerning their . . . Music, by Elsdon Best. New Zealand, Dominion Museum, Bulletin No. 8. Wellington, New Zealand: Whitecombe & Tombs, 1925.

The Head-Hunters of Western Amazonas: The Life and Culture of the Jibaro Indians of Eastern Ecuador and Peru, by Rafael Karsten. Societa Scientiarum Fennica, Commentations Humanarum Litterarum. VII.1. Helsingfors, 1935.

Kewa Tales, edited by John LeRoy. Vancouver, BC: University of British Columbia Press, 1985.

Kojiki, translated by Donald L. Philippi. Tokyo: University of Tokyo Press, 1968.

The Life and Hard Times of a Korean Shaman: Of Tales and the Telling of Tales, by Laurel Kendall. Honolulu: University of Hawaii Press, 1988.

Myths and Legends of Fiji and Rotuma, by A. W. Reed and Inez Hames. Wellington, New Zealand: A. H. Reed and A. W. Reed, 1967.

Native Mesoamerican Spirituality: Ancient Myths, Discourses, Stories, Doctrines, Hymns, Poems from Aztec, Yucatec, Quiche-Maya and Other Sacred Traditions, edited by Miguel Léon-Portilla, translations by Miguel Léon-Portilla et al. New York: Paulist Press, 1980.

Nihongi: Chronicles of Japan from the Earliest Times to A.D. 697, translated by A. G. Aston. 1896. Rutland, VT: Charles E. Tuttle Co., 1972, 1988.

Nisa: The Life and Words of a !Kung Woman, by Marjorie Shostak. New York: Vintage Books, 1983.

Pele and Hiiaka: A Myth from Hawaii, by Nathaniel B. Emerson. Honolulu, Honolulu Star-Bulletin, 1915.

The Sacred Pipe: Black Elk's Account of the Seven Rites of the Oglala Sioux, recorded and edited by Joseph Epes Brown, Norman: University of Oklahoma Press, 1953.

Sanapia: Comanche Medicine Woman, by David E. Jones. New York: Holt, Rinehart and Winston, 1972.

Tales of the North American Indians, selected and annotated by Stith Thompson. Bloomington, IN: Indiana University Press, 1929.

Yurok Myths, by A. L. Kroeber. Berkeley, CA: University of California Press, 1976.

Zuni Mythology, Volume 1, by Ruth Benedict. New York: Columbia University Press, 1953.

Bibliography

Introductory Texts

Mircea Eliade, *Shamanism: Archaic Techniques of Ecstasy,* 1951. Reprint, Princeton, NJ: Princeton University Press, 1964, 1974.

Åke Hultkrantz, *The Religions of the American Indians,* trans. Monica Setterwall. Berkeley, CA: University of California Press, 1979.

Weston La Barre, *The Ghost Dance: The Origins of Religion.* New York: Dell Publishing Company, 1970.

E. Thomas Lawson, *Religions of Africa.* San Francisco: Harper & Row, 1985.

Arnold Van Gennep, *The Rites of Passage,* trans. Monika B. Vizedom and Gabrielle L. Caffee. Chicago: The University of Chicago Press, 1960.

Works about Women in Shamanism and Tribal Religions

Paula Gunn Allen, *The Sacred Hoop: Recovering the Feminine in American Indian Traditions.* Boston: Beacon Press, 1986.

Diane Bell, *Daughters of the Dreaming.* Sydney, Australia: McPhee Grible/George Allen and Unwin, 1983.

Burr C. Brundage, *The Fifth Sun: Aztec Gods, Aztec World.* Austin, TX: University of Texas Press, 1979.

Carmen Blacker, *The Catalpa Bow.* London: George Allen & Unwin Ltd., 1975.

Rita M. Gross, "Tribal Religions: Aboriginal Australia." Pp. 37–58 in *Women in World Religions,* ed. Arvind Sharma. Albany, NY: State University of New York Press, 1987.

Joan Halifax, *Shamanic Voices: A Survey of Visionary Narratives.* New York: E. P. Dutton, 1979.

Åke Hultkrantz, "The Religion of the Goddess in North America." Pp. 202–16 in *The Book of the Goddess: Past and Present,* ed. Carl Olson. New York: Crossroad, 1989.

Phyllis Kaberry, *Aboriginal Woman: Sacred & Profane.* London: George Routledge & Sons, Ltd., 1939.

Laurel Kendall, *Shamans, Housewives, and Other Restless Spirits: Women in Korean Ritual Life.* Honolulu, HI: University of Hawaii Press, 1985, 1987.

I. M. Lewis, *Ecstatic Religion: An Anthropological Study of Spirit Possession and Shamanism.* Middlesex, England: Penguin Books, 1971.

Bruce Lincoln, *Emerging from the Chrysalis: Studies in Rituals of Women's Initiation.* Cambridge, MA: Harvard University Press, 1981.

Yolanda and Robert Murphy, *Women of the Forest.* New York: Columbia University Press, 1974; 2nd ed. 1985.

Kyoko Motomochi Nakamura, "The Significance of Amaterasu in Japanese Religious History." Pp. 176–

89 in *The Book of the Goddess: Past and Present,* ed. Carl Olson. New York: Crossroad, 1989.

Peggy Reeves Sanday, *Female Power and Male Dominance: On the Origin of Sexual Inequality.* Cambridge: Cambridge University Press, 1981.

Sabrina Sojourner, "From the House of Yemanja: The Goddess Heritage of Black Women." Pp. 57–63 in *The Politics of Women's Spirituality,* ed. Charlene Spretnak. Garden City, NY: Anchor Books, 1982.

Unspoken Worlds: Women's Religious Lives in Non-Western Cultures, ed. Nancy A. Falk and Rita M. Gross. San Francisco: Harper & Row, 1980.

Woman the Gatherer, ed. Frances Dahlberg. New Haven, CT: Yale University Press, 1981.

HINDUISM

Introduction

Hinduism is a term used to categorize a complex and diverse range of religious and philosophical practices followed by various ethnic and linguistic groups throughout South Asia (and wherever South Asians have migrated) over a period of several thousand years.

The earliest religious texts of Hinduism are the Vedas, a collection of hymns and prayers to various gods and goddesses as well as epic chants and magic spells that were, and indeed continue to be, recited during sacrifices and other rituals. These texts were composed by the Aryans, a nomadic people who began migrating into India around 1500 B.C.E. In India they found a high but declining agricultural society, and many of the Vedic hymns refer to their conquest of these people. This and other evidence suggests that the composition of these texts began sometime before the migration, ca. 1500 B.C.E., and did not conclude until ca. 1000 B.C.E.

In this period of Hinduism male gods predominated; the hereditary priesthood of the brahmans achieved great religious power as officiators at the sacrificial ceremonies that are the main religious activity; and the caste system was formulated.

As the Aryans became settled in India, their religious practices took a philosophical turn that led to the composition of the Upanishads (ca. ninth–fifth centuries B.C.E.). In these texts, one of the main ideas is to turn away from the outer sacrifice of Vedic ritualism to the inner sacrifice of a life of contemplation based on meditation and ascetic practice. These texts undercut the religious authority of the Vedic priests and gave it to those possessing spiritual insight, some of whom may be priests, but they may also be kings and women. Further, these texts articulate the related ideas of reincarnation and karma. Karma, which means action, refers to all the acts and interactions of daily life that are believed to have consequences both in this life and in future lives.

This period of religious ferment culminated in the founding of two great Indian religions in the sixth century B.C.E., Buddhism and Jainism, both of which challenged the religious authority of the Vedas and of the priesthood associated with them. For various reasons, over the next few centuries many people joined these new religions.

Indian political life also underwent transformations. Toward the end of the fourth century B.C.E. the Mauryan Empire was established in northern India. Under the Mauryan emperor Ashoka (ca. 269–232 B.C.E.) almost all of present-day India and Pakistan was briefly brought under one rule. After the breakdown of this empire in the next generation, no equally strong central government was established until the fourth century C.E. From about 150 B.C.E. to 200 C.E. India was a land of political and religious turmoil as well as a land subject to a series of foreign invasions.

During this time the religious tradition of the brahmans was redefining itself and creating a new class of religious literature that would provide detailed instructions on how to order one's life. One of the most important texts from this period is the *Manu Smriti,* the laws of Manu. The formulation of this text begins in the third century B.C.E. and was not fixed in the form we have it today until the fourth century C.E. This text reflects the new understanding of salvation (*moksha*), which is to achieve a final escape from the ceaseless round of birth and rebirth. This and other new Hindu religious texts formulate an ideal model of society to help and direct people toward salvation. The caste system, which had already been formulated in the Vedic period, consists of a hierarchy of *brāhmaṇa*s (the priestly class), *kshatriya*s (warriors, administrators), *vaishya*s (traders, farmers), and *shūdra*s (craftspeople and laborers). In this system each person has particular duties to society and to religious goals. The highest caste, the *brāhmaṇa*s, has the duty of religious ritual and study, particularly of the Vedas. The *kshatriya*s and the *vaishya*s have the duty of religious ritual and study along with their respective occupational duties. The *shūdra*s have the primary duty of service to the three higher castes and do not have access to the Vedas. This system is then merged with the chronological four stages of life (*ashramas*): students (a period of celibate study), householders (married and having children), forest dwellers (withdrawal from society), and renouncers (abandonment of all ties and possessions for life as a wandering ascetic).

This means that from birth onward a Hindu's religious and social roles and obligations are clear. Salvation, *moksha,* is to be obtained by fulfilling these obligations in order to reincarnate into the next highest caste. Being born a brahman is believed to make it easier to achieve salvation because their duty to religious practices puts them in closer touch with the spiritual life and because they have the highest ritual purity of all the castes. This system receives its fullest articulation in the laws of Manu, the *Manu Smriti.*

This is, however, a male-oriented system, and women are, in the main, limited to the stages of the householder. Their education takes place at home, under the supervision of the women of the family, and is directed toward the household tasks they will perform as wives and mothers. Eventually, Hindu women were encouraged to think of their husbands as their god; they were to quite literally devote themselves to their husbands. Apotheosis also extended to women who were viewed as a goddess in certain rituals and as the goddess Lakṣmī, the bringer of prosperity, in the home. Both instances point to the fluidity of the boundaries between human and divine in Hinduism, where the gods are very human, and some humans, especially ascetic sages, achieve godlike status.

Another form of literature that was also developing at this time is the epic, especially the *Mahābhārata* (composed between the fifth century B.C.E. and the fourth century C.E.) and the *Rāmāyana* (composed around the second century B.C.E.). These texts contain some of the best-known Hindu stories, legends, and myths, which, beside their entertainment value, provide guidelines for behavior that is socially and religiously appropriate. They were and continue to be publicly recited and performed all over South Asia, and the stories are known by all. Consequently, they are one of the main means of communicating the values of the religion to all Hindus. Given its size and its lengthy period of composition, the *Mahābhārata* offers complex and varied images of women, but, like the *Rāmāyana,* the emphasis is on woman as faithful wife.

Bhakti is a form of religious devotion that was first introduced into Hinduism in the *Bhagavad Gītā* (composed between the first century B.C.E.–first century C.E.) and which gradually led to a variety of bhakti movements throughout the centuries all over South Asia. Bhakti, which means passionate devotion, offers salvation to all, because its only requirement is the ability to feel love and devotion for god. This is in contrast to the traditional religious system controlled by the hereditary male priesthood of the brahmans, which emphasized the caste system, gender distinction, religious learning, and even the ability to make rich offerings. Krishna, the supreme god of the *Bhagavad Gītā*, while accepting many of the traditions of the brahmans, spreads open the door to the divine. In the form of a simple cow herder, Krishna becomes the focus of many bhakti movements, while other bhakti movements focus on other supreme gods such as Shiva. These various bhakti movements had two important consequences for Hindu women. First, several important bhaktas were women. This meant that women now had powerful religious role models whether they chose to emulate them or not. Second, the ideal devotee for these male gods was envisioned as female. This led to encouraging male devotees to imagine themselves as women longing for union with their beloved, in other words, longing for mystical union with god. Though idealizing and compartmentalizing women's emotional life, these movements also valorized women's feelings.

Around the fourth century C.E., new, powerful, and fierce goddesses (*devīs*) began to emerge on the fringes of orthodox belief and practice, from the village culture and possibly from among the indigenous non-Aryan peoples of India. These goddesses grew in popularity and eventually some of them were incorporated into the brahmanical tradition. An underlying unity among the Hindu goddesses is shown in the term *Mahādevī* ("great goddess"). This term represents the diverse manifestations of the Hindu goddesses as various aspects of this one, active, powerful, creatrix. She created the cosmos; she will destroy it; and she presently maintains it both in her pacific and her fierce forms, as when she is manifest as a warrior to do battle with a demon. Despite her awesome powers she is perceived by her devotees as present and responsive to their needs; she protects them from harm and grants blessings. Perhaps most importantly, she grants wisdom and liberation.

The Vedas

The earliest religious texts of the Hindus are the four *Veda*s, the best known of which is the *Rig Veda*. The other three *Veda*s all include hymns taken from the *Rig Veda*. The *Yajur* and *Sāma Veda*s are specifically concerned with the technical and formulaic aspects of sacrifice while the *Atharva Veda*, which was the last to be composed, is primarily concerned with magic and medicine.

RIG VEDA

CREATION

Indra and Vritra

Several different versions of creation exist in the *Rig Veda*. In the first selection the great warrior god Indra brings about creation through a cosmic battle. First he slays the dragon Vritra, and then he slays Vritra's mother, Dānu, the primordial dragon who controls the cosmic waters and is associated with the powers of chaos. On one level this hymn symbolizes the Aryan conquest of India. Scholars have speculated that the waters Indra sets free in this hymn refer to the irrigation works of the conquered agricultural people while archaeological remains indicate that the indigenous people worshipped a goddess or several goddesses. One can therefore speculate that in slaying Dānu, Indra is slaying the goddess of the conquered people.

Hymn XXXII

I will declare the manly deeds of Indra, the first that he achieved, the Thunder-wielder.
He slew the Dragon, then disclosed the waters, and cleft the channels of the mountain torrents.

He slew the Dragon lying on the mountain: his heavenly bolt of thunder Tvashtar fashioned.
Like lowing kine in rapid flow descending the waters glided downward to the ocean.

Impetuous as a bull, he chose the Soma, and in three sacred beakers drank the juices.

Maghavan grasped the thunder for his weapon, and smote to death this firstborn of the dragons.

When, Indra, thou hadst slain the dragons, firstborn, and overcome the charms of the enchanters,
Then, giving life to Sun and Dawn and Heaven; thou foundest not one foe to stand against thee.

Indra with his own great and deadly thunder smote into pieces Vritra, worst of Vritras.
As trunks of trees, what time the axe hath felled them, low on the earth so lies the prostrate Dragon.

He, like a mad weak warrior, challenged Indra, the great impetuous many-slaying Hero.

He, brooking not the clashing of the weapons, crushed—Indra's foe—the shattered forts in falling.

Footless and handless still he challenged Indra, who smote him with his bolt between the shoulders.
Emasculate yet claiming manly vigour, thus Vṛitra lay with scattered limbs dissevered.

There as he lies like a bank-bursting river, the waters taking courage flow above him.
The Dragon lies beneath the feet of torrents which Vṛitra with his greatness had encompassed.

Then humbled was the strength of Vṛitra's mother: Indra hath cast his deadly bolt against her.
The mother was above, the son was under, and like a cow beside her calf lay Dânu.

Rolled in the midst of never-ceasing currents flowing without a rest for ever onward,
The waters bear off Vṛitra's nameless body: the foe of Indra sank to during darkness.

Guarded by Abi stood the thralls of Dâsas, the waters stayed like kine held by the robber.

But he, when he had smitten Vṛitra, opened the cave wherein the floods had been imprisoned.

A horse's tail wast thou when he, O Indra, smote on thy bolt; thou, God without a second,
Thou hast won back the kine, hast won the Soma; thou hast let loose to flow the Seven Rivers.

Nothing availed him lightning, nothing thunder, hailstorm of mist which he had spread around him:
When Indra and the Dragon strove in battle, Maghavan gained the victory for ever.

Whom sawest thou to avenge the Dragon, Indra, that fear possessed thy heart when thou hadst slain him;
That, like a hawk affrighted through the regions, thou crossedst nine-and-ninety flowing rivers?

Indra is King of all that moves and moves not, of creatures tame and horned, the Thunder-wielder.
Over all living men he rules as Sovran, containing all as spokes within the felly.
[From *The Hymns of the Rgveda,* vol. 1, p. 43.]

The Birth of the Gods

The second hymn to describe creation tells of the birth of the gods without, however, giving primacy to either the female or male, though elsewhere in the *Rig Veda* Aditi is referred to as "the mother of the gods." (1.113.19)

Hymn LXXII

Let us with tuneful skill proclaim these generations of the Gods,
That one may see them when these hymns are chanted in a future age.
These Brahmaṇaspati produced with blast and smelting, like a smith.
Existence, in an earlier age of Gods, from Non-existence sprang.
Existence, in the earliest age of Gods, from Non-existence sprang. Thereafter were the regions born. This sprang from the Productive Power.
Earth sprang from the Productive Power; the regions from the earth were born.
Daksha was born of Aditi, and Aditi was Daksha's Child.
For Aditi, O Daksha, she who is thy Daughter, was brought forth.

After her were the blessed Gods born sharers of immortal life.
When ye, O Gods, in yonder deep close-clasping one another stood.
Thence, as of dancers, from your feet a thickening cloud of dust arose.
When, O ye Gods, like Yatis, ye caused all existing things to grow,
Then ye brought Sûrya forward who was lying hidden in the sea.
Eight are the Sons of Aditi who from her body sprang to life.
With seven she went to meet the Gods: she cast Mārtānda far away.
So with her Seven Sons Aditi went forth to meet the earlier age.
She brought Mārtānda thitherward to spring to life and die again.
[From *The Hymns of the Rgveda,* vol. 2, pp. 487–488.]

The Cosmic Sacrifice

In the following hymn creation is the product of the cosmic sacrifice of a man. The only female involvement in this process occurs in v. 5 with the birth of Virāj, the female creative principle.

Hymn XC

A thousand heads hath Purusha, a thousand eyes, a thousand feet.

On every side pervading earth he fills a space ten fingers wide.

This Purusha is all that yet hath been and all that is to be

The Lord of Immortality which waxes greater still by food.

So mighty is his greatness; yea, greater than this is Purusha.

All creatures are one-fourth of him, three-fourths eternal life in heaven.

With three-fourths Purusha went up: one-fourth of him again was here.

Thence he strode out to every side over what eats not and what eats.

From him Virâj was born; again Purusha from Virâj was born.

As soon as he was born he spread eastward and westward o'er the earth.

When Gods prepared the sacrifice with Purusha as their offering,

Its oil was spring, the holy gift was autumn; summer was the wood.

They balmed as victim on the grass Purusha born in earliest time.

With him the Deities and all Sâdhyas and Rshis sacrificed.

From that great general sacrifice the dripping fat was gathered up.

He formed the creatures of the air, and animals both wild and tame.

From that great general sacrifice Richas and Sâma-hymns were born;

Therefrom were spells and charms produced; the Yajus had its birth from it.

From it were horses born, from it all cattle with two rows of teeth;

From it were generated kine, from it the goats and sheep were born.

When they divided Purusha how many portions did they make?

What do they call his mouth, his arms? What do they call his thighs and feet?

The Brâhman was his mouth, of both his arms was the Râjanya made.

His thighs became the Vaisya, from his feet the Sûdra was produced.

The Moon was gendered from his mind, and from his eye the Sun had birth;

Indra and Agni from his mouth were born, and Vâyu from his breath.

Forth from his navel came mid-air; the sky was fashioned from his head;

Earth from his feet, and from his ear the regions. Thus they formed the worlds.

Seven fencing-sticks had he, thrice seven layers of fuel were prepared,

When the Gods, offering sacrifice, bound, as their victim, Purusha.

Gods, sacrificing, sacrificed the victim: these were the earliest holy ordinances.

The Mighty ones attained the height of heaven, there where the Sâdhas, Gods of old, are dwelling.

[From *The Hymns of the Rgveda*, vol. 1, pp. 517–520.]

HYMNS TO GODDESSES

Despite the great importance of goddesses in later Hinduism, most of the hymns in the *Rig Veda* are devoted to the male gods who dominate the early pantheon. While goddesses rarely received ritual offerings, there are a few hymns to various goddesses, though none of them have either the power or the popularity of a god such as Indra. In the main these goddesses are associated with natural phenomena.

The next two hymns (X:127 and VII:77) praise the sister goddesses, Night and Dawn. Night is perceived to be fearful, so the hymn invokes her protection. Dawn, on the other hand, is considered auspicious and a bringer of riches.

To Night

With all her eyes the goddess Night looks forth
  approaching many a spot:
She hath put all her glories on.

Immortal, she hath filled the waste, the goddess hath
  filled height and depth:
She conquers darkness with her light.

The Goddess as she comes hath set Dawn her Sister
  in her place:
And then the darkness vanishes.

So favor us this night, O thou whose pathways we
  have visited
As birds their nest upon the tree.

The villagers have sought their homes, and all that
  walks and all that flies,
Even the falcons fain for prey.

Keep off the she-wolf and the wolf; O Night, keep
  the thief away:
Easy be thou for us to pass.

Clearly hath she come nigh to me who decks the dark
  with richest hues:
O Morning, cancel it like debts.

These have I brought to thee like kine [= cattle]. O
  Night, thou Child of Heaven, accept
This laud as for a conqueror.
  [From *Selections from Vedic Hymns,* p. 1.]

To Dawn

She hath shone brightly like a youthful woman,
  stirring to motion every living creature.
Agni hath come to feed on mortals' fuel. She hath
  made light and chased away the darkness.

Turned to this All, far-spreading, she hath risen and
  shone in brightness with white robes about her.
She hath beamed forth lovely with golden colors,
  Mother of kine, Guide of the days she bringeth.

Bearing the gods' own Eye (= Sun), auspicious Lady,
  leading her Courser white (= Sun) and fair to look
  on,
Distinguished by her beams Dawn shines apparent,
  come forth to all the world with wondrous treasure.

Draw nigh with wealth and dawn away the foeman:
  prepare for us wide pasture free from danger.
Drive away those who hate us, bring us riches: pour
  bounty, opulent Lady, on the singer.

Send thy most excellent beams to shine and light us,
  giving us lengthened days, O Dawn, O Goddess,
Granting us food, thou who hast all things precious,
  and bounty rich in chariots, kine, and horses.

O Ushas, nobly-born, Daughter of Heaven, whom
  the Vasiṣthas with their hymns make mighty,
Bestow thou on us vast and glorious riches. Preserve
  us evermore, ye gods, with blessings.
  [From *Selections from Vedic Hymns,* p. 2.]

To Sarasvatī

Sarasvatī is a goddess whose influence and popularity increase in later Hinduism when she is honored as the goddess of learning and eloquence. The following excerpt from the *Rig Veda* emphasizes her earlier nature as a powerful river. In this hymn she is invoked particularly for the good luck she can confer as well as for the blessings of children and food.

To Sarasvatī

I sing a lofty song, for she is mightiest, most divine
  of Streams.
Sarasvatī will I exalt with hymns and lauds, and,
  Vasiṣṭha, Heaven and Earth.

When in the fulness of their strength the Purus dwell,
  Beauteous One, on thy two grassy banks,
Favor us thou who hast the Maruts for thy friends:
  stir up the bounty of our chiefs.

So may Sarasvatī auspicious send good luck; she, rich
  in spoil, is never niggardly in thought,

When praised in Jamadagni's way and lauded as
  Vasiṣṭha lauds.

We call upon Sarasvān, as unmarried men who long
  for wives,
As liberal men who yearn for sons.

Be thou our kind protector, O Sarasvān, with those
  waves of thine
Laden with sweets and dropping oil.

May we enjoy Sarasvān's breast, all-beautiful, that
  swells with streams,
May we gain food and progeny.
  [From *Selections from Vedic Hymns,* p. 35.]

ATHARVA VEDA

To Earth

In the *Rig Veda* earth is represented as part of a female/male pair, earth/sky, but in the following hymn from the *Atharva Veda* (XII:1) the earth is described as an independent deity.

Hymn to Goddess Earth

Truth, greatness, universal order (rita), strength, consecration, creative fervour (tapas), spiritual exaltation (brahma), the sacrifice, support the earth. May this earth, the mistress of that which was and shall be, prepare for us a broad domain.

The earth that has heights, and slopes, and great plains, that supports the plants of manifold virtue, free from the pressure that comes from the midst of men, she shall spread out for us, and fit herself for us!

The earth upon which the sea, and the rivers and the waters, upon which food and the tribes of men have arisen, upon which this breathing, moving life exists, shall afford us precedence in drinking!

The earth whose are the four regions of space, upon which food and the tribes of men have arisen, which supports the manifold breathing, moving things, shall afford us cattle and other possessions also!

The earth upon which of old the first men unfolded themselves, upon which the gods overcame the Asuras, shall procure for us (all) kinds of cattle, horses, and fowls, good fortune, and glory!

The earth that supports all, furnishes wealth, the foundation, the golden-breasted resting-place of all living creatures, she that supports Agni Vaisvânara (the fire), and mates with Indra, the bull, shall furnish us with property!

The broad earth, which the sleepless gods ever attentively guard, shall milk for us precious honey, and, moreover, besprinkle us with glory!

That earth which formerly was water upon the ocean (of space), which the wise (seers) found out by their skillful devices; whose heart is in the highest heaven, immortal, surrounded by truth, shall bestow upon us brilliancy and strength, (and place us) in supreme sovereignty!

That earth upon which the attendant waters jointly flow by day and night unceasingly, shall pour out milk for us in rich streams, and, moreover, besprinkle us with glory!

The earth which the Asvins have measured, upon which Vishnu has stepped out, which Indra, the lord of might, has made friendly to himself; she, the mother, shall pour forth milk for me, the son!

Thy snowy mountain heights, and thy forests, O earth, shall be kind to us! The brown, the black, the red, the multi-coloured, the firm earth, that is protected by Indra, I have settled upon, not suppressed, not slain, not wounded.

Into thy middle set us, O earth, and into thy navel, into the nourishing strength that has grown up from thy body; purify thyself for us! The earth is the mother, and I the son of the earth; Parganya is the father; he, too, shall save us!

The earth upon which they (the priests) inclose the altar (vedi), upon which they, devoted to all (holy) works, unfold the sacrifice, upon which are set up, in front of the sacrifice, the sacrificial posts, erect and brilliant, that earth shall prosper us, herself prospering!

Him that hates us, O earth, him that battles against us, him that is hostile towards us with his mind and his weapons, do thou subject to us, anticipating (our wish) by deed!

The mortals born of thee live on thee, thou supportest both bipeds and quadrupeds. Thine, O earth, are these five races of men, the mortals, upon whom the rising sun sheds undying light with his rays.

These creatures all together shall yield milk for us; do thou, O earth, give us the honey of speech!

Upon the firm, broad earth, the all-begetting mother of the plants, that is supported by (divine) law, upon her, propitious and kind, may we ever pass our lives!

* * *

Upon the earth men give to the gods the sacrifice, the prepared oblation; upon the earth mortal men live pleasantly by food. May this earth give us breath and life, may she cause me to reach old age!

* * *

Rock, stone, dust is this earth; this earth is supported, held together. To this golden-breasted earth I have rendered obeisance.

The earth, upon whom the forest-sprung trees ever stand firm, the all-nourishing, compact earth, do we invoke.

Rising or sitting, standing or walking, may we not stumble with our right or left foot upon the earth!

To the pure earth I speak, to the ground, the soil

that has grown through the brahma (spiritual exaltation). Upon thee, that holdest nourishment, prosperity, food, and ghee, we would settle down, O earth!

Purified the waters shall flow for our bodies; what flows off from us that do we deposit upon him we dislike: with a purifier, O earth, do I purify myself!

★ ★ ★

What, O earth, I dig out of thee, quickly shall that grow again: may I not, O pure one, pierce thy vital spot, (and) not thy heart!

Thy summer, O earth, thy rainy season, thy autumn, winter, early spring, and spring; thy decreed yearly seasons, thy days and nights shall yield us milk!

★ ★ ★

May this earth point out to us the wealth that we crave; may Bhaga (fortune) add his help, may Indra come here as (our) champion!

The earth upon whom the noisy mortals sing and dance, upon whom they fight, upon whom resounds the roaring drum, shall drive forth our enemies, shall make us free from rivals!

To the earth upon whom are food, and rice and barley, upon whom live these five races of men, to the earth, the wife of Parganya, that is fattened by rain, be reverence!

The earth upon whose ground the citadels constructed by the gods unfold themselves, every region of her that is the womb of all, Pragâpati shall make pleasant for us!

The earth that holds treasures manifold in secret places, wealth, jewels, and gold shall she give to me; she that bestows wealth liberally, the kindly goddess, wealth shall she bestow upon us!

The earth that holds people of manifold varied speech, of different customs, according to their habitations, as a reliable milch-cow that does not kick, shall she milk for me a thousand streams of wealth!

[From *Hymns of the Atharva-Veda*, pp. 199–207.]

The Upanishads

The *Upanishads* represent a new philosophical stream in the religious life of the Aryans who, by the time of their composition (ca. ninth to fifth centuries B.C.E.), were thoroughly assimilated to India. These texts reveal a shift in emphasis from the outer sacrifice of Vedic practices to the inner sacrifice of a life of contemplation. The existential base of early Indian religion shifts in these texts. The basis of all reality, the spirit of the universe, is identified as Brahman, not to be confused with the god Brahmā or the priesthood of *brāhmaṇas*. Within each individual there is the Ātman, or self, which comes from Brahman and which is capable of eternal and blissful union with Brahman. Hence the need for contemplation, meditation, and/or ascetic practices, all of which awaken the Ātman to its higher destiny.

In redefining the religion in this way, these texts also undercut the spiritual authority of the traditional Vedic priesthood, the brahmans. In these texts, people other than the priests, such as kings and women, have access to profound spiritual truths.

THE KENA UPANISHAD

In the following excerpt (14–28) the old Vedic gods do not know Brahman, and it is left up to Umā, the goddess of wisdom, to explain it to them.

Now, Brahma won a victory for the gods. Now, in the victory of this Brahma the gods were exulting. They bethought themselves: 'Ours indeed is this victory! Ours indeed is this greatness!'

Now, It understood this of them. It appeared to them. They did not understand It. 'What wonderful being (*yakṣa*) is this?' they said.

They said to Agni (Fire): 'Jātavedas, find out this — what this wonderful being is.'

'So be it.'

He ran unto It.

Unto him It spoke: 'Who are you?'

'Verily, I am Agni,' he said. 'Verily, I am Jātavedas.'
'In such as you what power is there?'
'Indeed, I might burn everything here, whatever there is here in the earth!'
It put down a straw before him. 'Burn that!'
He went forth at it with all speed. He was not able to burn it. Thereupon indeed he returned, saying: 'I have not been able to find out this—what this wonderful being is.'
Then they said to Vāyu (Wind): 'Vāyu, find out this—what this wonderful being is.'
'So be it.'
He ran unto It.
Unto him It spoke: 'Who are you?'
'Verily, I am Vāyu,' he said. 'Verily, I am Mātariśvan.'
'In such as you what power is there?'
'Indeed, I might carry off everything here, whatever there is here in the earth.'
It put down a straw before him. 'Carry that off!'
He went at it with all speed. He was not able to carry it off. Thereupon indeed he returned, saying:

'I have not been able to find out this—what this wonderful being is.'
Then they said to Indra: 'Maghavan ('Liberal'), find out this—what this wonderful being is.'
'So be it.'
He ran unto It. It disappeared from him.
In that very space he came upon a woman exceedingly beautiful, Umā, daughter of the Snowy Mountain (Himavat).
To her he said: 'What is this wonderful being?'
'It is Brahma,' she said. 'In that victory of Brahma, verily, exult ye.'
Thereupon he knew it was Brahma.
Therefore, verily, these gods, namely Agni, Vāyu, and Indra, are above the other gods, as it were; for these touched It nearest, for these and [especially] he [i. e. Indra] first knew It was Brahma.
Therefore, verily, Indra is above the other gods, as it were; for he touched It nearest, for he first knew It was Brahma.
[From *The Thirteen Principal Upanishads*, pp. 337–39.]

THE BRIHADĀRAṆYAKA UPANISHAD

The following three excerpts reveal the conversations between the sage Yajñāvalkya and various women. The first conversation (2.4) is with his wife, Maitreyī, whom he is about to leave behind as he enters the forest for a life of ascetic contemplation. Maitreyī shapes their conversation when she declines Yajñāvalkya's offer of material support and instead asks for his knowledge. In this way Maitreyī demonstrates a woman's desire for spiritual knowledge and Yajñāvalkya reveals a willingness to instruct women on a philosophically sophisticated level.

'Maitreyī!' said Yajñāvalkya, 'lo, verily, I am about to go forth from this state. Behold! let me make a final settlement for you and that Kātyāyanī.'
Then said Maitreyī: 'If now, sir, this whole earth filled with wealth were mine, would I be immortal thereby?'
'No,' said Yajñāvalkya. 'As the life of the rich, even so would your life be. Of immortality, however, there is no hope through wealth.'
Then said Maitreyī: 'What should I do with that through which I may not be immortal? What you know, sir—that, indeed, tell me!'
Then said Yajñāvalkya: 'Ah (*bata*)! Lo (*are*), dear (*priyā*) as you are to us, dear is what you say! Come, sit down. I will explain to you. But while I am expounding, do you seek to ponder thereon.'
Then said he: 'Lo, verily, not for love of the husband is a husband dear, but for love of the Soul (*Ātman*) a husband is dear.
Lo, verily, not for love of the wife is a wife dear,

but for love of the Soul a wife is dear.
Lo, verily, not for love of the sons are sons dear, but for love of the Soul sons are dear.
Lo, verily, not for love of the wealth is wealth dear, but for love of the Soul wealth is dear.
Lo, verily, not for love of Brahmanhood (*brahma*) is Brahmanhood dear, but for love of the Soul Brahmanhood is dear.
Lo, verily, not for love of Kshatrahood (*kṣatra*) is Kshatrahood dear, but for love of the Soul Kshatrahood is dear.
Lo, verily, not for love of the worlds are the worlds dear, but for love of the Soul the worlds are dear.
Lo, verily, not for love of the gods are the gods dear, but for love of the Soul the gods are dear.
Lo, verily, not for love of the beings (*bhūta*) are beings dear, but for love of the Soul beings are dear.
Lo, verily, not for love of all is all dear, but for love of the Soul all is dear.
Lo, verily, it is the Soul (*Ātman*) that should be seen,

that should be hearkened to, that should be thought on, that should be pondered on, O Maitreyī. Lo, verily, with the seeing of, with the hearkening to, with the thinking of, and with the understanding of the Soul, this world-all is known.

Brahmanhood has deserted him who knows Brahmanhood in aught else than the Soul.

Kshatrahood has deserted him who knows Kshatrahood in aught else than the Soul.

The worlds have deserted him who knows the worlds in aught else than the Soul.

The gods have deserted him who knows the gods in aught else than the Soul.

Beings have deserted him who knows beings in aught else than the Soul.

Everything has deserted him who knows everything in aught else than the Soul.

This Brahmanhood, this Kshatrahood, these worlds, these gods, these beings, everything here is what this Soul is.

It is—as, when a drum is being beaten, one would not be able to grasp the external sounds, but by grasping the drum or the beater of the drum the sound is grasped.

It is—as, when a conch-shell is being blown, one would not be able to grasp the external sounds, but by grasping the conch-shell or the blower of the conch-shell the sound is grasped.

It is—as, when a lute is being played, one would not be able to grasp the external sounds, but by grasping the lute or the player of the lute the sound is grasped.

It is—as, from a fire laid with damp fuel, clouds of smoke separately issue forth, so, lo, verily, from this great Being (*bhūta*) has been breathed forth that which is Rig-Veda, Yajur-Veda, Sāma-Veda, [Hymns] of the Atharvans and Aṅgirases, Legend (*itihāsa*), Ancient Lore (*purāṇa*), Sciences (*vidyā*), Mystic Doctrines (*upaniṣad*, Verses (*śloka*), Aphorisms (*sūtra*), Explanations (*anuvyākhyāna*), and Commentaries (*vyākhyāna*). From it, indeed, are all these breathed forth.

It is—as of all waters the uniting-point is the sea, so of all touches the uniting-point is the skin, so of all tastes the uniting-point is the tongue, so of all smells the uniting-point is the nostrils, so of all forms the uniting-point is the eye, so of all sounds the uniting-point is the ear, so of all intentions (*saṁkalpa*) the uniting-point is the mind (*manas*), so of all knowledges the uniting-point is the heart, so of all acts (*karma*) the uniting-point is the hands, so of all pleasures (*ānanda*) the uniting-point is the generative organ, so of all evacuations the uniting-point is the anus, so of all journeys the uniting-point is the feet, so of all the Vedas the uniting-point is speech.

It is—as a lump of salt cast in water would dissolve right into the water; there would not be [any] of it to seize forth, as it were (*iva*), but wherever one may take, it is salty indeed—so, lo, verily, this great Being (*bhūta*), infinite, limitless, is just a mass of knowledge (*vijñāna-ghana*).

Arising out of these elements (*bhūta*), into them also one vanishes away. After death there is no consciousness (*na pretya saṁjñā 'sti*). Thus, lo, say I.' Thus spake Yājñavalkya.

Then spake Maitreyī: 'Herein, indeed, you have bewildered me, sir—in saying (*iti*) "After death there is no consciousness"!'

Then spake Yājñavalkya: 'Lo, verily, I speak not bewilderment (*moha*). Sufficient, lo, verily, is this for understanding.

For where there is a duality (*dvaita*), as it were (*iva*), there one sees another; there one smells another; there one hears another; there one speaks to another; there one thinks of another; there one understands another. Where, verily, everything has become just one's own self, then whereby and whom would one smell? then whereby and whom would one see? then whereby and whom would one hear? then whereby and to whom would one speak? then whereby and on whom would one think? then whereby and whom would one understand? Whereby would one understand him by whom one understands this All? Lo, whereby would one understand the understander?'

[From *The Thirteen Principal Upanishads,* pp. 98–102.]

The following two excerpts (3.6 and 3.8) take place during a philosophical tournament held in the city of Videha under the sponsorship of King Janaka. One of the philosophers, a woman named Gārgī, questions Yājñavalkya about the nature of reality.

Then Gārgī Vācaknavī questioned him. 'Yājñavalkya,' said she, 'since all this world is woven, warp and woof, on water, on what, pray, is the water woven, warp and woof?'

'On wind, O Gārgī.'

'On what then, pray, is the wind woven, warp and woof?'

'On the atmosphere-worlds, O Gārgī.'

'On what then, pray, are the atmosphere-worlds woven, warp and woof?'

'On the worlds of the Gandharvas, O Gārgī.'

'On what then, pray, are the worlds of the Gandharvas woven, warp and woof?'

'On the worlds of the sun, O Gārgī.'

'On what then, pray, are the worlds of the sun woven, warp and woof?'

'On the worlds of the moon, O Gārgī.'

'On what then, pray, are the worlds of the moon woven, warp and woof?'

'On the worlds of the stars, O Gārgī.'

'On what then, pray, are the worlds of the stars woven, warp and woof?'

'On the worlds of the gods, O Gārgī.'

'On what then, pray, are the worlds of the gods woven, warp and woof?'

'On the worlds of Indra, O Gārgī.'

'On what then, pray, are the worlds of Indra woven, warp and woof?'

'On the worlds of Prajāpati, O Gārgī.'

'On what then, pray, are the worlds of Prajāpati woven, warp and woof?'

'On the worlds of Brahma, O Gārgī.'

'On what then, pray, are the worlds of Brahma woven, warp and woof?'

Yājñavalkya said: 'Gārgī, do not question too much, lest your head fall off. In truth, you are questioning too much about a divinity about which further questions cannot be asked. Gārgī, do not over-question.'

Thereupon Gārgī Vācaknavī held her peace.

[From *The Thirteen Principal Upanishads,* pp. 337–339.]

Undaunted, after a short respite, Gārgī continues her questioning. In this text, she is the only one to question Yājñavalkya twice.

Then [Gārgī] Vācaknavī said: 'Venerable Brahmans, lo, I will ask him [i.e. Yājñavalkya] two questions. If he will answer me these, not one of you will surpass him in discussions about Brahma.'

'Ask, Gārgī.'

She said: 'As a noble youth of the Kāśīs or of the Videhas might rise up against you, having strung his unstrung bow and taken two foe-piercing arrows in his hand, even so, O Yājñavalkya, have I risen up against you with two questions. Answer me these.'

Yājñavalkya said: 'Ask, Gārgī.'

She said: 'That, O Yājñavalkya, which is above the sky, that which is beneath the earth, that which is between these two, sky and earth, that which people call the past and the present and the future—across what is that woven, warp and woof?'

He said: 'That, O Gārgī, which is above the sky, that which is beneath the earth, that which is between these two, sky and earth, that which people call the past and the present and the future—across space is that woven, warp and woof.'

She said: 'Adoration to you, Yājñavalkya, in that you have solved this question for me. Prepare yourself for the other.'

'Ask, Gārgī.'

She said: 'That, O Yājñavalkya, which is above the sky, that which is beneath the earth, that which is between these two, sky and earth, that which people call the past and the present and the future—across what is that woven, warp and woof?'

He said: 'That, O Gārgī, which is above the sky, that which is beneath the earth, that which is between these two, sky and earth, that which people call the past and the present and the future—across space alone is that woven, warp and woof.'

'Across what then, pray, is space woven, warp and woof?'

He said: 'That, O Gārgī, Brahmans call the Imperishable (*akṣara*). It is not coarse, not fine, not short, not long, not glowing [like fire], not adhesive [like water], without shadow and without darkness, without air and without space, without stickiness, (intangible), odorless, tasteless, without eye, without ear, without voice, without wind, without energy, without breath, without mouth, (without personal or family name, unaging, undying, without fear, immortal, stainless, not uncovered, not covered), without measure, without inside and without outside.

It consumes nothing soever.

No one soever consumes it.

Verily, O Gārgī, at the command of that Imperishable the sun and the moon stand apart. Verily, O Gārgī, at the command of that Imperishable the earth and the sky stand apart. Verily, O Gārgī, at the command of that Imperishable the moments, the hours, the days, the nights, the fortnights, the months, the seasons, and the years stand apart. Verily, O Gārgī, at the command of that Imperishable some rivers flow from the snowy mountains to the east, others to the west, in whatever direction each flows. Verily, O Gārgī, at the command of that Imperishable men praise those who give, the gods are desirous of a sacrificer, and the fathers [are desirous] of the Manes-sacrifice.

Verily, O Gārgī, if one performs sacrifices and

worship and undergoes austerity in this world for many thousands of years, but without knowing that Imperishable, limited indeed is that [work] of his. Verily, O Gārgī, he who departs from this world without knowing that Imperishable is pitiable. But, O Gārgī, he who departs from this world knowing that Imperishable is a Brahman.

Verily, O Gārgī, that Imperishable is the unseen Seer, the unheard Hearer, the unthought Thinker, the unununderstood Understander. Other than It there is naught that sees. Other than It there is naught that

hears. Other than It there is naught that thinks. Other than It there is naught that understands. Across this Imperishable, O Gārgī, is space woven, warp and woof.

She said: 'Venerable Brahmans, you may think it a great thing if you escape from this man with [merely] making a bow. Not one of you will surpass him in discussions about Brahma.'

Thereupon [Gārgī] Vācaknavī held her peace.

[From *The Thirteen Principal Upanishads*, pp. 117–119.]

The Laws of Manu

Most great religious traditions formulate law books which are generally ideal representations of how things should be. Hinduism has its *Manu Smriti,* or laws of Manu, which was, and is, consulted by orthodox Hindus when they are in doubt as to correct procedure. The goal of this text is to codify Hindu religious law in all aspects of daily life.

The following excerpt from chapter three sets forth some of the laws regarding women: It forbids the sale of women into marriage, protects their rights to own separate property, and recommends that women be honored.

No father who knows (the law) must take even the smallest gratuity for his daughter; for a man who, through avarice, takes a gratuity, is a seller of his offspring.

But those (male) relations who, in their folly, live on the separate property of women, (e.g. appropriate) the beasts of burden, carriages, and clothes of women, commit sin and will sink into hell.

Some call the cow and the bull (given) at an Ârsha wedding 'a gratuity'; (but) that is wrong, since (the acceptance of) a fee, be it small or great, is a sale (of the daughter).

When the relatives do not appropriate (for their use) the gratuity (given), it is not a sale; (in that case) the (gift) is only a token of respect and of kindness towards the maidens.

Women must be honoured and adorned by their fathers, brothers, husbands, and brothers-in-law, who desire (their own) welfare.

Where women are honoured, there the gods are pleased; but where they are not honoured, no sacred rite yields rewards.

Where the female relations live in grief, the family soon wholly perishes; but that family where they are not unhappy ever prospers.

The houses on which female relations, not being duly honoured, pronounce a curse, perish completely, as if destroyed by magic.

Hence men who seek (their own) welfare, should always honour women on holidays and festivals with (gifts of) ornaments, clothes, and (dainty) food.

[From *The Laws of Manu*, chap. 3, pp. 84–85.]

The excerpts from chapters five and nine present the laws regarding the conduct of women. Women are defined as always dependent on men, and the text lists a wife's duties to her husband both while he is alive and after he is dead. Verses 33–37 of chapter nine specify the contribution of women (the soil) and men (the seed) to their children, stating that the male contribution is more important.

By a girl, by a young woman, or even by an aged one, nothing must be done independently, even in her

own house.

In childhood a female must be subject to her father,

in youth to her husband, when her lord is dead to her sons; a woman must never be independent.

She must not seek to separate herself from her father, husband, or sons; by leaving them she would make both (her own and her husband's) families contemptible.

She must always be cheerful, clever in (the management of her) household affairs, careful in cleaning her utensils, and economical in expenditure.

Him to whom her father may give her, or her brother with the father's permission, she shall obey as long as he lives, and when he is dead, she must not insult (his memory).

* * *

The husband who wedded her with sacred texts, always gives happiness to his wife, both in season and out of season, in this world and in the next.

Though destitute of virtue, or seeking pleasure (elsewhere), or devoid of good qualities, (yet) a husband must be constantly worshipped as a god by a faithful wife.

No sacrifice, no vow, no fast must be performed by women apart (from their husbands); if a wife obeys her husband, she will for that (reason alone) be exalted in heaven.

A faithful wife, who desires to dwell (after death) with her husband, must never do anything that might displease him who took her hand, whether he be alive or dead.

At her pleasure let her emaciate her body by (living on) pure flowers, roots, and fruit; but she must never even mention the name of another man after her husband has died.

Until death let her be patient (of hardships), self-controlled, and chaste, and strive (to fulfil) that most excellent duty which (is prescribed) for wives who have one husband only.

Many thousands of Brâhmanas who were chaste from their youth, have gone to heaven without continuing their race.

A virtuous wife who after the death of her husband constantly remains chaste, reaches heaven, though she have no son, just like those chaste men.

But a woman who from a desire to have offspring violates her duty towards her (deceased) husband, brings on herself disgrace in this world, and loses her place with her husband (in heaven).

Offspring begotten by another man is here not (considered lawful), nor (does offspring begotten) on another man's wife (belong to the begetter), nor is a second husband anywhere prescribed for virtuous women.

She who cohabits with a man of higher caste, forsaking her own husband who belongs to a lower one, will become contemptible in this world, and is called a remarried woman (parapûrvâ).

By violating her duty towards her husband, a wife is disgraced in this world, (after death) she enters the womb of a jackal, and is tormented by diseases (the punishment of) her sin.

She who, controlling her thoughts, words, and deeds, never slights her lord, resides (after death) with her husband (in heaven), and is called a virtuous (wife).

In reward of such conduct, a female who controls her thoughts, speech, and actions, gains in this (life) highest renown, and in the next (world) a place near her husband.

A twice-born man, versed in the sacred law, shall burn a wife of equal caste who conducts herself thus and dies before him, with (the sacred fires used for) the Agnihotra, and with the sacrificial implements.

Having thus, at the funeral, given the sacred fires to his wife who dies before him, he may marry again, and again kindle (the fires).

[From *The Laws of Manu,* chap. 5, 195–199.]

The husband, after conception by his wife, becomes an embryo and is born again of her; for that is the wifehood of a wife (gâyâ), that he is born (gâyate) again by her.

As the male is to whom a wife cleaves, even so is the son whom she brings forth; let him therefore carefully guard his wife, in order to keep his offspring pure.

No man can completely guard women by force; but they can be guarded by the employment of the (following) expedients:

Let the (husband) employ his (wife) in the collection and expenditure of his wealth, in keeping (everything) clean, in (the fulfilment of) religious duties, in the preparation of his food, and in looking after the household utensils.

Women, confined in the house under trustworthy and obedient servants, are not (well) guarded, but those who of their own accord keep guard over themselves, are well guarded.

Drinking (spirituous liquor), associating with wicked people, separation from the husband, rambling abroad, sleeping (at unseasonable hours), and dwelling in other men's houses, are the six causes of the ruin of women.

Women do not care for beauty, nor is their attention fixed on age; (thinking) '(It is enough that) he is a man,' they give themselves to the handsome and to the ugly.

Through their passion for men, through their mutable temper, through their natural heartlessness, they become disloyal towards their husbands, however carefully they may be guarded in this (world).

Knowing their disposition, which the Lord of

creatures laid in them at the creation, to be such, (every) man should most strenuously exert himself to guard them.

(When creating them) Manu allotted to women (a love of their) bed, (of their) seat and (of) ornament, impure desires, wrath, dishonesty, malice, and bad conduct.

For women no (sacramental) rite (is performed) with sacred texts, thus the law is settled; women (who are) destitute of strength and destitute of (the knowledge of) Vedic texts, (are as impure as) falsehood (itself), that is a fixed rule.

★ ★ ★

Thus has been declared the ever pure popular usage (which regulates the relations) between husband and wife; hear (next) the laws concerning children which are the cause of happiness in this world and after death.

Between wives (striyah) who (are destined) to bear children, who secure many blessings, who are worthy of worship and irradiate (their) dwellings, and between the goddesses of fortune (sriyah, who reside) in the houses (of men), there is no difference whatsoever.

The production of children, the nurture of those born, and the daily life of men, (of these matters) woman is visibly the cause.

Offspring, (the due performance of) religious rites, faithful service, highest conjugal happiness and heavenly bliss for the ancestors and oneself, depend on one's wife alone.

She who, controlling her thoughts, speech, and acts, violates not her duty towards her lord, dwells with him (after death) in heaven, and in this world is called by the virtuous a faithful (wife, sâdhvî).

But for disloyalty to her husband a wife is censured among men, and (in her next life) she is born in the womb of a jackal and tormented by diseases, the punishment of her sin.

Listen (now) to the following holy discussion, salutary to all men, which the virtuous (of the present day) and the ancient great sages have held concerning male offspring.

They (all) say that the male issue (of a woman) belongs to the lord, but with respect to the (meaning of the term) lord the revealed texts differ; some call the begetter (of the child the lord), others declare (that it is) the owner of the soil.

By the sacred tradition the woman is declared to be the soil, the man is declared to be the seed; the production of all corporeal beings (takes place) through the union of the soil with the seed.

In some cases the seed is more distinguished, and in some the womb of the female; but when both are equal, the offspring is most highly esteemed.

On comparing the seed and the receptable (of the seed), the seed is declared to be the more important; for the offspring of all created beings is marked by the characteristics of the seed.

Whatever (kind of) seed is sown in a field, prepared in due season, (a plant) of that same kind, marked with the peculiar qualities of the seed, springs up in it.

This earth, indeed, is called the primeval womb of created beings; but the seed develops not in its development any properties of the womb.

[From *The Laws of Manu*, chap. 9, pp. 229–334.]

The Epics

The epic literature of India remains a living tradition throughout South Asia and wherever Hindus have immigrated through its continual recitation and performance. The epics are the living repositories of the best-known Hindu stories and an important means of communicating the religious and social values of Hinduism, particularly as they relate to gender.

THE MAHĀBHĀRATA

The *Mahābhārata* is a huge text that was composed over several centuries (ca. fifth century B.C.E. to fourth century C.E.) and its best-known stories provide guidelines for appropriate social and religious behavior.

SHAKUNTALĀ

In the following selection Shakuntalā, a semi-divine woman living as an ascetic, chooses her own husband, a powerful king, who later betrays her and their son. Though Shakuntalā forcefully and publicly confronts the king on his obligations, it is not until a voice from above speaks in her favor that the king relents and acknowledges her rights. Even so, this story stands as an important example of the religious and social rights available to the faithful wife.

The episode begins when King Duḥṣanta is out hunting and comes upon a hermitage of ascetics and seers. Here he meets Shakuntalā, who tells him about her divine mother and her human father. The story of Shakuntalā's birth represents a frequent theme in Indian literature, in which ascetics become so powerful through the practice of austerities that they threaten the power of the gods. To offset this danger the gods often, as in this story, send an apsara, a divine woman, to seduce the ascetic and thereby reduce his power. This story is told by the narrator of the epic, Vaiśaṃpāyana.

Vaiśaṃpāyana said:

Thereupon the strong-armed king dismissed his councillors and went on alone. He did not find the seer of strict vows in the hermitage. Failing to find the seer and finding the hermitage empty, he spoke in a loud voice, thundering over the woodland: "Who is here?" Hearing his cry, a young maiden appeared, like Śrī incarnate, and came out of that hermitage, wearing the garb of a female hermit. No sooner had the black-eyed girl seen King Duḥṣanta than she bade him welcome and paid him homage. She honored him with a seat, with water to wash his feet, and a guest gift, and asked, O king, the overlord of men about his health and well-being.

After honoring him properly and inquiring about his health, she said with a faint smile, "What can I do?" The king, seeing that she had a flawless body and having been honored properly, replied to the sweet-spoken girl, "I have come to pay my worship to the venerable seer Kaṇva. Where has the reverend gone, my dear? Tell me, my pretty."

Śakuntalā said:

My reverend father has gone out of the hermitage to gather fruit. Wait a while, you will see him return.

Vaiśaṃpāyana said:

The king, having failed to find the seer, looked at the girl who had addressed him and saw that she had beautiful hips, a lustrous appearance, and a charming smile. She was radiant with beauty, with the sheen of austerities and the calm of self-restraint. The king now said to the maiden, as perfect of shape as of age. "Who are you? Whose are you? Why, fair-waisted girl, have you come to this wilderness? Endowed with such perfection of beauty? From where are you, my pretty? For one look at you, lovely, has carried my heart away! I want to know about you, tell me, my pretty."

At these words of the king in the hermitage she laughed and said in a very sweet voice. "I am regarded as the daughter of the venerable Kaṇva, Duḥṣanta, the great-spirited and famous ascetic and equable scholar of the Law."

Duḥṣanta said:

The reverend lord, whom the world worships, has never spilled his seed! The God Law himself might stray from his course, but not this saint of strict vows. How could you have been born his daughter, fair maiden? I have great doubts on this, pray dispel them!

Śakuntalā said:

Then listen, my king, how this story has come to me, and how this once came to be, and how in fact I became the hermit's daughter. One day a seer came here who raised questions about my birth, and hear how the reverend spoke to him, sire.

"Viśvāmitra, as you know," he said, "performed of yore such huge austerities that he bitterly mortified Indra himself, lord of the hosts of Gods. Fearful lest the ascetic, whose puissance had been set ablaze by his austerities, would topple him from his throne, the Sacker of Cities therefore spoke to Menakā. 'Menakā, you are distinguished in the divine talents of the Apsaras. Take my welfare to heart, beautiful woman, and do as I ask you, listen. That great ascetic Viśvāmitra, who possesses the splendor of the sun, has been performing awesome austerities that make my mind tremble. Menakā of the pretty waist, Viśvāmitra is your burden. This unassailable man of honed spirit is engaged in dreadful austerities; and lest he topple me from my throne, go to him and seduce him. Obstruct his asceticism, do me the ultimate favor! Seduce him with your beauty, youth, sweetness, fondling, smiles, and flatteries, my buxom girl, and turn him away from his austerities!'"

★ ★ ★

"Indra . . . gave orders to the ever-moving wind, and Menakā at once departed with the wind. Then Menakā, callipygous nymph, set timid eyes on Viśvāmitra, who, all his evil burned off by his austerities, was yet engaged in more in his hermitage. She greeted him and began to play in front of him. Off with the wind went her moonlight skirt, the fair-skinned nymph dropped to the ground embracing it, bashfully smiling at the wind. And so that strictest of seers saw Menakā nude, nervously clutching at her skirt, indescribably young and beautiful. And remarking the virtue of her beauty the bull among brahmins fell victim to love and lusted to lie with her. He asked her, and she was blamelessly willing.

"The pair of them whiled away a very long time in the woods, making love when the spirit seized them, and it seemed only a day. And on Menakā the hermit begot Śakuntalā, on a lovely tableland in the Himālayas, by the river Mālinī. Once the baby was born, Menakā abandoned her on the bank of the Mālinī; and, her duty done, she returned rapidly to Indra's assembly.

"Birds, seeing the baby lying in the desolate wilderness that was teeming with lions and tigers, surrounded her protectively on all sides. Lest beasts of prey, greedy for meat, hurt the little girl in the forest, the birds stood guard around Menakā's child. Then I chanced to come to the river to rinse my mouth and saw her lying in the deserted and lonely woods surrounded by birds. I took her home and adopted her as my daughter. In the decisions of Law they quote three kinds of fathers respectively: the one who begets the child's body, the one who saves its life, and the one who gives it food. And, since she had been protected by birds in the desolate wilderness, I gave her the name Śakuntalā. Thus, you should know, did Śakuntalā become my daughter, good friend, and innocently Śakuntalā thinks of me as her father."

In this manner did Kanva describe my birth to the great seer who had questioned him, and thus, overlord of men, should you know me for Kanva's daughter. For I think of Kanva as my father, never having known my own. So, sire, I have told you exactly as I have heard it.

Duhṣanta said:
And very clear is it that you are the daughter of a king, the way you told it, beautiful girl. Be my wife, buxom woman! Tell me, what can I do for you? Today I shall bring you golden necklaces, clothes, earrings wrought of gold, and sparkling gems from many countries, my pretty, and breast plates and hides. Today all my kingdom will be yours; be my wife, my pretty! Come to me, timid and lovely, according to the rite of the Gandharvas, for my girl of the lovely thighs, the Gandharva mode is cited as the best of marriage rites!

Śakuntalā said:
My father has gone out of the hermitage to gather fruits, O king. Wait a while. He himself will give me away to you.

Duhṣanta said:
I want you to love me, flawless girl of the beautiful hips! Here I stand for you, for my heart has gone out to you. Oneself is one's own best friend, oneself is one's only recourse. You yourself can lawfully make the gift of yourself. There are eight forms of marriage known in total as being lawful *brāhma, daiva, ārṣa, prājāpatya, āsura, gāndharva, rākṣasa,* and lastly *paiśāca.* Manu Svāyaṃbhuva has declared their lawfulness in this order of descent. The first four are recommended for a brahmin, you must know; the first six, innocent girl, are lawful for the baronage, in descending order. The *rākṣasa* mode is set forth for kings, the *āsura* marriage for commoners and serfs. Three of the five are lawful, the other two are held to be unlawful. The *paiśāca* and *āsura* forms are never to be perpetrated. Marriage can be done according to this rite, for such is known to be the course of the Law. *Gāndharva* and *rākṣasa* marriages are lawful for the baronage, have no fear of that—either one or the two mixed may be held, without a doubt. You are in love with me as I am in love with you, fair girl—pray become my wife by the rite of the Gandharvas!

Śakuntalā said:
If this is the course of the Law, and if I am my own mistress, then, chief of the Pauravas, this is my condition in giving myself in marriage, my lord. Give your own true promise to the secret covenant I make between us: the son that may be born from me shall be Young King to succeed you, great king, declare this to me as the truth!

If it is to be thus, Duhṣanta, you may lie with me.

Vaiśaṃpāyana said:
Without hesitation the king replied, "So shall it be! And I shall conduct you to my city, sweet-smiling woman, as you deserve. This I declare to you as my truth, my lovely." Having thus spoken, the royal seer took his flawlessly moving bride solemnly by the hand and lay with her. And he comforted her and departed, and said many times. "I shall send an escort for you, with footmen, horses, chariots, and elephants; and with that I shall take you to my castle, sweet-smiling Śakuntalā!"

* * *

When Duhṣanta had returned to his seat after making his promises to Śakuntalā, the woman with the lovely thighs gave birth to a son of boundless might, after bearing him for a full three years, O Janamejaya, a son radiant like a blazing fire, enriched with all the virtues of beauty and generosity, true scion of Duhṣanta.

* * *

Taking her lotus-eyed son, who was like the child of an Immortal, the radiant woman left the woodland that Duḥṣanta had known. She went with her son to the king, her son shining with the brilliance of the morning sun, and was recognized and admitted. Śakuntalā paid proper homage to her king and said, "This is your son, sire. Consecrate him as Young King! For he is the godlike son you have begotten on me, king. Now act with him as you promised, greatest of men. Remember the promise you made long ago when we lay together, man of fortune, in Kaṇva's hermitage!"

When the king heard these words of hers, he remembered very well, yet he said, "I do not remember. Whose woman are you, evil ascetic? I do not recall ever having had recourse to you, whether for Law, Profit, or Love. Go or stay, as you please, or do what you want!"

At these words the beautiful and spirited woman was overcome with shame and, stunned with grief, stood motionless like a tree trunk. Her eyes turned copper red with indignant fury, her pursed lip began to tremble, and from the corner of her eyes she looked at the king with glances that seemed to burn him. Yet, although driven by her fury, she checked her expression and controlled the heat that had been accumulated by her austerities. For a moment she stood in thought, filled with grief and indignation, and looking straight at her husband, she said angrily, "You known very well, great king! Why do you say without concern that you do not know, lying like a commoner? Your heart knows the truth of it!"

* * *

"Do not despise me, who have been a faithful wife, because I have come on my own. You fail to honor me with the guest gift that is due me, your wife, who have come to you of my own accord! Why do you slight me in your assembly as though I were a commoner? I am surely not baying in the desert—why don't you hear me? Duḥṣanta, if you do not do my word as I am begging you, your head will burst into a hundred pieces! A husband enters his wife and is reborn from her—thus the old poets know this as a wife's wifehood. The offspring that is born to a man who follows the scriptures saves with his lineage the forebears that died before. Svayaṃbhū himself has said that a son is a *putra* because he saves his father from the hell named Put. She is a wife who is handy in the house, she is a wife who bears children, she is a wife whose life is her husband, she is a wife who is true to her lord. The wife is half the man, a wife is better than his best friend, a wife is the root of Law, Profit, and Love, a wife is a friend in a man's extremity. They who have wives have rites, they who have wives have households, they who have wives are happy, they who have wives have luck. Sweet-spoken wives are friends in solitude, fathers in the rites of the Law, mothers in suffering. Even in the wilderness she means respite for the man who is journeying. A man with a wife is a trustworthy man. Therefore a wife is the best course. Only a faithful wife follows even a man who has died and is transmigrating, sharing a common lot in adversities, for he is forever her husband. A wife who has died before stands still and waits for her husband; and a good wife follows after her husband if he has died before. This, sire, is the reason why marriage is sought by man, where a husband finds a wife for now and eternity."

* * *

"In time past while you were going on a chase and were led off by a deer, you approached me, a young girl, in my father's hermitage. Urvaśī, Pūrvacitti, Sahajanyā, Menakā, Viśvācī, and Ghṛtācī are the six greatest Apsarās. And from among them it was the beautiful Apsarā Menakā, daughter of Brahmā, who came from heaven to earth and bore me by Viśvāmitra. The Apsarā Menakā gave birth to me on a peak of the Himālayas and abandoned me pitilessly and went, as if I were another's child. What evil deeds have I done before in another life that in my childhood I was abandoned by my kin, and now by you? Surely when you forsake me I shall go to my hermitage— but pray do not forsake your own son!"

Duḥṣanta said:

I do not know that this is my son you have born, Śakuntalā. Women are liars—who will trust your word? Menakā, your mother, was a merciless slut who cast you off like a faded garland on a peak of the Himālayas! Viśvāmitra, your merciless father, who born a baron, reached for brahminhood, was a lecher! Menakā is the first of the Apsarās, Viśvāmitra the first of the seers—how can you call yourself their daughter, speaking like a whore? Are you not ashamed to say such incredible things, especially in my presence? Off with you, evil ascetic! An ever-awesome seer, an Apsarā like Menakā—are related to you, a wretch that wears a hermit's garb! Your son is too big, and he is strong even while still a child; how can he have shot up like a *śāla* tree in such a short time? Your own birth is very humble, and you look like a slut to me. So Menakā happened to give birth to you from sheer lust? Everything you say is obscure to me, ascetic. I do not know you. Go where you want!

Śakuntalā said:

King, you see the faults of others that are small, like mustard seeds, and you look but do not see your own, the size of pumpkins! Menakā is one of the Thirty Gods, the Thirty come after Menakā! My birth is higher than yours, Duḥṣanta! You walk on earth, great king, but I fly the skies. See how we differ, like Mount Meru and a mustard seed! I can roam to the palaces of great Indra, of Kubera, of Yama, of Varuṇa; behold my power, king!

* * *

Tiger among kings, do not forsake your son, as you protect yourself, your word, and your Law, O lord of the earth. Do not stoop to deceit, lion among kings. The gift of one pond is better than a hundred wells, one sacrifice is more than a hundred ponds, one son more than a hundred sacrifices, one truth more than a hundred sons. A thousand Horse Sacrifices and truth were held in a balance, and truth outweighed all thousand. Speaking the truth, O king, may or may not be equaled by learning all *Vedas* and bathing at all sacred fords. There is no Law higher than truth, nothing excels truth; and no evil is bitterer on earth than a lie. Truth, O king, is the supreme Brahman, truth is the sovereign covenant. Do not forsake your covenant, king, the truth shall be your alliance.

If you hold with the lie, if you have no faith of your own in me, then I shall go. There is no consorting with one like you. Even without you, Duhṣanta, my son shall reign over the four-cornered earth crowned by the king of mountains!

Vaiśampāyana said:

Having said all this to the king, Śakuntalā departed. Then, a disembodied voice spoke from the sky to Duhṣanta, as he sat surrounded by his priests, chaplain teachers, and councillors. "The mother is the father's water sack—he is the father who begets the son. Support your son, Duhṣanta; do not reject Śakuntalā. The son who has seed saves from Yama's realm, O God among men. You have planted this child. Śakuntalā has spoken the truth. A wife bears a son by splitting her body in two; therefore, Duhṣanta, keep Śakuntalā's son, O king. This is ruin: what man alive will forsake a live son born from himself?

"Paurava, keep this great-spirited scion of Duhṣanta and Śakuntalā; for he is yours to keep, and so is our behest. And as you keep him, he will be known by the name of Bharata."

King Paurava heard the utterance of the celestials and, much delighted, spoke to his chaplain and councillors, "Listen, good sirs, to what the Envoy of the Gods has spoken! I myself knew very well he was my son. But if I had taken him as my son on her word alone, suspicion would have been rife among the people and he would never have been cleared of it."

The king, having thus cleared himself of all suspicions, through the words of the Envoy of the Gods, now happily and joyfully accepted his son, O Bhārata. He kissed him on the head and embraced him lovingly; and he was welcomed to the court by the brahmins and praised by the bards. The king upon touching his son became filled with the greatest joy; and, knowing his duty, he honored his wife according to it. His majesty made up to her and said, "The alliance I made with you was not known to my people; that is the reason why I argued, so that I might clear you, my queen. People would think that I had a bond with you because you are a woman, and that I had chosen this son for the kingdom. That is why I argued. And if you have spoken very harsh words to me in your anger, dear wide-eyed wife, it was out of love, and I forgive you, beautiful woman."

Thus spoke King Duhṣanta to his beloved queen, and he honored her, O Bhārata, with clothes, food, and drink. Thereupon King Duhṣanta invested his son by Śakuntalā with the name Bhārata and anointed him Young King.

[From *The Mahābhārata*, vol. 1, pp. 160–171.]

THE LOSS OF DRAUPADĪ

The next excerpt from the *Mahābhārata* relates the events surrounding the loss of Draupadī, the wife of the five Pāṇḍava brothers who are the heroes of the epic. Challenged to a game of dice, the eldest brother losses all restraint and gambles away everything he has including himself, his four brothers, and their joint wife, Draupadī. The excerpt begins with the demand of Duryodhana, the victor, that Draupadī be brought into the hall of the kings. When confronted, Draupadī shows her knowledge of the law (*dharma*) by asking whether her husband had first lost his own freedom before gambling away hers. She will argue that having first lost himself, he had lost the right to stake her because a slave does not own anyone else.

Draupadī is forceably dragged before the assembly of men, which the text makes clear is not the proper place for a virtuous woman. Further, she is menstruating, hence wearing "one garment." This is a time of pollution for Hindu women and for anyone who has contact with her. It is not, however, Draupadī's argument that saves her, but rather the appearance of evil omens. In response to these, the old king Dhritarāṣṭra, the father of her tormentor, Duryodhana, offers her three boons. His is the final authority, and thus he gives Draupadī a way out.

This excerpt defines the wife as the property of her husband, just as the younger brothers are the property of the eldest, but it also shows the protection the gods give to the faithful wife, e.g., she cannot be stripped of her skirt and ominous omens appear. Even though she does not carry the day, this excerpt also shows that it is acceptable for the faithful wife to speak publicly in her own defense. The following excerpt, which is told by the narrator Vaiśaṃpāyana, begins with Duryodhana's demand that Draupadī be brought before him.

"Go, usher, and bring me Draupadī here!
You have nothing to fear from the Pāṇḍavas.
The Steward is timid and speaks against it,
But never did he wish that *we* should prosper!"

The usher, a bard, at his master's word
Went quickly out upon hearing the king,
And he entered, a dog in a lion's den,
Crawling up to the Queen of the Pāṇḍavas.

The usher said:
Yudhiṣṭhira, crazed by the dicing game,
Has lost you to Duryodhana, Draupadī.
Come enter the house of Dhṛtarāṣṭra,
To your chores I must lead you, Yājñasenī!

Draupadī said:
How dare you speak so, an usher, to me?
What son of a king would hazard his wife?
The king is befooled and crazed by the game—
Was there nothing left for him to stake?

The usher said:
When nothing was left for him to stake,
Ajātaśatru wagered you.
Already the king had thrown for his brothers,
And then for himself—then, Princess, for you.

Draupadī said:
Then go to the game and, son of a bard, ask in the assembly, "Bhārata, whom did you lose first, yourself or me?" When you have found out, come and take me, son of a bard!

Vaiśaṃpāyana said:
He went to the hall and asked Draupadī's question. "As the owner of whom did you lose us?" so queries Draupadī. "Whom did you lose first, yourself or me?" But Yudhiṣṭira did not stir, as though he had lost consciousness, and made no reply to the bard, whether good or ill.

Duryodhana said:
Let Kṛṣṇā of the Pāñcālas [Draupadī] come here and ask the question herself. All the people here shall hear what she or he has to say.

* * *

[When Draupadī was brought before him Duryodhana said:]
"All right now, come, Pāñcālī [Draupadī], you're won!
Look upon Duryodhana, without shame!
You shall now love the Kurus, long-lotus-eyed one,
You've been won under Law, come along to the hall!"

In bleak spirits did she rise,
And wiped with her hand her pallid face.
In despair she ran where the women sat
Of the aged king, the bull of the Kurus.

And quickly the angry Duḥśāsana
Came rushing to her with a thunderous roar;
By the long-tressed black and flowing hair
Duḥśāsana grabbed the wife of a king.

The hair that at the concluding bath
Of the king's consecration had been sprinkled
With pure-spelled water, Dhṛtarāṣṭra's son
Now caressed with force, unmanning the Pāṇḍus.

Duḥśāsana, stroking her, led her and brought her,
That Kṛṣṇā of deep black hair, to the hall,
As though unprotected amidst her protectors,
And tossed her as wind tosses a plantain tree.

And as she was dragged, she bent her body
And whispered softly, "It is now my month!
This is my sole garment, man of slow wit,
You cannot take me to the hall, you churl!"

But using his strength and holding her down,
By her deep black locks, he said to Kṛṣṇā,
"To Kṛṣṇā and Jiṣṇu, to Hari and Nara,
Cry out for help! I shall take you yet!

"Sure, you be in your month, Yajñasena's daughter.
Or wear a lone cloth, or go without one!
You've been won at the game and been made a slave,
And one lechers with slaves as the fancy befalls!"

Her hair disheveled, her half skirt drooping,
Shaken about by Duḥśāsana,
Ashamed and burning with indignation.
She whispered again, and Kṛṣṇā [Draupadī] said,

"In the hall are men who have studied the books,
All follow the rites and are like unto Indras.
They are all my *gurus* or act for them:
Before their eyes I cannot stand thus!

"You ignoble fool of cruel feats,
Don't render me nude, do not debase me!
These sons of kings will not condone you,
Were Indra and Gods to be your helpmates!

"The king, son of Dharma, abides by the Law,
And the Law is subtle, for the wise to find out:
But even at his behest I would not
Give the least offense and abandon my virtue.

"It is *base* that amidst the Kaurava heroes
You drag me inside while I am in my month;
There is no one here to honor you for it,
Though surely they do not mind your plan.

"Damnation! lost to the Bhāratas
Is their Law and the ways of sagacious barons,
When all these Kauravas in their hall
Watch the Kuru Law's limits overstridden!

"There is no mettle in Drona and Bhīṣma,
Nor to be sure in this good man;
The chiefs of the elders amongst the Kurus
Ignore this dread Unlaw of this king."

As she piteously spoke the slim-waisted queen
Threw a scornful glance at her furious husbands
And inflamed with the fall of her sidelong glances,
The Pāṇḍavas, wrapped with wrath in their
    limbs.

Bhīṣma said:
As the Law is subtle, my dear, I fail
To resolve your riddle the proper way:
A man without property cannot stake another's—
But given that wives are the husband's chattels?

Yudhiṣṭhira may give up all earth
With her riches, before he'd give up the truth.
The Pāṇḍava said, "I have been won,"
Therefore I cannot resolve this doubt.

No man is Śakuni's peer at the dice,
And he left Yudhiṣṭhira his own choice.
The great-spirited man does not think he was
    cheating,
Therefore I cannot speak to the riddle.

Draupadī said:
In the meeting hall he was challenged, the king,
By cunning, ignoble, and evil tricksters
Who love to game; he had never much tried it.
Why then do you say he was left a choice?

Pure, the best of Kurus and Pāṇḍavas,
He did not wake up to the playing of tricks,
He attended the session and when he'd lost all,
Only then he agreed to hazard me.

They stand here, the Kurus, they stand in their hall,
Proud owners of sons and daughters-in-law:
Examine ye all this word of mine,
And resolve my riddle the proper way!

* * *

Ignoring those who caution him against dishonoring Draupadī, Duryodhana orders that she and her husbands be stripped.

Hearing this all the Pāṇḍavas shed their upper clothes and sat down in the assembly hall. Then Duhśāsana forcibly laid hold of Draupadī's robe, O king, and in the midst of the assembly began to undress her. But when her skirt was being stripped off, lord of the people, another similar skirt appeared every time. A terrible roar went up from all the kings, a shout of approval, as they watched that greatest wonder on earth. And in the midst of the kings Bhīma, lips trembling with rage, kneading hand in hand, pronounced a curse in a mighty voice: "Take to heart this word of mine, ye barons that live on this earth, a word such as never has been spoken before nor any one shall ever speak hereafter! May I forfeit my journey to all my ancestors, if I do not carry out what I say, if I not tear open in battle the chest of this

misbegotten fiend, this outcaste of the Bharatas, and drink his blood!"

* * *

Draupadī said:
I on whom the assembled kings set eye in the arena at my Bridegroom Choice, but never before or after, I am now brought into the hall! I whom neither wind nor sun have seen before in my house, I am now seen in the middle of the hall in the assembly of the Kurus. I whom the Pāṇḍavas did not suffer to be touched by the wind in my house before, they now allow to be touched by this miscreant. The Kurus allow—and methinks that Time is out of joint—their innocent daughter and daughter-in-law to be molested! What

greater humiliation than that I, a woman of virtue and beauty, now must invade the men's hall? What is left of the Law of the kings? From of old, we have heard, they do *not* bring law-minded women into their hall. This ancient eternal Law is lost among the Kauravas. How can I, wife of the Pāṇḍus, sister of Dhṛṣṭadyumna Pārṣata, and friend of Vāsudeva, enter the hall of the kings? Is the wife of the King Dharma whose birth matches his a slave or free? Speak, Kauravas, I shall abide by your answer. For this foul man, disgrace of the Kauravas, is molesting me, and I cannot bear it any longer, Kauravas! Whatever the kings think, whether I have been won or not, I want it answered, and I shall abide by the answer, Kauravas.

* * *

Karṇa said:
There are three who own no property,
A student, a slave, a dependent woman:
The wife of a slave, you are *his* now, my dear;
A masterless slave wench, you are now slave wealth!

Come in and serve us with your attentions:
That is the chore you have left in this house.
Dhṛtarāṣṭra's men, and not the Pārthas,
Are now your masters, child of a king!

Now quickly choose you another husband
Who will not gamble your freedom away:
For license with masters is never censured:
That is the slave's rule, remember it!

* * *

"You're lost, Duryodhana, shallow-brain,
Who in this hall of the bulls of the Kurus
Berated a woman most uncouthly,
And her a Draupadī, married by Law!"

Having spoken the wise Dhṛtarāṣṭra withdrew,
For he wished for the weal of his allies-in-law;
Kṛṣṇā Pāñcālī he pacified,
And thinking with insight, informed of the facts,

Dhṛtarāṣṭra said:
Choose a boon from me, Pāñcālī, whatever you

wish; for you are to me the most distinguished of my daughters-in-law, bent as you are on the Law!

Draupadī said:
If you give me a boon, bull of the Bharatas, I choose this: the illustrious Yudhiṣṭhira, observer of every Law, shall be no slave! Do not let these little boys, who do not know my determined son, say of Prativindhya when he happens to come in, "Here comes the son of a slave!" He has been a *king's* son, as no man has been anywhere. Spoiled as he is, he shall die, Bhārata, when he finds out that he has been a slave's son!

Dhṛtarāṣṭra said:
I give you a second boon, good woman, ask me! My heart has convinced me that you do not deserve only a single boon.

Draupadī said:
With their chariots and bows I choose Bhīmasena and Dhanaṃjaya, Nakula and Sahadeva, as my second boon!

Dhṛtarāṣṭra said:
Choose a third boon from us; two boons do not honor you enough. For of all of my daughters-in-law you are the best, for you walk in the Law.

Draupadī said:
Greed kills Law, Sir, I cannot make another wish. I am not worthy to take a third boon from you, best of kings. As they say, the commoner has one boon, the baron and his lady two, but three are the king's, great king, and a hundred the brahmin's. They were laid low, my husbands, but they have been saved; and they will find the good things, king, with their own good acts!

Karṇa said:
Of all the women of mankind, famous for their beauty, of whom we have heard, no one have we heard accomplished such a deed! While the Pārthas and the Dhārtarāṣṭras are raging beyond measure, Kṛṣṇā Draupadī has become the salvation of the Pāṇḍavas! When they were sinking, boatless and drowning, in the plumbless ocean, the Pāñcālī became the Pāṇḍavas' boat, to set them ashore!
[From *The Mahābhārata,* vol. 2, pp. 139–153.]

THE RĀMĀYAṆA

The second great epic of India is the *Rāmāyaṇa,* which was composed around the second century B.C.E. Tradition says it was the work of one man, the sage Valmīki. The story tells the adventures of Rāma, who has been unjustly exiled, and his wife Sītā. In popular Hinduism they are the supreme divine couple. Rāma is an incarnation of the great sky god Viṣṇu, and Sītā, though understood to be Viṣṇu's wife Lakṣmī, is clearly represented as the daughter of the earth. In the epic, Rāma and Sītā enact the ideal relationship between husband and wife. However, in this, the earliest *Rāmāyaṇa*, it is Rāma who is understood to be the deity, while Sītā is the ideal devotee who remains faithful to her god/husband no matter how unfair his actions may seem. She is the personification of the ideal Hindu wife, who is the source of her husband's prosperity.

RĀMA'S DEPARTURE FROM HOME

The following excerpt (II.24–29) describes Rāma's departure from home, during which he argues with both his mother (Kaushalya) and his wife as to whether they can accompany him. In the course of these discussions, the obligations of a Hindu wife to her husband are made clear.

Perceiving determined to honour his father's command, Kaushalya, bursting into tears, said to the supremely virtuous Ramachandra:—

"A stranger till to-day to hardship, how will that virtuous prince, beneficent to all, whom I bore to King Dasaratha, be able to subsist on a handful of corn? He whose servants live on hulled rice, how can Rama live on roots and fruits in the forest? Who will believe and who will not tremble on learning that the virtuous and beloved Kakutstha has been banished by the king? Assuredly a powerful destiny rules everything in the world since, despite being beloved by all, O Rama, thou art now to go to the forest! O Child, the fire of my grief fanned by the breath of thy departure, fed on the fuel of my lamentations and affliction, its sacred libations my sighs and tears, its columns of smoke my fears and groans evoked by thine absence, in its unparalleled intensity will certainly scorch and consume me, when I am deprived of thee, as, at the end of winter, the forest fire destroys the undergrowth! As a cow follows in the footsteps of its calf so shall I follow thee, O My Dear Child, wheresoever thou goest."

Hearing these words, that bull among men, Rama, answered his mother, who was overcome with sorrow, and said:—

"Deceived by Kaikeyi, when I have entered the forest, the king deserted by thee will surely die. To leave her consort is ever inauspicious for a woman, do not therefore commit this sin; banish this thought even from thy mind. As long as the king, my father, the offspring of Kakutstha, lives, submission is due to him; it is an unwritten law."

At these words the beautiful and tenderly cherished Kaushalya replied to Rama of blessed karma, "Let it be so!"

★ ★ ★

Suppressing his sobs, Rama replied to his mother, who was weeping, and said:—

"As long as she lives, a woman's God and master is her husband; further the king is thine absolute lord as well as mine. We are not without a master, by the king's grace; he is the wise director of his people. Moreover the virtuous Bharata, filled with goodwill to all beings, will always be devoted to thee, for it is his duty. Do not neglect anything that will prevent the king, in his paternal affliction, from suffering the least distress, lest he succumb to the violence of his grief. Exert thyself without ceasing to minister to the aged monarch. Even a pious woman given over to fasting and spiritual practices, were she the chief of the virtuous, is treading an evil path if she is not attentive to her lord. By obedience to her husband, a woman attains the highest heaven, even if she has failed to render due homage to the Gods. To be subject to her consort and seek to please him is the strict duty of a woman, laid down by the Veda and acknowledged by the world. O Queen, by the maintenance of the sacred fire with the aid of incense, do thou on my behalf invoke the Gods and cover the brahmins with consideration. Pass the time of waiting (for my return) in this wise. Chaste, serene, wholly devoted to thy consort, thou shalt thus attain thy highest desire on my return, should the most virtuous of kings survive!"

★ ★ ★

Having taken leave of his mother, Kaushalya, whose blessings he had received, Rama prepared to enter the forest, fixed in devotion to his duty, and that prince with his lustre illumined the royal highway, as it were, that was thronged with people, causing their hearts to beat by the charm of his qualities.

The illustrious Princess of Videha [Sītā] had no knowledge of what had taken place and was reflecting within herself on her association with her consort when enthroned. Having fulfilled her duties cheerfully by worshipping the Gods, in her gratitude, the princess, versed in her royal obligations, awaited her lord.

At that moment, Rama entered her luxurious abode that was filled with a happy throng, and he appeared distressed and advanced with his head bowed. Then Sita, perceiving him to be a prey to grief and fear, and anxious, trembling ran to meet her consort, whereupon beholding her, the virtuous Raghava was unable to conceal the suffering of his soul and gave way to sorrow.

★ ★ ★

"O Sita, my venerable father has banished me to the forest! O Thou, who art born of a noble family, O Thou, who art conversant with thy duty and dost follow the righteous path, know, O Janaki, for what reason I am going hence to-day.

"The king, faithful to his word, my Sire Dasaratha, formerly bestowed two boons on my mother, Kaikeyi. This day, as mine enthronement was to take place through the king's ministrations, she remembered the contract made with her and demanded, for its fulfilment, as was her right, that I should pass fourteen years in the Dandaka Forest and my father should install Bharata on the throne. I have come to see thee before leaving for the lonely forest. Do not speak in praise of me in Bharata's presence; in times of prosperity, men do not suffer the praise of their rivals gladly, therefore do not extol my virtues before him. Have a care never even to utter my name, so that it may prove possible for thee to live in peace with him. The king has finally conferred the regency on him; therefore thou must pay him every honour, O Sita, for he will be the sovereign.

★ ★ ★

At these words, Vaidehi, that sweet and gracious princess, her tender heart wounded, said to her lord: —

"O Offspring of a great king, O Rama, I am unable to show aught but contempt for what I hear! It is unworthy of a warrior, a prince skilled in the use of sword and lance! O Lord, what thou hast said is shameful and may not be endured! O Son of an illustrious monarch, a father, a mother, a brother, a son or a daughter-in-law enjoy the fruit of their merits and receive what is their due, a wife alone follows the destiny of her consort, O Bull among Men; therefore, from now on, my duty is clear, I shall dwell in the forest! For a woman, it is not her father, her son, nor her mother, friends nor her own self but the husband, who in this world and the next is ever her sole means of salvation. If thou dost enter the impenetrable forest to-day, O Descendant of Raghu, I shall precede thee on foot, treading down the spiky Kusha Grass. Relinquishing anger and envy, as water that is poured away on quenching one's thirst, take me with thee without hesitation, there is no fault in me that would warrant me being left alone by thee, O Hero! In truth whether it be in palaces, in chariots or in heaven, wherever the shadow of the feet of her consort falls, it must be followed! I have been fully instructed in my diverse duties by my mother and father, I have no need of instruction in what I have now to do, I shall enter into the deep forest, that is impassable, deserted by men, filled with wild beasts and frequented by tigers. I shall willingly dwell in the forest as formerly I inhabited the palace of my father, having no anxiety in the Three Worlds and reflecting only on my duties towards my lord. Ever subject to thy will, docile, living like an ascetic, in those honey-scented woodlands I shall be happy in thy proximity, O Rama, O Illustrious Lord. What are the rest of men to me? Undoubtedly I shall accompany thee to the forest to-day; none shall restrain me, O Mighty Prince, on this I am firmly resolved!

★ ★ ★

By the command of my revered parents, it is incumbent on me to accompany thee, O Rama; separated from thee I should immediately yield up my life. Assuredly when near thee, even the King of the Gods would not be able to bear me away by force, O Raghava. Deprived of her consort a woman cannot live, thou canst not doubt this truth where I am concerned. Indeed, O Sagacious Prince, formerly, in my father's house, the brahmins predicted that I should certainly have to dwell in the forest; since I heard the prophecies of those brahmins at home, I have ever dwelt on the idea of inhabiting a forest, O Mighty Hero. I shall fulfil the command to dwell in the forest without default, thou art my husband and I will accompany thee, O My Beloved, it cannot be otherwise. I shall conform to that decree and go with thee, the time has come to fulfil the prediction of the Twice-born. I know that this sojourn in the forest is assuredly replete with difficulties of every kind, but, O Hero, they do not touch those who are masters of their senses. When I was young, a pious and saintly woman in my father's house, in the presence of my mother, described the life in the forest! O Prince, formerly I often entreated thee to take me to the forest where I wished to live with thee; this is the moment to take me, O Raghava, may prosperity attend thee! It will please me greatly to follow one who is a hero to the forest. O Thou of pure soul, I shall remain sinless by following piously in the steps of my consort, for a husband is a God. If death overtakes me, I shall be happy forever with thee according to the instruction of the venerable brahmins. A woman, who in this life has been given by her parents to a man with the traditional blessing of water, belongs to him according to the law, even after death. For what reason wilt thou not take me with thee, I who am a devoted and faithful wife? O Kakutstha, it behoves thee to take me with thee, wretched woman that I am, who am devoted and faithful in prosperity and adversity and to whom joy and pain are one. If, despite my grief, thou wilt not take me to the forest, I shall seek death by poison, or cast myself into the fire or drown myself!"

[From *The Ramayana of Valmiki*, vol. 1, pp. 225–237.]

SĪTĀ'S BIRTH

In the following excerpt (II.117–118) Sītā, sometimes called Vaidehi, meets the woman ascetic Anasūyā and learns her story. Anasūyā states that the first obligation of a woman is to be devoted to her husband, an idea that Sītā seconds in her speech. Sītā then tells the story of her miraculous birth from the earth.

Raghava went away, accompanied by Vaidehi and Lakshmana. Reaching Atri's hermitage, he paid obeisance to him, and that blessed One received him as he were a son and offered him abundant hospitality, rendering the fortunate Saumitri and Sita equal honour. Thereafter the virtuous ascetic, who delighted in ministering to the welfare of all creatures, called his aged wife Anasuya, who had just come there, she who was revered by all, rich in asceticism and who lived a pious life, and he addressed her affectionately, saying: —

"Do thou welcome Videha's daughter!"

Thereafter Atri related the story of that virtuous female ascetic to Rama, saying: —

"Formerly a drought extending over a period of ten years burnt up the earth, whereupon this virtuous woman produced fruit and roots and, undergoing a rigid mortification enriched by pious observances, caused the River Jahnavi to flow here. For ten thousand years, she practised the most severe asceticism and, in virtue of her penances, dispelled the darkness, destroying the impediments in the path of the Sages. Solicited on behalf of the Gods, she brought ten nights into the compass of one! She should be venerated as a mother by thee, O Irreproachable One. Let Vaidehi find refuge with that ascetic who is revered by all, and, though old, is ever free from anger."

On the words of the Rishi, Raghava answered, "Be it so!" and, glancing at the virtuous Sita, said to her: —

"O Princess, thou hast heard what the Sage has said, this is best for thee; honour the saintly Anasuya without delay, whose deeds have brought her great renown in this world!"

Hearing Raghava speak thus, Sita, the illustrious Maithili, approached Atri's virtuous consort and reverently paid homage to the fortunate Anasuya, who was feeble, bent, her hair white with age, her limbs trembling like a palm tree agitated by the wind. Announcing her name, Sita made obeisance to the ascetic with her senses subdued and, glad at heart, with joined palms, enquired as to her welfare.

Seeing the virtuous Sita engaged in righteous acts, the aged Anasuya encouraged her with kindly words, saying: —

"By the grace of heaven, thou hast fulfilled thy duty! Forsaking wealth and comfort, of which thou art worthy, and thy kinsfolk, O Sita, thou didst accompany Rama in his exile in the forest! Those women, who are devoted to their husbands, whether it be in the city or the forest or if they be well or ill disposed towards them, attain the highest bliss. Whether he be a sinner or a slave to desire or poor, the husband is a God to a woman of noble sentiments. On reflection, I know of none who is a better friend than the husband, who protects his wife in all circumstances and is like unto asceticism, which is both salutary and imperishable. Undoubtedly those wicked women, who do not remain faithful to their consorts in adversity and only follow their passions, committing unworthy acts, ranging at will here and there, having forgotten their duty, fall into dishonour. But those, like thee, who are endowed with virtue, who look with detachment on prosperity and adversity in this world, go to the Celestial Regions. Thus, devoted to thy lord, virtuous and full of deference and obedience, carry out thy conjugal duties and thou wilt obtain merit and renown.

⋆ ⋆ ⋆

Anasuya having spoken thus, the selfless Vaidehi, full of reverence for her, addressed her in gentle tones, saying: —

"O Noble Lady, thy counsel is in no wise a source of wonder to me, for I know well, for such a woman her husband is her Guru. It is my conviction that the husband, whether he be of humble origin or without fortune, should unhesitatingly be obeyed by such as I am; how much more then if he be renowned for his virtues, compassionate, master of my heart and who is ever affectionate and manifests the tenderness of a mother and father to me! The mighty Rama bears himself to all the Queens as he does towards his mother; free from all sense of importance that hero like a devoted son treats all those women as his mothers on whom the king has even once bestowed a single glance! When departing for the lonely and fearful forest, Queen Kaushalya imparted certain instruction to me which I have inscribed on my heart, and, what my mother taught me when, witnessed by the fire, I gave my hand to Rama, I shall always remember. I have not forgotten any of those words; O Virtuous One, obedience to one's lord is the crowning discipline for a woman of noble birth! Savitri, having served her lord faithfully, is now highly honoured in heaven, and thou also, having followed this path in submission to thy husband, shalt enter paradise. Rohini, a pearl among women, who is a Goddess in the Celestial Regions, ever accompanies the moon. Thus many other women, who have been faithful to their consorts, are highly revered in the higher worlds for their virtuous conduct."

Anasuya rejoiced to hear Sita speak thus, and, kissing the brow of the Princess of Mithila, in order to please her spoke thus:—

"O Sita, in virtue of my pious observances, I have acqu'red great merit and, through these powers, I wish to confer a boon on thee. O Princess of Mithila, thy words have given me extreme satisfaction, now say what good I may do to thee!"

Hearing these words, Sita, surprised, answered smilingly:—

"My desires have already been fulfilled by thee!"

On this, that virtuous One was gratified in even greater measure and said:—

"O Sita, I will prepare a great joy for thee which will be to thine advantage! Here are divine gifts: a garland, jewels, apparel and a precious unguent and rare ointment to adorn thy person; all these will never fade and will become thee well! Thy body anointed with this celestial and rare paste, O Daughter of Janaka, will enhance the beauty of thy lord, as Lakshmi increases the glory of the imperishable Vishnu!"

Thereupon the princess accepted the robes, paste and ornaments, gifts of love to her from the female ascetic, and the illustrious Sita, having received these tokens of affection from Anasuya with joined palms sat down beside her. As Sita was thus sitting near her, Anasuya, who was firm in her vows, questioned her on those things that were near to her heart.

* * *

Then Sita obediently answered, saying:—

"Hear me and I will relate it all to thee. There was a King of Mithila, full of valour, named Janaka, who rejoiced in observing the duties of a warrior and ruled the world with justice.

"When he was ploughing the land intended for sacrifice, I emerged from the earth like a daughter. At that time, the monarch was engaged in scattering handfuls of soil and, beholding me covered with dust, was astonished. Being without issue, full of tenderness, he placed me on his lap, saying, 'This shall be my daughter', and, in great affection, adopted me. Thereupon a voice resembling that of a human being rang out, saying, 'O King, verily she is thy daughter!'

"The king rejoiced in my possession and, through it, his prosperity increased."

[From *The Ramayana of Valmiki*, vol. I, pp. 431–434.]

SĪTĀ'S ORDEAL BY FIRE

At the heart of the *Rāmāyaṇa* is the capture of Sītā by the demon Rāvana and her eventual rescue by Rāma. The following excerpt (VI.116–118) relates the first meeting of Sītā and Rāma after he had killed her abductor. Rāma repudiates Sītā, which requires her to give evidence of her virtue in a public setting. Sītā's word and even her ordeal by fire are not enough; divine intervention is required.

Hearing that his consort, who had dwelt long in the titan's abode, had come, rage, joy and grief overwhelmed Raghava, the slayer of his foes and, beholding Sita in the palanquin, Rama, in order to test

her, dissembling his happiness, said to Bibishana:—

"O Supreme Lord of the Titans, O My Friend who ever rejoiced in my victories, bring Vaidehi nearer to me."

At Raghava's command, the righteous Bibishana caused the crowd to disperse, whereupon titans clad in armour, wearing turbans, with drums and bamboo staves in their hands began to move about driving away the warriors, bears, monkeys and titans, who, scattering, stood apart some way off. And as they were being driven away, a tremendous clamour arose resembling the roar of the sea buffeted by the winds.

Seeing them dispersing, whilst confusion was created amongst them, Rama in affection for them, grew indignant at their departure and, highly incensed, with a glance that seemed as if it would consume him, addressed the exceedingly intelligent Bibishana in terms of reproach, saying:—

"Why, disregarding me, dost thou harass them, are they not my people? Her conduct, not raiment, walls, seclusion or other royal prohibitions, are a woman's shield. In times of calamity, peril, war, the Swyamvara or the nuptual ceremony, it is not forbidden to behold a woman unveiled. It is not prohibited to look upon a woman who has fallen into distress and difficulty, above all in my presence. Therefore, leaving the palanquin, let Vaidehi come hither on foot so that the dwellers in the woods may see her at my side."

Hearing Rama's words, Bibishana became thoughtful and conducted Sita to him reverently, whilst Lakshmana, Sugriva and also Hanuman, hearing Rama speak thus, were saddened.

Then Maithili, confused and shrinking within herself, approached her lord accompanied by Bibishana; and it was with astonishment, delight and love that Sita, whose husband was a god, gazed on Rama's gracious appearance, she whose own face was still beautiful. Beholding the countenance of her dearly loved lord, whom she had not seen for so long and which was as radiant as the full moon when it rises, she cast aside all anxiety and her own face became as fair as the immaculate orb of the night.

* * *

Beholding Maithili standing humbly beside him, Rama gave expression to the feelings he had concealed in his heart, saying:—

"O Illustrious Princess, I have re-won thee and mine enemy has been defeated on the battlefield; I have accomplished all that fortitude could do; my wrath is appeased; the insult and the one who offered it have both been obliterated by me. To-day my prowess has been manifested, to-day mine exertions have been crowned with success, to-day I have fulfilled my vow and am free. As ordained by destiny the stain of thy separation and thine abduction by that fickle-minded titan has been expunged by me, a mortal. Of what use is great strength to the vacillating, who do not with resolution avenge the insult offered to them?

"To-day Hanuman is plucking the fruit of his glorious exploits, and Sugriva, who is valiant in war and wise in counsel, with his army is reaping the harvest of his exertions! Bibishana too is culling the fruits of his labours, he who cast off a brother, who was devoid of virtue, to come to me."

When Sita heard Rama speak in this wise, her large doe-like eyes filled with tears and, beholding the beloved of his heart standing close to him, Rama, who was apprehensive of public rumour, was torn within himself. Then, in the presence of the monkeys and the titans, he said to Sita, whose eyes were as large as lotus petals, her dark hair plaited, and who was endowed with faultless limbs:—

"What a man should do in order to wipe out an insult, I have done by slaying Ravana for I guard mine honour jealously! Thou wert re-won as the southern region, inaccessible to man, was re-gained by the pure-souled Agastya through his austerities. Be happy and let it be known that this arduous campaign, so gloriously terminated through the support of my friends, was not undertaken wholly for thy sake. I was careful to wipe out the affront paid to me completely and to avenge the insult offered to mine illustrious House.

"A suspicion has arisen, however, with regard to thy conduct, and thy presence is as painful to me as a lamp to one whose eye is diseased! Henceforth go where it best pleaseth thee, I give thee leave, O Daughter of Janaka. O Lovely One, the ten regions are at thy disposal; I can have nothing more to do with thee! What man of honour would give rein to his passion so far as to permit himself to take back a woman who has dwelt in the house of another? Thou hast been taken into Ravana's lap and he has cast lustful glances on thee; how can I reclaim thee, I who boast of belonging to an illustrious House? The end which I sought in re-conquering thee has been gained; I no longer have any attachment for thee; go where thou desirest! This is the outcome of my reflections, O Lovely One! Turn to Lakshmana or Bharata, Shatrughna, Sugriva or the Titan Bibishana, make thy choice, O Sita, as pleases thee best. Assuredly Ravana, beholding thy ravishing and celestial beauty, will not have respected thy person during the time that thou didst dwell in his abode."

On this, that noble lady, worthy of being addressed in sweet words, hearing that harsh speech from her beloved lord, who for long had surrounded her with every homage, wept bitterly, and she resembled a creeper that has been torn away by the trunk of a great elephant.

* * *

Hearing these harsh words from the wrathful Raghava, causing her to tremble, those fearful utterances, which till that time had never been heard by her and were now addressed to her by her lord in the presence of a great multitude, Maithili, the daughter of Janaka, overwhelmed with shame, pierced to the heart by that arrow-like speech, shed abundant tears. Thereafter, wiping her face, she addressed her husband in gentle and faltering accents, saying:—

"Why dost thou address such words to me, O Hero, as a common man addresses an ordinary woman? I swear to thee, O Long-armed Warrior, that my conduct is worthy of thy respect! It is the behaviour of other women that has filled thee with distrust! Relinquish thy doubts since I am known to thee! If my limbs came in contact with another's, it was against my will, O Lord, and not through any inclination on my part; it was brought about by fate. That which is under my control, my heart, has ever remained faithful to thee; my body was at the mercy of another; not being mistress of the situation, what could I do? If despite the proofs of love that I gave thee whilst I lived with thee, I am still a stranger to thee, O Proud Prince, my loss is irrevocable!

"When, in Lanka, thou didst dispatch the great warrior Hanuman to seek me out, why didst thou not repudiate me then? As soon as I had received the tidings that I had been abandoned by thee, I should have yielded up my life in the presence of that monkey, O Hero! Then thou wouldst have been spared useless fatigue on mine account and others lives would not have been sacrificed, nor thine innumerable friends exhausted to no purpose. But thou, O Lion among Men, by giving way to wrath and by thus passing premature judgement on a woman, hast acted like a worthless man.

"I have received my name from Janaka, but my birth was from the earth and thou hast failed to appreciate fully the nobility of my conduct, O Thou who are well acquainted with the nature of others. Thou hast had no reverence for the joining of our hands in my girlhood and mine affectionate nature, all these things hast thou cast behind thee!"

Having spoken thus to Rama, weeping the while, her voice strangled with sobs, Sita addressed the unfortunate Lakshmana, who was overwhelmed with grief, saying:—

"Raise a pyre for me, O Saumitri, this is the only remedy for my misery! These unjust reproaches have destroyed me, I cannot go on living! Publicly renounced by mine husband, who is insensible to my virtue, there is only one redress for me, to undergo the ordeal by fire!"

Hearing Vaidehi's words, Lakshmana, the slayer of hostile warriors, a prey to indignation, consulted Raghava with his glance and by Rama's gestures he understood what was in his heart, whereupon the valiant Saumitri, following his indications, prepared the pyre,

None amongst his friends dared to appeal to Rama, who resembled Death himself, the Destroyer of Time; none dared to speak or even to look upon him.

Thereafter Vaidehi, having circumambulated Rama, who stood with his head bowed, approached the blazing fire and, paying obeisance to the Celestials and brahmins, Maithili, with joined palms, standing before the flames, spoke thus:—

"As my heart has never ceased to be true to Raghava, do thou, O Witness of all Beings, grant me thy protection! As I am pure in conduct, though Rama looks on me as sullied, do thou, O Witness of the Worlds, grant me full protection!"

With these words, Vaidehi circumambulated the pyre and with a fearless heart entered the flames.

And a great multitude were assembled there, amongst which were many children and aged people who witnessed Maithili entering the fire. And, resembling gold that has been melted in the crucible, she threw herself into the blazing flames in the presence of all. That large-eyed lady, entering the fire, who is the Bearer of Sacrificial Offerings, appeared to those who watched her to resemble a golden altar. That fortunate princess entering the fire, which is nourished by oblations, seemed, in the eyes of the Rishis, Devas and Gandharvas, to resemble a sacrificial offering.

Then all the women cried out:— 'Alas!' on seeing her, like a stream of butter hallowed by the recitation of mantras, fall into the flames, and she appeared to the Three Worlds, the Gods, the Gandharvas and the Danavas like a goddess smitten by a curse and cast down from heaven into hell. Then, as she entered the flames, a great and terrible cry rose from the titans and the monkeys.

[From *The Ramayana of Valmiki*, vol. 3, pp. 333–338.]

The gods intervene (VI.120) and tell Rāma that he really is a god who has incarnated on earth to dispell evil and Sītā is really the goddess Lakṣmī, the goddess of good fortune. The god of fire then puts out the fire surrounding Sītā and says to Rāma:

"Here is Vaidehi [Sītā], O Rama, there is no sin in her! Neither by word, feeling or glance has thy lovely consort shown herself to be unworthy of thy noble qualities. Separated from thee, that unfortunate one was borne away against her will in the lonely forest by Ravana, who had grown proud on account of his power. Though imprisoned and closely guarded by titan women in the inner apartments, thou wast ever the focus of her thoughts and her supreme hope. Surrounded by hideous and sinister women, though tempted and threatened, Maithili never gave place in her heart to a single thought for that titan and was solely absorbed in thee. She is pure and without taint, do thou receive Maithili; it is my command that she should not suffer reproach in any way."

These words filled Rama's heart with delight and he, the most eloquent of men, that loyal soul, reflected an instant within himself, his glance full of joy. Then the illustrious, steadfast and exceedingly valiant Rama, the first of virtuous men, hearing those words addressed to him, said to the Chief of the Gods: —

"On account of the people, it was imperative that Sita should pass through this trial by fire; this lovely woman had dwelt in Ravana's inner apartments for a long time. Had I not put the innocence of Janaki to the test, the people would have said: — 'Rama, the son of Dasaratha is governed by lust!' It was well known to me that Sita had never given her heart to another and that the daughter of Janaka, Maithili, was ever devoted to me. Ravana was no more able to influence that large-eyed lady, whose chastity was her own protection, than the ocean may pass beyond its bournes. Despite his great perversity, he was unable to approach Maithili even in thought, who was inaccessible to him as a flame. That virtuous woman could never belong to any other than myself for she is to me what the light is to the sun. Her purity is manifest in the Three Worlds; I could no more renounce Maithili, born of Janaka than a hero his honour. It behoveth me to follow your wise and friendly Counsel, O Gracious Lords of the World."

Having spoken thus, the victorious and extremely powerful Rama, full of glory, adored for his noble exploits, was re-united with his beloved and experienced the felicity he had merited.

[From *The Ramayana of Valmiki*, vol. 3, pp. 341–342.]

The Bhakti (Devotion) Movements

Bhakti is a form of religious devotion that focuses on one god, most often Shiva or Krishna, as the great god who created all the other gods and everything and everyone else that exists. In contradistinction to orthodox Hinduism, bhakti movements usually offer salvation to everyone, regardless of their caste. They are able to do this because the only requirement for salvation is a whole-hearted and passionate devotion to god. Often this devotion is described in terms of a woman's emotions as she waits, longing for the return of her beloved. This emphasis on female emotions caused many of the male poet/saints to try to identify with women and their emotions in order to approach god. Often they assumed a female voice in their songs. Perhaps because of this emphasis on women's experience several women themselves rose to prominence as poet/saints, though not without a struggle.

MAHĀDEVĪYAKKA

The following selections were written by a twelfth-century woman who lived in southern India, Mahādevīyakka. For her, Shiva, whom she refers to in her poems as "lord white as jasmine," is the supreme god. As is often the case, her songs provide some biographical details, such as her need to struggle against the values of the secular world in order to pursue union with Shiva. We know that she was an ardent devotee of Shiva from at least the age of ten and considered him to be her true husband. The local king, however, fell in love with her, and she was required to marry him. It was a difficult marriage in which Mahādevīyakka objected to her husband's lack of faith and his sensuality. After a few years she left her husband, discarded her social position and obligations along with her clothes, and began to wander, looking for Shiva, dressed only in her long hair. Eventually she arrived at Kalyāṇa, a center of Shiva worship, where she was initially rejected by the leading male saint because of her nudity. He asks her why, if she is so pure, she bothers covering her nakedness with her long hair. She replies:

> Till the fruit is ripe inside
> the skin will not fall off.

Mahādevīyakka is said to have died in her twenties.

I saw the haughty Master
for whom men, all men,
are but women, wives.

I saw the Great One
who plays at love
with Śakti,
original to the world,

I saw His stance
and began to live.
        [From *Speaking of Śiva*, p. 120.]

He bartered my heart,
    looted my flesh,
    claimed as tribute
    my pleasure,
    took over
all of me.

I'm the woman of love
for my lord, white as jasmine.
        [From *Speaking of Śiva*, p. 125.]

Other men are thorn
under the smooth leaf.
I cannot touch them,
go near them, nor trust them,
nor speak to them confidences.

Mother,
because they all have thorns
in their chests,
        I cannot take
any man in my arms but my lord
        white as jasmine.
        [From *Speaking of Śiva*, p. 125.]

Husband inside,
lover outside.
I can't manage them both.

This world
and that other,
cannot manage them both.

O lord white as jasmine

I cannot hold in one hand
both the round nut
and the long bow.
        [From *Speaking of Śiva*, p. 127.]

People,
male and female,
blush when a cloth covering their shame
comes loose.
        When the lord of lives
lives drowned without a face
in the world, how can you be modest?

When all the world is the eye of the lord,
onlooking everywhere, what can you
cover and conceal?
        [From *Speaking of Śiva*, p. 131.]

I love the Beautiful One
    with no bond nor fear
    no clan no land
    no landmarks
    for his beauty.

So my lord, white as jasmine, is my husband.

Take these husbands who die,
    decay, and feed them
    to your kitchen fires!
        [From *Speaking of Śiva*, p. 134.]

RĀDHĀ AND KRISHNA

During the fourteenth to seventeenth centuries a devotional movement (bhakti) spread across northern and eastern India that had Krishna as the supreme god. In this tradition Krishna is the playful lover, the simple cowherder to whom women, especially the *gopis* or cowherders, are irresistibly drawn. These young women abandon husbands, homes, and honor to be with Krishna. By giving up all that is valued in the everyday world these women represent the ideal devotee who, out of love for god, foresakes everything else. Among them, it is Rādhā who is greatly loved by Krishna. The following songs, which are taken from a Bengali collection, tell of their love. The erotic nature of the songs is purposeful. Just as Rādhā demonstrates the full-hearted longing one should feel toward god, Krishna demonstrates his desire for union with his devotees. All the songs end with a signature line in which the author identifies him or herself and occasionally includes a comment on the poem.

Fingering the border of her friend's sari, nervous
  and afraid,
sitting tensely on the edge of Krishna's couch,

as her friend left she too looked to go
but in desire Krishna blocked her way.

He was infatuated, she bewildered;
he was clever, and she naive.

He put out his hand to touch her; she quickly
  pushed it away.
He looked into her face, her eyes filled with tears.

He held her forcefully, she trembled violently
and hid her face from his kisses behind the edge
  of her sari.

Then she lay down, frightened, beautiful as a doll;
he hovered like a bee round a lotus in a painting.

Govinda-dāsa says, Because of this
drowned in the well of her beauty,
Krishna's lust was changed.
    [From *In Praise of Krishna*, p. 11.]

As water to sea creatures,
  moon nectar to *chakora* birds,
  companionable dark to the stars—
my love is to Krishna.

My body hungers for his
  as mirror image hungers
  for twin of flesh.

His life cuts into my life
  as the stain of the moon's rabbit
  engraves the moon.

As if a day when no sun came up
  and no color came to the earth—
that's how it is in my heart when he goes away.

Vidyāpati says Cherish such love
and keep it young, fortunate girl.
    [From *In Praise of Krishna*, p. 17.]

My friend, I cannot answer when you ask me to
  explain
what has befallen me.
Love is transformed, renewed,
each moment.
He has dwelt in my eyes all the days of my life,
yet I am not sated with seeing.
My ears have heard his sweet voice in eternity,
and yet it is always new to them.
How many honeyed nights have I passed with him
in love's bliss, yet my body
wonders at his.
Through all the ages
he has been clasped to my breast,
yet my desire
never abates.
I have seen subtle people sunk in passion
but none came so close to the heart of the fire.

Who shall be found to cool your heart,
says Vidyāpati.
    [From *In Praise of Krishna*, p. 18.]

The next two songs describe the terrors Rādhā must overcome in order to find Krishna. These are the terrors of the devotee who must leave the well-traveled path in order to find his or her own highly personal relationship with the divine.

O Mādhava, how shall I tell you of my terror?
I could not describe my coming here
if I had a million tongues.
When I left my room and saw the darkness

I trembled:
I could not see the path,
there were snakes that writhed round my
  ankles!

I was alone, a woman; the night was so dark,
the forest so dense and gloomy,
and I had so far to go.
The rain was pouring down—
which path should I take?
My feet were muddy
and burning where thorns had scratched them.
But I had the hope of seeing you, none of it
     mattered,
and now my terror seems far away . . .
When the sound of your flute reaches my ears
it compels me to leave my home, my friends,
it draws me into the dark toward you.

I no longer count the pain of coming here,
says Govinda-dāsa.
     [From *In Praise of Krishna*, p. 21.]

This dark cloudy night
he'll not come to me . . .
But yes, he is here!

He stands dripping with rain
in the courtyard. O my heart!

What virtue accrued in
another life has brought me
such bliss? I who
fear my elders and dare not go out to him?
I who torment him? I see

his sorrow and deep love
and I am tormented.
I would set fire to my house
for him, I would bear
the scorn of the world.

He thinks his sorrow is joy,
when I weep he weeps.

When it comes to know such depth of love
the heart of the world will rejoice,
says Chandidāsa.
     [From *In Praise of Krishna*, p. 22.]

The next song describes the pain of separation, the feeling of being cut off from god after one had known the bliss of union.

When they had made love
she lay in his arms in the *kunja* grove.
Suddenly she called his name
and wept—as if she burned in the fire of
separation.
     The gold was in her *anchal*
     but she looked afar for it!
—Where has he gone? Where has my love gone?
O why has he left me alone?

And she writhed on the ground in despair,
only her pain kept her from fainting.
Krishna was astonished
and could not speak.

Taking her beloved friend by the hand,
Govinda-dāsa led her softly away.
     [From *In Praise of Krishna*, p. 23.]

In the following songs Rādhā describes what she has given up in loving Krishna and yet how irresistible is his call.

To her friend:

O, why did I go to the Yamunā river? There
the moon apple of Nanda's eye lay waiting
under the *kadamba* tree.
The honey of his look, the radiance
of his body—these
were the bait and the snare he laid:
and my eyes lit there like birds
and at once were trapped,
and my heart leapt like a doe into his nets

leaving the cage of my breast empty,
and goaded by his glance,
my pride, that wild elephant,
which I had kept
chained night and day in my mind, broke loose
and escaped me.
     At the first note of his flute
down came the lion gate of reverence for elders,
down came the door of *dharma*,
my guarded treasure of modesty was lost,
I was thrust to the ground as if by a thunderbolt.

Ah, yes, his dark body poised
in the *tribhanga* pose
shot the arrow that pierced me;
no more honor, my family
lost to me,
my home at Vraja
lost to me.
Only my life is left—and my life too
Is only a breath that is leaving me.

So says Jagadānandap-dāsa.
[From *In Praise of Krishna*, p. 28.]

To her friend:

How can I describe his relentless flute,
which pulls virtuous women from their homes
and drags them by their hair to Shyām
as thirst and hunger pull the doe to the snare?
Chaste ladies forget their lords,
wise men forget their wisdom,
and clinging vines shake loose from their trees,
hearing that music.
Then how shall a simple dairymaid withstand its
  call?

Chandidāsa says, Kālā the puppetmaster leads the dance.
[From *In Praise of Krishna*, p. 29.]

To her friend:

My mind is not on housework.
Now I weep, now I laugh at the world's
censure.
        He draws me—to become
an outcast, a hermit woman in the woods!
He has bereft me of parents, brothers, sisters,
my good name. His flute
took my heart—
his flute, a thin bamboo trap enclosing me—
a cheap bamboo flute was Rādhā's ruin.
That hollow, simple stick—
fed nectar by his lips, but issuing
poison . . .

If you should find
a clump of jointed reeds,
pull off their branches!
Tear them up by the roots!
Throw them
        into the sea.

Dvija Chandidāsa says, Why the bamboo?
Not it but Krishna enthralls you: him you cannot uproot.
[From *In Praise of Krishna*, p. 30.]

MĪRĀBĀĪ

Mīrābāī (ca. 1500–1550) is one of the best-known saints in all of India. She was born in Rajasthan, in northern India, and, like Mahādevīyakka, she thought of god as her true husband. Consequently, her arranged marriage to an Indian prince was an unhappy one. Mīrā's devotions to god and her associations with various religious devotees so angered her husband's family that they tried to poison her. Eventually she ran away to join a company of Krishna worshippers in Brindavan, the center of Krishna worship. Again like Mahādevīyakka, she is rejected by the leading male saint of the time, who refuses even to speak with her because he has vowed never to speak to a woman. Mīrā makes the point that there is only one man in Brindavan, Krishna, because all true devotees are female in relation to god.

Bhaktis cultivate a highly personal relationship with their god in which they often concentrate on particular aspects of the god. In Mīrā's case her poems frequently emphasize Krishna's dark skin and his feat of having once lifted a mountain in order to protect his followers. Often she calls him Hari, lord.

Life without Hari is no life, friend,
And though my mother-in-law fights,
  my sister-in-law teases,
  the *rana* is angered,

A guard is stationed on a stool outside,
  and a lock is mounted on the door,
How can I abandon the love I have loved
  in life after life?

Mira's Lord is the clever Mountain Lifter:
    Why would I want anyone else?
                          [Caturvedi, no. 42]
    [From *Songs of the Saints of India,* p. 134.]

I saw the dark clouds burst,
    dark Lord,
Saw the clouds and tumbling down
In black and yellow streams
    they thicken,
Rain and rain two hours long.
See —
    my eyes see only rain and water,
    watering the thirsty earth green.
Me —
    my love's in a distant land
    and wet, I stubbornly stand at the door,
For Hari is indelibly green,
    Mira's Lord,
And he has invited a standing,
    stubborn love.
                          [Caturvedi, no. 82]
    [From *Songs of the Saints of India,* p. 135.]

I have talked to you, talked,
    dark Lifter of Mountains,
About this old love,
    from birth after birth.
Don't go, don't,
    Lifter of Mountains,
Let me offer a sacrifice — myself —
    beloved,
        to your beautiful face.
Come, here in the courtyard,
    dark Lord,
The women are singing auspicious wedding songs;
My eyes have fashioned
    an altar of pearl tears,
And here is my sacrifice:
    the body and mind
Of Mira,
    the servant who clings to your feet,
        through life after life,
            a virginal harvest for you to reap.
                          [Caturvedi, no. 51]
    [From *Songs of the Saints of India,* p. 138.]

The Great Goddess

DURGĀ

Around the fourth century C.E. new, powerful, and fierce goddesses (*devīs*) began to emerge on the fringes of orthodox belief and practice from the village culture and possibly from among the indigenous non-Aryan peoples of India. These goddesses gained a popularity that continues to this day. One of the best-known stories about such a goddess is the myth of Durgā slaying the buffalo demon. This demon threatens even the might of the gods who call upon Durgā to save them from the chaos it represents. By slaying the demon, Durgā restores order to the cosmos.

In some versions of the story Durgā exists independently, but the *Mārkaṇḍeya Devīmāhātmya Purāṇa,* from which the following excerpt is taken, says that Durgā was created from the energies of the various male gods in order to fight the buffalo demon who could only be destroyed by a female. Like her Greek counterpart, Athena, Durgā is a war goddess who is not born from a womb. As the following description of the battle shows, Durgā, called Caṇḍika and Ambikā in this text, is a ferocious warrior.

When his army was being destroyed in this manner, the demon Mahiṣa himself, in the form of a buffalo, terrorized the troops of the goddess. Some of them he beat with his snout, others he trampled with his hooves, still others he lashed with his tail, while some were ripped to shreds by his horns. Some were thrown to the ground by his bellowing and the speed of his charge while others were felled by the gusts of his panting breath. After felling her troops, the demon rushed to attack the lion that was with the great goddess. At this Ambikā became enraged. The mighty, virile buffalo, whose hooves pounded the earth, also grew furious, smashing the lofty mountains with his horns and bellowing aloud. Trampled by his violent sallies, the earth was shattered, and the ocean, lashed by his hairy tail, overflowed on all sides. Shaken by his slashing horns, the troops were utterly dispersed. Mountains tumbled by the hundreds from the sky, struck down by the wind of his snorting breath.

When she saw this great demon attacking, swelling with rage, Caṇḍikā then became furious enough to destroy him. She threw her noose and lassoed the great Asura. Thus trapped in that mighty battle, he abandoned his buffalo shape and became a lion. At the moment Ambikā cut off its head, a man appeared, sword in hand. As soon as Ambikā cut down that man along with his sword and shield, the demon became a huge elephant. With a roar he dragged the goddess's lion along with his trunk, but while he was pulling the lion, she cut off his trunk with her sword. Then the great demon resumed his wondrous buffalo shape, causing all three worlds with their moving and unmoving creatures to tremble.

Provoked by this, Caṇḍikā, mother of the world, guzzled her supreme liquor, laughing and red-eyed. And the Asura, puffed up with pride in his own strength and bravery, bellowed aloud and tossed mountains at Caṇḍikā with his horns. Pulverizing those mountains that were hurled at her with arrows sent aloft, the goddess, excited by anger, her mouth red with liquor, cried out to him and his invincible troop, "Roar and bellow, but only as long as I drink the mead, you fool! In a moment the gods will be howling at you when you die by my hand!" So speaking, the goddess flew up and trod on his throat with her foot, piercing him with her spear. Crushed by her foot, overcome by the power of that goddess, the demon came half-way out of his own mouth. Still battling in this way, he was felled by the goddess who cut off his head with her mighty sword. So that demon Mahiṣa, his army and his allies, who had so distressed the three worlds, were all annihilated by the goddess.

At Mahiṣa's death, all the gods and demons, mankind and all creatures living in the three worlds cried "Victory!" And when the entire army of the lamenting Daityas was annihilated, the whole host of the gods went into exultant rapture. The gods and the great celestial seers praised that goddess, while Gandharva lords sang aloud and hosts of Apsarases danced.

[From *Devī-Māhātmya,* pp. 237–38.]

KĀLĪ

A later battle in this text introduces the goddess Kālī. These two goddesses, Durgā and Kālī, are often interchanged. In the following excerpt, during the heat of battle, Durgā, called Ambikā, gives birth to Kālī.

As they had been commanded, the Daityas, led by Caṇḍa and Muṇḍa, formed a four-fold army and sallied forth, their weapons raised aloft. They saw the goddess, smiling slightly, positioned on her lion atop the great golden peak of a mighty mountain. When they saw her, they made zealous efforts to seize her, while other demons from the battle approached her with bows and swords drawn. Then Ambikā became violently angry with her enemies, her face growing black as ink with rage. Suddenly there issued forth from between her eyebrows Kālī, with protruding fangs, carrying a sword and a noose, with a mottled, skull-topped staff, adorned with a necklace of human skulls, covered with a tiger-skin, gruesome with shriveled flesh. Her mouth gaping wide, her lolling tongue terrifying, her eyes red and sunken, she filled the whole of space with her howling. Attacking and killing the mighty demons, she devoured the armed force of the enemies of the gods. Seizing with one hand the elephants with their back-riders, drivers, warriors and bells, she hurled them into her maw. In the same way she chewed up warriors with their horses, chariots and charioteers, grinding them up most horribly with her teeth. One she grabbed by the hair of the head, another by the nape of the neck, another she trod underfoot while another she crushed against her chest. The mighty striking and throwing weapons loosed by those demons she caught in her mouth and pulverised in fury. She ravaged the entire army of powerful evil-souled Asuras; some she devoured while others she trampled; some were slain by the sword, others bashed by her skull-topped club, while other demons went to perdition crushed by the sharp points of her teeth.

Seeing the sudden demise of the whole Daitya army, Caṇḍa rushed to attack that most horrendous goddess Kālī. The great demon covered the terrible-eyed goddess with a shower of arrows while Muṇḍa hurled discuses by the thousands. Caught in her mouth, those weapons shone like myriad orbs of the sun entering the belly of the clouds. Then howling horribly, Kālī laughed aloud malevolently, her maw gaping wide, her fangs glittering, awful to behold. Astride her huge lion, the goddess rushed against Caṇḍa; grabbing his head by the hair, she decapitated him with her sword. When he saw Caṇḍa dead, Muṇḍa attacked, but she threw him too to the ground, stabbing him with her sword in rage. Seeing both Caṇḍa and the mighty Muṇḍa felled, the remains of the army fled in all directions, overcome with fear.

Grabbing the heads of the two demons, Kālī approached Caṇḍikā and shrieked, cackling with fierce, demoniac laughter, "I offer you Caṇḍa and Muṇḍa as the grand victims in the sacrifice of battle. Now you yourself will kill Śumbha and Niśumbha!" Witnessing this presentation of the two great Asuras, the eminent Caṇḍikā spoke graciously to Kālī, "Since you have captured Caṇḍa and Muṇḍa and have brought them to me, O goddess, you will be known as Cāmuṇḍā!" . . .

So speaking, the honorable goddess Caṇḍikā of fierce mettle vanished on the spot before the eyes of the gods. And all the gods, their enemies felled, performed their tasks without harassment and enjoyed their shares of the sacrifices. When Śumbha, enemy of the gods, world-destroyer, of mighty power and valor, had been slain in battle and the most valiant Niśumbha had been crushed, the rest of the Daityas went to the netherworld.

In such a way, then, does the divine goddess, although eternal, take birth again and again to protect creation. This world is deluded by her; it is begotten by her; it is she who gives knowledge when prayed to and prosperity when pleased. By Mahākālī is this entire egg of Brahmā pervaded, lord of men. At the awful time of dissolution she takes on the form of Mahāmārī, the great destructress of the world. She is also its unborn source; eternal, she sustains creatures in time. As Lakṣmī, or Good Fortune, she bestows wealth on men's homes in times of prosperity. In times of disaster she appears as Misfortune for their annihilation. When the goddess is praised and worshiped with flowers, incense, perfume and other gifts, she gives wealth, sons, a mind set upon Dharma, and happiness to all mankind.

[From *Devī-Māhātmya*, pp. 238–240.]

PĀRVATĪ

The goddess Pārvatī is a complex figure. While ever the faithful wife of her husband, the great god Shiva, the stories surrounding her describe an independent and willful individual who sets her mind on winning Shiva for her husband not through feminine wiles but through ascetic practices. Pārvatī is often called by other names, such as Umā and Kālī. These are goddesses who can be understood as also married to Shiva or as different aspects of the same great goddess. In the following excerpt from the *Śiva Śatarudra Purāṇa*, Shiva is also called by many different names such as Śankara and Rudra. This excerpt tells of Shiva's testing of Pārvatī's ascetic practices (*tapas*).

Desiring Śankara for her husband, she went to the deep forest with two companions and practised pure *tapas;* Śiva, skilled in various sports, sent the Seven Seers to the site of Pārvatī's *tapas* to examine her asceticism in person. Arriving there, these sages performed their inspection scrupulously, but even with their utmost efforts they were unable to distract her. They returned to Śiva, bowed, and told him what had happened. Thus having accomplished their task, they returned respectfully to Svarloka.

After the seers had gone home, lord Śankara, the begetter, decided to investigate Śiva's [Pārvatī's] behavior himself. The mighty lord, who had himself become a serene ascetic through the appeasement of desire took the form of a *brahmacārin,* this our most wondrous lord. In the body of an ancient brahmin, glowing with his own luster, the luminous one who carried a staff and umbrella was happy at heart. Thus bearing the body of a matted-haired ascetic, Śambhu Śankara who is kind to his devotees went at once with great joy to the forest of the mountain daughter.

There he saw the goddess standing at a fire altar surrounded by her companions, pure like an auspicious digit of the moon. When Śambhu, who is loyal to his devotees, saw the goddess, he approached her eagerly in a friendly manner. When she saw him coming, this marvelous and splendid brahmin, his body covered with fine hair, his aspect serene, with a staff and animal skin, in the person of an aged *brahmacārin* with matted hair carrying a water jar, she worshiped him most graciously with all the offerings of *pūjā.* After joyfully honoring the *brahmacārin,* the goddess Pārvatī inquired respectfully about his health, "Who are you who have come here in the form of a *brahmacārin?* Where have you come from to brighten this forest? Speak, O choicest of those who know the Veda!"

Thus questioned by Pārvatī, the twice-born *brahmacārin* graciously replied at once in order to test Śiva's intentions, "Be assured that I am a twice-born *brahmacārin.* I am an ascetic, going where I please, a benefactor who gives help to others."

As he said this, Śankara the *brahmacārin* who is kind to his devotees stood at her side concealing his true nature. "What can I say, great goddess? There is nothing more to be said. A great perversion is going on here, I see, conduct that will bring disaster. For in your early youth when you should be enjoying fine pleasures and the attentions of others, you are doing *tapas* to no purpose at all! Who are you? Whose daughter are you? Why are you practising *tapas* in this lonely forest, *tapas* that is hard to master even for self-controlled seers?"

At these words, the supreme goddess began to laugh and replied politely to the excellent *brahmacārin,* "Hear my whole story, O wise brahmin *brahmacārin.* I was born in the land of Bharata, in the house of Himavat. Before that I was born in the House of Dakṣa as the maiden Satī, beloved of Śankara. When my father insulted me about my husband, I abandoned by body through Yoga. In this birth, O twice-born one, I won Śiva again by my great merit, but after reducing Manmatha to ashes, he abandoned me and went away. When Śankara left my father's house to do *tapas,* I was ashamed. So I came here for *tapas* myself, following the word of my *guru.* With mind, speech and action I have chosen Śankara as my lord.

"All this is the truth I speak and not a lie. Yet I realize my purpose is most difficult to obtain. How am I to succeed? In any case, it is because of my heart's desire that I am now practising *tapas.* Disregarding all the other gods who are headed by Indra, leaving aside even Viṣṇu and Brahmā, I want in truth to win for my husband only the one who holds the Pināka!"

When he heard these determined words of Pārvatī, O seer, the matted-haired Rudra said this with a smile, "What an idea you have in your head, goddess, daughter of Himācala! Abandoning the gods for Rudra, you practise *tapas!* I am well acquainted with this Rudra, so listen to what I say. He has a bull on his banner. He is not a normal man. His hair is unkempt. He is always alone by himself. Above all, he is indifferent to the world. Therefore do not yoke your mind to this Rudra! Your lovely form, goddess, is wholly opposite to that of Hara. What you propose offends me; but you are free to do as you choose."

After saying this, Rudra in his *brahmacārin* form continued to ridicule himself in various ways before her in order to test her. When she heard the brahmin's untoward words, the goddess Pārvatī, greatly provoked, answered him who was reviling Śiva, "This much I am sure of, that there is someone here who deserves to be killed, even though he appears at the moment to be inviolable. You must be some imposter who has come here in the guise of a *brahmacārin* in order to insult Śiva! Now I am angry with you, fool! You cannot possibly know Śiva, for your face is turned away from him. It infuriates me that I have honored you! On earth, one who insults Śiva has all the merit he has accumulated since birth reduced to ashes. And one who so much as touches a despiser of Śiva must perform expiation. Fie on you, dirty thief! Vile man, I know this Śiva whom you have described. He is the supreme lord! He adopts various forms through illusion so that you cannot know him definitively. Yet Rudra, granter of my wishes, beloved of the virtuous, is utterly without alteration!"

After Śiva, the goddess, had said this, she recited the truth about Śiva, describing Rudra as the unmanifest Brahman who is without characteristics. After listening to the goddess' words, the twice-born *brahmacārin* started once again to speak, but the mountain-born Śivā, turning her face away from any further abuse of Śiva, her mind's fancy fixed on him, spoke quickly to her companion:

"Stop this horrid brahmin from speaking out as he wishes, friend, or he will once again insult Śiva! The sin of one who reviles Śiva is not his alone, but those who listen to the insult also share in the guilt. Anyone, without exception, who reviles Śiva is to be killed by his servants. A brahmin who does so is to be shunned; one should leave his company at once. This wicked man is again going to speak ill of Śiva, but because he is a brahmin, he is not to be killed. He is, however, to be ignored and avoided at all costs. Let us leave this place at once and go somewhere else immediately so we will not have to converse further with this idiot!"

After Umā had said this . . . seer, and just as she was lifting one foot to go, Śiva appeared before her and caught hold of her garment. Assuming his divine form as it appears to those who meditate on him, Śiva made himself visible to Śivā and spoke to her while her face was still turned away from him.

"If you leave me, where will you go? O Śivā, I will not leave you alone. I have tested you, blameless woman, and find you firmly devoted to me. I came to you in the form of a *brahmacārin* and said to you many things, all out of desire for your own welfare. I am profoundly pleased with your special devotion. Tell me what your heart desires! There is nothing you do not deserve! Because of your *tapas,* I shall be your servant from this moment on. Due to your loveliness, each instant without you lasts an Age. Cast off your modesty! Become my wife forevermore! Come, beloved. I shall go to my mountain at once, together with you."

Śivā became overjoyed at hearing these words of the lord of the gods and abandoned immediately all the hardships of *tapas.* Trembling at the sight of Śiva's celestial form, Śivā kept her face modestly turned down and replied respectfully to the lord, "If you are pleased with me and if you have compassion for me, then be my husband, O lord of the gods"

Thus addressed by Śivā, Śiva took her hand according to custom and went to Mt. Kailāsa with her. Having won her husband, the mountain-born girl performed the divine offices for the gods.

[From *Devī-Māhātmya,* pp. 161–164.]

LAKSMĪ

A continuing theme in Hinduism is the battle between various demons and the gods. The well-known myth of the Churning of the Ocean of Milk has the hard-presseed gods appeal to the great god Viṣṇu for help against the demons. Viṣṇu tells them how to churn the ocean of milk in order to release an empowering nectar that will enable the gods to overcome the demons. Many other things arise from this churning, including the great goddess Śrī, also called Lakṣmī, the goddess of good fortune and prosperity.

The following excerpts from this myth are taken from the *Viṣṇu Purāṇa*. They tell of Lakṣmī's birth after which she immediately goes to Viṣṇu (Hari), thereby identifying herself as his wife. The myth then continues with a lengthy exposition of their complementary aspects.

After this, the goddess Śrī of vibrant beauty arose from this milk, standing in a blossoming lotus with a lotus in her hand. With joy the great seers assembled there praised her with the Śrīsūkta; and the Gandharvas, led by Viśvāvasu, sang before her while the throngs of Apsarases, led by Ghṛtācī danced. The Ganges and other rivers approached her with their waters for bathing. The elephants of the four quarters holding up golden vessels of pure water bathed the goddess, the great mistress of all the worlds. The ocean in bodily form gave her a wreath of unfading lotuses, while Viśvakarman wrought ornaments for her body. Wearing celestial garlands and garments, bathed and adorned with decorations, with all the gods looking on, she went to Hari's chest. While resting on Hari's chest, Lakṣmī made the gods know instant supreme bliss just by looking at the two of them, O Maitreya.

★ ★ ★

The eternal Śrī, loyal to Viṣṇu, is the mother of the world. Just as Viṣṇu pervades the universe, O excellent brahmin, so does she. Viṣṇu is meaning; Śrī is speech. She is conduct; Hari is behavior. Viṣṇu is knowledge; she is insight. He is Dharma; she is virtuous action.

Viṣṇu is the creator; Śrī is creation. She is the earth and Hari earth's upholder. The eternal Lakṣmī is contentment, O Maitreya; the blessed lord is satisfaction. Śrī is wish, the lord desire. He is the sacrifice, she the fee. The goddesss is the offering of butter, Janārdana the sacrificial cake. At the sacrifice, Lakṣmī is the women's hut, Madhusūdana the sacrificial site. Lakṣmī is the altar, Hari the sacrificial pole. Śrī is the firewood, the lord the sacred grass. The lord has the nature of the Sāma Veda; the lotus-born Śrī is the *udgītha*. Lakṣmī is the *svāhā* cry; Jagannātha Vāsudeva is the oblation-eating fire.

Śauri the lord is Śankara, and Lakṣmī is Gaurī, excellent brahmin. Keśava is the sun, Maitreya, and the lotus-dwelling goddess is its light. Viṣṇu is the host of the Fathers, Padmā the *svādhā* offering of constant nourishment. Śrī is the sky; Viṣṇu, the Self of everything, is wide-open space. Śrī's husband is the moon; its beauty is the constant Śrī. Lakṣmī is fortitude, enacted in the world, Hari the all-pervading wind. Govinda is the ocean, O brahmin; Śrī is the shore, great seer.

Lakṣmī bears the form of Indrānī, while Madhusūdana is Indra, her spouse, among the gods. The discus-bearing Viṣṇu is Yama personified; the lotus-dwelling Lakṣmī is his wife. Śrī is prosperity; the god who possesses Śrī is the lord of wealth himself. Illustrious Lakṣmī is Gaurī; Keśava is Varuṇa himself. Śrī is the host of gods, chief brahmin, and Hari is lord of the host.

He who bears a mace in his right hand is reliability, O excellent twice-born one; Lakṣmī is power. Lakṣmī is the instant, the lord the wink of an eye. He is the hour; she is the second. Lakṣmī is light; he is the lamp. Hari is everything and lord of everything as well. Śrī, mother of the world, is a forest creeper while Viṣṇu is a tree. Śrī is the starry night; the god who carries mace and discus is the day. Viṣṇu, granter of wishes, is the bridegroom; the lotus-dwelling goddess is the bride.

Appearing in the form of a male river is the lord, while Śrī takes form as a female river. The lotus-eyed god is a banner; the lotus-dweller is a flag. Lakṣmī is desire, O Maitreya, and Jagannātha Nārāyaṇa is greed. Together Lakṣmī and Govinda are passion and love.

What more is there to tell? In summary, let it be said that among gods, beasts and human beings, Hari is all that is known as male, and Śrī all that is known as female. There is nothing more beyond these two!

[From *Classical Hindu Mythology*, pp. 97–99.]

THREE HYMNS TO THE GODDESS

The following excerpts from three hymns of praise to the Goddess, taken from the *Devī-Māhātmya* section of the *Mārkaṇḍeya Purāṇa,* are sung by the gods. They reveal her many aspects, from the beautiful and benign all-loving mother to the bloodthirsty, avenging protectress.

You are Svāhā, you are Svadhā, you are the exclamation Vaṣat, having speech as your very soul.

You are the nectar of the gods, O imperishable, eternal (*nityā*) one; (you) abide having the threefold syllabic moment (*mātrā*) as your very being.

(You are) the half-*mātrā*, steadfast, eternal, which cannot be uttered distinctly.

You are she; you are Sāvitrī (the Gāyatrī *mantra*); you are the Goddess, the supreme mother.

By you is everything supported, by you is the world created;

By you is it protected, O Goddess, and you always consume (it) at the end (of time).

At (its) emanation, you have the form of creation; at (its) protection, (you have) the form of steadiness;

Likewise at the end of this world, (you have) the form of destruction, O you who consist of the world!

You (*bhavatī*) are the great knowledge (*mahāvidyā*), the great illusion (*mahāmāyā*), the great insight (*mahāmedhā*), the great memory,

And the great delusion, the great Goddess (*mahādevī*), the great demoness.

And you are the primordial material (*prakṛti*) of everything, manifesting the triad of constituent strands,

The night of destruction, the great night, and the terrible night of delusion.

You are Śrī, you the queen (*īśvarī*), you modesty, you intelligence (*buddhī*), characterized by knowing;

Modesty, well-being, contentment, too, tranquillity and forebearance are you.

Terrible with your sword and spear, likewise with cudgel and discus,

With conch and bow, having arrows, sling, and iron mace as (your) weapons,

Gentle, more gentle than other gentle ones, exceedingly beautiful,

You are superior to the high and low, the supreme queen.

Whatever and wherever anything exists, whether it be real or unreal, O (you) who have everything as your very soul,

Of all that, you are the power (*śakti*); how then can you be (adequately) praised?

By you, the creator of the world, the protector of the world, who (also) consumes the world

Is brought under the influence of sleep (*nidrā*); who here is capable of praising you?

[From *Devī-Māhātmya,* pp. 290–291.]

O Goddess, you are insight, knowing the essence of all scripture, you are Durgā, a vessel upon the ocean of life (that is so) hard to cross, devoid of attachments.

(You are) Śrī, whose sole abode is in the heart of Kaiṭabha's foe (Viṣṇu) you are Gaurī, whose abode is made with the one who is crowned with the moon (Śiva).

Slightly smiling, spotless, like the orb of the full moon, as pleasing as the lustre of the finest gold (is your face).

* * *

O Goddess, may you, the supreme one, be gracious to life; enraged, you (can) destroy (whole) families in a trice.

This is now known, since the extensive power of the Asura Mahiṣa has been brought to an end.

Honored are they among nations, riches are theirs, honors are theirs, and their portion of *dharma* does not fail,

Fortunate are they, with devoted children, servants, and wives, on whom you, the gracious one, always bestow good fortune.

O Goddess, a virtuous man always attentively performs all righteous actions on a daily basis,

And then he goes to heaven by your grace: are you not thus the bestower of rewards on the three worlds, O Goddess?

O Durgā, (when) called to mind, you take away fear from every creature; (when) called to mind by the healthy, you bestow an exceedingly pure mind.

O you who destroy poverty, misery, and fear, who other than you is always tender-minded, in order to work benefits for all?

Since these (foes) are slain, the world attains happiness; although they have committed (enough) sin to remain in hell for a long time,

Your disposition, O Goddess, calms the activity of evil-doers, and this incomprehensible form (of yours) is unequalled by others,

And (your) valor is the slayer of those who have robbed the gods of their prowess: thus was compassion shown by you even towards enemies.

With what may this prowess of yours be compared? Where is there (such a) form, exceedingly charming (yet) striking fear into enemies?

Compassion in mind and severity in battle are seen

in you, O Goddess, granter of boons even upon the triple world.

This whole triple world was rescued by you, through the destruction of (its) enemies; having slain (them) at the peak of battle,

The hosts of enemies were led to heaven by you, and our fear, arising from the frenzied foes of the gods, was dispelled: hail to you!

With (your) spear protect us, O Goddess! And with (your) sword protect (us), O Ambikā!

Protect us with the sound of (your) bell, and with the twang of your bow-string!

In the east protect (us) and in the west, O Caṇḍikā; protect (us) in the south

By the wielding of your spear, likewise in the north, O queen.

With your gentle forms which roam about in the triple world,

And with the exceedingly terrible ones, protect us, and also the earth.

And with the weapons, O Ambikā, sword, and spear, and club, and the rest,

Which lie in your sprout(-like) hands, protect (us) on every side.

[From *Devī-Māhātmya,* pp. 294–295.]

Hail to the Goddess, hail eternally to the auspicious (*śivā*) great Goddess!

Hail to Prakṛti, the auspicious! We, restrained, bow down to her.

To the terrible one, hail! To the eternal Gaurī, the supportress, hail!

And to the moonlight, to the blissful one having the form of the moon, hail eternally!

To the auspicious one (are we) bowed down; to growth, to success do we offer praise, alleluia!

To Nairṛti, to the Lakṣmī of kings, to you, Śarvāṇī, hail, hail!

To Durgā, the inaccessible further shore, the essential one who accomplishes all,

To fame, likewise the black one (*kṛṣṇā*), the smoky one, hail eternally!

To the one who is exceedingly gentle and exceedingly terrible (are we) bowed down: hail, hail!

Hail to the support of the world, to the Goddess (who is) action: hail, hail!

The Goddess who is known as Viṣṇumāyā in all creatures,

Hail to her, hail to her, hail to her: hail, hail!

The Goddess who is designated "consciousness" in all creatures,

Hail to her, hail to her, hail to her: hail, hail!

The Goddess who abides in all creatures in the form of intelligence,

Hail to her, hail to her, hail to her: hail, hail!

The Goddess who abides in all creatures in the form of sleep,

Hail to her, hail to her, hail to her: hail, hail!

The Goddess who abides in all creatures in the form of hunger,

Hail to her, hail to her, hail to her: hail, hail!

The Goddess who abides in all creatures in the form of shadow,

Hail to her, hail to her, hail to her: hail, hail!

The Goddess who abides in all creatures in the form of power,

Hail to her, hail to her, hail to her: hail, hail!

The Goddess who abides in all creatures in the form of thirst,

Hail to her, hail to her, hail to her: hail, hail!

The Goddess who abides in all creatures in the form of patience,

Hail to her, hail to her, hail to her: hail, hail!

The Goddess who abides in all creatures in the form of birth,

Hail to her, hail to her, hail to her: hail, hail!

The Goddess who abides in all creatures in the form of modesty,

Hail to her, hail to her, hail to her: hail, hail!

The Goddess who abides in all creatures in the form of tranquillity,

Hail to her, hail to her, hail to her: hail, hail!

The Goddess who abides in all creatures in the form of faith,

Hail to her, hail to her, hail to her: hail, hail!

The Goddess who abides in all creatures in the form of loveliness,

Hail to her, hail to her, hail to her: hail, hail!

The Goddess who abides in all creatures in the form of Lakṣmī,

Hail to her, hail to her, hail to her: hail, hail!

The Goddess who abides in all creatures in the form of activity,

Hail to her, hail to her, hail to her: hail, hail!

The Goddess who abides in all creatures in the form of memory,

Hail to her, hail to her, hail to her: hail, hail!

The Goddess who abides in all creatures in the form of compassion,

Hail to her, hail to her, hail to her: hail, hail!

The Goddess who abides in all creatures in the form of contentment,

Hail to her, hail to her, hail to her: hail, hail!

The Goddess who abides in all creatures in the form of mother (*mātṛ*),

Hail to her, hail to her, hail to her: hail, hail!

The Goddess who abides in all creatures in the form of error,

Hail to her, hail to her, hail to her: hail, hail!

She who is the governess of the senses in all creatures,

And constantly in the elements, to the Goddess of pervasiveness, hail, hail!

She who abides, having pervaded this whole world in the form of mind,

Hail to her, hail to her, hail to her: hail, hail!

Praised of yore by the gods because refuge was desired, similarly praised by the lord of gods day after day,

May she, the queen, the cause of what is bright, accomplish for us bright things, auspicious things:

may she destroy misfortunes.

She, the ruler (*īśā*), is now reverenced by us, the gods, who are tormented by haughty demons.

And at this very moment, she who has been called to mind by us, whose bodies are prostrated in devotion (*bhakti*), destroys all (our) misfortunes.

[From *Devī-Māhātmya*, pp. 295–298.]

Sources

Classical Hindu Mythology: A Reader in the Sanskrit Purāṇas, ed. and trans. Cornelia Dimmitt and J. A. B. van Buitenen. Philadelphia: Temple University Press, 1978.

Devī-Māhātmya: The Crystallization of the Goddess Tradition, by Thomas B. Coburn. Delhi: Motilal Banarsidass, 1984.

Hymns of the Atharva-Veda, Together with Extracts from the Ritual Books and the Commentaries, trans. Maurice Bloomfield. Delhi: Motilal Banarsidass, 1964. First published by Oxford University Press, 1897.

The Hymns of the Ṛgveda, translated with a popular commentary by Ralph T. H. Griffith. 1889. Vols. 1 and 2 complete in two volumes. Varanasi: Chowkhamba Sanskrit Series Office, 1971.

In Praise of Krishna: Songs from the Bengali, trans. Edward C. Dimock, Jr., and Denise Levertov, with an introduction and notes by Edward C. Dimock, Jr. Garden City, NY: Anchor Books, Doubleday, 1967.

The Laws of Manu, translated with extracts from seven commentaries by G. Bühler. Delhi: Motilal Banarsidass, 1964. First published by Oxford University Press, 1886.

The Mahābhārata: Vol. 1, The Book of the Beginning, trans. and ed. J. A. B. van Buitenen. Chicago and London: University of Chicago Press, 1973.

The Mahābhārata: Vol. 2, The Book of the Assembly Hall, The Book of the Forest, trans. and ed. J. A. B. van Buitenen. Chicago and London: University of Chicago Press, 1975.

The Ramayana of Valmiki. 3 vols. Trans. Hari Prasad Shastri. 3rd ed. London: Shanti Sadan, 1953–59.

Selections from the Vedic Hymns, trans. Daniel Smith. Berkeley, CA: McCutchon Pub., 1968.

Songs of the Saints of India, text and notes by John Stratton Hawley, translations by J. S. Hawley and Mark Juergensmeyer. New York and Oxford: Oxford University Press, 1988.

Speaking of Śiva, translated with an introduction by A. K. Ramanujan. Baltimore: Penguin Books, 1973.

The Thirteen Principal Upanishads, translated from the Sanskrit by Robert Ernest Hume. 2d ed. rev. London and New York: Oxford University Press, 1931.

Bibliography

Introductory Textbooks

Ainslie T. Embree, *The Hindu Tradition.* New York: Vintage Books, 1966, 1972.

Thomas J. Hopkins, *The Hindu Religious Tradition.* Belmont, CA: Wadsworth Publishing Co., 1971.

Wendy Doniger O'Flaherty, *Hindu Myths: A Sourcebook Translated from the Sanskrit.* Harmondsworth, England: Penguin Books Ltd., 1975, 1978

Works on Women in Hinduism

A. S. Altekar, *The Position of Women in Hindu Civilisation from Prehistoric Times to the Present Day.* Benares: The Culture Publication House, Benares Hindu University, 1938.

Lynn Bennett, *Dangerous Wives and Sacred Sisters: Social and Symbolic Roles of High-Caste Women in Nepal.* New York: Columbia University Press, 1983.

The Divine Consort: Radha and the Goddesses of India, ed. John Stratton Hawley and Donna Marie Wulff. Boston: Beacon Press, 1982, 1986.

Doranne Jacobson and Susan S. Wadley, *Women in India: Two Perspectives.* New Delhi: Manohar, 1977.

Frédérique Apffel Marglin, "Female Sexuality in the Hindu World." Pp. 39–60 in *Immaculate & Powerful: The Female in Sacred Image and Social Reality,* ed. Clarissa W. Atkinson, Constance H. Buchanan, and Margaret R. Miles. Harvard Women's Studies in Religion Series. Boston: Beacon Press, 1987.

David Kinsley, *Hindu Goddesses: Visions of the Divine Feminine in the Hindu Religious Tradition.* Berkeley, CA: University of California Press, 1986, 1988.

Prabhati Mukherjee, *Hindu Women—Normative Models.* New Delhi: Orient Longman, 1978.

Unspoken Worlds: Women's Religious Lives in Non-Western Cultures, ed. Nancy A. Falk and Rita M. Gross. San Francisco: Harper & Row, 1980. Contains several articles on women in Hinduism.

Women, Religion and Social Change, ed. Yvonne Yazbeck Haddad and Ellison Banks Findly. Albany, NY: State University of New York Press, 1985.

Katherine K. Young, "Hinduism." Pp. 59–103 in *Women in World Religions,* ed. Arvind Sharma. Albany, NY: State University of New York, 1987.

BUDDHISM

Introduction

Buddhism begins with the life of its founder Gautama of the Śākya tribe, called the Buddha (a title meaning "the enlightened one"), who lived from 566–486 B.C.E. The traditional account of his life is that he was born the son of a king. At the time of his birth a holy man predicted that he would either rule the world or would renounce the world. In order to ensure his glorious future as a great king, the Buddha's father brought him up in luxury and prevented him from seeing anything unpleasant. When he was about twenty-nine years old, however, he had a profound religious experience that changed his life. This experience is represented by the story of his four visions, which occurred when the Buddha travelled outside the palace grounds. Here he encountered four different aspects of human experience he had never seen before: He saw a sick man, an old man, a dead man, and, finally, the Buddhist solution to these, the wandering ascetic. Profoundly shaken by the transitoriness and the suffering endemic to all existence, the Buddha decided to leave home and become a wandering ascetic.

After practicing extreme forms of asceticism he realized that the middle path between asceticism and the worldly life is the better way. This is what Buddhists call Buddhism, the Middle Way, which is based on the Eight-fold Path attributed to the Buddha. This path is a model for a moderate life that emphasizes meditation as a way to change one's conscious perception of the world. In other words, an enlightened person sees the world differently from one who is still bound by desire and suffering. This is an important theme in Buddhist literature and one that appears frequently in the selections that follow. Enlightened beings are released from the wheel of existence; they are beyond death and rebirth.

Importantly, the ideal for Buddhism was and is monastic life which involves celibacy. Often in world religion women gain power when they give up their sexuality, and this is the case in Buddhism.

The Buddha established a religious community that practiced his ideas, and he continued to preach and shape the community until his death at age 80, 45 years later. The center of this community are the monks and nuns who have renounced worldly life: they are celibate, they eat only one meal a day, they go out and beg for their food from the laity, and they spend most of the year wandering from place to place in order not to become attached to one spot. Their goal is to reach enlightenment in this life. Included in this community are the lay supporters, who gain merit by giving to the community. This merit helps the laity to be reborn in a position deemed to be more favorable to spiritual progress. The lay supporters adopt five precepts: not to take any life (animal or human), not to steal, no illicit sex, not to lie, and no intoxicating substances.

The early tradition emphasized the human qualities of the Buddha, making the point that enlightenment is open to all sentient beings who strive for it. In time, however, the tradition began to change, and the Buddha was described in more transcendent terms. One consequence of this is that as the Buddha is increasingly represented as less human and more divine, achieving a direct, personal enlightenment experience is seen as less of a human possibility. Now the emphasis is placed on acquiring merit in order to win a rebirth that will lead to enlightenment, or to be reborn in a particular Buddhist heaven. The Buddha is now represented (iconographically and textually) as a divinity and as such can be worshipped and appealed to.

These and other changes and innovations in doctrine occuring around the first century before the Common Era lead to the development of two distinct but friendly schools of Buddhism. The first is Theravāda, or Southern Buddhism, which maintains its connection to early

Buddhism especially through its religious ideal of the *arhat,* an enlightened being who achieves a personal and final enlightenment. Upon their death they are set free from the wheel of existence and cease to exist. They will not reincarnate. The other school is Mahāyāna, or Northern Buddhism. This school understands itself to contain the estoeric doctrine of the Buddha, the teachings he did not preach publicly. Its religious ideal is the *bodhisattva,* an enlightened being who postpones final personal enlightenment in order to continue to reincarnate and help all other beings to achieve enlightenment.

In the early tradition the idea existed that there had been previous Buddhas, beings who in past ages achieved enlightenment just like Gautama Buddha. From this it follows that there will be future Buddhas, like Maitreya, who are presently residing in various heavens awaiting the time for their incarnation. In addition, there are other worlds and heavens that have their own Buddhas, such as Amitābha. These Buddhas have superhuman qualities, and in fact their prominence tends to displace the historical Buddha. Instead of the monastic model of the life of the Buddha, the alternative is to seek rebirth in the heaven of a particular celestial Buddha through devotion to that Buddha. This tradition emphasizes contemplation, visualization and, most importantly, the recitations of the name of a particular celestial Buddha such as Amitābha. This had great appeal to a laity that, for various reasons, could not or would not become monks or nuns.

A new school of Buddhism, variously called Esoteric Buddhism, Vajrayāna, and/or Tantra began sometime around the fifth century. This movement had its roots in the popular religion of northern India, which contained many magical and shamanistic features as well as the worship of goddesses. All these elements are incorporated into Tantric practices. This form of Buddhism stresses enlightenment in one lifetime in contradistinction to the idea of gradual enlighten-ment over several lifetimes that had developed in some sects of Mahāyāna and Theravāda. Tantra, with its vivid sexual images and use of forbidden substances such as wine and meat in rituals, challenged the Buddhist establishment. It emphasizes individual visionary experiences, and its ideal type is the *siddha.* This is an enlightened being who is usually a homeless wanderer, often acts like a madman to point out the duplicity of social life, and frequently travels with a female consort. One of the most famous beings of this type was Padmasambhava who, according to tradition, subdued all the demons of Tibet thereby allowing Buddhism to take root. Other types of *siddha*s are Marpa, who lived as a married man and had great magical powers and was the teacher of Milarepa, who lived as a celibate hermit. There were and are women *siddha*s, but most often the tradition is described from the male point of view. Eventually this movement was institutionalized into mainstream Buddhism.

Theravāda

Theravāda or Southern Buddhism, is the oldest surviving school of Buddhism. This form of Buddhism spread south from northern India to Sri Lanka and eventually east to Burma, Thailand, Cambodia, and Laos. Its ideal type is the *arhat,* a monk or nun who has achieved enlightenment. This means that monastic women can achieve positions of prominence and prestige, but this opportunity declines over time along with the decline of the order of nuns.

All the philosophical texts, sermons, stories, myths, and rules of early Buddhism were col-lected into what is called the Pāli Canon. According to tradition it was first written down in the first century B.C.E. in Ceylon (today called Sri Lanka), although additional material con-tinued to be added until at least the fifth century C.E. In its various forms this body of literature is the accepted canon of most Buddhists, including followers of Mahāyāna and Tantric Buddhism, and several of the excerpts that follow are taken from it.

The two biographical works on the Buddha, which are regarded as sacred books by most Buddhists, were composed somewhat later (between the first century B.C.E. and the first century C.E.) than most of the Pāli Canon; but they, like the Pāli Canon itself, are based on earlier oral materials. Consequently, the order of the excerpts in this section is not chronological. Rather, it begins with a creation story written in the fifth century C.E. and is followed by excerpts from the biographies of the Buddha. The remaining excerpts are taken from various books of the Pāli Canon and include a folktale about the Buddha, the story of the first ordination of women, and a selection of poems written by Buddhist nuns.

CREATION

The creation story of the Buddhists is similar to the Hindu creation story in that both stories share the Indian belief that the life of the universe is cyclical: It comes into being, destroys itself, and comes into being again, in the endless turning of the wheel of existence. The following excerpt is taken from chapter 13 of the *Visuddhi-Magga,* written by Buddhaghoṣa in Ceylon during the fifth century C.E. In it the earth is formed gradually. Beings of light are then attracted to it and begin to eat pieces of it. As a consequence of this primal meal distinctions arise: handsome and ugly, female and male, possessions. Because of its emphasis on the cyclical nature of existence, this story does not emphasize one sex over the other; both participate in the creation of the world as we know it. The division into sexes is seen as part of the process, even though this division has negative consequences. In the later Tantric tradition of Buddhism highly trained adepts attempt to reverse this process of creation in their meditational practices in order to arrive at a purer, non-earthly and androgynous form.

Now after the lapse of another long period, a great cloud arises. And first it rains with a very fine rain. . . . After the water has thus been massed together by the wind, it dwindles away, and by degrees descends to a lower level. As the water descends, the Brahma-heavens reappear in their places, and also the four upper heavens of sensual pleasure. When it has descended to its original level on the surface of the earth, mighty winds arise, and they hold the water helplessly in check, as if in a covered vessel. This water is sweet, and as it wastes away, the earth which arises out of it is full of sap, and has a beautiful color, and a fine taste and smell, like the skimmings on the top of thick rice-gruel.

Then beings, who have been living in the Heaven of the Radiant Gods, leave that existence, either on account of having completed their term of life, or on account of the exhaustion of their merit, and are reborn here on earth. They shine with their own light and wander through space. Thereupon, as described in the Discourse on Primitive Ages, they taste that savory earth, are overcome with desire, and fall to eating it ravenously. Then they cease to shine with their own light, and find themselves in darkness. When they perceive this darkness, they become afraid. Thereupon, the sun's disk appears, full fifty leagues

in extent, banishing their fears and producing a sense of divine presence. On seeing it, they are delighted and overjoyed, saying, "Now we have light; and whereas it has banished our fears and produced a sense of divine presence [sura-bhāva], therefore let it be called suriya [the sun]." Hence they named it suriya. After the sun has given light throughout the day, it sets. Then they are alarmed again, saying, "The light which we had has perished." Then they think: "It would be well if we had some other light." Thereupon, as if divining their thoughts, the disk of the moon appears, forty-nine leagues in extent. On seeing it, they are still more delighted and overjoyed, and say, "As if divining our wish [chanda], has it arisen: therefore is it canda [the moon]." And therefore they named it canda. When thus the sun and the moon have appeared, the constellations and the stars arise. From that time on night and day succeed each other, and in due course the months and half-months, seasons and years. . . .

Now after these beings have begun to eat the savory earth, by degrees some become handsome and some ugly. Then the handsome despise the ugly, and as the result of this despising, the savoriness of the earth disappears, and the bitter pappaṭaka plant grows up. In the same manner that also disappears, and the padālatā plant grows up. In the same way that also disappears, and rice grows up without any need of cultivation, free from all husk and red granules, and exposing the sweet-scented naked rice-grain. Then pots appear for the rice, and they place the rice in the pots, and place these pots on the tops of stones. And flames of fire spring up of their own accord, and cook the rice, and it becomes rice-porridge resembling the jasmine flower, and needing the addition of no broth or condiments, but having any desired flavor. Now when these beings eat this material food, the excrements are formed within them, and in order that they may relieve themselves, openings appear in their bodies, and the virility of the man, and the femininity of the woman. Then the woman begins to meditate excessively on the man, and the man on the woman, and as a result of this excessive meditation, the fever of lust springs up, and they have carnal connection. And being tormented by the reproofs of the wise for their low conduct, they build houses for its concealment. And having begun to dwell in houses, after a while they follow the example of some lazy one among themselves, and store up food. From that time on the red granules and the husks envelop the rice-grains, and wherever a crop has been mown down,

it does not spring up again. Then these beings come together, and groan aloud, saying, "Alas! wickedness has sprung up among men; for surely we formerly were made of mind." The full account of this is to be supplied from the Discourse on Primitive Ages.

Then they institute boundary lines, and one steals another's share. After reviling the offender two or three times, the third time they beat him with their fists, with clods of earth, with sticks, etc. When thus stealing, reproof, lying, and violence have sprung up among them, they come together, and say, "What if now we elect some one of us, who shall get angry with him who merits anger, reprove him who merits reproof, and banish him who merits banishment. And we will give him in return a share of our rice." When, however, the people of this, our world-cycle came to this decision, our Blessed One, who was at the time a Future Buddha, was of all these beings the handsomest, the most pleasing of appearance, possessing the greatest influence and wisdom, and able to raise up and put down. Then they all came to him, and having gained his assent, they elected him their chief. . . .

[From *Visuddhi-Magga*, chap. 13, pp. 324–327 in *Buddhism in Translations*.]

THE BIOGRAPHY OF THE BUDDHA

The two major biographies of the Buddha are the *Lalitavistara* and the *Buddhacarita*. Both were composed in India between the first century B.C.E. and the first century C.E., a period that saw the rise of the Mahāyāna school of Buddhism. The *Lalitavistara,* which is a Mahāyāna text, emphasizes the miraculous nature of the Buddha and refers to him as "the Bodhisattva," a being of infinite compassion. Its author or authors are unknown.

The *Buddhacarita* was written by Aśvaghoṣa, a Buddhist monk. In contrast to the *Lalitavistara,* it is a courtly poem, written partly to impress educated Indians in order to convert them to Buddhism. In it the Buddha is referred to as the Blessed One. Both texts cover the main events of the Buddha's life: his miraculous birth, the death of his mother, his marriage, life in his father's palace, the four visions that prompt him to turn away from a worldly life, and, after great effort, his enlightenment.

The following two selections from the *Buddhacarita* represent women as sexual temptresses, a point of view often assumed by celibate clergies around the world. These two incidents from the life of the Buddha are meant to demonstrate that the Buddha is so spiritually advanced that not even such alluring women can arouse him. They also, however, provide sacred evidence for the fact that women, willingly or no, are seductive and therefore monks must restrict their contact with them. In the first incident, following the instructions of the king, the women of the palace attempt to distract the Buddha from the spiritual path.

As if somewhat frightened, the women made gestures designed to cause rapture with brows, looks and blandishments, with laughter, frolicking and movements.

But what with the king's command, and the prince's [the Buddha] gentleness and the power of intoxication and love, they soon abandoned timidity.

Then surrounded by the women, the prince wandered through the garden, like an elephant through the Himalayan forest, accompanied by a herd of females.

In that lovely grove he shone with the women in attendance on him, like Vivasvat surrounded by Apsarases in the pleasaunce of Yibhrāja.

Then some of the young women there, pretending to be under the influence of intoxication, touched him with their firm, rounded, close-set, charming breasts.

One made a false stumble and clasped him by force with her tender arm-creepers, which hung down loosely from her drooping shoulders.

Another, whose mouth with copper-coloured lower lip smelt of spirituous liquor, whispered in his ear, "Listen to a secret."

Another, who was all wet with unguents, said as if commanding him, "Make a line here", in the hope of winning the touch of his hand.

Another repeatedly let her blue garments slip down under the pretext of intoxication, and with her girdle partly seen she seemed like the night with the lightning flashing.

Some walked up and down so as to make their golden zones tinkle and displayed to him their hips veiled by diaphanous robes.

Others grasped mango-boughs in full flower and leaned so as to display bosoms like golden jars.

Another lotus-eyed damsel came from a lotus-bed with a lotus and stood by the side of the lotus-faced prince as if she were Padmaśrī.

Another sang a sweet song with gesticulations to bring out the sense, reproving his indifference, as it were, with looks that said, "You deceive yourself."

Another imitated him by drawing the bow of her brows on her fair countenance and making gestures in mimicry of his solemnity.

A damsel with fine rounded breasts and earrings shaking with her laughter mocked him out loud, saying, "Finish it, Sir."

Similarly, as he was retreating, some bound him with ropes of garlands, and others restrained him with words that were like ankuses but were softened with innuendoes.

Another in order to bring about an argument seized a mango-spray and asked, stuttering with intoxication, "Whose flower now is this?"

One of them, modelling her gait and outward appearance on those of a man, said to him, "Sir, you have been conquered by women, conquer this earth now!". . .

Thus these young women, to whose minds love had given free rein, assailed the prince with wiles of every kind.

But despite such allurements the prince firmly guarded his senses, and in his perturbation over the inevitability of death, was neither rejoiced nor distressed.

[From *The Buddhacarita*, chap. 4.]

The second selection from the *Buddhacarita* takes place approximately six years later, a few days before the Buddha's enlightenment. The author, Aśvaghoṣa, uses the arrival of the courtesan Amrapālī as the occasion for the Buddha to make a speech about the power of women to distract men from the spiritual life. In the end, however, the Buddha honors Amrapālī by accepting the invitation to her home.

After passing one night there, the Śrīghana [the Buddha] moved on to the city of Vaiśālī and abode in a glorious grove in the domain of Amrapālī.

The courtesan Amrapālī, hearing the Teacher was there mounted a modest equipage and went forth with great joy.

She wore diaphanous white garments and was without garlands or body-paint, like a woman of good family at the time of worshipping the gods.

In the pride of her beauty, she attracted by her united charms the minds and the wealth of the Licchavi nobles.

Self-assured in her loveliness and glory, like a forest goddess in beauty, she descended from her chariot and quickly entered the grove.

The Blessed One, seeing that her eyes were flashing and that she was a cause of grief to women of family, commanded His disciples with voice like a drum: —

"This is Amrapālī approaching, the mental fever of those whose strength is little; do you take your stand on knowledge, controlling your minds with the elixir of awareness.

Better is the neighbourhood of a snake or of an enemy with drawn sword, than that of woman for the man who is devoid of awareness and wisdom.

Whether sitting or lying down, whether walking

or standing, or even when portrayed in a picture, woman carries away men's hearts.

Even if they be afflicted by disaster (*vyasana*), or fling their arms about weeping, or be burnt with dishevelled hair, yet women are pre-eminent in power.

Making use of extraneous things, they deceive by many adventitious (*āhārya*) qualities, and concealing their real qualities they delude fools.

By seeing woman as impermanent, suffering, without self and impure, the minds of the adepts are not overcome on looking at her.

With minds well accustomed to these temptations (*ālaya*), like cattle to their pastures, how can men be deluded when attacked by the pleasures of the gods?

Therefore taking the arrows of mystic wisdom, grasping the bow of energy in your hands and girding on the armour of awareness, think well on the idea of the objects of sense.

It is better to sear the eyes with red-hot iron pins than to look on woman's rolling eyes with misdirected awareness.

If at the moment of death your mind be subject to passion, it binds you helplessly and takes you to a rebirth among animals or in Hell.

Therefore recognize this danger and do not dwell on the external characteristics (*nimitta*); for he sees truly, who sees in the body only Matter (*rūpa*)."

★ ★ ★

While He thus instructed the disciples who had not proceeded to the end of the matter, Amrapālī, seeing Him, drew near with folded hands.

Seeing the Seer seated with tranquil mind under a tree, she deemed herself highly favoured by His occupation (*paribhoga*) of the grove.

Then with great reverence, setting her eyes, restless as they were, in order, she did obeisance to the Sage with her head, which was like a *campaka* flower fully opened.

Then when she had seated herself in accordance with the Omniscient's directions, the Sage addressed her with words suited to her understanding: —

"This your intention is virtuous and your mind is steadfast by purification; yet desire for the Law is hard to find in a woman who is young and in the bloom of her beauty.

What cause is there for wonder that the Law should attract men of intelligence (*dhīmat*?) or women who are afflicted by misfortune (*vyasana*) or are self-controlled (*ātmavat*) or ill?

But it is extraordinary that in the world solely devoted (*ekarasa*) to the objects of sense a young woman, by nature weak in comprehension and unsteady in mind, should entertain the idea of the Law.

Your mind is turned to the Law, that is your real wealth (*artha*); for since the world of the living is transitory, there are no riches outside the Law.

Health is borne down by illness, youth cut short by age, and life snatched away by death, but for the Law there is no such calamity (*vipat*).

Since in seeking (for pleasure) one obtains only separation from the pleasant and association with the unpleasant, therefore the Law is the best path.

Dependence on others is great suffering, self-dependence the highest bliss; yet, when born in the race of Manu, all females are dependent on others.

Therefore you should come to a proper conclusion, since the suffering of women is excessive by reason equally of their dependence on others and of childbirth."

Young in years, but not like the young in disposition, intelligence and gravity, she listened joyfully to these words of the Great Sage.

Through the Tathāgata's preaching of the Law, she cast aside the condition of mind that was given up to the lusts, and despising the state of being a woman and turning aside from the objects of sense, she felt loathing for her means of livelihood.

Then entirely prostrating her slender body, like a mango-branch laden with blossom, she fixed her eye with devotion on the Great Sage and again stood with purified sight for the Law.

The woman, though modest by nature, yet ever spurred on by longing for the Law, joined her hands like a clump of lotuses (*paṅkajākara*) and spoke with gently uttered voice: —

"O Holy One, You have attained the goal and soothe suffering in the world. Deign in company with Your disciples to make the time of alms-seeking fruitful for me who am ripe for the fruit (?, *phalabhūta*), in order that I may receive a sermon."

Then the Blessed One, seeing her to be so devoted, and knowing animate beings to be dependent on food, gave His consent by silence and announced His intention to her with a gesture (*vikāra*).

He, Who possessed the supreme Law and an eye, that discerned occasions (*kṣaṇakṛtyavat*?), rejoiced exceedingly in the vessel of the Law, . . . knowing that the best gain is by faith, He praised her.

[From *The Buddhacarita,* chap. 22.]

In the following selection from chapter 18 of the *Lalitavistara* it has been six years since the Buddha, here called the Bodhisattva, rejected the women of the palace and left home. During this time he practiced a severe form of asceticism, eating only one juniper berry, one grain of rice, and one sesame seed each day. At the prompting of his dead mother, who descends from heaven to speak to him, the Buddha decides on a more moderate path between the severe asceticism he had been practicing and the worldly life of pleasure he had led as a prince. To this end, he accepts food from some young village women. In the process of accepting food from these women the Buddha begins a reconciliation with females from all realms of existence: human (living and dead), divine, and animal.

When the Bodhisattva had first begun to practice austerities, ten young village girls came to see him. They had continued to honor and to serve him, although it was the five men of good family who generally attended on him, giving him the juniper berry, grain of rice, or sesame seed. The names of the ten girls were: Balā, Balaguptā, Supriyā, Vijayasenā, Atimuktakamalā, Sundarī, and Kumbhakārī, Uluvillikā, Jātilikā, and Sujātā.

These young girls now prepared several kinds of food which they offered to the Bodhisattva. He partook of them and thereafter regularly sought alms in the village, so that he regained his color and his strength, and became known as the beautiful śramaṇa [ascetic], the great śramaṇa.

* * *

[The text shifts briefly to the first person in order to have the Buddha tell his story and then returns to the third person.]

O monks, the saffron garments which I had worn for six years had become extremely worn. And, monks, this came to my mind: "How fine it would be if I were to find something with which to cover myself."

At that time, O monks, Rādhā, a girl who had served Sujātā, daughter of the head villager, had just died. After being wrapped in a hemp cloth, she was taken to a corner of the cemetery, where she was left. I noticed this dusty rag, and stepping close with my left foot, I stretched out my right hand and bent over to take the cloth away. At that motion the earth gods called out to the gods of the air: "What an astonishing thing, friends! How extraordinary! Here is the descendent of a great royal family, who not only has abandoned the sovereignty of a Cakravartin [world conqueror], but now stoops down for a dusty cloth!"

* * *

In the meantime, O monks, the Bodhisattva thought again: "I have found a dust-covered cloth. It would now be good to find some water!" At once the gods struck the ground powerfully with their hands and on the very spot, a pond appeared. Today this pond is still called Pāṇihatā, Struck with the Hands.

* * *

When the Bodhisattva, being quite weary, thought to step out of the pond, the demon Pāpīyān, out of envy, raised the edges of the pond by magic. But on the shore of this pond stood a large kakubha tree, and the Bodhisattva, as was the custom at that time, spoke to the goddess of this tree to propitiate her. He then asked her to bend down a branch of the tree, and when she had lowered the branch, the Bodhisattva pulled himself out of the water. Once out of the water, he sat under the kakubha tree and sewed the cloth, fashioning it into a monk's garment. Today, this place is still called Pāṁsukūlasīvana, The Sewing of the Dust-Covered Cloth.

* * *

In the middle of the night, the gods had spoken to Sujātā, the daughter of Nāndika, head of the village of Uruvilvā, saying: "Sujātā, the one for whom you have made many offerings has ceased the practice of mortifications, and is now ready to receive pure and abundant food. Formerly you prayed: 'After partaking of the food prepared by me, may the Bodhisattva attain perfect, supreme, and complete Enlightenment.' Now do what must be done."

O monks, upon hearing this, Sujātā, daughter of Nāndika the head villager, immediately took the milk of a thousand cows, drew from it seven times the purest cream, and poured this cream together with the freshest and newest rice into an earthen pot which she put on a new fireplace. And in the midst of this special food, as she prepared it, there appeared auspicious signs: a śrīvatsa, a svastika, a nandyāvarta, a lotus, a vardhamāna, and other signs of blessing.

Then Sujātā thought: "Since such signs appear, there can be no doubt: after taking this food, the Bodhisattva will obtain the perfect, supreme, and complete Enlightenment." Previously, a sage who knew the signs, who knew the rules for understanding the marks of the body, had come to the village and had prophesied that Immortality would be attained there.

* * *

Then, monks, the Bodhisattva went to the home of Sujātā, daughter of the head villager, and sat upon the seat prepared for him. O monks, Sujātā offered the Bodhisattva a golden bowl filled with milk and honey. At that moment, the Bodhisattva thought: "Now that Sujātā has offered such food to me, there can be no doubt: after partaking of it, I will attain the perfect, supreme, and complete Enlightenment of a Buddha."

As the Bodhisattva accepted the food from Sujātā, he asked her: "My sister, what should I do with the golden bowl?" and she replied: "Take it with you." To which the Bodhisattva replied: "I have no need of such a bowl." To this Sujātā answered: "Then do with it what you please. I do not give food to anyone without also giving a bowl."

So taking the bowl of food with him, the Bodhisattva left Uruvilvā, and later in the morning arrived near the Nairañjanā, the river of the nāgas. Placing the bowl and his garments to one side, he entered the river to refresh himself.

* * *

Emerging from the water, the Bodhisattva looked for a place to seat himself along the shore, and a daughter of the nāgas [a species of snake] who resided in the Nairañjanā river came from deep below and offered him a resplendent lion throne. Seating himself, the Bodhisattva ate his fill of the soup of milk and honey, thinking with kindness of Sujātā, the daughter of the head villager. When he had eaten as much as he needed he threw the golden bowl into the river, without thought of attachment. No sooner had he thrown the bowl into the water than Sāgara, a king of the nāgas, feeling faith and respect arise within him, took up the bowl and carried it to his abode, saying: "This bowl is worthy of homage!"

[The Buddha then prepares for his enlightenment.]

[From *Lalitavistara,* chap. 18 in *The Voice of the Buddha,* vol. 1, pp. 404–409.]

THE ORDINATION OF THE FIRST NUNS

The following passage on the first ordination of women in Buddhism makes several points. First, the Buddha is reluctant to ordain women. Second, they require a male intermediary in the form of Ānanda, a leading disciple of the Buddha, to argue on their behalf. Third, once the Buddha agrees to their ordination, he lists eight conditions, which include placing the order of nuns under the rule of the order of monks. Finally, the Buddha predicts the decline of his teachings as a consequence of the ordination of women. Some scholars view this excerpt as an interpolation by the monks designed to bring the nuns under their control, and not as the words of the Buddha.

Mahā–Pajāpatī the Gotamid, the woman asking the Buddha for ordination, is the Buddha's aunt, the sister of his mother, who raised him after the death of his mother.

At that time The Buddha, The Blessed One, was dwelling among the Sakkas at Kapilavatthu in Banyan Park. Then drew near Mahā–Pajāpatī the Gotamid to where The Blessed One was; and having drawn near and greeted The Blessed One, she stood respectfully at one side. And standing respectfully at one side, Mahā–Pajāpatī the Gotamid spoke to The Blessed One as follows:

"Pray, Reverend Sir, let women retire from household life to the houseless one, under the Doctrine and Discipline announced by The Tathāgata."

"Enough, O Gotamid, do not ask that women retire from household life to the houseless one, under the Doctrine and Discipline announced by The Tathāgata."

And a second time Mahā–Pajāpatī the Gotamid spoke to The Blessed One. . . .

And a third time Mahā–Pajāpatī the Gotamid spoke to The Blessed One. . . .

Then thought Mahā–Pajāpatī the Gotamid, "The Blessed One permitteth not that women retire from household life to the houseless one, under the Doctrine and Discipline announced by The Tathāgata";

and she was sorrowful, sad, and tearful, and wept. And saluting The Blessed One, and keeping her right side toward him, she departed.

Then The Blessed One, after dwelling at Kapila-vatthu as long as he wished, departed on his wanderings toward Vesālī; and wandering from place to place, he came to where Vesālī was. And there The Blessed One dwelt at Vesālī, in Great Wood, in Pagoda Hall.

Then Mahā-Pājapatī the Gotamid had her hair cut off, put on yellow garments, and with a number of Sakka women departed towards Vesālī; and going from place to place, she drew near to where Vesālī was, and Great Wood, and Pagoda Hall. And Mahā-Pājapatī the Gotamid with swollen feet, and covered with dust, sorrowful, sad, and tearful, stood weeping outside in the entrance porch.

Now the venerable Ānanda saw Mahā-Pājapatī the Gotamid with swollen feet, and covered with dust, sorrowful, sad, and tearful, stand weeping outside in the entrance porch. And he spoke to Mahā-Pājapatī the Gotamid as follows:

"Wherefore dost thou, O Gotamid, with swollen feet, and covered with dust, sorrowful, sad, and tearful, stand weeping outside in the entrance porch?"

"Because, alas! O Ānanda, reverend sir, The Blessed One permitteth not that women retire from household life to the houseless one, under the Doctrine and Discipline announced by The Tathāgata."

"In that case, O Gotamid, stay thou here a moment, and I will beseech The Blessed One that women retire from household life to the houseless one, under the Doctrine and Discipline announced by The Tathāgata."

Then the venerable Ānanda drew near to where The Blessed One was; and having drawn near and greeted The Blessed One, he sat down respectfully at one side. And seated respectfully at one side, the venerable Ānanda spoke to The Blessed One as follows:

"Reverend Sir, here this Mahā-Pājapatī the Gotamid with swollen feet, and covered with dust, sorrowful, sad, and tearful, stands weeping outside in the entrance porch, and says that The Blessed One permitteth not that women retire from household life to the houseless one, under the Doctrine and Discipline announced by The Tathāgata. Pray, Reverend Sir, let women retire from household life to the houseless one, under the Doctrine and Discipline announced by The Tathāgata."

"Enough, Ānanda, do not ask that women retire from household life to the houseless one, under the Doctrine and Discipline announced by The Tathāgata."

And a second time the venerable Ānanda spoke to The Blessed One. . . .

And a third time the venerable Ānanda spoke to The Blessed ones. . . .

Then the venerable Ānanda spoke to The Blessed One as follows:

"Are women competent, Reverend Sir, if they retire from household life to the houseless one, under the Doctrine and Discipline announced by The Tathāgata, to attain to the fruit of conversion, to attain to the fruit of once returning, to attain to the fruit of never returning, to attain to saintship?"

"Women are competent, Ānanda, if they retire from household life to the houseless one, under the Doctrine and Discipline announced by The Tathāgata, to attain to the fruit of conversion, to attain to the fruit of once returning, to attain to the fruit of never returning, to attain to saintship."

"Since, then, Reverend Sir, women are competent, if they retire from household life to the houseless one, under the Doctrine and Discipline announced by The Tathāgata, to attain to the fruit of conversion, to attain to the fruit of once returning, to attain to the fruit of never returning, to attain to saintship, consider, Reverend Sir, how great a benefactress Mahā-Pājapatī the Gotamid has been. She is the sister of the mother of The Blessed One, and as foster-mother, nurse, and giver of milk, she suckled The Blessed One on the death of his mother. Pray, Reverend Sir, let women retire from household life to the houseless one, under the Doctrine and Discipline announced by The Tathāgata."

"If, Ānanda, Mahā-Pājapatī the Gotamid will accept eight weighty regulations, let it be reckoned to her as her ordination: —

"A priestess of even a hundred years' standing shall salute, rise to meet, entreat humbly, and perform all respectful offices for a priest, even if he be but that day ordained. This regulation shall be honored, esteemed, revered, and worshiped, and is not to be transgressed as long as life shall last.

"A priestess shall not keep residence in a district where there are no priests. This regulation shall be honored, esteemed, revered, and worshiped, and is not to be transgressed as long as life shall last.

"On each half-month a priestess shall await from the congregation of the priests the appointing of fast-day, and some one to come and administer the admonition. This regulation shall be honored, esteemed, revered, and worshiped, and is not to be transgressed as long as life shall last.

"At the end of residence a priestess shall invite criticism in both congregations in regard to what has been seen, or heard, or suspected. This regulation shall be honored, esteemed, revered, and worshiped, and is not to be transgressed as long as life shall last.

"If a priestess be guilty of serious sin, she shall undergo penance of half a month toward both the congregations. This regulation shall be honored, esteemed, revered, and worshiped, and is not to be transgressed as long as life shall last.

"When a female novice has spent her two years in the practice of the six rules, she shall seek ordination from both the congregations. This regulation shall be honored, esteemed, revered, and worshiped, and is not to be transgressed as long as life shall last.

"A priestess shall not revile or abuse a priest in any manner. This regulation shall be honored, esteemed, revered, and worshiped, and is not to be transgressed as long as life shall last.

"From this day on the priestesses shall not be allowed to reprove the priests officially, but the priests shall be allowed to reprove the priestesses officially. This regulation shall be honored, esteemed, revered, and worshiped, and is not to be transgressed as long as life shall last.

"If, Ananda, Mahā-Pajāpatī the Gotamid will accept these eight weighty regulations, let it be reckoned to her as her ordination."

Then the venerable Ānanda, when he had received from The Blessed One these eight weighty regulations, drew near to Mahā-Pajāpatī the Gotamid; and having drawn near, he spoke to Mahā-Pajāpatī the Gotamid as follows:

"If now, O Gotamid, you will accept eight weighty regulations, it shall be reckoned to you as your ordination:

* * *

"Just as, O Ānanda, reverend sir, a woman or a man, youthful, young, and fond of ornament, having bathed his head, and obtained a wreath of blue lotuses, or a wreath of jasmine flowers, or a wreath of ati-muttaka flowers, would take it up with both hands, and place it on the head, the noblest part of the body; in exactly the same way do I, O Ānanda, reverend sir, take up these eight weighty regulations, not to be transgressed as long as life shall last."

Then the venerable Ānanda drew near to where The Blessed One was; and having drawn near and greeted The Blessed One, he sat down respectfully at one side. And seated respectfully at one side, the venerable Ānanda spoke to The Blessed One as follows:

"Mahā-Pajāpatī the Gotamid, Reverend Sir, has accepted the eight weighty regulations; the sister of the mother of The Blessed One has become ordained."

"If, Ānanda, women had not retired from household life to the houseless one, under the Doctrine and Discipline announced by The Tathāgata, religion, Ānanda, would long endure; a thousand years would the Good Doctrine abide. But since, Ānanda, women have now retired from household life to the houseless one, under the Doctrine and Discipline announced by The Tathāgata, not long, Ānanda, will religion endure; but five hundred years, Ānanda, will the Good Doctrine abide. Just as, Ānanda, those families which consist of many women and few men are easily overcome by burglars, in exactly the same way, Ānanda, when women retire from household life to the houseless one, under a doctrine and discipline, that religion does not long endure. Just as, Ānanda, when the disease called mildew falls upon a flourishing field of rice, that field of rice does not long endure, in exactly the same way, Ānanda, when women retire from household life to the houseless one, under a doctrine and discipline, that religion does not long endure. Even as, Ānanda, when the disease called rust falls upon a flourishing field of sugar-cane, that field of sugar-cane does not long endure, in exactly the same way, Ānanda, when women retire from household life to the houseless one, under a doctrine and discipline, that religion does not long endure. And just as, Ānanda, to a large pond a man would prudently build a dike, in order that the water might not transgress its bounds, in exactly the same way, Ānanda, have I prudently laid down eight weighty regulations, not to be transgressed as long as life shall last."

[From *Culla-Vagga,* X.1, pp. 324–330.]

POEMS OF BUDDHIST NUNS

The following poems are taken from the *Therīgāthā* ("Songs of the Sisters") and are traditionally attributed to Buddhist nuns thought to have lived during the time of the Buddha. Each one is preceded by the name of the poet. The majority are poems celebrating the spiritual accomplishment of enlightenment, which is referred to as being "released." The first three poems especially indicate that the author's enlightenment arose directly from her experience as a woman.

Muttā

I am well-released, properly released by my release by means of the three crooked things, by the mortar, pestle, and my crooked husband. I am released from birth and death; that which leads to renewed existence has been rooted out.

[From *The Elders' Verses,* vol. 2, *Therīgāthā,* p. 2.]

Somā

That place, hard to gain, which is to be attained by the seers, cannot be attained by a woman with two-finger-intelligence (= very little intelligence).

What (harm) could the woman's state do to us, when the mind is well-concentrated, when knowledge exists for someone rightly having insight into the doctrine?

Everywhere enjoyment of pleasure is defeated; the mass of darkness (of ignorance) is torn asunder; thus know, evil one, you are defeated, death.

[From *The Elders' Verses,* vol. 2, *Therīgāthā,* p. 7.]

Vimalā, the former courtesan

Intoxicated by my (good) complexion, my figure, beauty, and fame, haughty because of my youth, I despised other women.

Having decorated this body, very variegated, deceiving fools, I stood at the brothel door, like a hunter having spread out a snare,

showing my ornamentation. Many a secret (place) was revealed. I did various sorts of conjuring, laughing at (= mocking?) many people.

Today (that same) I, having wandered for alms with shaven head, clad in the outer robe, am seated at the foot of a tree, having obtained (the stage of) non-reasoning.

All ties, those which are divine and those which are human, have been cut out. Having annihilated all the āsavas [desires], I have become cool, quenched.

[From *The Elders' Verses,* vol. 2, *Therīgāthā,* p. 11.]

In the following poems nuns are shown to be teachers as well as disciples.

Uttamā

Four or five times I went out from my cell, not having obtained peace of mind, being without self-mastery over the mind.

(That same) I went up to a bhikkhunī who was fit-to-be-trusted by me. She taught me the doctrine, the elements of existence, the sense-bases, and the elements.

Having heard her doctrine as she instructed me, for seven days I sat in one and the same cross-legged position, consigned to joy and happiness. On the eighth (day) I stretched forth my feet, having torn asunder the mass of darkness (of ignorance).

[From *The Elders' Verses,* vol. 2, *Therīgāthā,* p. 7.]

Candā

Formerly I fared ill, a widow, without children. Without friends and relations I did not obtain food or clothing.

Taking a bowl and stick, begging from family to family, and being burned by cold and heat, I wandered for seven years.

But having seen a bhikkhunī who had obtained food and drink, approaching her I said, "Send me forth into the houseless state."

And (that same) Paṭācārā, in pity, sent me forth; then having exhorted me, she urged me towards the highest goal.

Having heard her utterance, I took her advice. The noble lady's exhortation was not in vain; I have the triple knowledge; (I am) without āsavas [desires].

[From *The Elders' Verses,* vol. 2, *Therīgāthā,* p. 15.]

Vijayā

Four or five times I went forth from my cell, not having obtained peace of mind, being without self-mastery over the mind.

Having approached a bhikkhunī, having honoured her, I questioned (her). She taught me the doctrine, and the elements, and sense-bases,

the four noble truths, the faculties, and the powers, the constituents of enlightenment and the eight-fold way for the attainment of the supreme goal.

Having heard her utterance, taking her advice, in the first watch of the night I recollected that I had been born before.

In the middle watch of the night I purified the deva-eye. In the last watch of the night I tore asunder the mass of darkness (of ignorance).

And I then dwelt suffusing the body with joy and happiness. On the seventh (day) I stretched forth my feet, having torn asunder the mass of darkness (of ignorance).

[From *The Elders' Verses,* vol. 2, *Therīgāthā,* p. 19.]

Kisāgotamī speaks of the pains that exist in a woman's life.

Kisāgotamī

The state of having noble friends has been described by the sage with reference to the world; resorting to noble friends, even a fool would be wise.

Good men are to be resorted to; thus the wisdom of those who resort to them increases. Resorting to good men one would be released from all pains.

One should know pain, and the uprising of pain, and (its) cessation, and the eight-fold way, even the four noble truths.

The state of women has been said to be painful by the charioteer of men-who-are-to-be-tamed [the Buddha]; even the state of being a co-wife is painful; some, having given birth once,

even cut their throats; (some) tender ones take poisons; gone into the midst of people-killers (= in hell with murderers?) both (groups) suffer misfortunes.

Going along, about to bring forth, I saw my husband dead; having given birth on the path, (I had) not yet arrived at my own house.

Two sons dead and a husband dead upon the path for miserable (me); mother and father and brother were burning upon one pyre.

O miserable woman, with family annihilated, immeasurable pain has been suffered by you; and your tears have been shed for many thousands of births.

Then I saw the flesh of my sons eaten in the midst of the cemetery; with my family destroyed, despised by all, with husband dead, I attained the undying.

The noble eight-fold way leading to the undying has been developed by me; quenching has been realized; I have looked at the doctrine as a mirror.

I have my dart cut out, my burden laid down; that which was to be done has been done by me. The therī Kisāgotamī, with mind completely released, has said this.

[From *The Elders' Verses*, vol. 2, *Therīgāthā*, p. 24.]

Mahāyāna

Mahāyāna, or Northern Buddhism, took shape as a separate school of Buddhism in northern India beginning in the first century B.C.E. This form of Buddhism spread north to Tibet and east to China, Korea, and Japan.

Mahāyāna distinguishes itself from Theravāda in several ways. Most importantly, its religious ideal is represented by the Bodhisattva, a being of infinite compassion, who can be female or male, divine or human. This leaves the path of spiritual accomplishment open to women, though, as the excerpts show, not without a struggle.

The following three excerpts come from the early period of Mahāyāna Buddhism (first century B.C.E.-third century C.E.) in India. All were translated from the original Sanskrit into Tibetan, Chinese, and Japanese and are among the most well-known of Mahāyāna texts.

AN ISSUE OF GENDER

The first excerpt is chapter seven of the Vimalakīrti Sūtra, which was composed between the first century B.C.E. and the second century C.E. This chapter discusses the illusory nature of all beings, human and otherwise, and the attitude a Bodhisattva should take toward these illusory beings. The discussion is carried on as a dialogue between Mañjuśrī, a celestial Bodhisattva, and Vimalakīrti, a lay Bodhisattva. Their discussion is interrupted by an unnamed goddess, who causes a rain of flowers to fall. Also present is one of the Buddha's best known disciples, Śāriputra, who takes exception to the presence of the goddess and enters into an argument with her. In response to Śāriputra's challenge, the goddess changes herself into a male form and changes Śāriputra into a female form. In this way the goddess dramatizes the chapter's theme of the illusory nature of all beings and negates the theory that the female gender precludes spiritual achievement.

Mañjuśrī: What is the great compassion of a bodhisattva?

Vimalakīrti: It is the giving of all accumulated roots of virtue to all living beings.

Mañjuśrī: What is the great joy of the bodhisattva?

Vimalakīrti: It is to be joyful and without regret in giving.

Mañjuśrī: What is the equanimity of the bodhisattva?

Vimalakīrti: It is what benefits both self and others.

Mañjuśrī: To what should one resort when terrifed by fear of life?

Vimalakīrti: Mañjuśrī, a bodhisattva who is terrifed by fear of life should resort to the magnanimity of the Buddha.

Mañjuśrī: Where should he who wishes to resort to the magnanimity of the Buddha take his stand?

Vimalakīrti: He should stand in equanimity toward all living beings.

Mañjuśrī: Where should he who wishes to stand in equanimity toward all living beings take his stand?

Vimalakīrti: He should live for the liberation of all living beings.

Mañjuśrī: What should he who wishes to liberate all living beings do?

Vimalakīrti: He should liberate them from their passions.

Mañjuśrī: How should he who wishes to eliminate passions apply himself?

Vimalakīrti: He should apply himself appropriately.

Mañjuśrī: How should he apply himself, to "apply himself appropriately"?

Vimalakīrti: He should apply himself to productionlessness and to destructionlessness.

Mañjuśrī: What is not produced? And what is not destroyed?

Vimalakīrti: Evil is not produced and good is not destroyed.

Mañjuśrī: What is the root of good and evil?

Vimalakīrti: Materiality is the root of good and evil.

Mañjuśrī: What is the root of materiality?

Vimalakīrti: Desire is the root of materiality.

Mañjuśrī: What is the root of desire and attachment?

Vimalakīrti: Unreal construction is the root of desire.

Mañjuśrī: What is the root of unreal construction?

Vimalakīrti: The false concept is its root.

Mañjuśrī: What is the root of the false concept?

Vimalakīrti: Baselessness.

Mañjuśrī: What is the root of baselessness?

Vimalakīrti: Mañjuśrī, when something is baseless, how can it have any root? Therefore, all things stand on the root which is baseless.

Thereupon, a certain goddess who lived in that house, having heard this teaching of the Dharma of the great heroic bodhisattvas, and being delighted, pleased, and overjoyed, manifested herself in a material body and showered the great spiritual heroes, the bodhisattvas, and the great disciples with heavenly flowers. When the flowers fell on the bodies of the bodhisattvas, they fell off on the floor, but when they fell on the bodies of the great disciples, they stuck to them and did not fall. The great disciples shook the flowers and even tried to use their magical powers, but still the flowers would not shake off. Then, the goddess said to the venerable Śāriputra, "Reverend Śāriputra, why do you shake these flowers?"

Śāriputra replied. "Goddess, these flowers are not proper for religious persons and so we are trying to shake them off."

The goddess said, "Do not say that, reverend Śāriputra. Why? These flowers are proper indeed! Why? Such flowers have neither constructual thought nor discrimination. But the elder Śāriputra has both constructual thought and discrimination.

"Reverend Śāriputra, impropriety for one who has renounced the world for the discipline of the rightly taught Dharma consists of constructual thought and discrimination, yet the elders are full of such thoughts. One who is without such thoughts is always proper.

"Reverend Śāriputra, see how these flowers do not stick to the bodies of these great spiritual heroes, the bodhisattvas! This is because they have eliminated constructual thoughts and discriminations.

"For example, evil spirits have power over fearful men but cannot disturb the fearless. Likewise, those intimidated by fear of the world are in the power of forms, sounds, smells, tastes, and textures, which do not disturb those who are free from fear of the passions inherent in the constructive world. Thus, these flowers stick to the bodies of those who have not eliminated their instincts for the passions and do not stick to the bodies of those who have eliminated their instincts. Therefore, the flowers do not stick to the bodies of these bodhisattvas, who have abandoned all instincts.

Then the venerable Śāriputra said to the goddess, "Goddess, how long have you been in this house?"

The goddess replied, "I have been here as long as the elder has been in liberation."

Śāriputra said, "Then, have you been in this house for quite some time?"

The goddess said, "Has the elder been in liberation for quite some time?"

At that, the elder Śāriputra fell silent.

The goddess continued, "Elder, you are 'foremost of the wise!' Why do you not speak? Now, when it is your turn, you do not answer the question."

Śāriputra: Since liberation is inexpressible, goddess, I do not know what to say.

Goddess: All the syllables pronounced by the elder have the nature of liberation. Why? Liberation is neither internal nor external, nor can it be apprehended apart from them. Likewise, syllables are neither internal nor external, nor can they be apprehended anywhere else. Therefore, reverend Śāriputra, do not point to liberation by abandoning speech! Why? The holy liberation is the equality of all things!

Śāriputra: Goddess, is not liberation the freedom from desire, hatred, and folly?

Goddess: "Liberation is freedom from desire, hatred, and folly" — that is the teaching for the excessively proud. But those free of pride are taught that the very nature of desire, hatred, and folly is itself liberation.

Śāriputra: Excellent! Excellent, goddess! Pray, what have you attained, what have you realized, that you have such eloquence?

Goddess: I have attained nothing, reverend Śāriputra. I have no realization. Therefore I have such eloquence. Whoever thinks, "I have attained! I have realized!" is overly proud in the discipline of the well taught Dharma.

Śāriputra: Goddess, do you belong to the disciple-vehicle, to the solitary-vehicle, or to the great vehicle?

Goddess: I belong to the disciple-vehicle when I teach it to those who need it. I belong to the solitary-vehicle when I teach the twelve links of dependent origination to those who need them. And, since I never abandon the great compassion, I belong to the great vehicle, as all need that teaching to attain ultimate liberation. . . .

Reverend Śāriputra, I have been in this house for twelve years, and I have heard no discourses concerning the disciples and solitary sages but have heard only those concerning the great love, the great compassion, and the inconceivable qualities of the Buddha. . . .

Śāriputra: Goddess, what prevents you from transforming yourself out of your female state?

Goddess: Although I have sought my "female state" for these twelve years, I have not yet found it. Reverend Śāriputra, if a magician were to incarnate a woman by magic, would you ask her, "What prevents you from transforming yourself out of your female state?"

Śāriputra: No! Such a woman would not really exist, so what would there be to transform?

Goddess: Just so, reverend Śāriputra, all things do not really exist. Now, would you think, "What prevents one whose nature is that of a magical incarnation from transforming herself out of her female state?"

Thereupon, the goddess employed her magical power to cause the elder Śāriputra to appear in her form and to cause herself to appear in his form. Then the goddess, transformed into Śāriputra, said to Śāriputra, transformed into a goddess, "Reverend Śāriputra, what prevents you from transforming yourself out of your female state?"

And Śāriputra, transformed into the goddess, replied, "I no longer appear in the form of a male! My body has changed into the body of a woman! I do not know what to transform!"

The goddess continued, "If the elder could again change out of the female state, then all women could also change out of their female states. All women appear in the form of women in just the same way as the elder appears in the form of a woman. While they are not women in reality, they appear in the form of women. With this in mind, the Buddha said, 'In all things, there is neither male nor female.'"

Then, the goddess released her magical power and each returned to his ordinary form. She then said to him, "Reverend Śāriputra, what have you done with your female form?"

Śāriputra: I neither made it nor did I change it.

Goddess: Just so, all things are neither made nor changed, and that they are not made and not changed, that is the teaching of the Buddha.

Śāriputra: Goddess, where will you be born when you transmigrate after death?

Goddess: I will be born where all the magical incarnations of the Tathāgata are born.

Śāriputra: But the emanated incarnations of the Tathāgata do not transmigrate nor are they born.

Goddess: All things and living beings are just the same; they do not transmigrate nor are they born!

Śāriputra: Goddess, how soon will you attain the perfect enlightenment of Buddhahood?

Goddess: At such time as you, elder, become endowed once more with the qualities of an ordinary individual, then will I attain the perfect enlightenment of Buddhahood.

Śāriputra: Goddess, it is impossible that I should become endowed once more with the qualities of an ordinary individual.

Goddess: Just so, reverend Śāriputra, it is impossible that I should attain the perfect enlightenment of Buddhahood! Why? Because perfect enlightenment stands upon the impossible. Because it is impossible, no one attains the perfect enlightenment of Buddhahood.

Śāriputra: But the Tathāgata has declared: "The Tathāgatas, who are as numerous as the sands of the Ganges, have attained perfect Buddhahood, are attaining perfect Buddhahood, and will go on attaining perfect Buddhahood."

Goddess: Reverend Śāriputra, the expression, "the Buddhas of the past, present and future," is a conventional expression made up of a certain number of syllables. The Buddhas are neither past, nor present, nor future. Their enlightenment transcends the three times! But tell me, elder, have you attained sainthood?

Śāriputra: It is attained, because there is no attainment.

Goddess: Just so, there is perfect enlightenment

because there is no attainment of perfect enlightenment.

Then the Licchavi Vimalakīrti said to the venerable elder Śāriputra, "Reverend Śāriputra, this goddess has already served ninety-two million billion Buddhas.

She plays with the superknowledges. She has truly succeeded in all her vows. She has gained the tolerance of the birthlessness of things. She has actually attained irreversibility. She can live wherever she wishes on the strength of her vow to develop living beings."
[From *The Holy Teaching of Vimalakīrti*, pp. 56–63.]

Can Women Achieve Enlightenment?

The following excerpt is from chapter eleven of the *Lotus Sūtra,* one of the best known and earliest works of Mahāyāna Buddhism. It was composed in India between the first and third centuries C.E. and is similar to the *Vimalakīrti Sūtra* in several ways. First, the protagonist is a semidivine but nameless female (the daughter of Sāgara), while the other main characters remain Mañjuśrī (Mañgusrî), the celestial Bodhisattva, and Śāriputra, the disciple of the Buddha. Second, this story also questions whether or not women can achieve liberation, which this text appears to answer negatively. Third, it also involves a change of sex. The excerpt begins with the Bodhisattva Prajñākūta questioning the celestial Bodhisattva Mañjuśrī.

What law hast thou preached, or what Sûtra, in showing the path of enlightenment, so that those who are there with you have conceived the idea of enlightenment? that, once having gained a safe ford, they have been decisively established in omniscience?

Mañgusrî answered: In the bosom of the sea I have expounded the Lotus of the True Law and no other Sûtra. Pragñâkûta said: That Sûtra is profound, subtle, difficult to seize; no other Sûtra equals it. Is there any creature able to understand this jewel of a Sûtra or to arrive at supreme, perfect enlightenment? Mañgusrî replied: There is, young man of good family, the daughter of Sâgara, the Nâga-king, eight years old, very intelligent, of keen faculties, endowed with prudence in acts of body, speech, and mind, who has caught and kept all the teachings, in substance and form, of the Tathâgatas, who has acquired in one moment a thousand meditations and proofs of the essence of all laws. She does not swerve from the idea of enlightenment, has great aspirations, applies to other beings the same measure as to herself; she is apt to display all virtues and is never deficient in them. With a bland smile on the face and in the bloom of an extremely handsome appearance she speaks words of kindliness and compassion. She is fit to arrive at supreme, perfect enlightenment. The Bodhisattva Pragñâkûta said: I have seen how the Lord Sâkyamuni, the Tathâgata, when he was striving after enlightenment, in the state of a Bodhisattva, performed innumerable good works, and during many Aeons never slackened in his arduous task. In the whole universe there is not a single spot so small as a mustard-seed where he has not surrendered his

body for the sake of creatures. Afterwards he arrived at enlightenment. Who then would believe that she should have been able to arrive at supreme, perfect knowledge in one moment?

At that very moment appeared the daughter of Sâgara, the Nâga-king, standing before their face. After reverentially saluting the feet of the Lord she stationed herself at some distance and uttered on that occasion the following stanzas:

Spotless, bright, and of unfathomable light is that ethereal body, adorned with the thirty-two characteristic signs, pervading space in all directions.

He is possessed of the secondary marks and praised by every being, and accessible to all, like an open market-place.

I have obtained enlightenment according to my wish; the Tathâgata can bear witness to it; I will extensively reveal the law that releases from sufferance.

Then the venerable Sâriputra said to that daughter of Sâgara, the Nâga-king: Thou hast conceived the idea of enlightenment, young lady of good family, without sliding back, and art gifted with immense wisdom, but supreme, perfect enlightenment is not easily won. It may happen, sister, that a woman displays an unflagging energy, performs good works for many thousands of Aeons, and fulfils the six perfect virtues (Pâramitâs), but as yet there is no example of her having reached Buddhaship, and that because a woman cannot occupy the five ranks, viz. 1. the rank of Brahma; 2. the rank of Indra; 3. the rank of a chief guardian of the four quarters; 4. the rank of Kakravartin; 5. the rank of a Bodhisattva incapable of sliding back.

Now the daughter of Sâgara, the Nâga-king, had at the time a gem which in value outweighed the whole universe. That gem the daughter of Sâgara, the Nâga-king, presented to the Lord, and the Lord graciously accepted it. Then the daughter of Sâgara, the Nâga-king, said to the Bodhisattva Pragñâkûta and the senior priest Sâriputra: Has the Lord readily accepted the gem I presented him or has he not? The senior priest answered: As soon as it was presented by thee, so soon it was accepted by the Lord. The daughter of Sâgara, the Nâga-king, replied: If I were endowed with magic power, brother Sâriputra, I should sooner have arrived at supreme, perfect enlightenment, and there would have been none to receive this gem.

At the same instant, before the sight of the whole world and of the senior priest Sâriputra, the female sex of the daughter of Sâgara, the Nâga-king, disappeared; the male sex appeared and she manifested herself as a Bodhisattva, who immediately went to the South to sit down at the foot of a tree made of seven precious substances, in the world Vimala (i.e. spotless), where he showed himself enlightened and preaching the law, while filling all directions of space with the radiance of the thirty-two characteristic signs and all secondary marks. All beings in the Saha-world beheld that Lord while he received the homage of all, gods, Nâgas, goblins, Gandharvas, demons, Garudas, Kinnaras, great serpents, men, and beings not human, and was engaged in preaching the law. And the beings who heard the preaching of that Tathâgata became incapable of sliding back in supreme, perfect enlightenment. And that world Vimala and this Saha-world shook in six different ways. Three thousand living beings from the congregational circle of the Lord Sâkyamuni gained the acquiescence in the eternal law, whereas three hundred thousand beings obtained the prediction of their future destiny to supreme, perfect enlightenment.

Then the Bodhisattva Pragñâkûta and the senior priest Sâriputra were silent.

[From *Saddharma-Puṇḍarīka*, pp. 250–254.]

KUAN YIN, A FEMALE BODHISATTVA

The second excerpt from the *Lotus Sūtra* is taken from the Chinese translation of chapter twenty-four. In the Sanskrit version this chapter discusses the celestial Bodhisattva Avalokiteśvara, a male deity whose name means "all seeing." In the Chinese version two important differences are evident: the name was mistranslated as Kuan Yin, "all hearing," and the deity is female. The following chapter is the main textual source concerning this popular female Bodhisattva and enumerates her many powers. In Japan she is called Kannon.

Then the Bodhisattva Inexhaustible Knowledge [Akṣayamati] rose from his seat, circumambulated me [the Buddha] with his hands folded, and said: "Lord, why is the Bodhisattva Kuan-[shih]-yin called Kuan-[shih]-yin?"

I spoke to the Bodhisattva Inexhaustible Knowledge: "Good son, if the unlimited hundreds of millions of living beings who undergo great suffering hear the Bodhisattva Kuan-yin and with concentration call out the name Bodhisattva 'Kuan-yin,' then they will experience that sound [of the name] and all will be liberated. If one retains the name of this Bodhisattva Kuan-yin, then even if thrown into an immense fire, one will not be burned because of this Bodhisattva's great power. If there is a great river which is raging and one calls out this name, one will reach a safe [shallow] spot. If the hundreds of millions of living beings who seek gold, silver, lapis lazuli, tortoise shell, agate, coral, amber, and other precious jewels embark on the great seas and meet with ominous gales which blow their ships, casting them down to the land of demons [Rakṣas], if even one individual in their midst calls out the name 'Bodhisattva Kuan-yin,' all will be saved from the demons. That is why this Bodhisattva is called 'Kuan-yin.'

"If there is someone who should be punished and calls out the name 'Bodhisattva Kuan-yin,' the one who holds the sword over him would have his sword destroyed and the person [to be punished] would be freed. If the three thousand great world systems were filled with spirits [Yakṣas] and demons [Rakṣas] who wished to torment them and these [Yakṣas and Rakṣas] heard the people calling out the name 'Bodhisattva Kuan-yin,' these evil spirits could not even see them with their evil eyes, let alone harm them. Supposing someone whether innocent or guilty, were handcuffed, chained, or bound, if one calls out the name of the Bodhisattva Kuan-yin these [bonds] will be broken and he will be freed.

"Supposing there is a thousand great world systems where there are robbers and there is a chief merchant who is in charge of the other merchants who carry precious jewels on a hazardous road. One person among them calls out, 'Good sons, do not be afraid. You should all concentrate and call out the name Bodhisattva Kuan-yin. This Bodhisattva can bring fearlessness to all living beings. You should call out the name and you will then be freed from these robbers.' All the merchants then called out, 'Praise to the Bodhisattva Kuan-yin!' Because they called this name, they will be saved.

"Inexhaustible Knowledge, the Bodhisattva Mahāsattva Kuan-yin's magnificent spiritual powers are like this. If living beings are intensely passionate and yet they always revere the Bodhisattva Kuan-yin, they will be able to give up their desire. If they are intensely hateful yet they always revere the Bodhisattva Kuan-yin, they will give up their hatred. If they are greatly disillusioned yet they always revere the Bodhisattva Kuan-yin, they will give up their disillusionment.

"Inexhaustible Knowledge, because of the immense benefits of the Bodhisattva Kuan-yin's power, living beings should always concentrate on this Bodhisattva. If a woman wishes to have a son and worships and pays homage to the Bodhisattva Kuan-yin, she will have a virtuous and wise son. If she wishes to have a daughter, again she will give birth to an exceptionally refined daughter who has past virtuous habits [from former lives] and whom everyone will cherish.

★ ★ ★

By means of various appearances, this Bodhisattva moves about in various lands saving living beings. Therefore, you should concentrate and revere the Bodhisattva Kuan-yin. This Bodhisattva, a great being, can bring fearlessness to those who are in imminent danger and are frightened. Therefore, in this profane world all call this Bodhisattva the giver of fearlessness [Abhayaṃdada]."

[From *Women in Buddhism,* pp. 256–260.]

A BUDDHIST QUEEN

The third text from the early period of Mahāyāna Buddhism is the *Śrīmālā Sūtra,* which was written in south India in the third century C.E. This excerpt is from the first chapter. In it the Buddha predicts Queen Śrīmālā's future enlightenment and describes the Buddha land, or heaven, that she will rule over.

The queen . . . spoke these verses before her retinue and Chandra:
    It is said that the voice of a Buddha is most rare in the world. If this saying be true, I must serve thee.
    If the Lord Buddha may come for the sake of the world, may he, with compassion, come here on behalf of the teaching for me!
At that very instant, the Lord approached in the space [in front], and she saw the inconceivable body of the Buddha seated there, emitting pure light rays. Queen Śrīmālā and her retinue respectfully bowed with folded hands at their heads, and she praised the best of speakers:
    Lord, there is nothing comparable to your bodily form and glory. I bow to you, the Lord of the world, matchless and incomparable.

★ ★ ★

May the Lord now protect me and quicken the seed of enlightenment. May the *muni* benefit me in this and subsequent lives.
The Lord spoke forth: "Queen, in your former lives I have made you practice toward enlightenment; and in future lives I shall assist you." Queen Śrīmālā prayed: "Whatever the merit I have performed in this and in other lives, by that merit, Lord, may I always see you, assisting me."
Thereupon, Queen Śrīmālā along with all her lady attendants and entire retinue bowed to the feet of the Lord. The Lord prophesied to Queen Śrīmālā amid the assembled group that she would attain the incomparable right perfected enlightenment.
    "Queen, by reason of your virtuous root formed of the merits accumulated by praising the genuine qualities of the Tathāgata, you, for incalculable aeons, will experience perfect sovereignty among gods and men. In all your lives you will not fail

to see me. Just as you now praise me face to face, so you will continue praising. And you will also make offerings to innumerable Buddha Lords.

"After 20,000 aeons you will become the Tathāgata-Arhat-Samyaksambuddha Samanta-prabha. At that time, in your Buddha land there will be no evil destiny. Besides, at that time the sentient beings will stay on the path of ten virtuous actions; those beings will not have sickness or old age or disagreeable disturbances; and even the names of the path of unvirtuous actions will not be mentioned.

"Any sentient being born in that Buddha land will surpass the Paranirmitavaśavartin deities in pleasure; glory of shape and color; splendor in the sense objects of form, sound, odor, smell, tangibles; and ecstasy of that sentient being in all enjoyments.

"Queen, any sentient beings born in that Buddha land will also be installed in the Great Vehicle. Accordingly, Queen, at that time the beings who have created virtuous roots will all gather in that Buddha land."

While Queen Śrīmālā was hearing the sublime prophecy, uncountable gods and men were inspired to be born in that Buddha land. And the Lord prophesied that all of them would be born in that world-region.

[From *The Lion's Roar of Queen Śrīmālā*, pp. 59–64.]

LADY NIJŌ'S AUTOBIOGRAPHY

Lady Nijō (1258–?) was a court lady and a concubine of a retired Japanese emperor. After being expelled from court, she became a wandering Buddhist nun in 1289. In the following selection from her journal she details the hard transition from her former luxurious life to her present ascetic life.

Toward the end of the second month I set out from the capital at moonrise. I had given up my home completely, yet my thoughts quite naturally lingered on the possibility of return, and I felt that the moon reflected in my fallen tears was also weeping. How weak-willed I was! These thoughts occupied my mind all the way to Ōsaka Pass, the place where the poet Semimaru once lived and composed the poem that ends, "One cannot live forever in a palace or a hut." No trace of his home remained. I gazed at my reflection in the famous clear spring at the pass and saw a pathetic image of myself attired down to the tips of my walking shoes in this unfamiliar traveling nun's habit.

* * *

After several days I arrived at Red Hill Lodge in Mino province, where I stopped for the night, weary and lonely from the days I had spent in unaccustomed travel. The lodge was managed by two sisters whose skill as entertainers, especially their sensitive playing of the *koto* and the *biwa*, reminded me of the past. When I ordered some *sake* and asked them to play for me, I noticed that the elder sister appeared troubled. She attended closely to her *biwa* playing, yet I could tell that she was on the verge of tears, and I guessed that we were very much alike. She must have wondered too about the tears that stained my dark sleeves, so out of keeping for a nun, for she composed this poem and passed it to me on a little *sake* cup stand:

I wonder what emotion
Caused you to resolve upon
The life of a wandering
Wisp of smoke from Fuji.

I was moved by her unexpected sympathy to write in reply:

Smoldering flames of love
Sent forth the smoke
From Fuji's Peak
In the Suruga Range.

I was reluctant to leave even this kind of a friend, but of course I could not remain indefinitely, and so once again I set forth.

* * *

I had left the capital late in the second month intending to push myself hard on my journeys, yet I was so unused to traveling that my progress was slow. Now the third month had already begun. A bright moon rose early, flooding the night sky just as it did in the capital, and once again His Majesty's image floated through my mind. Within the sacred precincts of the Atsuta Shrine cherry trees bloomed in rich profusion. For whom were they putting on this brilliant display?

Blossoms glow against spring sky
Near Narumi Lagoon,
How long now before
Petals scatter among pines.

I wrote this on a slip of paper and tied it to the branch of a cryptomeria tree in front of the shrine.

For a week I remained in prayer at the shrine before resuming my travels. As I approached the Narumi tidelands I glanced back at the shrine and saw patches of the scarlet fence that surrounded it gleaming through the mist. I struggled to suppress the tears that welled up.

Have pity on me, O gods
Enshrined by braided strands
My fate has twisted now to grief.

Following the moon across the Kiyomi Barrier, my mind was filled with troubles from the past and fears about the future as numerous as the grains of white sand on the vast beach that stretched before my eyes.

★ ★ ★

Late that month I arrived at the island of E no Shima, a fascinating place that is not easy to describe. It is separated from the mainland by a stretch of sea, and has many grottoes, in one of which I found shelter with a pious mountain ascetic who had been practicing austerities for many years. Senju Grotto, as it was called, was a humble yet charming dwelling, with fog for a fence and bamboo trees for screens. The ascetic made me feel welcome and presented me with some shells of the area, whereupon I opened the basket my companion carried, took out a fan from the capital, and offered it to him.

"Living here as I do, I never hear news from the capital," he said. "Certainly things like this aren't brought to me by the wind. Tonight I feel as though I've met a friend from the distant past." My own feelings quite agreed.

It was quiet with no one around and no special event taking place, yet I could not sleep a wink that night. I lay upon my mattress of moss brooding on the great distance I had traveled and the cloak of worries that covered me, and I wept quietly into my sleeve. Then I decided to go outside and look around. The horizon was lost in a haze that might have been clouds, waves, or mist; but the night sky high above was clear, and the brilliant moon hung motionless. I felt as though I had actually journeyed two thousand *li*. From the hills behind the grotto I heard the heart-rending cries of monkeys and felt an anguish so intense it seemed new. I had undertaken this solitary journey with only my thoughts and my grief in hopes that it would dry my tears. How distressing to have come so far and yet to have the worries of the world still cling to me.

A roof of cedar branches,
Pine pillars, bamboo blinds,
If only these could screen me
From this world of sorrow.

[From *The Confessions of Lady Nijō*, pp. 181–186.]

ZEN STORIES

The following excerpts are taken from *101 Zen Stories*, a collection of Japanese anecdotes, some of which were written down as early as the thirteenth century. They reflect the intense "being-in-the-momentness" of Zen practice, especially as its relates to women.

If You Love, Love Openly

Twenty monks and one nun, who was named Eshun, were practicing meditation with a certain Zen master.

Eshun was very pretty even though her head was shaved and her dress plain. Several monks secretly fell in love with her. One of them wrote her a love letter, insisting upon a private meeting.

Eshun did not reply. The following day the master gave a lecture to the group, and when it was over, Eshun arose. Addressing the one who had written her, she said: "If you really love me so much, come and embrace me now."

[From *Zen Flesh, Zen Bones*, p. 9.]

Gisho's Work

Gisho was ordained as a nun when she was ten years old. She received training just as the little boys did. When she reached the age of sixteen she traveled from one Zen master to another, studying with them all.

She remained three years with Unzan, six years with Gukei, but was unable to obtain a clear vision. At last she went to the master Inzan.

Inzan showed her no distinction at all on account of her sex. He scolded her like a thunderstorm. He cuffed her to awaken her inner nature.

Gisho remained with Inzan thirteen years, and then she found that which she was seeking!

In her honor, Inzan wrote a poem:

This nun studied thirteen years under my guidance.
In the evening she considered the deepest koans,
In the morning she was wrapped in other koans.
The Chinese nun Tetsuma surpassed all before her,
And since Mujaku none has been so genuine as this Gisho!
Yet there are many more gates for her to pass through.
She should receive still more blows from my iron fist.

After Gisho was enlightened she went to the province of Banshu, started her own Zen temple, and taught two hundred other nuns until she passed away one year in the month of August.

[From *Zen Flesh, Zen Bones,* pp. 36–37.]

Incense Burner

A woman of Nagasaki named Kame was one of the few makers of incense burners in Japan. Such a burner is a work of art to be used only in a tearoom or before a family shrine.

Kame, whose father before her had been such an artist, was fond of drinking. She also smoked and associated with men most of the time. Whenever she made a little money she gave a feast inviting artists, poets, carpenters, workers, men of many vocations and avocations. In their association she evolved her designs.

Kame was exceedingly slow in creating, but when her work was finished it was always a masterpiece. Her burners were treasured in homes whose womenfolk never drank, smoked, or associated freely with men.

The mayor of Nagasaki once requested Kame to design an incense burner for him. She delayed doing so until almost half a year had passed. At that time the mayor, who had been promoted to office in a distant city, visited her. He urged Kame to begin work on his burner.

At last receiving the inspiration, Kame made the incense burner. After it was completed she placed it upon a table. She looked at it long and carefully. She smoked and drank before it as if it were her own company. All day she observed it.

At last, picking up a hammer, Kame smashed it to bits. She saw it was not the perfect creation her mind demanded.

[From *Zen Flesh, Zen Bones,* pp. 67–68.]

Fire-Poker Zen

Hakuin used to tell his pupils about an old woman who had a teashop, praising her understanding of Zen. The pupils refused to believe what he told them and would go to the teashop to find out for themselves.

Whenever the woman saw them coming she could tell at once whether they had come for tea or to look into her grasp of Zen. In the former case, she would serve them graciously. In the latter, she would beckon to the pupils to come behind her screen. The instant they obeyed, she would strike them with a fire-poker.

Nine out of ten of them could not escape her beating.

[From *Zen Flesh, Zen Bones,* p. 76.]

POEMS OF THE NUN RYŌNEN GENSO

The following excerpts are a brief autobiographical sketch and a poem of the famous Japanese Zen nun Ryōnen Genso (1646–1711). Among other things, these excerpts reveal that the issue of being a woman, especially a beautiful woman, was still seen as an impediment to monastic life.

Before she became a nun, Ryōnen had served at the Japanese Court, married, and had several children. She was a well-educated court lady, whose poems, paintings, and calligraphy were greatly admired. After ten years of marriage, and probably with the permission of her husband, Ryōnen became a nun. Following the incidents recounted below, Ryōnen was accepted by the Zen master Haku-ō, became his leading pupil, and had her enlightenment experience confirmed by him (a traditional Zen practice). In later years, she became the abbot of her own monastery and was famous for her scholarship and good deeds, such as providing education for children in the surrounding villages.

When I was young I served Yoshino-kimi, the grand-daughter of Tōfukumon'in, a disciple of the imperial temple Hōkyō-ji. Recently she passed away; although I know that this is the law of nature, the transience of the world struck me deeply, and I became a nun. I cut my hair and dyed my robes black and went on pilgrimage to Edo. There I had an audience with the monk Haku-ō of the Obaku Zen sect. I recounted to him such things as my deep devotion to Buddhism since childhood, but Haku-ō replied that although he could see my sincere intentions, I could not escape my womanly appearance. Therefore I heated up an iron and held it against my face, and then wrote as my brush led me:

Formerly to amuse myself at court I would burn
      orchid incense;

Now to enter the Zen life I burn my own face.
The four seasons pass by naturally like this,
But I don't know who I am amidst the change.
   In this living world
the body I give up and burn
   would be wretched
if I thought of myself as
anything but firewood.
      [From *The Art of Zen*, p. 95.]

In the autumn of my sixty-sixth year, I've already
      lived a long time—
The intense moonlight is bright upon my face.
There's no need to discuss the principles of *kōan* study;
Just listen carefully to the wind outside the pines and
      cedars.
      [From *The Art of Zen*, p. 99.]

Tantra

Tantric Buddhism, also called Vajrayāna, is a later development of Mahāyāna Buddhism, though it also traces itself back to the teachings of the Buddha. Tantric practices, which began to spread throughout northern India around the fifth century C.E., influenced both Hinduism and Buddhism. These practices emphasize female deities and utilize sexual imagery, holding out the promise of magical powers. Theoretically, Tantric Buddhism gives women a religious status equal to men. It has elaborate rituals and it advocates the use of mystical syllables and phrases called mantras. Today its best known practitioners are exiled Tibetan Buddhists.

WISDOM AS FEMININE

Prajñā, wisdom, is central to all forms of Buddhism because it is the essential element of the enlightenment experience. Wisdom is developed and grows through the continuing practice of the Buddhist virtues and meditation. The *prajñāpāramitā* ("perfection of wisdom") texts of the Mahāyāna school of Buddhism, as their name suggests, discuss at length the means of attaining or perfecting wisdom, which leads to the elimination of all dualities, that is, enlightenment. It is the achievement of wisdom that enables the Bodhisattva to maintain the consciousness of the ultimate reality of enlightenment while functioning and aiding those whose consciousness is bounded by the illusions of worldly reality.

Prajñā is often conceived of as a goddess, especially in the Tantric tradition, and is frequently called "the Mother of all the Buddhas." Tantric Buddhism further emphasizes the need for the union of wisdom (conceived of as female) with means (conceived of as male).

In the following excerpt from a Mahāyāna text Śāriputra, one of the leading disciples of the historical Buddha and the one referred to as most wise, describes and praises wisdom.

Sariputra: The perfection of wisdom, O Lord, is the accomplishment of the cognition of the all-knowing. The perfection of wisdom is the state of all-knowledge.

The Lord: So it is, Sariputra, as you say.

Sariputra: The perfection of wisdom gives light, O Lord. I pay homage to the perfection of wisdom! She is worthy of homage. She is unstained, and the entire world cannot stain her. She is a source of light, and from everyone in the triple world she removes darkness, and leads them away from the blinding darkness caused by defilements and wrong views. In her we can find shelter. Most excellent are her works. She makes us seek the safety of the wings of enlightenment. She brings light to the blind, so that all fear and distress may be forsaken. She has gained the five eyes, and she shows the path to all beings. She herself is an organ of vision. She disperses the gloom and darkness of delusion. She guides to the Path those who have strayed on to a bad road. She is identical with all-knowledge. She never produces any dharma, because she has forsaken the residues relating to both kinds of coverings, those produced by defilement and those produced by the cognizable. She does not stop any dharma. Herself unstopped and unproduced is the perfection of wisdom. She is the Mother of the Bodhisattvas, on account of the emptiness of own-marks. As the donor of the jewel of all the Buddha-dharmas she brings about the ten powers of a Tathagata. She cannot be crushed. She protects the unprotected, with the help of the four grounds of self-confidence. She is the antidote to birth-and-death. She has a clear knowledge of the own-being of all dharmas, for she does not stray away from it. The perfection of wisdom of the Buddhas, the Lords, sets in motion the wheel of Dharma.

[From *Ashtasāhasrikā* VII, 170–171; p. 146 in *Buddhist Texts Through the Ages*.]

The next excerpt is also a Mahāyāna text that describes and praises wisdom.

Homage to Thee, Perfect Wisdom,
Boundless, and transcending thought!
All Thy limbs are without blemish,
Faultless those who Thee discern.

Spotless, unobstructed, silent,
Like the vast expanse of space;
Who in truth does really see Thee
The Tathagata perceives.

As the moonlight does not differ
From the moon, so also Thou
Who aboundst in holy virtues,
And the Teacher of the world.

Those, all pity, who came to Thee,
Buddha-dharmas heralding,
They will win with ease, O Gracious!
Majesty beyond compare.

Pure in heart, when once they duly
Look upon Thee, surely then
Their complete success is certain,—
O Thou, fruitful to behold!

To all heroes who of others
Have the welfare close at heart
Thou a mother, who does nourish,
Who gives birth, and who gives love.

Teachers of the world, the Buddhas
Are Thine own compassionate sons;
Then art Thou, O Blessed Lady.
Grandam thus of beings all

All th'immaculate perfections
At all times encircle Thee,
As the stars surround the crescent,
O Thou blameless holy one!

Those in need of light considering,
The Tathagatas extol
Thee, the Single One, as many,
Multiformed and many-named.

As the drops of dew in contact
With the sun's rays disappear,
So all theorizings vanish,
Once we have obtained Thee.

When as fearful Thou appearest
Thou engender'st fear in fools;
When benignly Thou appearest
Comes assurance to the wise.

How will one who no affection
Has for Thee, though yet Thy Lord,
Have, O Mother, greed and loathing
For the many other things?

Not from anywhere Thou comest,
And to nowhere doest Thou go;
In no dwelling place have sages
Ever apprehended Thee.

Not to see Thee in this manner
Is to have attained to Thee,
Gaining thus the final freedom,—
O how wonderful is this!

One indeed is bound who sees Thee;
One who sees not bound is too.
One again is freed who sees Thee;
One who sees not freed is too.

Wonderful, profound, illustrious,
Hard Thou art to recognize.
Like a mock show Thou art seen, and
Yet Thou art not seen at all.

By all Buddhas, Single Buddhas,
By Disciples courted, too,
Thou the one path to salvation,
There's no other, verily.

Saviours of the world, from pity,
So that men might understand,
Speak of Thee, observing custom,

Yet of Thee they do not speak.

Who is able here to praise Thee,
Lacking signs and featureless?
Thou the range of speech transcending,
Not supported anywhere.

In such words of current language
Constantly we laud Thee, whom
None of our acclaim concerneth;
So we reach beatitude.

By my praise of Perfect Wisdom
All the merit I may rear,
Let that make the world devoted
To this wisdom without peer.
    [From *Rāhulabhadra, Prajñāpāramitāstotra,* pp. 147–
149 in *Buddhist Texts Through the Ages.*]

The following two excerpts are taken from Tantric texts. The first is an advanced visualization to be performed during meditation, and the second, while emphasizing wisdom and using very esoteric language, also brings out the union of wisdom with means (*upāya*).

One should envisage in one's own heart the syllable DHĪḤ set upon a lunar disk, and with the rays that emerge from it one should arouse all gurus and Buddhas and Bodhisattvas and drawing them in before oneself, one should envisage them as sitting there in their various positions. Then one should mentally confess one's sins and rejoice at such merit as has accrued, take the threefold refuge, rouse the thought of enlightenment, dedicate merit and beg for pardon. Next one should develop friendliness, compassion, sympathetic joy and even-mindedness. Then with these words one should meditate the Void: "I possess in my essence the adamantine nature which is knowledge of the Void." Next one should envisage that syllable DHĪḤ which is set on the lunar disk, as transformed into the Lady Prajñāpāramitā. She bears a head-dress of twisted hair; she has four arms and one face. With two of her hands she makes the gesture of expounding the dharma and she is adorned with various jewelled ornaments. She blazes like the colour of gold and in her (second) left hand she holds a blue lotus with a Prajñāpāramitā-book upon it. She wears various garments both below and above and with her (second) right hand she makes the gesture of fearlessness. She is seated cross-legged on the lunar disk and on a red lotus. Envisaging her thus, one should perform the act of identification: "Such as is the Lady Prajñāpāramitā, even so am I. Such as am I, even so is the Lady Prajñāpāramitā." Next one

should set out the mantras: at the throat OM DHĪḤ, on the tongue OM GĪH and on the ears OM JRĪḤ.

Then in one's own heart one should imagine a red eight-petalled lotus, which arises from the syllable ĀḤ and is complete with pericarp and filament, and upon the pericarp and petals of this lotus one should mentally inscribe in yellow these words:

the eastern petal:	HOMAGE
on the south-eastern petal:	TO THE LADY
on the southern petal:	PRAJÑĀPĀRAMITĀ
on the south-western petal:	WHOSE VIRTUE IS IMMORTALITY
on the western petal:	WHO RESPONDS TO LOVING DEVOTION
on the north-western petal:	WHO IS REPLETE WITH THE KNOWLEDGE OF ALL THE TATHAGATAS
on the northern petal:	WHO IS LOVING TOWARDS ALL
on the north-eastern petal:	OM DHĪḤ

Then

on the eastern side of the pericarp:	ŚRU
on the south-eastern side:	TI
on the southern side:	SMR̥
on the south-western side:	TI
on the western side:	VI
on the north-western side:	JA

on the northern side: YE
on the north-eastern side: SVĀHĀ

Having thus set out these mantra-words, one should recite them and meditate upon them—for a day, or for a week, for six months or a year. Thereby one becomes possessed of wisdom.

[From *Sādhanamālā,* pp. 252–254 in *Buddhist Texts Through the Ages.*]

Candālī blazes at the navel,
She burns the Five Tathagatas,
She burns Locana and the others,
AHAM is burned and the Moon is melted.

Canda is explained as Wisdom, that is to say the left vein, Ālī is explained as Means, that is to say the right vein, Candālī means these two united in accordance with one's master's word.

The word 'navel' indicates the centre and the centre here is Avadhūtī, and here Candālī burns. She burns with the great fire of passion the five skandhas of the person, and earth and the other four elements of the material world. And when AHAM (= I) is burned, which means when such notions as I and mine are consumed, then there flows and arises the knowledge of great bliss.

By no one may the Innate be explained,
In no place may it be found,
It is known of itself by merit,
And by due attendance on one's master.

[From *Hevajratantra,* pp. 254–255 in *Buddhist Texts Through the Ages.*]

FEMALE AND MALE SYMBOLS

Tantric practices can be extremely esoteric and often possess a rich symbolism whose meaning is obscure to the uninitiated. The following excerpt is from a short, extremely esoteric ceremony taken from the *Kālachakra Tantra,* a teaching traditionally ascribed to the Buddha, which became widely known in India during the tenth century C.E. In this ceremony the disciple is initiated into the meaning and practice of the vajra ("thunderbolt") and the bell. These two are the primary symbols of Tantric Buddhism, representing the duality of being. Both are charged with power. The bell is a female symbol, representing wisdom. The vajra, or thunderbolt, is a male symbol, representing skillful means. When combined in perfect balance they lead to enlightenment. Practitioners often manipulate these two, one in each hand, during their meditation.

Vajra and Bell Initiation

Again, mandala is offered to the lama, undifferentiable from the Vajra Speech of Kālachakra, as a present for the vajra and bell initiation that cleanses the two channels.

Offer mandala.

To the lama, personal deity, and Three Jewels I offer in visualization
The body, speech, mind, and resources of myself and others,
Our collections of virtue in the past, present, and future,
And the wonderful precious mandala with the masses of Samantabhadra's offerings.
Accepting them through your compassion, please bless me into magnificence.

Idam guru-ratna-mandalakam niryātayāmi. [I offer this jewelled mandala to the guru.]

The *Sūtra of Teaching to Nanda on Entry to the Womb (tshe dang ldan pa dga' bo mngal do 'jug pa bstan pa, āyushmannandagarbhābhāvakrāntinirdesha)* says that in our bodies there are eighty thousand channels. In Mantra, the count of the channels is seventy-two thousand. Among these, the main channels are three—the right, left, and central channels. Among these, a practitioner is seeking to make use of the central one.

When the right and left channels—*rasanā* and *lalanā*—are active, conceptions of subject and object are generated. Hence, in order to purify the right and left channels, the students make supplication to receive the vajra and bell initiations.

Make supplication three times with:

Om hūm hoh vijñānā-jñānā-svabhāve, karuṇā-prajñā-ātmake vajra-vajra-ghaṇṭe savyetarakarayor mama vajrasatvah saprajño dadātu hum hūm phaṭ. [Oṃ hūṃ hoh please may Vajrasattva together with [his] Wisdom Woman bestow the vajra and vajra-bell that have a nature of consciousness and exalted wisdom [and] an essence of compassion and wisdom in my right hand and other hand huṃ hūṃ phaṭ.]

Then, the student's right and left channels and the substances of the initiation, vajra and bell, are generated as [two sets of] Kālachakra and his consort, Vishvamātā. Therefore, listen carefully to the ritual instructions and imagine the process as indicated.

Clear away [obstructors] from the student and from the vajra and bell [with the six syllables, oṃ āh hūṃ hoh haṃ kshah and water from the conch] and purify them. With:

Oṃ shūnyatā-jñāna-vajra-svabhāvātmako 'haṃ [I have the essential nature of indivisible emptiness and wisdom,] you and the vajra bell turn into emptiness. From within emptiness, your right channel and the vajra which is the initiation substance [each appear as] hūṃ [which transform into] vajras, from which are generated blue Kālachakras with one face and two hands holding vajra and bell; they are embraced by Vishvamātās holding a curved knife and a skull. Your left channel and the bell [each appear as] phrem [which transform into] curved knives, from which are generated yellow Vishvamātās with one face and two hands holding a curved knife and skull; they are embraced by Kālachakra. At the forehead of these two is oṃ; at the neck āh; at the heart hūṃ, and at the navel hoh. Light, emitted from the hūṃ at their heart, draws in Wisdom Beings like the meditated ones.

Jah hūm bam hoh hi. [Be summoned, enter, become fused with, be pleased, and become of the same taste.]

They become of one taste with their respective Pledge Beings.

Oṃ ā ī ṛ ū ḹ pañcha-dhātu-vishodhani svāhā. [Oṃ ā ī ṛ ū ḹ be founded in the purification of the five constituents.] The Mothers confer initiation on the deities of the initiation substances. The Father Deity [Kālachakra] is seal-impressed by Akshobhya, and the Mother Deity [Vishvamātā] is seal-impressed by Vajrasattva.

Make offering [to those deities] with:

Gandhaṃ pushpaṃ dhūpaṃ dīpaṃ akshate naividye lāsye hāsye vādye nṛtye gītye kāme pūja kuru kuru svāhā. [Make offering with perfume, flowers, incense, lamps, fruit, food, lower robe, smiles, music, dance, singing, and touch svāhā.]

The Father Deity and Mother Deity become absorbed; upon being melted by the fire of great desire they become the vajra and bell that are the initiation substances. Light rays from the heart of the lama who is not different from the principal deity draw in the initiation deities—Father and Mother Conquerors, Sons, and Daughters—filling the expanse of space.

Vajra-bhairava ākarshaya jah. [Vajra Frightful One, summon jah.]

Make offering with:

Gandhaṃ pushpaṃ dhūpaṃ dīpaṃ akshate naividye lāsye hāsye vādye nṛtye gītye kāme pūja kuru kuru svāhā. [Make offering with perfume, flowers, incense, lamps, fruit, food, lower robe, smiles, music, dance, singing, and touch svāhā.]

Make a supplication:

Just as Vajradhara bestowed
Initiations, sources of good qualities,
On the Buddhas for the sake of protecting transmigrating beings,
So please also bestow such here.

Then:

The Conquerors in space—Fathers and Mothers—make the intention to confer initiation. The Bodhisattvas make expressions of auspiciousness. Rūpa-vajrā and so forth make offering, and a rain of flowers and so forth descend. Male and Female Wrathful Ones expel obstructors. The principal Father Deity and Mother Deity in the mandala that has been achieved, holding vajra and bell, confer initiation.

The Vajra Worker raises up the vajra and bell. Auspiciousness is expressed with:

Through an auspiciousness dwelling in the hearts of all the sentient,
The essence of all, the supreme lord of all lineages,
Progenitor of all the sentient, the great bliss,
May you have today auspiciousness at the supreme conferral of initiation.

Through the Buddha possessing perfection like a gold mountain,
Protector of the three worlds who has abandoned the three defilements,
With a face like the broad petals of a lotus,
May you have today the auspiciousness of pacification.

Through the highest supreme unwavering teaching set forth by him,

Renowned in the three worlds, worshipped by gods
    and humans,
Most excellent of doctrine, pacifying all beings,
May you have today the auspiciousness of pacification.

Through the excellent spiritual community, rich
    with the auspiciousness of having heard the
    doctrine,

Place of worship by humans, gods, and demi-gods,
Highest supreme of assemblies, knowing con-
    science, and the foundation of glory,
May you have today the auspiciousness of pacifi-
    cation.
[From *The Kālachakra Tantra,* pp. 298–304.]

THE GODDESS TĀRĀ

In her many forms Tārā is the most popular deity of Tibetan Buddhism. She is a goddess
and a female Buddha, known as the Great Protector. The following excerpt is taken from
the beginning of the *Tārā Tantra,* written by Tāranathā (b. 1575), the great historian of Tibetan
Buddhism.

The first part tells of a previous incarnation of Tārā, before she became a goddess, when
she was a woman and made a vow to remain female until the end of time as we know it. The
rest of the excerpt offers examples of her powers and her mercy. This list of her abilities also
demonstrates to her devotees that she is available to all people, no matter what their occupation or class may be.

Long ago, in an age before which there was nothing
else, the Victorious One, the Tathāgata Dundubhiśvara came into existence and was known as the
Light of the Various Worlds. The Princess "Moon of
Wisdom" had the highest respect for his teaching, and
for ten million, one hundred thousand years, she made
offerings to this Enlightened One, his attendant
Śrāvakas and to countless members of the Sangha of
Bodhisattvas. The offerings she prepared each day
were in value comparable to all the precious things
which filled a distance of twelve yojanas in each of
the ten directions, leaving no intermediate spaces un-
filled. Finally, after all this she awoke to the first concepts of Bodhi-Mind. At that time some monks said
to her, "It is as a result of these, your roots of virtuous
actions, that you have come into being in this female
form. If you pray that your deeds accord with the
teachings, then indeed on that account you will
change your form to that of a man, as is befitting."
After much discourse she finally replied, "In this life
there is no such distinction as "male" and "female",
neither of "self-identity", a "person" nor any perception (of such), and therefore attachment to ideas of
"male" and "female" is quite worthless. Weak-minded
worldlings are always deluded by this." And so she
vowed, "There are many who wish to gain enlightenment in a man's form, and there are but few who wish
to work for the welfare of sentient beings in a female
form. Therefore may I, in a female body, work for
the welfare of beings right until Samsāra has been
emptied."

Then she remained in the palace for ten million and
one hundred thousand years in a state of meditation,
wisely applying her mind to the five sensual pleasures.
As a result of this she gained success in the realisa-
tion that dharmas are non-originating and also perfected the meditation known as "Saving All Sentient
Beings", by the power of which, every morning she
released ten million and one hundred thousand beings
from (the bondage of) their worldly minds. As long
as all of them were not fully instructed in this steadfast course, she would take no nourishment at all. This
same policy was followed each evening when she set
a like number of beings on the same path. Then her
former name was changed and she became known as
the Saviouress. Then the Tathāgatha Dundubhiśvara
prophesies: "As long as you can possibly continue
manifesting such supreme Bodhi, you will be exclusively known as 'Goddess Tārā'".

* * *

Now follow, culled from annals and stories, some
accounts of Noble Arya Tārā's mercy, perfections and
her promises. They will be in the form of a discourse.
She is the Protectress from the Fear of Enemies. A
Kṣatriya from the land of Odiviśa awakened one day
in a grove where he had fallen asleep, and found
himself surrounded by a host of a thousand enemy
soldiers, all brandishing their swords at him. He
recalled having heard that Tārā was the Protectress
against the Sixteen Fears, and as he had no other

(divinity) in which to seek refuge, he thought he would go to the Goddess as his defence. At the same instant at which he called out her name, the Noble Lady herself appeared before him, arriving from the skies. From underneath her feet whirlwinds carried the soldiers off into the ten directions, and so the man was able to arrive safely in his own country.

She is the Protectress from the Fear of Lions. A wood-gatherer went off into the forest and there he came face to face with a ravenous lioness which held him in her jaws and prepared to eat him. His hope faded away. Terrified and scared he begged Tārā to come to his assistance, and she suddenly appeared before him, clothed in leaves. She pulled him from the lioness' jaws and set him down safely in the city market-place.

She is the Protectress from the Fear of Elephants. A twelve-year old girl went one day to the forest to gather flowers, and there she was confronted with a fierce elephant named Kuni, who bound her in his trunk and started to crush her with his tusks. Remembering Tārā's name, the girl earnestly begged her to help and Tārā brought the elephant under control. The creature then put the girl up on a stone ledge and saluted her with its trunk, and leading her away, took her to the town's market-place. Then it took her to the council chambers, the Temple and around the King's palace. The King heard of this girl and her great stock of merits and took her as his Queen.

She is the Protectress from the Fear of Fire. A certain householder hated his enemy (neighbour) and one night set fire to his house. The latter started to flee but could not get free — at that instant he called out, "Tārā, O Mother Tārā!" A beautiful blue cloud arose above the house, and from it fell a continual shower of rain, like a yoke, on the house itself, completely quenching the flames.

She is the Protectress from the Fear of Poisonous Snakes. Once, in a certain city lived a prostitute who was given a necklace of five hundred pearls. She contacted a merchant about its sale and wished to go to his house at midnight. Leaving her house, and while on the road there, she happened to grasp an acacia branch around which was coiled a poisonous snake which seized her around her body. By her mere recollection of Arya Tārā, the snake was transformed into a flower garland in which form it remained for seven days. Thereafter it lost its white venom and proceeded into the river, so it is said.

She is the Protectress from the Fear of Brigands. A man from Gujarat, known as Bharukcha, was a very wealthy trader. On the way to the land of Maru with about a thousand camels and half that number of bulls, all fully laden, he found that his path went through the territory of a bandit gang which was situated in the midst of a veritable wilderness. All the previous traders who had gone there had been slain, and their flesh, blood and bones were scattered in the four directions. A myriad of these traders had been impaled on wooden stakes and the robbers who behaved like devils even ate their flesh. The (chief) trader was absolutely terrified, and as he had no other protector he begged Tārā to help him. She immediately arose in the phantom form of "Tārā the Heroine", holding aloft a sword and accompanied by a huge army, Tārā banished the bandits to a remote land and brought the dead back to life. Accordingly, when the robbers had been scattered into isolation the trader happily set off and again arrived at the Bharukcha clan.

She is the Protectress from Prison Walls. A leader of a robber band went to the subterranean treasury of the king. There he found a jug of beer which he drank, and being a bit befuddled he went to sleep. However, he was seen and seized by the king's men who flung him into a dungeon, bound up. There he underwent various sufferings. Bereft of any other protector he prayed to Tārā and a five-coloured bird descended from the sky, loosened his bonds and caused the dungeon door to open by itself. Having thus been freed and once again at large, he returned to his own country. (That night) in a dream, a beautiful girl adorned with all types of ornaments arose and said to him, "If you recall my kind deed to you then you and your followers must relinquish your thieving ways!" And so it happened that the robber and his five hundred accomplices gave up their lives of crime and did many virtuous deeds instead.

* * *

She is the Protectress from the Fear of Poverty. A Brahmin who was extremely poor and suffering considerably as a result, one day in a narrow street came upon a stone image of Tārā and he poured out an account of how his troubles had arisen. Pointing out a site near a shrine she said that it would be changed into a treasure trove. Then, exactly as had been indicated, he found many golden vessels filled with pearls and silver vessels filled with various jewels. It is said that within a week all the sufferings due to his poverty had been resolved. Also there was once a poor farmer who invoked Noble Tārā and supplicated her. She appeared in the form of a maiden clothed in leaves and prophesied that he should go eastwards. He did just this and, sleeping in the desert one night, he was awakened by the sound of tinkling bells and saw a green horse, ornamented with bells pawing at the sand. In a flash the horse vanished and the farmer, digging in the furrow made by the horse's hoof, found first of all a silver door, then one made of gold, then one of crystal, one of lapis lazuli, and finally one made up of seven precious gems. In the underground kingdom (to which the door led) he became king over many Nagas and Asuras, and experienced many of his dearest wishes. When he re-emerged from the door to the hold in the ground and had arrived back in his own country he found that in the meantime three kings had occupied the throne, so it is said.

[From *The Origin of the Tārā Tantra*, pp. 11–20.]

THE BIOGRAPHY OF YESHE TSOGYEL

This excerpt is taken from chapter three of the biography of Yeshe Tsogyel, traditionally believed to have lived during the eighth century. Yeshe Tsogyel was an early practitioner of Buddhism in Tibet and the disciple and companion of Padmasambhava, one of Tibet's greatest teachers (in this text he is called Pema Jungne). This biography reflects the early days of Buddhism in Tibet, when the new faith had not yet taken root.

In the following excerpt Yeshe Tsogyel struggles to avoid marriage, preferring to lead a life devoted to religious practices. She meets Padmasabhava, who aids her and delivers a speech on the nature of tantra and the importance of women.

When the hordes of suitors descended upon Kharchen, my parents and their officials held council upon the question of my marriage. It was unanimously decided that excepting a claim from the Emperor I should be given to no one, because the disappointment of the unlucky suitors would surely be the cause of strife. This decision was made public, and the suitors dispersed each to his own home.

Soon after, Prince Pelgyi Zhonnu of Kharchu arrived to beg for my hand, bringing three hundred horses and mule loads of gifts. At the same time Prince Dorje Wongchuk of Zurkhar appeared with a similar load of treasure. For my parents to give me to one would leave the other dissatisfied, so I was asked to make my own choice.

'I will go with neither of them.' I insisted. 'If I was to go I would be guilty of incarcerating myself within the dungeon of worldly existence. Freedom is so very hard to obtain. I beg you, my parents, to consider this.'

Although I begged them earnestly, my parents were adamant. 'There are no finer palaces in the known world than the residences of these two princes,' my father told me. 'You are totally lacking in filial affection. I would be unable to give away such a savage as you in either China or Hor. I will give you to one of these princes.

'My daughter tells me that she is not inclined to go with either of you,' he told the rival suitors. 'So if I give her to one of you and the other disputes it she will stay with me. You are both familiar with competition; when I send her outside whoever lays hands on her first can have her. But the loser must not quarrel. If either of you fight over her, I will petition the Emperor to punish you.'

Then he decked me in fine brocades and gave me one hundred horse loads of chattels and provisions to take with me, and I was involuntarily led out of the house. The instant I stepped outside the rivals rushed towards me, and Kharchupa's official, Śāntipā, reaching me first, caught me by the breast and attempted to lead me away. However, I braced my legs against a boulder so that my feet sank into it like mud. To move me was like trying to move a mountain, and no one succeeded. Then those fiendish officials took a lash of iron throns, and stripping me naked they began to whip me. I explained to them:

This body is the result of ten thousand years of effort;
If I cannot use it to gain enlightenment
I will not abuse it with the pain of samsaric existence.
You may be the noblest and most powerful in Kharchu
But you lack the equipment to gain a day of wisdom.
So kill me; I care not.

The official called Śāntipā answered me.

Girl, you have beautiful body that is rotten within;
Your fair skin creates turbulence within the Prince's heart;
Like a dry bean you are smooth on the outside but hard within;
Give up this foolishness and become Princess of Kharchu.

I replied:

This precious human body is hard to obtain
But to gain a body like yours is easy—
Your sinful body is not even human.
Why should I go with you to become Princess of Kharchu?

Then again the officials whipped me with a lash of iron thorns, until my back was a bloody pulp, and unable to bear the physical pain I stood up and accompanied them. That evening the master and his servants camped at Drakda, and out of joy they danced and sang. I was profoundly depressed and wept tears of blood. Although many plans passed through my mind, no opportunity of escape presented itself. My voice breaking with grief I sang this agonised plaint to the Buddhas of the ten directions.

Alas! Buddhas and Bodhisattvas of the ten directions,
  protectors of beings,
The guardians possessing compassion and magical
  power,
The eye of awareness and magical legions,
Now is the time to fulfil your compassionate pledges.
My pure thoughts whiter than the glacial snows
Have become blacker than the shale of this alien devil;
Take pity on me!
My righteous thoughts as precious as gold
Have now less worth than the bronze of this alien
  devil;
You protectors with the Eye of Awareness, show
  understanding!

My pure aspiration, a wish-fulfilling gem,
Has less value now than the stone of this alien devil;
You magicians show your magical skill.
I hoped to reach *nirvāṇa* in one body in this lifetime
But this alien devil has pulled me into the mire of
  saṃsāra;
Quickly arrest my fate, compassionate lords.

Even as I made this prayer the men appeared to fall into a drunken stupor and slept. Then I fled, fled faster than the wind. Crossing many passes and valleys, I travelled south. The following morning my former captors were angry and shamefaced. They searched for me fruitlessly in every direction, and having searched Kharchen thoroughly to no avail they returned to Kharchu.

★ ★ ★

After my escape, I Tsogyel, lived in the valley of Womphu Taktsang, sustaining myself upon fruit and clothing myself with the fibre of the cotton tree. But Zurkharpa, the unsuccessful suitor, heard rumour of where I had gone and sent three hundred men to search for me. They found me and forcibly brought me back to their master.

Finally the emperor hears about Yeshe Tsogyel, and he demands her for his wife.

I arrived in Samye escorted by the King's envoy of welcome, decked in ornaments of precious stones and dressed in silk brocades suited to my new rank. The King celebrated our marriage with a three-month feast. Then due to my faith in the *Buddha-dharma he appointed me custodian of the dharma.* Scholars taught me letters and grammar, knowledge of the five arts and sciences, and both secular and religious accomplishments. A mere indication was sufficient for me to grasp whatever I was taught.

One day the King again invited the Great Master Pema Jungne to visit him. He prepared a jewelled-encrusted throne for him, and when the Master was seated offered him a great *ganackra feast, piling before him a mountain of material wealth. To make a formal mandala offering,* he arranged pieces of gold upon a silver *mandala* tray, and pieces of turquoise upon a golden *mandala* tray. The elements of the silver *mandala* represented his empire. He offered the Four Districts of Central Tibet and Tsang as Mount Meru; China, Jang and Kham as the eastern continent and its two satellite islands; he offered Jar, Kongpo and Bhutan as the southern continent and its two islands; and he offered Hor, Mongolia and the Northern Plains (Jangthang) as the northern continent and its two islands.

Further, represented by the turquoise, he offered me, his queen, as an offering of sensual gratification. Then he made his request: 'O Great Rimpoche, in this *mandala* I offer everything within my power. Through your great compassion you hold in your care all creatures, men and gods, in every form and at all times. Please grant me the special instruction through which I can attain Buddhahood instantaneously, relying upon the effort of this one body in this single lifetime. Grant me the extraordinary teaching of the Tantra, the sacred word beyond *karma* and cause and effect.' And he prostrated before the Guru nine by nine times in supplication.

The Great Guru replied with these verses:

Listen! The tantric mysteries are said to be secret
Not because the Tantra is immoral but because it is
  closed
Closed to the narrow-minded adherents of lesser
  paths.
And there is no irony in your *karma,* O King!
You have intelligence, intuitive insight and a broad
  mind;
  You will not alter your faith or renege on your
  samaya;

And you will attend to the tantric Lama with
  devotion.
This Great Being is free of any germ of desire,
The aberrations of lust are absent;
But woman is a sacred ingredient of the Tantra,
A qualified Awareness Dākinī is necessary;
She must be of good family, faithful and honour
  bound,
Beautiful, skilful in means, with perfect insight,
Full of kindness and generosity;
Without her the factors of maturity and release are
  incomplete,
And the goal of tantric practice is lost from sight.
However, throughout this Kingdom of Tibet
There are many practitioners of the Tantra,
But as many reach their goal as there are stars in the
  day sky.
In view of that, O King,

To you I will open the door of tantric practice.

Completing his address to the King, the Guru
assumed the form of Vajradhara, and remained in that
state. The King prostrated until his forehead was
bruised, and then he offered the five sacred ingredients, including myself to the Guru, who was
exceedingly pleased.

*Thereafter the Guru installed Tsogyel as his Consort and
Lady, and gave her initiation and empowerment, and then
as mystic partners they went first to Chimphju Geu to perform secret yoga.*

*Thus ends the third chapter in which is described how
Tsogyel recognised impermanence and encountered the Master.*

SAMAYA ITHI GYA GYA GYA!
  [From *Sky Dancer: The Secret Life and Songs of the
Lady Yeshe Tsogyel*, pp. 15–24.]

A FEMALE DISCIPLE OF MILAREPA

One of the most beloved and best known works of Tibetan Buddhism is the "Hundred
Thousand Songs of Milarepa," poems and stories attributed to the great teacher Milarepa
(1040–1123). The following excerpt contains the story of one of Milarepa's leading women
disciples, Sahle Aui. It tells how she met Milarepa and convinced him to accept her as a disciple,
and of her eventual spiritual accomplishment.

The Jetsun Milarepa went for alms to Ngogang
from the Belly Cave of Nya Non. He stayed at La
Shin for half a day, and then proceeded to Nagchar.
On his way there he met a pretty young girl about
sixteen years of age, with dark eyebrows and gleaming hair, well-dressed and well adorned. . . .
  Soon after, the girl visited the Jetsun, bringing a
friend with her. She gave Milarepa a nugget of gold,
and sang:

Please listen to me,
Great Repa Yogi, the accomplished one.
When I look at human lives
They remind me of dew on grass.
Thinking thus, my heart is full of grief.

When I see my friends and relatives,
They are as merchants passing in the street.
Thinking thus, my heart is grieved and sad.

★ ★ ★

Because of my good deeds in former lives,
I was born this time a human being.
My past life drives me from behind,
Cooking and household duties pull me on.
I draw closer to death every minute.
This decaying body
At any time may fall.
My breath, like morning-fog,
At any time may disappear.
Thinking thus, I cannot sleep.
Thinking thus, my heart is sad.

Oh, my Father Jetsun,
For the sake of Dharma I visit you.
Pray bless, protect, and pity me,
And grant me the holy Teachings!

[Impressed by her spiritual conviction, Milarepa
grants her initiation.]
  A sacramental offering was then made on a grand

scale. The Jetsun ordained her as a Geninma in accordance with the general Buddhist Rules, initiated her into the esoteric Tantric Order, and gave her many verbal instructions. He then named her "Sahle Aui," and ordered her to meditate. In a very short time she gained good Experiences and merits, and learned to meditate alone. The Jetsun then said to her, "I am very pleased with your faith and perseverance; the Experiences and Realizations that you have now gained will enable you to meditate independently in solitude. You should go now into the mountains and meditate by yourself.

* * *

Milarepa then set out for Nya Non to learn the whereabouts of his female disciple, Sahle Aui. On the way he met some monks who told him that Sahle Aui was still meditating in the cave to which she had first gone. They said that she never spoke or moved her body, but sat still like a dead corpse all the time. They believed that she must have gone astray in her meditation. Milarepa thought, "To absorb oneself in Samadhi like that is a good thing and not a hindrance." He then went toward the girl's abode. Meanwhile, in an illumination, Sahle Aui also saw the Jetsun coming, so she went to the edge of the valley to welcome him.

After making obeisances and inquiring after his health, Sahle Aui sat down to one side quietly, without uttering a word. In order to examine her meditation experience, Milarepa sang:

Oh, Sahle Aui, the hermit
Who took the Dharma to her heart,
With faith and veneration
You first relied on your Guru;
And through his blessings
Your mind has ripened.
Sipping the heavenly nectar of the Skillful Path
A real knowledge of Dharma has grown in you.
Without sloth and laziness in your devotion
The Warm-Experience that all saints have had
Has now grown within you.

* * *

Presenting her inner Experience to the Jetsun, Sahle Aui sang:

You ripened the unripened,
You emancipated those who were not free.

You made me realize that all
Manifestations in the outer world
Are unreal and magic-like.
I have thus seen the Mother of the Illuminating Dharmata,
I have thus realized that flowing thoughts
Are phantom-like projections;
As waves rise from the sea
They will vanish into it again.
All doubts, errors, and
Temptations in the world
Are thus wiped out!
Following the clear Path
I have gained true knowledge,
Understanding what the Tantras mean.
Truth of the lesser path should not
Be taken for the higher.
By craving it one cannot reach Buddhahood.
I now sincerely ask you, my Guru,
To instruct me in the Tantra.

* * *

I am a woman aspiring to Nirvana
Who, from Voidness and Compassion would n'er depart.
Free from conceit and arrogance,
I shall e'er be glad to learn the Doctrine.
Ever in you I trust as in the Buddha.
With all Dākinīs caroling with me,
This is my song to you, my gracious Guru.

The Jetsun, very much pleased, said, "You have gained good understanding and Experiences from your meditation. It is indeed difficult to win Realization like this. Although you have now entered the Path of the Omniscient Ones, you should still remain and meditate in solitude."

Obeying this injunction Sahle Aui again meditated in the hermitage. Later on she became one of the four foremost yoginī disciples of the Jetsun. During her lifetime she performed a great service to the Dharma and benefited many sentient beings. The story of her life may be found in a book written by Ngan Tson Dunba Shun Chub Jhalbo.

This is the story of Sahle Aui.
[From The *Hundred Thousand Songs of Milarepa*, vol. 2, pp. 408–420.]

CÖD RITUAL

Machig Lapdron (eleventh century) is one of the most famous women in Tibetan Buddhism. She is primarily known for the creation of the Cöd ritual, a tantric practice in which the celebrant, under the supervision of a guru, mentally cuts up his or her own body and offers it to the deities. This practice is said to facilitate the eradication of ego. Its practice continues today among highly trained adepts.

AUM!

[THE *YOGIC* DANCE WHICH DESTROYETH ERRONEOUS BELIEFS]

Now visualize thyself as having become, instantaneously,
The Goddess of the All-Fulfilling Wisdom,
Possessed of the power of enlarging thyself to the vastness of the Universe,
And endowed with all the beauties of perfection;
[Then] blow the human thigh-bone trumpet loudly,
And dance the Dance which Destroyeth Erroneous Beliefs.

Phaṭ!

I, the *yogin,* who practise the Dauntless Courage,
Devoting my thought and energy wholly to the realizing that *Nirvāṇa* and the *Sangsāra* are inseparable,
Am dancing this measure on [the forms of] spiritual beings who personify the self;
May I [be able to] destroy the *sangsāric* view of duality.
Come to the Dance, ye revered *Gurus* of the Root Faith;
Come, ye Heroes and Heroines, as innumerable as the drops of the Ocean;
Come to the Dance, ye Sky-Traversing Ones, who wander everywhere:
May this zealous devotion [of mine] be successful; vouchsafe your blessings upon it.

[THE *YOGIC* DANCE OF THE FIVE DIRECTIONS]

* * *

[THE *YOGIN*'S RESOLUTION]

Phaṭ!

O! the unenlightened mind, which looketh upon the apparent as being the Real,
May it be thoroughly subdued [by me] in virtue of religious practices;
And thus in order to master and thoroughly comprehend the true nature of the Real,
I resolve to free myself of all hope and of all fear.

[Instructions to the *yogin:*] Now, in performing the sacrifice, imagine thy body to be constituted of every desirable [worldly] thing.

[THE DEDICATION OF THE ILLUSORY BODY IN SACRIFICE]

Phaṭ!

This illusory body, which I have held to be so precious,
I dedicate [in sacrifice] as a heaped-up offering,
Without the least regard for it, to all the deities that constitute the visualized assembly;
May the very root of self be cut asunder.
Phaṭ!

* * *

[THE VISUALIZING OF THE CORPSE AND WRATHFUL GODDESS]

Phaṭ!

Then imagine this body, which is the result of thine own *karmic* propensities,
To be a fat, luscious-looking corpse, huge [enough to embrace the Universe],
Then [saying] *Phaṭ!* visualize the radiant Intellect; which is within thee,
As being the Wrathful Goddess and as standing apart [from thy body],
Having one face and two hands and holding a knife and a skull.
Think that she severeth the head from the corpse,
And setteth it, as a skull [like an enormous cauldron], over three skulls placed like legs of a tripod embracing the Three Regions,
And cutteth the corpse into bits and flingeth them inside the skull as offerings to the deities.
Then think that by [the mystic power of] the rays of the three-syllable *mantras, Aum, Āh, Hūṃ,* and *Hā, Hō, Hrī,*
The offerings are wholly transmuted into *amrita,* sparkling and radiant.

[Instructions to the *yogin:*] Repeat the above *mantras* several times, and think that thereby the impurities [of the body offered in the mystic sacrifice] have been purged away and the offering as a whole hath been transmuted into *amrita* [elixir] and that the *amrita* hath been increased into universe-filling quantities [for the good of all beings].

* * *

[THE OFFERING OF THE SACRIFICIAL FEAST TO SPIRITUAL BEINGS]

Phaṭ!

Be ye *sangsāric* or *non-sangsāric,* ye Eight Orders of Spirits, ye elementals and non-human beings,

And ye mischievous and malignant hosts of flesh-eating sprites who would mislead [the devotee],

On the outspread human-hide, covering all the World Systems,

Heaped up flesh, blood, and bones have been laid out, as a [sacrificial] offering.

If I consider these to be 'mine' or as being 'I', I will thereby manifest weakness.

Ungrateful would ye all be should ye not enjoy the offering most heartily.

If ye be in haste, bolt it down uncooked;

If ye have leisure, cook and eat it, piece by piece;

And leave not a bit the size of an atom behind.

[THE DEDICATING OF THE MERIT OF THE ACT OF SACRIFICE]

Phaṭ!

Ah! when one hath uncoiled, and become emancipated from, the concepts of 'pious' and 'impious',

There should not remain the least trace of hopes and fears;

Yet, in accordance with the unerring working of the interdependent chain [of causes and effects],

May the stream of the accumulation of merits be dedicated to the Realm of Truth and be inexhaustible.

Phaṭ!

In virtue of the merits arising from this crude, illusory gift of mine own body,

May all accumulated *karmic* obligations and unpaid balances of the aeons be paid and cleared.

When the Real Truth of the *Dharma* illuminateth my nature,

May all of you [i.e. the unenlightened deities and elementals at the feast] be born [as humans] and become my first disciples.

Thereupon, may the Uncreated Essence of the Pure, Unborn Mind

Arise in the nature of the three,—deities, men, and elementals;

And, avoiding the path of the misleading belief in the reality of the 'I' [or Egoism],

May their principle of consciousness be thoroughly saturated with the moisture of Love and Compassion.

As for myself, may I complete my ascetic practices successfully,

And [be enabled to] regard pleasure and pain with equanimity,

And to realize the *Sangsāra* and *Nirvāṇa* as being indistinguishable.

Triumphing over all Directions, may I be enabled to serve every being with whom I have come into contact.

Thus may my divine mission be crowned with success,

And may I attain to the Body of Glory.

Phaṭ!

[Here endeth the Rite for Eradicating the *Sangsāric* Self.]

[From *Tibetan Yoga and Secret Doctrines,* pp. 301–319.]

Sources

The Art of Zen: Paintings and Calligraphy by Japanese Monks, 1600–1925, by Stephen Addiss. New York: Harry N. Abrams, 1989.

The Buddhacarita, by Aśvaghoṣa, translated by E. H. Johnston. 1936. New Delhi: Motilal Banarsidas, 1972, 1984.

Buddhism in Translations, trans. Henry Clarke Warren. 1896. New York: Atheneum, 1962.

Buddhist Texts Through the Ages, ed. Edward Conze. 1954. New York: Harper & Row, 1964.

The Confessions of Lady Nijō, trans. Karen Brazell. Stanford: Stanford University Press, 1973, 1976.

The Elders' Verses, vol. 2, *Therīgāthā,* trans. K. R. Norman. London: Pali Text Society, 1971.

The Holy Teaching of Vimalakīrti: A Mahāyāna Scripture, trans. Robert A. F. Thurman. University Park, PA, and London: Pennsylvania State University Press, 1976.

The Hundred Thousand Songs of Milarepa, vol. 2, trans. Garma C. C. Chang. Boulder, CO, and London: Shambhala Publications, 1962, 1977.

The Kālachakra Tantra, trans. Jeffrey Hopkins. London: Wisdom Publications, 1985.

The Lion's Roar of Queen Śrīmālā, trans. Alex Wayman and Hideko Wayman. New York and London: Columbia University Press, 1974.

The Origin of the Tārā Tantra, by Jo-Nan Taranatha, translated and edited by David Templeman. Dharamsala: Library of Tibetan Works and Archives, 1981.

Sky Dancer: The Secret Life and Songs of the Lady Yeshe Tsogyel, trans. Keith Dowmad. London: Routledge & Kegan Paul, 1984.

Suddharma-Pundarīka or The Lotus of the True Law, trans. H. Kern. New York: Dover Publications, 1963. Reprint of vol. 21 of *The Sacred Books of the East,* ed. F. Max Müller. Oxford: Clarendon Press, 1884.

Tibetan Yoga and Secret Doctrines, ed. W. Y. Evans-Wentz. London and New York: Oxford University Press, 1935, 1958, 1967.

The Voice of the Buddha: The Beauty of Compassion, vol. 1, translated into English by Gwendolyn Bays from the French of Edouard Foucaux. Berkeley, CA: Dharma Publishing, 1983.

Women in Buddhism: Images of the Feminine in Mahāyāna Tradition, by Diana Y. Paul. Berkeley, CA: University of California Press, 1979, 1985.

Zen Flesh, Zen Bones, compiled by Paul Reps. Garden City, NY: Anchor Books, n.d.

Bibliography

Introductory Textbooks

Richard H. Robinson and Willard L. Johnson, *The Buddhist Religion: A Historical Introduction.* 3rd. ed. Belmont, CA: Wadsworth Publishing Company, 1970, 1982.

Richard Gombrich, *Theravāda Buddhism: A Social History from Ancient Benares to Modern Colombo.* New York: Routledge & Kegan Paul, 1988.

Though their indices do not show it, both these books have meaningful discussions of women in Buddhism, especially nuns, dispersed throughout their pages.

Works on Women in Buddhism

Tsultrim Allione, *Women of Wisdom.* London: Routledge & Kegan Paul, 1984.

Nancy Auer Falk, "The Case of the Vanishing Nuns: The Fruits of Ambivalence in Ancient Indian Buddhism." In *Unspoken Worlds: Women's Religious Lives in Non-Western Cultures,* ed. Nancy A. Falk and Rita M. Gross. San Francisco: Harper & Row, 1980.

Nancy Schuster Barnes, "Buddhism." In *Women in World Religions,* ed. Arvind Sharma. New York: State University of New York Press, 1987.

Feminine Ground: Essays on Women and Tibet, ed. Janice D. Willis. Ithaca, NY: Snow Lion Publications, 1989, 1987.

Lenore Friedman, *Meetings with Remarkable Women: Buddhist Teachers in America.* Boston: Shambhala, 1987.

I. B. Horner, *Women Under Primitive Buddhism.* 1930. New Delhi: Motilal Banarsidass, 1975.

Edward Kamens, *The Buddhist Poetry of the Great Kamo Priestess.* Ann Arbor, MI: Center for Japanese Studies, University of Michigan, 1990.

Anne C. Klein, "Primordial Purity and Everyday Life: Exalted Female Symbols and the Women of Tibet." In *Immaculate & Powerful: The Female in Sacred Image and Social Reality,* ed. Clarissa W. Atkinson, Constance H. Buchanan, and Margaret Miles. Boston: Beacon Press, 1985.

Paula Richman, "The Portrayal of a Female Renouncer in a Tamil Buddhist Text." In *Gender and Religion: On the Complexity of Symbols,* ed. Caroline Walker Bynum, Stevan Harrell, and Paula Richman. Boston: Beacon Press, 1986.

Barbara Ruch, "The Other Side of Culture in Medieval Japan." Pp. 500–543 in *The Cambridge History of Japan,* vol. 3. Cambridge: Cambridge University Press, 1990.

Katheryn A. Tsai, "The Chinese Buddhist Monastic Order for Women: The First Two Centuries." In *Women in China: Current Directions in Historical Scholarship,* ed. Richard W. Guisso and Stanley Johannesen. Youngstown, OH: Philo Press, 1981.

Janice D. Willis, "Nuns and Benefactresses: The Role of Women in the Development of Buddhism." In *Women, Religion and Social Change,* ed. Yvonne Yazbeck Haddad and Ellison Banks Findly. Albany, NY: State University of New York Press, 1985.

CONFUCIANISM

Introduction

Confucianism began in the works of its founder, Confucius (551–479 B.C.E.), especially the *Analects,* a well-known collection of Confucius's conversations with his pupils and his advice to rulers. Later, two more collections of teachings attributed to Confucius were gathered together, the *Great Learning* and the *Doctrine of the Mean.* Additionally, Confucius himself took as authoritative the classical texts of Ancient China: The *Book of Changes,* the *Book of Rites,* the *Book of Songs,* the *Book of History,* the *Book of Music,* and the *Spring and Autumn Annals* (which he may also have written), and he is said to have edited or made additions to another five. Consequently, they are often referred to as the Confucian Classics and are considered the source of all wisdom. They are the core texts of Chinese culture and as such reveal commonly-held beliefs about the nature of the universe and the appropriate roles for human beings, male and female.

The underlying notion in all these texts is that the cosmos is orderly because it is based on relationships that are hierarchical and harmonious. In his attempt to duplicate this order in earthly matters Confucius emphasized these three things: relationship, hierarchy, and harmony. These are best understood in the cosmic relationship of heaven and earth, in which heaven, a male principle, dominates and sustains the earth, a female principle. The hierarchy is clear: heaven dominates the earth; and yet the harmony and balance inherent in this relationship is revealed by the orderly course of nature. In the human realm, this pattern for relationship is expressed primarily through the ideal Confucian family in which the husband rules over the wife, the father over the son. The family is the main building block of the Confucian state, and it is in the family that women's primary roles as wife and mother are established. This idea received additional expression and support in the concept that there are two principles existing in all things: yin/yang, the passive/active, the female/male. For instance, individual women and men contain yin and yang within them, and good health and tranquillity are believed to derive from the harmonious blending of the two.

CREATION

The following creation story (from later Confucianism—11th century C.E.), begins with the non-ultimate (non-being) and the great ultimate (being). It is the latter that generated yang (the male) and then yin (the female); from the interaction of these two all else comes into being.

Chou Tun-Yi
An Explanation of the Diagram of the Great Ultimate

The Non-ultimate! And also the Great Ultimate (*T'ai-chi*). The Great Ultimate through movement generates the yang. When its activity reaches its limit, it becomes tranquil. Through tranquillity the Great Ultimate generates the yin. When tranquillity reaches its limit, activity begins again. Thus movement and tranquillity alternate and become the root of each other, giving rise to the distinction of yin and yang, and these two modes are thus established.

By the transformation of yang and its union with yin, the five agents of water, fire, wood, metal, and earth arise. When these five material-forces (*chi*) are distributed in harmonious order, the four seasons run their course.

The five agents constitute one system of yin and yang, and yin and yang constitute one Great Ultimate. The Great Ultimate is fundamentally the Non-ultimate. The five agents arise, each with its specific nature.

When the reality of the Non-ultimate and the essence of yin and yang and the five agents come into mysterious union, integration ensues. The heavenly principle (*ch'ien*) constitutes the male element, and the earthly principle (*k'un*) constitutes the female element.

The interaction of these two material forces engenders and transforms the myriad things. The myriad things produce and reproduce, resulting in an unending transformation.

It is man alone who receives [the material forces] in their highest excellence, and therefore he is most intelligent. His corporeal form appears, and his spirit develops consciousness. The five moral principles of his nature (humanity, righteousness, decorum, wisdom, and good faith) are aroused by, and react to, the external world and engage in activity; good and evil are distinguished and human affairs take place.

The sage orders these affairs by the principles of the Mean, correctness, humanity, and righteousness, considering tranquillity to be the ruling factor. Thus he establishes himself as the ultimate standard for man. Hence the character of the sages is "identical with that of Heaven and earth; his brilliance is identical with that of the sun and moon; his order is identical with that of the four seasons; and his good and evil fortunes are identical with those of heavenly and earthly spirits." The gentleman cultivates these moral qualities and enjoys good fortune, whereas the inferior man violates them and suffers evil fortune.

Therefore it is said: "The yin and the yang are established as the way of heaven; the elements of strength and weakness as the way of earth; and humanity and righteousness as the way of man." It is also said there: "If we investigate into the cycle of things, we shall understand the concepts of life and death." Great is the *Book of Changes!* Herein lies its excellence!

[From *Sources of Chinese Tradition,* vol. 1, pp. 458–459.]

The Classics

THE BOOK OF CHANGES

People were expected to harmonize with this cosmic order, especially with regard to gender roles. One of the earliest sources for these notions of yin/yang is the *Book of Changes,* an ancient book of divination which, because of its continuous use as a source of prophecy, has had, and continues to have, a profound influence on Chinese thought and religious life. Tradition tells us that the core of the *Book of Changes* existed as early as the second millennium B.C.E. In the twelfth century B.C.E. King Wen and his son the Duke of Chou added to it and later Confucius is said to have edited it and to have added a commentary. It is based on sixty-four figures of six horizontal lines, called hexagrams, each of which is composed of two trigrams of various names and meanings. Therefore, each hexagram is first understood and named as a whole, then divided into its two trigrams, and lastly a meaning is attributed to each line. The following selections are taken from the first two readings, "The Creative," which is yang (male) and represents heaven, and "The Receptive," which is yin (female) and represents earth. Together, through their complementary opposition, they represent creation. Some of the additional commentary on each one is attributed to Confucius. These selections encapsulate notions about yin/yang, female/male, that have influenced Chinese thought for centuries, both Confucian and Taoist. Given its traditional connection to Confucius, it is included here among the works he influenced.

Ch'ien—The Creative

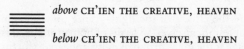

above CH'IEN THE CREATIVE, HEAVEN

below CH'IEN THE CREATIVE, HEAVEN

The first hexagram is made up of six unbroken lines. These unbroken lines stand for the primal power, which is light-giving, active, strong, and of the spirit. The hexagram is consistently strong in character, and since it is without weakness, its essence is power or energy. Its image is heaven. Its energy is represented as unrestricted by any fixed conditions in space and is therefore conceived of as motion. Time is regarded as the basis of this motion. Thus the hexagram includes also the power of time and the power of persisting in time, that is, duration.

The power represented by the hexagram is to be interpreted in a dual sense—in terms of its action on the universe and of its action on the world of men. In relation to the universe, the hexagram expresses the strong, creative action of the Deity. In relation to the human world, it denotes the creative action of the holy man or sage, of the ruler or leader of men, who through his power awakens and develops their higher nature.

THE JUDGMENT

The Creative works sublime success,
Furthering through perseverance.

According to the original meaning, the attributes [sublimity, potentiality of success, power to further, perseverance] are paired. When an individual draws this oracle, it means that success will come to him from the primal depths of the universe and that everything depends upon his seeking his happiness and that of others in one way only, that is, by perseverance in what is right.

★ ★ ★

Applied to the human world, these attributes show the great man the way to notable success: "Because he sees with great clarity causes and effects, he completes the six steps at the right time and mounts toward heaven on them at the right time, as though on six dragons." The six steps are the six different positions given in the hexagram, which are represented later by the dragon symbol. Here it is shown that the way to success lies in apprehending and giving actuality to the way of the universe [*tao*], which, as a law running through end and beginning, brings about all phenomena in time. Thus each step attained forthwith becomes a preparation for the next. Time is no longer a hindrance but the means of making actual what is potential.

The act of creation having found expression in the two attributes sublimity and success, the work of conservation is shown to be a continuous actualization and differentiation of form. This is expressed in the two terms "furthering" (literally, "creating that which accords with the nature of a given being") and "persevering" (literally, "correct and firm"). "The course of the Creative alters and shapes beings until each attains its true, specific nature, then it keeps them in conformity with the Great Harmony. Thus does it show itself to further through perseverance."

In relation to the human sphere, this shows how the great man brings peace and security to the world through his activity in creating order: "He towers high above the multitude of beings, and all lands are united in peace."

★ ★ ★

THE IMAGE

The movement of heaven is full of power.
Thus the superior man makes himself strong and
    untiring.

Since there is only one heaven, the doubling of the trigram Ch'ien, of which heaven is the image, indicates the movement of heaven. One complete revolution of heaven makes a day, and the repetition of the trigram means that each day is followed by another. This creates the idea of time. Since it is the same heaven moving with untiring power, there is also created the idea of duration both in and beyond time, a movement that never stops nor slackens, just as one day follows another in an unending course. This duration in time is the image of the power inherent in the Creative.

With this image as a model, the sage learns how best to develop himself so that his influence may endure. He must make himself strong in every way, by consciously casting out all that is inferior and degrading. Thus he attains that tirelessness which depends upon consciously limiting the fields of his activity.

THE LINES

Nine at the beginning means:
Hidden dragon. Do not act.

★ ★ ★

Here this creative force is still hidden beneath the earth and therefore has no effect. In terms of human affairs, this symbolizes a great man who is still unrecognized. Nonetheless he remains true to himself. He does not allow himself to be influenced by outward success or failure, but confident in his strength, he bides his time. Hence it is wise for the man who consults the oracle and draws this line to wait in the calm strength of patience. The time will fulfill itself. One need not fear lest strong will should not prevail; the main thing is not to expend one's powers prematurely in an attempt to obtain by force something for which the time is not yet ripe.

Nine in the second place means:
Dragon appearing in the field.
It furthers one to see the great man.

Here the effects of the light-giving power begin to manifest themselves. In terms of human affairs, this means that the great man makes his appearance in his chosen field of activity. As yet he has no commanding position but is still with his peers. However, what distinguishes him from the others is his seriousness of purpose, his unqualified reliability, and the influence he exerts on his environment without conscious effort. Such a man is destined to gain great influence and to set the world in order. Therefore it is favorable to see him.

Nine in the third place means:
All day long the superior man is creatively active.
At nightfall his mind is still beset with cares.
Danger. No blame.

A sphere of influence opens up for the great man. His fame begins to spread. The masses flock to him. His inner power is adequate to the increased outer activity. There are all sorts of things to be done, and when others are at rest in the evening, plans and anxieties press in upon him. But danger lurks here at the place of transition from lowliness to the heights. Many a great man has been ruined because the masses flocked to him and swept him into their course. Ambition has destroyed his integrity. However, true greatness is not impaired by temptations. He who remains in touch with the time that is dawning, and with its demands, is prudent enough to avoid all pitfalls, and remains blameless.

Nine in the fourth place means:
Wavering flight over the depths.
No blame.

A place of transition has been reached, and free choice can enter in. A twofold possibility is presented to the great man: he can soar to the heights and play an important part in the world, or he can withdraw into solitude and develop himself. He can go the way of the hero or that of the holy sage who seeks seclusion. There is no general law to say which of the two is the right way. Each one in this situation must make a free choice according to the inner law of his being. If the individual acts consistently and is true to himself, he will find the way that is appropriate for him. This way is right for him and without blame.

Nine in the fifth place means:
Flying dragon in the heavens.
It furthers one to see the great man.

Here the great man has attained the sphere of the heavenly beings. His influence spreads and becomes visible throughout the whole world. Everyone who sees him may count himself blessed. Confucius says about this line:

Things that accord in tone vibrate together. Things that have affinity in their inmost natures seek one another. Water flows to what is wet, fire turns to what is dry. Clouds (the breath of heaven) follow the dragon, wind (the breath of earth) follows the tiger. Thus the sage arises, and all creatures follow him with their eyes. What is born of heaven feels related to what is above. What is born of earth feels related to what is below. Each follows its kind.

Nine at the top means:
Arrogant dragon will have cause to repent.

When a man seeks to climb so high that he loses touch with the rest of mankind, he becomes isolated, and this necessarily leads to failure. This line warns against titanic aspirations that exceed one's power. A precipitous fall would follow.

When all the lines are nines, it means:
There appears a flight of dragons without heads.
Good fortune.

When all the lines are nines, it means that the whole hexagram is in motion and changes into the hexagram K'un, THE RECEPTIVE, whose character is devotion. The strength of the Creative and the mildness of the Receptive unite. Strength is indicated by the flight of dragons, mildness by the fact that their heads are hidden. This means that mildness in action joined to strength of decision brings good fortune.

K'un—The Receptive

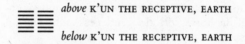
above K'UN THE RECEPTIVE, EARTH

below K'UN THE RECEPTIVE, EARTH

This hexagram is made up of broken lines only. The broken line represents the dark, yielding, receptive primal power of yin. The attribute of the hexagram is devotion; its image is the earth. It is the perfect complement of THE CREATIVE—the complement, not the opposite, for the Receptive does not combat the Creative but completes it. It represents nature in contrast to spirit, earth in contrast to heaven, space as against time, the female-maternal as against the male-paternal. However, as applied to human affairs, the principle of this complementary relationship is found not only in the relation between man and woman, but also in that between prince and minister and between father and son. Indeed, even in the individual this duality appears in the coexistence of the spiritual world and the world of the senses.

But strictly speaking there is no real dualism here, because there is a clearly defined hierarchic relationship between the two principles. In itself of course the Receptive is just as important as the Creative, but the attribute of devotion defines the place occupied by this primal power in relation to the Creative. For the Receptive must be activated and led by the Creative; then it is productive of good. Only when it abandons this position and tries to stand as an equal side by side with the Creative, does it become evil. The result then is opposition to and struggle against the Creative, which is productive of evil to both.

THE JUDGMENT

The Receptive brings about sublime success,
Furthering through the perseverance of a mare.
If the superior man undertakes something and tries
to lead,
He goes astray;
But if he follows, he finds guidance.
It is favorable to find friends in the west and south,
To forego friends in the east and north.
Quiet perseverance brings good fortune.

The four fundamental aspects of the Creative—
"sublime success, furthering through perseverance"—
are also attributed to the Receptive. Here, however,
the perseverance is more closely defined: it is that of
a mare. The Receptive connotes spatial reality in contrast to the spiritual potentiality of the Creative. The
potential becomes real and the spiritual becomes
spatial through a specifically qualifying definition.
Thus the qualification, "of a mare," is here added
to the idea of perseverance. The horse belongs to earth
just as the dragon belongs to heaven. Its tireless roaming over the plains is taken as a symbol of the vast
expanse of the earth. This is the symbol chosen
because the mare combines the strength and swift-
ness of the horse with the gentleness and devotion
of the cow.
Only because nature in its myriad forms corresponds with the myriad impulses of the Creative
can it make these impulses real. Nature's richness lies
in its power to nourish all living things; its greatness
lies in its power to give them beauty and splendor.
Thus it prospers all that lives. It is the Creative that
begets things, but they are brought to birth by the
Receptive. Applied to human affairs, therefore, what
the hexagram indicates is action in conformity with
the situation. The person in question is not in an independent position, but is acting as an assistant. This
means that he must achieve something. It is not his
task to try to lead—that would only make him lose
the way—but to let himself be led. If he knows how
to meet fate with an attitude of acceptance, he is sure
to find the right guidance. The superior man lets
himself be guided; he does not go ahead blindly, but
learns from the situation what is demanded of him
and then follows this intimation from fate.

★ ★ ★

THE IMAGE

The earth's condition is receptive devotion.
Thus the superior man who has breadth of
character
Carries the outer world.

Just as there is only one heaven, so too there is only
one earth. In the hexagram of heaven the doubling
of the trigram implies duration in time, but in the
hexagram of earth the doubling connotes the solid-
ity and extension in space by virtue of which the earth
is able to carry and preserve all things that live and
move upon it. The earth in its devotion carries all
things, good and evil, without exception. In the same
way the superior man gives to his character breadth,
purity, and sustaining power, so that he is able both
to support and to bear with people and things.

THE LINES

Six at the beginning means:
When there is hoarfrost underfoot,
Solid ice is not far off.

Just as the light-giving power represents life, so the
dark power, the shadowy, represents death. When the
first hoarfrost comes in the autumn, the power of
darkness and cold is just at its beginning. After these
first warnings, signs of death will gradually multiply,
until, in obedience to immutable laws, stark winter
with its ice is here.
In life it is the same. After certain scarcely noticeable
signs of decay have appeared, they go on increasing
until final dissolution comes. But in life precautions
can be taken by heeding the first signs of decay and
checking them in time.

Six in the second place means:
Straight, square, great.
Without purpose,
Yet nothing remains unfurthered.

The symbol of heaven is the circle, and that of earth
is the square. Thus squareness is a primary quality of
the earth. On the other hand, movement in a straight
line, as well as magnitude, is a primary quality of the
Creative. But all square things have their origin in a
straight line and in turn form solid bodies. In mathematics, when we discriminate between lines, planes,
and solids, we find that rectangular planes result from
straight lines, and cubic magnitudes from rectangular
planes. The Receptive accommodates itself to the
qualities of the Creative and makes them its own.
Thus a square develops out of a straight line and a
cube out of a square. This is compliance with the laws
of the Creative; nothing is taken away, nothing added.
Therefore the Receptive has no need of a special purpose of its own, nor of any effort; yet everything turns
out as it should.
Nature creates all beings without erring: this is its
straightness. It is calm and still: this is its foursquare-
ness. It tolerates all creatures equally: this is its
greatness. Therefore it attains what is right for all
without artifice or special intentions. Man achieves
the height of wisdom when all that he does is as self-
evident as what nature does.

Six in the third place means:
Hidden lines.
One is able to remain persevering.
If by chance you are in the service of a king,
Seek not works, but bring to completion.

If a man is free of vanity he is able to conceal his abilities and keep them from attracting attention too soon: thus he can mature undisturbed. If conditions demand it, he can also enter public life, but that too he does with restraint. The wise man gladly leaves fame to others. He does not seek to have credited to himself things that stand accomplished, but hopes to release active forces; that is, he completes his works in such a manner that they may bear fruit for the future.

Six in the fourth place means:
A tied-up sack. No blame, no praise.

The dark element opens when it moves and closes when at rest. The strictest reticence is indicated here. The time is dangerous, because any degree of prominence leads either to the enmity of irresistible antagonists if one challenges them or to misconceived recognition if one is complaisant. Therefore a man ought to maintain reserve, be it in solitude or in the turmoil of the world, for there too he can hide himself so well that no one knows him.

Six in the fifth place means:
A yellow lower garment brings supreme good fortune.

Yellow is the color of the earth and of the middle; it is the symbol of that which is reliable and genuine.

The lower garment is inconspicuously decorated — the symbol of aristocratic reserve. When anyone is called upon to work in a prominent but not independent position, true success depends on the utmost discretion. A man's genuineness and refinement should not reveal themselves directly; they should express themselves only indirectly as an effect from within.

Six at the top means:
Dragons fight in the meadow.
Their blood is black and yellow.

In the top place the dark element should yield to the light. If it attempts to maintain a position to which it is not entitled and to rule instead of serving, it draws down upon itself the anger of the strong. A struggle ensues in which it is overthrown, with injury, however, to both sides. The dragon, symbol of heaven, comes to fight the false dragon that symbolizes the inflation of the earth principle. Midnight blue is the color of heaven; yellow is the color of the earth. Therefore, when black and yellow blood flow, it is a sign that in this unnatural contest both primal powers suffer injury.

When all the lines are sixes, it means:
Lasting perseverance furthers.

When nothing but sixes appears, the hexagram of THE RECEPTIVE changes into the hexagram of THE CREATIVE. By holding fast to what is right, it gains the power of enduring. There is indeed no advance, but neither is there retrogression.
[From *The I Ching,* pp. 1–15.]

The following hexagram, number 37, entitled "The Family," is a model for the ideal Confucian family life. Confucius believed that only out of the harmonious and hierarchical arrangement of the family could an orderly society develop. In order to achieve this, the children and the wife must be firmly under the control of the father because, according to this hexagram, all order and harmony stems from him.

Chia Jên—The Family [The Clan]

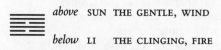

above SUN THE GENTLE, WIND

below LI THE CLINGING, FIRE

This hexagram represents the laws obtaining within the family. The strong line at the top represents the father, the lowest the son. The strong line in the fifth place represents the husband, the yielding second line the wife. On the other hand, the two strong lines in the fifth and the third place represent two brothers, and the two weak lines correlated with them in the fourth and the second place stand for their respective wives. Thus all the connections and relationships within the family find their appropriate expression. Each individual line has the character according with its place. The fact that a strong line occupies the sixth place — where a weak line might be expected indicates very clearly the strong leadership that must come from the head of the family. The line is to be considered here not in its quality as the sixth but in its quality as the top line. THE FAMILY shows the laws operative within the household that, transferred to outside life, keep the state and the world in order. The influence that goes out from within the family is represented by the symbol of the wind created by fire.

THE JUDGMENT

THE FAMILY. The perseverance of the woman furthers.

The foundation of the family is the relationship between husband and wife. The tie that holds the family together lies in the loyalty and perseverance of the wife. Her place is within (second line), while that of the husband is without (fifth line). It is in accord with the great laws of nature that husband and wife take their proper places. Within the family a strong authority is needed; this is represented by the parents. If the father is really a father and the son a son, if the elder brother fulfills his position, and the younger fulfills his, if the husband is really a husband and the wife a wife, then the family is in order. When the family is in order, all the social relationships of mankind will be in order.

Three of the five social relationships are to be found within the family—that between father and son, which is the relation of love, that between husband and wife, which is the relation of chaste conduct, and that between elder and younger brother, which is the relation of correctness. The loving reverence of the son is then carried over to the prince in the form of faithfulness to duty; the affection and correctness of behavior existing between the two brothers are extended to a friend in the form of loyalty, and to a person of superior rank in the form of deference. The family is society in embryo; it is the native soil on which performance of moral duty is made easy through natural affection, so that within a small circle a basis of moral practice is created, and this is later widened to include human relationships in general.

THE IMAGE

Wind comes forth from fire:
The image of THE FAMILY.
Thus the superior man has substance in his words
And duration in his way of life.

Heat creates energy: this is signified by the wind stirred up by the fire and issuing forth from it. This represents influence working from within outward. The same thing is needed in the regulation of the family. Here too the influence on others must proceed from one's own person. In order to be capable of producing such an influence, one's words must have power, and this they can have only if they are based on something real, just as flame depends on its fuel. Words have influence only when they are pertinent and clearly related to definite circumstances. General discourses and admonitions have no effect what-

soever. Furthermore, the words must be supported by one's entire conduct, just as the wind is made effective by its duration. Only firm and consistent conduct will make such an impression on others that they can adapt and conform to it. If words and conduct are not in accord and not consistent, they will have no effect.

THE LINES

Nine at the beginning means:
Firm seclusion within the family.
Remorse disappears.

The family must form a well-defined unit within which each member knows his place. From the beginning each child must be accustomed to firmly established rules of order, before ever its will is directed to other things. If we begin too late to enforce order, when the will of the child has already been over-indulged, the whims and passions, grown stronger with the years, offer resistance and give cause for remorse. If we insist on order from the outset, occasions for remorse may arise—in general social life these are unavoidable—but the remorse always disappears again, and everything rights itself. For there is nothing more easily avoided and more difficult to carry through than "breaking a child's will."

Six in the second place means:
She should not follow her whims.
She must attend within to the food.
Perseverance brings good fortune.

The wife must always be guided by the will of the master of the house, be he father, husband, or grown son. Her place is within the house. There, without having to look for them, she has great and important duties. She must attend to the nourishment of her family and to the food for the sacrifice. In this way she becomes the center of the social and religious life of the family, and her perseverance in this position brings good fortune to the whole house.

In relation to general conditions, the counsel given here is to seek nothing by means of force, but quietly to confine oneself to the duties at hand.

Nine in the third place means:
When tempers flare up in the family,
Too great severity brings remorse.
Good fortune nonetheless.
When woman and child dally and laugh,
It leads in the end to humiliation.

In the family the proper mean between severity and indulgence ought to prevail. Too great severity toward one's own flesh and blood leads to remorse. The wise thing is to build strong dikes within which complete freedom of movement is allowed each individual. But in doubtful instances too great severity, despite occasional mistakes, is preferable, because it preserves discipline in the family, whereas too great weakness leads to disgrace.

> Six in the fourth place means:
> She is the treasure of the house.
> Great good fortune.

It is upon the woman of the house that the well-being of the family depends. Well-being prevails when expenditures and income are soundly balanced. This leads to great good fortune. In the sphere of public life, this line refers to the faithful steward whose measures further the general welfare.

> Nine in the fifth place means:
> As a king he approaches his family.

> Fear not.
> Good fortune.

A king is the symbol of a fatherly man who is richly endowed in mind. He does nothing to make himself feared; on the contrary, the whole family can trust him, because love governs their intercourse. His character of itself exercises the right influence.

> Nine at the top means:
> His work commands respect.
> In the end good fortune comes.

In the last analysis, order within the family depends on the character of the master of the house. If he cultivates his personality so that it works impressively through the force of inner truth, all goes well with the family. In a ruling position one must of his own accord assume responsibility.

[From *The I Ching,* pp. 153–157.]

THE BOOK OF SONGS

The *Book of Songs* is an anthology of poems or songs, some of which may date from the Shang Dynasty (1751–1112 B.C.E.). Some are folk songs, while others were used at the ceremonies and banquets of the aristocracy. The first selection describes a new bride serving her husband's ancestors. The wig in the last stanza is only worn on these occasions.

See, she gathers white aster
By the pools, on the little islands.
See, she uses it
At the rituals of her prince and lord.

See, she gathers white aster
Down in the ravine.

See, she uses it
In the ancestral hall of prince and lord.

Her tall wig nods
At dawn of night, while she plies her task.
With tall wig gently swaying
Here she comes back to her room.

[From *The Book of Songs,* p. 90.]

Though ancestor worship is usually strictly patriarchal, the following legend of a dynasty begins with a woman who gets pregnant through a god. It very quickly, however, becomes her son's story.

She who in the beginning gave birth to the people,
This was Chiang Yüan.
How did she give birth to the people?
Well she sacrificed and prayed
That she might no longer be childless.
She trod on the big toe of God's footprint,
Was accepted and got what she desired.
Then in reverence, then in awe

She gave birth, she nurtured;
And this was Hou Chi.

Indeed, she had fulfilled her months,
And her first-born came like a lamb
With no bursting or rending,
With no hurt or harm.
To make manifest His magic power

God on high gave her ease.
So blessed were her sacrifice and prayer
That easily she bore her child.

Indeed, they put it in a narrow lane;
But oxen and sheep tenderly cherished it.
Indeed, they put it in a far-off wood;
But it chanced that woodcutters came to this wood.
Indeed, they put it on the cold ice;
But the birds covered it with their wings.
The birds at last went away,
And Hou Chi began to wail.

Truly far and wide
His voice was very loud.
Then sure enough he began to crawl;

Well he straddled, well he reared,

To reach food for his mouth.
He planted large beans;
His beans grew fat and tall.
His paddy-lines were close set,
His hemp and wheat grew thick,
His young gourds teemed.

Truly Hou Chi's husbandry
Followed the way that had been shown.
He cleared away the thick grass,
He planted the yellow crop.
It failed nowhere, it grew thick,
It was heavy, it was tall,
It sprouted, it eared,
It was firm and good,
It nodded, it hung—
He made house and home in T'ai.
[From *The Book of Songs,* pp. 241–242.]

A second poem is also about her.

Holy is the Closed Temple,
Vast and mysterious;
Glorious was Chiang Yüan,
Her power was without flaw.
God on high succoured her;
Without hurt, without harm,
Fulfilling her months, but not late,
She bore Hou Chi,
Who brought down many blessings,
Millet for wine, millet for cooking, the early planted
    and the late planted,

The early ripening and the late ripening, beans and
    corn.
He took possesion of all lands below,
Setting the people to husbandry.
They had their millet for wine, their millet for
    cooking,
Their rice, their black millet.
He took possession of all the earth below,
Continuing the work of Yü.
[From *The Book of Songs,* pp. 269–270.]

The next poem celebrates the wedding of Chuang Chiang, which took place in 757 B.C.E.
While much of the poem defines her in terms of her male relations, she stands out as a proud
and independent figure.

A splendid woman and upstanding;
Brocade she wore, over an unlined coat,
Daughter of the Lord of Ch'i,
Wife of the Lord of Wei,
Sister of the Crown Prince of Ch'i,
Called sister-in-law by the Lord of Hsing,
Calling the Lord of T'an her brother-in-law.

Hands white as rush-down,
Skin like lard,
Neck long and white as the tree-grub,
Teeth like melon seeds,
Lovely head, beautiful brows.

Oh, the sweet smile dimpling,
The lovely eyes so black and white.

This splendid lady takes her ease;
She rests where the fields begin.
Her four steeds prance,
The red trappings flutter.
Screened by fans of Pheasant-feather she is led to
    Court.
Oh, you Great Officers, retire early,
Do not fatigue our lord.

Where the water of the river, deep and wide,
Flows northward in strong course,

In the fish-net's swish and swirl
Sturgeon, snout-fish leap and lash.
Reeds and sedges tower high.

All her ladies are tall-coiffed;
All her knights, doughty men.
[From *The Book of Songs*, p. 80.]

What follows is the last part of a poem describing the building of a house. It ends with a prediction of the children to be born in that house and describes how differently the girl will be raised from the boy.

Well levelled is the courtyard,
Firm are the pillars,
Cheerful are the rooms by day,
Softly gloaming by night,
A place where our lord can be at peace.

Below, the rush-mats; over them the bamboo-mats.
Comfortably he sleeps,
He sleeps and wakes
And interprets his dreams.
'Your lucky dreams, what were they?'
'They were of black bears and brown,
Of serpents and snakes.'

The diviner thus interprets it:
'Black bears and brown
Mean men-children.
Snakes and serpents

Mean girl-children.'

So he bears a son,
And puts him to sleep upon a bed,
Clothes him in robes,
Gives him a jade sceptre to play with.
The child's howling very lusty;
In red greaves shall he flare,
Be lord and king of house and home.

Then he bears a daughter,
And puts her upon the ground,
Clothes her in swaddling-clothes,
Gives her a loom-whorl to play with.
For her no decorations, no emblems;
Her only care, the wine and food,
And how to give no trouble to father and mother.
[From *The Book of Songs*, pp. 283–284.]

THE BOOK OF RITES

The *Book of Rites* is the latest of the classical texts of China, and it serves as an instruction on correct and proper behavior in a ritual context. Confucius recommended its study in order to ritualize, or make correct, all human interactions. It is a text that goes a long way toward defining women as subject to men, because it is quite specific about behavior that, in order to be harmonious, must be hierarchical. This means the female always defers to the male: when she is a child it is her father; then her husband; and later her son.

The following excerpts are taken from book ten, "The Pattern of the Family." The first two set out the obligations of both the son and his wife to his parents.

The sovereign and king orders the chief minister to send down his (lessons of) virtue to the millions of the people.

Sons, in serving their parents, on the first crowing of the cock, should all wash their hands and rinse their mouths, comb their hair, draw over it the covering of silk, fix this with the hair-pin, bind the hair at the roots with the fillet, brush the dust from that which is left free, and then put on their caps, leaving the ends of the strings hanging down. They should then put on their squarely made black jackets, knee-covers, and girdles, fixing in the last their tablets. From the left and right of the girdle they should hang their articles for use: — on the left side, the duster and handkerchief, the knife and whetstone, the small spike, and the metal speculum for getting fire from the sun; on the right, the archer's thimble for the thumb and the armlet, the tube for writing instruments, the knife-case, the larger spike, and the borer for getting fire from wood. They should put on their leggings, and adjust their shoe-strings.

(Sons') wives should serve their parents-in-law as they served their own. At the first crowing of the cock, they should wash their hands, and rinse their mouths; comb their hair, draw over it the covering of silk, fix this with the hair-pin, and tie the hair at the roots with the fillet. They should then put on the jacket, and over it the sash. On the left side they should hang the duster and handkerchief, the knife and whetstone, the small spike, and the metal speculum to get fire with; and on the right, the needle-case, thread, and floss, all bestowed in the satchel, the great spike, and the borer to get fire with from wood. They will also fasten on their necklaces, and adjust their shoe-strings.

Thus dressed, they should go to their parents and parents-in-law. On getting to where they are, with bated breath and gentle voice, they should ask if their clothes are (too) warm or (too) cold, whether they are ill or pained, or uncomfortable in any part; and if they be so, they should proceed reverently to stroke and scratch the place. They should in the same way, going before or following after, help and support their parents in quitting or entering (the apartment). In bringing in the basin for them to wash, the younger will carry the stand and the elder the water; they will beg to be allowed to pour out the water, and when the washing is concluded, they will hand the towel. They will ask whether they want anything, and then respectfully bring it. All this they will do with an appearance of pleasure to make their parents feel at ease. (They should bring) gruel, thick or thin, spirits or must, soup with vegetables, beans, wheat, spinach, rice, millet, maize, and glutinous millet,—whatever they wish, in fact; with dates, chestnuts, sugar and honey, to sweeten their dishes; with the ordinary or the large-leaved violets, leaves of elm-trees, fresh or dry, and the most soothing rice-water to lubricate them; and with fat and oil to enrich them. The parents will be sure to taste them, and when they have done so, the young people should withdraw.

[From *The Texts of Confucianism, Sacred Books of the East,* vol. 27, pp. 449–451.]

If a son have two concubines, one of whom is loved by his parents, while he himself loves the other, yet he should not dare to make this one equal to the former whom his parents love, in dress, or food, or the duties which she discharges, nor should he lessen his attentions to her after their death. If he very much approves of his wife, and his parents do not like her, he should divorce her. If he do not approve of his wife, and his parents say, 'she serves us well,' he should behave to her in all respects as his wife,—without fail even to the end of her life.

[From *The Texts of Confucianism, Sacred Books of the East,* vol. 27, p. 457.]

Other sections define how women and men should behave toward each other.

The men should not speak of what belongs to the inside (of the house), nor the women of what belongs to the outside. Except at sacrifices and funeral rites, they should not hand vessels to one another. In all other cases when they have occasion to give and receive anything, the woman should receive it in a basket. If she have no basket, they should both sit down, and the other put the thing on the ground, and she then take it up. Outside or inside, they should not go to the same well, nor to the same bathing-house. They should not share the same mat in lying down; they should not ask or borrow anything from one another; they should not wear similar upper or lower garments. Things spoken inside should not go out, words spoken outside should not come in. When a man goes into the interior of the house, he should not whistle nor point. If he have occasion to move in the night, he should use a light; and if he have no light, he should not stir. When a woman goes out at the door, she must keep her face covered. She should walk at night (only) with a light; and if she have no light, she should not stir. On the road, a man should take the right side, and a woman the left.

[From *The Texts of Confucianism, Sacred Books of the East,* vol. 27, pp. 454–455.]

The observances of propriety commence with a careful attention to the relations between husband and wife. They built the mansion and its apartments, distinguishing between the exterior and interior parts. The men occupied the exterior; the women the interior. The mansion was deep, and the doors were strong, guarded by porter and eunuch. The men did not enter the interior; the women did not come out into the exterior.

Males and females did not use the same stand or rack for their clothes. The wife did not presume to hang up anything on the pegs or stand of her husband; nor to put anything in his boxes or satchels; nor to share his bathing-house. When her husband had gone out (from their apartment), she put his pillow in its case, rolled up his upper and under mats, put them in their covers, and laid them away in their proper receptacles. The young served the old; the low served the noble; — also in this way.

As between husband and wife, it was not until they were seventy, that they deposited these things in the same place without separation. Hence though a concubine were old, until she had completed her fiftieth year, it was the rule that she should be with the husband (once) in five days. When she was to do so, she purified herself, rinsed her mouth and washed, carefully adjusted her dress, combed her hair, drew over it the covering of silk, fixed her hair-pins, tied up the hair in the shape of a horn, brushed the dust from the rest of her hair, put on her necklace, and adjusted her shoe-strings. Even a favourite concubine was required in dress and diet to come after her superior. If the wife were not with the husband, a concubine waiting on him would not venture to remain the whole night.

When a wife was about to have a child, and the month of her confinement had arrived, she occupied one of the side apartments, where her husband sent twice a day to ask for her. If he were moved and came himself to ask about her, she did not presume to see him, but made her governess dress herself and reply to him.

When the child was born, the husband again sent twice a day to inquire for her. He fasted now, and did not enter the door of the side apartment. If the child were a boy, a bow was placed on the left of the door; and if a girl, a handkerchief on the right of it. After three days the child began to be carried, and some archery was practised for a boy, but not for a girl.

[From *The Texts of Confucianism, Sacred Books of the East,* vol. 27, pp. 470–472.]

The text then gives information on the extensive rituals for the birth of a son. This is followed by a guide for the education of children and a brief summary of a boy's life and a girl's life.

When the child was able to take its own food, it was taught to use the right hand. When it was able to speak, a boy (was taught to) respond boldly and clearly; a girl, submissively and low. The former was fitted with a girdle of leather; the latter, with one of silk.

At six years, they were taught the numbers and the names of the cardinal points; at the age of seven, boys and girls did not occupy the same mat nor eat together; at eight, when going out or coming in at a gate or door, and going to their mats to eat and drink, they were required to follow their elders: — the teaching of yielding to others was now begun; at nine, they were taught how to number the days.

At ten, (the boy) went to a master outside, and stayed with him (even) over the night. He learned the (different classes of) characters and calculation; he did not wear his jacket or trousers of silk; in his manners he followed his early lessons; morning and evening he learned the behaviour of a youth; he would ask to be exercised in (reading) the tablets, and in the forms of polite conversation.

At thirteen, he learned music, and to repeat the odes, and to dance the *ko* (of the duke of Kâu). When a full-grown lad, he danced the hsiang (of king Wû). He learned archery and chariot-driving. At twenty, he was capped, and first learned the (different classes of) ceremonies, and might wear furs and silk. He danced the tâ hsiâ (of Yü), and attended sedulously to filial and fraternal duties. He might become very learned, but did not teach others; — (his object being still) to receive and not to give out.

At thirty, he had a wife, and began to attend to the business proper to a man. He extended his learning without confining it to particular subjects. He was deferential to his friends, having regard to the aims (which they displayed). At forty, he was first appointed to office; and according to the business of it brought out his plans and communicated his thoughts. If the ways (which he proposed) were suitable, he followed them out; if they were not, he abandoned them. At fifty, he was appointed a Great officer, and laboured in the administration of his department. At seventy, he retired from his duties. In all salutations of males, the upper place was given to the left hand.

A girl at the age of ten ceased to go out (from the women's apartments). Her governess taught her (the arts of) pleasing speech and manners, to be docile and obedient, to handle the hempen fibres, to deal with the cocoons, to weave silks and form fillets, to learn (all) woman's work, how to furnish garments, to watch the sacrifices, to supply the liquors and sauces, to fill the various stands and dishes with pickles and brine, and to assist in setting forth the appurtenances for the ceremonies.

At fifteen, she assumed the hair-pin; at twenty, she was married, or, if there were occasion (for the delay), at twenty-three. If there were the betrothal rites, she became a wife; and if she went without these, a concubine. In all salutations of females, the upper place was given to the right hand.

[From *The Texts of Confucianism, Sacred Books of the East,* vol. 27, pp. 476–479.]

The last excerpt is from chapter forty-one, entitled "The Meaning of the Marriage Ceremony." It sets forth the purpose of marriage and the obligations upon all parties, especially the wife, and the establishment of these obligations in ancient times by the queen and son of heaven (the emperor). It concludes that harmony between husband and wife leads to harmony in nature.

The ceremony of marriage was intended to be a bond of love between two (families of different) surnames, with a view, in its retrospective character, to secure the services in the ancestral temple, and in its prospective character, to secure the continuance of the family line. Therefore the superior men, (the ancient rulers), set a great value upon it. . . .

The father gave himself the special cup to his son, and ordered him to go and meet the bride; it being proper that the male should take the first step (in all the arrangements). The son, having received the order, proceeded to meet his bride. Her father, who had been resting on his mat and leaning-stool in the temple, met him outside the gate and received him with a bow, and then the son-in-law entered, carrying a wild goose. After the (customary) bows and yieldings of precedence, they went up to the hall, when the bridegroom bowed twice and put down the wild goose. Then and in this way he received the bride from her parents.

After this they went down, and he went out and took the reins of the horses of her carriage, which he drove for three revolutions of the wheels, having handed the strap to assist her in mounting. He then went before, and waited outside his gate. When she arrived, he bowed to her as she entered. They ate together of the same animal, and joined in sipping from the cups made of the same melon; thus showing that they now formed one body, were of equal rank, and pledged to mutual affection.

The respect, the caution, the importance, the attention to secure correctness in all the details, and then (the pledge of) mutual affection,—these were the great points in the ceremony, and served to establish the distinction to be observed between man and woman, and the righteousness to be maintained between husband and wife. From the distinction between man and woman came the righteousness between husband and wife. From that righteousness came the affection between father and son; and from that affection, the rectitude between ruler and minister. Whence it is said, 'The ceremony of marriage is the root of the other ceremonial observances.' . . .

Rising early (the morning after marriage), the young wife washed her head and bathed her person, and waited to be presented (to her husband's parents), which was done by the directrix, as soon as it was bright day. She appeared before them, bearing a basket with dates, chestnuts, and slices of dried spiced meat. The directrix set before her a cup of sweet liquor, and she offered in sacrifice some of the dried meat and also of the liquor, thus performing the ceremony which declared her their son's wife.

The father and mother-in-law then entered their apartment, where she set before them a single dressed pig,—thus showing the obedient duty of (their son's) wife.

Next day, the parents united in entertaining the young wife, and when the ceremonies of their severally pledging her in a single cup, and her pledging them in return, had been performed, they descended by the steps on the west, and she by those on the east,—thus showing that she would take the mother's place in the family.

Thus the ceremony establishing the young wife in her position; (followed by) that showing her obedient service (of her husband's parents); and both succeeded by that showing how she now occupied the position of continuing the family line:—all served to impress her with a sense of the deferential duty proper to her. When she was thus deferential, she was obedient to her parents-in-law, and harmonious with all the occupants of the women's apartments; she was the fitting partner of her husband, and could carry on all the work in silk and linen, making cloth and silken fabrics, and maintaining a watchful care over the various stores and depositories (of the household).

In this way when the deferential obedience of the wife was complete, the internal harmony was secured; and when the internal harmony was secured, the long continuance of the family could be calculated on. Therefore the ancient kings attached such importance (to the marriage ceremonies).

Therefore, anciently, for three months before the marriage of a young lady, if the temple of the high ancestor (of her surname) were still standing (and she had admission to it), she was taught in it, as the public hall (of the members of her surname); if it were no longer standing (for her), she was taught in the public hall of the Head of that branch of the surname to which she belonged;—she was taught there the virtue, the speech, the carriage, and the work of a wife. When the teaching was accomplished, she offered a sacrifice (to the ancestor), using fish for the victim, and soups made of duckweed and pondweed. So was she trained to the obedience of a wife.

Anciently, the queen of the son of Heaven divided the harem into six palace-halls, (occupied) by the 3 ladies called fû-zăn, the 9 pin, the 27 shih-fû, and the

81 yü-khî. These were instructed in the domestic and private rule which should prevail throughout the kingdom, and how the deferential obedience of the wife should be illustrated; and thus internal harmony was everywhere secured, and families were regulated. (In the same way) the son of Heaven established six official departments, in which were distributed the 3 kung, the 9 khing, the 27 tâ fû, and the 81 sze of the highest grade. These were instructed in all that concerned the public and external government of the kingdom, and how the lessons for the man should be illustrated; and thus harmony was secured in all external affairs, and the states were properly governed.

It is therefore said, 'From the son of Heaven there were learned the lessons for men; and from the queen, the obedience proper to women.' The son of Heaven directed the course to be pursued by the masculine energies, and the queen regulated the virtues to be cultivated by the feminine receptivities. The son of Heaven guided in all that affected the external administration (of affairs); and the queen, in all that concerned the internal regulation (of the family). . . .

Therefore when the lessons for men are not cultivated, the masculine phenomena in nature do not proceed regularly; — as seen in the heavens, we have the sun eclipsed. When the obedience proper to women is not cultivated, the feminine phenomena in nature do not proceed regularly; — as seen in the heavens, we have the moon eclipsed. Hence on an eclipse of the sun, the son of Heaven put on plain white robes, and proceeded to repair what was wrong in the duties of the six official departments, purifying everything that belonged to the masculine sphere throughout the kingdom; and on an eclipse of the moon, the queen dressed herself in plain white robes, and proceeded to repair what was wrong in the duties of the six palace-halls, purifying everything that belonged to the feminine sphere throughout the kingdom. The son of Heaven is to the queen what the sun is to the moon, or the masculine energy of nature to the feminine. They are necessary to each other, and by their interdependence they fulfil their functions.

[From *The Texts of Confucianism, Sacred Books of the East,* vol. 27, pp. 429–434.]

Early Confucianism

CONFUCIUS

Confucius taught men to become a *chün tzu,* a gentleman, by having them develop *jen,* virtue. They developed this through *li,* rites and music and by following the *tao,* the way, especially the way of the ancients, and by filial piety.

When it came to women, Confucius and the tradition that developed around his teachings had little to offer them. In its connection to Chinese ancestor worship, Confucianism maintains the patriarchal dominance of the male, leaving women to seek what comfort they can from the ancestral shrines of their family-in-law. Confucianism was the tradition of the literati, the learned administrators and teachers of China, which was closed to women. Confucius's one statement about women in the *Analects* is pretty close to this tradition's attitude toward women:

Women and people of low birth are very hard to deal with. If you are friendly with them, they get out of hand, and if you keep your distance, they resent it. (Arthur Waley, trans., *The Analects of Confucius,* book 17, verse 25, pp. 216–217.)

For Confucius women had a primary role as wife to her husband and daughter-in-law to her husband's parents. Her sphere of activity was the private realm of the home. The gentleman, on the other hand, cultivated his nature in the home but then moved out into the world, preferably into politics. For Confucius, women, like yin, must remain in a subordinate position to the male, be it father, husband, or son.

BIOGRAPHY OF CONFUCIUS

The following excerpt is from the earliest biography of Confucius, which was written by the great Chinese historian Ssu ma Ch'ien (145–90 B.C.E.). While Ssu ma Ch'ien had a great deal of respect for Confucius, he was more concerned with presenting the man than the legend. Consequently there are none of the miraculous incidents usually found in the biographies of religious heroes. Not surprisingly, since Confucianism is very much a religion for men, the biography contains few women: Only Confucius's mother and a brief incident with the Queen of Wei are mentioned. There is no reference to Confucius's wife or when he married her, although the biography concludes with a list of his male descendants.

Ancestry, Childhood, and Youth (551–523 B.C.E.)

Confucius was born in the town of Tsou, in the county of Ch'angping, in the country of Lu. His early ancestor was K'ung Fangshu (who was a ninth-generation descendant of a king of Sung and the fourth-generation ancestor of Confucius). Fangshu was the father of Pohsia, and Pohsia was the father of Shuliang Ho. Ho was the father of Confucius by extra-marital union with a girl of the Yen family [named Yen Chentsai]. She prayed at the hill Nich'iu and begat Confucius in answer to her prayer, in the twenty-second year of Duke Hsiang of Lu (551 B.C.). There was a noticeable convolution on his head at his birth, and that was why he was called "Ch'iu" (meaning a "hill"). His literary name was Chungni, and his surname was K'ung. ("Confucius" means "K'ung the Master").

Soon after Confucius was born, his father died, and was buried at Fangshan, which was in Eastern Lu (in Shantung). Therefore Confucius was in doubt as to the place of his father's tomb, because his mother had concealed the truth from him. When he was a child, he used to play at making sacrificial offerings and performing the ceremonies. When Confucius' mother died, he buried her temporarily, for caution's sake, in the Street of the Five Fathers, and it was not until an old woman, the mother of Wanfu of Tsou, informed him of the whereabouts of his father's grave, that he buried his parents together at Fangshan. . . .

[From *The Wisdom of Confucius*, pp. 55–58.]

Confucius then began a life of wandering from kingdom to kingdom in the hope of finding a ruler who would implement his ideas.

[H]e passed through P'u where he stayed for over a month and then returned to Wei. He stopped at the home of Chu Poyu (a cultured old gentleman whom Confucius respected). The Queen Nancia of Wei sent a message to Confucius, saying, "The gentlemen of foreign countries who do us the honor of visiting our country and wish to be friends of our King always see me. May I have the pleasure of your company?" Confucius tried to decline but could not get out of it. The Queen saw Confucius from behind a curtain of linen. Confucius entered and kowtowed facing north, and the Queen made a double curtsy from behind the curtain, and her jade hangings jingled. After the interview, Confucius said, "I did not intend to see her, but during the interview, we saw each other with perfect decorum." Tselu was greatly displeased (for Nancia was notoriously loose in her morals), and Confucius swore an oath, saying, "If I had done anything wrong, may Heaven strike me! May Heaven strike me!"

Confucius stayed for over a month at Wei. One day the Duke was riding in a carriage with the Queen, the eunuch Yung Chu acting as the driver and Confucius following behind in a second carriage (or occupying the second driver's seat). Thus they paraded through the streets, attracting the people's attention, and Confucius remarked, "I have never yet seen people attracted by virtuous scholars as they are by beautiful women." Confucius regarded this as a disgrace and left Wei for Ts'ao. That year (495 B.C.) Duke Ting of Lu died.

[From *The Wisdom of Confucius*, pp. 69–70.]

THE GREAT LEARNING

The brief essay entitled *The Great Learning* has had a tremendous and enduring influence on Confucianism. Its authorship and date of composition remain uncertain though it is generally attributed to Confucius's pupil Tseng-tzu. However, the basic ideas appear to go back go Confucius. Its main theme is that of self-cultivation, even though it is addressed to the ruler and his officials. The point of the text is that the problems rulers face in governing are the same as those individuals face in trying to live a moral life.

In the following excerpt we see Confucius's ideas about the interconnectedness of all things at work: correct relationships between individuals will lead to a peaceful and harmonious country. This system requires women to remain in the private sphere of the family while men cultivate themselves within the family and then move out into the public sphere.

What is meant by "The regulation of one's family depends on the cultivation of his person," is this: — Men are partial where they feel affection and love; partial where they despise and dislike; partial where they stand in awe and reverence; partial where they feel sorrow and compassion; partial where they are arrogant and rude. Thus it is that there are few men in the world who love, and at the same time know the bad qualities of *the object of their love,* or who hate, and yet know the excellences of *the object of their hatred.*

Hence it is said, in the common adage, "A man does not know the wickedness of his son; he does not know the richness of his growing corn."

This is what is meant by saying that if the person be not cultivated, a man cannot regulate his family.

The above eighth chapter of commentary explains cultivating the person and regulating the family.

What is meant by "In order rightly to govern his State, it is necessary first to regulate his family," is this: — It is not possible for one to teach others, while he cannot teach his own family. Therefore, the ruler, without going beyond his family, completes the lessons for the State. There is filial piety: — therewith the sovereign should be served. There is fraternal submission: — therewith elders and superiors should be served. There is kindness: — therewith the multitude should be treated.

In the Announcement to K'ang, it is said, "Act as if you were watching over an infant." If a mother is really anxious about it, though she may not hit *exactly the wants of her infant,* she will not be far from doing so. There never has been *a girl* who learned to bring up a child, that she might afterwards marry.

From the loving *example* of one family, a whole State becomes loving, and from its courtesies, the whole State becomes courteous, while, from the ambition and perverseness of the one man, the whole State may be led to rebellious disorder; — such is the nature of the influence. This verifies the saying, "Affairs may be ruined by a single sentence; a kingdom may be settled by its one man."

Yaou and Shun led on the empire with benevolence, and the people followed them. Këë and Chow led on the empire with violence, and the people followed them. The orders which these issued were contrary to the practices which they loved, and so the people did not follow them. On this account, the ruler must himself be possessed of the *good* qualities, and then he may require them in the people. He must not have *the bad qualities* in himself, and then he may require that they shall not be in the people. Never has there been a man, who, not having reference to his own character and wishes in dealing with others, was able effectually to instruct them.

Thus we see how the government of the State depends on the regulation of the family.

[From *The Life and Teachings of Confucius,* pp. 273–275.]

THE DOCTRINE OF THE MEAN

An equally brief and equally significant text of early Confucianism as well as neo-Confucianism is *The Doctrine of the Mean.* Like *The Great Learning,* it is also of uncertain date and authorship, though it is traditionally said to be the work of Confucius's grandson, Tzu Ssu. It advocates achieving the moral life through practicing moderation and sincerity. Indeed, these reflect the cosmic order so that in perfecting oneself, one achieves a profound sense of participation in the cosmic order.

The following excerpt lists the five primary relationships of Confucianism and their attendant obligations. Essentially, women only participate as wives.

"The duties of universal obligation are five, and the virtues wherewith they are practised are three. The duties are those between sovereign and minister, between father and son, between husband and wife, between elder brother and younger, and those belonging to the intercourse of friends. Those five are the duties of universal obligation. Knowledge, magnanimity, and energy, these three, are the virtues universally binding. And the means by which they carry *the duties* into practice is singleness.

"Some are born with the knowledge *of those duties;* some know them by study; and some acquire the knowledge after a painful feeling of their ignorance. But the knowledge being possessed, it comes to the same thing. Some practise them with a natural ease; some from a desire for their advantages; and some by strenuous effort. But the achievement being made, it comes to the same thing."

The Master said, "To be fond of learning is to be near to knowledge. To practise with vigour is to be near to magnanimity. To possess the feeling of shame is to be near to energy.

"He who knows these three things knows how to cultivate his own character. Knowing how to cultivate his own character, he knows how to govern other men. Knowing how to govern other men, he knows how to govern the empire with all its States and families.

"All who have the government of the empire with its States and families have nine standard rules to follow; — viz. the cultivation of their own characters; the honouring of men of virtue and talents; affection towards their relatives; respect towards the great ministers; kind and considerate treatment of the whole body of officers; dealing with the mass of the people as children; encouraging the resort of all classes of artisans; indulgent treatment of men from a distance; and the kindly cherishing of the princes of the States.

[From *The Life and Teachings of Confucius*, pp. 300–301.]

THE MENCIUS

The *Mencius* is a collection of the teachings of the Confucian philosopher Mencius (371–289 B.C.E.), traditionally referred to as the Second Sage, Confucius being the first. It was compiled by his students and, like the *Analects,* it was written in the form of dialogues.

In the following excerpt Mencius supports the rules of propriety between women and men.

Shun-yu K'wăn said, "Is it the rule that males and females shall not allow their hands to touch in giving or receiving anything?" Mencius replied, "It is the rule." "If a man's sister-in-law be drowning," asked K'wăn, "shall he rescue her by the hand?" [Mencius] said, "He who would not [so] rescue his drowning sister-in-law would be a wolf. For males and females not to allow their hands to touch in giving and receiving is the [general] rule; to rescue by the hand a drowning sister-in-law is a peculiar exigency.

[From *Mencius*, 4 B/17 in *The Life and Works of Mencius*, p. 246.]

In another excerpt Mencius denies the greatness of two men mentioned by the king and instead suggests that they were more like women. He does this by talking about the rituals associated with sons and daughters, rituals he supports. (The two men in question tried to please their rulers in order to obtain power. Mencius's point is that they should have helped the ruler to rule correctly rather than seeking their own ends.)

King Ch'un said [to Mencius], "Are not Kung-sun Yen and Chang E really great men? Let them once be angry, and all the princes are afraid; let them live quietly, and the flames of trouble are extinguished throughout the kingdom.

Mencius said, "How can they be regarded as great men? Have you not read the Ritual [usages]; —'At the capping of a young man, his father admonishes him. At the marrying away of a daughter, her mother admonishes her, accompanying her to the door, and cautioning her in these words, "You are going to your home. You must be respectful; you must be cautious.

Do not disobey your husband." [Thus,] to look upon compliance as their correct course is the rule for concubines and wives.

[From *Mencius*, 3 B/2 in *The Life and Works of Mencius*, p. 217.]

In the following excerpt Mencius emphasizes that a man must be correct in his own behaviour before he can influence the behavior of others, especially his wife and children.

Mencius said, "If a man do not himself walk in the right way, it will not be walked in [even] by his wife and children. If he order others but not according to the right way, he will not be able to get the obedience [even] of his wife and children."

[From *Mencius*, 3 B/2 in *The Life and Works of Mencius*, p. 370.]

Pan Chao, A Female Scholar

One woman who rose to prominence on the basis of her scholarship was Pan Chao (first century C.E.), the only woman ever to be appointed to the post of historian to the Imperial Court of China and the most famous woman scholar in Chinese history. Her extant works include two memorials to the throne, four narrative poems, and an essay on the education of women. This last work became a standard textbook for women.

Pan Chao was born into a leading family of Confucian scholars where she received her education. Her marriage was short-lived because of the early death of her husband, after which Pan Chao returned to her father's home where she continued her scholarly activities. Since she probably lived until she was seventy, she is also honored for her long and respectable widowhood. (In later centuries Confucian women were not free to remarry). When the emperor Ho, who had appointed her as court historian, died (105 C.E.) the empress Teng became regent for her infant son and often consulted with Pan Chao on matters of state.

The following excerpts are from her Lesson for Women, which defines the duties and responsibilities of a Confucian woman; primarily, this meant to fulfill her role as wife. Marriage was a sacred duty enjoined on both men and women so that they might have children who would continue the rites for the ancestors. The only advantage Pan Chao seeks for women is that girls receive the same education as boys, an idea that received no support in China until fairly recent times.

Lessons for Women

INSTRUCTIONS IN SEVEN CHAPTERS
FOR A WOMAN'S ORDINARY WAY OF LIFE
IN THE FIRST CENTURY A.D.

Introduction

I, the unworthy writer, am unsophisticated, unenlightened, and by nature unintelligent, but I am fortunate both to have received not a little favor from my scholarly father, and to have had a (cultured) mother and instructresses upon whom to rely for a literary education as well as for training in good manners. More than forty years have passed since at the age of fourteen I took up the dustpan and the broom in the Ts'ao family. During this time with trembling heart I feared constantly that I might disgrace my parents, and that I might multiply difficulties for both the women and the men (of my husband's family). Day and night I was distressed in heart, (but) I labored without confessing weariness. Now and hereafter, however, I know how to escape (from such fears).

Being careless, and by nature stupid, I taught and

trained (my children) without system. Consequently I fear that my son Ku may bring disgrace upon the Imperial Dynasty by whose Holy Grace he has unprecedentedly received the extraordinary privilege of wearing the Gold and the Purple, a privilege for the attainment of which (by my son, I) a humble subject never even hoped. Nevertheless, now that he is a man and able to plan his own life, I need not again have concern for him. But I do grieve that you, my daughters, just now at the age for marriage, have not at this time had gradual training and advice; that you still have not learned the proper customs for married women. I fear that by failure in good manners in other families you will humiliate both your ancestors and your clan. I am now seriously ill, life is uncertain. As I have thought of you all in so untrained a state, I have been uneasy many a time for you. At hours of leisure I have composed in seven chapters these instructions under the title, "Lessons for Women." In order that you may have something wherewith to benefit your persons, I wish every one of you, my daughters, each to write out a copy for yourself.

From this time on everyone of you strive to practise these (lessons).

Chapter I
Humility

On the third day after the birth of a girl the ancients observed three customs: (first) to place the baby below the bed; (second) to give her a potsherd with which to play; and (third) to announce her birth to her ancestors by an offering. Now to lay the baby below the bed plainly indicated that she is lowly and weak, and should regard it as her primary duty to humble herself before others. To give her potsherds with which to play indubitably signified that she should practise labor and consider it her primary duty to be industrious. To announce her birth before her ancestors clearly meant that she ought to esteem as her primary duty the continuation of the observance of worship in the home.

These three ancient customs epitomize a woman's ordinary way of life and the teachings of the traditional ceremonial rites and regulations. Let a woman modestly yield to others; let her respect others; let her put others first, herself last. Should she do something good, let her not mention it; should she do something bad, let her not deny it. Let her bear disgrace; let her even endure when others speak or do evil to her. Always let her seem to tremble and to fear. (When a woman follows such maxims as these,) then she may be said to humble herself before others.

Let a woman retire late to bed, but rise early to duties; let her not dread tasks by day or by night. Let her not refuse to perform domestic duties whether easy or difficult. That which must be done, let her finish completely, tidily, and systematically. (When a woman follows such rules as these,) then she may be said to be industrious.

Let a woman be correct in manner and upright in character in order to serve her husband. Let her live in purity and quietness (of spirit), and attend to her own affairs. Let her love not gossip and silly laughter. Let her cleanse and purify and arrange in order the wine and the food for the offerings to the ancestors. (When a woman observes such principles as these,) then she may be said to continue ancestral worship.

No woman who observes these three (fundamentals of life) has ever had a bad reputation or has fallen into disgrace. If a woman fail to observe them, how can her name be honored; how can she but bring disgrace upon herself?

Chapter II
Husband and Wife

The Way of husband and wife is intimately connected with *Yin* and *Yang*, and relates the individual to gods and ancestors. Truly it is the great principle of Heaven and Earth, and the great basis of human relationships. Therefore the "Rites" honor union of man and woman; and in the "Book of Poetry" the "First Ode" manifests the principle of marriage. For these reasons the relationship cannot but be an important one.

If a husband be unworthy then he possesses nothing by which to control his wife. If a wife be unworthy, then she possesses nothing with which to serve her husband. If a husband does not control his wife, then the rules of conduct manifesting his authority are abandoned and broken. If a wife does not serve her husband, then the proper relationship (between men and women) and the natural order of things are neglected and destroyed. As a matter of fact the purpose of these two (the controlling of women by men, and the serving of men by women) is the same.

Now examine the gentlemen of the present age. They only know that wives must be controlled, and that the husband's rules of conduct manifesting his authority must be established. They therefore teach their boys to read books and (study) histories. But they do not in the least understand that husbands and masters must (also) be served, and that the proper relationship and the rites should be maintained.

Yet only to teach men and not to teach women, is that not ignoring the essential relation between them? According to the "Rites," it is the rule to begin to teach children to read at the age of eight years, and by the age of fifteen years they ought then to be ready for cultural training. Only why should it not be (that girls' education as well as boys' be) according to this principle?

Chapter III
Respect and Caution

As *Yin* and *Yang* are not of the same nature, so man and woman have different characteristics. The distinctive quality of the *Yang* is rigidity; the function of the *Yin* is yielding. Man is honored for strength; a woman is beautiful on account of her gentleness. Hence there arose the common saying: "A man though born like a wolf may, it is feared, become a weak monstrosity; a woman though born like a mouse may, it is feared, become a tiger."

Now for self-culture nothing equals respect for others. To counteract firmness nothing equals compliance. Consequently it can be said that the Way of respect and acquiescence is woman's most important principle of conduct. So respect may be defined as nothing other than holding on to that which is permanent; and acquiescence nothing other than being liberal and generous. Those who are steadfast in devotion know that they should stay in their proper places; those who are liberal and generous esteem others, and honor and serve (them).

If husband and wife have the habit of staying together, never leaving one another, and following each other around within the limited space of their own rooms, then they will lust after and take liberties with one another. From such action improper language will arise between the two. This kind of discussion may lead to licentiousness. Out of licentiousness will be born a heart of disrespect to the husband. Such a result comes from not knowing that one should stay in one's proper place.

Furthermore, affairs may be either crooked or straight; words may be either right or wrong. Straightforwardness cannot but lead to quarreling; crookedness cannot but lead to accusation. If there are really accusations and quarrels, then undoubtedly there will be angry affairs. Such a result comes from not esteeming others, and not honoring and serving (them).

(If wives) suppress not contempt for husbands, then it follows (that such wives) rebuke and scold (their husbands). (If husbands) stop not short of anger, then they are certain to beat (their wives). The correct relationship between husband and wife is based upon harmony and intimacy, and (conjugal) love is grounded in proper union. Should actual blows be dealt, how could matrimonial relationship be preserved? Should sharp words be spoken, how could (conjugal) love exist? If love and proper relationship both be destroyed, then husband and wife are divided.

Chapter IV
Womanly Qualifications

A woman (ought to) have four qualifications: (1) womanly virtue; (2) womanly words; (3) womanly bearing; and (4) womanly work. Now what is called womanly virtue need not be brilliant ability, exceptionally different from others. Womanly words need be neither clever in debate nor keen in conversation. Womanly appearance requires neither a pretty nor a perfect face and form. Womanly work need not be work done more skillfully than that of others.

To guard carefully her chastity; to control circumspectly her behavior; in every motion to exhibit modesty; and to model each act on the best usage, this is womanly virtue.

To choose her words with care; to avoid vulgar language; to speak at appropriate times; and not to weary others (with much conversation), may be called the characteristics of womanly words.

To wash and scrub filth away; to keep clothes and ornaments fresh and clean; to wash the head and bathe the body regularly, and to keep the person free from disgraceful filth, may be called the characteristics of womanly bearing.

With whole-hearted devotion to sew and to weave; to love not gossip and silly laughter; in cleanliness and order (to prepare) the wine and food for serving guests, may be called the characteristics of womanly work.

These four qualifications characterize the greatest virtue of a woman. No woman can afford to be without them. In fact they are very easy to possess if a woman only treasure them in her heart. The ancients had a saying: "Is Love afar off? If I desire love, then love is at hand!" So can it be said of these qualifications.

Chapter V
Whole-hearted Devotion

Now in the "Rites" is written the principle that a husband may marry again, but there is no Canon that authorizes a woman to be married the second time. Therefore it is said of husbands as of Heaven, that as certainly as people cannot run away from Heaven, so surely a wife cannot leave (a husband's home).

If people in action or character disobey the spirits of Heaven and of Earth, then Heaven punishes them. Likewise if a woman errs in the rites and in the proper mode of conduct, then her husband esteems her lightly. The ancient book, "A Pattern for Women," (*Nü Hsien*) says: "To obtain the love of one man is the crown of a woman's life; to lose the love of one man is to miss the aim in woman's life." For these reasons a woman cannot but seek to win her husband's heart. Nevertheless, the beseeching wife need not use flattery, coaxing words, and cheap methods to gain intimacy.

Decidedly nothing is better (to gain the heart of a husband) than whole-hearted devotion and correct manners. In accordance with the rites and the proper mode of conduct, (let a woman) live a pure life. Let her have ears that hear not licentiousness; and eyes that see not depravity. When she goes outside her own home, let her not be conspicuous in dress and manners. When at home let her not neglect her dress. Women should not assemble in groups, nor gather together, (for gossip and silly laughter). They should not stand watching in the gateways. (If a woman follows) these rules, she may be said to have whole-hearted devotion and correct manners.

If, in all her actions, she is frivolous, she sees and hears (only) that which pleases herself. At home her hair is dishevelled, and her dress is slovenly. Outside the home she emphasizes her femininity to attract attention; she says what ought not to be said; and she looks at what ought not to be seen. (If a woman does such as) these, (she may be) said to be without whole-hearted devotion and correct manners.

Chapter VI
Implicit Obedience

Now "to win the love of one man is the crown of a woman's life; to lose the love of one man is her eternal disgrace." This saying advises a fixed will and a whole-hearted devotion for a woman. Ought she then to lose the hearts of her father- and mother-in-law?

There are times when love may lead to differences of opinion (between individuals); there are times when duty may lead to disagreement. Even should the husband say that he loves something, when the parents-in-law say "no," this is called a case of duty leading to disagreement. This being so, then what about the hearts of the parents-in-law? Nothing is better than an obedience which sacrifices personal opinion.

Whenever the mother-in-law says, "Do not do that," and if what she says is right, unquestionably the daughter-in-law obeys. Whenever the mother-in-law says, "Do that," even if what she says is wrong, still the daughter-in-law submits unfailingly to the command.

Let a woman not act contrary to the wishes and the opinions of parents-in-law about right and wrong; let her not dispute with them what is straight and what is crooked. Such (docility) may be called obedience which sacrifices personal opinion. Therefore the ancient book, "A Pattern for Women," says: "If a daughter-in-law (who follows the wishes of her parents-in-law) is like an echo and a shadow, how could she not be praised?"

Chapter VII
Harmony with Younger Brothers- and Sisters-in-law

In order for a wife to gain the love of her husband, she must win for herself the love of her parents-in-law. To win for herself the love of her parents-in-law, she must secure for herself the good will of younger brothers- and sisters-in-law. For these reasons the right and the wrong, the praise and the blame of a woman alike depend upon younger brothers- and sisters-in-law. Consequently it will not do for a woman to lose their affection.

They are stupid both who know not that they must not lose (the hearts of) younger brothers- and sisters-in-law, and who cannot be in harmony with them in order to be intimate with them. Excepting only the Holy Men, few are able to be faultless. Now Yen Tzu's greatest virtue was that he was able to reform. Confucius praised him (for not committing a misdeed) the second time. (In comparison with him) a woman is the more likely (to make mistakes).

Although a woman possesses a worthy woman's qualifications, and is wise and discerning by nature, is she able to be perfect? Yet if a woman live in harmony with her immediate family, unfavorable criticism will be silenced (within the home. But) if a man and woman disagree, then this evil will be noised abroad. Such consequences are inevitable.

[From *Pan Chao*, pp. 82–89.]

Biographies of Chinese Women

The *Lieh Nü* (*Biographies of Women*) was composed by the first-century B.C.E. Confucian scholar Liu Hsiang. The virtues attributed to women in this text later became actual social and legal restrictions on women. In other words, the ideal behavior represented in this text became required behavior for women.

The following excerpt is taken from the chapter entitled "Biographies Illustrating the Correct Deportment of Mothers." The most famous of these is the biography of Mencius's mother (he is called Meng-tzu in this text), who is considered the ideal model for motherhood. Since Mencius's father died while Mencius was still quite young, his mother raised him by herself with full devotion to him. Her first concern was his education; later she advised him about his wife; and, finally, she enumerated the duties of a woman.

She was the mother of Meng K'o of Tsou; her honorary title was "Meng Mu." She was living near a graveyard when Meng-tzu was small and he enjoyed going out to play as if he were working among the graves. He enthusiastically built up the graves and performed burials. His mother said "This is not the place for me to keep my son." Then she departed and dwelt beside a market place. Since he enjoyed playing as if his business were that of the merchant and bargainer, his mother again said, "This is not the place for me to live with my son." She once more moved her abode and dwelt beside a schoolhouse. He [Meng-tzu] amused himself by setting up the instruments of worship and by bowing politely to those coming and going. Meng Mu said, "Truly my son can dwell here." Thereafter they dwelt there and as Meng-tzu grew up he learned the six liberal arts. In the end he attained fame as a great scholar. . . .

While Meng-tzu was young yet, he was studying at school. When he returned home, Meng Mu, who was weaving, asked him, saying, "How much have you learned?" Meng-tzu said, "About as usual." Meng Mu took up a knife and cut the web of her loom. Meng-tzu was frightened and asked the reason for her doing that. Meng Mu said, "Your being remiss in your studies is like my cutting the web of my loom. Now, the Superior Man learns that he may establish a reputation; he investigates that he may broaden his knowledge. Therefore if you remain inactive, you will be peaceful; if you arouse yourself, you will keep harm away. If you now abandon your studies, you will not avoid becoming a privy servant and will be without means of freeing yourself from your misfortune. What difference is there [in your studying] and my weaving? I spin thread that we may have food. If the woman abandons her weaving when she is half way through, how shall she clothe her husband and how shall he grow without grain to eat? Just as the woman who abandons what she has to eat, so the man who fails in his cultivation of virtue, if he does not become a thief or robber, will become a captive or slave." Meng-tzu, having become frightened, studied diligently morning and evening without respite. He served his teacher, Tzu Ssu, and consequently became the most famous scholar of the whole nation. . . .

After Meng-tzu had married, he was about to enter [his wife's] private room and saw her disrobed within. As Meng-tzu was displeased, he immediately departed without entering. His wife apologized to Meng Mu and asked to depart. She said, "I have learned about the state of matrimony and it does not include [the sharing of] one's private room. Today when I secretly yielded to laziness in my own room, my husband saw me. At once he became displeased and treated me as a guest concubine. The rules of conduct of the wife demand that she not stay over night as a guest. I ask to return to my father and mother." For this reason, Meng Mu summoned her son and said to him, "It is proper etiquette when one is about to enter a door to ask who is within and thus one attains to proper respect. When one is about to enter a hall, he should raise his voice so as to warn those within. If one is about to enter the door of a room, the glance should be cast down, lest one see another's fault. Today you did not observe the rules of etiquette and yet you found fault with the etiquette of your wife. Are you not far from right conduct?" Meng-tzu thanked her and retained his wife. . . .

While Meng-tzu was living in Ch'i, he had an air of sadness about him. Meng Mu noticed it and said, "Son, how is it that you have an air of sadness about you?" Meng-tzu replied, "I have not." Another day when at leisure at home, he was leaning against a pillar and sighing. Meng Mu saw him and said, "The other day you seemed to have a sad appearance but you said you were not sad. Today you are leaning against a pillar and sighing. Why are you doing that?" Meng-tzu replied, "I, K'o, have learned that the Superior Man is first qualified and then receives his position. He does not attempt to attain it unfairly and then receive a reward nor does he covet honors and emoluments. If the nobles do not listen, he does not force himself upon his superiors; if they listen to his teachings but do not follow him, then he does not set foot in their court. Today, the Tao is not followed in the state of Ch'i and I desire to depart but my mother is old. That is why I am sad." Meng Mu said, "Now the proper conduct of a woman is found in her skill in preparing the five foods, fermenting wine, caring for her husband's parents, and making clothes and that is all. A woman's duty is to care for the household and she should have no desire to go abroad. The *Book of Changes* says, 'She provides sustenance and avoids going out.' The *Book of Songs* says:

"'For her no decorations, no emblems;
Her only care the wine and food.'

This means that it does not belong to the woman to determine anything herself but she has the three obediences. Therefore, when young, she has to obey her parents; when married, she has obey her husband; when her husband is dead, she obeys her son. This is proper etiquette. Now my son has reached maturity and I am old. Do you act according to righteousness and I shall act according to the rules of propriety."

[From *The Position of Women in Early China*, pp. 39–42.]

The next excerpt is from the chapter entitled "Biographies of the Virtuous and Wise." In it a queen educates her husband on what makes a talented minister by comparing a particular minister's accomplishments to her own accomplishments among the concubines (*mei jen*).

Chi, née Fan was the wife of King Chuang of Ch'u. When King Chuang ascended the throne, he liked to hunt wild animals. Fan Chi admonished him [about this] but he did not stop, [so] then she would not eat the flesh of birds and animals. The King reformed his ways and was diligent in governmental affairs.

The King usually listened at court and left off late. Chi descended to the palace to meet him and said, "How is it that you stopped so late? Have you become tireless?" The King said, "When I converse with talented men, I do not know weariness." Chi said, "The King speaks of talented men. Who, I pray?" [The King] said, "Yü Ch'iu Tzu." Chi covered her mouth and laughed. The King said, "How is it that Chi is laughing?" She said, "Yü Ch'iu Tzu is capable but only capable; he is not yet loyal." The King said, "Why do you say that?" She replied, saying, "I [your wife] have looked after dusting and hairdressing for eleven years and have sent out men to Cheng and Wei to search for Mei Jen to send in before the King. Today, the concubines more capable than I are two; and those of the same class as I seven. And yet, how can I but desire to monopolize the favors of the King? I have learned that in the hall there should be many women and thereby [the King] may tell of their ability. I cannot let my private [desires] obstruct the public [good] and I desire the King to see more and understand men's ability. Now, Yü Ch'iu Tzu has been minister of Ch'u for more than ten years but those whom he has introduced [for office] were either his sons, younger brothers, or men of his tribe. I have not heard that he advanced the capable or retired the unfit. This cuts off the superior man and obstructs the road [of advancement] for the talented ones. To know [a man] of ability, and not to bring that one forward is disloyalty; not to know ability, is ignorance. Was it not all right that I should laugh at this?" The King was pleased [with her answer]. The next day, the King, using Chi's words, made the matter known to Yü Ch'iu Tzu. Ch'iu Tzu, not knowing what to reply, left his seat. On this account when he had gone to his home, he ordered messengers to meet Sun Shu-ao and recommend him. The King used him as Overseer of the Officials and he ruled Ch'u for three years but King Chuang became head of the feudal princes. The Annals of Ch'u say: "The feudal reign of King Chuang was by the strength of Fan Chi." . . .

The Sung says: Fan Chi was humble, yielding, and had no envy. She presented and advanced Mei Jen to dwell with her in the same place. By such means she criticized Ch'iu Tzu's obstructing the road for worthy men. Ch'iang of Ch'u used her words, and by her merit and skill afterwards became the feudal lord.

[From *The Position of Women in Early China*, pp. 56–58.]

The next excerpt is from the chapter entitled "Biographies of the Chaste and Obedient." In it a widow chooses death rather than acting incorrectly.

Po-chi was the daughter of Duke Hsüan of Lu, and the younger sister of Duke Ch'eng. Her mother, who was called Miu Chiang, would give Po-chi in marriage to Duke Kung of Sung. Duke Kung did not come personally to welcome the bride and Po-chi was vexed by the command of her mother and father [to go anyway] but she went on.

★ ★ ★

When Po-chi had been married to Duke Kung for ten years, the Duke died and Po-chi was a widow. Once in the time of Duke Ch'eng, Po-chi found herself at night in a house that had caught fire. Those nearby cried, "Lady, flee the fire!" Po-chi said, "The rule for women is that when the Matron and Governess are not present, they do not leave the house at night. I await the coming of the Matron and Governess." The Matron arrived but the Governess did not come as yet. The bystanders cried, "Lady, flee from the fire!" Po-chi said, "The rule for women is that when the Governess has not come, no one can leave the house at night. To transgress a rule of righteousness in order to save one's life is not so good as to keep the rule of righteousness and to die in doing so." Afterwards she continued to stay there until the fire reached her and she died. The *Ch'un Ch'iu* related in detail her affair as the virtuous Po-chi who caused chastity to be the virtue of women. Thus did Po-chi fulfil to the utmost the duty of wifehood. At that time among the nobles who heard of it, there was no one who did not grieve for her, and they judged that while a dead person could not be made to live again, wealth could be restored. The ministers called a meeting at Shan-yüan and indemnified Sung for its loss. The *Ch'un Ch'iu* praised this action. *The Man of Noble Sentiments* says: This is propriety that if the woman does not find her governess, she does not go out of the house at night. In going out she must carry a light: This was said of Po-chi. *The Book of Songs* says:

"Be very careful in your conduct,

Be correct in your manners."

Po-chi could be said not to have failed in her deportment.

The Sung says: Po-chi was single-hearted and the observance of propriety was her one thought. The palace took fire at night when the matron and the governess were not at hand. She awaited the fire and died but her heart did not repent it. The *Ch'un Ch'iu* praised her and related her story in detail.

[From *The Position of Women in Early China*, pp. 103–106.]

The final excerpt is from the chapter entitled "Biographies of Pernicious and Depraved Women." It is one example among many of a woman who resists the strictures of polygamy, thereby becoming a famous villainess.

Chiang of Hsüan was the daughter of the Marquis of Ch'i and the wife of Duke Hsüan of Wei. In the beginning Duke Hsüan's wife, I-Chiang, gave birth to Chi-tzu who was made crown prince. Duke Hsüan also took a wife from the state of Ch'i and called her Chiang of Hsüan. She gave birth to [two sons], Shou and Shuo, and when I-Chiang died, Chiang of Hsüan wished to establish Shou as crown prince. Then she planned with Shou's younger brother to get rid of Chi-tzu. When the Duke was sending Chi-tzu to Ch'i, Chiang of Hsüan secretly ordered some strong soldiers to wait for him at the border and kill him. She said, "When a man arrives with four horses and a yak's tail standard, then you must kill him." Shou heard of this and told the crown prince, saying, "The crown prince should flee from here." Chi-tzu said, "I cannot do so for if I disobey my father's orders, then of what use am I as a son?" Shou reckoned that the crown prince would certainly go [to Ch'i]. Therefore he drank with the crown prince [until he was drunk] and having stolen his yak's tail standard, departed and the robbers killed him. Chi-tzu sobered up and searched for his yak's tail standard without finding it. He hurriedly went out to pursue Shou but he was

dead already. Chi-tzu sorrowed over Shou who had died for him and spoke to the robbers saying, "I am the one whom you desired to kill. What fault did this man commit? I beg you to kill me." The robbers killed him then and since the two sons were dead, Shuo was made the crown prince. Duke Hsüan died and Shuo was put on the throne as Duke Hui. In the end he had no descendants and there was disorder [in the state] for five generations until the time of Duke Tai and afterwards there was peace. *The Book of Songs* says:

"A man like this,
Of whom no good word is said."

This could be said of her.

The Sung says: Chiang of Duke Hsüan of Wei planned ruin for the crown prince and desired to establish [her own son] Shou in his place. She secretly arranged with strong soldiers [to do this]. Shou then died and together with him the crown prince. Ultimately Wei went to ruin and for five generations there was no peace. This disaster started from Chiang.

[From *The Position of Women in Early China*, pp. 192–193.]

Neo-Confucianism

While Confucius himself tended to downplay the role of the spirits in human life in favor of proper conduct and proper relationship, the Neo-Confucian movement that began in the Sung dynasty (960–1279 C.E.) had definite metaphysical and cosmological interests drawn mainly from the *Book of Changes*. Prior to this revival the new Buddhist religion (which had begun to enter China in the first century) and Taoism occupied the prominent place in Chinese religious life. Consequently, Neo-Confucianism was a successful attempt to regain the earlier prominence of Confucianism as the leading religious and philosophical school of China. Many of its writings are also concerned with self-discipline and the control of desire. This had a direct bearing on the lives of women, since women were seen as the stimulators of male desire. The end result was to place a greater emphasis on women's chastity, especially that of widows, who were pressured into not remarrying.

CHU HSI

More than any other individual, it was Chu Hsi (1130–1200 C.E.) who defined Neo-Confucianism. His lasting influence is measured by his editions of and commentaries on the works of Confucius and Mencius, which were the required texts in public education and for the civil service examinations from 1313–1912 C.E. He taught that the cosmos and humanity were one, that everything and everyone has what he called the Great Ultimate within it. One of his major works is the *Chin-ssu lu* (*Reflections on Things at Hand*). This is an anthology of Neo-Confucian thought which continues to provide enduring guidelines for Confucianists. In it Chu Hsi frequently refers to the hexagrams of the *I Ching*. The following excerpt is taken from chapter 6 of the *Chin-ssu lu,* entitled "The Way to Regulate the Family." As the excerpt demonstrates, the regulation of family life remains at the core of Neo-Confucian thought as it did in earlier Confucianism, and this is where guidelines for women are most frequently found.

"In dealing with the troubles caused by one's mother, one should not be too firm." In dealing with his mother, the son should help her with mildness and gentleness so she will be in accord with righteousness. If he disobeys her and the matter fails, it will be his fault.

Is there not a way to obey with ease? If one goes forward with his strength and abruptly resists or defies her, the kindness and love between mother and son will be hurt. That will be great harm indeed. How can he get into her heart and change her? The way lies in going backward, bending his will to obey, and following his mother so that her personal life will be correct and matters well managed. The way for strong ministers to serve weak rulers is similar to this.

* * *

The text of the second lowest, undivided line of the *kuei-mei* [marriage of a maiden] hexagram says that correctness and tranquillity should be maintained. This principle is not out of accord with the normal and correct relationship between husband and wife. People today consider indecent liberties and improper intimacies as normal and therefore consider correctness and tranquillity as abnormal, without realizing that these are the normal and lasting ways of the relationship between husband and wife.

Tranquillity and correctness are the ways to enable husband and wife to live together for a long time,

whereas indecent liberties and improper intimacies result in disrespect and cause husband and wife to drift apart. (Yeh Ts'ai, *Chin-ssu lu chi-chieh,* 6:3)

Most people today are careful in choosing sons-in-law but careless in selecting daughters-in-law. Actually the character of sons-in-law is easy to see but that of daughters-in-law is difficult to know. The choice of a daughter-in-law is very important. Why should it be neglected.

Male persons are usually outside the home. Their character can easily be seen in their speech and their dealing with others. Female persons confine themselves to their own private quarters. It is difficult to know their character. Furthermore, taking a daughter-in-law in marriage is to continue the family line. Some ancient people predicted whether a family would prosper or decline on the basis of the virtuous or vicious character of the daughter-in-law. The matter is of utmost importance. Should the choice be neglected? (Chand Po-hsing, *Chin-ssu lu chi-chieh,* 6:4a)

* * *

FURTHER QUESTION: Confucius regarded Kung-yeh Ch'ang as inferior to Nan Yung and therefore gave his brother's daughter to Nan Yung in marriage and his own daughter to Kung-yeh Ch'ang. Why?
ANSWER: This is to judge the Sage by one's own

selfish mind. Anyone who avoids suspicion is internally deficient. The Sage was perfectly impartial. Why should he have to avoid suspicion? In giving one's daughter in marriage, one seeks a match according to her qualifications. If, as we may suppose, one's brother's daughter is not very beautiful, one must select a young man of corresponding quality to match her, and if one's own daughter is beautiful, he must select a young man of good talents to match her. Why should one avoid any suspicion? In the case of Confucius, it may have been that the ages of the daughters and the pupils did not match or that the marriages took place at different times. We do not know any of these facts. To think that Confucius did what he did in order to avoid suspicion is greatly mistaken. Even a worthy does not do things in order to avoid suspicion. How much less does a sage!

When Master Ch'eng referred to the difference in age and the difference in dates of marriage, he did so as one way of answering someone's question. It does not mean that these were the actual facts. Probably both pupils were good enough men to be entrusted with the daughters. Perhaps he saw Kung-yeh Ch'ang first and gave his own daughter in marriage, and later saw that Nan Yung was also a good man and gave his brother's daughter in marriage to him. Judging from Master Ch'eng's explanation, perhaps Confucius' daughter, being older, was married first and his brother's daughter later. (Chu Hsi, *Chu Tzu yü-lei*, 28:1b)

QUESTION: According to principle, it seems that one should not marry a widow. What do you think?

ANSWER: Correct. Marriage is a match. If one takes someone who has lost her integrity to be his own match, it means he himself has lost his integrity.

FURTHER QUESTION: In some cases the widows are all alone, poor, and with no one to depend on. May they remarry?

ANSWER: This theory has come about only because people of later generations are afraid of starving to death. But to starve to death is a very small matter. To lose one's integrity, however, is a very serious matter.

A married woman should follow only one husband throughout her life. To marry again is to lose integrity. (Yeh Ts'ai, *Chin-ssu lu chi-chieh*, 6:5–6)

The injunction not to marry a widow is intended for a superior man. How can an inferior man of the street be expected not to do so? Some people think that Master Ch'eng's words are extreme, but they are not. They express only a common principle. If a woman sacrifices her integrity because of fear of hunger, how different is she from the minister who surrenders to the enemy because of fear of battle? When a widow remarries, she is ashamed. If one does a thing knowing it to be shameful, what else will he not do? (Wang Fu, *Tu Chin-ssu lu,* p. 35)

* * *

[Chu Hsi speaks of his own upbringing.]

Father was kindhearted and altruistic but at the same time firm and decisive. In his daily associations with the young and the lowly, he was always careful lest he hurt them. But if they violated any moral principle, he would not give in. Not a day passed when he did not inquire whether those who served him were adequately fed and clothed.

He married Miss Hou. My mother was known for filial piety and respectfulness in serving her parents-in-law. She and father treated each other with full respect as guests are treated. Grateful for her help at home, father treated her with even greater reverence. But mother conducted herself with humility and obedience. Even in small matters, she never made decisions alone but always asked father before she did anything. She was humane, altruistic, liberal, and earnest. She cared for and loved the children of my father's concubines just as she did her own. My father's cousin's son became an orphan when very young, and she regarded him as her own.

She was skillful in ruling the family. She was not stern, but correct. She did not like to beat servants but, instead, looked upon little servants as her own children. If we children should scold them, she would always admonish us, saying, "Although people differ in noble and humble stations, they are people just the same. When you grow up, can you do the same thing?" Whenever father got angry, she always gently explained the matter to him. But if we children were wrong, she would not cover up. She often said, "Children become unworthy because a mother covers up their wrongdoings so the father is unaware of them."

Mother had six sons. Only two are still living. Her love and affection for us were of the highest degree. But in teaching us she would not give in a bit. When we were only several years old, sometimes we stumbled when we walked. People in the family would rush forward to hold us, for fear we might cry. Mother would always scold us with a loud voice and say, "If you had walked gently, would you have stumbled?" Food was always served us by her side. If we swallowed the sauces, as we often did, she would immediately shout and stop us, saying, "If you seek to satisfy your desires when you are young, what will you do when you grow up?" Even when we gave orders to others, we were not allowed to scold in harsh language. Consequently my brother and I are not particular in our food and clothing, and do not scold people in harsh language. It is not that we are this way by nature but that we were taught to be like this. When we quarreled with others, even though we were right, she would not take sides with us. She said, "The trouble is that one cannot bend and not that one cannot stretch out." When we were somewhat older, we were always told to keep company with good teachers and friends. Although we were poor, whenever someone wanted to invite a guest, she would gladly make preparations for it.

When mother was seven or eight, she read an ancient poem, which says,

Women do not go out of doors at night.
If they do, they carry a lighted candle.

From then on, she never went outside the gate of her living quarters after dark. As she grew up, she loved literature but did not engage in flowery compositions. She considered it vastly wrong for present-day women to pass around literary compositions, notes, and letters (Mao Hsing-lai, *Chin-ssu lu chi-chu*, 6:10a).

[From *Reflections on Things at Hand*, pp. 171–181.]

The next two excerpts are also from the *Chin-ssu lu.*

Between man and woman, there is an order of superiority and inferiority, and between husband and wife, there is the principle of who leads and who follows. This is a constant principle. If people are influenced by feelings, give free rein to desires, and act because of pleasure, a man will be driven by desires and lose his character of strength, and a woman will be accustomed to pleasure and forget her duty of obedience. Consequently, there will be misfortune and neither will be benefited.

[From *Reflections on Things at Hand*, p. 202.]

* * *

MASTER LIEN-HSI [CHOU TUN-I] SAID: There is a foundation for the government of the world. It is the ruler's person. There is a model for the government of the world. It is the family. The foundation must be correct. To make the foundation correct, there is no other way than to make the heart sincere. The model must be good. In order for the model to be good, there is no other way than to maintain harmony among kin. It is difficult to govern a family whereas it is easy to govern the world, for the family is near while the world is distant. If members of the family are separated, the cause surely lies with women. This is why the hexagram *k'uei* [to part] follows the hexagram *chia-jen* [family], for "When two women live together, their wills move in different directions." This was why Yao, having put his empire in order, gave his two daughters in marriage to Shun in order to test him and see whether the throne should be given to him. Thus it is that, in order to see how a ruler governs his empire, we observe the government of his family. In order to see how he governs his family, we observe how he governs himself. To be correct in one's person means to be sincere in one's heart. And to be sincere in one's heart means to turn back from evil activities.

[From *Reflections on Things at Hand*, p. 272.]

Lady Hong's Memoir

Before the common era, Confucianism spread to Korea and Japan and later throughout Southeast Asia. The following excerpt is from the memoirs of an eighteenth-century Korean aristocrat, Lady Hong, who describes the execution of her husband, the Crown Prince, which took place in 1762. According to her description of their life together, the prince had always been an eccentric, who suffered from a bad relationship with his father the King. She documents his descent into madness through displays of erratic behavior and the random slaying of innocent people. While the situation she describes is extreme, especially the conflicts between her duty to her husband, her King, her father, and her son, her attitude throughout the ordeal remains Confucian.

Lady Sonhui [the mother of the prince], who had viewed with despair the prince's growing wild behaviour, now reached the conclusion that she could not help him any more. Moreover, a letter he sent to Princess Hwawan, who was not acceding to his request, was so horrible that no one would have dared to repeat the words in it. He even said that he would get to her at the upper palace by going through a gutter. He was increasingly determined to kill Prince Yongsong. However, no one succeeded in bringing Prince Yongsong to the court, and only his official robe, his ceremonial robes for his audience with the king, his military uniform, his utensils for daily use and the ceremonial strings decorated with jade for his ceremonial robe, together with a gold crown and belt, were brought in. The prince had all these burnt and destroyed. Prince Yongsong's death now seemed imminent. Since Lady Sonhui felt there could be no further doubt that the prince's actions had reached a quite intolerable extreme, and not because she merely wished to save Prince Yongsong's life, she decided to advise the king to put the prince to death.

Between 2 and 3 July 1762, the prince tried in vain to get to the upper palace through a gutter. Frightful rumours abounded, which completely exaggerated the facts. The prince was so disturbed that all his actions were the product of madness. Thus, when he lost his senses and was possessed by anger, he insisted that he had to do it and said, 'I would go and do so with sword in hand.' I do not think he would have behaved like this even for one minute had he been in his right mind. His fate was so strange and cruel, that he had to experience things hitherto unknown, even from ancient times, and was not destined to live out his allotted span. Did heaven create such a disaster in order to make him suffer like that? Oh heaven, how can you inflict such things on the world?

Lady Sonhui felt unable to blame her sick son, but recognized that she could no longer rely on him. Since he was her only son and her only support in the world, she would never have made such a recommendation as this to the king, if the situation had not reached such a critical stage. It was Lady Sonhui's lifelong torment that her son's condition had developed because he was unable to receive the king's favour, and that the king was never able to overcome his prejudice. Even when the prince's affliction became so severe that he could not recognise his parents, she still hesitated to offer any advice to the king because of her own feelings towards the prince. Yet all the time she was alarmed that he might become involved in some unimaginable disaster, being in such a state that he was totally unaware of what he was doing. And what would happen then to the four-hundred-year-old dynasty? She therefore decided that it was right to protect the king, even though this meant that the prince should not continue to live, in view of the fact

that his illness was so critical and that the royal grandson was a blood relative of the three royal ancestors. It was for these reasons that she concluded there was no other way to protect the kingdom, even though her love for the prince knew no bound.

On 4 July 1762 she wrote to me, saying, 'Since the rumours about what happened last night were so much more serious than anything I have heard before, I felt I would rather have been dead than have heard them. If I must live, it is only right for me to protect the kingdom and save the royal grandson, although I do not think I shall be able to face you again for the rest of my life.' This was the full extent of her note, and I wept as I held her letter in my hand, not knowing the great tragedy that would occur that day.

On the morning of that same day, the king was in the Kwan'gwang-ch'ong Hall at Kyonghyon-dang Mansion, and was just about to seat himself on the throne to hold audience. Lady Sonhui approached him and said weeping, 'Since the prince's illness has become quite critical and his case is hopeless, it is only proper that you should protect yourself and the royal grandson, in order to keep the kingdom at peace. I request that you eliminate the prince, even though such a suggestion is outrageous and a sin against humanity.' She added, 'It would be terrible for a father to do this in view of the bond of affection between father and son; but it is his illness which is to be blamed for this disaster, and not the prince himself. Though you eliminate him, please exert your benevolence to save the royal grandson, and allow him and his mother to live in peace.'

It was impossible for me, as the prince's wife, to admit that she was right, but the situation was completely hopeless. It would have been proper for me to have followed the prince in death, but I could not bring myself to do so because of the royal grandson, and I lamented the cruel necessity of continuing to live.

When the king received Lady Sonhui's recommendation, he did not give himself time to think over the decision, but hurriedly ordered a procession to Ch'angdok Palace. Lady Sonhui herself, having made a supreme sacrifice of her love for the benefit of the state, was totally distraught, beating her breast with her hands. She went to Yangdok-dang Hall where she used to live, and lay there without food, presenting an example of suffering rarely seen since ancient times.

[From *Memoirs of a Korean Queen*, pp. 92–94.]

Meanwhile it was getting dark and he [the prince] hurried to the king, who was seated in the Hwin-yong-jon Shrine, grasping a sword in his hand. There the king finally took the decision to kill the prince, striking the floor (in his anger). It is impossible for me to describe the sight. Alas, it was most tragic! As soon as the prince had left me I could hear the angry voice of the king, so I sent someone to keep watch under the wall of the Hwinyong-jon Shrine, which is not far from where I was at the Toksong-hap Pavilion, and this person reported to me that the prince was already prostrating himself, with his royal robe taken off. I realized immediately that it was a situation of the utmost gravity and felt my heart torn asunder. Since it was pointless to stay there, I went to the royal grandson. Neither of us knew what to do, and we remained together, embracing each other. At about four o'clock it was reported that a eunuch had come to ask for the large grain box from the kitchen outside the Taejo-jon Mansion. This request was hard to understand, and put us in such a fluster that we could not readily obey the order. The royal grandson, guessing that matters had reached a climax, went inside the gate to the king and said, 'Please save my father!'

The king very sternly said, 'Go away!' Whereupon the royal grandson came and sat down in the prince's anteroom. I doubt that anyone, from the beginning of the world, has experienced such feelings as I did then. After I had seen the royal grandson out, I felt as if heaven and earth had collided and the sun and the moon had gone into eclipse, and I had no further wish to remain in this world. I tried to kill myself with a sword, but I could not succeed: there were people around me who snatched it away. A second attempt was also fruitless, since I could not find anything sharp enough. I went and stood under the Konbok Gate, which leads to the Hwinyong-jon Shrine through the Sungmun-dang Hall, but could not see anything. I could only hear the king banging his sword against the floor, and the prince saying, 'Father, father, please do not do this! I know I did wrong, but from now on I will do my reading and whatever you wish me to do. I will do just as you wish!' Once again I felt my heart torn apart, and my vision blurred. It was no use struggling, or beating my breast with my hands.

With his physical courage and manly strength, why did the prince not resist going into the grain box, when he was forced to do so? Instead, he simply submitted to be put in. At first he tried to run away, but he could not fight his way out in such circumstances. How could heaven bring him to this? [The grain box was then buried in the earth. This type of execution may have been prompted by the desire not to spill royal blood.]

Though I was wailing under the gate, in the grip of a bitter and unprecedented sorrow, there was no response. Since the crown prince was already dethroned, it would be difficult for his wife and children to stay at court. Also, I was worried about keeping the royal grandson out there, in case something might happen. Therefore, sitting at the gate, I wrote a memorial to the king saying, 'In view of your feelings, it is impossible for us to remain at court, and it would be most inappropriate to keep the royal grandson here, since he shares his father's guilt. Therefore, we beg permission to go to my family's house, and I entreat Your Highness to extend your favour to the royal grandson and to protect him.' I had great trouble finding a eunuch to hand the note to the king.

Before long my brother came and said, 'You are not to stay at the court, since you have been demoted to commoner status, and you have been instructed to return home. We have brought the palanquin for you and another palanquin without a top for the royal grandson.' We wept bitterly and embraced one another. I was assisted through the Ch'onghwi Gate to the Chosung-jon Mansion, where the palanquin was waiting at the guard gate. Governess Yun accompanied me in the palanquin, which was carried by court guards and followed by a crowd of court maids — an unheard of sight. I had fainted when I got into the palanquin, but was revived by Governess Yun massaging me. When I reached home, I was laid down to rest in a room opposite the main room, while the royal grandson was brought in escorted by my uncle and brother, and the royal grandson's wife and Ch'ongyon were brought in a palanquin sent from the home of the former. It was such a distressing sight that I felt I could not go on living! However, on reconsideration, I concluded that I had not been successful in killing myself before and that I could not leave the royal grandson to endure such agony alone, for then there would be no one to help him to fulfil his promise. So I continued to suffer the pain of living out my cruel life, and calling on heaven for help. I do not think that anyone since ancient times can have led such a bitter existence.

When I met the royal grandson at my old home I found him most distressed at undergoing such a dreadful experience while still so young. Since I was very worried that he might fall sick from shock, I tried to hide my own true feelings and said, 'Though what has happened is really terrible, it is the will of heaven. Take great care of yourself and be good, and then the state will be peaceful and you will be able to repay royal favours. I know you must be very upset, but take care of yourself so that you come to no harm.'

Since father could not leave the court, and my brother too held a government post which meant staying at court, there was no one at home but my uncle and two of my mother's brothers to attend the royal grandson. They looked after him, attending him day and night, while my youngest brother, who used to play with the royal grandson whenever he came to court as a child, slept in the male guest room together with him. After about a week the board minister, Kim Si-mok, and his son, Kim Ki-dae, came to visit us at home. Since our house was quite cramped, and all the court maids belonging to the royal grandson and his wife were there, we rented the house of Yi Kyong-ok (an official of the *Hongmun'gwan*) which was situated outside the south wall of our house, and Madame Kim, the wife of the board minister, came there with her daughter-in-law to attend upon the royal grandson's wife. A hole was made in the fence, and they came in and went out through that.

Then father, who had been removed from office and had been staying for some time in the eastern suburbs while the king disposed of the prince's body, was reinstated as senior vice president of the council when the situation was completely hopeless. On hearing the news about the prince, father rushed in a frenzy into the court and fainted on his arrival. The royal grandson, who heard of this while in the prince's attendance room, sent tranquillizing drugs for my father to take. On regaining consciousness, he too had no further desire to live but, like me, he was concerned to look after the royal grandson so that he might not follow in the prince's footsteps. The gods of heaven and earth can bear witness to his utter devotion to the good of the kingdom. Though it was his cruel fate to continue to live, he could hardly do so with equanimity in view of what had happened.

O Yu-son and Pak Song-won came to our gate to request the royal grandson to prostrate himself on a mat and ask for punishment. Of course, it was proper for him to do so, but as he was too young he remained in the small back room. I had been unable to see father since I came home, which made me feel even worse,

but the next day father returned with the royal instructions. My son and I shed bitter tears and embraced father as he delivered the king's instructions that I should protect and look after the royal grandson. Even in my overwrought condition I was much moved at hearing this royal edict. I congratulated the royal grandson on obtaining the king's favour, covering his head and saying, 'As your father's wife and son, both of us have borne up against this disaster. So we should never reproach or blame anyone, but only lament our own misfortunes. It is the royal favour alone that has saved our lives on this occasion, and the king is the only one on whom we can rely in the future. Therefore, I wish you to do your best to obey the king, repay his favour, and fulfil your filial duty to your father, by steadying your mind and, most importantly, by leading a good life.' I expressed my gratitude for the royal favour and told father, 'Please tell the king that I owe the rest of my life to him and that I am at his command.' I did not speak deceitfully, since while it was unfortunate that the prince had ever begun to demonstrate such peculiar behaviour patterns, no one was to blame that they developed to the stage they did. For I had no grudge against the king and never dared to blame him.

When father came home from the court he clasped the royal grandson to him, weeping, and comforted him, saying, 'The king is right—be sage and wise so that you can repay his royal favour, and fulfil your filial duty to your father.' Then he returned to court again.

[From *Memoirs of a Korean Queen*, pp. 96–99.]

Folktales and Stories

"A CURE FOR JEALOUSY"

The following tale offers an example of how a Confucian gentleman handles a difficult wife and in the process humiliates women who do not live up to the Confucian ideal of a wife.

The young scholar Hsien-yüan of Changchou was childless at thirty. His wife, a woman of the Chang clan, was abnormally jealous, and Hsien-yüan was too afraid of her to take a second wife who might bear him the sons he wanted. Chancellor Ma of the Grand Secretariat, the presiding official at Hsien-yüan's degree examination, felt sorry for the young man and presented him with a concubine. First Wife Chang was furious at this intrusion into her family affairs and swore to repay Chancellor Ma in kind.

It happened around then that Chancellor Ma lost his own wife. So Lady Chang found a country

woman widely known for her bad temper and bribed a go-between to persuade Ma to make the shrew his new first wife. The Chancellor saw through Chang's scheme but proceeded with the betrothal. On the wedding day the trousseau included a five-colored club for the purpose of beating husbands. It was an heirloom that had been in the country woman's family for three generations.

When the wedding ceremony ended, Ma's host of concubines offered their respects. The new first wife asked who all these women were, and they told her that they were concubines. The bride lashed out,

"What social law sanctions concubines in the household of a dignified chancellor?" She took the club to attack the women, but Chancellor Ma ordered them to seize it and beat the wife instead. She fled to her room cursing and crying, while the concubines created such a din with gongs and drums that her sobs could not be heard.

The new wife then declared that she would do away with herself. Promptly offering her a knife and a rope, the attendants said, "The master has been expecting you to try something like this. So he has given us these dreadful things to present to you." At that the concubines beat upon wooden drums and chanted the mantra so that her soul would ascend quickly to paradise. They made such a racket that the first wife's ravings about taking her own life were not heard.

Chancellor Ma's new first wife was basically a woman of dignity. Realizing that she had exhausted her bluffs and threats, she conquered her anger and called for the Chancellor. Putting on a proper expression when he entered her room, she said, "My lord, you are truly a man! The tricks I have been using were handed down from my great-grandmother—effective, perhaps, for intimidating the spineless men of this world, but not the way to treat you, my lord. I want to serve you from now on. And I hope that you for your part will treat me according to propriety."

"If it can be so," replied the Chancellor, "so be it." And they saluted one another again as bride and groom. Chancellor Ma ordered the concubines to apologize by knocking their heads to the floor. Then he put his first wife in charge of all money and gems and of the account books for their fields and dwellings. And in a month's time the Ma household was orderly and harmonious. There was no criticism from inside or out.

Now Chang, the first wife of Hsien-yüan, having sent one of her followers to Chancellor Ma's wedding, learned all about the confrontation between the first wife and the concubines. "Why didn't she beat them with her club?" asked Chang.

"She was overpowered."

"Why didn't she curse and cry?"

"The noise of their drums and the clamor of their voices drowned her out."

"Why didn't she threaten suicide?"

"They had knife and rope all ready, and they sang the mantra for rebirth to bid her farewell."

"What did the new first wife do then?"

"She submitted to good form and gave in."

Enraged, Lady Chang exclaimed, "For the world to have such a good for nothing woman! She has spoiled everything."

Now when Chancellor Ma had first presented the concubine to Hsien-yüan, Hsien-yüan's classmates prepared lamb and wines and went to congratulate him. As soon as everyone at the party was feeling mellow, Lady Chang began abusing the guests from behind a screen. Everyone bore her insults impassively, except for one classmate who was a habitual drunkard. He stepped forward, seized Lady Chang by the hair, and slapped her. "If you show respect to my elder brother Hsien-yüan, you are my sister-in-law," he said; "otherwise you are my enemy. Your husband was childless, and that is why his examiner and patron, Chancellor Ma, presented him with a concubine. He was thinking of the future of your ancestral line. One word more, and you die under my fist!" The other guests rushed forward and pulled the man off her so that she could escape. But she was humiliated, for her skirts were torn and some clothing was damaged, nearly exposing parts of her body.

Lady Chang had been nicknamed the Female Demon. With her ferocious pride badly hurt by the turn of events, her hatred of Chancellor Ma increased. She expressed it by doing everything she could to make life miserable for the concubine he had presented. But the concubine, who still received secret instructions from the Chancellor, remained compliant and agreeable. Though she was now a part of the household, she never exchanged a word with Hsien-yüan. For this reason Lady Chang stopped short of having her put to death.

In a short while Chancellor Ma personally presented one hundred pieces of silver to Hsien-yüan. "Next spring," he told his protégé, "there will be a triennial examination for the highest degree. Take this for your expenses and go to the capital now, so that you can spend the next few months in study."

Hsien-yüan accepted the gift and went home to tell Lady Chang that he was leaving. Since she had been worried that he would become intimate with the concubine, the first wife was only too glad to bid him goodbye. As Hsien-yüan was boarding the boat to the capital, however, one of Chancellor Ma's servants intercepted him and took him to Ma's own home. There in the seclusion of the back gardens, the young man pursued his studies in peace.

At the same time, Chancellor Ma sent a go-between to persuade Lady Chang that she should take advantage of Hsien-yüan's absence and sell the concubine. "That's what I'd like to do," said Lady Chang, "but it must be to a buyer in a remote place, so there will be no problems later on." "No problem at all," said the go-between.

Presently a cloth seller from Shensi province came to see Lady Chang. He was ugly and bearded but carried three hundred pieces of silver. Chang summoned the young concubine, who pleased the traveling salesman no end. The bargain was struck, but Lady Chang was not satisfied until she had stripped the gown and shoes from the concubine. Now poorly clothed, without even a hairpin in the way of finery, the concubine was put into a bamboo sedan chair and taken off. As the porters carried her over the north bridge, she cried out, "I won't go so far away," and she jumped into the water. (However, a small boat darted out, picked up the concubine, and ferried her to Ma's rear garden, where she joined Hsien-yüan.)

When Lady Chang heard that the girl had drowned, she fell into a state of fright and confusion. Then the salesman from Shensi burst in on her and raged: "I bought a live woman, not a dead one. You sold her without making the situation clear to her. How dare you force a good woman to do something mean? You have taken advantage of a simple traveler. Give me back my money." Having no defense, Lady Chang returned his three hundred pieces of silver.

The following day a man and a woman, white-headed and tattered, appeared at Lady Chang's house. "Chancellor Ma took our daughter and presented her to your household as a concubine," they wailed. "Where is she now? If she lives, return her. If she is dead, return the body." Lady Chang had no answer. The two old parents knocked their heads against Lady Chang, ready to give up their own lives. They threw plates and smashed bowls until not an article in the household was left unbroken. They would not leave until Chang gave them money and her neighbors interceded and begged them to go.

Another day, four or five fierce constables from the county magistrate came carrying the official crimson arrest warrant. "This is a case involving human life," they said. "We must conduct the culprit Chang to appear before the magistrate." They threw their iron chains on the table with a resounding clang. Lady Chang asked the reason, but they would say nothing. When she offered them money, however, they told her that a certain concubine's parents had reported the suspicious death of their daughter.

Lady Chang was now terrified, and she wished that her husband were at home to deal with these things so that she, a lone woman, would not be shamed and made to stand up in court. She keenly regretted her bad treatment of her husband, her violence toward the concubine, the mistakes she had made, and the helplessness of being a woman. She was torn between resentment and remorse when someone dashed up wearing the white mourning cap. "Master Hsien-yüan has died suddenly at the Lu Kou Bridge," he shouted. "I am the muleteer; I came straightaway to tell you."

Lady Chang was too shaken to speak. "We had better go," said the constables to each other, "since there has been a death in the family." Lady Chang went to prepare her costume for the funeral. A few days later the constables came again, and Chang engaged a lawyer to assist her. She pawned her trousseau and sold the house to bribe the court clerk to delay her case. This gave her a respite, but now she was bankrupt and could not even buy food.

Again the go-between arrived and said, "Madame is in such straits—and without a son to raise in widowhood!"

Lady Chang was so distressed that she went to a blind fortune teller. The woman cast Chang's horoscope and said, "It is your fate to wive two men. Wearing gold and pearl, you will marry again."

After hearing this, Lady Chang summoned the go-between and told her, "I would be willing to remarry; destiny cannot be avoided. But since I am arranging my own marriage, I must see the groom first." The go-between brought a handsome, splendidly dressed young man for her inspection. "That is Master So-and-So," she said.

The delighted Lady Chang put off her widow's weeds and married the youth before the end of the forty-nine-day mourning period. As the couple were performing the wedding ritual of sharing the cup, an ugly woman wielding a large club rushed out of the house. "I am the formal wife and mistress here!" she screeched. "How dare you come into my home as a concubine! I won't allow it!" She beat Lady Chang severely, and Lady Chang regretted having been deceived by the go-between even as she realized that this was exactly how she had treated Hsien-yüan's concubine. "Is that the will of heaven?" she wondered. Her tears fell silently.

Guests and friends finally persuaded the first wife to stop. "Let the young master consummate the wedding," they said, "and save the complaints for tomorrow."

Several youths holding wedding candles escorted Lady Chang to the bedroom. No sooner was the screen raised than lo! Hsien-yüan himself was sitting grandly upon the bed. Certain that he was reappearing as a ghost, Lady Chang fell to the ground in a faint. When she returned to consciousness, she pleaded through her tears, "Do not think I have betrayed you, my lord; truly I had no choice."

With a laugh Hsien-yüan waved his hand. "Have no fear. Have no fear," he said. "Your two marriages are still one marriage." Then he put her on the bed and told her how she had been taken in by Chancellor Ma's scheme. At first she could not believe it, but soon everything became clear to her. She felt remorse and shame, and from then on she reformed her conduct. In fact, both Lady Chang and the country woman whom Chancellor Ma had married turned to the paths of virtue and became worthy wives forever after.

[From the *Chiu Hsiao Shuo* in *Chinese Fairy Tales and Fantasies,* pp. 140–145.]

"THE MASTER AND THE SERVING MAID"

The next tale offers a curious twist on the issue of a woman's chastity.

To decide right and wrong, we have only tradition and law to go by. And yet there are cases where people single-mindedly follow their convictions without the approval of tradition or sanction of law.

In my own clan there was a serving maid named Liu Ch'ing. When she was seven her master ordered that she be given in marriage to a young servant named Yi Shou. When she was sixteen a day was set for the wedding. But suddenly Yi Shou ran away because of some gambling debts, and for a long time there was no news of him. The master was ready to match Liu Ch'ing with another servant, but she swore to die before she would agree.

Liu Ch'ing was rather appealing, and the master himself tried to interest her in becoming his concubine. Again she swore to die before she would agree. The master sent an older woman to talk her into it. The woman told her, "Even if you're not going to give up on Yi Shou, you might as well accept the master for now. Meanwhile we'll do all we can to find Yi Shou and marry you to him. If you refuse, you'll be sold away to some remote area and lose all chance of seeing Yi Shou again."

For a few days Liu Ch'ing cried silently. Then with head bowed low, she offered her pillow to the master. But she kept insisting that the search for Yi Shou go on. Three or four years later, Yi Shou returned to accept his fate and settle his debts. True to his word, the master ordered the nuptials.

After the wedding the serving maid resumed her duties, but she never exchanged another word with the master. She promptly avoided his slightest approach. He had her whipped and gave Yi Shou money to coerce her, but she firmly refused any relations with the master. In the end the master had no choice but to send them away with his blessing.

As Liu Ch'ing was getting ready to leave, she placed a small box before the master's mother. Then she departed, touching her head to the floor in respectful submission. When the box was opened, they found all the personal gifts the master had made her over the years. Not a thing was missing.

Later Yi Shou became a peddler, while Liu Ch'ing took in sewing to survive. But she had no regrets to her dying day.

When I was living at home, Yi Shou was still trading in brass and ceramic utensils. His hair had gone white. I asked him about his wife. "Dead," he replied.

Strange! this serving maid neither chaste nor unchaste, both chaste and unchaste! I see no way to unriddle it, so I made this record for more learned gentlemen to judge.

[From the *Hsiu Ch'i Hsieh* in *Chinese Fairy Tales and Fantasies*, pp. 137–139.]

YINGYING

The following excerpt is taken from a story written by Yüan Zhen (779–831 C.E.) based on the life of a young woman named Cui Yingying, who was born in 784 C.E. This story was, and continues to be, the inspiration for a particular genre of literature, called Yingying or West chamber literature, which reworks the story in a variety of ways that reveal the social mores of their time. Yüan Zhen, however, wrote a didactic story that warns young people about the pitfalls of sexual passion, especially young men attracted to women who seem to possess an immortal beauty. These women, such as Yingying, in this version called Miss Ts'ui, are often referred to as *yao* (witch) or as *huli* (fox). Both these terms suggest willful women who initiate sex, as Miss Ts'ui does after initially rejecting her lover, instead of demurely waiting to fulfill a man's desire—they are the personifications of immoral women. When a friend of Yingying's lover, having read her moving final letter, asked the lover why he had broken with her, the lover replied by accusing her of being such a witch, a *yao* (glossed over in this translation).

The Story of Ying-ying

During the Chen-yüan period (785–804) there lived a young man named Chang. He was agreeable and refined, and good-looking, but firm and self-contained, and capable of no improper act. When his companions included him in one of their parties, the others could all be brawling as though they would never get enough, but Chang would just watch tolerantly without ever taking part. In this way he had got to be twenty-two years old without ever having had relations with a woman. When asked by his friends, he explained, "Teng T'u-tzu was no lover, but a lecher. I am the true lover—I just never happened to meet the right girl. How do I know that? It's because all things of outstanding beauty never fail to make a permanent impression on me. That shows I am not without feelings." His friends took note of what he said.

Not long afterward Chang was traveling in P'u, where he lodged a few miles east of the city in a monastery called the Temple of Universal Salvation. It happened that a widowed Mrs. Ts'ui had also stopped there on her way back to Ch'ang-an. She had been born a Cheng; Chang's mother had been a Cheng, and when they worked out their common ancestry, this Mrs. Ts'ui turned out to be a rather distant aunt on his mother's side.

This year Hun Chen died in P'u, and the eunuch Ting Wen-ya proved unpopular with the troops, who took advantage of the mourning period to mutiny. They plundered the citizens of P'u, and Mrs. Ts'ui, in a strange place with all her slaves and chattels, was terrified, having no one to turn to. Before the mutiny Chang had made friends with some of the officers in P'u, and now he requested a detachment of soldiers to protect the Ts'ui family. As a result all escaped harm. In about ten days the Imperial Commissioner of Enquiry Tu Ch'üeh came with full power from the throne and restored order among the troops.

Out of gratitude to Chang for the favor he had done them, Mrs. Ts'ui invited him to a banquet in the central hall. She addressed him, "Your widowed aunt with her helpless children would never have been able to escape alive from these rioting soldiers. It is no ordinary favor you have done us; it is rather as though you had given my son and daughter their lives, and I want to introduce them to you as their elder brother so that they can express their thanks." She summoned her son Huan-lang, a very attractive child of ten or so. Then she called her daughter, "Come out and pay your respects to your brother, who saved your life." There was a delay; then word was brought that she was indisposed and asked to be excused. Her mother exclaimed in anger, "Your brother Chang saved your life. You would be a slave if it were not for him—how can you give yourself airs?"

After a while she appeared, wearing an everyday dress and no makeup on her smooth face, except for a remaining spot of rouge. Her hair coils straggled down to touch her eyebrows. Her beauty was extraordinary, so radiant it took the breath away. Startled, Chang made her a deep bow as she sat down beside her mother. Because she had been forced to come out against her will, she looked angrily straight ahead, as though unable to endure the company. Chang asked her age. Mrs. Ts'ui said, "From the seventh month of the fifth year of the reigning emperor to the present twenty-first year," it is just sixteen years."

Chang tried to make conversation with her, but she would not respond, and he had to leave after the meal was over. From this time on Chang was infatuated but had no way to make his feeling known to her. She had a maid named Hung-niang with whom Chang had managed to exchange greetings several times, and finally he took the occasion to tell her how he felt. Not surprisingly, the maid was alarmed and fled in confusion. Chang was sorry he had said anything, and when she returned the next day he made shame-faced apologies without repeating his request. The maid said, "Sir, what you said is something I would not dare repeat to my mistress or let anyone else know about it. But you know very well who Miss Ts'ui's relatives are; why don't you ask for her hand in marriage, as you are entitled to do because of the favor you did them?"

Chang said, "From my earliest years I have never been one to make any improper connections. Whenever I have found myself in the company of young women, I would not even look at them, and it never occurred to me that I would be trapped in any such way. But the other day at the dinner I was hardly able to control myself, and in the days since, I walk without knowing where I am going and eat without hunger—I am afraid I cannot last out another day. If I were to go through a regular matchmaker, taking three months and more for the exchange of betrothal presents and names and birthdates—you might just as well look for me among the dried fish in the shop. Can't you tell me what to do?"

The maid replied, "Miss Ts'ui is so very strict that not even her elders could suggest anything improper to her. It would be hard for someone in my position to say such a thing. But I have noticed she writes a lot. She is always reciting poetry to herself and is moved by it for a long time after. You might see if you can seduce her with a love poem. That is the only way I can think of."

Chang was delighted and on the spot composed two stanzas of Spring Verses which he handed over to her. That evening Hung-niang came back with a note on colored paper for him, saying, "By Miss Ts'ui's instructions."

The title of her poem was "Bright Moon on the Night of the Fifteenth":

I await the moon in the western chamber
Where the breeze comes through the half-opened
    door.
Sweeping the wall the flower shadows move:
I imagine it is my lover who comes.

Chang understood the message: that day was the fourteenth of the second month, and an apricot tree was in bloom next to the wall east of the Ts'ui's courtyard. It would be possible to climb it.

On the night of the fifteenth Chang used the tree as a ladder to get over the wall. When he came to the western chamber, the door was ajar. Inside, Hung-niang was asleep on a bed. He awakened her, and she asked, frightened, "How did you get here?"

"Miss Ts'ui's letter told me to come," he said, not quite accurately. "You go tell her I am here."

In a minute Hung-niang was back, "She's coming! She's coming!"

Chang was both happy and nervous, convinced that success was his. Then Miss Ts'ui appeared in formal dress, with a serious face, and began to upbraid him, "You did us a great kindness when you saved our lives, and that is why my mother entrusted my young brother and myself to you. Why then did you get my silly maid to bring me that filthy poem? You began by doing a good deed in preserving me from the hands of ravishers, and you end by seeking to ravish me. You substitute seduction for rape—is there any great difference? My first impulse was to keep quiet about it, but that would have been to condone your wrongdoing, and not right. If I told my mother, it would amount to ingratitude, and the consequences would be unfortunate. I thought of having a servant convey my disapproval, but feared she would not get it right. Then I thought of writing a short message to state my case, but was afraid it would only put you on your guard. So finally I composed those vulgar lines to make sure you would come here. It was an improper thing to do, and of course I feel ashamed. But I hope that you will keep within the bounds of decency and commit no outrage."

As she finished speaking, she turned on her heel and left him. For some time Chang stood, dumbfounded. Then he went back over the wall to his quarters, all hope gone.

A few nights later Chang was sleeping alone by the veranda when someone shook him awake. Startled, he rose up, to see Hung-niang standing there, a coverlet and pillow in her arms. She patted him and said, "She is coming! She is coming! Why are you sleeping?" And she spread the quilt and put the pillow beside his. As she left, Chang sat up straight and rubbed his eyes. For some time it seemed as though he were still dreaming, but nonetheless he waited dutifully. Then there was Hung-niang again, with Miss Ts'ui leaning on her arm. She was shy and yielding, and appeared almost not to have the strength to move her limbs. The contrast with her stiff formality at their last encounter was complete.

This evening was the night of the eighteenth, and the slanting rays of the moon cast a soft light over half the bed. Chang felt a kind of floating lightness and wondered whether this was an immortal who visited him, not someone from the world of men. After a while the temple bell sounded. Daybreak was near. As Hung-niang urged her to leave, she wept softly and clung to him. Hung-niang helped her up, and they left. The whole time she had not spoken a single word. With the first light of dawn Chang got up, wondering was it a dream? But the perfume still lingered, and as it got lighter he could see on his arm traces of her makeup and the teardrops sparkling still on the mat.

For some ten days afterwards there was no word from her. Chang composed a poem of sixty lines on "An Encounter with an Immortal" which he had not yet completed when Hung-niang happened by, and he gave it to her for her mistress. After that she let him see her again, and for nearly a month he would join her in what her poem had called the "western chamber," slipping out at dawn and returning stealthily at night. Chang once asked what her mother thought about the situation. She said, "She knows there is nothing she can do about it, and so she hopes you will regularize things."

Before long Chang was about to go to Ch'ang-an, and he let her know his intentions in a poem. Miss Ts'ui made no objections at all, but the look of pain on her face was very touching. On the eve of his departure he was unable to see her again. Then Chang went off to the west. A few months later he again made a trip to P'u and stayed several months with Miss Ts'ui.

She was a very good calligrapher and wrote poetry, but for all that he kept begging to see her work, she would never show it. Chang wrote poems for her, challenging her to match them, but she paid them little attention. The thing that made her unusual was that, while she excelled in the arts, she always acted as though she were ignorant, and although she was quick and clever in speaking, she would seldom indulge in repartee. She loved Chang very much, but would never say so in words. At the time she was subject to moods of profound melancholy, but she never let on. She seldom showed on her face the emotions she felt. On one occasion she was playing her cither alone at night. She did not know Chang was listening, and the music was full of sadness. As soon as he spoke, she stopped and would play no more. This made him all the more infatuated with her.

Some time later Chang had to go west again for

the scheduled examinations. It was the eve of his departure, and though he had said nothing about what it involved, he sat sighing unhappily at her side. Miss Ts'ui had guessed that he was going to leave for good. Her manner was respectful, but she spoke deliberately and in a low voice, "To seduce someone and then abandon her is perfectly natural, and it would be presumptuous of me to resent it. It would be an act of charity on your part if, having first seduced me, you were to go through with it and fulfill your oath of lifelong devotion. But in either case, what is there to be so upset about in this trip? However, I see you are not happy and I have no way to cheer you up. You have praised my cither playing, and in the past I have been embarrassed to play for you. Now that you are going away, I shall do what you so often requested."

She had them prepare her cither and started to play the prelude to the "Rainbow Robe and Feather Skirt." After a few notes, her playing grew wild with grief until the piece was no longer recognizable. Everyone was reduced to tears, and Miss Ts'ui abruptly stopped playing, put down the cither, and ran back to her mother's room with the tears streaming down her face. She did not come back.

Next morning Chang went away. The following year he stayed on in the capital, having failed the examinations. He wrote a letter to Miss Ts'ui to reassure her, and her reply read roughly as follows:

I have read your letter with its message of consolation, and it filled my childish heart with mingled grief and joy. In addition you sent me a box of ornaments to adorn my hair and a stick of pomade to make my lips smooth. It was most kind of you; but for whom am I to make myself attractive? As I look at these presents my breast is filled with sorrow.

Your letter said that you will stay on in the capital to pursue your studies, and of course you need quiet and the facilities there to make progress. Still it is hard on the person left alone in this far-off place. But such is my fate, and I should not complain. Since last fall I have been listless and without hope. In company I can force myself to talk and smile, but come evening I always shed tears in the solitude of my own room. Even in my sleep I often sob, yearning for the absent one. Or I am in your arms for a moment as it used to be, but before the secret meeting is done I am awake and heartbroken. The bed seems still warm beside me, but the one I love is far away.

Since you said goodbye the new year has come. In the spring Ch'ang-an is a city of pleasure with chances for love everywhere. I am truly fortunate that you have not forgotten me and that your affection is not worn out. Loving you as I do, I have no way of repaying you, except to be true to our vow of lifelong fidelity.

Our first meeting was at the banquet, as cousins.

Then you persuaded my maid to inform me of your love; and I was unable to keep my childish heart firm. You made advances, like that other poet, Ssu-ma Hsiang-ju; I failed to repulse them as the girl did who threw her shuttle. When I offered myself in your bed, you treated me with the greatest kindness, and I supposed, in my innocence, that I could always depend on you. How could I have foreseen that our encounter could not possibly lead to something definite, that having disgraced myself by coming to you, there was no further chance of serving you openly as a wife? To the end of my days this will be a lasting regret—I must hide my sighs and be silent. If you, out of kindness, would condescend to fulfill my selfish wish, though it came on my dying day it would seem a new lease on life. But if, as a man of the world, you curtail your feelings, sacrificing the lesser to the more important, and look on this connection as shameful, so that your solemn vow becomes dispensable, still my true love will not vanish though my bones decay and my frame dissolve: in wind and dew it will seek out the ground you walk on. My love in life and death is told in this. I weep as I write, for feelings I cannot express. Take care of yourself, a thousand times over, take care of your dear self.

This bracelet of jade is something I wore as a child: I send it to serve as a gentleman's belt pendant. Like jade may you be invariably firm and tender; like a bracelet may there be no break between what came before and what is to follow. Here are also a skein of tangled thread and a tea roller of mottled bamboo. These things have no intrinsic value, but they are to signify that I want you to be true as jade, and your love to endure unbroken as a bracelet. The spots on the bamboo are like the marks of my tears, and my unhappy thoughts are as tangled as the thread: these objects are symbols of my feelings and tokens for all time of my love. Our hearts are close, though our bodies are far apart and there is no time I can expect to see you. But where the hidden desires are strong enough, there will be a meeting of spirits. Take care of yourself, a thousand times over. The springtime wind is often chill; eat well for your health's sake. Be circumspect and careful, and do not think too often of my unworthy person.

Chang showed her letter to his friends, and in this way word of the affair got around.

* * *

[Asked for an explanation, Chang] said, "It is a general rule that those women endowed by Heaven with great beauty invariably either destroy themselves or destroy someone else. If this Ts'ui woman were to meet someone with wealth and position, she would use the favor her charms gain her to be cloud and rain or dragon or monster—I can't imagine what she might turn into. Of old, Emperor Hsin of the Shang and King Yu of the Chou were brought low by women, in spite of the size of their kingdoms and the extent of their power; their armies were scattered, their persons butchered, and down to the present day their names are the objects of ridicule. I have no inner strength to withstand this evil influence. That is why I have resolutely suppressed my love."

At this statement everyone present sighed deeply.

Over a year later Ts'ui was married, and Chang for his part had taken a wife. Happening to pass through the town where she was living, he asked permission of her husband to see her, as a cousin. The husband spoke to her, but Ts'ui refused to appear. Chang's feelings of hurt showed on his face, and she was told about it. She secretly sent him a poem:

Emaciated, I have lost my looks,
Tossing and turning, too weary to leave my bed.
It's not because of others I am ashamed to rise,
For you I am haggard and before you ashamed.

She never did appear. Some days later when Chang was about to leave, she sent another poem of farewell:

Cast off and abandoned, what can I say now,
Whom you loved so briefly long ago?
Any love you had then for me
Will do for the one you have now.

After this he never heard any more about her. His contemporaries for the most part conceded that Chang had done well to rectify his mistake. I have often mentioned it among friends so that, forewarned, they might avoid doing such a thing, or if they did, that they might not be led astray by it. In the ninth month of a year in the Chen-yüan period (785–804) when an official, Li Shen, was passing the night in my house in Ching-an Street, the conversation touched on the subject. He found it most extraordinary and composed a "Song of Ying-ying" to commemorate the affair. Ts'ui's child-name was Ying-ying, and Li Shen used it for his poem.

[From "Yuan Chen and 'The Story of Ying-ying,'" pp. 93–103.]

Sources

The Book of Songs: The Ancient Chinese Classic of Poetry, trans. Arthur Waley. New York: Grove Press, 1987.

Chinese Fairy Tales and Fantasies, translated and edited by Moss Roberts, with the assistance of C. N. Tay. New York: Pantheon Books, 1979.

The I Ching or Book of Changes, the Richard Wilhelm translation rendered into English by Cary F. Baynes. 1950. 2d ed. Princeton, NJ: Princeton University Press, 1967.

The Life and Teachings of Confucius, by James Legge. London: N. Trübner & Co., 1867.

The Life and Works of Mencius, by James Legge. Vol. 2 or *The Chinese Classics,* trans. James Legge. London: N. Trübner & Co., 1875.

Memoirs of a Korean Queen, by Lady Hong. Edited, introduced, and translated by Choe-Wall Yang-hi. London: KPI Ltd., 1985, 1987.

Pan Chao: Foremost Woman Scholar of China, First Century A.D., by Nancy Lee Swann. 1932. New York: Russell & Russell, 1968.

The Position of Women in Early China According to Lieh Nu Chuan "The Biographies of Chinese Women," by Alber Richard O'Hara. Taipei, Taiwan: Mei Ya Publications, Inc., 1971.

Reflections on Things at Hand: The Neo-Confucian Anthology Compiled by Chu Hsi and Lü Tsu-ch'ien, trans. Wing-tsit Chan. New York: Columbia University Press, 1967.

Sources of Chinese Tradition, ed. W. Theodore de Bary, et al. Vol. 1. New York: Columbia University Press, 1964.

The Texts of Confucianism, trans. James Legge. Vols. 27 and 28 of *The Sacred Books of the East,* ed. F. Max Müller. Oxford: Clarendon Press, 1885.

The Wisdom of Confucius, edited and translated with noted by Lin Yutang. New York: Random House, Inc., 1938.

"Yüan Chen and 'The Story of Ying-Ying,'" trans. James R. Hightower. *Harvard Journal of Asiatic Studies* 33 (1973): 93–103.

Bibliography

Introductory Texts

Wing-tsit Chan, translator and compiler, *A Source Book in Chinese Philosophy.* Princeton, NJ: Princeton University Press, 1963.

Arthur Waley, *The Analects of Confucius.* 1938. New York: Vintage Books, 1989.

Works on Women and Confucianism

Allison H. Black, "Gender and Cosmology in Chinese Correlative Thinking." In *Gender and Religion: On the Complexity of Symbols,* ed. Caroline

Walker Bynum, Stevan Harrell, and Paula Richman. Boston: Beacon Press, 1986.

Martina Deuchler, "The Tradition: Women During the Yi Dynasty." Pp. 1–47 in *Virtues in Conflict,* ed. Sandra Matielli. Seoul, 1977.

Richard W. Guisso and Stanley Johannesen, *Women in China: Current Directions in Historical Scholarship* Youngstown, OH: Philo Press, 1981.

Stevan Harrell, "Men, Women, and Ghosts in Taiwanese Folk Religion." Pp. 97–116 in *Gender and Religion: On the Complexity of Symbols,* ed. Caroline Walker Bynum, Stevan Harrell, and Paula Richman. Boston: Beacon Press, 1986.

Theresa Kelleher, "Confucianism." In *Women in World Religions,* ed. Arvind Sharma. Albany, NY: State University of New York Press, 1987.

Olga Lang, *Chinese Family and Society.* New Haven, CT: Yale University Press, 1946.

Edward H. Schafer, *The Divine Woman: Dragon Ladies and Rain Maidens.* San Francisco: North Point Press, 1980.

Margery Wolf and Roxane Witke, *Women in Chinese Society.* Stanford, CA: Stanford University Press, 1975.

TAOISM

Introduction

The semilegendary figure of Lao Tzu is traditionally credited with the founding of Taoism in the sixth century B.C.E. According to this tradition Lao Tzu decided to seek the life of a recluse far from the paths of civilization. On his way out of the city a gatekeeper asked him to share his wisdom, and Lao Tzu complied by composing the *Tao Te Ching* and leaving it with the guard.

This text is rich in paradox and mystical insight. It accepts Chinese cosmological beliefs such as the harmonious nature of the cosmos and the relationship of yin/yang. In general, the text recommends that individuals model themselves after nature, which demonstrates this cosmic harmony, by pursuing a passive quietism and mystical union with the Tao (understood to be the ground of all being). Much of the text is directed to political leaders, who are advised to become sages, to rule without force or coercion, by being passive and by harmonizing their natures with the Tao. If they do this, then the people will automatically submit to their rule. At the same time, the *Tao Te Ching* also lends itself to the ideal of the sage as recluse, someone who has left society to pursue self-cultivation in harmony with nature.

Taoism also drew on indigenous religious practices associated with shamanism, such as trance and dream experiences, breathing techniques, healing, herbology, etc. As the tradition continued to develop it added magical techniques, exorcism, and dietary restrictions to its practices while its main goal became the search for immortality. Alchemy and carefully regulated sexual intercourse were thought to be ways to achieve immortality, which for the Taoists essentially means the ability to prolong life in the physical body.

Taoism affirms the social/philosophical position of women, saying that the weakness and passivity that are part of women's nature represent yin and are good and should be emulated by men. When Taoism organized into an official religious system it reflected the cosmic balancing of yin and yang by having women fulfill lay religious offices, although most of these offices were held by men. Additionally, there were some convents in which women pursued the goals of Taoism in a communal setting.

Despite the positive value ascribed to yin (the feminine principle), Taoism, like so many other religions, is a tradition predominently shaped by and for men. Tellingly, the rich biographical tradition of Taoism is dominated by men; very few biographies of women Taoists exist. Also, women's roles in the biographies of Taoist men are generally quite passive. In the case of Taoist stories and folktales women are frequently spiritualized, so that the tales depict encounters of real men with otherworldly women. This situation is somewhat aggravated by the problems of translation; until fairly recently most translators were men who, in choosing selections to translate, often favored men, thus reducing even further sources on Taoist women in translation. This, of course, can be said of all religious traditions.

The Early Sages

LAO TZU

BIOGRAPHY

The following biography of Lao Tzu, called Master Lao, was written by Hsieh Tao-hang (581–618 C.E.), a Sui dynasty scholar and government minister. When, in the first century

B.C.E., the great Chinese historian Ssu-ma Ch'ien attempted to write about Lao Tzu's life he found only conflicting legends. There is simply no historical basis for Lao Tzu who, nonetheless, remained an extremely important religious figure as the purported author of the *Tao Te Ching*. The following biography stresses the cosmic dimensions of Lao Tzu by beginning with the creation of the world and makes no attempt to provide personal details. Perhaps because Lao Tzu the man is lost in the mists of time, his is one of the few biographies of a founder of a religion that does not provide important information about women in the formative period of the tradition.

After the Thâi Kî (or Primal Ether) commenced its action, the earliest period of time began to be unfolded. The curtain of the sky was displayed, and the sun and moon were suspended in it; the four-cornered earth was established, and the mountains and streams found their places in it. Then the subtle influences (of the Ether) operated like the heaving of the breath, now subsiding and again expanding; the work of production went on in its seasons above and below; all things were formed as from materials, and were matured and maintained. There were the (multitudes of the) people; there were their rulers and superiors.

As to the august sovereigns of the highest antiquity, living as in nests on trees in summer, and in caves in winter, silently and spirit-like they exercised their wisdom. Dwelling like quails, and drinking (the rain and dew) like newly-hatched birds, they had their great ceremonies like the great terms of heaven and earth, not requiring to be regulated by the dishes and stands; and (also) their great music corresponding to the common harmonies of heaven and earth, not needing the guidance of bells and drums.

By and by there came the loss of the Tâo, when its Characteristics took its place. They in their turn were lost, and then came Benevolence. Under the Sovereigns and Kings that followed, now more slowly and anon more rapidly, the manners of the people, from being good and simple, became bad and mean. Thereupon came the Literati and the Mohists with their confused contentions; names and rules were everywhere diffused. The 300 rules of ceremony could not control men's natures; the 3000 rules of punishment were not sufficient to put a stop to their treacherous villanies. But he who knows how to cleanse the current of a stream begins by clearing out its source, and he who would straighten the end of

a process must commence with making its beginning correct. Is not the Great Tâo the Grand Source and the Grand Origin of all things?

The Master Lâo was conceived under the influence of a star. Whence he received the breath (of life) we cannot fathom, but he pointed to the (plum-) tree (under which he was born), and adopted it as his surname; we do not understand whence came the musical sounds (that were heard), but he kept his marvellous powers concealed in the womb for more than seventy years. When he was born, the hair on his head was already white, and he took the designation of 'The Old Boy' (or Lâo-tze). In his person, three gateways and two (bony) pillars formed the distinctive marks of his ears and eyes; two of the symbols for five, and ten brilliant marks were left by the wonderful tread of his feet and the grasp of his hands. From the time of Fû-hsî down to that of the Kâu dynasty, in uninterrupted succession, dynasty after dynasty, his person appeared, but with changed names. In the times of kings Wǎn and Wû he discharged the duties, (first), of Curator of the Royal Library, and (next), of the Recorder under the Pillar. Later on in that dynasty he filled different offices, but did not change his appearance. As soon as Hsüan Nî saw him, he sighed over him as 'the Dragon,' whose powers are difficult to be known. Yin (Hsî), keeper of the (frontier) gate, keeping his eyes directed to every quarter, recognised 'the True Man' as he was hastening into retirement. (By Yin Hsî he was prevailed on) to put forth his extraordinary ability, and write his Book in two Parts,—to lead the nature (of man) back to the Tâo, and celebrating the usefulness of 'doing nothing.' The style of it is very condensed, and its reasoning deep and far-reaching.

[From *The Texts of Taoism*, pp. 311–314.]

TAO TE CHING

Creation

The following two excerpts from the *Tao Te Ching* define the Tao as being beyond ordinary comprehension and further explain that it is the origin of all that is: the Tao, which is female, manifested as the female and male principle, yin and yang, leading to the creation of the cosmos.

The Tào that can be trodden is not the enduring and unchanging Tào. The name that can be named is not the enduring and unchanging name.

(Conceived of as) having no name, it is the Originator of heaven and earth; (conceived of as) having a name, it is the Mother of all things.

Always without desire we must be found
If its deep mystery we would sound;
But if desire always within us be,
Its outer fringe is all that we shall see.

Under these two aspects, it is really the same; but as development takes place, it receives the different names. Together we call them the Mystery. Where the Mystery is the deepest is the gate of all that is subtle and wonderful.

[From *The Way of Life,* I.1, p. 47.]

The Tào produced One; One produced Two; Two produced Three; Three produced All things. All things leave behind them the Obscurity (out of which they have come), and go forward to embrace the Brightness (into which they have emerged), while they are harmonised by the Breath of Vacancy.

[From *The Way of Life,* I.42, p. 85.]

The Tao as Female

While Lao Tzu uses several images to describe the Tao, such as "the uncarved block" and "the babe," most of his images are those associated with the female such as "the valley" and "water." He speaks directly of the female in the following excerpts.

Who knows his manhood's strength,
Yet still his female feebleness maintains;
As to one channel flow the many drains,
All come to him, yea, all beneath the sky.
Thus he the constant excellence retains; —
The simple child again, free from all stains.

Who knows how white attracts,
Yet always keeps himself within black's shade,
The pattern of humility displayed,
Displayed in view of all beneath the sky;
He in the unchanging excellence arrayed,
Endless return to man's first state has made.

Who knows how glory shines,
Yet loves disgrace, nor e'er for it is pale;
Behold his presence in a spacious vale,
To which men come from all beneath the sky.
The unchanging excellence completes its tale;
The simple infant man in him we hail.

[From *The Way of Life,* I.28, p. 71.]

The valley spirit dies not, aye the same;
The female mystery thus do we name.
Its gate, from which at first they issued forth,
Is called the root from which grew heaven and earth.
Long and unbroken does its power remain,
Used gently, and without the touch of pain.

[From *The Way of Life,* I.6, p. 51.]

The following excerpt describes one who knows the Tao, a sage, in female terms, such as being like a valley and like muddy water (yin is dark as well as moist).

The skilful masters (of the Tào) in old times, with a subtle and exquisite penetration, comprehended its mysteries, and were deep (also) so as to elude men's knowledge. As they were thus beyond men's knowledge, I will make an effort to describe of what sort they appeared to be.

Shrinking looked they like those who wade through a stream in winter; irresolute like those who are afraid of all around them; grave like a guest (in awe of his host); evanescent like ice that is melting away; unpretentious like wood that has not been fashioned into anything; vacant like a valley, and dull like muddy water.

Who can (make) the muddy water (clear)? Let it be still, and it will gradually become clear. Who can secure the condition of rest? Let movement go on,

and the condition of rest will gradually arise.

They who preserve this method of the Tâo do not wish to be full (of themselves). It is through their not being full of themselves that they can afford to seem worn and not appear new and complete.

[From *The Way of Life*, I.15, pp. 58–59.]

THE CHUANG TZU

The *Chuang Tzu*, named after the man Chuang Tzu (fl. c. 319 B.C.E.), who is quoted throughout the text, uses humor and paradox to break down the conventional values of the world and to create new values. The text expresses the idea that we are so fixed in the notions of what is right and what is wrong that we cannot really see anything for what it actually is.

The following excerpt demonstrates Chuang Tzu's radical approach, which flies in the face of the formal attitude of Confucianism, especially with regard to mourning. At the same time, he also manages to express feelings for his wife.

Chuang Tzu's wife died. When Hui Tzu went to convey his condolences, he found Chuang Tzu sitting with his legs sprawled out, pounding on a tub and singing. "You lived with her, she brought up your children and grew old," said Hui Tzu. "It should be enough simply not to weep at her death. But pounding on a tub and singing—this is going too far, isn't it?"

Chuang Tzu said, "You're wrong. When she first died, do you think I didn't grieve like anyone else? But I looked back to her beginning and the time before she was born. Not only the time before she was born, but the time before she had a body. Not only the time before she had a body, but the time before she had a spirit. In the midst of the jumble of wonder and mystery a change took place and she had a spirit. Another change and she had a body. Another change and she was born. Now there's been another change and she's dead. It's just like the progression of the four seasons, spring, summer, fall, winter.

"Now she's going to lie down peacefully in a vast room. If I were to follow after her bawling and sobbing, it would show that I don't understand anything about fate. So I stopped."

[From *Chuang Tzu*, p. 113.]

In the following excerpt a woman sage obliquely describes her method of teaching.

Nan-po Tzu-k'uei said to the Woman Crookback, "You are old in years and yet your complexion is that of a child. Why is this?"

"I have heard the Way!"

"Can the Way be learned?" asked Nan-po Tzu-k'uei.

"Goodness, how could that be? Anyway, you aren't the man to do it. Now there's Pu'liang-Yi—he has the talent of a sage but not the Way of a sage, whereas I have the Way of a sage but not the talent of a sage. I thought I would try to teach him and see if I could really get anywhere near to making him a sage. It's easier to explain the Way of a sage to someone who has the talent of a sage, you know. So I began explaining and kept at him for three days, and after that he was able to put the world outside himself. When he had put the world outside himself, I kept at him for seven days more, and after that he was able to put things outside himself. When he had put things outside himself, I kept at him for nine days more, and after that he was able to put life outside himself. After he had put life outside himself, he was able to achieve the brightness of dawn, and when he had achieved the brightness of dawn, he could see his own aloneness. After he had managed to see his own aloneness, he could do away with past and present, and after he had done away with past and present, he was able to enter where there is no life and no death. That which kills life does not die; that which gives life to life does not live. This is the kind of thing it is: there's nothing it doesn't send off, nothing it doesn't welcome, nothing it doesn't destroy, nothing it doesn't complete. Its name is Peace-in-Strife. After the strife, it attains completion."

[From *Chuang Tzu*, pp. 78–79.]

Chuang Tzu also emphasized that individuals need to harmoniously balance yin and yang. The following excerpt, which describes the cosmic manifestation of conflict between these two principles, also hints at the impact of such a conflict within an individual.

When the yin and yang go awry, then heaven and earth see astounding sights. Then we hear the crash and roll of thunder, and fire comes in the midst of rain and burns up the great pagoda tree. Delight and sorrow are there to trap man on either side so that he has no escape. Fearful and trembling, he can reach no completion. His mind is as though trussed and suspended between heaven and earth, bewildered and lost in delusion. Profit and loss rub against each other and light the countless fires that burn up the inner harmony of the mass of men. The moon cannot put out the fire, so that in time all is consumed and the Way comes to an end.

[From *Chuang Tzu*, p. 132.]

In the next excerpt Chuang Tzu's description of a sage notes his femaleness.

Chien Wu said to Lien Shu, "I was listening to Chieh Yü's talk—big and nothing to back it up, going on and on without turning around. I was completely dumbfounded at his words—no more end than the Milky Way, wild and wide of the mark, never coming near human affairs!"

"What were his words like?" asked Lien Shu.

"He said that there is a Holy Man living on faraway Ku-she Mountain, with skin like ice or snow, and gentle and shy like a young girl. He doesn't eat the five grains, but sucks the wind, drinks the dew, climbs up on the clouds and mist, rides a flying dragon, and wanders beyond the four seas. By concentrating his spirit, he can protect creatures from sickness and plague and make the harvest plentiful. I thought this was all insane and refused to believe it."

"You would!" said Lien Shu. "We can't expect a blind man to appreciate beautiful patterns or a deaf man to listen to bells and drums. And blindness and deafness are not confined to the body alone—the understanding has them too, as your words just now have shown. This man, with this virtue of his, is about to embrace the ten thousand things and roll them into one. Though the age calls for reform, why should he wear himself out over the affairs of the world? There is nothing that can harm this man. Though flood waters pile up to the sky, he will not drown. Though a great drought melts metal and stone and scorches the earth and hills, he will not be burned. From his dust and leavings alone you could mold a Yao or a Shun! Why should he consent to bother about mere things?

[From *Chuang Tzu*, pp. 27–28.]

Techniques for Immortality

Women, or aspects of the feminine, often appear in stories and instructions about Taoist techniques to achieve immortality. These appearances reflect the strongly feminine (yin) element in the Tao itself. Since most of these texts were written by and for men, they stress the male adept's need not only to be in touch with the feminine but to internalize it.

TWO ALCHEMICAL TEXTS

The following excerpt from the Taoist Canon (*Tao tsang*) is a guide to an elaborate alchemical visualization practiced by Taoist adepts. The goal of the visualization is to absorb the essences of the sun and moon, which can transform the adept's body into a vehicle for immortality. The visualization involves seeing the Jade Woman, a celestial guardian of divine secrets, and eventually visualizing sexual union with her.

The Technique of the Mystic Realized One

Actualize sun or moon within the mouth. In the white light of day actualize the sun; in the middle of the night actualize the moon. It is also permissible to actualize [either one] when it is neither [plainly] daytime nor nighttime so that a decisive distinction can be made as to whether it is to be sun or moon. The sun's color is red. The moon's color is yellow. The sun has nine rays of purple light. The moon has ten rays of white light. Cause sun or moon to stand opposite the mouth, nine feet away from it. The light rays should be directed towards the mouth, with the rays straight as bowstrings so that they will enter into the mouth. Next, actualize a young woman as present within the sun or moon." A purple cap is placed on her head, and she has a cloak and skirt of vermilion damask. She calls herself the Jade Woman of the Cinnabar Aurora of the Highest Mysteries of the Greatest Mystery. Her taboo-name is Binding Coil (*Ch'an-hsüan*) and her agnomen is Secret Realized (*Mi-chen*). From her mouth she exhales a red pneuma which fills the space between the light-rays from sign or moon completely. It combines with them until rays and auroral glow are both used up, then gushes into one's own mouth. One masters it and gulps it down. Actualize the woman also as exhaling it in sequence; activate it nine times ten. After these have been gulped down, actualize a conscious command to the phosphor of sun or moon to press intimately close upon one's own face, and command that the Jade Woman's mouth press a kiss upon your own mouth, causing the liquor of the pneuma to come down into the mouth. One then conjures her inaudibly: "Jade Woman, Living Germ of Sun and Moon, Conserving Spirit of the Luminous Hall, Purple Realized One of the Grand Aurora, Binding Coil, generated spontaneously from the Barrens in the Prior Age, whose agnomen is Secret Realized One, whose head is capped with the Numinous Crown of the Purple-flowered Lotus, and whose body is cloaked in a multicolored damask cloak and a Flying Skirt of Vermilion Cinnabar, who emerges from the sun and enters the moon. Lit by Heaven! Subtly fragrant! May your mouth emit the orange pneuma to irrigate my Three Primes. May my face gaze upon the Sky Well. Make my white-souls compliant. Give definition to my cloud-souls. May the mystic liquor move in streams. May the foetal germ grow to completion. May the Five Stores generate efflorescence. Open my

pupils in reverse to my face, that I may inspect and rein the myriad numina, the Supervisor of Destiny, and the "flying transcendents." This done, actualize the salival liquor from the mouth of the Jade Woman, commanding it to gush into one's own mouth. Then, having rinsed it with the liquor, proceed to swallow it. Stop only after nine times ten passages. [Then], in quieting the heart, in making thoughts resonant and activating them, there need no longer be any limit set on most of one's strivings. If one is actualizing the sun, he does not actualize the moon. If one is actualizing the moon, he does not actualize the sun. It is only essential that he should actualize them both impartially. If one misses the time for taking the dose, he should actualize the two phosphors as returning to the Luminous Hall—the sun on the left, the moon on the right. Command lights and flashes of sun and moon to radiate jointly with the pupils of the eyes, reflecting the two pneumas in the four [directions], so that they may gush freely through one. One may also actualize sun and moon regularly as in place in the Luminous Hall, without waiting for the regular taking of the dose from [one of] the two phosphors of sun and moon, and thus exploit them concurrently. Perform these things for five years and the Jade Woman of Greatest Mystery will come down to you, and lie down to take her ease with you. The Jade Woman of Greatest Mystery can also divide her shape to make several tens of Jade Women who will be responsible for your urgent errands. This is the ultimate in accumulating resonance, in knotting germinal essences together, in transmuting life, and in seeing germinal essences as simulacra. In the end, it is a miraculous response to your resonance. The Most High Realized Magistrates employ the Way of the Sun's Aurora and the Technique of Draining the Two Phosphors to bring men into communication with the numina, to summon the Realized Ones, to embody their lives in gemmy refulgence, to bind the myriad spirits in service and to command them, and finally to rise up into the chambers of the divine kings. The Way which was taught to Yü of Hsia long ago by the Realized Person of Mount Chung—that was precisely the technique of the Mystic Realized One. However, this is no more than an excerpted outline; and indeed we lack anything about the affairs of Binding Coil.

[From "The Jade Woman of Greatest Mystery," pp. 393–396.]

The following two excerpts are from the fourth-century alchemical text, the *Nei P'ien*, written by Ko Hung (ca. 280–340 C.E.). These two excerpts are among the rare stories about Taoist females, and the first is reminiscent of the practice of female infanticide through abandonment. The point of the story is that the profound alchemical practices of the Taoists are simple enough or natural enough for a child, even a female child. It is also a play on Lao Tzu's description in the *Tao Te Ching* of the Tao as a baby.

Ch'en Shih of Ying-ch'uan, also known as Chung-kung and Chief of T'ai-ch'iu, was a sincere scholar. In compiling his *Notes on Strange Things that I have Learned,* he says that a man of his district by the name of Chang Kuang-ting once fled his place when disaster struck. Having a daughter of four unable to walk or wade streams, whom he could not carry, he planned to abandon her. She would undoubtedly die of hunger, but he did not want her bones to lie uncovered. It happened that at the entrance to the village there was a large, old grave mound in the top of which had once been dug a hole. Attaching a rope to a large pot, he lowered his daughter into the tomb, where he left her with a few months' supply of dry food and drink and fled to await better times. Three years later he managed to return home and wished to gather up his daughter's bones for burial. When he went and looked, there was his daughter still sitting in the tomb. On seeing her parents, she recognized them and was very happy, but the parents at first were fearful that it was her ghost. Only when they had entered the tomb and approached her did they realize that she was not dead. When asked where she had procured food, she replied that when her supplies were first exhausted she became very hungry. On noticing a creature in the corner that stretched its neck and swallowed its breath, she tried doing the same thing, and gradually she became less and less hungry. She had continued to practice this every day. The clothes which had been left for her when her parents had departed were naturally still in the tomb, for, since she had not moved about, they were not worn out. Therefore she did not suffer from the cold. When her father sought the creature which she had mentioned, it proved to be a large tortoise. At first, on leaving the tomb and eating starches, her stomach hurt and she was nauseated, but after a while she became used to them. This proves that tortoises are in possession of a method leading to immortality; it constitutes evidence that when a processor imitates them he can live as long as they do.

[From *Alchemy, Medicine, Religion*, pp. 57–58.]

The second excerpt shows a woman's successful attainment of immortality in the wilds of nature and its loss when she is returned to civilization.

Under Emperor Ch'eng of the Han, hunters in the Chung-nan mountains [W of Ch'ang-an] saw a naked person whose body was covered with black hair. They wanted to capture this individual, but it passed over pits and valleys like a thoroughbred and could not be overtaken. Then they did some spying in the region, surrounded the place, and captured it. When they had established that it was a woman, she was questioned, and replied, "I was originally a Ch'in concubine. Learning that with the arrival of bandits from the East the King of Ch'in would surrender and the palace would be burned, I became frightened and ran away to the mountains where I famished for the lack of food. I was on the point of dying when an old man taught me how to eat the leaves and fruits of pines. At first it was bitter and unpleasant, but I gradually grew used to it until it produced lack of hunger and thirst. In the winter I suffered no cold, and in summer I felt no heat."

Calculation showed that this woman, having been the concubine of Prince Ying of Ch'in, was more than two hundred years old in the time of Emperor Ch'eng. When she was brought back to the court to be fed starches, the first odor from them nauseated her for several days, but then she became reconciled to them. After about two years of this new life, her body lost its hair, and she turned old and died. If she had not been caught, she would have become a genie.

[From *Alchemy, Medicine, Religion*, p. 194.]

A BIOGRAPHY

The following story and its commentary explain some Taoist breathing and fasting techniques for the attainment of immorality. Both these techinques refer to being in the womb, thereby evoking earlier images of the Tao as a babe and as feminine. In other words, one who seeks to be immortal (a *hsien*) must become like a babe and rest in the feminine or in the Tao. The story is translated from another work by Ko Hung (ca. 280–340 C.E.), the *Shen Hsien Chuan,* a collection of biographies, along with his commentary on the techniques it describes.

Wang Chên

Wang Chên was a native of Shang-tang [in Shansi]. At the age of seventy-nine he began to study Tao, practising the art of womb-breathing and abstaining from food for more than thirty years. His appearance was youthful, his complexion fine. He could walk as fast as a galloping horse, and his muscular power was equal to the combined strength of several men. Wu Ti of the Wei dynasty [i.e. Ts'ao Ts'ao] having heard of his fame, summoned him to an interview and found that he looked like a man of thirty or thereabouts; but suspecting trickery, he had searching inquiries made in his village, and obtained the same account from many different persons who had known Wang Chêng from their boyhood. It was agreed that he was at that time four hundred years old. Wu Ti was then convinced that he was a man of Tao, and paid him much honour and respect. . . . His outward appearance still continued impervious to age, until at last he ascended Mount Nü-chi and left the world to become a hsien.

Breathing exercises, so we are told, form one of the essential means of attaining hsienship. A note by Ko Hung on the subject will not therefore be out of place:

Those who have acquired the art of womb-breathing are able to inhale and exhale the air independently of the nose and mouth, like the foetus in the womb. . . . When you are beginning to learn how to control your breath, you take in the air through the nose and hold it while you count your heart-beats. When you have counted 120, let the air out very gently through the mouth. During this process, care should be taken that the passage of the air either way is quite inaudible to yourself, and more should go in than comes out. A good test is to place a piece of swan's down at the aperture of the nostrils, and see that it does not stir when the breath is expelled. Practice will enable the number of heart-beats to be gradually increased, until at last you can hold your breath while you count a thousand. When this number is reached, the aged become rejuvenated, getting steadily younger day by day. This breathing exercise should be performed only in a period of "live air", not in a period of "dead air" . . . A day and a night are divided into twelve periods of two hours each: the six periods from midnight to midday are "live air" periods, and the six from midday to midnight are "dead air" periods. Breathing exercises performed in a "dead air" period are useless.

"Womb-eating" has an analogous meaning, namely, being nourished, like the foetus, otherwise than by ordinary food and drink. In exercising the breath it is most essential that much food be not eaten; for raw vegetables, fat meat, and the like, cause the breath to become strong and hard to retain. Anger should also be avoided, because if one gets angry the breath is disturbed and will not flow in abundance, or else it may set up a cough. Thus there are very few who are able to perform these exercises. My great-uncle Ko Hsüan, whenever he was thoroughly intoxicated or the weather was very hot, used to lie down at the bottom of a deep pool and only emerge after a day had passed—a feat which was only rendered possible by his faculty of retaining the breath and of womb-respiration.

[From *A Gallery of Chinese Immortals,* pp. 69–70.]

Female Sages

Dispersed throughout Taoist literature are occasional stories of female sages. In general, Taoist sages turned their backs on society and its values, so the marginal position of most of these women is typical of all Taoist sages, and stories about sages tend to stress the fantastic elements.

SUN BU-ER

POEMS

Sun Bu-er was a twelfth-century female Taoist sage. She married and had three children before completely devoting herself to Taoist practices at the age of fifty-one. Eventually she developed her own following of students. The excerpts from her poems are rich in the alchemical imagery that describes the transformative power of the Tao, especially its ability to so profoundly change people that they become immortal.

Cutting off the Dragon
(For women only.)

When stillness climaxes, it can produce movement;
Yin and yang mold each other.
Grab the jade tiger in the wind.
Catch the gold bird in the moon.
Keep your eyes on the incubation process,
Keep your mind on the course of following and
    reversing.
When the magpie bridges are crossed,
The alchemical energy returns to the furnace.
    [From *Immortal Sisters,* p. 31.]

Projecting the Spirit

There is a body outside the body,
Which has nothing to do with anything produced by
    magical arts.
Making this aware energy completely pervasive
Is the living, active, unified original spirit.
The bright moon congeals the gold liquid,
Blue lotus refines jade reality.
When you've cooked the marrow of the sun and
    moon,
The pearl is so bright you don't worry about poverty.
    [From *Immortal Sisters,* p. 52.]

Ingestion of the Medicine

The great forge produces mountains and waters,
Containing therein the potential of creation.
In the morning, greet the energy of the sun;
At night, inhale the vitality of the moon.
In time the elixir can be culled;
With the years, the body naturally lightens.
Where the original spirit comes and goes,
Myriad apertures emit radiant light.
    [From *Immortal Sisters,* pp. 47–48.]

Flying

At the right time, just out of the valley,
You rise lightly into the spiritual firmament.
The jade girl rides a blue phoenix,
The gold boy offers a scarlet peach.
One strums a brocade lute amidst the flowers,
One plays jewel pipes under the moon.

One day immortal and mortal are separated,
And you coolly cross the ocean.
    [From *Immortal Sisters,* p. 56.]

Facing a Wall

All things finished,
You sit still in a little niche.
The light body rides on violet energy,
The tranquil nature washes in a pure pond.
Original energy is unified, yin and yang are one;
The spirit is the same as the universe.
When the work is done, you pay court to the Jade
    Palace;
A long whistle gusts a misty gale.
    [From *Immortal Sisters,* p. 50.]

The Womb Breath
(The same for men and women.)

If you want the elixir to form quickly,
First get rid of illusory states.
Attentively guard the spiritual medicine;
With every breath return to the beginning of the
    creative.
The energy returns, coursing through the three
    islands;
The spirit, forgetting, unites with the ultimate.
Coming this way and going this way,
No place is not truly so.
    [From *Immortal Sisters,* p. 37.]

Carrying Out Practice
(The first part is applicable to both men and women;
    the last part is for the use of women alone.)

Gather the breath into the point where the spirit is
    frozen,
And living energy comes from the east.
Don't get stuck on anything at all,
And one energy will come back to the terrace.
The darkness should go down the front,
The light induced up the back.
After a shower, a peal of thunder
Rumbles at the top of the mountain and the bottom
    of the sea.
    [From *Immortal Sisters,* p. 28.]

Gathering the Mind
(The same for men and women.)

Before our body existed,
One energy was already there.
Like jade, more lustrous as it's polished,

Like gold, brighter as it's refined.
Sweep clear the ocean of birth and death,
Stay firm by the door of total mastery.
A particle at the point of open awareness,
The gentle firing is warm.
[From *Immortal Sisters,* p. 24.]

BIOGRAPHY

Legend and history blend in the following description of Sun Bu-er's life (called Sun Pu-erh in this text) taken from the sixteenth-century novel *Seven Taoist Masters,* author unknown. In the first excerpt Sun Pu-erh has received instruction from her husband's teacher, Wang Ch'ung-yang, and she now wants to devote herself fully to Taoist practices.

Wang Ch'ung-yang finished speaking, smiled, and asked Sun Pu-erh, "To which vehicle do you aspire?" Sun Pu-erh replied, "Your student aspires to the Great Vehicle." Wang Ch'ung-yang said, "You have ambitious aspirations, but I don't know whether you have the discipline and perseverance to pursue that path." Sun Pu-erh said, "Sir, my aspirations are not ambitious, but my will is strong. I am willing to sacrifice everything to attain the Great Vehicle."

Wang Ch'ung-yang then said, "Those who cultivate the Tao must find a place that is conducive to training. Certain places are filled with power, and training at these power places will enhance one's progress. There is a power hidden in the city of Loyang, and the gods have ordained that an immortal will emerge from there. One need merely cultivate oneself there for ten to twelve years, and immortality will be attained. Are you willing to go?" Sun Pu-erth said, "I am willing to go anywhere if that is what is required to cultivate the Great Vehicle." Wang Ch'ung-yang looked at Sun Pu-erh and then shook his head. "You cannot go." Sun Pu-erh said, "I am willing to do anything. I am willing to die, if necessary." Wang Ch'ung-yang said, "Dying is a waste if it achieves no purpose. To simply throw your life away is to rob yourself of the chance to become an immortal. Loyang is more than a thousand miles away. You will meet with perils along the way. You will be the target of men who desire your beauty. They will rape you and molest you. And rather than be shamed, you would take your own life before they touch you. Now, is that not wasting your life to no purpose? Not only will you not achieve immortality but you will throw away what was given to you by Heaven. That is why I said you cannot go."

Sun Pu-erh left the meditation hall and went directly to the kitchen. Telling the servants to leave, she filled a wok with cooking oil, heated the oil until

it was hot, and then poured in cold water. The oil sizzled, and sparks of hot liquid shot out of the wok. Sun Pu-erh closed her eyes and let the liquid hit her face, burning the skin in numerous places; even after healing, the burns would leave scars and marks all over her face. She then returned to Wang Ch'ung-yang and said, "Look at my ugly face. Now will you allow me to travel to Loyang?" Wang Ch'ung-yang clapped his hands and said, "I have never seen one as determined as you are or willing to sacrifice so much. I did not come to Shantung Province in vain. You shall go to Loyang."

Wang Ch'ung-yang then taught Sun Pu-erh the methods of internal alchemy. He showed her how to immerse fire in water, how to unite *yin* and *yang,* and how to conceive and nourish the spirit. When he was satisfied that Sun Pu-erh remembered and understood the instructions, he said, "Remember, hide your knowledge. Do not let people know you are a seeker of the Tao. After you have finished the Great Alchemical Work, then you may reveal yourself and teach others. In the meantime, let your face heal. Do not even let your servants know of your plans. Leave as soon as you are ready. You need not come to say farewell to me. We shall meet again soon at the celebration of the ripening of the immortal peach."

Sun Pu-erh thanked Wang Ch'ung-yang and left the meditation hall. On her way back to her room, she ran into a servant, who screamed when she saw the lady's face. When the servant recovered her wits, she asked Sun Pu-erh, "Lady, what has happened to your face?" Sun Pu-erh said, "I was cooking a snack for the teacher, and by mistake I added water to the cooking oil. I did not get out of the way in time, and the sizzling liquid shot into my face. It is nothing serious." Sun Pu-erh locked herself in her room for the next few days and reviewed Wang Ch'ung-yang's instructions.

When Ma Tan-yang returned home, the servants at once told him about his wife's accident in the kitchen. Ma Tan-yang went to Sun Pu-erh's room, saw her face, and consoled her. Gently he said, "You should have been more careful. Let the servants do the cooking. The lady of the house should not be working in the kitchen. Now your beautiful face is ruined with scars." Sun Pu-erh stared at Ma Tan-yang and cackled madly. "Are you the messenger of the Empress of Heaven? Have you come to invite me to attend the celebrations in heaven? If so, let's get going!" She opened the window and jumped out. Pretending to slip, she deliberately fell and lay on the ground, groaning. Ma Tan-yang ran out, put his arms around her and helped her up. Sun Pu-erh laughed and cried like a mad woman. Ma Tan-yang escorted her back to her room and then went to Wang Ch'ung-yang.

Seeing his teacher, Ma Tan-yang said, "Sir, my wife has gone mad. She has lost her mind. She is talking nonsense, and she laughs and cries for no reason." Wang Ch'ung-yang said, "If she is not mad, how can she become an immortal?" Ma Tan-yang did not understand Wang Ch'ung-yang's remark. He was about to ask his teacher what it meant when Wang Ch'ung-yang waved his hand and told him to leave. Sadly, Ma Tan-yang went back to his room.

Sun Pu-erh's pretended insanity succeeded in getting Ma Tan-yang and everyone else in the mansion to leave her alone. She reviewed Wang Ch'ung-yang's instructions repeatedly until she could perform them naturally and effortlessly. A month passed, and Sun Pu-erh looked at her face in the mirror. Scars and pockmarks dotted her face. Since she had not combed her hair for a month, she was no longer the beautiful wife of a wealthy merchant. Sun Pu-erh was delighted. She was now ready to make the journey to Loyang. With a piece of charcoal she smeared her face and her clothing. Looking like a mad beggar-woman, she ran out into the living room, laughed wildly, and rushed out the front door. A servant tried to stop her, but she bit the girl in the arm. Yelping in pain, the servant let go of her. The other servants alerted Ma Tan-yang. He hurried to the living room, but was told that the lady had already left the house. Ma Tan-yang and the servants searched the town and the immediate countryside for Sun Pu-erh, but they could not find her.

Knowing that Ma Tan-yang would search for her, Sun Pu-erh had hidden herself inside a haystack on a nearby farm. She heard the voices of the servants and her husband and continued to conceal herself until it was dark. When everything was silent, she quietly slipped out and walked toward Loyang. Along the way, she slept in abandoned temples and caves. She obtained her food from begging, and when people asked who she was, she acted insane and uttered nonsense. In this way, people left her alone, and eventually she arrived safely at Loyang.

[From *Seven Taoist Masters,* pp. 54–59.]

In the next excerpt Sun Pu-erh, after twelve years of seclusion and practice, has achieved immortality, and, as a way of teaching, she displayed her power to the villagers. Afterwards, she returned to her husband and instructed him.

Sun Pu-erh lived in the city of Loyang for twelve years. She attained the Tao and acquired powerful magical abilities. One day she said to herself, "I have lived in Loyang for a long time. Now I have attained the Tao, I should demonstrate the powers of the Tao to the people." Sun Pu-erh took two withered branches and blew at them softly. Instantly the two branches were transformed into a man and a woman. The woman resembled Sun Pu-erh, and the man appeared to be a handsome man in his thirties. The couple went to the busiest streets of the city and started laughing, embracing, and teasing each other. Loyang was the center of learning and culture in those days, and such shameful behaviors in public between a man and a woman in public was not tolerated. Yet despite reprimands from the city officials and the teachers of the community, the couple continued their jesting and playing day after day. Even after the guards escorted them away from the city they were found back in the busy streets the next day.

When the prominent members of the community saw that their efforts to banish the couple from the city were in vain they took counsel among themselves and approached the mayor, saying, "Many years ago, a mad woman took refuge in an abandoned house at the edge of the city. We took pity on her and gave her food when she begged. Now she is not only forgetting our kindness to her but has become a nuisance to public peace and decency. We would like to ask you to arrest this shameless couple and burn them in public. We have come to this last resort because they have ignored our pleas and our threats." One of the more powerful community leaders added, "Sir, as the leader of this city you are responsible for the good behavior of our citizens. You must do something about this shameless couple." Not wanting to offend the powerful citizens of the community, the mayor issued a decree and had it posted throughout the city. It read: "Madness is the result of losing reason. Without reason all actions become irrational. For a man and woman to embrace and tease each other in public is to break the rules of propriety. If they exhibit such shameful behavior during the day there is nothing they cannot do at night. The streets of the city are not places for jesting. To display such offensive behavior in public is abominable. We have asked them to leave, but they have refused. We have banished them from the city, but they have returned. There is only one thing left for us to do. We shall arrest them and burn them in public. Thus we can rid ourselves of these evil characters."

Together with the city guards, community leaders, and a large crowd, the mayor walked toward the abandoned house at the edge of the city where the man and the mad woman were reported to be staying. As they approached the house the mayor said, "Let everyone carry along some dry wood or twigs. We shall pile them around the house and burn the abominable place, together with the mad woman and the shameless man." The crowds piled dry branches around the building and set them on fire. Flames and smoke engulfed the building. Suddenly the grey smoke turned into a multicolored haze and the mad woman was seen seated on a canopy of clouds, flanked by the man and woman whom the people had seen jesting in the streets. Sun Pu-erh said to the crowds below, "I am a seeker of the Tao. My home is in Shantung Province, and my name is Sun Pu-erh. Twelve years ago I arrived in Loyang. I disguised myself as a mad woman so that I might pursue the path of the Tao in peace. I have finally attained the Tao, and today I shall be carried into the heavens by fire and smoke. I transformed two branches into a man and a woman so that circumstances would lead you here to witness the mystery and the powers of the Tao. In return for your kindness and hospitality to me through the years I shall give you this couple. They will be your guardians, and I shall see to it that your harvests will be plentiful and your city protected from plagues and natural disasters." Sun Pu-erh gave the man and woman a push and they fell onto the crowd below. Instantly the couple was transformed back into their original form. The crowd picked up the two branches, but when they looked up at the sky all they saw was a small black figure growing smaller and smaller as it flew higher and higher. The figure became a black dot, and finally the black dot disappeared. The crowds bowed their heads in respect and dispersed. For the next five years, Loyang enjoyed a prosperity that was unmatched by any town in China. Its countryside yielded bountiful harvests, and livestock was healthy and plentiful. The rains came at the appropriate times, and the city and its surrounding region seemed to be immune to natural disasters. In gratitude to Sun Pu-erh the citizens built a shrine to her. In it was a statue of her likeness, and beside her stood statues of the man and woman she had created from two branches. The shrine was named the Three Immortals' Shrine. It was said that those who presented offerings with sincerity received blessings from the three immortals.

After Sun Pu-erh ascended to the heavens she returned to the earthly realm. She wondered about the progress of Ma Tan-yang [her husband] and decided to offer help if needed.

When Sun Pu-erh appeared at the Ma mansion the servants could not believe that the lady of the mansion was back. They ran to tell Ma Tan-yang, and he hurried out to greet his wife. He welcomed her home and said, "Friend in the Tao, you must have suffered much these years." Sun Pu-erh replied, "We who cultivate the Tao must bear whatever hardships beset us. Otherwise we will not be able to attain the Tao." That night, Ma Tan-yang invited Sun Pu-erh to meditate with him. Sun Pu-erh maintained her meditation position through the night, but Ma Tan-yang could not. The next morning Ma Tan-yang said to Sun Pu-erh, "Friend in the Tao, your meditation skills are much more advanced than mine." Sun Pu-erh said, "Brother, I can see that your magical powers do not seem to be as strong as they could be." Ma Tan-yang said, "You are mistaken. My magical powers are strong. I can transform stones into silver pieces. Let me show you." Sun Pu-erh said, "I can transform stones into gold, but I do not wish to do so, for gold and silver are material things that we must leave behind. Therefore it is not important whether they can be turned into silver or gold. Let me tell you a story." Then Sun Pu-erh related to Ma Tan-yang a story about Immortals Lü Tung-pin and Chung-li Ch'üan.

When Immortal Lü Tung-pin was studying with his teacher Chung-li Ch'üan, Chung-li Ch'üan gave him a large and heavy sack to carry. Immortal Lü carried the sack for three years without complaint or resentment. At the end of three years, Chung-li Ch'üan told Immortal Lü to open the sack. He said to Immortal Lü, "While you were carrying the sack these years, did you know what was inside?" Immortal Lü replied, "Yes, I knew that the sack was filled with stones." Chung-li Ch'üan then said, "Do you know that the rocks that you've been carrying around all these years could be turned into gold? Because you have shown sincerity and humility and have never uttered a word of complaint, I shall teach you how to turn these stones into gold if you wish." Immortal Lü asked Chung-li Ch'üan, "When these stones have been transformed into gold, will they be identical to real gold?" Chung-li Ch'üan replied, "No, gold that has been transformed from stones or other objects will only last for five hundred years. After that, they will return to their original form." Immortal Lü said, "Then I do not wish to learn the techinques of turning stones into gold. If the gold is not permanent, then what I do now will have harmful effects five hundred years later. I would rather be ignorant of a technique which may potentially harm people." Hearing Lü Tung-pin's reply, Chung-li Chüan said, "Your foundations are stronger than mine. Your level of enlightenment will be higher than mine. As you have enlightened me, I now realize that this technique of turning stones to gold or silver or precious gems is not worth learning and not worth teaching."

After hearing Sun Pu-erh's story, Ma Tan-yang felt ashamed and said no more. Next day, Sun Pu-erh invited Ma Tan-yang to take a bath in a tub of boiling water. Ma Tan-yang looked at the bubbling water, tested it with his finger, and exclaimed, "This water is so hot that I almost burned my finger. How can I sit in it and take a bath?" Sun Pu-erh jumped into the tub of boiling water as if it had been merely lukewarm. Turning to Ma Tan-yang, she said, "Brother, after all these years you should have cultivated a body that is impervious to heat and cold. How is it that you have not made much progress in

your training?" Ma Tan-yang said, "I do not know. We received the same instructions from the same teacher. How come your meditation skill, your magical powers, and your physical development surpass mine by far?" Sun Pu-erh dried herself, put on fresh clothes and explained to Ma Tan-yang, "These twelve years I have lived in hardship. My training was done under the most adverse of conditions. Moreover, since I had to beg and live in the most meager of shelters, my body and mind were not distracted or dulled by comfortable living. You, on the other hand, lived in a comfortable house, had servants to tend your needs, and did not meet with hardships. Therefore your senses, your mind, and your body became lazy, and you did not train as hard as I did."

Ma Tan-yang said to Sun Pu-erh, "You are right. I shall leave this place and travel. I shall seek the Tao in my journeys." Late that night Ma Tan-yang changed into Taoist robes and slipped out of his mansion. The next morning Sun Pu-erh summoned the servants and told them to sell the property and distribute the money and household goods to the needy, for she knew that Ma Tan-yang would never return to his mansion and his lands again.

[From *Seven Taoist Masters*, pp. 120–125.]

FROM THE LIEH TZU

The following tale is taken from the Taoist classic, the *Lieh Tzu,* named after a semilegendary sage and is traditionally dated to the fourth century B.C.E. Actually it is a Neo-Taoist text, which recent scholarship has dated to the third century C.E. The brief tale describes the unique magical abilities of a female Taoist sage.

Ch'in Ch'ing turned to a friend and said:
'Once a woman named Erh of Han ran out of provisions while travelling East to Ch'i. She entered the capital through the Concord Gate, and traded her songs for a meal. When she left, the lingering notes curled round the beams of the gate and did not die away for three days; the by-standers thought that she was still there.

'She passed an inn, where the landlord insulted her. She therefore wailed mournfully in long-drawn-out notes; and all the people in the quarter, old and young, looked at each other sadly with the tears dripping

down their faces, and could not eat for three days. They hurried after her and brought her back; and again she sang them a long ballad in drawn-out notes. The people of the whole quarter, old and young, could not help skipping with joy and dancing to handclaps, forgetting that they had been sad just before. Afterwards they sent her away with rich presents.

'That is why even today the people of Concord Gate are good singers and funeral wailers, taking as their example the memory of Erh's singing.

[From *The Book of Lieh-tzu,* p. 109.]

TWO TALES FROM THE LIEH HSIEN CHUAN

The following brief story is a variant of Mao Nü's story, quoted above from the alchemical text, the *Nei P'ien*. This version was translated from the *Lieh Hsien Chuan,* a collection of

Taoist biographies. The translator believes this story to have been written down by 30 B.C.E. The Ch'in dynasty fell in 207 B.C.E.

Mao Nü

Mao Nü ["Hairy Woman"] . . . has been seen by hunters on Mount Hua-yin [this is Mt. Hua, the Sacred Peak of the West, not far from Ch'ang-an] for many generations. Her body is covered with hair. She professes to be one of the ladies from Ch'in Shih Huang's palace who, during the troubles that attended the downfall of the Ch'in dynasty, became a wandering fugitive and took refuge on the mountain. There she encountered the Taoist recluse Ku Ch'un, who taught her to eat pine-needles. In consequence of this diet she became immune from cold and hunger, and her body was so etherealized that it seemed to fly along. For over 170 years the mountain grotto in which she makes her abode has resounded to the thrumming of a lute.

[From *Lieh Hsien Chuan* in *A Gallery of Chinese Immortals,* p. 35.]

Another excerpt from the *Lieh Hsien Chuan* tells the story of a male sage who eventually teaches one of his wives about the path to immortality.

Wên Pin

Wên Pin was a villager of T'ai-ch'iu . . . who made his living as a vendor of straw sandals. He took a number of wives, turning them away after thirty years or so. At a later period, one of his former wives, who had now passed the age of ninety, saw Wên Pin again. He was still in the full vigour of manhood, and the old lady wept, and pleaded with him to take her back. Wên Pin excused himself, saying: "It wouldn't do; but could you perhaps meet me at the altar west of the village pavilion, at daybreak on the first of the first moon?" Accordingly, the old lady, accompanied by her grandson, travelled over ten *li* by night and sat by the altar waiting for Pin. In a short time he arrived and was greatly surprised to see her. —"So you really love Tao, then?" he said. "Had I known that before, I should never have sent you away." He then instructed her to swallow chrysanthemum petals, *ti fu . . . ,* certain epiphytes of the mulberry, and pine-seeds. Thus increasing her store of vital energy, she too became rejuvenated, and was seen for more than a hundred years afterwards.

[From *Lieh Hsien Chuan* in A Gallery of Chinese Immortals, p. 53.]

Female Deities

QUEEN MOTHER OF THE WEST

One of the most important and complex female deities of Taoism is the Queen Mother of the West. She possesses the peaches of immortality, which means that she can confer immortality. The following story from the *Han Wu ku-shih* (composed between the second and sixth centuries) describes the famous meeting between her and the Han Dynasty emperor Wu Ti. As in many of the stories about meetings between mortal men and celestial women, it is the women who journey to earth.

An earlier but shorter version of this story, preserved in the *Lieh-tzu,* has the Queen Mother of the West visiting another ruler, King Mu. She seems to have been a pre-Taoist divinity that was gradually assimilated by the Taoists. In the process her powers were greatly enhanced, and, during the Han Dynasty, when she receives a partner, the King Father of the East, they are attributed with the creation of the cosmos. Her essential function, though, is to confer eternal life on her devotees, and in this context she was popular with all classes of people.

The Queen Mother sent her messenger to tell the emperor that she would be visiting him on the seventh day of the seventh month. When the appointed day came, the emperor swept the inner parts of the palace and lit the lamp of the nine decorated branches. On the seventh day of the seventh month he kept vigil in the hall of the Reception of Flowery Delights. At the exact hour of midday he suddenly saw that there were green birds arriving from the west and roosting in front of the hall. . . .

That night, at the seventh division of the clock, there was not a cloud in the sky; it was dark, as if one might hear the sound of thunder, and stretching to the edge of the heavens there was a purple glow. By and by the Queen Mother arrived. She rode in a purple carriage, with the daughters of jade riding on each side; she wore the sevenfold crown upon her head; the sandals on her feet were black and glistening, embellished with the design of a phoenix; and the energies of new growth were like a cloud. There were two green birds, like crows, attending on either side of the Mother. When she alighted from her carriage the emperor greeted her and bowed down, and invited her to be seated. He asked for the drug of deathlessness, and the Queen said "Of the drugs of long, long ago, there were those such as the Purple Honey of the Blossoms of the centre, the Scarlet honey of the Mountains of the clouds, or the Golden juice of the fluid of jade. . . . But the emperor harbours his desires and will not let them go, and there are many things for which his heart still yearns; he may not yet attain the drug of deathlessness."

Then the Queen drew out seven peaches; two she ate herself and five she gave to the emperor. . . . She stayed with him until the fifth watch, and although she discussed matters of this world, she was not willing to talk of ghosts or spirits; and with a rustle she disappeared. . . .

Once she had gone the emperor was saddened for a long time.

[From *Ways to Paradise*, pp. 117–118.]

THE GODDESS OF THE LO RIVER

The following poem was written by Ts'ao Chih (192–232 C.E.), the brother of the emperor. It contains an elaborate description of the goddess of the Lo River, who appears to the poet as he is traveling home. Though they long for each other, they inhabit different worlds, and their love cannot be consummated. The poem reflects some of the ancient shamanistic poems of China in which deities were encouraged to join in sexual union with their human devotees. Such unions between humans and divinities, while fraught with peril, could confer spiritual power. The images in the poem also reveal the prevailing ideals for female beauty and demeanor.

Leaving the capital
To return to my fief in the east,
Yi Barrier at my back,
Up over Huan-yüan,
Passing through T'ung Valley,
Crossing Mount Ching;
The sun had already dipped in the west,
The carriage unsteady, the horses fatigued,
And so I halted my rig in the spikenard marshes,
Grazed my team of four at Lichen Fields,
Idling a while by Willow Wood,
Letting my eyes wander over the Lo.
Then my mood seemed to change, my spirit grew
    restless;
Suddenly my thoughts had scattered.
I looked down, hardly noticing what was there,
Looked up to see a different sight,
To spy a lovely lady by the slopes of the riverbank.

I took hold of the coachman's arm and asked, "Can you see her? Who could she be—a woman so beautiful!"

The coachman replied, "I have heard of the goddess of the River Lo, whose name is Fu-fei. What you see, my prince—is it not she? But what does she look like? I beg you to tell me!"

And I answered:

Her body soars lightly like a startled swan,
Gracefully, like a dragon in flight,
In splendor brighter than the autumn
    chrysanthemum,
In bloom more flourishing than the pine in spring;
Dim as the moon mantled in filmy clouds,
Restless as snow whirled by the driving wind.
Gaze far off from a distance:

She sparkles like the sun rising from morning mists;
Press closer to examine:
She flames like the lotus flower topping the green
    wave.
In her a balance is struck between plump and frail,
A measured accord between diminutive and tall,

With shoulders shaped as if by carving,
Waist narrow as though bound with white cords;
At her slim throat and curving neck
The pale flesh lies open to view,
No scented ointments overlaying it,
No coat of leaden powder applied.
Cloud-bank coiffure rising steeply,
Long eyebrows delicately arched,
Red lips that shed their light abroad,
White teeth gleaming within,
Bright eyes skilled at glances,
A dimple to round off the base of the cheek—
Her rare form wonderfully enchanting,
Her manner quiet, her pose demure.
Gentle-hearted, broad of mind,
She entrances with every word she speaks. . . .

★ ★ ★

Desiring that my sincerity first of all be known,
I undo a girdle-jade to offer as pledge.
Ah, the pure trust of that lovely lady,
Trained in ritual, acquainted with the Odes;
She holds up a garnet stone to match my gift,
Pointing down into the depths to show where we
   should meet.
Clinging to a lover's passionate faith,
Yet I fear that this spirit may deceive me;
Warned by tales of how Chiao-fu was abandoned,
I pause, uncertain and despairing;
Then, stilling such thoughts, I turn a gentler face
   toward her,
Signaling that for my part I abide by the rules of ritual.
The spirit of the Lo, moved by my action,
Paces to and fro uncertainly,
The holy light deserting her, then reappearing,
Now darkening, now shining again;
She lifts her light body in the posture of a crane,
As though about to fly but not yet taking wing.

★ ★ ★

Then the god Ping-yi calls in his winds,
The River Lord stills the waves,
While P'ing-i beats a drum,
And Nü-kua offers simple songs.
Speckled fish are sent aloft to clear the way for her
   carriage,
Jade bells are jangled for accompaniment;

Six dragon-steeds, solemn, pulling neck to neck,
She rides the swift passage of her cloudy chariot.
Whales dance at the hubs on either side,
Water birds flying in front to be her guard.
And when she has gone beyond the northern
   sandbars,
When she has crossed the southern ridges,
She bends her white neck,
Clear eyes cast down,
Moves her red lips,
Speaking slowly;
Discussing the great principles that govern friendship,
She complains that men and gods must follow
   separate ways,
Voices anger that we cannot fulfill the hopes of youth,
Holding up her gauze sleeve to hide her weeping,
Torrents of teardrops drowning her lapels.
She laments that our happy meeting must end forever,
Grieves that, once deparated, we go to different lands.

"No way to express my unworthy love,
   I give you this bright earring from south of the
      Yangtze.
   Though I dwell in the Great Shadow down under
      the waters,
   My heart will forever belong to you, my prince!"

Then suddenly I could not tell where she had gone;
To my sorrow the spirit vanished in darkness, veil-
   ing her light.
With this I turned my back on the lowland, climbed
   the height;
My feet went forward but my soul remained behind.
Thoughts taken up with the memory of her image,
I turned to look back, a heart full of despair.
Hoping that the spirit form might show itself again,
I embarked in a small boat to journey upstream,
Drifting over the long river, forgetting to return,
Wrapped in endless remembrances that made my
   longing greater.
Night found me fretful, unable to sleep;
Heavy frosts soaked me until the break of day.
I ordered the groom to ready the carriage,
Thinking to return to my eastern road,
But though I seized the reins and lifted up my whip,
I stayed lost in hesitation and could not break away.
   [From *Chinese Rhyme-Prose*, pp. 56–60.]

Folktales

"LI CHI SLAYS THE SERPENT"

The following tale can be read as a Taoist satire of the Confucian attitude toward woman: a young girl, while mouthing Confucian views about daughters, demonstrates great physical courage and ingenuity.

Li Chi Slays the Serpent

In Fukien, in the ancient state of Yüeh, stands the Yung mountain range, whose peaks sometimes reach a height of many miles. To the northwest there is a cleft in the mountains once inhabited by a giant serpent seventy or eighty feet long and wider than the span of ten hands. It kept the local people in a state of constant terror and had already killed many commandants from the capital city and many magistrates and officers of nearby towns. Offerings of oxen and sheep did not appease the monster. By entering men's dreams and making its wishes known through mediums, it demanded young girls of twelve or thirteen to feast on.

Helpless, the commandant and the magistrates selected daughters of bondmaids or criminals and kept them until the appointed dates. One day in the eighth month of every year, they would deliver a girl to the mouth of the monster's cave, and the serpent would come out and swallow the victim. This continued for nine years until nine girls had been devoured.

In the tenth year the officials had again begun to look for a girl to hold in readiness for the appointed time. A man of Chianglo county, Li Tan, had raised six daughters and no sons. Chi, his youngest girl, responded to the search for a victim by volunteering. Her parents refused to allow it, but she said, "Dear parents, you have no one to depend on, for having brought forth six daughters and not a single son, it is as if you were childless. I could never compare with Ti Jung of the Han Dynasty, who offered herself as a bondmaid to the emperor in exchange for her father's life. I cannot take care of you in your old age; I only waste your good food and clothes. Since I'm no use to you alive, why shouldn't I give up my life a little sooner? What could be wrong in selling me to gain a bit of money for yourselves?" But the father and mother loved her too much to consent, so she went in secret.

The volunteer then asked the authorities for a sharp sword and a snake-hunting dog. When the appointed day of the eighth month arrived, she seated herself in the temple, clutching the sword and leading the dog. First she took several pecks of rice balls moistened with malt sugar and placed them at the mouth of the serpent's cave.

The serpent appeared. Its head was as large as a rice barrel; its eyes were like mirrors two feet across. Smelling the fragrance of the rice balls, it opened its mouth to eat them. Then Li Chi unleashed the snake-hunting dog, which bit hard into the serpent. Li Chi herself came up from behind and scored the serpent with several deep cuts. The wounds hurt so terribly that the monster leaped into the open and died.

Li Chi went into the serpent's cave and recovered the skulls of the nine victims. She sighed as she brought them out, saying, "For your timidity you were devoured. How pitiful!" Slowly she made her way homeward.

The king of Yüeh learned of these events and made Li Chi his queen. He appointed her father magistrate of Chiang Lo county, and her mother and elder sisters were given riches. From that time forth, the district was free of monsters. Ballads celebrating Li Chi survive to this day.

[From *Sou Shen Chi* in *Chinese Fairy Tales and Fantasies*, pp. 129–131.]

HO HSIEN KU, A FEMALE IMMORTAL

The Eight Immortals figure prominently in popular Taoism, and Ho Hsien Ku is the only female among them. (Another, however, Lan Ts'ai Ho, is sometimes represented as female, sometimes as male.) While there may be some historical basis for a few of the men, the popular cycle of tales associated with all eight began during the T'ang dynasty (618–907 C.E.) and continued to develop until the Yuan dynasty (1260–1368 C.E.) when they reached their fullest official form.

Ho Hsien Ku is said to have achieved immortality through her ascetic practices, but in the following tale she is an abused servant girl who passes a test of her generosity by the other seven immortals.

How Ho Hsien Ku Became an Immortal

An old woman owned a small farm at the foot of Mi-Lo Shan. She had never completed a full day's work and had no intention of doing so. As the years progressed she had become lazier and lazier, spending most of the day maliciously gossiping with her neighbours or giving abrupt orders to her servant.

Her latest servant was a young, beautiful and generous hearted girl called Ho Hsien Ku. However hard she worked the old woman was never satisfied. She continually harangued, scolded and punished the helpless girl. Ho Hsien Ku's day began at five o'clock in the morning and rarely finished before midnight.

Besides clearing the house and preparing the food she had to plant and reap the crops and feed and care for the animals. Ho Hsien Ku did this without complaint in return for food and lodgings, but at night, when she fell exhausted on to her straw mattress, she silently wept herself to sleep.

One day the old woman set off to visit her cousin, leaving the young girl to guard the house. Ho Hsien Ku placed a small wicker chair outside the front door and sat down with her sewing basket to repair the old woman's clothes.

Through the haze of the hot afternoon sun, she saw seven figures moving slowly towards her. As they drew closer, she saw their ragged clothes, gaunt faces and downcast eyes. The beggars eventually gathered around her. One stepped forward and in pleading tones addressed Ho Hsien Ku. 'Could you please help us. We have not eaten a morsel of food in five days and now we are starving. Could you spare us a bowl of rice.'

Ho Hsien Ku was moved by their distress. If she had had the choice, she would have given the beggars all the food in the house but she was hesitant. The old woman meticulously checked the amount of food in the house each day. If a handful of rice or a spoonful of oil was missing, she would beat the girl mercilessly. But Ho Hsien Ku could not turn the beggars away. She would rather be beaten black and blue than let these unfortunate ragged men starve by the roadside.

She beckoned the beggars to rest on the straw mats in front of the house then went into the kitchen to boil a pan of rice. Ten minutes later each beggar had a bowl of rice in his hands which he devoured eagerly and gratefully. The rice gave them renewed strength and after thanking Ho Hsien Ku profusely, the beggars wandered in the direction of the nearest town. No sooner had they disappeared from view, when the old woman returned home. Without acknowledging Ho Hsien Ku, she marched straight into the kitchen to check the rice, noodles, eggs, fish, oil and wood. Ho Hsien Ku sat trembling outside the door and within a few minutes a piercing scream of anger came from the kitchen. The old woman ran from the kitchen brandishing a wooden broom.

'You thief, you ungrateful wretch! What have you done with my rice? Have you eaten it or sold it?' she demanded as she held the girl's arm with a vise-like grip.

Holding back her tears, Ho Hsien Ku recounted the whole story but the old woman had a heart like iron. 'I have no pity for these dirty beggars. You either find them and bring them back to me or I will beat your legs till you can no longer walk.'

The old woman loosened her grip on Ho Hsien Ku's arm, just enough for Ho Hsien Ku to break free and dash after the beggars. She eventually caught up with them as they were resting by the dusty roadside. Standing breathlessly before them she pleaded desperately.

'I am sorry to ask you this, but could you return with me to prove to my mistress that you ate the rice. If you do not come she will beat me black and blue.'

The beggars were only too willing to help the girl who had taken pity on them and they returned home with her. The old woman was still in a furious temper when they arrived.

'How dare you eat the food that belongs to a poor old woman,' she screamed. 'I demand that you vomit every morsel on the floor in front of me. If you don't, I will make sure that nobody in this district offers you food or water. You deserve to starve.'

The beggars had no choice but to do as they were told. One by one they vomited the noodles on to the packed earth floor in front of the house. The old woman then turned to Ho Hsien Ku and demanded vehemently, 'Eat every single noodle that has been vomited. This is the price you have to pay for feeding dirty beggars.'

She pushed the tearful and frightened Ho Hsien Ku to the floor and the helpless girl was forced to put a handful of the vomited noodles into her mouth. As soon as the noodles touched her tongue she felt her body become lighter and lighter. She felt her legs rise from the ground and her body began to float away from the spiteful old woman, away from the home where she had suffered so miserably.

The old woman began to panic and turned round to demand an explanation from the beggars, but they too had risen high above the house. She caught a last glimpse of the beggars before they disappeared into the clouds and her servant, Ho Hsien Ku, was in their midst.

The Seven Immortals had come to earth to test the young girl's character and she had proved herself worthy of immortality. Because she had endured suffering without complaint and given to the poor without thought for herself, she could work alongside the Immortals for eternity.

[From *The Eight Immortals of Taoism*, pp. 130–132.]

SUPERNATURAL WIVES—TWO TALES

A common motif in Taoist tales is the supernatural wife. Most often this is a celestial woman of great beauty who for various reasons marries a mortal man, thereby transforming his life to one of graciousness, luxury, and tranquility. Sometimes the husbands make mistakes and loose their divine wives, but in other tales, such as the one that follows, the wife takes her earthly husband up to heaven with her. In other words, she confers immortality on him. While idealized and romantic, these tales also suggest the transformative value of women on men's lives.

A Supernatural Wife

A certain Mr. Chao, of Ch'ang-shan lodged in a family of the name of T'ai. He was very badly off, and falling sick was brought almost to death's door. One day they moved him into the verandah so that it might be cooler for him; and when he awoke from a nap, lo! a beautiful girl was standing by his side.

"I am come to be your wife," said the girl in answer to his question as to who she was; to which he replied that a poor fellow like himself did not look for such luck as that, adding that, being then on his death-bed he would not have much occasion for the services of a wife. The girl said she could cure him, but he told her he very much doubted that.

"And even," continued he, "should you have any good prescription, I have not the means of getting it made up."

"I don't want medicine to cure you with," rejoined the girl, proceeding at once to rub his back and sides with her hand, which seemed to him like a ball of fire. He soon began to feel much better and asked the young lady what her name was, in order as he said, that he might remember her in his prayers.

"I am a spirit," replied she, "and you, when alive under the Han dynasty as Ch'u Sui-liang, were a benefactor of my family. Your kindness being engraven on my heart, I have at length succeeded in my search for you and am able in some measure to repay you."

Chao was dreadfully ashamed of his poverty-stricken state, and afraid that his dirty room would spoil the young lady's dress. But she made him show her in and accordingly he took her into his apartment, where there were neither chairs to sit upon, nor signs of anything to eat, saying, "You might, indeed, be able to put up with all this, but you see my larder is empty and I have absolutely no means of supporting a wife."

"Don't be alarmed about that," cried she, and in another moment he saw a couch covered with costly robes, the walls papered with a silver-flecked paper, and chairs and tables appear, the latter laden with all kinds of wine and exquisite viands. They then began to enjoy themselves and lived together as husband and wife, many people coming to witness these strange things, and being all cordially received by the young lady, who in her turn always accompanied Mr. Chao when he went out to dinner anywhere.

One day there was an unprincipled young graduate among the company, which she seemed immediately to become aware of and, after calling him several bad names, she struck him on the side of the head, causing his head to fly out of the window while his body remained inside. And there he was, stuck fast, unable to move either way until the others interceded for him and he was released. After some time visitors became too numerous and if she refused to see them they turned their anger against her husband. At length, as they were sitting together drinking with some friends at the Tuan-yang festival, a white rabbit ran in, whereupon the girl jumped up and said, "The doctor has come for me"; then, turning to the rabbit, she added, "You go on: I'll follow you."

So the rabbit went away, and then she ordered them to get a ladder and place it against a high tree in the back yard, the top of the ladder overtopping the tree. The young lady went up first and Chao close behind her, after which she called out to anybody who wished to join them to make haste up. None ventured to do so with the exception of a serving-boy belonging to the house, who followed after Chao. And thus they went up, up, up, up, until they disappeared in the clouds and were seen no more.

However, when the bystanders came to look at the ladder, they found it was only an old door-frame with the panels knocked out; and when they went into Mr. Chao's room, it was the same old, dirty, unfurnished room as before. So they determined to find out all about it from the serving-boy when he came back, but this he never did.

[From *Taoist Tales*, pp. 98–99.]

The following story represents women on three levels. The first is the earthly woman, the mother whose skill supports her family and, through her filial youngest son, establishes the prosperity of the family. The second woman is an ambiguous figure who is partly of the earth and partly of the heavens; she can be read as either a Taoist sage living alone in the wilderness or an immortal. She functions as a tester and, for those who pass her tests, a helper. The fairies are the third level of women in the story. They are celestial beings, one of whom is drawn down to the earth by the skills of the earthly mother.

The Piece of Chuang Brocade

Long, long ago there lived a Tanpu—an old Chuang woman—in a valley at the bottom of a high mountain. Her husband was dead, and she lived in a hut with her three sons. The first was called Leme, the second Letuie and the third Leje.

Her people were famous for weaving brocade, so much so that there is a particular kind known as Chuang brocade. But this Tanpu had a special gift. The flowers, plants, birds and animals she wove on her brocade were as lifelike as could be. She could always sell her brocade—it was made into waistcoats, quilt covers and bedspreads. In fact, the whole family of four lived on the labour of her hands.

One day, the Tanpu went to town to sell some brocade and buy rice with the money from it. But in the town she saw an extraordinarily beautiful coloured picture in one of the shops. It was a picture of an ideal estate, with tall buildings, a wonderful garden, vast fruitful fields, an orchard, a vegetable garden and a fish pond. All the animals you could want were there—fat chickens, ducks, cattle and sheep. Tanpu gazed and gazed at the picture. Somehow it made her feel very happy. She fell so much in love with it that finally she bought it. But of course this meant that she couldn't buy so much rice.

All the way back she kept on stopping by the road-side to look at her picture. "Oh," she murmured to herself, "if only I could live in such an estate!"

When she got home she showed the picture to her sons. They also liked it very much.

"Wouldn't it be wonderful, Leme, if we could live in such an estate!" the Tanpu said to the eldest son.

"That's an idle dream, Ami." Leme pooh-poohed the idea.

"If only we could live in such an estate, Letuie!" the Tanpu said to her second son.

"Only in the next world, Ami." Letuie also pooh-poohed it.

Then the Tanpu frowned and said to the third son, "Leje, I swear I shall die of disappointment if I can't live in such an estate." And she sighed a great sigh.

Leje thought it over. Then he said, trying to comfort his mother, "Ami, you can weave very well and the patterns you weave on your Chuang brocade are as lifelike as can be. Why don't you weave a copy of this picture? Looking at it all the time will be nearly as good as if you were living in that place."

The Tanpu meditated a few second and smacked her lips. "You're right!" she said. "I must weave such a brocade, or I'll die of disappointment."

So she bought silk yarn of every colour, set her loom up, and began to weave the picture into a brocade. . . .

She wove and wove. By the third year she finished the brocade.

Oh, how beautiful was that piece of Chuang brocade!

There it all was. Grand building, with blue-tiled roofs, green walls, red pillars and yellow gates. In front of the building was a lovely garden where beautiful flowers blossomed and goldfish swished their tails in a pond. On the left was an orchard where song-birds of every kind perched on the fruit trees, laden with red and orange fruits. On the right lay a vegetable garden where green and yellow vegetables grew plenteously. Behind the buildings was a vast grassy enclosure where sheep and cattle grazed, and chickens and ducks pecked at worms. A sheep-fold, a cattle byre and coops for the chickens and ducks could be seen on the meadow. At the foot of the hill, not far from the buildings, stretched broad fields golden with maize and rice. A clear river flowed in front of the estate and a red sun shone in the sky.

"Oh, oh, how beautiful it is!" exclaimed the three sons.

The Tanpu stretched herself, and rubbed her blood-shot eyes. Her lips parted in a smile, and then widened into a joyous laugh.

And then, all of a sudden, a great wind blew from the west. And swish! away went the brocade, out of the door, up to the sky, straight towards the east.

The Tanpu chased after it like a flash, waving her hands, and shouting at the top of her voice. But it vanished in a twinkling of an eye.

The poor Tanpu fainted outside the door.

The three brothers helped her into the house and laid her on the bed. She came to herself slowly after they had given her some ginger broth to sup. "Leme, go to the east and find me my brocade. It means more than life to me," she said to the eldest son.

Leme nodded his head, put on his straw sandals, and made for the east. After a month's travel he came to a mountain pass.

There was a stone house at the pass, with a stone horse standing at its right side. Its mouth was open, as if it wanted to eat some red berries which grew beside it. In front of the house sat a white-haired old woman, who spoke to Leme when she saw him. "Where are you going, my son?" she asked.

"I'm searching for a piece of Chuang brocade," answered Leme. "My mother has spent three years weaving it. It was blown to the east by a great gust of wind."

"The brocade was taken away by the fairies of the Sun Mountain in the east," said the old woman. "They want to use it as a pattern for their weaving, because it was so well woven. But it is very difficult to get there. First you have to knock two of your teeth out and put them into my stone horse's mouth so that it will be able to move and eat the red berries. When it has eaten ten berries you can mount it. It will take you to the Sun Mountain. On the way you must first pass the Flame Mountain, which burns fiercely. When the horse goes through the fire you must endure the burning heat with your teeth clenched. If you utter one word of complaint you will be burned to ashes. Then you will come to a big, stormy sea where waves full of floating ice will lash you. You must clench your teeth and must not shudder. The slightest shudder and you will sink to the bottom of the sea. When you have crossed the icy sea you will be able to go to the Sun Mountain and bring back your mother's brocade."

Leme felt his teeth and thought of the burning fire and the lashing, icy waves. He went white as a ghost.

The old woman looked at him and laughed, "You can't bear it, my son. Don't go. I'll give you a small iron box of gold. You can go home and live happily."

She fetched a small iron box of gold out from the stone house, and Leme took it and went away.

As he went back he thought to himself, "I shall be able to live very well with this box of gold. But I shan't take it home. Spending it all on myself will be better than spending it on four people." So he decided not to go home but went instead to the big city.

The Tanpu grew thinner and thinner. She waited for two months. But still Leme did not come back. "Letuie, go to the east, and bring me back my Chuang brocade. It is all my life to me," she said to her second son.

Letuie nodded, put on his straw sandals and headed for the east. A month later, he met the old woman sitting by the door of the stone house at the mountain pass. The old woman told him the things she had told his brother. Letuie touched his teeth, and thought of the burning fire and the lashing waves. He, too, went white as a ghost.

The old woman gave him a small iron box of gold. He took it and, like his brother, decided not to go back home but instead went to the big city.

The Tanpu waited for another two months on her bed. She got as thin as a piece of dry firewood. Every day she looked out of the door and wept. Her eyes, already bloodshot, finally became blind from crying.

Then one day, Leje said to his mother, "Ami, maybe my brothers have met with some accident on the way and therefore have not come back. Let me go. I'll bring you back the brocade."

"All right, Leje. You go." The Tanpu agreed, after thinking it over. "But take good care of yourself on the way. The neighbours will look after me."

Leje put on his straw sandals, threw out his chest and set off in big strides towards the east. It took him only half a month to get to the mountain pass. There he met the old woman sitting in front of the stone house.

The old woman told him the same things as she had told his two brothers, and said, "My son, your brothers have both gone home with a small box of gold. You may have one too."

"No, I want to get the brocade back," Leje replied. He immediately bent down and picked up a stone and knocked two of his teeth out. He put them into the mouth of the stone horse, and the big stone horse came to life and ate ten red berries. Leje jumped on its back, caught hold of its mane and dug his heels into its flanks. The horse lifted its head and neighed. And klop, klop, it galloped off towards the east.

In three days and three nights he came to the Flame Mountain. Red flames surged around him and the horse. His skin hissed in the fire. Bending low on his horse he endured it with his teeth clenched tight. It took him half a day to go through the Flame Mountain and reach the big sea. Cold waves with pieces of ice clinking in them rolled at him. Leje was cold and bruised with ice. But bending low on his horse and gritting his teeth he endured it all. Half a day later he reached the opposite shore, where the Sun Mountain stood. The kind sun shone warmly on him. How comforting it was!

From a gorgeous mansion on the top of the mountain there rang out the sound of girlish singing and merry laughter.

Leje dug his heels in again, the stone horse reared up, and in less than no time they reached the mansion. He jumped down from his horse and went in through the door. There in the hall were many beautiful fairies weaving away. And in the centre of the hall hung the Tanpu's brocade for them to copy.

They were all very startled when they saw Leje stride in. He told them what he had come for. "Very well," one of the fairies said, "we'll finish weaving it tonight and you can have it tomorrow. Will it please you to wait here for a night?"

Leje consented and the fairies brought him many delicious fruits. He was quite exhausted and fell asleep on a chair. When dusk fell, the fairies hung up a pearl, which shone like a lamp, to light the hall. They went on weaving all night by the light of the pearl.

One fairy, dressed all in red, seemed very clever and quick, and finished her piece first. When she came to compare her work with the Tanpu's, she found that the Tanpu's brocade was much better done, with its fiery red sun, crystal-clear fish pond, bright red flowers and lifelike cattle and sheep.

"Wouldn't it be wonderful if I could live in this Chuang brocade," murmured the fairy to herself. And as the other fairies had still not finished their pieces, she picked up some silk thread, and embroidered a picture of herself on the Tanpu's brocade, standing by the fish pond, looking at the red flowers.

It was already late in the night when Leje woke up. The fairies had all gone to their beds to sleep. Under the shining pearl, he saw the Tanpu's brocade on the table. "Suppose they won't give me the brocade tomorrow? I must not delay longer. My dear Ami has been sick for such a long, long time. Better if I take the brocade and go now," thought he.

So he took the brocade, folded it up and put it next his heart. Out he went, jumped on his horse, and dug his heels in. And klop, klop, the stone horse galloped off in the moonlight.

Bending over his horse with his teeth clenched, Leje first crossed the sea again and then the Flame Mountain, and soon reached the mountain pass.

There was the old woman, standing in front of the stone house, who said smiling, "Dismount, my son." Leje dismounted. The old woman took out his teeth from the stone horse's mouth and put them back in Leje's mouth. The stone horse again stood motionless beside the red-berry bush.

The old woman fetched him a pair of deerskin shoes. "Here, my son," she said. "Put these shoes on and go home quickly. Your Ami is dying!"

He put on the shoes and got home in a trice. The Tanpu, groaning weakly, lay on the bed like a piece of tinder. It really seemed as though she was dying that minute.

"Ami, Ami!" called Leje, rushing over to the bed. He took the brocade out from next his heart and spread it before her. It gleamed so brightly that the Tanpu's sight came back to her. She got up from the bed immediately and gazed with smiling eyes at the brocade, the brocade she had taken three years to weave. "Oh, my youngest son," she said, "it's too dark in here. Let's take it out in the sunlight."

Mother and son went outside and spread the brocade lovingly on the ground. And whoo-oo-oo-oo, a fragrant breeze sprang up and drew the brocade out and out, bigger and bigger, until it covered a wide, wide area.

Their little hut had disappeared in it. Instead, what should they see but big, magnificent buildings! Around them lay a garden, an orchard, a vegetable garden, fields, cattle and sheep—just exactly like the pattern on the brocade.

Suddenly the Tanpu saw a girl in red standing by the fish pond, looking at the flowers. Off went the Tanpu to her, and found she was the fairy in red, who had been brought here because she had embroidered herself into the brocade.

The Tanpu asked her to live with them in the big buildings.

She also asked her poor neighbours to come and live in her beautiful estate because they had looked after her when she was ill.

Leje married the beautiful fairy in red. They lived very happily together.

One day two beggars came to the gate of the beautiful estate. Who should they be but Leme and Letuie? Yes, they had gone to the big city with the gold they got from the old woman, but they had eaten and drunk it all away. Now they were reduced to beggary.

When they came to the beautiful estate and saw the Tanpu, Leje, and his lovely wife singing happily in the garden, they thought of the past, and were terribly ashamed, so much so that they picked up their begging sticks and crept away again.

[From *Taoist Tales*, pp. 45–51.]

STAR WOMEN

The following tale was composed by the tenth century, and it contains several common motifs, such as the studious boy interrupted at his work by an otherworldly visitation and the celestial women, literally, star-women, who confer wisdom. The Lady is probably the Mystic Woman of the Nine Heavens who is the guardian of esoteric knowledge about the stars. Through her daughters and other celestial teachers she confers knowledge on three young men.

When Scholar Yao, Notary to the Autocrat in T'ang, was relieved of his office, he dwelt in the left [part] of the city of P'u [old city in Hopei]. He had one son, and two collateral nephews, each with a distinct surname. When they had reached the years of manhood, all were uncouth dullards, and quite unworthy of him. Yao's son was older than the other two youths, and Yao was concerned that he was not studious. Despite daily admonishment and censure, they all wandered about, lazy and unregenerate. Accordingly he plaited floss-grass to make a dwelling for them on the sunlit side of Mount T'iao, hoping that, cut off from extraneous affairs, they would devote themselves to the arts and sciences. There, in the thick depths of the wooded ravines, the din and dust would not penetrate. On the day when he was to send them off, Yao gave them warning: "Each season I will test what you are capable of, and if your studies have not progressed, it will be switching and scourging for you! You must exert yourselves at this!" But when they arrived in the mountains, the two youths did not once open up a scroll, but occupied themselves only with splitting and hewing, painting and plastering. So it went for several months. Then the elder said to the other two, "Now the time for testing has come, but neither of you has attended to his books, and I fear for you!" The two lads paid him no attention at all, but the elder applied himself to his books most assiduously. One evening [a lady appears]. . . . The lady's years were something over thirty. In air and attitude she was relaxed and self-controlled, and when she looked up and down like a divinity one could not tell at all what sort of person she might be. "Do you have homes and houses?" she asked the three youths, and when each of the three youths said that he had not, she returned, "I have three daughters, distinguished in manners, and immaculate in virtue, who would be suitable mates for you three young lords." The three youths gave salutations and thanks. But the Lady did not leave— she stayed, and for each of the three youths she founded a cloister. In a twitch and a blink whole halls and extensive galleries were all built and arrayed in order. The following day coaches arrived there. Their guests were resplendent, their suite was gorgeous, surpassing a community of royal relatives. Carts and costumes were dazzling and coruscating: the light flowing from them lit up the land, and their perfumes filled the mountain valleys. Three girls descended from the carts. All were seventeen or eighteen years. The Lady conducted the three girls up into the hall, and then invited the three youths to their seats, where wine and rich viands were set out, with fruits and nuts, of kinds not often found in this world, in plenty and even superfluity—and most of them never encountered by them before. All was beyond anything the three youths might naturally expect. The Lady indicated how each of the three girls was to be paired

with her lord. When the three youths retired from their mats, with salutations and thanks, there were then several tens of maids, like divine transcendents, to escort them, and that evening they exchanged the nuptial bowls.

The Lady said to the three youths: "What men treat seriously is life; what they desire is honor. Now before a hundred days have been lost to mankind, I shall bring life to you, lords, enduring beyond this world, and position far beyond that of any mortal magnate." The three youths saluted once more and gave thanks, but were anxious lest their ignorance be a hindrance and their dull wits an obstacle. The Lady said, "Do not be anxious, milords, for this is a simple thing!" Then she enjoined her manager on earth, commanding him to summon K'ung Hsüan-fu. In a moment Master K'ung came, equipped with hat and sword. The Lady approached the staircase, and Hsüan-fu presented himself with a respectful salutation. Standing erect, the Lady asked if she might impose a slight task on him, addressing him thus: "My three sons-in-law desire to study. Will you guide them, milord?" Then Hsüan-fu gave commands to the three youths. He showed the chapter titles of the Six Registers to them with his finger—and they awoke to an understanding of their overall meaning without missing a single detail, thoroughly conversant with all as if they had always been rehearsing them. Then Hsüan-fu gave thanks, and departed. Now the Lady commanded Chou Shang-fu to show them "The Mystic Woman's Talisman and Secret Esoterica of the Yellow Pendants." The three youths acquired these too without missing anything. She sat and spoke with them again, and found that their studious penetration of all the civil and military arts was now as far-reaching as that of a Heavenly Person. Inspecting each other, the three youths were aware that now their air and poise were balanced and expansive, while their spiritual illumination was uninhibited and buoyant— they were in all respects equipped to become Commanders or Ministers. Afterwards Yao despatched a boy of his household with a supply of provisions. Such was his amazement when he arrived that he ran off. Yao asked the reason for this, and he replied with word of the richness of houses, grounds, curtains and hangings, and the abundance of lovely and ravishing beings. Yao spoke to his family in astonishment: "This is surely an enchantment of mountain ghosts!" He hurriedly summoned his three sons, but as the three youths were about to go, the Lady warned them: "Take care against leakage or disclosure, lest you bring about the application of a flogging with switches! Let there be no speaking of this!" When his three sons arrived, Yao too was amazed at the precocious expression of soul and psyche, and the relaxation and courtliness of informed replies. "All of my three sons," said Yao, "must have been suddenly possessed by ghostly beings!" He asked them desperately what was the source of this, but they said nothing. Then he flogged them several tens of times. Unable to bear the pain, they set forth everything from beginning to end. At that, Yao had them immured in a detached place. Now he had an important pedagogue as a long-term boarder, and he summoned him and spoke to him of this. The pedagogue said in surprise, "Most unusual! Most unusual! What were you doing to chastise your three sons, milord? The three youths had been instructed that if they did not divulge this matter they would surely become lords or ministers — in nobility far beyond any mortal magnate. That they have let it out was their destiny." When Yao asked him about the reason for this, he said, "I observe that none of the stars 'Weaving Woman,' 'Minx Woman' and 'Attentive Woman' are lit up. This means that these three woman-stars have come down among men, and were going to bring fortune to your three sons. Since they have now divulged one of the master-keys of Heaven, the three youths will be lucky to escape

calamity!" That night the pedagogue took Yao out to inspect the three stars, and the stars were without light. Yao then released his three sons and sent them back to the mountain. When they arrived, the three women were cold and distant, as if they did not recognize them. The Lady scolded them: "You young men did not heed my words and since you have divulged a master-key of Heaven, we must say good-bye here and now." She then made them drink a hot liquid, and when the three youths had drunk they were as benighted and uncouth as before — they did not know a single thing.

"The three woman-stars," said the pedagogue to Yao, "are still among men, and indeed are not far from this part of the country." He addressed himself closely to his intimates about their location, and someone said that it was the household of Chang Chia-chen in Ho-tung, in which there were afterwards three generations of commanders and ministers.

[From *Pacing the Void*, pp. 139–142.]

Sources

Alchemy, Medicine, Religion in the China of A.D. 320: The Nei P'ien of Ko Hung, trans. James R. Ware. Cambridge, MA, and London: M.I.T. Press, 1966.
The Book of Lieh-tzu, trans. A. C. Graham. 1960; London: John Murray, 1973.
Chinese Fairy Tales and Fantasies, by Moss Roberts. New York: Pantheon Books, 1979.
Chinese Rhyme-Prose: Poems in the Fu Form from the Han and Six Dynasties Periods, translated and with an introduction by Burton Watson. New York and London: Columbia University Press, 1971.
Chuang Tzu: Basic Writings, trans. Burton Watson. New York: Columbia University Press, 1964.
The Eight Immortals of Taoism: Legends and Fables of Popular Taoism, translated and edited by Kwok Man Ho and Joanne O'Brien. New York: Penguin, 1990.
A Gallery of Chinese Immortals, selected biographies translated from Chinese sources by Lionel Giles. London: John Murray, 1948.
Immortal Sisters: Secrets of Taoist Women, translated and edited by Thomas Cleary. Boston and Shaftesbury: Shambhala, 1989.
"The Jade Woman of Greatest Mystery," by Edward H. Schafer. *History of Religion* 17/3–4 (1978): 393–396.
Pacing the Void: T'ang Approaches to the Stars, by Edward H. Schafer. Berkeley, Los Angeles, and London: University of California Press, 1977.
Seven Taoist Masters: A Folk Novel of China, trans. Eva Wang. Boston and Shaftesbury: Shambhala, 1990.

Taoist Tales, edited with an introduction by Raymond Van Over. New York and Ontario: New American Library, 1973.
The Texts of Taoism, trans. James Legge. Volume 40 of *The Sacred Books of the East,* ed. F. Max Müller. London: Oxford University Press, 1891, 1927.
The Way of Life, by Lao Tzu, a new translation of the *Tao Te Ching* by R. B. Blakney. New York and Ontario: New American Library, 1955.
Ways to Paradise: The Chinese Quest for Immortality, by Michael Loewe. London: George Allen and Unwin, 1979.

Bibliography

Introductory Textbooks

Judith M. Boltz, *A Survey of Taoist Literature: Tenth to Seventeenth Centuries.* Berkeley, CA: Institute of East Asian Studies, University of California, 1987.
Arthur Waley, *The Way and Its Power: A Study of the Tao Te Ching.* New York: Grove Press, Inc., 1958.
Holmes Welch, *Taoism: The Parting of the Way.* Boston: Beacon Press, 1957, 1965.

Works on Women and Taoism

Emily M. Ahern, "The Power and Pollution of Chinese Women." In *Women in Chinese Society,* ed. Margery Wolf and Roxanne Witke. Stanford, CA: Stanford University Press, 1975.

Roger T. Ames, "Taoism and the Androgynous Ideal." In *Women in China: Current Directions in Historical Scholarship,* ed. Richad W. Guisso and Stanley Johannesen. Youngstown, OH: Philo Press, 1981.

Alison H. Black, "Gender and Cosmology in Chinese Correlative Thinking." In *Gender and Religion: On the Complexity of Symbols,* eds. Caroline Walker Bynum, Stevan Harrell, and Paula Richman. Boston: Beacon Press, 1986.

Ellen Marie Chen, "Tao as the Great Mother and the Influence of Motherly Love in the Shaping of Chinese Philosophy." *History of Religion,* 14/1 (1974): 51–64.

Barbara Reed, "Taoism." In *Women in World Religions,* ed. Arvind Sharma. Albany, NY: State University of New York Press, 1987.

Edward H. Schafer, *The Divine Woman: Dragon Ladies and Rain Maidens.* San Francisco: North Point Press, 1980.

ALTERNATIVE RELIGIOUS MOVEMENTS

Introduction

Most of the people discussed in this chapter led lives surrounded by controversy and were dogged by scandal either in their own lives or in the lives of their followers (Blavatsky, Eddy, Gurdjieff). This has often contributed to their neglect by serious scholars, though a new generation of scholars is beginning to give them the attention they deserve as important shapers of modern religious history. All, except for Ann Lee, have followers to this day.

The movements represented in this chapter are particularly meaningful for the study of women in religion because women were prominent, when not actually instrumental, in their founding; and women participated, and continue to participate, in these movements in large numbers. Indeed, women often greatly outnumber men.

Dissenting Christian Movements

Many religious movements grew out of the European Reformation and opposed the official state churches with their "true" churches. These radical and mystical forms of Protestantism emphasized the personal and individual experience of God, or the Holy Spirit, which empowered both women and men to preach and did away with an ordained clergy. Its adherents often saw their form of Christianity as a return to the early, egalitarian Christianity practiced by Jesus and the apostles. In these groups women eagerly took up active religious roles.

THE QUAKERS

WOMEN'S RIGHT TO PREACH

The Quakers, or the Religious Society of Friends, arose in the 1650s in England under the inspiration of their first leader, George Fox (1624–1691). They emphasized individual religious experience, which can lead to preaching by any Friend, female or male. The only authority was the direct inspiration they received from God, and therefore they rejected offical ecclesiastical and civil authority for which they were persecuted, especially in New England by the Puritans.

Margaret Fell (1614–1702) was an early convert (in 1648) and preacher who married George Fox in 1669. She is known as the "mother" of the Society, not only because she was Fox's wife, but for her own formidable organizational abilities, her fortitude in prison, and her writings. The following excerpt is from *Women's Speaking Justified, Proved and Allowed of by the Scriptures,* which she wrote while serving a four-year prison sentence as a result of religious persecution. This is a theological proof for the equal religious status of women based on biblical authority. In her text, "the Apostle" refers to Paul.

Whereas it hath been an Objection in the minds of many, and several times hath been objected by the Clergy, or Ministers, and others, against Women's speaking in the Church; and so consequently may be taken, that they are condemned for meddling in the things of God; the ground of which Objection, is taken from the Apostles words, which he writ in his first Epistle to the *Corinthians,* chap. 14, vers. 34, 35. And also what he writ to *Timothy* in the first Epistle; chap. 2, vers. 11, 12. But how far they wrong the

404 AN ANTHOLOGY OF SACRED TEXTS BY AND ABOUT WOMEN

Apostles intentions in these Scriptures, we shall show clearly when we come to them in their course and order. But first let me lay down how God himself hath manifested his Will and Mind concerning women, and unto women.

And first, when *God created Man in his own Image: in the Image of God created he them, Male and Female: and God blessed them, and God said unto them, Be fruitful, and multiply: And God said, behold, I have given you of every Herb, etc. Gen.* 1. Here God joins them together in his own Image, and makes no such distinctions and differences as men do; for though they be weak, he is strong; and as he said to the Apostle, *His Grace is sufficient,* and his *strength is made manifest in weakness,* 2 Cor. 12.9. And such hath the Lord chosen, even *the weak thing of the world, to confound the things which are mighty and things which are despised, hath God chosen to bring to nought things that are,* I. Cor. 1. And God hath put no such difference between Male and Female as men would make.

★ ★ ★

And now to the Apostles words, which is the ground of the great Objection against Women's speaking: And first, I Cor. 14. let the Reader seriously read that Chapter, and see the need and drift of the Apostle in speaking these words: for the Apostle is there exhorting the *Corinthians* unto charity, and to desire Spiritual gifts, and not to speak in an unknown tongue, and not to be Children in understanding, but to be Children in malice, but in understanding to be men; and that the spirits of the Prophets should be subject to the Prophets, for God is not the author of Confusion, but of Peace. And then he saith, *Let your Women keep silence in the Church, etc.*

Where it doth plainly appear that the women, as well as others, that were among them, were in confusion, for he saith, *How is it Brethen? When ye come together, every one of you hath a Psalm, hath a Doctrine, hath a Tongue, hath a revelation, hath an Interpretation? Let all things be done to edifying.* Here was no edifying, but all was in confusion speaking together: Therefore he saith, *If any man speak in an unknown tongue, let it be by two, or at most by three, and that by course and let one interpret, but if there be no Interpreter, let him keep silence in the Church.* Here the Man is commanded to keep silence as well as the woman, when they are in confusion and out of order.

[From *Womens Speaking Justified*, pp. 3, 8.]

WOMEN'S MEETINGS

The Quakers held two kinds of meetings: meetings for worship and meetings for business such as the registering of births, marriages and deaths as well as to aid Friends in need. The Meetings for Business were held monthly for a town, quarterly for a county, and yearly for a state or nation. In 1670 George Fox instituted independent Women's Meetings for Business, which gave women official roles in the administration of the society. A correspondence sprang up between various Women's Meetings, and the following excerpt is from the yearly meeting held at York on April 28, 1688. In it the women describe the presence of God among them and their confidence that God approves of what they are doing. They also give advice on how Quaker women should conduct themselves, do their work, and how to go about marrying.

A TESTIMONY for the Lord and his Truth, given forth by the women friends, at their yearly meeting, at York, being a tender salutation of love, to their friends and sisters, in the several monthly meetings, in this county, and elsewhere, greeting.

Dear friends and sisters,

We, being met together in the fear of the Lord, to wait upon him for his ancient power, to order us, and, in his wisdom and counsel, to guide us in our exercise relating to church affairs: It hath pleased him to break in among us in a glorious manner, to our great satisfaction, and he hath filled our meeting with his living presence, and crowned our assembly with his heavenly power, and opened the fountain of life unto us, and caused the streams of his love freely to flow among us, and run from vessel to vessel, to the gladding of our hearts, which causeth living praise, and hearty thanksgiving to be rendered unto him, who alone is worthy. And, friends, we hereby signify to you, that there hath been many living testimonies delivered among us from the divine openings of the spirit of life, in many brethren and sisters, whereby we are fully satisfied that the Lord is well pleased with this our service, and doth accept our sacrifices and free-will offerings, and returns an answer of peace unto our bosoms, which is greatly our reward.

★ ★ ★

And now to you young women, whom our souls love, and whom the Lord delighteth to do good unto, and hath visited with the tastes of his love, be you ordered by him in all things, that, in your modest and chaste behaviour, your comely and decent dresses in your apparel, and in all other things you may be good examples to others.

★ ★ ★

And, friends, be not concerned in reference to marriage out of God's fear, but first wait to know your Maker to become your husband and the bridegroom of your souls, then you will come to know that you are not your own, but that he must have the ordering and disposing of you, in soul, body and spirit, which are all his; for he, being the only one unto you, and the chiefest of ten thousand among you, will be your beloved and your friend. Oh! friends, this state is happy, and blessed are they that attain it, and live in it; the Lord is not unmindful of them, but in his own time . . . can provide meet helps for them; then will your marriage be honourable, being orderly accomplished with the assent of parents, and the unity of friends, and an honour to God, and comfort to your own souls: then husbands and children are a blessing in the hands of the Lord, and you will arise in your day, age and generation, as mothers in Israel, as those holy ancients whose living testimonies reacheth unto us, and blessed memories liveth with us according to our measures; as Lydia open hearted

to God and one to another . . . careful to do one another good, as Deborah concerned in the commonwealth of Israel, and as Jael zealous for the truth, who was praised above women. And you, friends, who are under the present concern, and in your day's work, do it not negligently, not with careless minds, but be you diligent in every of your women's meetings, to take the care upon them, and so far as may answer truth, do you endeavour that nothing be practised among you, but what tends to God's honour, and one another's comfort; let nothing be indulged or connived at in any, whereby truth is dishonoured, and let that be cherished and encouraged in all wherewith truth is honoured; and these our testimonies cast not carelessly into a corner, but some time peruse them, and mark well the wholesome advice therein; that our travel may be answered; the Lord honoured, and you reap the benefit; and let a record be kept from month to month, and from year to year, of the Lord's dealing with us, and mercy to us, to future ages; that from age to age, and one generation to another, his own works may praise him, to whom all praises do belong, and be ascribed both now and for ever.

From our yearly meeting at York, the 28th of the 4th month, 1688.

Signed on the behalf of the meeting by Catharine Whitton, Mary Waite, Judith Boulby, Deborah Winn, Elizabeth Sedman, Eliz. Beckwith, Frances Taylor, Mary Lindley.

[From Epistle from the Womens Yearly Meeting at York, 1688, pp. 3–9.]

The Shakers

ANN LEE – GOD AS MOTHER AND FATHER

Ann Lee (1736–1784) was the founder of the American Shakers, a group that referred to themselves as the United Society of Believers in Christ's Second Appearing. The Shakers originated in 1747 in England as a breakaway group from the Quakers. The name Shaker was used to describe the unusual practices of the Believers, who held highly emotional services in which people danced, spoke in tongues, shouted, sang, or just generally shook with emotion.

Ann Lee was born into a poor, working-class family in Manchester, England, where she eventually become involved with the English Shakers. She married and had four children, all of whom died when very young. Lee saw the loss of her children and the pain she had suffered while giving birth as a punishment for sexual desire. This negative view of sexuality was confirmed for her in a vision she had in 1770 in which it was revealed to her that sexuality had been the cause of the expulsion from Eden and that only by giving up sex could human beings be reconciled to God. Hence the emphasis on celibacy among the Shakers. In 1774 she and eight of her followers left for America. She was persecuted and suffered brutal beatings, which contributed to her premature death in 1784.

Ann Lee understood her womanhood as an essential part of her ministry as did her followers. This is particularly clear in her formulation of God as both mother and father, with a tendency to emphasize God as mother. Since all believers had been children with mothers, Lee built upon this common experience in developing the notion that the mystical motherhood of God could be felt as a personal reality. Believers saw Ann Lee, whom they called Mother Ann, as their spiritual mother through whom they had been reborn to a new life into "Christlife." Further, they believed that just as God's spirit had incarnated in male form through Christ, God's spirit now was incarnated in the female form of Mother Ann.

This theology, combined with celibacy, the shared labor of both sexes, and the emphasis on the religious experience of each individual led to an extraordinarily egalitarian community in which leadership at every level was equally shared between women and men.

Ann Lee was illiterate and she left no writings. The following two excerpts are from *Summary Views,* a work written by the Elder Calvin Green, a prominent Shaker leader of the 1820s and 1830s. The first excerpt presents the Shaker understanding of God as both Mother and Father. The second excerpt shows how this theological understanding was carried through in their understanding of the equalitarian roles of women and men in the true church. Note the centrality of celibacy for the equal status of women.

To have just conceptions of the real character of that Divine PRINCIPLE or BEING whom we call GOD, it is necessary to understand the nature of his attributes, which stand in perfect correspondence with each other, and which are fully displayed in his Word and Works, and clearly manifest his Divine perfections. "For the invisible things of him from the creation of the world are clearly seen, being understood by the things that are made." (Rom. i. 20.)

It is certainly most reasonable and consistent with infinite Wisdom, that the image and likeness of God should be most plainly manifested in man, who was made the most noble part of the natural creation. Accordingly we read, "And God said, Let us make man in our image, after our likeness. So God created man in his own image; in the image of God created he him; male and female created he them." Hence it must appear evident that there exists in the DEITY, the likeness of male and female, forming the unity of that creative and good principle from which proceeds the work of *Father and Mother,* manifested in *Power* to create, and *Wisdom* to bring forth into proper order, all the works of God. If it were not so, then man, who was created male and female, as father and mother, could not, with any propriety, be said to show forth the image and likeness of God. But the manifestation of Father and Mother in the Deity, being spiritual, does not imply two *Persons,* but two *Incomprehensibles,* of one substance, from which proceed all Divine power and life.

[FOOTNOTE.] This shows something essentially different from "three distinct persons in one God," all in the masculine gender, as established by a council of catholic bishops in the fourth century,

and which has been the prevailing creed among their blind and bigoted followers to this day.

The Almighty is manifested as proceeding from everlasting, as the *first Source* of all power, and the *fountain* of all good, the *Creator* of all good beings, and is the ETERNAL FATHER; and the Holy Spirit of Wisdom, who was the *Co-worker* with him, from everlasting, is the ETERNAL MOTHER, the *bearing Spirit* of all the works of God. This is according to the testimony of her own inspiration. (See Prov. viii; and iii. 17, 18, 19.)

★ ★ ★

As the true church of Christ, which is his body, is composed of male and female, as its members; and as there must be a correspondent spiritual union between the male and female, to render the church complete, as a spiritual body; so it is essentially necessary that such a spiritual union should exist in the head of that body, which is Christ; otherwise there could be no source from which such a correspondent, spiritual union could flow to that body. It must be admitted by every reasonable person, that the order of man cannot be complete without the woman. If so, then the church cannot exist, in its proper order, without male and female members; for, "neither is the man without the woman, nor the woman without the man, in the Lord." (1 Cor. xi. 11.) And it would be very unreasonable to suppose that the body of Christ should be more complete and perfect, in its order, than the head. This would give the body a superiority over the head.

This spiritual union between the male and female,

in the body and in the head of the church, is that which the apostle calls a *great mystery*. (Eph. v. 32.) And indeed it is a great mystery to the lost children of man, who seem to have no conception of any other union between the male and female, than that which is natural, according to the order of the flesh. Nor do they seem to know any other design in the creation of the female, nor any other essential use for her than that of carnal enjoyment in a sexual union, and the production of offspring through that medium. But the work of Christ, being a spiritual work, the union must therefore be spiritual; and it is impossible for souls to come into this work, and enjoy this union, unless the Spirit of Christ become their life.

Since then, Christ must appear in every female, as well as in every male, before they can be saved; and since that Divine Spirit has appeared in one man, whom God has chosen as the Captain of our salvation, and an example of righteousness to all men; is it not reasonable and consistent that the same anointing power (which is Christ) should also appear in a woman, and distinguish her as a leader, and an example of righteousness to all women?

It may be asked, How can Christ appear in a woman? With the same propriety we might ask, how can Christ appear in a man? Christ is a Spirit: "The Lord is that Spirit." (2 Cor. iii. 17.) In that Spirit is contained the only power of salvation. If Christ could not appear in a man, then no man could be saved; so also, if Christ could not appear in a woman, then no woman could be saved. Christ first appeared in Jesus of Nazareth, by which he was constituted the head of the new and spiritual creation of God. The Spirit of Christ was in the primitive church; and the Spirit of Christ is also in every one of his true and faithful followers. The Spirit of Christ is the same, whether revealed in man, woman or child.

[From *The Shakers,* pp. 214–216.]

Christian Science

MARY BAKER EDDY—ON GENESIS

Mary Baker Eddy (1821–1910) is one of the very few woman founders of a thriving and important religious movement. She was raised in rural New Hampshire in the tradition of the American Puritanism she never really abandoned. Her early life was filled with suffering and loss as well as frequent bouts of ill health. In 1866 she experienced a spiritual healing which she attributed to reading about one of Jesus' healings in the Gospel of Matthew. This led to her understanding that Jesus had knowledge of a "science" that was the foundation of all his works and that through understanding this science Jesus' works, such as healing, were repeatable. She elaborates on these points in *Science and Health with Key to the Scriptures,* which was published in 1875. In 1879 she and her followers founded the Church of Christ, Scientist. Her last major achievement was the founding in 1908 of *The Christian Science Monitor,* a highly respected national newspaper.

The following excerpts from *Science and Health with Key to the Scriptures* are taken from Baker's exegesis of Genesis 1–3, in which she expresses her view of the ultimate unreality of materiality, belief in which is the main cause of suffering. This anti-material stance also affects her theory of gender, which is that gender is mental, not material. She adds to her theories about gender that the ideal man corresponds to intelligence and truth, while the ideal woman corresponds to life and love. Notice also, in this context, her discussion of the feminine and masculine aspects of God. Of particular interest is her lack of significant comments on Eve's punishment to bring forth children in great pain. This is connected to her belief that God does not permit any human suffering.

Genesis i. 1.   In the beginning God created the heaven and the earth.

The infinite has no beginning. This word *beginning* is employed to signify *the only,*—that is, the eternal verity and unity of God and man, including, the universe. The creative Principle—Life, Truth, and Love—is God. The universe reflects God. There is but one creator and one creation. This creation consists of the unfolding of spiritual ideas and their identities, which are embraced in the infinite Mind and forever reflected. These ideas range from the infinitesimal to infinity, and the highest ideas are the sons and daughters of God.

* * *

Genesis i. 12.   And the earth brought forth grass, and herb yielding seed after his kind, and the tree yielding fruit, whose seed was in itself, after his kind: and God saw that it was good.

God determines the gender of His own ideas. Gender is mental, not material. The seed within itself is the pure thought emanating from divine Mind. The feminine gender is not yet expressed in the text. *Gender* means simply *kind* or *sort,* and does not necessarily refer either to masculinity or femininity. The word is not confined to sexuality, and grammars always recognize a neuter gender, neither male nor female. The Mind or intelligence of production names the female gender last in the ascending order of creation. The intelligent individual idea, be it male or female, rising from the lesser to the greater, unfolds the infinitude of Love.

* * *

Genesis i. 27.   So God created man in His own image, in the image of God created He him; male and female created He them.

To emphasize this momentous thought, it is repeated that God made man in His own image, to reflect the divine Spirit. It follows that *man* is a generic term. Masculine, feminine, and neuter genders are human concepts. In one of the ancient languages the word for *man* is used also as the synonym of *mind.* This definition has been weakened by anthropomorphism, or a humanization of Deity. The word *anthropomorphic,* in such a phrase as "an anthropomorphic God," is derived from two Greek words, signifying *man* and *form,* and may be defined as a mortally mental attempt to reduce Deity to corporeality. The life-giving quality of Mind is Spirit, not matter. The ideal man corresponds to creation, to intelligence, and to Truth. The ideal woman corresponds to Life and to Love. In divine Science, we have not as much authority for considering God masculine, as we have for considering Him feminine, for Love imparts the clearest idea of Deity.

* * *

Genesis ii. 21, 22.   And the Lord God [Jehovah, Yawah] caused a deep sleep to fall upon Adam, and he slept: and He took one of his ribs, and closed up the flesh instead thereof; and the rib, which the Lord God [Jehovah] had taken from man, made He a woman, and brought her unto the man.

Here falsity, error, credits Truth, God, with inducing a sleep or hypnotic state in Adam in order to perform a surgical operation on him and thereby create woman. This is the first record of magnetism. Beginning creation with darkness instead of light,— materially rather than spiritually,— error now simulates the work of Truth, mocking Love and declaring what great things error has done. Beholding the creations of his own dream and calling them real and God-given, Adam—*alias* error—gives them names. Afterwards he is supposed to become the basis of the creation of woman and of his own kind, calling them *mankind,*—that is, a kind of man.

But according to this narrative, surgery was first performed mentally and without instruments; and this may be a useful hint to the medical faculty. Later in human history, when the forbidden fruit was bringing forth fruit of its own kind, there came a suggestion of change in the *modus operandi,*—that man should be born of woman, not woman again taken from man. It came about, also, that instruments were needed to assist the birth of mortals. The first system of suggestive obstetrics has changed. Another change will come as to the nature and origin of man, and this revelation will destroy the *dream* of existence, reinstate reality, usher in Science and the glorious fact of creation, that both man and woman proceed from God and are His eternal children, belonging to no lesser parent.

* * *

Genesis iii. 11, 12.   And He said, Who told thee that thou wast naked? Hast thou eaten of the tree, whereof I commanded thee that thou shouldst not eat? And the man said, The woman whom Thou gavest to be with me, she gave me of the tree, and I did eat.

Here there is an attempt to trace all human errors directly or indirectly to God, or good, as if He were the creator of evil. The allegory shows that the snake-talker utters the first voluble lie, which beguiles the woman and demoralizes the man. Adam, *alias mortal error,* charges God and woman with his own dereliction, saying, "The woman, whom Thou gavest me, is responsible." According to this belief, the rib taken from Adam's side has grown into an evil mind, named *woman,* who aids man to make sinners more rapidly than he can alone. Is this an help meet for man?

Materiality, so obnoxious to God, is already found in the rapid deterioration of the bone and flesh which came from Adam to form Eve. The belief in material life and intelligence is growing worse at every step, but error has its suppositional day and multiplies until the end thereof.

Truth, cross-questioning man as to his knowledge of error, finds woman the first to confess her fault. She says, "The serpent beguiled me, and I did eat;"

as much as to say in meek penitence, "Neither man nor God shall father my fault." She has already learned that corporeal sense is the serpent. Hence she is first to abandon the belief in the material origin of man and to discern spiritual creation. This hereafter enabled woman to be the mother of Jesus and to behold at the sepulchre the risen Saviour, who was soon to manifest the deathless man of God's creating. This enabled woman to be first to interpret the Scriptures in their true sense, which reveals the spiritual origin of man.

★ ★ ★

Genesis iii. 16. Unto the woman He said, I will greatly multiply thy sorrow and thy conception: in sorrow thou shalt bring forth children; and thy desire shall be to thy husband, and he shall rule over thee.

Divine Science deals its chief blow at the supposed material foundations of life and intelligence. It dooms idolatry. A belief in other gods, other creators, and other creations must go down before Christian Science. It unveils the results of sin as shown in sickness and death. When will man pass through the open gate of Christian Science into the heaven of Soul, into the heritage of the first born among men? Truth is indeed "the way."

[From *Science and Health with Key to the Scriptures,* pp. 502–535.]

WOMAN'S SUFFRAGE MOVEMENT

THE WOMAN'S BIBLE

Elizabeth Cady Stanton (1815–1902) was a woman of phenomenal energy: She gave birth to and raised seven children while actively working in temperance, antislavery, and women's rights organizations. Not surprisingly, she was one of the first women to be vocal about the burden of running a household and raising children. Stanton often referred to the frequent use of the Bible in defense of what she opposed: slavery, intemperance, and the subjection of women. She especially felt that Christianity could and did exert a powerful influence on women's domestic situation.

In 1870 the Church of England began work on a revised Bible translation which was unfavorably received, and Stanton felt the time was ripe for women to set to work on those sections of the Bible that dealt directly with women. To this end she organized a committee of women scholars. The result of this committee, *The Woman's Bible,* published in 1895, was fiercely criticized.

The first excerpt from *The Woman's Bible* is Numbers 12, with Elizabeth Cady Stanton's comments on it. The second is Revelations 12, and the commentator is Stanton's colleague, Matilda Joslyn Gage (1826–1898), a woman as much interested in women's rights as she was in the occult (note her reference to Madame Blavatsky).

Numbers xii.

And Miriam and Aaron spake against Moses because of the Ethiopian woman whom he had married.

2 And they said, Hath the Lord indeed spoken only by Moses? hath he not spoken also by us? And the Lord heard it.

3 (Now the man Moses was very meek, above all the men which were upon the face of the earth.)

5 And the Lord came down in the pillar of the cloud and stood in the door of the tabernacle and called Aaron and Miriam, and they both came forth.

6 And He said, Hear now my words: If there be a prophet among you, I, the Lord, will make myself known unto him in a vision, and will speak unto him in a dream.

8 With him will I speak mouth to mouth, even apparently, and not in dark speeches; and the similitude of the Lord shall he behold; wherefore then were ye not afraid to speak against my servant Moses?

9 And the anger of the Lord was kindled against them; and He departed.

10 And the cloud departed from off the tabernacle; and, behold, Miriam became leprous, white as snow; and Aaron looked upon Miriam, and behold, she was leprous.

11 And Aaron said unto Moses, Alas, my lord, I beseech thee, lay not the sin upon us, wherein we have done foolishly, and wherein we have sinned.

13 And Moses cried unto the Lord, saying Heal her now, O God, I beseech thee.

15 And Miriam was shut out from the camp seven days; and the people journeyed not till Miriam was brought in again.

Here we have the first mention of Moses's second marriage, but the name of the woman is not given, though she is the assigned cause of the sedition. Both Aaron and Miriam had received a portion of the prophetic genius that distinguished Moses, and they naturally thought that they should have some share in the government, at least to make a few suggestions, when they thought Moses made a blunder. Miriam was older than Moses, and had at this time the experience of 120 years. When Moses was an infant on the River Nile, Miriam was intrusted by his parents to watch the fate of the infant in the bulrushes and the daughter of Pharaoh in her daily walks by the river side. It was her diplomacy that secured the child's own mother for his nurse in the household of the King of Egypt.

It is rather remarkable, if Moses was as meek as he is represented in the third verse, that he should have penned that strong assertion of his own innate modesty. There are evidences at this and several other points that Moses was not the sole editor of the Pentateuch, if it can be shown that he wrote any part of it. Speaking of the punishment of Miriam, Clarke in his commentaries says it is probable that Miriam was chief in this mutiny; hence she was punished while Aaron was spared. A mere excuse for man's injustice; had he been a woman he would have shared the same fate. The real reason was that Aaron was a priest. Had he been smitten with leprosy, his sacred office would have suffered and the priesthood fallen into disrepute.

As women are supposed to have no character or sacred office, it is always safe to punish them to the full extent of the law. So Miriam was not only afflicted with leprosy, but also shut out of the camp for seven days. One would think that potential motherhood should make women as a class as sacred as the priesthood. In common parlance we have much fine-spun theorizing on the exalted office of the mother, her immense influence in moulding the character of her sons; "the hand that rocks the cradle moves the world," etc., but in creeds and codes, in constitutions and Scriptures, in prose and verse, we do not see these lofty paeans recorded or verified in living facts. As a class, women were treated among the Jews as an inferior order of beings, just as they are to-day in all civilized nations. And now, as then, men claim to be guided by the will of God.

In this narrative we see thus early woman's desire to take some part in government, though denied all share in its honor and dignity. Miriam, no doubt, saw the humiliating distinctions of sex in the Mosaic code and customs, and longed for the power to make the needed amendments. In criticising the discrepancies in Moses's character and government, Miriam showed a keen insight into the common principles of equity and individual conduct, and great self-respect and self-assertion in expressing her opinions — qualities most lacking in ordinary women.

Evidently the same blood that made Moses and Aaron what they were, as leaders of men, flowed also in the veins of Miriam. As daughters are said to be more like their fathers and sons like their mothers, Moses probably inherited his meekness and distrust of himself from his mother, and Miriam her self-reliance and heroism from her father. Knowing these laws of heredity, Moses should have averted the punishment of Miriam instead of allowing the full force of God's wrath to fall upon her alone. If Miriam had helped to plan the journey to Canaan, it would no doubt have been accomplished in forty days instead of forty years. With her counsel in the cabinet, the people might have enjoyed peace and prosperity, cultivating the arts and sciences, instead of making war on other tribes, and burning offerings to their gods. Miriam was called a prophetess, as the Lord had, on some occasions, it is said, spoken through her, giving messages to the women. After their triumphal escape from Egypt, Miriam led the women in their songs of victory. With timbrels and dances, they chanted that grand chorus that has been echoed and re-echoed for centuries in all our cathedrals round the globe. Catholic writers represent Miriam "as a type of the Virgin Mary, being legislatrix over the Israelitish women, especially endowed with the spirit of prophecy."

[From *The Woman's Bible,* pp. 101–113.]

Revelation xii.

And there appeared a great wonder in heaven; a woman clothed with the sun, and the moon under her feet, and upon her head a crown of twelve stars:

2 And she being with child travailed in birth.

3 And there appeared another wonder in heaven; and behold a great red dragon, having seven heads and ten horns, and seven crowns upon his heads.

4 And his tail drew the third part of the stars of heaven, and the dragon stood before the woman to devour her child as soon as it was born.

5 And she brought forth a man child, that was caught up unto God.

6 And the woman fled into the wilderness, where she hath a place prepared of God.

13 And when the dragon saw that he was cast unto the earth, he was wroth with the woman, and went to make war with the remnant of her seed.

The constellation Draco, the Great Serpent, was at one time the ruler of the night, being formerly at the very centre of the heavens and so large that it was called the Great Dragon. Its body spread over seven signs of the Zodiac, which were called its seven heads. So great a space did it occupy, that, in mystic language, it "drew a third part of the stars from heaven and cast them to the earth." Thuban, in its tail, was formerly the pole-star, or "judge of the earth." It approached much nearer the true pole than Cynosura, the present pole-star, which is one and a half degrees distant and will never approach nearer than twelve minutes, while Thuban was only ten minutes distant.

At an early day serpents were much respected; they were thought to have more "pneuma" or spirit than any other living thing and were termed "fiery." For this cause high initiates were called "naga," or serpents of wisdom; and a living serpent was always carried in the celebration of the mysteries. During the brilliant eighteenth and nineteenth Egyptian dynasties, Draco was a great god; but when this constellation lost its place in the heavens, and Thuban ceased to be the guiding sidereal Divinity, it shared the fate of all the fallen gods. "The gods of our fathers are our devils," says an Arabic proverb. When Re-Veilings was written, Draco had become a fallen angel representing evil spirituality. By precessional motion the foot of Hercules rests upon its head, and we find it depicted as of the most material color, red.

Colors and jewels are parts of astrology; and ancient cities, as Ectabana, were built and colored after the planets. The New Jerusalem of Re-Veilings is purely an astrological city, not to be understood without a knowledge of mystic numbers, letters, jewels and colors. So, also, the four and twenty elders of Re-Veilings are twenty-four stars of the Chaldean Zodiac, "counsellors" or "judges," which rose and set with it. Astrology was brought into great prominence by the visit of the magi, the zodiacal constellation Virgo, the "woman with a child," ruling Palestine, in which country Bethlehem is situated. The great astronomer and astrologer, Ptolemy, judged the character of countries from the signs ruling them, as to this day is done by astrologers.

The woman attacked by the great red dragon, Cassiopea, was known as Nim-Makh, the Mighty Lady. For many centuries, at intervals of about three hundred years, a brilliant star suddenly appeared in this constellation, remaining visible a few months, then as suddenly disappearing. In mystic phraseology this star was a child. It was seen A.D. 945, A.D. 1264, and was noted by Tycho Brahe and other astronomers in 1562, when it suddenly became so brilliant that it could be seen at midday, gradually assuming the appearance of a great conflagration, then as gradually fading away. Since thus caught up to the throne of God, this star-child has not again appeared, although watched for by astronomers during the past few years. The Greeks, who borrowed so much from the Egyptians, created from this book the story of Andromeda and the monster sent by Neptune to destroy her, while Madame Blavatsky says that St. John's dragon is Neptune, a symbol of Atlantaean magi.

The crown of twelve stars upon the head of the apocalyptic woman are the twelve constellations of the Zodiac. Clothed with the sun, woman here represents the Divinity of the feminine, its spirituality as opposed to the materiality of the masculine; for in Egypt the sun, as giver of life, was regarded as feminine, while the moon, shining by reflected light, was looked upon as masculine. With her feet upon the moon, woman, corresponding to and representing the soul, portrays the ultimate triumph of spiritual things over material things—over the body, which man, or the male principle, corresponds to and represents.

"There was war in heaven." The wonderful progress and freedom of woman, as woman, within the last half century, despite the false interpretation of the Bible by the Church and by masculine power, is the result of this great battle; and all attempts to destroy her will be futile. Her day and hour have arrived; the dragon of physical power over her, the supremacy of material things in the world, as depicted by the male principle, are yielding to the spiritual, represented by woman. The eagle, true bird of the sun and emblem of our own great country, gives his wings to her aid; and the whole earth comes to help her against her destroyer.

And thus must Re-Veilings be left with much truth untouched, yet with the hope that what has been written will somewhat help to a comprehension of this greatly misunderstood yet profoundly "sacred" and "secret" book, whose true reading is of such vast importance to the human race.

[From *The Woman's Bible,* pp. 181–183.]

Occultism and Esotericism

Occultism refers to diverse movements that have in common a desire to learn and manipulate the secret workings of the universe, workings that cannot be recognized by the instruments or knowledge of modern science. In this way occultism can be distinguished from esotericism, which tends to emphasize the philosophical and mystical implications of such secret workings rather than attempt to control them. Underlying all these movements is the general belief that the cosmos is a web of interdependent relationships that can be understood by various means such as esoteric knowledge and different forms of divination such as astrology and tarot cards. Participants in these movements pursue an individualistic path of spiritual development; each person learns for her or himself.

The earliest occult movements in the West can be traced to the early centuries of the Common Era and continue unabated to the present, though at different times and in different places one aspect dominated others, for instance alchemy or magic. In modern times occultism often blended with spiritualism, especially in the nineteenth century. Spiritualism postulates the existence of another, supernatural world in addition to the real world. Breaching the boundaries between these two worlds is their main goal, and this is done through seances and trances mainly to contact the dead. Most of the "spirit" teachers contacted by occultists are believed to have once been living beings.

Women have been important to such movements in three ways. First, some women were able to achieve leadership roles. Second, women participated in these movements in large numbers. Third, ideas about the "true" spiritual nature of women proliferated in ways that both complemented and contended with the nascent feminist movement.

THE THEOSOPHICAL SOCIETY

The Theosophical Society was founded in 1875 in New York City by the Russian aristocrat Helena P. Blavatsky, referred to as HPB by Theosophists, and the American lawyer and journalist Colonel Henry S. Olcott. In a brief period of time it became an international movement of great spiritual and political power and was itself the source of several other significant occult movements, such as Alice Bailey's Arcane School, Rudolf Steiner's Anthroposophy and Krishnamurti. In Asia the Society was active in the Indian Independence Movement and in the international revival of Buddhism. In Europe and America the Society spread the religious and philosophical ideas of Asia. Its purpose was to be a society that investigated and integrated the ideas of science, religion, and philosophy in an environment of universal brotherhood without distinction as to race, creed, sex, caste, or color.

The Society believes in a hidden or esoteric knowledge that can lead individuals to enlightenment, or salvation, who pursue a path seeking such knowledge by learning the secret law of the universe.

Helena Petrovna Blavatsky—The Secret Doctrine

At about the age of eighteen Helena Petrovna Blavatsky (1831–1891) left her native Russia, abandoning her husband of less than a year, and began a life of travel and study. She was, by all reports, an independent and tempestuous woman, who alternately shocked and fascinated her contemporaries. Many of the details of her life remain undocumented. She received more than her fair share of slander, so it is difficult to describe her life, especially her early years, with any degree of accuracy other than to say that she showed an early and sustained interest in occultism and did indeed travel throughout the world seeking spiritual knowledge. When she arrived in New York in 1873 she became involved with the spiritualism movement but was critical of it. She was more interested in the philosophical aspects of spirituality and eventually found people with similar interests such as Col. Olcott, with whom she founded The Theosophical Society.

Blavatsky described herself as a transmitter, not an originator, of spiritual doctrine that was given to her by spiritual masters, highly evolved beings with whom she communicated psychically. She believed it was her obligation to pass these teachings on to the world.

The Secret Doctrine, one of the major works of occultism of the nineteenth century, was published in two volumes in 1888. According to Blavatsky it was based on, or a translation from, "The Stanzas of Dzyan," a purportedly ancient religious text that remains unknown to scholars. This is believed to be the sourcebook for all religions; in other words, it is believed to be the earliest and most esoteric religious book in the world from which all the religions of the world arose.

The following excerpt is from the first volume, and it explains creation beginning from a female "eternal parent." In her commentary on this stanza HPB refers to this eternal parent as space. This parent is impregnated by light and gives birth to a son in an ongoing evolutionary process.

Cosmic Evolution

*In Seven Stanzas translated
from the Book of Dzyan.*

STANZA I.

1. THE ETERNAL PARENT WRAPPED IN HER EVER INVISIBLE ROBES HAD SLUMBERED ONCE AGAIN FOR SEVEN ETERNITIES.

2. TIME WAS NOT, FOR IT LAY ASLEEP IN THE INFINITE BOSOM OF DURATION.

3. UNIVERSAL MIND WAS NOT, FOR THERE WERE NO AH-HI TO CONTAIN IT.

4. THE SEVEN WAYS TO BLISS WERE NOT. THE GREAT CAUSES OF MISERY WERE NOT, FOR THERE WAS NO ONE TO PRODUCE AND GET ENSNARED BY THEM.

5. DARKNESS ALONE FILLED THE BOUNDLESS ALL, FOR FATHER, MOTHER AND SON WERE ONCE MORE ONE, AND THE SON HAD NOT AWAKENED YET FOR THE NEW WHEEL, AND HIS PILGRIMAGE THEREON.

★ ★ ★

STANZA III.

1. . . . THE LAST VIBRATION OF THE SEVENTH ETERNITY THRILLS THROUGH INFINITUDE. THE MOTHER SWELLS, EXPANDING FROM WITHIN WITHOUT, LIKE THE BUD OF THE LOTUS.

2. THE VIBRATION SWEEPS ALONG, TOUCHING WITH ITS SWIFT WING THE WHOLE UNIVERSE AND THE GERM THAT DWELLETH IN DARKNESS: THE DARKNESS THAT BREATHES OVER THE SLUMBERING WATERS OF LIFE. . . .

3. DARKNESS RADIATES LIGHT, AND LIGHT DROPS ONE SOLITARY RAY INTO THE MOTHER-DEEP. THE RAY SHOOTS THROUGH THE VIRGIN EGG. THE RAY CAUSES THE ETERNAL EGG TO THRILL, AND DROP THE NON-ETERNAL GERM, WHICH CONDENSES INTO THE WORLD-EGG.

4. THEN THE THREE FALL INTO THE FOUR. THE RADIANT ESSENCE BECOMES SEVEN INSIDE, SEVEN OUTSIDE. THE LUMINOUS EGG, WHICH IN ITSELF IS THREE, CURDLES AND SPREADS IN MILK-WHITE CURDS THROUGHOUT THE DEPTHS OF MOTHER, THE ROOT THAT GROWS IN THE DEPTHS OF THE OCEAN OF LIFE.

5. THE ROOT REMAINS, THE LIGHT REMAINS, THE CURDS REMAIN, AND STILL OEAOHOO IS ONE.

6. THE ROOT OF LIFE WAS IN EVERY DROP OF THE OCEAN OF IMMORTALITY, AND THE OCEAN WAS RADIANT LIGHT, WHICH WAS FIRE, AND HEAT, AND MOTION. DARKNESS VANISHED AND WAS NO MORE; IT DISAPPEARED IN ITS OWN ESSENCE, THE BODY OF FIRE AND WATER, OR FATHER AND MOTHER.

7. BEHOLD, OH LANOO! THE RADIANT CHILD OF THE TWO, THE UNPARALLELED REFULGENT GLORY: BRIGHT SPACE SON OF DARK SPACE, WHICH EMERGES FROM THE DEPTHS OF THE GREAT DARK WATERS. IT IS OEAOHOO THE YOUNGER, THE ★ ★ ★ HE SHINES FORTH AS THE SON; HE IS THE BLAZING DIVINE DRAGON OF WISDOM; THE ONE IS FOUR, AND FOUR TAKES TO ITSELF THREE, AND THE UNION PRODUCES THE SAPTA, IN WHOM ARE THE SEVEN WHICH BECOME THE TRIDASA (OR THE HOSTS AND THE MULTITUDES). BEHOLD HIM LIFTING THE VEIL AND UNFURLING IT FROM EAST TO WEST. HE SHUTS OUT THE ABOVE, AND LEAVES THE BELOW TO BE SEEN AS THE GREAT ILLUSION. HE MARKS THE PLACES FOR THE SHINING ONES, AND TURNS THE UPPER INTO A SHORELESS SEA OF FIRE, AND THE ONE MANIFESTED INTO THE GREAT WATERS.

[FROM *The Secret Doctrine,* pp. 27–29.]

Commentaries

ON THE SEVEN STANZAS AND THEIR TERMS, ACCORDING TO THEIR NUMERATION, IN STANZAS AND SLOKAS.

STANZA I.

1. "THE ETERNAL PARENT (Space), WRAPPED IN HER EVER INVISIBLE ROBES, HAD SLUMBERED ONCE AGAIN FOR SEVEN ETERNITIES (*a*)."

The "Parent Space" is the eternal, ever present cause of all—the incomprehensible DEITY, whose "invisible robes" are the mystic root of all matter, and of the Universe. Space is the *one eternal thing* that we can most easily imagine, immovable in its abstraction and un-influenced by either the presence or absence in it of an objective Universe. It is without dimension, in every sense, and self-existent. Spirit is the first differentiation from THAT, the causeless cause of both Spirit and Matter. It is, as taught in the esoteric catechism, neither limitless void, nor conditioned fulness, but both. It was and ever will be. . . .

Thus, the "Robes" stand for the noumenon of un-differentiated Cosmic Matter. It is not matter as we know it, but the spiritual essence of matter, and is co-eternal and even one with Space in its abstract sense. Root-nature is also the source of the subtle invisible properties in visible matter. It is the Soul, so to say, of the ONE infinite Spirit. The Hindus call it Mulaprakriti, and say that it is the primordial substance, which is the basis of the Upadhi or vehicle of every phenomenon, whether physical, mental or psychic. It is the source from which Akâsa radiates.

(a) By the Seven "Eternities," aeons or periods are meant. The word "Eternity," as understood in Chris-tian theology, has no meaning to the Asiatic ear, ex-cept in its application to the ONE existence; nor is the term sempiternity, the eternal only in futurity, any-thing better than a misnomer. Such words do not and cannot exist in philosophical metaphysics, and were unknown till the advent of ecclesiastical Christian-ity. The Seven Eternities meant are the seven periods, or a period answering in its duration to the seven periods, of a Manvantara, and extending throughout a Maha-Kalpa or the "Great Age"—100 years of Brahmâ—making a total of 311,040,000,000,000 of years; each year of Brahmâ beings composed of 360 "days," of the same number of "nights" of Brahmâ (reckoned by the Chandrayana or lunar year); and a "Day of Brahmâ" consisting of 4,320,000,000 of mortal years. These "Eternities" belong to the most secret calculations, in which, in order to arrive at the true total, every figure must be 7^x (7 to the power of x); x varying according to the nature of the cycle in the subjective or real world.

[From *The Secret Doctrine,* pp. 35–36.]

RUDOLF STEINER

Rudolf Steiner (1861–1925) was born in Hungary, educated in Austria, and lived in Ger-many and Switzerland. He was a man with many interests: a significant scholar and editor of Goethe, a philosopher, an innovative educator, dramatist, and builder, to list just a few of his interests. For a while he was a member of the Theosophical Society, but in 1913 he founded his own group, the Anthroposophical Society, which was devoted to human wisdom. Though his goal was to have his teachings supersede religion, he maintained an esoteric understanding of Christianity, somewhat under the influence of Rosicrucian traditions, in which he included ideas about karma and reincarnation. He developed a form of spiritual discipline that he believed would help people to see the spiritual core of all reality for themselves.

The following excerpt is taken from a lecture Steiner gave in Berlin on October 23, 1905, for women only. (An earlier lecture on the same topic was given to men only.) In this lecture Steiner emphasizes the participation of women in the Theosophical Society (this is before his break with the Society in 1912) and traces the separation of the sexes in occult matters to the Freemasons, an occult order of builders he traces back to the Temple of Solomon. He then explains the originally female nature of human beings (an interesting variation on a story in Plato's *Symposium*), and elaborates on the occult meaning of Adam and Eve.

The things which we wish to discuss today have not hitherto been discussed in front of women. Therefore, it is a rather bold step I am taking to speak about these things to you. However, particular occult currents make it necessary.

Within these currents there are some things of an intimate nature which, up to a short while ago, could not be mentioned in the presence of women, because the occult brotherhood, whose task it was to nurture these intimate things, had a strict rule, to admit no women members. What they had to do in the world might not be done in co-operation with the female element. Until just recently, this rule has been strictly adhered to. Nowadays, the sole possibility of creating a balance between the two sexes exists only in the Theosophical Society. Here is indeed the only place where these things are discussed in front of women.

Now we ask: Why has this separation of the sexes

come about—which has taken such a grotesque form in the Lodges of Freemasonry? If one wants to understand why this segregation really became habitual, one has to use a rather grotesque metaphor: When two powers are at war with each other, it would be very foolish if the general of one side were to reveal his plan of campaign to the enemy general, before the battle started. It would be the same as handing over one's weapons to the enemy, if one were to enlist women in the Freemasons. For it is a matter of war for the Freemasons, a war indeed against the female spirit, a matter of sharp opposition to the female spirit as such. This war was necessary, yes, occult Freemasonry was founded precisely for this purpose. Therefore it was the custom to speak about occult matters to the two sexes separately.

* * *

The whole fertilising and fructifying force by which a new person is created, used to be combined in one sex. Then the human being was separated into male and female. Which sex can best lay claim to the generative power? It is the female. Therefore Zeus, who was worshipped as the progenitor of the human race, was portrayed in the oldest [versions of] Greek mythology as having female breasts. Zeus, as a superhuman being, was nearer to the female sex. The female sex was thus the first, the earlier one, and at that time had the power in itself of producing the complete human individual. This generative power lay within a human being of undivided sex, who approximated, in its outward physical form, more towards the female. In this single-sexed human being, the fertilising [principle] was wisdom, the spirit itself; and the fertilising of the female spirit by inspired wisdom is a later recapitulation of this. This human being of the single-sex era was the result of the fertilisation by the Divine Spirit of the substance produced in the woman.

Now you understand what it was by which a woman could give birth to a human being. Physically, there is first of all a woman, who is fertilised from above. It was the Divine Spirit in woman which was the fertilising principle. When the separation of the sexes happened, the differentiation started in the transformation of the female's spiritual organs of fertilisation into organs of wisdom. The masculine power that the woman had in herself turned the creative force into organs of wisdom. So half the generative force stayed with the woman; the creative

physical forces stayed with the man. As a result of this separation, the spinal cord and the brain with the nerve branches appeared, as portrayed in the Tree of Life and the Tree of Knowledge. The organ of wisdom is formed in the vertebrae by the spinal cord and its extension into the brain. From that time on, there is a duality in man; namely, the two trees of the biblical record, the Tree of Knowledge and the Tree of Life.

And now the new beings adapt themselves to the change. The individuals who had previously been female did not all subsequently take on the female form. The female side—the capacity to produce human beings—withdrew from one section and left behind, in substitution, the power to fertilise in a quite different way. Physical nature had divided itself into what fertilised and what needed to be fertilised. Spiritual nature, too, had similarly divided itself. In female individuals the spirit acquired male character and colouring; in the male the spirit had a female character. That is still the female within man.

The biblical legend shows this very clearly. As is known, the man having two sexes was forbidden to eat from the Tree of Knowledge. The power with which Jehovah had invested mankind was: to make his wisdom work in the woman. 'Thou shalt not eat of the Tree of Knowledge' means the same as 'Thou shalt not separate off the force of fertilisation and make it independent.' For Jehovah's power, the fertilising power, would thereby be lost to the woman. When woman ate from the Tree of Knowledge, she thereby laid the basis for becoming independent in respect of wisdom, thereby ceasing to remain a mere tool of Jehovah as he had planned. But thus she lost, along with Jehovah's power, the power to fertilise herself through wisdom as well. By eating [from the Tree of Knowledge] and giving the apple to man, she wiped this power out. Thus woman became dependent on man. It was Lucifer who led mankind along this path in order to make him independent. Jehovah was against this, and forbade man to eat from the Tree of Knowledge for that reason. However the woman did eat and gave to the man. The man ate too, so that the punishment decreed by Jehovah ensued. New bodies have to come into existence, which will work out the Karma of previous existence; death and [re-] birth come into the world. Woman is now no longer fertile through herself, but has become barren. And with fertilisation coming from outside, the possibility of this kind of death enters the world.

[From *The Temple Legend*, pp. 247–252.]

ASTROLOGY AND TAROT

While neither astrology or tarot is a religion, they were and remain a popular means of disseminating the religious ideas of the Theosophical Society as well as of other occult groups. Both are rich in gender imagery and interpretations of that imagery, which, while often quite muddled, tend to stay within the familiar range of the female as the passive support or helpmeet to the active male. The frequent use of these symbol systems for purposes of divination leads to a tacit acceptance of their meanings. In this way, occult ideas about gender coalesce with the preexisting ideas of very diverse individuals. In the main, occult ideas about gender differences do not favor actual women. Although they often advance the spiritual superiority of women, they promote unrealistic and unattainable, to say nothing of possibly undesirable, models of womanhoood.

ALAN LEO

Astrology underwent a revival in England beginning in the 1880s mainly through the influence of the Theosophical Society. While most of Blavatsky's discussions of cosmology were tinged with astrological references, it was not until Alan Leo (1860–1917) joined the Theosophical Society in 1890 that astrology became a part of the Theosophical course of study. Leo's influence on modern astrology has been enormous. Prior to him astrology had been limited to predictions about the future. Leo changed all that by emphasizing its esoteric meaning within the teachings of the Theosophical Society, and he also profited from popularizing astrology to the general public. Leo actually had an astrological workshop in which he employed nine people. This enabled him to maintain correspondence courses, publish books and periodicals on astrology, run an astrological society, and advise clients. He also was the first astrologer to sell prefabricated horoscopes by mailing clients standard interpretations based on their date of birth. Through his correspondence courses and publications he brought the study of astrology within the reach of masses of people.

Even though he was twice prosecuted by the police for fortune telling, Leo was a great success and one of the very few astrologers to make his living exclusively through astrology. The growing Theosophical Society, with its many chapters throughout the world, helped spread his name and publications. Henceforth, anyone who wanted to learn astrology read Leo; and in this way his ideas about astrology, filtered through a theosophical lens, came to dominate modern astrology in Europe and the United States.

Ideas about gender and astrology go back at least to the great Greek synthesizer Ptolemy (fl. 127–48 C.E.), whose *Tetrabiblos* remains the classical work on astrology. Briefly stated, astrology utilizes the zodiac, an integrated system of twelve constellations referred to by astrological signs such as Aries, Taurus, and so on, and the planets, including the sun and the moon. Both the astrological signs of the zodiac and the planets are divided by gender: alternating signs are male and female (e.g., Aries is male, Taurus is female, and so on). Planets such as the moon and Venus are female, and the sun and Mars are male. Leo calls such gender distinctions among the signs "polarity," explaining that "polarity refers to the division of the signs into two groups. The odd signs are all positive male day signs, and the even are negative female night signs. They refer to the duality shown everywhere in nature. Thus the words *positive, male,* and *day* convey precisely the same idea only expressed differently and refer to the force or life side of things; the words *negative, female,* and *night* signify the material or form side" (*How to Judge a Nativity,* p. 16). Here we are presented with the familiar duality of female as negative and dark, while male is positive and light.

Leo elaborates on these ideas in the following excerpt taken from his *The Art of Synthesis,* a guide to interpreting horoscopes, where he discusses the meanings of the sun and the moon in the horoscope. Exoterically the sun represents men, particularly the father, the husband, and authority figures. The moon represents women, particularly the mother and the wife. From the esoteric point of view, both the sun and the moon represent aspects of the self, and, not surprisingly, it is the male sun that represents the higher self while the female moon represents the lower self.

The Sun, Life-Giver

At the centre of our solar system is the Sun, the giver of life and light to the whole system. It is the principal influence throughout the whole science of Astrology, and is, until a certain stage is reached in evolution, the representative of the SELF.

★ ★ ★

From the Central Sun, which itself is triple, arise Seven Beings or Holy Ones, who send forth Their Rays or forces into Seven Solar systems; and our Sun represents one of these Rays. In the New Testament we read that Jesus said: I and my Father are one; and, I ascend unto my Father and your Father,—showing that He and those who followed Him belonged to the same 'Star' or 'Father' in the same planetary realm; and this is the astrological explanation of the statement: In my Father's house are many mansions.

★ ★ ★

The Sun is the giver of the life-principle, or the breath of life, and when manifesting in the physical world the Sun represents the specialised life or 'Prana' in each separated individual. In all degrees of manifestation the Sun is the giver of life, spiritually, mentally, and physically, and it is therefore of vital and primary importance in all study of Astrology. It is the representative of the One Life that permeates *all things;* and therefore careful study of the Sun and all that it denotes in a nativity is necessary before a sound judgment can be given.

From a physical and mundane standpoint the Sun is the giver of light by day, and the Moon by night. It is the breath of life, governing the inbreathing and the outbreathing.

From the standpoint of the feelings the Sun governs the heart, with its sensations and emotions, and gives life to these feelings, from the fiercest passion up to the purest love and friendship.

From a mental standpoint the Sun is the heart and Wisdom, the life of the intelligence, the self-conscious centre on the plane of the mind.

★ ★ ★

From an earthly standpoint, and a physical or material conception of things, the life permeating through each sign of the Zodiac is the animal life, which must be redeemed by the triune spiritual essences coming from the Sun direct as Will, Wisdom, and Activity. Man is made in the image of God, and in Him eternally lives and moves and has his being, though plunged into matter and confined by 'the circle of necessity'—the Zodiac. For the time he is dominated by the animal life, which he draws from the form side of existence; and only when ignorance has been overcome by experience and his birthright, his divine inheritance, is gradually realised, does he turn and begin to 'reverse his spheres.'

Thus, and thus only, does he rule his stars, *i.e.,* the planetary influences, which govern the *form* side of his existence only. Then the Christ or Christos is born in him, and the solar rays vivify and awaken the sleeping self that has been so long buried in matter. Thenceforward his task is to 'put the Moon under his feet,' to rise from the thraldom of the lower self and to be crowned by the Sun. The whole story is that of the prodigal son, who after eating the husks of personal illusions returns to his father, the individual or higher self, asking nothing but to be a servant; yet for him is prepared the joyous feast. In the story of St George and the Dragon again is repeated the struggle between the higher and the lower self, the SUN and the MOON, the Spirit and the Soul; the soul bowing down to the animal and inclining to the pleasures of the senses, until regenerated by the spirit and drawn from the selfishness and limitation of Saturn into the expansive and compassionate influence of Jupiter.

[From *The Art of Synthesis,* pp. 28–34.]

The Moon, Mother

The Moon is the great moulder of form. She is the Queen Mother of the heavens, the Virgin Mary of the Roman Catholics, and has chief rule over the earth and the zodiac: while the Sun is king over the solar system and the planetary spheres.

The Moon makes all forms as plastic as clay, and susceptible to every influence that is collected and transmitted by it to the forms it governs; hence the lunar orb is the most important factor in all things that are generated. . . .

The Moon's influence varies so greatly, according to the sign in which it is located at birth and the planet with which it is in closest aspect, that it is not a very easy task to give a definite account of it apart from sign and aspect. It is usually considered moderately cold and moist, and to be feminine, negative, receptive, plastic, magnetic, fruitful, and changeable.

★ ★ ★

The influence of the Moon over the feelings, according to its position by sign, has already been referred to. Everything outside the realm of intellect, from the lowest animal instinct up to the higher emotion, is very largely swayed by the Moon. The older and more highly evolved the soul, the weaker will be this influence, and the more will it be under the control of the will; and *vice versâ*, the younger the soul from the evolutionary point of view, the more is it the slave of lunar attraction and the less is it able to resist passions and appetites rushing upon it from without or surging up from within. This question of the degree of evolutionary status gained by the soul and innate at birth is by no means easy to read in the horoscope, and yet very important issues obviously hang upon it; in fact the whole question of personal morality is here involved. Broadly speaking, young souls and those who are very unevenly developed in some department of human nature seem to have many bad aspects, especially from malefics, the planets not dignified, and the benefics neither prominent nor strong; while the older and more highly evolved souls tend to reverse these conditions.

[From *The Art of Synthesis,* pp. 38–51.]

EVANGELINE ADAMS

In the United States it was Evangeline Adams (1865–1932) who became the great popularizer of astrology. Like Alan Leo, she made her living from astrology, published several popular books on the subject (several of which are still in print), and was arrested in 1914 for fortune telling. In her case, though, the trial gave her an enormous amount of publicity, especially when she was acquitted for having shown the astronomical basis of astrology and by successfully interpreting the horoscope of the judge's son in court. Judge Freschi made the distinction that while fortune-telling violates the law "every astrologer is not a fortune-teller. I believe that there is a line of distinction between the person who pretends to be able to read the future and tell with postiveness what will or shall happen and the one who merely reads a sign as indicating what ought to happen but in particular to make it plain that he is not attempting to predict future events" (*New York Criminal Reports,* vol. 23, 11 December 1914, p. 343.)

Most of Adams's desriptions of the signs are directed toward men, but from time to time she makes some telling remarks about the different effects the signs have on women and men. The following excerpts are from her book, *Astrology for Everyone.*

Aries

The Aries man shines in comparison with many of his brothers. There is nothing common or vulgar about his feelings for members of the opposite sex. He is ardent, demonstrative, even passionate; but always with admiration, usually with worship, in his heart. And he must not be disturbed in this attitude. He must fancy himself the protector, the savior. He must be, as indeed he is, Sir Galahad, the Pure in Heart.

Aries women are no less idealistic than the Aries men. They, too, scorn the common and the vulgar. But in their relations with those they love, they are beset by dangers which are peculiar to them. Men in the rôle of saviors are not unattractive to the women they love. Women in the same rôle rather wear on the men they insist on saving. Men as leaders have always commanded the admiration of womankind. Women as leaders have been accepted rather recently and somewhat reluctantly by mankind!

★ ★ ★

Aries women are naturally very romantic. They are given to sudden enthusiasms. They are even violent in the expression of their affections, and do not create an atmosphere of rest, tranquillity, or serenity. You should remember these tendencies of the women of your sign, and try to cultivate some of the softer feminine qualities which are useful in holding the admiration which your brilliant nature is bound to attract.

If a man, you have a natural gift for political or public work. You would make an excellent military leader in time of war. In less troubled times, you should succeed in any sort of executive position connected with machinery. You ought to be a fine railroad man. Your pioneer nature makes you a wonderful starter of enterprises. See to it that you are a good finisher.

If a woman, you must guard against being too dictatorial in your relations with men. Forget that you are the pioneer, the leader—at least, appear to forget it. Men will be attracted to you by the brilliant rays of your favoring Sun. Don't let them be driven away by the over-aggressiveness of the war-like Mars.

[From *Astrology for Everyone*, pp. 31–37.]

Gemini

If he is a man he will adopt a profession or a business in which quickness of mind and extreme mental facility are the chief requirements for success; and during business hours, he will use all of the strength of character which he possesses to the furtherance of the work on which he is engaged. After business hours, he will turn his active mind to some artistic or literary pursuit, quite different perhaps from the interest which has filled his day, but which in some way improves his equipment for his daily task.

If the Gemini subject is a woman, she will contrive to make her high mental gifts take the place of natural aptitude in the performance of her domestic duties. Gemini women are not natural housewives but they usually possess the ability and adaptability essential to success in planning or running a home. This task performed, and for the Gemini woman it is a task— she can then satisfy her longing for a more strictly intellectual career in some activity which will make her a more interesting companion or a more successful mate.

[From *Astrology for Everyone*, p. 54.]

Virgo

If you are a woman, you are chaste and devoted, but inclined to be undemonstrative, even cold. You are more intellectual than emotional. You do not yearn for children, although you make the most conscientious of mothers.

If a man, develop expertness in theoretical or practical mechanics; and you will have success in pursuits where your analytical powers come into play. You have a gift for building, manufacturing, farming and mining. You do well in real estate. Virgo people make good accountants; some win success as teachers and writers.

★ ★ ★

If you are a woman, you should learn to be more natural in your attitude toward the man you love. Don't be overcritical. See their good side as well as their bad, and confine your conversation so far as possible to the former. Show the man you love that you have an emotional side as well as a practical one!

[From *Astrology for Everyone*, pp. 92–97.]

Sagittarius

If a Sagittarian finds a member of the opposite sex who really understands the fine qualities which lie below his blunt and often brusque exterior, he makes an ideal husband. He resents jealousy and restriction; but his anger, though quick, is seldom long-lived; and he never cherishes a grudge. If he is sure that the woman of his choice is dealing openly and squarely with him, he will expand and develop. His flirtations, if they occur, are bound to be public ones and of slight importance.

The Sagittarian woman possesses most of these traits, both good and bad. If they follow their splendid intuition, they make excellent wives—provided always that they subdue their tendencies to bluntness in dealing with their husbands. They must be frank, because it is their nature, but they must be tactful, too.

[From *Astrology for Everyone*, p. 128.]

A. E. Waite

Arthur Edward Waite (1857–1941) was born in New York but moved to England with his mother when he was very young. He remained there for most of his life. Waite was both a serious scholar of occultism and a practitioner. For a while he was a member of the Theosophical Society and afterwards of the magical order called the Golden Dawn. This group was heavily influenced by Rosicrucian traditions, and its members included the poet William Butler Yeats and the scholar of religion Evelyn Underhill. Waite eventually founded his own branch of the Golden Dawn, abandoned much of its Egyptian influence, and focused on esoteric Christian mysticism and rituals, which often involved Kabbalist teachings. These influences are demonstrated in his interpretations of the Tarot cards.

Today Waite is best known for his creation, along with the artist Pamela Coleman-Smith, of the most popular Tarot deck. Divinization through decks of cards is as old as cards themselves in both the East and the West. For instance, the oldest extant European cards are from a Tarot deck designed for Charles VI of France in 1392. The origin of such cards are uncertain, but recent scholarship has shown that they share the symbolism of Hellenistic initiation rites as well as of astrology and alchemy. Waite's updating of the symbolism and the interpretation of the Tarot led to its becoming a popular form of divination, often in ways quite contrary to his mystical intentions.

The following excerpts are taken from Waite's discussion of the major arcana, the twenty-two picture cards distinguished from the fifty-six cards of the minor arcana, which are divided into four suits, much like modern playing cards. Waite describes each card and interprets its meaning. Significantly, sexual symbolism is frequent, because certain cards are gender specific and indeed appear in pairs, for instance cards numbers 1 and 2, the Magician and the High Priestess. The Magician is equated with spirit while the High Priestess is equated with the Law, the Word, and the Secret Church, all material manifestations of Spirit, and with the mother. No such father symbolism attends the Magician. Card number 6, the Lovers, spiritualizes the union of female and male and reinterprets Eve's participation in the fall and eventually in redemption.

I. The Magician

A youthful figure in the robe of a magician, having the countenance of divine Apollo, with smile of confidence and shining eyes. Above his head is the mysterious sign of the Holy Spirit, the sign of life, like an endless cord, forming the figure 8 in a horizontal position ∞. About his waist is a serpent-cincture, the serpent appearing to devour its own tail. This is familiar to most as a conventional symbol of eternity, but here it indicates more especially the eternity of attainment in the spirit. In the Magician's right hand is a wand raised towards heaven, while the left hand is pointing to the earth. This dual sign is known in very high grades of the Instituted Mysteries; it shews the descent of grace, virtue and light, drawn from things above and derived to things below. The suggestion throughout is therefore the possession and communication of the Powers and Gifts of the Spirit. On the table in front of the Magician are the symbols of the four Tarot suits, signifying the elements of natural life, which lie like counters before the adept, and he adapts them as he wills. Beneath are roses and lilies, the *flos campi* and *lilium convallium,* changed into garden flowers, to shew the culture of aspiration. This card signifies the divine motive in man, reflecting God, the will in the liberation of its union with that which is above. It is also the unity of individual being on all planes, and in a very high sense it is thought, in the fixation thereof. With further reference to what I have called the sign of life and its connexion with the number 8, it may be remembered that Christian Gnosticism speaks of rebirth in Christ as a change "unto the Ogdoad." The mystic number is termed Jerusalem above, the Land flowing with Milk and Honey, the Holy Spirit and the Land of the Lord. According to Martinism, 8 is the number of Christ.

II. The High Priestess

She has the lunar crescent at her feet, a horned diadem on her head, with a globe in the middle place, and a large solar cross on her breast. The scroll in her hands is inscribed with the word *Tora,* signifying the Greater Law, the Secret Law and the second sense of the Word. It is partly covered by her mantle, to shew that some things are implied and some spoken. She is seated between the white and black pillars—J. and B.—of the mystic Temple, and the veil of the Temple is behind her: it is embroidered with palms and pomegranates. The vestments are flowing and gauzy, and the mantle suggests light—a shimmering radiance. She has been called Occult Science on the threshold of the Sanctuary of Isis, but she is really the Secret Church, the House which is of God and man. She represents also the Second Marriage of the Prince who is no longer of this world; she is the spiritual Bride and Mother, the daughter of the stars and the Higher Garden of Eden. She is, in fine, the Queen of the borrowed light, but this is the light of all. She is the Moon nourished by the milk of the Supernal Mother.

In a manner, she is also the Supernal Mother herself—that is to say, she is the bright reflection. It is in this sense of reflection that her truest and highest name in bolism is *Shekinah*—the co-habiting glory. According to Kabalism, there is a *Shekinah* both above and below. In the superior world it is called *Binah*, the Supernal Understanding which reflects to the emanations that are beneath. In the lower world it is *Malkuth*—that world being, for this purpose, understood as a blessed Kingdom—that with which it is made blessed being the Indwelling Glory. Mystically speaking, the *Shekinah* is the Spiritual Bride of the just man, and when he reads the Law she gives the Divine meaning. There are some respects in which this card is the highest and holiest of the Greater Arcana.

[From *Pictorial Key to the Tarot,* pp. 72–79.]

VI. The Lovers

The sun shines in the zenith, and beneath is a great winged figure with arms extended, pouring down influences. In the foreground are two human figures, male and female, unveiled before each other, as if

Adam and Eve when they first occupied the paradise of the earthly body. Behind the man is the Tree of Life, bearing twelve fruits, and the Tree of the Knowledge of Good and Evil is behind the woman; the serpent is twining round it. The figures suggest youth, virginity, innocence and love before it is contaminated by gross material desire. This is in all simplicity the card of human love, here exhibited as part of the way, the truth and the life. It replaces, by recourse to first principles, the old card of marriage, which I have described previously, and the later follies which depicted man between vice and virtue. In a very high sense, the card is a mystery of the Covenant and Sabbath.

The suggestion in respect of the woman is that she signifies that attraction towards the sensitive life which carries within it the idea of the Fall of Man, but she is rather the working of a Secret Law of Providence than a willing and conscious temptress. It is through her imputed lapse that man shall arise ultimately, and only by her can he complete himself. The card is therefore in its way another intimation concerning the great mystery of womanhood.

[From *Pictorial Key to the Tarot,* pp. 92–95.]

MAGIC

DION FORTUNE

Dion Fortune (1890–1946) was a leading and very influential English occultist, who was a member of the Theosophical Society and an early student of pychoanalysis. Her interest in magic led her to briefly join the magical order of the Golden Dawn, but she eventually left to establish her own group, the Fraternity of the Inner Light, which still exists today and has itself led to five additional associated groups. She wrote numerous and highly regarded books on the occult and magic, including very popular novels that contain fictionalized descriptions of magical practices and theory.

While accepting prevailing ideas about men being active and women being passive in the ordinary world, Fortune emphasized women's occult powers on the "astral," where such gender roles were reversed. For Fortune the astral was the realm where the magician does her or his work and consequently is the more important realm. In her novel *The Sea Priestess,* Fortune expresses these ideas through her heroine, Vivien Le Fay Morgan, an incarnation of Morgan Le Fey, who Fortune traces back to the legendary land of Atlantis. In the following excerpt Morgan explains these and other things to a young man (Wilfred) she hopes will assist her in certain rituals.

And she told me that each man had it in him, by virtue of his manhood, to be a priest and each woman by virtue of her womanhood had it in her to be a priestess; for the Source of All Life created the worlds by dividing Its Unmanifest Unity into the manifesting Duality, and we that are created show forth in our

beings the uncreate Reality. Each living soul has its roots in the Unmanifest and draws thence its life, and by going back to the Unmanifest we find fulness of life.

But because we are limited and imperfect beings we cannot show forth the Infinite in Its totality; and because we are imprisoned upon the plane of form we can only conceive the Formless as far as minds habituated to form can imagine it. "And that," said Morgan le Fay, "is not very far, and the mathematicians go furthest. But we who are men and women, Wilfred, and who want to know God as He manifests in Nature—we see the luminous countenance of the Eternal in the beautiful forms of the gods. And in that way," she said, "we learn more, and can do more, than if we strive after abstract essences that elude us."

★ ★ ★

And she told me that in every being there are two aspects, the positive and the negative; the dynamic and the receptive; the male and the female; and this is shown forth in rudimentary form even in the physical body. In normal folk one of these is dominant and one is recessive, and this determines the sex; but though the recessive one is latent, it is nevertheless there, as is well known to those who study the anomalies of development and disease—and as is still better known to those who study the anomalies of the soul.

But the ancients did not concern themselves with anomalies, but said that the soul was bisexual, and that as one or the other aspect manifested in the world of form, the alternative aspect was latent in the world of spirit; and if we look into our own hearts we shall see how true this is, for each of us has two sides to his nature—the side that is forth-flowing by its own dynamism, and the side that lies latent, awaiting inspiration, and that comes not forth unless it is evoked. "And this," said she, "is the greater side of each one of us; and in a man it is his spiritual nature, and in a woman it is her dynamic will."

Then she told how in some the two sides of their nature came near to equilibrium, not in any physical or instinctual anomaly, but in temperament; for an anomaly is due to the repression of the dominant factor, whereas in that of which she spoke it was the two-sided soul that was finding expression through the higher self, and this was due to the work of initiation in past lives.

★ ★ ★

"Why are you taking all this trouble over me, Morgan le Fay? I am certain it is not for my own sweet sake, quite apart from your repeated assurance that priestesses have no preferences in these matters."

"Because, Wilfred, if you and I can do this thing, we break trail for those who come after us, and we shall bring back into modern life something that has been lost and forgotten and that is badly needed."

"That something being—?"

"The knowledge of the subtle, magnetic relationship between a man and a woman, and the fact that it is part of a larger whole. Do you remember how you felt in the cave—that I was all women and you were all men? Do you remember how our personalities stood aside and we were just channels of force—the positive and negative forces out of which creation is built? And how, when this happened, primordial powers rushed through us straight from the Unmanifest, and it was a tremendous thing? This was what was aimed at by the temple-trained priestesses and the hetaerae, and it is what is lacking in our modern understanding of these things."

[From *The Sea Priestess*, pp. 174–181.]

ALEISTER CROWLEY

The name Aleister Crowley is synonymous with magic, especially magical practices of the darker sort. Crowley (1875–1947) was a significant figure not only in occult circles but in the larger world as well, mainly because his erratic and eccentric behavior, flashes of brillance, and general showmanship brought him an enormous amount of attention. He remains, however, an elusive figure. His writings are purposely obscure, and even dedicated followers disagree as to what should be taken seriously and what was meant ironically.

Crowley was a members of the Golden Dawn but left when he was unable to take control of that group. He then began travelling with his wife Rose, and it was in Egypt that Rose went into a trance while Crowley was performing a ritual to the Egyptian god Thoth. Rose, in trance, dictated *The Book of the Law*, which convinced Crowley he was the Anti-Christ. He then founded his own order and began to write extensive commentaries on the revelation that came through Rose as well as about magic in general. Despite the importance of Rose in his life, Crowley left some very damning statements about women, such as the following excerpt from *The Book of Wisdom or Folly*.

My Son, I charge thee, howsoever thou beest provoked thereunto, tell not the Truth to any Woman. For this is that which is written: Cast not thy Pearls before Swine, lest they turn again and rend thee. Behold, in the Nature of Woman is no Truth, nor Apprehension of Truth, nor Possibility of Truth; only, if thou entrust this Jewel unto them, they forthwith use it to thy Loss and Destruction. But they are aware of thine own Love of Truth, and thy Respect thereunto; so therefore they tempt thee, flattering with their Lips, that thou betray thyself to them. And they feign falsely, with every Wile, and cast about for thy Soul, until either in Love, or in Wrath, or in some other Folly thereof, thou speak Truth, profaning thy Sanctuary. So was it ever, and herein I call to my Witness Samson of Timnath, that was lost by this Error. Now for any Woman any Lie sufficeth; and think not in thine Extremity that Truth is mighty, and shall prevail, as it doth with any Man; for with a Woman her whole Craft and Device is to persuade thee of this, so that thou utter the Secret of thy Soul, and become her Prey. But so long as thou nourish her with her own Food of Falsity, thou are secure.

[From *The Book of the Wisdom of Folly*, p. 133.]

G. I. GURDJIEFF—MEETINGS WITH REMARKABLE MEN

G. I. Gurdjieff (1877?–1949) was born in Southern Russia where, as a gifted young boy, he was trained for both the Orthodox priesthood and medicine. In 1894 he left home to search for esoteric knowledge and spent the next twenty years travelling through Inner Asia and the Middle East. His autobiographical work, *Meetings with Remarkable Men* (published posthumously in 1963), describes some of the people he met during this time. In 1913, in Moscow, he began to teach and gather followers until the Russian Revolution drove him eventually to France, where he established his institute, which attracted leading artists and intellectuals from Europe and the United States. Essentially, Gurdjieff developed a system for the development of consciousness based on a harmonious blending of mind, body, and feeling. An important part of his system of training includes his "science of movements," in which dance is used to heighten consciousness.

Two women are mentioned in *Meetings with Remarkable Men* in the context of the story of Prince Yuri Lubovedsky; they are his sister, Princess Lubovedsky, and the woman they both help, Vitvitskaïa, who Gurdjieff represents as a model of womanhood. The interaction between the two women is particularly interesting, as Vitvitskaïa's life is changed from one of degradation to one of spiritual accomplishment and respect.

To illustrate the character of the inner world of Vitvitskaïa—this woman who had stood on the brink of moral ruin and who later, thanks to the aid of persons with ideas who chanced to cross the path of her life, became, I may boldly say, such as might serve as an ideal for every woman—I will confine myself here to telling about only one aspect of her many-sided inner life.

Among other interests she was particularly drawn to the science of music. The seriousness of her attitude towards this science may be shown clearly by a conversation we had during one of the expeditions of our group.

* * *

She began as follows:
'I do not remember whether there was anything in music that touched me inwardly when I was still quite young, but I do remember very well how I thought about it. Like everybody else I did not wish to appear ignorant and, in praising or criticizing a piece of music, I judged it only with my mind. Even when I was quite indifferent to the music I heard, if my opinion was asked about it, I expressed a view, for or against, according to the circumstances.

'Sometimes when everyone praised it I spoke against it, using all the technical words I knew, so that people should think I was not just anyone, but an educated person who could discriminate in everything. And sometimes I condemned it in unison with others, because I thought that, if they criticized it, there was doubtless something in it which I did not know about, for which it should be criticized. But if I praised a piece of music, it was because I assumed that the composer, whoever he might be, having been occupied with this matter all his life, would not let any composition see the light if it did not deserve it. In short, in either praising or blaming, I was always insincere with myself and with others, and for this I felt no remorse of conscience.

'Later, when that good old lady, the sister of Prince Lubovedsky, took me under her wing, she persuaded me to learn to play the piano. "Every well-educated, intelligent woman," she said, "should know how to play this instrument." In order to please the dear old lady, I gave myself up wholly to learning to play the piano, and in six months I did indeed play so well that I was invited to take part in a charity concert. All our acquaintants present praised me to the skies and expressed astonishment at my talent.

'One day, after I had been playing, the prince's sister came over to me and very seriously and solemnly told me that, since God had given me such a talent, it would be a great sin to neglect it and not let it develop to the full. She added that, as I had begun to work on music, I should be really educated in this field, and not just play like any Mary Smith, and she therefore thought that I should first of all study the theory of music and, if necessary, even take an examination.

'From that day on she began sending for all kinds of books on music for me, and she even went to Moscow herself to buy them. Very soon the walls of my study were lined with enormous bookcases filled to overflowing with all kinds of musical publications.

'I devoted myself very zealously to studying the theory of music, not only because I wished to please my benefactress but also because I myself had become greatly attracted to this work, and my interest in the laws of music was increasing from day to day. My books, however, were of no help to me, for nothing whatsoever was said in them either about what music is, or on what its laws are based. They merely repeated in different ways information about the history of music, such as: that our octave has seven notes, but the ancient Chinese octave had only five; that the harp of the ancient Egyptians was called *tebuni* and the flute *mem;* that the melodies of the ancient Greeks were constructed on the basis of different modes such as the Ionian, the Phrygian, the Dorian and various others; that in the ninth century polyphony appeared in music, having at first so cacophonic an effect that there was even a case of premature delivery of a pregnant woman, who suddenly heard in church the roar of the organ playing this music; that in the eleventh century a certain monk, Guido d'Arezzo, invented solfege, and so on and so forth. Above all, these books gave details about famous musicians, and how they had become famous; they even recorded what kind of neckties and spectacles were worn by such and such composers. But as to what music is, and what effect it has on the psyche of people, nothing was said anywhere.

'I spent a whole year studying this so-called theory of music. I read almost all my books and finally became definitely convinced that this literature would give me nothing; but my interest in music continued to increase. I therefore gave up all my reading and buried myself in my own thoughts.

'One day, out of boredom, I happened to take from the prince's library a book entitled *The World of Vibrations,* which gave my thoughts about music a definite direction. The author of this book was not a musician at all, and from the contents it was obvious that he was not even interested in music. He was an engineer and mathematician. In one place in his book he mentioned music merely as an example for his explanation of vibrations. He wrote that the sounds of music are made up of certain vibrations which doubtless act upon the vibrations which are also in a man, and this is why a man likes or dislikes this or that music. I at once understood this, and I fully agreed with the engineer's hypotheses.

'All my thoughts at that time were absorbed by these interests and, when I talked with the prince's sister, I always tried to turn the conversation to the subject of music and its real significance. As a result she herself became interested in this question, and we pondered over it together and also began to make experiments.'

* * *

Vitvitskaïa died in Russia from a cold she caught while on a trip on the Volga. She was buried in Samara. I was there at the time of her death, having been called from Tashkent when she fell ill.

Recalling her now, when I have already passed the half-way mark of my life and have been in almost all countries and seen thousands of women, I must confess that I never have met and probably never will meet another such woman.

[From *Meetings with Remarkable Men,* pp. 127–134.]

Neopaganism

Neopaganism is a term used to define a great variety of religious movements that began in the late nineteenth century in Europe and the United States. Generally the term refers to people who have revived the worship of the pre-Christian pagan deites of Europe, although I apply the same term to the followers of Santeria and Voodoo, who worship African deities along with Christian saints. In addition to the possibilities of goddess worship, of particular importance to the religious life of women has been the revival of Witchcraft and the development of the Women's Spirituality Movement.

MATILDA JOSLYN GAGE—WOMAN, CHURCH, AND STATE

Matilda Joslyn Gage (1826–1898) was one member of the triumvirate of the Woman's Suffrage Movement of the nineteenth century along with Elizabeth Cady Stanton and Susan B. Anthony. She and Stanton wrote the three volume *The History of Woman Suffrage,* with Anthony's assistance as organizer. Her home was a station on the underground railroad, and she was an early advocate of rights of Native Americans (she was made an honorary member of the Council of Matrons of the Iroquois). She spoke out on a range of women's issues that many, including feminists of her day, felt were best left alone, such as the problems of women prisoners, revising rape laws, and equal pay for equal work.

Gage was the only leading feminist of her time who maintained that the position of women had not been steadily improving through history, but rather that in the past it had been much better than it was now. She was the first American feminist to articulate the theory of prehistoric matriarchies, which she believed were egalitarian, woman-centered societies that worshiped female deities. She was also the first to document the persecution of the witches and to analyze it as an attempt by the patriarchy to destroy female culture. Gage devoted much of the last years of her life to studying goddess worship and the position of women in the earliest societies.

She had a deep interest in Theosophy and the occult, and some of this is revealed in her commentaries in *The Woman's Bible,* which are on Revelations. In the following excerpt from her chapter on witchcraft in *Woman, Church, and State* (published 1893) Gage reveals the historical persecution of the witches in all its brutality and offers her own interpretation of who these women might have been, based on her knowledge of occultism. Notice especially her reference to Blavatsky.

Whatever the pretext made for witchcraft persecution we have abundant proof that the so-called "witch" was among the most profoundly scientific persons of the age. The church having forbidden its offices and all external methods of knowledge to woman, was profoundly stirred with indignation at her having through her own wisdom, penetrated into some of the most deeply subtle secrets of nature: and it was a subject of debate during the middle ages if learning for woman was not an additional capacity for evil, as owing to her, knowledge had first been introduced in the world. In penetrating into these arcana, woman trenched upon that mysterious hidden knowledge of the church which it regarded as among its most potential methods of controlling mankind. Scholars have invariably attributed magical knowledge and practices to the church, popes and prelates of every degree having been thus accused. The word "magic" or "wisdom," simply meaning superior science, was attributed in the highest degree to King Solomon, who ruled even the Elementals by means of his magic ring made in accord with certain natural laws. He was said to have drawn his power directly from God. Magi were known as late as the X century of this era. Among their powers were casting out demons, the fearless use of poisons, control of spirits and an acquaintance with many natural laws unknown to the world at large. During the present century, the Abbe Constant (Eliphas Levi), declared the Pentagram to be the key of the two worlds, and if rightly understood, endowing man with infinite power. The empire of THE WILL over the astral light is symbolized in magic by the Pentagram, the growth of a personal will being the most important end to be attained in the history of man's evolution. The opposition of the church to this growth of the human will in mankind, has ever been the most marked feature in its history. Under WILL, man decides for himself, escaping from all control that hinders his personal development.

It is only an innate and natural tendency of the soul to go beyond its body to find material with which to clothe the life that it desires to give expression to. The soul can and must be trained to do this consciously. You can easily see that this power possessed *consciously* will give its possessor power to work magic.

Ignorance and the anathemas of the church against knowledge to be gained through an investigation of the more abstruse laws of nature, have invested the word "magic" with terror. But magic simply means knowledge of the effect of certain natural, but generally unknown laws; the secret operation of natural causes, according to Bacon and other philosophers; consequences resulting from control of the invisible powers of nature, such as are shown in the electrical appliances of the day, which a few centuries since would have been termed witchcraft. Seeking to compel the aid of spirits, was understood as magic at an early day. Lenormant says the object of magic in Chaldea, was to conjure the spirits giving minute description of the ancient formula. Scientific knowledge in the hands of the church alone, was a great element of spiritual and temporal power, aiding it in more fully subduing the human will. The testimony of the ages entirely destroys the assertion sometimes made that witchcraft was merely a species of hysteria. Every discovery of science is a nearer step towards knowledge of the laws governing "the Accursed Sciences," as everything connected with psychic power in possession of the laity was termed by the church. "Her seven evidences for possession" included nearly all forms of mesmerism. All modern investigations tend to prove what was called witchcraft, to have been in most instances the action of psychic laws not yet fully understood.

★ ★ ★

"Magic" whether brought about by the aid of spirits or simply through an understanding of secret natural laws, is of two kinds, "white" and "black," according as its intent and consequences are either evil or good, and in this respect does not differ from the use made of the well known laws of nature, which are ever of good or evil character, in the hands of good or evil persons. To the church in its powerful control of the human will, must be attributed the use of "black magic," in its most injurious form. Proof that knowledge of the mysterious laws governing ordinary natural phenomena still exists even among civilized people, is indubitable. Our American Indians in various portions of the continent, according to authorities, also possess power to produce storms of thunder, lightning and rain.

A vast amount of evidence exists, to show that the word "witch" formerly signified a woman of superior knowledge.

★ ★ ★

Besides the natural psychics who formed a large proportion of the victims of this period, other women with a natural spirit of investigation made scientific discoveries with equally baleful effect upon themselves; the one fact of a woman's possessing knowledge serving to bring her under the suspicion and accusation of the church. Henry More, a learned Cambridge graduate of the seventeenth century wrote a treatise on witchcraft explanatory of the term "witch" which he affirmed simply signified a wise, or learned woman. It meant "uncommon" but not unlawful knowledge or skill. It will assist in forming an opinion to know that the word "witch" is from *wekken,* to prophesy a direct bearing upon the psychic powers of many such persons. The modern Slavonian or Russian name for witch, *vjedma,* is from the verb "to know" signifying much the same as Veda. Muller says *Veda* means the same as the wise, "wisdom." The Sanskrit word *Vidma* answers to the German *wir wissen,* which literally means "we know." A Russian name for the witch *Zaharku,* is derived from the verb *Znat,* to know. A curious account of modern Russian belief in witchcraft is to be found in Madame Blavatsky's *Isis Unveiled.* The German word *Heke,* that is, witch, primarily signified priestess, a wise or superior woman who in a sylvan temple worshiped those gods and goddesses that together governed earth and heaven. Not alone but with thousands of the people for whom she officiated she was found there especially upon Walpurgis Night, the chief Hexen (witch) Sabbat of the north. A German scholar furnished this explanation.

The German word Heke, (witch) is a compound word from "hag" and "idisan" or "disan." Hag means a beautiful landscape, woodland, meadow, field, altogether. Idisen means female deities, wise-women. Hexen-Sabbat, or Walpurgis Night is May twelfth. Perfume and avocation—originally the old gods—perverted by the priests. It is a remnant of the great gathering to worship the old deities, when Christianity had overshadowed them. A monument of the wedding of Woden or Odin with Freia—Sun and Earth at spring time.

The Saxon festival "Eostre," the christian Easter, was celebrated in April, each of these festivals at a time when winter having released its sway, smiling earth giving her life to healing herbs and leaves, once more welcomed her worshipers. In the south of Europe, the month of October peculiarly belonged to the witches. The first of May, May-day, was especially devoted by those elementals known as fairies, whose special rites were dances upon the green sward, leaving curious mementoes of their visits in the circles known as "Fairies Rings." In reality the original meaning of "witch" was a wise woman. So also the word *Sab* means sage or wise, and *Saba* a host or congregation; while *Bac, Boc* and *Bacchus* all originally signified book. *Sabs* was the name of the day when the Celtic Druids gave instruction and is the origin of our words Sabbath and Sunday. But the degradation of learning, its almost total loss among christian nations, an entire change in the signification of words, owing to ignorance and superstition led to the strangest and most infamous results. The earliest doctors among the common people of christian Europe were women who had learned the virtues and use of herbs. The famous works of Paracelsus were but compilations of the knowledge of these "wise women" as he himself stated. During the feudal ages women were excellent surgeons, wounded warriors frequently falling under their care and to the skill of these women were indebted for recovery from dangerous wounds. Among the women of savage races to much greater extent than among the men, a knowledge of the healing powers of plants and herbs is to this day found. But while for many hundred years the knowledge of medicine, and its practice among the poorer classes was almost entirely in the hands of women and many discoveries in science are due to them, yet an acquaintance of herbs soothing to pain, or healing in their qualities, was then looked upon as having been acquired through diabolical agency. Even those persons cured through the instrumentality of some woman, were ready when the hour came to assert their belief in her indebtedness to the devil for her knowledge. Not only were the common people themselves ignorant of all science, but their brains were filled with superstitious fears, and the belief that knowledge had been first introduced to the world through woman's obedience to the devil. In the fourteenth century the church decreed that any woman who healed others without having duly studied, was a witch and should suffer death; yet in that same century, 1527, at Basle, Paracelsus threw all his medical works, including those of Hippocrates and Galen into the fire, saying that he knew nothing except what he had learned from witches.

[From *Woman, Church and State,* pp. 100–104.]

ROBERT GRAVES—THE WHITE GODDESS

One of the most influential books for the modern goddess movement is Robert Graves's (1895–1985) erudite and eccentric *The White Goddess,* first published in 1946 and then expanded in 1966. Graves survived the trenches of World War I to become an internationally acclaimed poet, novelist, scholar, translator, and mythographer. *The White Goddess* reflects this diverse background, and it is a difficult book, being what he called "a historical grammar of poetic myth." For Graves the purpose of all true poetry is the religious invocation of the Goddess, and Graves suggests that the cult of the Goddess has continued, though often obscurely and even without the conscious knowledge of the poet, in poetry.

In the first excerpt from *The White Goddess* Graves elaborates upon two points, the single but infinitely variable theme found in certain ancient poetic myths and A. E. Housman's notion that a true poem is one that makes your hair stand on end. The theme is the story of the battle between the rival gods of the waxing and waning year and their relationship to the Goddess. This is a very ancient and widespread story that represents agricultural renewal. Graves considers Housman's test for true poetry a sound one because it is a physical reaction stimulated by the mixed emotions of exaltation and dread brought on by the presence of the Goddess.

The Theme, briefly, is the antique story, which falls into thirteen chapters and an epilogue, of the birth, life, death and resurrection of the God of the Waxing Year; the central chapters concern the God's losing battle with the God of the Waning Year for love of the capricious and all-powerful Threefold Goddess, their mother, bride and layer-out. The poet identifies himself with the God of the Waxing Year and his Muse with the Goddess; the rival is his blood-brother, his other self, his weird. All true poetry—true by Housman's practical test—celebrates some incident or scene in this very ancient story, and the three main characters are so much a part of our racial inheritance that they not only assert themselves in poetry but recur on occasions of emotional stress in the form of dreams, paranoiac visions and delusions. The weird, or rival, often appears in nightmare as the tall, lean, dark-faced bed-side spectre, or Prince of the Air, who tries to drag the dreamer out through the window, so that he looks back and sees his body still lying rigid in bed; but he takes countless other malevolent or diabolic or serpent-like forms.

The Goddess is a lovely, slender woman with a hooked nose, deathly pale face, lips red as rowan-berries, startlingly blue eyes and long fair hair; she will suddenly transform herself into sow, mare, bitch, vixen, she-ass, weasel, serpent, owl, she-wolf, tigress, mermaid or loathsome hag. Her names and titles are innumerable. In ghost stories she often figures as 'The White Lady', and in ancient religions, from the British Isles to the Caucasus, as the 'White Goddess'. I cannot think of any true poet from Homer onwards who has not independently recorded his experience of her. The test of a poet's vision, one might say, is the accuracy of his portrayal of the White Goddess and of the island over which she rules. The reason why the hairs stand on end, the eyes water, the throat is constricted, the skin crawls and a shiver runs down the spine when one writes or reads a true poem is that a true poem is necessarily an invocation of the White Goddess, or Muse, the Mother of All Living, the ancient power of fright and lust—the female spider or the queen-bee whose embrace is death. Housman offered a secondary test of true poetry: whether it matches a phrase of Keats's, 'everything that reminds me of her goes through me like a spear'. This is equally pertinent to the Theme. Keats was writing under the shadow of death about his Muse, Fanny Brawne; and the 'spear that roars for blood' is the traditional weapon of the dark executioner and supplanter.

Sometimes, in reading a poem, the hairs will bristle at an apparently unpeopled and eventless scene described in it, if the elements bespeak her unseen presence clearly enough: for example, when owls hoot, the moon rides like a ship through scudding cloud, trees sway slowly together above a rushing waterfall, and a distant barking of dogs is heard; or when a peal of bells in frosty weather suddenly announces the birth of the New Year.

Despite the deep sensory satisfaction to be derived from Classical poetry, it never makes the hair rise and the heart leap, except where it fails to maintain decorous composure; and this is because of the difference between the attitudes of the Classical poet, and of the true poet, to the White Goddess. This is not to identify the true poet with the Romantic poet. 'Romantic', a useful word while it covered the re-introduction into Western Europe, by the writers of verse-romances, of a mystical reverence for woman, has become tainted by indiscriminate use. The typical Romantic poet of the nineteenth century was physically degenerate, or ailing, addicted to drugs and melancholia, critically unbalanced and a true poet only in his fatalistic regard for the Goddess as the mistress who commanded his destiny. The Classical poet, however gifted and industrious, fails to pass the test because he claims to be the Goddess's master—she is his mistress only in the derogatory sense of one who lives in coquettish ease under his protection. Sometimes, indeed, he is her bawdmaster: he attempts to heighten the appeal of his lines by studding them with 'beauties' borrowed from true poems.

[From *The White Goddess*, pp. 24–25.]

The second excerpt from *The White Goddess* elaborates on the three aspects of the Goddess: the maiden, the mature woman, and the hag or crone, and her relationship to the male. In it Graves also supports the theory of an early matriarchy that preceded the present patriarchal system.

Skelton in his *Garland of Laurell* thus describes the Triple Goddess in her three characters as Goddess of the Sky, Earth and Underworld:

> *Diana in the leavës green,*
> *Luna that so bright doth sheen,*
> *Persephone in Hell.*

As Goddess of the Underworld she was concerned with Birth, Procreation and Death. As Goddess of the Earth she was concerned with the three seasons of Spring, Summer and Winter: she animated trees and plants and ruled all living creatures. As Goddess of the Sky she was the Moon, in her three phases of New Moon, Full Moon, and Waning Moon. This explains why from a triad she was so often enlarged to an ennead. But it must never be forgotten that the Triple Goddess, as worshipped for example at Stymphalus, was a personification of primitive woman—woman the creatress and destructress. As the New Moon or Spring she was girl; as the Full Moon or Summer she was woman; as the Old Moon or Winter she was hag.

* * *

In Europe there were at first no male gods contemporary with the Goddess to challenge her prestige or power, but she had a lover who was alternatively the beneficent Serpent of Wisdom, and the beneficent Star of Life, her son. The Son was incarnate in the male demons of the various totem societies ruled by her, who assisted in the erotic dances held in her honour. The Serpent, incarnate in the sacred serpents which were the ghosts of the dead, sent the winds. The Son, who was also called Lucifer or Phosphorus ('bringer of light') because as evening-star he led in the light of the Moon, was reborn every year, grew up as the year advanced, destroyed the Serpent, and won the Goddess's love. Her love destroyed him, but from his ashes was born another Serpent which, at Easter, laid the *glain* or red egg which she ate; so that the Son was reborn to her as a child once more. Osiris was a Star-son, and though after his death he looped himself around the world like a serpent, yet when his fifty-yard long phallus was carried in procession it was topped with a golden star; this stood for himself renewed as the Child Horus, son of Isis, who had been both his bride and his layer-out and was now his mother once again. Her absolute power was proved by a yearly holocaust in her honour as 'Lady of the Wild Things', in which the totem bird or beast of each society was burned alive.

The most familiar icon of Aegean religions is therefore a Moon-woman, a Star-son and a wise spotted Serpent grouped under a fruit-tree—Artemis, Hercules and Erechtheus. Star-son and Serpent are at war; one succeeds the other in the Moon-woman's favour, as summer succeeds winter, and winter succeeds summer; as death succeeds birth and birth succeeds death. The Sun grows weaker or stronger as the year takes its course, the branches of the tree are now loaded and now bare, but the light of the Moon is invariable. She is impartial: she destroys or creates with equal passion. The conflict between the twins is given an ingenious turn in the Romance of *Kilhwych and Olwen*: Gwyn ('White') and his rival Gwythur ap Greidawl ('Victor, son of Scorcher') waged perpetual war for Creiddylad (*alias* Cordelia), daughter of Lludd (*alias* Llyr, *alias* Lear, *alias* Nudd, *alias* Nuada, *alias* Nodens), each in turn stealing her from the other, until the matter was referred to King Arthur. He gave the ironical decision that Creiddylad should be returned to her father and that the twins should 'fight for her every first of May, until the day of doom', and that whichever of them should then be conqueror should keep her.

There are as yet no fathers, for the Serpent is no more the father of the Star-son than the Star-son is of the Serpent. They are twins, and here we are returned to the single poetic Theme. The poet identifies himself with the Star-son, his hated rival is the Serpent; only if he is writing as a satirist, does he play the Serpent. The Triple Muse is woman in her divine character: the poet's enchantress, the only theme of his songs. It must not be forgotten that Apollo himself was once a yearly victim of the Serpent: for Pythagoras carved an inscription on his tomb at Delphi, recording his death in a fight with the local python—the python which he was usually supposed to have killed outright. The Star-son and the Serpent are still mere demons, and in Crete the Goddess is not even pictured with a divine child in her arms. She is the mother of all things; her sons and lovers partake of the sacred essence only by her grace.

[From *The White Goddess*, pp. 386–388.]

NEOPAGAN RITUALS

Ritual activity is at the heart of contemporary Neopaganism. As the following selections show, these rituals tend to be highly creative and inclusive of both the personal and political experiences of participants.

RITUAL TO THE GODDESS

The following ritual, taken from Margot Adler's study of Neopaganism, *Drawing Down the Moon*, was created by Ed Fitch. It provides a framework for opening a sacred circle in which both women and men can then shape their own worship.

Pagan Ritual for General Use

A circle should be marked on the floor, surrounding those who will participate in the ceremony. An altar is to be set up at the center of the circle. At the center of the altar shall be placed an image of the Goddess, and an incense burner placed in front of it. Behind the image should be a wand fashioned from a willow branch. Candles should be set upon the altar . . . a total of five, since one is to be set at each quarter and one will remain on the altar during the rite.

When all the people are prepared they shall assemble within the circle. The woman acting as priestess shall direct the man who acts as priest to light the candles and incense. She shall then say:

> The presence of the noble Goddess extends every-
> where.
> Throughout the many strange, magical,
> And beautiful worlds.
> To all places of wilderness, enchantment, and
> freedom.

She then places a candle at the north and pauses to look outwards, saying:

> The Lady is awesome.
> The Powers of death bow before Her.

The person closest to the east takes a candle from the altar and places it at that quarter, saying:

> Our Goddess is a Lady of Joy.
> The winds are Her servants.

The person closest to the south takes a candle from the altar and places it at that quarter, saying:

> Our Goddess is a Goddess of Love.
> At Her blessings and desire
> The sun brings forth life anew.

The person closest to the west takes a candle from the altar and places it at that quarter, saying:

> The seas are the domains of our Serene Lady.
> The mysteries of the depths are Hers alone.

The priest now takes the wand, and starting at the north, draws it along the entire circle clockwise back to the north point, saying:

> The circle is sealed, and all herein
> Are totally and completely apart
> From the outside world,
> That we may glorify the Lady whom we adore.
> Blessed Be!

All repeat: Blessed Be!

The priest now holds the wand out in salute towards the north for a moment and then hands it to the priestess, who also holds it out in salute. She motions to the group to repeat the following lines after her:

> As above, so below . . .
> As the universe, so the soul.
> As without, so within.
> Blessed and gracious one,
> On this day do we consecrate to you
> Our bodies,
> Our minds,
> And our spirits.
> Blessed Be!

Now is the time for discussion and teaching. Wine and light refreshments may be served. When the meeting has ended, all will stand and silently meditate for moment. The priestess will then take the wand and tap each candle to put it out, starting at the north and going clockwise about the circle, while saying:

> Our rite draws to its end.
> O lovely and gracious Goddess,
> Be with each of us as we depart.

The circle is broken!

[From *Drawing Down the Moon*, pp. 470–472.]

A Separation Ritual

The following very personal ritual was created by Heather Whiteside to help her through her divorce. It is a particularly powerful ritual in that divorce and the loss of relationship are an increasingly common experience for which traditional religions can offer little solace, something this ritual does very well.

After five years of deepening friendship and two and a half years of marriage, it is difficult to realize that the relationship is better ended. Lives become so interwined with time that it is painful to have to pull out the knots and unravel the old, flawed pattern to begin to weave anew. Since deciding to end my mar-

riage, I've been through some dark days and darker moods; even knowing that it was the right decision and action to leave, the pain and grief have still seemed overwhelming. It has been only the comfort and healing energy of woman friends that has seen me through this time of mourning; and it has been only through symbolic enactments and rituals that I've begun to clear my mind and life of the past.

At the full moon, I began a triad of rituals, designed to help me understand and come to terms with my decisions, actions, and emotions. These included: a ritual of self affirmation, the creation of an herbal charm to "heal a broken heart", and a candle spell to ease the pain of separation.

The first ritual was in affirmation of myself and of the rightness of my decision to end the relationship; it also served to release the rage I had felt toward my partner during the time that our relationship, as we knew it, was dying. I lit candles on my altar, and after gazing into the flames to relax and center myself, meditated on the reasons why I could no longer stay in the marriage. I then stated aloud the affirmations which I had meditated on:

My primary energy is drawn toward women; my deepest emotions and strongest beliefs center around them. (He did not understand.)

I am an artist who creates images of women, strong women alone and strong women together — but never with men. (He was confused) by the woman-identified sensibility and the sensuality of my truest art.

I rejoice in my physical being, in the transformation of plump, fragile weaknesses into the muscle of my runner's angular strength. (He felt that his masculinity was threatened.)

I realize that I have goals and ambitions that I must and will achieve. (AND THEY ARE NOT HIS.)

The second ritual involved creating a charm to heal a broken heart, a small work of ritual art to help me move through the relationship, through its ending, and into a new space. The charm used a circle of blue cloth, containing Angelica root, Rose buds, and Bay Laurel; a cloth heart, some ashes, and a copper coin; this was drawn up into a pouch and tied with a white ribbon.

The circle of cloth was sewn from six triangles of blue velvet, three the light blue of dawn and three midnight dark. The seams were embroidered with alternating patterns; first a floral design in green, pink and yellow, and then a design of sun gold and moon silver stitching. I lavished attention on the cloth to invest it with my energy.

Angelica root is an herb sacred to the goddess Sophia; I knew that I needed wisdom to deal with my situation, and so the herb was to invoke the Goddess. Angelica root also maintains or restores peace and harmony.

Roses are a flower of love, but also of transforma-tion and change. The five petals of the rose flower stand for the Wiccan pentacle, to ground and center my emotions.

Bay Laurel is for luck and help in difficult situations.

The cloth heart was actually composed of three other hearts; the innermost being a heart cut from the hem of my wedding dress — this was cut into two pieces and sewn together again with blue thread. Next was a casing of white felt, also sewn with blue, and the outer heart was of red velvet. These are a broken heart which is healed, a pure white heart released of pain, and a red heart capable of love and passion again.

The ashes were from a copy of the marriage certifi-cate. The power of fire is transforming energy; while the flames took the paper to ashes, I was released from the bonds that the paper had stood for.

The copper coin was included to draw new love to me, when it is time for such.

When the charm was completed, I charged it with the energy of the four elements. I breathed upon it to give it the power of air; passed it through a candle flame to charge it with fire; sprinkled it with water to charge with that elemental force; and dipped it in salt to charge with earth.

The final ritual was a three-day candle spell for separation, to be able to part the relationship with more ease.

I took two identical white candles, and on one I inscribed the biological symbol for female, a penta-gram with my own name; while on the other I incised a male symbol, a pentagram, and my husband's name. I placed these candles close together on my altar, lit them and some ritual incense, and meditated on what the relationship and the marriage had meant to me and on how I would like to see the affair transformed into new friendship now. Then I moved the candles away a little from each other, and continued to move them further apart each day for three days. While doing this I chanted:

"Warm was the passion, cold is now the heart; let (name) and (name) painlessly part.
Come the fire of friendship and alliance instead in the name of Sophia, goddess of wisdom
So mote it be."

On the third day, after the candles were at their furthest point apart, I let them burn all the way down.

On my altar, the last candle has just flickered out; this ritual of separation and of healing is over. The circle is open but not broken.

Blessed Be.

[From "A Separation Ritual," by Heather White-side. In *Womanspirit,* Fall Equinox Issue, 1982, p. 43.]

RITUAL AND POLITICAL ACTION

In the following excerpt Starhawk, a Neopagan witch, describes the ritual elements of political action.

In the summer of 1981, several of us from different groups within the Pagan community decided to take part in the blockade of the Diablo Canyon Nuclear Power Plant, which was constructed close to an earthquake fault in an ecologically sensitive area of the California Coast. Fifteen years of opposition, including two previous occupations of the plant grounds by members of the Abalone Alliance, had not deterred the Pacific Gas and Electric company from proceeding. Testing and operating licenses had been delayed for over a year during the freeze on licensing after the nuclear accident at Three Mile Island, but that summer Reagan was pushing hard for nuclear power and licensing was imminent.

The Abalone Alliance is organized into small, autonomous groups called affinity groups. Members of each affinity group decide together how they want to participate in each action, though all are unified by a commitment to nonviolence. Our group, called Matrix, particularly wanted to bring our knowledge of ritual and group energy to the blockade.

The blockade was called early in September, after the security clearance was granted, the last step before licensing. I spent nearly three weeks on blockade altogether, was arrested twice, and each time spent about four days in the women's jail.

The blockade became a crucial experience in my understanding not only of the theory, but also of the actual practice of political/spiritual work based on the principle of power-from-within.

★ ★ ★

The Diablo blockade was an initiation: a journey through fear, a descent into the dark, and a return with knowledge and empowerment from within; a death and rebirth that began with a stripping process and promises something at the end.

For me, the journey that began in despair now reaches a place of hope and a sense of empowerment.

★ ★ ★

Because alone no one can dream the dark into love. We need each other for that. We need all the power we can raise together.

These are not comforting times in which to make promises; the stakes are too high, we are playing with forms of death from which there may be no return, and all the endings are still uncertain.

We can only begin.

Take hands; for we are the circle of rebirth. If there is to be renewal, it begins with us. We can touch — through these words, these pages. We can know the dark, and dream it into a new image.

As life, friends. As source.

[From *Dreaming the Dark,* pp. xiv–xvi.]

SANTERIA — SPELLS

Santeria is an African religious tradition that utilizes some of the symbolism and rituals of Roman Catholicism. It developed among the Yoruba people who were brought to Cuba in the nineteenth century to work in the sugarcane fields. They preserved their Yoruba deities, called *orisha*s, but also found correspondences between these deities and particular Catholic saints; they equally often call on the *orisha* or the equivalent saint — deity and saint are seen as one and the same. Since Santeria was primarily the religion of an oppressed people, it has kept many of its secrets, but enough is known to reveal an elaborate and highly detailed religious system involving sacrifice, divination, possession, and initiation. From Cuba Santeria spread throughout the Caribbean and into North and South America. Today it continues to thrive throughout these areas.

While most followers of Santeria also consider themselves Catholics, women find greater religious expression in Santeria than in Catholicism when they act as mediums or organize a group ritual or simply gain a sense of control over their lives by performing one of the many spells available to them.

The excerpts are some common spells collected by Migene González-Wippler, which involve the following Yoruba deities (*orisha*):

Oshún—goddess of love and marriage

Elegguá, god who opens and closes all doors

Yemayá, the goddess of the moon.

As with most of the rituals of Santeria, they are a means for resolving the problems of everyday life, such as romantic relationships.

For Love

A common practice to win somebody's favors is to tie five of his or her hairs with five hairs from the person who is casting the spell. The hairs are placed in the form of a cross in the center of a small bread roll, which is then buried in a flower-pot filled with four different types of earth. A sprig of rue is planted in the pot in the name of Oshún, asking her that in the same way the rue grows inside the pot, so will love grow in the heart of the victim for the person who desires him or her.

For Love

This spell is known as "the drunken coconut." It is an offer to Elegguá to enlist his aid in winning the love of a person. One starts by sawing off the top of a coconut and throwing away its milk. The empty coconut shell is filled with caramels, gum-drops, and five types of liquor. Several essences are also added to the mixture, namely, *esencia de menta, de amor, dominante, vencedora,* and *sígueme.* A cigar is lit in Elegguá's name and the smoke is blown inside the coconut shell. The top of the shell is replaced before the smoke can be dispersed, and the two parts of the coconut are sealed together with the wax from a candle bought in a church. The coconut symbolizes the head of the person who is being bewitched. A white candle is lit in Elegguá's honor during five consecutive days asking the orisha for the love of the person desired.

To Get Married

The name of the person desired is written on a piece of paper, which is then placed at the bottom of a small glass bowl. Over the paper are arranged five small hooks. The bowl is filled with honey and offered to Oshún, patroness of marriage, being careful to taste the honey at the moment of the offer. A yellow candle is lit in the orisha's honor during five days, asking her to propitiate the marriage. It is helpful to purchase a small image of the saint prior to the ceremony.

To Get Married

This spell was designed to force a reluctant man into marriage. The main ingredient of the spell is the man's sperm, which must be gathered surreptitiously in a small wad of cotton without him knowing what it is intended for. The cotton is formed into a wick by rolling it between the fingers until some of it protrudes from the rest of the cotton. This crude wick is used in an oil lamp that requires the following ingredients:

a large lily bulb	*aceite de amor*
aceite de coco	*aceite amarra hombre*
aceite de menta	*aceite de lirio*
aceite intranquilo	cantharides
acijte yo poedo y to no	quicksilver

The top of the lily is removed with a knife and the bulb is hollowed by removing most of its meat, ensuring that the outer cortex is intact. At the bottom of the cavity is placed a piece of parchment with the man's name written across it in the form of a cross. The quicksilver is added with the intention that in the same way this liquid runs, so will the man run to the woman who wants him. The cantharides are believed to fill the man with desire for the woman who is bewitching him. A little of each of the oils is added until the bulb is almost filled. The cotton wad is placed on top of the oil, floating over the liquid until it is saturated with it. A short invocation is said to Oshún, asking that she intercede and force the man into marrying the petitioner. The lamp is lit every night at nine during five nights while repeating the invocation to Oshún. According to the santeros, this spell never fails.

To Dominate a Husband

The name of the husband is written on a piece of paper and placed inside a medium-sized, black or dark bottle, together with a used personal article, some ammonia, *esencia dominante, esencia amanza guapo, esencia de menta,* and some of her urine. The bottle is closed tightly and hid in a place where the victim will not find it. Every time the husband becomes restless or troublesome in any way, his wife simply shakes the bottle several times. This simple act activates the magical ingredients inside the bottle and gives her complete domination over her husband.

For Fertility

A pomegranate is bought in the name of Yemayá, the beautiful Yoruba moon goddess. She is the patroness of motherhood and it is usually wise to enlist her aid in matters of fertility.

The pomegranate is cut in halves, which are both covered with honey. A piece of paper with the name of the petitioner is placed between the two halves of the pomegranate, which are then put back together again. Yemayá is then invoked and asked that in the same way the pomegranate is rich in health and seeds, so will the petitioner be healthy and fruitful. A blue candle is burned in Yemayá's honor every day for a month, starting with the first day of the menstruation cycle. It is not uncommon that women making this offer to this lovely goddess become pregnant during this month.

[From *Santería,* pp. 153–161.]

VOODOO—MAMA LOLA

Voodoo is also an African religious tradition that is heavily influenced by Roman Catholicism. It developed among the various West African peoples who worked in the cane fields of Haiti, where it came under the influence of Catholic rituals and symbols. Theologically, though, it remains a polytheistic African religion with a complex cosmology. Much like Santeria, Voodoo maintains its original African deities, which are equated with Christian saints. It too emphasizes initiation and spirit possession. Voodoo also played a significant part in the organization of the 1804 revolt that led to Haiti becoming the first Black republic in the Western Hemisphere.

The main concerns of Voodoo are the everyday problems of life from relationships to sickness, which Voodoo priests seek to cure. Both women and men are priests, and the following excerpt is taken from Karen McCarthy Brown's book *Mama Lola,* a study of a Voodoo priestess living in the Haitian community in Brooklyn, New York. In the excerpt Alourdes (Mama Lola) describes being called by the spirits. This begins to happen after she survives two major sicknesses and involves the dreams of her sister-in-law, her mother, as well as her own dreams, and two trips back to Haiti from New York City.

One day somebody tell me, "Beatrice want to see you." Beatrice my sister-in-law. Sunday afternoon, I got clothes on me, and I go there. When I first come to New York, I live in her house. But we don't get along too good, and I don't see her for a long time. Long time. You know me, I don't go to people I know to ask or beg for nothing! So I see her, I just say, "Aunt Bebe, people tell me you was asking for me. What happen . . . my mother? . . . Something happen in my family?"

She say, "No, nothing don't happen in your family. I want to see you because I got a dream about you." I say, "Oh, yeah? It very serious?" She say, "I don't know if it serious or not."

She say, "I dream I see a mountain man on Forty-second Street." She say, in that dream, she have to cross that street, and everybody standing, just waiting for the light. She look at that man. She say, "They got mountain man in New York, too?" When they give

the green light, she just walk. And one lady walking behind her say, "Hey, Madame! Madame! Madame! That man call you." Bebe say, "What man?" When she turn her head, she see the mountain man.

She went to the mountain man, and she tell the mountain man, "Hi," and he say, "Hi, Cousin." And Bebe say, "You want to speak to me?" And he say, "Yes, Cousin." And he tell Bebe, "Did you know Philo?" Bebe say, "Philo? Yeah." "Did you know Alourdes?" Bebe say, "Yes, I know Alourdes. She my sister-in-law."

And that man say: "When she come into New York, why she don't dress like me, jean pants and jean shirt? If she dress like me, she was well dressed, right?" And Bebe say, "I don't know." And the mountain man say, "Tell Alourdes if she dress like me, everything going to be beautiful!" Bebe say, "Really?" and that man walk maybe three or four step, and Bebe don't see him no more, and boom! the clock—rrrrrrrrrrrrrrr—and she say, "What time is it?"

It was six-thirty in the morning, and when she wake up, Bebe say, "Ahhhh! I understand that dream. I understand. I have to see Alourdes to explain her that." Because she know my mother have spirit, you know, so she say maybe Alourdes's mother' spirit come and talk to me. Maybe that man . . . maybe that Kouzen Zaka.

When Alourdes heard her sister-in-law's dream, she understood what she had to do. She had to go back to Haiti for the kind of treatment no hospital in the United States could provide.

★ ★ ★

Alourdes told her mother about Kouzen Zaka's message, and Philo said that even though she had not heard from Alourdes, she had known something was wrong. She also had had an important dream. In Philo's dream, Alourdes came back home with her arm in a cast, as if it had been broken. In the dream, Alourdes entered the house and, without saying a word to her mother, went straight to the altar to pray. After some time, she arose, turned her back on her mother, and, still silent, walked out the door. Philo had this dream about a month before Alourdes's return to Haiti, and it bothered her so much that she even discussed it with the neighbors.

On one of the first days Alourdes was home, the warrior spirit Ogou possessed her mother, and the message he delivered was not one Alourdes wanted to hear. "Papa Ogou come in my mother' head, and he tell me I'm suppose to see with card, you know . . . do spirit work . . . help people. That I don't like!" Although Alourdes's mother was very poor, she had quite a reputation as a manbo in Port-au-Prince. For a short period, Philo had even served as a counselor to François Duvalier, before he became president of Haiti and the ugly parts of his character revealed themselves. Nevertheless, Alourdes believed that little of her mother's healing knowledge or talent had rubbed off on her. "I say, 'Oh, boy! How I'm going to do that?' Because to help people you got to know a lot'a thing. I say, 'How I going to put all that in my head?' My mother tell me, 'You'll manage; don't you worry!'"

Initiation into the Vodou priesthood involves an elaborate set of rituals, the core of which is a long period of seclusion in which a person is said to kouche (literally, to lie down or go to sleep). These rituals are commonly referred to as "taking the ason," that is, taking up the beaded rattle that is said to give priests and priestesses a certain amount of leverage in working with the spirits.

Papa Ogou in my mother' head say I have to take the ason. You know, my mother don't have no ason. But Papa Ogou say I have to, because my father' family serve with the ason, so I have to take the ason for protection. I serve two kind of spirit, from my father' family and from my mother' family.

The initiation rituals for Alourdes could not take place right away. Money had to be saved for drummers, sacrificial animals, food and drink for the spirits. Several sets of ritual clothing had to be sewn. Thus on this first visit only a simple ritual called a lave têt (a headwashing) was performed. The headwashing was a pwomès (promise) Alourdes made to the spirits, indicating that she had heard their request and intended to honor it. The ritual also "cooled" the restive spirits in Alourdes's head and "fed" and strengthened them. After two weeks, she returned to New York. But before she left, she promised the spirits that she would return to Haiti to kouche as soon as she had seven hundred dollars.

During this time Alourdes drew on skills acquired during the short visit with her mother, on her awakening memory, and on the help of the spirits, who began to speak to her more directly through her dreams.

My mother teach me a lot'a thing. She show me how to read card. My mother start to show me; then, after that, I dream and the spirit finish . . . they finish show me how to read card in that dream. She teach me about senmp—you know, herb. My mother know a lot about herb, a whole lot! Also, I begin to remember. Since I little girl, I watch her, and now I remember a lot'a thing.

My mother tell me, "Now you going to see the real person. Somebody come in your house, they happy—you know, dancing, drinking—even they do that, you going to see if they sad. If they got something bad inside them, you going to see that."

Finally, when Alourdes had saved seven hundred dollars, she returned to Haiti to take the ason.

Second time I go back to Haiti, my life was not good. Not real bad like before, but not good. Second time I go, I pass one month in Haiti . . . nine day inside that little room where they kouche me. Then I a manbo. When I come back to New York, people pouring all over me! People who lose job, I make them find job. People who sick, I treat them. Their husband or wife leave them, I make that person come back. After I come back from Haiti second time, I did not have to work outside again.

[From Mama Lola, pp. 73–77.]

Sources

The Art of Synthesis, by Alan Leo. 1912. Reprint, Edinburgh: International Publishing Co., 1949.

Astrology for Everyone: What It Is and How It Works, by Evangeline Adams. 1931. Reprint, New York: Dell Publishing Co., 1972.

The Book of Wisdom of Folly, in the Form of an Epistle of 666 the Great Wild Beast to his Son 777, being the Equinox Volume III No. vi., by The Master Therion (Aleister Crowley). Chico, CA: L. A. Brock, n.d.

Drawing Down the Moon: Witches, Druids, Goddess-Worshippers, and Other Pagans in America Today, by Margot Adler. 1979. Rev. and expanded edition. Boston: Beacon Press, 1986.

Dreaming the Dark: Magic, Sex and Politics, by Starhawk. Boston: Beacon Press. 1982.

Epistle from the Womens Yearly Meeting at York, 1688. Los Angeles: William Andrews Clark Memorial Library, University of California, 1979.

How to Judge a Nativity, by Alan Leo. 1912. Reprint, Rochester, VT: Destiny Books, 1983.

Mama Lola: A Voodoo Priestess in Brooklyn, by Karen McCarthy Brown. Berkeley, CA: University of California Press, 1991.

Meetings with Remarkable Men, by G. I. Gurdjieff. 1963. New York: E. P. Dutton, 1969.

New York Criminal Reports, vol. 32, Dec. 11, 1914.

Pictorial Key to the Tarot, by Arthur Edward Waite. 1910. Reprint, New York: Causeway Books, 1972.

Santería: African Magic in Latin America, by Migene Gonzáles-Wippler. 1973. Reprint, Bronx, NY: Original Products, 1981.

Science and Health with Key to the Scriptures, by Mary Baker Eddy. Boston: Allison V. Stewart, 1914.

The Sea Priestess, by Dion Fortune. 1938. Reprint, York Beach, ME: Samuel Weiser, 1978.

The Secret Doctrine, Vols. 1 and 2, by H. P. Blavatsky. 1888. Facsimile edition. Los Angeles: The Theosophy Co., 1964.

"A Separation Ritual," by Heather Whiteside. In *Womanspirit,* Fall Equinox issue, 1982.

The Shakers: Two Centuries of Spiritual Reflection, ed. Robley Edward Whitson. Ramsey, NJ: Paulist, 1983.

The Temple Legend: Freemasonry and Related Occult Movements, by Rudolf Steiner. Translated by John M. Wood. London: Rudolf Steiner Press, 1985.

The White Goddess: A Historical Grammar of Poetic Myth, by Robert Graves. 1948. Amended and enlarged edition, New York: Farrar, Straus and Giroux, 1966.

Woman, Church and State: The Original Exposé of Male Collaboration Against the Female Sex, by Matilda Joslyn Gage. 1893. Reprint, Watertown, MA: Persephone Press, 1980.

The Woman's Bible, by Elizabeth Cady Stanton and the Revising Committee. 1895. Reprint, Seattle, WA: Coalition Task Force on Women and Religion, 1974.

Womens Speaking Justified, by Margaret Fell. 1667. Facsimile edition. The Augustan Reprint Society, Publication No. 194. Los Angeles: William Andrews Clark Memorial Library, University of California, 1979.

Bibliography

Introductory Works

Sydney E. Ahlstrom, *A Religious History of the American People.* 1972. Garden City, NY: Doubleday & Company, 1975.

Edward Deming Andrews, *The People Called Shakers.* 1953. New York: Dover Publications, 1963.

Nevill Drury, *Dictionary of Mysticism and the Occult.* San Francisco: Harper & Row, 1985.

Mircea Eliade, *Occultism, Witchcraft, and Cultural Fashions: Essays in Comparative Religions.* Chicago: University of Chicago Press, 1976.

Michael Gomes, *The Dawning of the Theosophical Movement.* Wheaton, IL: The Theosophical Publishing House, 1987.

Ellic Howe, *Urania's Children: The Strange World of the Astrologers.* London: William Kimber & Co., 1967.

T. M. Luhrmann, *Persuasions of the Witch's Craft: Ritual Magic in Contemporary England.* Cambridge, MA: Harvard University Press, 1989.

Geoffrey F. Nuttall, *The Holy Spirit in Puritan Faith and Experience.* Oxford: Basil Blackwell, 1946.

The Occult in America: New Historical Perspectives, ed. Howard Kerr and Charles L. Crow. Chicago: University of Chicago Press, 1983.

Robert F. Thompson, *Flash of the Spirit: African and Afro-American Art and Philosophy.* New York: Vintage Books, 1984.

Texts on Women and Alternative Religious Movements

Margaret Hope Bacon, *Mothers of Feminism: The Story of Quaker Women in America.* San Francisco: Harper & Row, 1989.

Mary Farrell Bednarowski, "Women in Occult America," *Journal of the American Academy of Religion* 177–195.

Diana Burfield, "Theosophy and Feminism: Some Explorations in Nineteenth Century Biography." Pp. 27–56 in *Women's Religious Experience,* ed. Pat Holden. London & Canberra: Croom Helm, 1983.

Cynthia Eller, "Relativizing the Patriarchy: The Sacred History of the Feminist Spirituality Movement." *History of Religion* 30/3 (1991): 279–295.

Mary K. Greer, "Women of the Golden Dawn," *Gnosis Magazine* 21 (Fall 1991): 56–63.

Nancy A. Hardesty, *Women Called to Witness: Evangelical Feminism in the 19th Century.* Nashville, TN: Abingdon Press, 1984.

Journal of Feminist Studies in Religion 5/1 (Spring 1989) Special Section on Neopaganism.

Diane Mariechild, *A Feminist Guide to Psychic Development.* Trumansburg, NY: The Crossing Press, 1981.

Penelope Washbourn, *Seasons of Woman.* San Francisco: Harper & Row, 1979.

Women & Religion in America, ed. Rosemary Radford Ruether and Rosemary Skinner Keller. 2 vols. San Francisco: Harper & Row, 1981, 1983.

INDEX OF NAMES

INDEX OF SUBJECTS

ACKNOWLEDGMENTS

The editor and publisher gratefully acknowledge permission to reprint copyrighted material from the following:

Judaism

Augsburg Fortress Publishers for selections from *Maenads, Martyrs, Matrons, Monastics,* by Ross Kraemer, copyright © 1988 Fortress Press. Used by permission of Augsburg Fortress.

Brown University for selections from "The Beruriah Traditions," by David Goodblatt in *Persons and Institutions in Early Rabbinic Judaism,* ed. by William Scott Green, published by Scholars Press, 1977, copyright © 1977 by William Scott Green.

The Jewish Publication Society for selections from *Tanakh: The Holy Scriptures,* copyright © 1985 by The Jewish Publication Society.

Paulist Press for selections from *The Zohar,* by D. C. Mott. Used by permission of Paulist Press.

Random House, Inc. and Crown Publishers for selections from *A Treasury of Jewish Folklore,* ed. by Nathan Ausubel, copyright © 1948 by Crown Publishers.

Random House, Inc. and Schocken Books for selections from *The Essential Philo,* ed. by Nahum N. Glatzer, copyright © 1971 by Schocken Books Inc.

Yale University Press for selections from *The Mishnah: A New Translation,* by Jacob Neusner, © 1988 by Yale University.

Christianity

Augsburg Fortress Publishers for selections reprinted from the following: *Luther's Works,* vol. 54, edited by Theodore G. Tappert, copyright © 1967 Fortress Press; *Women of the Reformation in France and England,* by Roland H. Bainton, copyright © 1973 Augsburg Publishing House; *Women of the Reformation in Germany and Italy,* by Roland H. Bainton, copyright © 1971 Augsburg Publishing House. Used by permission of Augsburg Fortress.

The Catholic University of America Press for selections from *Saint Gregory of Nyssa: Ascetical Works,* translated by Virginia Woods Callahan, copyright © 1967 by The Catholic University of America Press, Inc.

Concordia Publishing House for selections from *Luther's Works,* vol. 1, edited by Jaroslav Pelikan, copyright © 1958 Concordia Publishing House. Reprinted by permission of Concordia Publishing House.

Dover Publications, Inc. for selections from *The Malleus Maleficarum of Heinrich Kramer and James Sprenger,* translated by Rev. Montague Summers.

Doubleday for selections from *The Confessions of St. Augustine,* by John K. Ryan, copyright © 1960 by Doubleday, a division of Bantam Doubleday Dell Publishing Group, Inc. Used by permission of Doubleday, a division of Bantam Doubleday Dell Publishing Group, Inc.

HarperCollins Publishers Inc. for excerpts from *The Nag Hammadi Library,* by James M. Robinson, copyright © 1978 by E. J. Brill. Reprinted by permission of HarperCollins Publishers.

The National Council of the Churches of Christ in the USA for selections from the New Revised Standard Version of the Bible, copyright © 1989 by the Division of Christian Education of the National Council of the Churches of Christ in the USA and used by permission.

Paulist Press for selections from the following: *Catherine of Siena: The Dialogue,* translated by Suzanne Noffke, O.P., copyright © 1980 by The Missionary Society of St. Paul the Apostle in the State of New York; *Francis and Clare: The Complete Works,* translated by Regis J. Armstrong, O.F.M. Cap., and Ignatius C. Brady, O.F.M., copyright © 1982 by The Missionary Society of St. Paul the Apostle in the State of New York; *Hildegard of Bingen,* by Mother Columba Hart and Jane Bishop, copyright © 1990 by the Abbey of Regina Laudis: Benedictine Congregation Regina Laudis of the Strict Observance, Inc. Used by permission of Paulist Press.

Persea Books, Inc. for excerpts from *The Book of the City of Ladies,* by Christine de Pizan, translated by Carl Jeffrey Richards, copyright © 1982 by Persea Books, Inc.

Penguin Books Ltd. for selections from *The Alexiad of Anna Comnena,* pp. 463–467, translated by E. R. A. Sewter (Penguin Classics, 1969), copyright © E. R. A. Sewter, 1969 (Harmondsworth, England: 1969). Reproduced by permission of Penguin Books Ltd.

The University Press of America for selections from *A Lost Tradition: Women Writers of the Early Church,* by Patricia Wilson-Kastner, G. Ronald Kastner, Ann Millin, Rosemary Rader, and Jeremiah Reedy, copyright © 1981 by University Press of America, Inc.

Westminster/John Knox Press for selections from *Calvin: Institutes of the Christian Religion,* vols. XX and XXI: The Library of Christian Classics, edited by John T. McNeill and translated by Ford Lewis Battles, copyright © 1955 W. L. Jenkins. Used by permission of Westminster/John Knox Press.

Islam

Mouton de Gruyter for permission to reprint from *A Reader on Islam,* ed. Arthur Jeffrey, copyright © 1962 by Mouton & Co., Publishers.

Macmillan Publishing Company for permission to reprint from *The Koran Interpreted,* A. J. Arberry, translator, copyright © 1955 by George Allen & Unwin, Ltd.

Oxford University Press for selections from *The Life of Muhammad,* trans. by A. Guillaume.

Pantheon Books, a division of Random House, Inc. for permission to reprint from *Arab Folktales,* by Inea Bushnaq, copyright © 1986 by Inea Bushnaq.

Paulist Press for selections from *Ibn Al-'Arabi: The Bezels of Wisdom,* translated by R. W. J. Austin, copyright © 1980 by The Missionary Society of St. Paul the Apostle in the State of New York. Used by permission of Paulist Press.

Penguin Books Ltd. for selections from *Muslim Saints and Mystics,* by Farid al-Din Attar, translated by A. J. Arberry (Harmondsworth, England: Arkana, 1990), pp. 40–51, copyright © 1966 A. J. Arberry. Reproduced by permission of Penguin Books Ltd.

Ancient Near East, Greece, and Rome

The Continuum Publishing Company for permission to reprint from *The Aeneid,* by Vergil, copyright © 1964 by Frederick Ungar Publishing Company, Inc.

Farrar, Straus & Giroux, Inc. and Curtis Brown, Ltd. for excerpts from *The Golden Ass,* by Robert Graves. Copyright © 1951 by Robert Graves, renewal copyright © 1979 by Robert Graves. Reprinted by permission of Farrar, Straus & Giroux, Inc. and Curtis Brown, Ltd.

Harcourt Brace Jovanovich, Inc. for excerpts from *The Antigone of Sophocles: An English Version,* by Dudley Fitts and Robert Fitzgerald, copyright © 1939 by Harcourt Brace Jovanovich, Inc. and renewed 1967 by Dudley Fitts and Robert Fitzgerald, reprinted by permission of the publisher.

Harvard University Press and the Loeb Classical Library for permission to reprint excerpts from the following: *Livy,* vol. 9, trans. Evan T. Sage, Cambridge, Mass.: Harvard University Press, 1967. Lucretius, *De Rerum Natura,* trans. W. H. D. Rouse, revised by Martin Ferguson Smith, 2d ed, Cambridge, Mass.: Harvard University Press, 1982. Ovid, *Fasti,* vol. 5, trans. by Sir James George Frazer, Cambridge, Mass.: Harvard University Press, 1976. Philostratus and Eunapius, *The Lives of the Sophists,* trans. by Wilmer Cave Wright, Cambridge, Mass.: Harvard University, 1968. Pliny, *Natural History,* vol. 2, trans. by H. Rackham, Cambridge, Mass.: Harvard University Press, 1969. Plutarch, *Moralia,* vol. 5, trans. Frank Cole Babbitt, Cambridge, Mass.: Harvard University Press, 1969.

Prentice Hall for selections from Hugh Lloyd-Jones, *The Eumenides by Aeschylus,* copyright © 1970, pp. 38–39, 52–53, 58, 60–61. Reprinted by permission of Prentice Hall, Englewood Cliffs, New Jersey.

Princeton University Press for the following: selections from Barnes, Jonathan, editor, *The Complete Works of Aristotle,* volume one, copyright © 1984 by Princeton University Press; Pritchard, James, editor, *Ancient Near Eastern Texts Relating to the Old Testament,* copyright © 1969 by Princeton University Press; Pritchard, James, editor, *The Ancient Near East: Volume I, An Anthology of Texts and Pictures,* copyright © 1958 by Princeton University Press. Reprinted by permission of Princeton University Press.

Northern European Paganism

Bantam Books, a division of Bantam Doubleday Dell Publishing Group, Inc. for selections from *Beowulf and Other Old English Poems,* by Constance Hieatt, translator. Translation copyright © 1967, 1982.

Indiana University Press for selections from *New Readings on Women in Old English Literature,* ed. Helen Damico and Alexandra Hennessey Olsen. Copyright © 1990 by Indiana University Press.

Thomas Kinsella for selections from *The Tain,* published by Oxford University Press, copyright © 1969 Thomas Kinsella.

New York University Press for selections from *Njál's Saga,* trans. by Carl F. Bayerschmidt and Lee M. Hollander, copyright © 1955 by The American-Scandinavian Foundation.

Oxford University Press for selections from *An Anthology of Old English Poetry,* by Charles W. Kennedy, copyright © 1960 by Oxford University Press, Inc.; renewed 1988 by Elizabeth D. Kennedy. Reprinted by permission of the publisher.

Pantheon Books, a division of Random House, Inc., for selections from *The Complete Grimm's Fairy Tales,* by Jakob Ludwig Karl and Wilhelm Karl Grimm, trans. Margaret Hunt. Copyright © 1944 by Pantheon Books Inc. and renewed 1972 by Random House, Inc. Reprinted by permission of Pantheon Books, a division of Random House, Inc.

Random House, Inc. and Alfred A. Knopf, Inc. for selections from the following: *The Complete Works of Tacitus,* by Tacitus, ed. by M. Hadas, trans. by A. Church and Wm. Brodribb. Copyright © 1942 and renewed 1970 by Random House, Inc. Reprinted by permission of Random House, Inc. *Le Morte D'Arthur,* by Sir Thomas Malory, translated by Keith Baines. Copyright © 1967 by Keith Baines. Reprinted by permission of Clarkson N. Potter, Inc., a division of Crown Publishers, Inc.

University of California Press for selections from the following: *Mabinogi and Other Medieval Welsh Tales,* trans. Patrick K. Ford, copyright © 1977 by The Regents of the University of California. Snorri Sturluson, *Prose Edda of Snorri Sturluson,* ed. and trans. by Jean Young. Copyright © 1964 The Regents of the University of California.

University of Pennsylvania Press for selections from *Poems of the Vikings: The Elder Edda,* trans. by Patricia Terry.

Shamanism and Tribal Religions

Columbia University Press for a selection from *Zuni Mythology,* by Ruth Benedict, copyright © 1935 by Columbia University Press, New York. Reprinted by permission from the publisher.

Bantam Doubleday Dell Publishing Group, Inc. for selections from *African Folklore,* by Richard Dorson. Copyright © 1972 by Richard M. Dorson. Used by permission of Doubleday, a division of Bantam Doubleday Dell Publishing Group, Inc.

Harvard University Press for selections reprinted by permission of the publishers from *Nisa: The Life and Words of a !Kung Woman,* by Marjorie Shostak, Cambridge, Mass.: Harvard University Press, copyright © 1981 by Marjorie Shostak.

David Hawkes for selections reprinted from *Ch'u Tz'ü: The Songs of the South: An Ancient Chinese Anthology,* trans. by David Hawkes, Oxford: Clarendon Press, 1959. Available in revised edition *The Songs of the South,* published by Penguin Books, 1985.

Holt, Rinehart and Winston, Inc. for excerpts from *Sanapia: Commanche Medicine Woman,* by David E. Jones, copyright © 1972 by Holt, Rinehart and Winston, Inc., reprinted by permission of the publisher.

Middle American Research Institute of Tulane University for selections from *The Book of Counsel: The Popol Vuh of the Quiche Maya of Gautemala,* by Munro S. Edmonson.

The Oxford University Press for selections from *Conversations with Ogotemmêli: An Introduction to Dogon Religious Ideas,* by Marcel Griaule, copyright © 1965 by International African Institute.

Paulist Press for selections reprinted from *Native American Spirituality,* edited by Miguel Leon-Portilla, copyright © 1980 by The Missionary Society of St. Paul the Apostle in the State of New York. Used by permission of Paulist Press.

Penguin USA for selections from *Book of the Hopi,* by Frank Waters. Copyright © 1963 by Frank Waters. Used by permission of Viking Penguin, a division of Penguin Books USA Inc.

Routledge & Kegan Paul Ltd. for selections from *Djanggawul: An Aboriginal Religious Cult of North-Eastern Arnhem Land,* by Ronald M. Berndt, copyright © 1953.

University of British Columbia Press for selections from John LeRoy, editor, *Kewa Tales* (Vancouver: UBC Press, 1985), pp. 41–46, 89–91. Copyright © University of British Columbia Press. All rights reserved.

University of California Press for selections from *Yurok Myths,* translated and edited by Grace Buzaljko, copyright © 1976 by The Regents of the University of California.

University of Hawaii Press for selections from *The Life and Hard Times of a Korean Shaman: Of Tales and the Telling of Tales,* by Laurel Kendall, copyright © 1988 by the University of Hawaii Press.

University of Oklahoma Press for selections from *The Sacred Pipe,* recorded and edited by Joseph Epes Brown, copyright © 1953 by the University of Oklahoma Press.

The University of Tokyo Press for selections from *Kojiki,* trans. Donald L. Philippi.

University of Washington Press for selections from Edwin Grant Burrows, *Flower in My Ear,* copyright © 1985 by the University of Washington Press.

Hinduism

Doubleday for selections from *In Praise of Krishna,* by Edward Dimock and Denise Levertov. Copyright © 1967 by The Asia Society, Inc. Used by permission of Doubleday, a division of Bantam Doubleday Dell Publishing Group, Inc.

McCutchan Publishing Corporation, Berkeley, CA 94102 for selections from David Smith, *Selections from Vedic Hymns.* Permission granted by the publisher.

Motilal Banarsidass for selections from *Devī-Māhātmya: The Crystallization of the Goddess Tradition,* by Thomas B. Coburn.

The Oxford University Press for selections from *Songs of the Saints of India,* by J. S. Hawley and M. Juergensmeyer, copyright © 1988.

Penguin Books Ltd. for selections from *Speaking of Śiva,* trans. A. K. Ramanujan, Baltimore, MD, pp. 120, 125, 127, 131, and 134. Copyright © 1973 by A. K. Ramanujan. Reproduced by permission of Penguin Books Ltd.

Shanti Sadan for selections from *The Ramayana of Valmiki,* trans. H. P. Shastri. Copyright © 1953 by Shanti Sadan.

Temple University Press for selections from *Classical Hindu Mythology,* edited by Cornelia Dimmitt and J. A. B. van Buitenen. Copyright © 1990 by Temple University. Reprinted by permission of Temple University Press.

University of Chicago Press for selections reprinted from *The Mahābhārata,* vol. I, trans. and ed. by J. A. B. van Buitenen. Copyright © 1973 by The University of Chicago Press.

Buddhism

Harry N. Abrams, Inc. for selections from *The Art of Zen,* by Stephen Addiss (New York: Harry N. Abrams, Inc., 1989) copyright © 1989 by Stephen Addiss.

Carol Publishing Group for selections from *The Hundred Thousand Songs of Milarepa,* edited and translated by Garma C. C. Chang, copyright © 1962 by Oriental Studies Foundation. Published by arrangement with Carol Publishing Group.

Columbia University Press for selections from *The Lion's Roar of Queen Śrīmālā,* by Alex Wayman and Hideko Wayman, copyright © 1974 by Columbia University Press. Used by permission of Columbia University Press.

Dharma Publishing for selections from *Voice of the Buddha: The Beauty of Compassion,* translated into English from the French of Edouard Foucaux by Gwendolyn Bays, copyright © 1983 by Dharma Publishing.

Doubleday for selections from *The Confessions of Lady Nijō,* by Lady Nijō, translation by Karen Brazel, translation copyright © 1973 by Karen Brazel. Used by permission of Doubleday, a division of Bantam, Doubleday, Dell Publishing Group, Inc.

Grove Press, Inc. for selections from *Bankei Zen,* by Peter Haskel, copyright © 1984 by Peter Haskel and Yoshito Hakeda. Reprinted by permission of Grove Weidenfeld, a division of Wheatland Corporation.

Library of Tibetan Works and Archives for selections from *The Origin of the Tārā Tantra,* by Jo-Nan Taranatha, translated and edited by David Templeman, copyright © 1981 by the Library of Tibetan Works and Archives.

Motilal Banarsidass Publishers Pvt. Ltd. for selections from *The Buddhacarita,* by Aśvaghoṣa, translated by E. H. Johnston.

The Oxford University Press for selections from *Tibetan Yoga and Secret Doctrines,* ed. by W. Y. Evans-Wentz.

The Pali Text Society for selections from *The Elders' Verses II: Therigatha,* translated by K. R. Norman, copyright © 1971 by the Pali Text Society.

Diana Y. Paul for selections from *Women in Buddhism: Images of the Feminine in Mahāyāna Tradition,* by Diana Y. Paul, copyright © 1979 by Diana Y. Paul.

Penguin Books Ltd. for selections from *Sky Dancer: The Secret Life and Songs of the Lady Yeshe Tsogyel,* trans. Keith Dowman, published by Routledge & Kegan Paul, 1984, copyright © 1984 Keith Dowman, pp. 15–24.

Pennsylvania State University Press for selections from *The Holy Teaching of Vimalakīrti,* translated by R. A. F. Thurman (University Park and London: The Pennsylvania State University Press, 1976), pp. 56–63, copyright © 1976 by The Pennsylvania State University. Reproduced by permission of the publisher.

Charles E. Tuttle Co., Inc. of Tokyo, Japan for selections from *Zen Flesh, Zen Bones,* by Paul Reps.

Wisdom Publications for selections from *Kālachakra Tantra, Rite of Initiation,* by His Holiness the Dalai Lama, translated and edited by Jeffrey Hopkins, copyright © 1985, rev. 1989, by Jeffrey Hopkins and Tenzin Gyatso, the Fourteenth Dalai Lama.

Confucianism

Columbia University Press for selections from the following: *Reflections on Things at Hand: The Neo-Confucian Anthology Compiled by Chu Hsi and Lü Tsu-ch'ien,* trans. Wing-tsit Chan. Copyright © 1967. *Sources of Chinese Tradition,* ed. Theodore de Bary, vol. 1. Copyright © 1960 by Columbia University.

Grove Press for selections from *The Book of Songs: The Ancient Chinese Classic of Poetry,* trans. by Arthur Waley.

Harvard Journal of Asiatic Studies, for selections from "Yüan Chen and 'The Story of Ying-Ying,'" by James Hightower, vol. 33, 1973.

KPI Ltd. for selections from *Memoirs of a Korean Queen, Lady Hong,* trans. Choe-WaIl Yang-hi. Copyright © 1985 Yang-hi Choe-Wall.

Pantheon Books for selections from *Chinese Fairy Tales and Fantasies,* by Moss Roberts. Copyright © 1979 by Moss Roberts. Reprinted by permission of Pantheon Books, a division of Random House, Inc.

Princeton University Press for selections from Wilhelm, Richard, trans. *The I Ching or Book of Changes,* rendered into English by Cary F. Baynes, Bollingen Series XIX. Copyright © 1950, 1967, renewed 1977 by Princeton University Press. Excerpt, pp. 1–15, 153–157 reprinted by permission of Princeton University Press.

Random House, Inc. for selections from *The Wisdom of Confucius,* by Confucius, trans. by Lin Yutang, copyright © 1938 and renewed 1966 by Random House, Inc. Reprinted by permission of Random House, Inc.

Taoism

Columbia University Press for selections from the following: *Chinese Rhyme-Prose: Poems in the Fu Form from the Han and Six Dynasties Periods,* trans. by Burton Watson. Copyright © 1966. *Chuang Tzu: Basic Writings,* trans. Burton Watson. Copyright © 1964, Columbia University Press.

John Murray (Publishers) Ltd. for selections from the following: *The Book of Lieh-Tzu,* translated by A. C. Graham, and *A Gallery of Chinese Immortals,* translated by Lionel Giles.

MIT Press for selections from *Alchemy, Medicine, Religion in the China of A.D. 320: The Nei P'ien of Ko Hung (Pao-p'u tzu),* trans. by James R. Ware. Copyright © 1966 by the Massachusetts Institute of Technology.

Pantheon Books for selections from *Chinese Fairy Tales and Fantasies,* by Moss Roberts. Copyright © 1979 by Moss Roberts, reprinted by permission of Pantheon Books, a division of Random House, Inc.

Penguin Books USA and Random Century Group for selections from *Taoist Tales,* by Raymond Van Over. Copyright © 1973 by Raymond Van Over. Used by permission of New American Library, a division of Penguin Books USA Inc.

Penguin Books USA and Random Century Group for selections from *Eight Immortals of Taoism,* by Kwok Man Ho and Joanne O'Brien. Copyright © 1990 by Kwok Man Ho and Joanne O'Brien. Introduction copyright © 1990 by Martin Palmer. Used by permission of New American Library, a division of Penguin Books USA Inc.

Random House, Inc. and Alfred A. Knopf, Inc. for selections from *Chinese Fairy Tales and Fantasies,* translated and edited by Moss Roberts, copyright © 1979 by Moss Roberts. Reprinted by permission of Pantheon Books, a division of Random House, Inc.

Shambhala Publications, Inc. for selections from the following: *Immortal Sisters: Secrets of Taoist Women,* translated and edited by Thomas Cleary. Copyright © 1989 by Thomas Cleary. *Seven Taoist Masters: A Folk Novel of China,* translated by Eva Wong. Copyright © 1990 by Eva Wong. Reprinted by arrangement with Shambhala Publications, Inc., 300 Massachusetts Avenue, Boston, MA 02115.

University of California Press for selections from *Pacing the Void: T'ang Approaches to the Stars,* by Edward Schafer. Copyright © 1977 The Regents of the University of California.

University of Chicago Press for selections from "The Jade Woman of Greatest Mystery," by Edward Schafer in *History of Religion,* 17, nos. 3–4, 1978. Copyright © 1978 by The University of Chicago.

Alternative Religious Movements

Beacon Press for selections from *Dreaming the Dark,* by Starhawk. Copyright © 1982, 1988 by Miriam Simos. Reprinted by permission of Beacon Press.

Farrar, Straus & Giroux, Inc. for excerpts from *The White Goddess,* by Robert Graves. Copyright © 1948 by International Authors N.V. Renewal copyright © 1975 by Robert Graves. Reprinted by permission of Farrar, Straus & Giroux, Inc. and Curtis Brown, Ltd.

Original Publications for selections from *Santería: African Magic in Latin America,* by Migene González-Wippler. Copyright © 1987 Original Publications.

Paulist Press for selections from *The Shakers: Two Centuries of Spiritual Reflection,* ed. by Robley Edward Whitson. Copyright © 1983 by Robley Edward Whitson. Used by permission of Paulist Press.

Penguin Books USA Inc. for selections from *Drawing Down the Moon,* by Margot Adler. Copyright © 1979 by Margot Adler. Used by permission of Viking Penguin, a division of Penguin Books USA Inc. *Meetings with Remarkable Men,* by G. I. Gurdjieff. Copyright © 1963 by Editions Janus. Used by permission of the publisher, Dutton, an imprint of New American Library, a division of Penguin Books USA Inc.

Rudolf Steiner Press for selections from *The Temple Legend,* by Rudolf Steiner, trans. by John M. Wood. Copyright © 1985 Rudolf Steiner Press, London.

The Society of Inner Light for selections from *The Sea Priestess,* by Dion Fortune.

University of California Press for selections from *Mama Lola: A Voodoo Priestess in Brooklyn,* by Karen Brown. Copyright © 1991 The Regents of the University of California.